Community Matters
A Reader for Writers

Second Edition

Marjorie Ford
Stanford University

Elizabeth Schave Sills
The Health Trust

PEARSON
Longman

New York San Francisco Boston
London Toronto Sydney Tokyo Singapore Madrid
Mexico City Munich Paris Cape Town Hong Kong Montreal

Senior Vice President and Publisher: *Joseph Opiela*
Senior Acquisitions Editor: *Lynn M. Huddon*
Marketing Manager: *Deborah Murphy*
Senior Supplements Editor: *Donna Campion*
Production Manager: *Denise Phillip*
Project Coordination, Text Design, and Electronic Page Makeup: *WestWords, Inc.*
Cover Design Manager: *Wendy Ann Fredericks*
Cover Designer: *Maria Ilardi*
Cover Photo: *Top:* David Young-Wolff/PictureQuest/PhotoEdit; *Bottom left:* Patrick Robert/Corbis/Sygma; *and Bottom right: Free the Children*, Photo by Alam Rahman
Photo Researcher: *WestWords, Inc.*
Senior Manufacturing Buyer: *Alfred C. Dorsey*
Printer and Binder: *R.R. Donnelley and Sons*
Cover Printer: *Lehigh Press, Inc.*

For permission to use copyrighted material, grateful acknowledgment is made to the copyright holders on pp. 595–600, which are hereby made part of this copyright page.

Library of Congress Cataloging-in-Publication Data

Ford, Marjorie (Marjorie A.)
    Community matters : a reader for writers / Marjorie Ford, Elizabeth Schave Sills.--2nd ed.
        p. cm.
    ISBN 0-321-20783-1 (pbk.)
1. Readers--Social sciences 2. Community life--Problems, exercises, etc. 3. English language--Rhetoric--Problems, exercises, etc. 4. Report writing--Problems, exercises, etc. 5. Readers--Community life. 6. College readers. I. Sills, Elizabeth Schave. II. Title.

PE1127.S6F67 2004
808'.0427--dc22

                                2004007616

Please visit us at http://www.ablongman.com

ISBN 0-321-20783-1

1 2 3 4 5 6 7 8 9 10—DOC—07 06 05 04

Contents

3 Research Writing   51

4 Writing About the Community: Resources   83

5 A Sense of Place   113

Memories of Place, Identity, and Community

"The foreignness almost seemed literal; often I didn't understand what the people in my grandmother's house were saying, and often what I said was not understood."

"This was a garden, a wonderful thing to look at in the spring. But bit by bit, after the monkey left, the garden began to take over itself."

"In the shadow of impending chaos, the café is filled with a sense of not just preserving less troubled times, but of continuing a strong cultural tradition rooted in words."

Complexities of Family Life Today

Community Projects That Support Children and Families

player. So the satisfaction that comes from being novel is tempered by the fact that there is no communal standard by which to form a meaningful judgment, no cultural practice."

"Not an art exhibition in the conventional sense, partly an impromptu memorial, partly a rescue effort, and partly a testimonial of support for those who were actually doing the rescuing, it became a rallying point for the neighborhood and the community at large."

9 Work   427

Reconciling Personal Values and Workplace Expectations

"For at the time I had already made up my mind that imperialism was an evil thing and the sooner I chucked my job and got out of it the better."

"To her question of what I planned to do, I replied that I would get a job on the streetcars. She rejected the proposal with: 'They don't accept colored people on the streetcars.'"

"Three programmers, the network guy, me—fifty-eight years of collective technical experience—and the idea of helping people with a computer is a first for any of us."

Revealing the Economic Divide

"Until economic development in Mexico has diminished the underlying need for migration. . . . the emphasis in the United States should be on making sure that all workers, regardless of their nationality, are paid decent wages and protected from exploitation."

"Guilt, you may be thinking warily. Isn't that what we're supposed to feel? But guilt doesn't go anywhere near far enough; the appropriate notion is shame—shame at our own dependency. In this case, on the unpaid labor of others."

"The potential now exists to transform the role that the civic sector plays in society, and to transform the way the nonprofit and corporate

tion fractions of patients receiving chemotherapy with the children squabbling in the background."

Solving Today's Health Care Issues

"Perhaps the most controversial way to use schools to prevent obesity has been undertaken not by academics and health professionals but by parents, teachers, and school administrators, who have in recent years fought a high-stakes guerilla war with the fast-food companies that have come to dominate the school nutrition scene.

"The bottom line from this multitude of studies: if you belong to no groups but decide to join one, you cut your risk of dying over the next year if half . . . less connected Americans are feeling worse."

"True freedom means the freedom of political communities to protect the values they hold most dear, and it is that freedom that we need to exercise with regard to the biotechnology revolution today."

Building Communities to Address Health Issues

"I have tried to voice some of my feelings and thoughts about the travesty of prosthesis, the pain of amputation, the function of cancer in a profit economy, my confrontation with mortality, the strength of women loving and the power and rewards of self-conscious living."

"A few weeks ago, I had thought MSFers were exercising some kind of false modesty when they balked at being called heroes, but now I understand that they are merely experiencing what it is to be full alive. This is disalienation, the antithesis of the programmed numbness that life in a modern industrial city can be, commuting alone to anonymous work with strangers."

"'Though our Sadako is no longer with us, her spirit lives on, a symbol of peace for all the children of the world!'"

Preface

All who serve, serve life. What we serve is something worthy of our attention, of our commitment of our time and our lives. Serving is not about fixing life, outwitting life, manipulating life, controlling life, or struggling to gain mastery over life. When we serve, we discover that life is holy.

Naomi Remen

Community Matters: A Reader for Writers presents a unique approach to the teaching of writing. We came to the project from two different disciplines: as a writing instructor and as a program director for a non-profit organization. Because of our professional experiences, our values are rooted in questions about how to create and support effective communities. Combining our insights, expertise, and ideals, our vision has been to create a book that will encourage students to think critically and creatively about the social, political, and philosophical issues that are shaping the communities to which they belong, while helping them to build a personally engaged community within their writing classroom.

Community Matters is designed as a rhetoric-reader for writing instructors who are interested in the theme of community and civic participation, as well as traditional and nontraditional teaching methods, including experiential learning and service learning. This approach to teaching writing will help to create bridges between those organizations that support and respond to community issues and the academic community with its focus on analysis, argument, and research. The text's emphasis on reflection will help students to make connections between their academic experiences and their role in the community.

Community Matters has two parts. Chapters 1–4 inform students about the fundamentals of reading, writing, and research, including academic and field research, while also providing guidelines for structuring community writing and reflections. Chapters 5–10 present a series of selected readings through thematic topics: a sense of place, family, education, culture, work, and health. Each chapter is divided into three sub-sections. The first readings focus on tradition, the second set introduces current issues, while the third grouping features community action projects that are designed to have a significant impact on improving the quality of community life. These chapters offer a variety of writing styles and genres, including literary essays, arguments, proposals, memoirs, poems, and short stories. Because of the text's emphasis on social action and community development, many of the thematic selections have never been anthologized in composition readers, and some have been written especially for this text.

Distinctive Features of this Book

We have designed the *thematic features* to introduce students to a range of issues that contribute to a definition of community while also providing guidelines for developing critical thinking and reading skills. The *writing features* present readings and writings as integrated processes, while also emphasizing the importance of argument and rhetoric. The *apparatus features* guide students into analytical and expressive ways of understanding, thinking, and writing about the thematic selections.

Thematic Features

- Introduce a variety of readings, activities, and strategies that will help students to understand their communities, from the most personal to the most public.

- Develop an extended definition as well as an awareness of community in its many faces and forms.

- Encourage students to explore and think critically about how social assumptions, institutions, and values strengthen our communities while sometimes leading to social conflict and misunderstanding.

- Identify and develop values and strategies that can help communities to solve social problems and effect change.

- Encourage within the format of a traditional thematic reader a type of experiential learning that is grounded in the classroom experience as well as in experiences within the larger community.

Writing Features

- Present reading and writing as linked processes.
- Support a process-based writing pedagogy.
- Place a special emphasis on the role of audience.
- Provide strategies for creating effective writing groups.
- Discuss and clarify techniques for academic, web-based, and field research.
- Provide guidelines for community-based writing projects.

- Support a rhetoric-based approach to writing and thinking critically that emphasizes the fundamental importance of the relationships between reader, writer and content.

Apparatus Features

- Author notes for all of the selections.
- Reading analysis questions for all of the selections ("Reading Matters").
- Writing prompts for all of the selections ("Writing Matters").
- End of chapter questions that encourage comparative analysis and community-based writing activities.
- URLs for Web sites related to thematic selections.
- Visual materials that help to deepen the thematic presentation.

New to this Edition

- A new "Health" chapter raises issues of importance to today's students, such as how genetics will change our health, how the American diet is leading to dangerously obese children as well as adults, and how women and technology are changing medical treatment.

- Over 30% new readings in the book, including such provocative and engaging selections as "Getting Close to the Machine" by Ellen Ullman; "In The Strawberry Fields" by Eric Schlosser; "Evaluation" by Barbara Ehrenreich; "The Tennis Partner" by Abraham Verghese; "Flatland America: What Can Be Done?" by Greg Crister; and "The Cancer Journals" by Audre Lorde.

- New students writing that exemplifies writing techniques and community action as well as reflection projects completed by writers using the first edition of *Community Matters*.

- Two Web sites for each selection ("Revelant Web Sites") to help students explore sites that are relevant to the themes of their reading selections.

- More emphasis on writing as rhetorically shaped with persuasion as the key goal.

- The Instructors Manual for the Second Edition of *Community Matters* is divided into three parts. Part I provides teaching ideas, additional writing assignments, and worksheets, and new students essays. Part II offers advice on how to develop writing courses that include community service activities as well as examples of syllabi that integrate community writing. Part III features a range of articles that will be helpful to an instructor teaching community service writing.

Acknowledgments

We are grateful to the many people who helped to inform our understanding of community and who supported us during the process of creating and developing *Community Matters*. First we thank our reviewers for their insightful questions and their various perspectives: Ann George, Northwestern Community College; Andrew Haggerty, Broome County Community College; Deborah Reese, Armstrong Atlantic State University; Kathleen J. Ryan, West Virginia University; Kathy Wright, Northern Illinois University.

At Longman Publishers we would like to thank Lynn Huddon for being a champion of this project and sharing our vision. We would also like to acknowledge the team who supported us during the production of the book: editorial assistant, Esther Hollander; production manager, Denise Phillip; project editor, Jami Darby; permissions editor, Marcy Lunetta; supplements editor, Donna Campion; and marketing manager, Deborah Murphy.

Next we would like to thank those individuals who wrote articles specifically for this text: Mark Applebaum, Estella Habal, and Pamela Michael. For reading numerous drafts and for his insights and support, we thank Jon Ford.

We thank the many students in our classes at Stanford University and DeAnza College who worked with the manuscript and offered crucial feedback as it was being shaped. We are especially grateful to those students who wrote new pieces for this edition, including Melissa Burns, Vanya Choumanova, and Elizabeth Derse. We thank our friends and colleagues in the community. At Stanford University, we thank Marvin Diogenes, Pat Fobair, Charles Junkerman, and Hilton Obenzinger. We also thank our friends and colleagues at The Health Trust for their support and their vision.

We thank our close friends and mentors: Ingrid Abrash, Mark Applebaum, Nancy Bryant, Pamela Culp, Joan Friedman, Gale Hilton, Olivia Hurd, Lansing Moran, and Cathy Young. Finally, we thank our families: Jon Ford, Maya Ford, Michael Ford, Barbara Klein, Douglas Schave, Richard Schave, Rebecca Sills, Robin Sills, Robert Sills, and Jonathan Sills for their excellent advice and for their love.

Marjorie Ford   Elizabeth
Schave Sills

Introduction

In a democratic society we must live cooperatively, and serve the community in which we live, to the best of our ability. For our own success to be real, it must contribute to the success of others.

Eleanor Roosevelt

We have designed *Community Matters* as a resource. We hope that it will inspire you and help you explore your role in the many communities that shape your life and encourage you to rethink your definition and understanding of the word *community*. We hope, too, that as you become engaged in thinking critically and creatively about the characteristics of the communities in your own life, you will also develop insights into the role that you want to take in shaping the communities to which you belong.

Communities are complex; oftentimes they reflect our sense of place, our values, our commitments, our strengths, and our weaknesses. Communities exist in neighborhoods, in family units, in the workplace, in classrooms, in cyberspace, and in cultural celebrations. In his recent book, *Almost Home*, Professor of Public Policy David L. Kirp offers a relevant perspective on the way that individuals bring meaning to the idea of community:

> There is a ton of prose on the idea of community, and mostly it is passionately opinionated. Community is praised and damned—a haven in a heartless world or a prison of conformity; a place where habits of the heart are nurtured or a seedbed of intolerance; a place to which you can't return or else a place from which you'd gladly flee. *The word community itself is a Rorschach blot upon which myriad hopes and fears are projected.*

As we move into the new millennium, our communities are rapidly being transformed by technology and the international economy. We are at a turning point in history when our dependence and trust in communities as growing more essential, yet we face many new issues and unanswered questions about the future of our communities. What will be the continuing impact of the changing family unit? How can we help to rebuild communities that have been destroyed by natural disasters, poverty, or war? What efforts can we make as a society to ensure that there is equal access to technology, information, and education? How are service and volunteerism developing into an essential aspect of our economy and well-being? How are the realities of the global marketplace affecting our relationships with people from cultures that have values that are different from our own?

1

Searching for answers to these types of complex questions has engaged the minds of many fine thinkers. Aspiring to find equitable solutions—balancing competing needs and interests—is at the core of our democratic process. As Alexis De Tocqueville, whose political philosophy helped to frame the American Constitution, wrote in *Democracy in America:* "In democratic countries, knowledge of how to combine is the mother of all forms of knowledge; on its progress depends that of all the others." Democracy and community are therefore linked through the foundation of our country's political traditions. As citizens we have an opportunity to effect change in the many communities to which we belong. Through our involvement in a number of different communities, we can gain knowledge and develop understanding. With such perspective we can make informed decisions that will help to improve the quality of life in our immediate communities and in our nation.

Think for a moment about what community means to you personally. Try to remember the community stories that have captured your imagination. Was there a family story whose meaning guided you as you were growing up? Which historical or contemporary leaders do you look to for inspiration? How have the media influenced your memories of community stories? Are there myths or religious stories that shape your attitudes about the importance of community? The power of a community's particular and sometimes universal stories, with their heroines, heroes, ordinary people, and villains, can capture a community's imagination and conscience while presenting ethical dilemmas. These community stories can encourage members to reconsider their values and norms, to interpret and possibly redefine their role in the community and its role and goals.

Reading, Researching, and Writing

Community Matters is organized into 10 chapters. Chapters 1 to 4 provide you with guidelines for developing your reading, writing, and research skills and will help you to begin to write for the communities that influence your life. We have included several examples of writing assignments to introduce you to the way that you will be applying and integrating the writing concepts and the thematic concerns presented in this text. Some of the writing assignments provide you with an opportunity to do writing for the community. Through writing for the community, you will experience aspects of community life that may be unfamiliar. These "real-world" writing projects will present you with new writing challenges and new audiences; in some cases members of the community will be reading and evaluating your writing along with your instructor. Writing for the community may engage your sense of civic responsibility, deepen your understanding of complex community issues, and provide you with opportunities to address issues and develop solutions. Through reflecting on these writing experiences, you can also refine your critical thinking skills as well as your understanding of your own values and writing style.

Preview of Writing Assignments

- Interview people in your community about their opportunities in school. Write about what you have learned about how school can function as a community. Compare and contrast your own experiences with those of the people you interviewed.

- Write an essay about a public event that you have attended. What did you learn about the community? Did you experience the event as political? Cultural? Social? How did the event help you to clarify your own values? Use specific examples to clarify your main ideas.

- Write an essay that explores a work situation that forced you to rethink and reevaluate your own values and the importance of community. What did you learn from the situation? Were you changed by the experience? How and why?

The Thematic Readings

The reading selections are organized into six thematic chapters (Chapters 5 to 10). These chapters introduce you to various community issues and provide you with a wealth of opportunity to exercise your active reading and critical thinking skills. Each chapter examines a significant aspect of community, a particular area in human endeavor where communities are found. The chapter themes include: "A Sense of Place," "Family," "Education," "Culture," "Work," and "Health." All chapters have been divided into three sections. The first section places the theme in the context of experience and reflection. The second section provides a more analytical perspective through the voices of social theorists, historians, and professionals in the field. The third section presents action-based community projects that have helped to transform communities in specialized and vital ways. While some of the readings may challenge your assumptions and beliefs, your understanding of the meaning of the word *community* will grow richer and more complex as you continue to read and think about the selections. In thinking about communities that are different from your own, you may find that you can also see and value your own community in new ways.

We have included highlights from the featured readings to give you a preview of what issues and questions you will explore in the pages to follow:

- In "The Invisible Riot," social critic Mike Davis discusses the political and economic conditions that set the stage for the Los Angeles riots that left the downtown community a "modern high rise ghost town."

- In "The Olympic Games," international travel writer Pico Iyer examines how his own identity has been changed through his many encounters with the international quality of life in the Information Age. He draws conclusions about how new communities are being shaped in urban centers all over the world.

- In "How to YA/YA in Your Neighborhood," Claudia Barker tells the success story of a nonprofit after-school community art program for youth in downtown New Orleans that has become nationally and internationally known.

- The casebook "The One Thousand Paper Cranes" explores the impact of a young girl's dream for world peace.

Your definition of community has been and will continue to be shaped by your values and experiences as an individual and a community member. We hope that the reading and writing resources in *Community Matters* will inform and inspire you. We hope, too, that they will help you to understand how "community matters" in your own life.

Reading

Reading can challenge us to learn, whether it takes place in the classroom, in the privacy of one's bedroom, in response to a community debate, or in the process of solving a challenge at work. Reading can connect us to new communities: through work projects, in chat rooms, at book clubs, or through participating in producing a newsletter, a fact sheet, or publicity for a community organization. As you study the selections in this text, we encourage you to think about reading in the broadest sense, to think about how reading in the "real world" can enhance your academic studies, to think about how reading can bring you pleasure and can help to make you a more resourceful member of your community.

Reading Actively

Reading and writing help us to learn about ourselves, to discover and create meaning through the language that we use in response to the texts that we read. When we read a text, we are engaged in bringing its meaning to life in our minds. The reading process involves a dialogue between inner worlds—preconceived ideas, feelings, and experiences—and the voice of the text. This imaginative dialogue between mind and text can help to clarify your own thoughts and feelings. To become engaged in "active reading" you need to be writing about what you are reading. Always have a pencil or a pen with you when you sit down to study a reading selection in *Community Matters* and when you are reading for your other college courses as well. Underline passages that interest you, images that seem especially descriptive and compelling, and facts and examples that provide clear support. If you disagree with the writer, make note of your position in the margins of your text. If you have questions about the text, write them down so that you can go back to them once you have finished the reading selection. Perhaps what you are reading will bring up memories; note those in the margins, too. Any imaginative dialogue with a text that you are reading can be developed, clarified, and intensified through underlining key passages and writing notes or questions in the margins.

Through reading, you will learn about the issues, the people, and the worlds represented in a text. For example, "Viet Kieu," a memoir included in *Community Matters,* features an extended conversation between a tour guide in Vietnam and a Vietnamese American who is returning to his homeland for a summer trip. Their dialogue can be seen as an extended example of analytical and critical thinking as the two men are actively questioning one another's values and, at the same time, thinking about their own assumptions about their life goals. While this selection exhibits critical thinking, the young men's revelations may remind you of ways in which you have had to change to adjust to life in a new country, or they may give you insights into issues that immigrants to the United States often face.

All of the reading selections in *Community Matters* provide challenging opportunities for you to practice your critical thinking and reading skills. The readings will also foster your personal growth as you come to better understand the issues that shape the lives of people in your own communities and in communities that are different from your own.

Reading As a Process

The reading strategies presented in this chapter will help you to discover meaning and find satisfaction in the challenges of reading. Before studying these strategies, think about the expectations you have of reading. What strategies do you already use to read effectively? Considering the questions and issues that follow will help you to clarify your approach to reading and will guide you in developing a reading process that works for you.

Reflecting on Your Reading Process

When is reading pleasurable for you? When is reading a challenge for you?

What do you like to read: magazines, newspapers, short stories, novels, memoirs, historical accounts, poetry?

Do you read and concentrate differently when you are reading "schoolwork" rather than when you are reading for pleasure or for escape?

What is the longest period of time that you can concentrate on your reading?

Do you have a place where you feel comfortable reading? Why do you like reading there?

Do you use any prereading strategies? For example, after looking at a title, do you ask yourself questions about what you think you will be reading or what you expect to learn from the text? Do you ask yourself questions about where the author was born, where he or she grew up, and what political and social values he or she respects?

Do you like to underline the text you are reading to keep track of the author's main ideas? If there is something that you don't understand, do you write questions to yourself so that you can go back later and find answers to your questions? Do you make notes to yourself about ideas that interest you so that you can locate them again more easily?

Do you refer to a dictionary as you read? Do you try to use new words that you discover in your reading?

Do you try to talk about things that you have read with your friends or your family?

Practicing the reading process presented in this chapter will help you to improve your reading skills. At the same time, you will be building your confidence as a reader as well as your ability to focus and concentrate on the text that you are reading. We suggest a four-stage reading process that will teach you how to articulate and clarify your responses and to develop a reasoned analysis and interpretation of the text that you are reading. Your reading process will vary depending on the complexity of what you are reading.

Prereading Stage

Prereading refers to a method of previewing what you will be reading. Asking yourself questions about the following characteristics of a text before you begin to read it will prepare you to absorb more from your assignment.

What does the title suggest about the selection?   The title can give you insight into the selection's topic. Ask yourself if the selection's subject matter is one that interests you. What do you already know about the topic?

What is the author's background?   Where was the author born? Where does the writer live? Is the writer male or female? The answers to these questions will determine how much of a challenge it may be for you to understand the perspective likely to be presented in the reading and how much background information you will need to research as you study the text.

Where and when was the text originally published?   Was the selection written within the past five years, ten years, or in a more distant past? If what you are planning to read is modern, you are more likely to be able to relate to the ideas and references used by the author. If the selection was written many years ago, however, some words and expressions may be unfamiliar, as will some of the allusions to historical figures or works. If this is the case, don't feel discouraged or frustrated. You will be able to understand the piece, but you also will need to do some research to find the information you need. You can locate background information by checking in dictionaries, in encyclopedias, or on the Internet.

What does the selection's apparent organization tell you?   Bold headings and subsections divide the ideas into parts for you. Graphic design features and visuals help to support and clarify meanings of the text. The works cited and Internet references, footnotes, and appendixes provide you with information on the sources that the author used to construct the book that you are reading.

Who was the intended audience for the selection?   What interests, beliefs, knowledge, and assumptions would the intended audience have? Typical audiences include college professors in a particular subject, classmates, the college campus community, local or national newspaper readers, employers, technicians, professionals in a specific field, and community organizations.

What is the form or genre of the selection?   Every selection you read has a particular form with standard characteristics. Identifying the form will help you to understand, interpret, and evaluate its meaning and purpose. After you note what kind of form the writer is using, consider what assumptions and expectations one can reasonably have of such forms, and the type of reading approach each requires. Typical forms of writing include journal entries, e-mail conversations, brochures, field notes, interviews, newsletters, newspaper articles, reviews, web sites, grant proposals, arguments, and research analysis.

Skimming

At this stage of the reading process you should just plunge in and read the work quickly to get an overall sense of its meaning. As you are reading, check off or star a few key passages and put a question mark by an idea, a detail, or a word that seems confusing. Don't be concerned at this stage about what you don't yet understand; instead, try to become engaged with the energy and issues in the text.

An immediate and unstructured written response to what you have just read can help you to develop your interest in the text and deepen your response to it. A quick response often contains a synthesis of what you think the author meant to convey as well as the personal thoughts and experiences that you bring to the reading. As you write your response, consider the following issues: *What was the main point of the selection? What was the author's purpose? Did you have a strong emotional or intellectual response to it? How did reading the selection challenge you? What didn't you understand after your first reading?* If you disagree with one or more of the points the author is making, you might write your response in a letter form, "talking back" to the writer. Alternatively, you might want to write spontaneously about what you are thinking when you finish reading.

Share your quick responses with your class or in small groups. Spend some time discussing how to account for the differences in the responses. *Did aspects of your personal experiences and background lead you to respond to the work in a particular way? Did some members of the group have specialized knowledge that helped them and you to see more deeply into the text? What key words, references, cultural customs, or values might you need to understand to deepen your comprehension and response to the work?* Although there is a lot of room for variation in individual responses to any work, each interpretation must be based on an accurate reading of the text itself.

Study Stage

None of us studies everything that we read. Often we skim newspapers or magazines just to get the main idea. We may read a novel for pleasure. Most college reading assignments do need to be studied carefully. The strategies that follow will help you to read more closely and accurately in order to analyze and interpret a text that you are reading.

Developing your concentration skills   You can build your concentration skills by actively trying to get deeply involved in what you are reading. Study in a place where there are no distractions. Put yourself on a reading schedule that paces you to read progressively longer pieces of text. Periodically, after several paragraphs or a page, look up from your reading and think of a question to ask yourself about what you've just read, write a question in the margins of your text, or make a quick summary of what you have been reading. If you find that your mind is wandering from your reading, take a short break and go back to your work with a more refreshed mind.

Using the dictionary   The dictionary is an invaluable source of information for readers doing careful textual analysis. (Use a substantial dictionary, a hardback, desk-sized edition or go online, where you will find a wide range of excellent dictionaries and encyclopedias.) While dictionaries will help you to find definitions of words you don't know or have never seen in print, it is also helpful to look up words you recognize, but that don't seem to quite make sense in a given context of your reading. Sometimes a partial knowledge of a complex word can lead to a misunderstanding of the meaning of an entire passage. It is always worthwhile to study a word that is confusing you; explore all of its given meanings—the etymologies and the examples of contextual uses. Get into the habit of referring to your dictionary frequently.

Marking the text   In the study stage, marking becomes even more focused and detailed. Writing in the margins and underlining individual words and sentences will help to increase your engagement with what you are reading. This can make concentrating on what you are trying to absorb and understand easier. Underscore passages you consider especially important, such as topic sentences or key word phrases. Make notes to yourself, pointing out essential facts, representative examples, central statements of cause and effect or comparison, and thesis statement ideas for future reference or for possible inclusion in an essay. Also consider underlining passages that give the selection tone and voice. In this case circle ironic statements, metaphors, and highly descriptive narrative or persuasive sections. Write questions to yourself about the text. Agree or disagree with it. Prepare yourself to discuss the text with other readers, especially those whom you think may have had a different response to the text than you had.

In the following example one of our students, Jason Loomis, has annotated pages from the "Digital Divide," one of the reading selections in Chapter 7 on page 310. Note that Loomis's annotation includes brief summaries of key sentences and concepts. Translating these concepts into his own words helped Loomis better understand the passage he was reading.

Jason Loomis   Loomis 1

Annotation of a passage from *"Digital Divide"*

computers change how education works across the nation

brings up many issues that must be addressed

differences between students with and without access to technology

education now, more than ever, depends on money rather than intelligence and other such characteristics

differing experience for students with differing amounts of access to technology

This is the educational essence of the digital divide.

The arena of education in our nation is being altered by the introduction of computer and connectivity technology—the "wiring" of our schools. As this technology is introduced into the classroom, it can alter the way students are taught. It is important, therefore, to explore some of the fundamental concerns about introducing this technology, as well as its educational applications. There is an increasing disparity between schools and students with and without significant access to this technology, but access to technology itself is only one of many issues involved. In the world of today, more than at any time in the past century, much of a student's educational experience depends on that student's socioeconomic background. It has nothing to do with the student's intelligence, learning ability, or industriousness. Rather, it has to do with whether the student has access to technology, access to the information made available by that technology, and access to educators trained in integrating that technology and information into the educational experience.

U.S. public education encompasses many different realities, depending on many variables, including state requirements and curricula, educator licensing requirements, and the funding available to schools. In the area of computer and communications technologies, though, there are some commonalities. The majority of public

---

Loomis 2

schools have many differences in requirements and funding but many share a common lack of available technology and funding allocated to technology many schools don't have the money for technology lack of integration with curriculum, lack educators have it hard enough, but are now expected to learn technology too teachers expected to convey technology to students when they are struggling with it themselves teachers don't think training is adequate computers not effective w/out people who can use them well	schools still don't have directly allocated funds for telecommunications and don't have adequate infrastructure to support the technology being touted and dispensed by the computer industry and the government. Of the remaining schools, most do not have adequate funds for the maintenance and support of the equipment that they have managed to obtain. Even if adequate provision has been made for this (and it rarely is), the seemingly insurmountable obstacle of integrating this mass of equipment into a meaningful curriculum—including the significant teacher training required—still looms large.

Educators nationwide are faced with a set of continuing challenges, including overcrowded classrooms, poorly maintained facilities, uneven support, and insufficient pay scales and benefits packages. Now, in addition to their continuing mandated education requirements, teachers find themselves in the position of having to learn a wide variety of new technology-related skills to meet the social expectations of the Information Age: the use of computers, the use of a variety of software packages on computers, the use of the Internet, and elementary troubleshooting techniques to offset the lack of comprehensive technical support. They are also expected to be able to convey this knowledge to their students, a group (like educators) ranging from the technophilic to the technophobic. Elena McFadden, a first grade teacher at Hoover Elementary School in Redwood City, California, is, in many ways, a typical educator trying to do her best with limited resources. "I took the computer class that teachers are required to take for their credentials, and I don't feel I received any training adequate to making me able to teach computers any better than when I walked into the class," Ms. McFadden noted. "You can't buy a bunch of computers and not train teachers to use them, and expect education and learning to go on." |

Paraphrasing   Writing a paraphrase of a text will help you to pay close attention to what you are reading and to understand it better. Paraphrasing is also helpful in research writing when you don't want to quote long pieces of text yet need to include a key portion of an author's work. To paraphrase, put the main concepts of the text into your own words and sentence structure without changing the fundamental meaning of the original material, leaving out figurative language and lengthy examples. Searching for synonyms and altering sentence structure will help you to rephrase the text without changing its basic content. If you find yourself having difficulty putting the idea of your source into your own language, this may be because you do not understand a key word or phrase in the original. Keep a good dictionary and thesaurus nearby to refer to when paraphrasing.

Summarizing   Any text, from a paragraph to an entire book, can be summed up in a few well-chosen phrases or sentences. A summary is different from a paraphrase, for in a summary you restate the source's main ideas and overall perspective, capturing the essence of the original passage in as few words as possible. The challenge becomes to avoid leaving out the most significant ideas while cutting out much of the supporting material such as secondary ideas, references and quotations, examples, long case studies, and statistical analyses. The best summaries are written using your own voice, while also capturing the tone of the original.

In the following example Jason Loomis has written a summary of two of the concluding paragraphs of the "Digital Divide."

Summary:
It has been suggested that opportunities can be limited for those without (the money for) technology regardless of motivation. To make matters worse, publicly accessible technology resources are often inadequate and unhelpful.

. . . Most of us have become convinced that, for better or worse, a person must exhibit a certain level of technological aptitude in order to be of value in the workplace. Facility with computer and connectivity technology is a set of skills that employers look for in potential employees and that institutes of higher education look for in potential students. A lack of proficiency in these skills can be a bar to entry into either of these areas.

It is no longer enough for driven, economically disadvantaged people to spend hours at either a local or school library, teaching themselves what they need to know in order to succeed. In this age, when library economic resources are generally not even back to the level that they were a generation ago, it is ever more difficult for the economically disadvantaged to make use of what resources there are. Those computers that are put into libraries for public access are generally slow, outdated, and overburdened. Software availability is usually limited, decreasing the utility of those machines that are available to young people trying to increase their chances of success in the Information Age.

Outlining   Making an outline of the major ideas in a reading selection will help you develop perspective on what you have read and can help you to better understand and remember the selection's structure and point of view.

This strategy can also help to focus your thinking, organize your understanding of what you have read, and prepare you for exams. In a sense, an outline is a kind of summary, but one designed to more clearly represent the structure of points and subpoints (supports) in the work studied. Outlines vary in complexity from a simple sequential list of major ideas to more elaborate schemas using Roman numerals, alphabetical letters, and so forth.

Reflective Response Stage

When you are in the study stage of reading, your main concern is to develop an ongoing understanding of each section. After your close reading is complete, you will want to think more about the selection's overall meaning and to understand how the parts of the text work together to create complex meanings or stages of an argument. After you have analyzed the meaning of a text, you may wish to move on to evaluating the work, and finally to writing a synthesis of it, in which you systematically compare it to other texts to place it within a larger body of ideas. In writing a critical reflective response or when integrating a text as a source within a research paper, often you will find yourself using all three of these strategies as we explain them next.

Analysis Analysis demands that you go beyond simply finding the "main idea," which you did in making a summary. It involves looking for patterns of thought and language that support the dominant tone and meaning of the work. Begin by thinking about how literal, metaphorical, and persuasive strategies are affecting the text's meaning. Then compare the written record of your reactions at this stage of the reading process with your written responses to the first reading of the text. At this stage you will probably find that your ideas have deepened considerably and that you have a more comprehensive view of the work than you did initially. You can analyze a work in several ways. Different readers will put emphasis on different conventions and techniques. For example, some readers may prefer to do a stylistic analysis, looking at the way the writer uses devices such as sentence structure, word choice, and figurative language to create meaning. Other readers will pay closer attention to larger structural strategies such as comparison, narration, definition, and classification. Some readers, particularly when analyzing argumentative writing, may prefer to analyze by examining a series of points, ideas, or types of evidence used to support ideas.

Focusing Your Analysis

What is the purpose of your analysis?

What point (thesis) do you want to make about the selection?

What content and passages in the text do you want to refer to?

How will you back up your analysis with additional support such as authority, facts, and personal experience?

What aspects of the selection's structure will you focus on: the use of language, the use of sentence structure or syntax, the use of evidence and logic, the use of organizational strategies such as narration or comparison, or the use of tone or irony?

How will you shape your introduction to engage your reader's interest in your analysis?

How can your conclusion extend your thesis idea into a more general perspective?

Have you used a standard form of documentation to integrate quotations from the text you are analyzing? (Check an MLA or APA handbook or web site for details about documentation.)

Evaluative response Evaluation, or examining the strengths and weaknesses of a reading to decide whether it meets your intellectual standards and needs, is at the heart of both argumentative writing and research writing. It is necessary to evaluate the arguments of others for sound or fallacious reasoning and to evaluate your sources for your papers to make sure that they are relevant and reliable. Evaluation of a text usually occurs in conjunction with the kind of analysis discussed in the previous box. For example, if you analyze an essay for its stylistic techniques and their role in creating the meaning of the essay, you may need to follow up your analysis with an evaluation of the success or failure of the strategies you have analyzed.

You need to be especially careful when you write an evaluation of a piece of writing. A good evaluation uses fair criteria, so you will need to be sensitive to the writer's intentions, to the audience of the selection, and to the exact nature of what you are reading and reflecting upon. Be clear and consistent about your criteria for evaluation and your expectations.

Evaluating What You Have Read

What is your overall response to the values, ideas, and emotional stance presented in the work?

Do the values of this selection reflect or illuminate key issues of concern both to you as an individual and to your community? If so, which ones?

Did the author present accurate and convincing evidence to support his or her conclusions and recommendations?

After finishing the text, did you want to read more by this writer, or to follow up the thread of the argument or theme of the work by reading thematically related works by other writers? Why?

Would you recommend the work to other readers?

What criteria will you use to evaluate the text? Why are these criteria appropriate and related to the writer's purpose and audience?

Responding through synthesis   Synthesis integrates analysis and evaluation. It brings together several works in order to examine and reflect upon their underlying ideas, to weigh the distinctions between solutions presented, and to work not just to decide which work is "best" but rather what is most workable in each for the purpose of creating a new and improved idea. Synthesis is what takes place in any form of creative group collaboration: in writing, the performing arts, business, or science. Synthesis is a process in which a number of individuals engaged in a common enterprise freely contribute ideas and then work together to combine them into a new and powerful product, concept, or course of action.

When you are writing a synthesis, first consider the ideas of a number of writers you have studied. Eliminate those ideas that seem inappropriate or irrelevant; use the ideas of more recent or sophisticated writers to support an argument or course of action.

Developing a Synthesis

Prior to writing your paper, have you reread all your sources, making sure you understand their major arguments?

Have you taken notes on your sources' key passages?

Do you fully understand the points of similarity and distinction between the sources you have read and intend to write about?

Have you done some preliminary evaluation of the compared key ideas of the paper, noting relative strengths and weaknesses of each?

Do you have a plan for the sequential set of links or relationships between key workable ideas in your final synthesis?

Do you have an effective introduction, thesis, and conclusion for your paper?

Can you develop a series of arguments to support your own vision of a workable idea or solution derived from your synthesis of the ideas in the readings you have analyzed in your paper?

Have you used the proper research format to introduce and to document quotations, summaries, and paraphrases from your sources?

Reading Images

In *Community Matters* we have integrated a variety of visual images such as photographs, drawings, murals, and posters into the thematic chapters. Some of the images accompany the original pieces and others were selected because they contribute to the chapter topics. A strong photograph or visual image, film, or television program draws you in, inspiring you to find out more about the subject matter and to better understand its meaning. Although some theorists believe that the traditional act of reading is passé in this electronic age, the perceptual and critical thinking process for decoding, analyzing, interpreting, and evaluating materials that involve images along with printed words or even with no words at all is not so different from book reading as it might seem. Whether you are reading a book, watching a film, viewing a television show, or scrolling through web pages, you need to pay close attention to all of the clues for meaning available. You will need to look for patterns of imagery, symbols, significant character interaction, plotlines, and crucial meaning statements, whether in the form of speeches by characters, key bits of dialogue, or voice-overs (in the case of a film).

Whether reading a book, viewing a film, or examining an Internet site, you also need to know something about the author (director/screenwriter, in the case of a film, or, in the case of many web pages, the organization that has produced the page and its objectives). You need to know how this work builds on other works by the same writer or organization and the cultural assumptions and traditions (of writing, filmmaking, or multimedia) from which the work issues.

Finally, whether you are reading a book, looking at a photograph, watching a film or TV show, or even cruising the Internet, you need to create the opportunity for a second reading or viewing, to get closer to the work through repeated exposure to grasp its full significance and to make interpretations and connections with other similar works. While this is easier and cheaper to do with a book, you can always watch a film a second time, take notes, videotape a TV show, or, in the case of Web pages, bookmark the page or save it for instant replay later on. In nonprint media or multimedia you have to learn to "read" visual images for intellectual suggestions and emotional impact, just as you examine the words in a written text closely for their connotations or shadings of meaning. In multimedia, in a way similar to any illustrated text, you need to be alert to a complex interplay between words, images, and even sounds.

What makes a person a good reader, interpreter, and judge of visual images and electronic media is precisely the kind of habits of good study that an experienced reader brings to a book. You need to resist both the passive mood many people can sink into in front of TV sets as well as the "surfing" mentality that involves clicking rapidly and restlessly from one link to another on the Internet. When studying media, writing can be an especially helpful way to develop critical responses. Try keeping a journal of media you watch and respond actively to the media, using the kind of entries suggested previously in the section on the reader's journal: preliminary responses and entries, interpretive entries, and evaluative entries for a repeated viewing of material that looks interesting. In this way, you can become a full reader—sensitive to the world of books as well as an able critic of the electronic media that surround us daily, which may seem at times to overwhelm our abilities to respond or even to take a position. Don't let that happen to you.

As you continue to read and reread a text, to study its visual images if you encounter them, you will find yourself becoming better able to understand it from more perspectives, identifying with different ideas, perceiving different qualities as more important or dominant, and creating relationships between the individual text and other works that you have read and studied. The varying ways in which you respond to an essay, story, or book reflect your growing process of understanding both the text and yourself as a reader.

Relevant Web Sites

Oxford English Dictionary <http://www.oed.com>

The online version of the *Oxford English Dictionary.*

New York Times Books <http://www.nytimes.com/books/home/>

A searchable archive of 50,000 book reviews since 1980. This site includes bestseller lists, access to first chapters, book news, and book forums.

The English Server <http://www.eserver.org>

Links to library resources including audio and video recordings of scholarly presentations, nonfiction book texts, community bulletin boards, calls for papers, texts on literacy, cultural theory, drama, feminism, film and TV, language, poetry, and rhetoric.

America Reads <http://www.ed.gov/inits/americareads/>

This web site highlights former President Clinton's reading initiative and contains information about how to get involved in ensuring that every child can read well by the third grade.

2   Writing

In *Community Matters* we present writing both as a personal or "writer-based" process and as a public or "real-world" process. Writing often begins with expressive writing: writing for oneself to articulate and clarify thoughts and feelings. Making one's thoughts public through writing then initiates a connection between the writer and his or her audience. Writing can empower us. As writers, we can effect change within ourselves and the communities to which we belong. The Greek rhetorician Aristotle believed that all writing that was "public" in nature had, in addition to a purpose, three main qualities that needed to be in balance with one another for the work to be persuasive: a strong sense of pathos, or appeal to the beliefs and deep feelings of the reader or audience; a sense of ethos, or the way the writer projects himself or herself as believable and worth of our trust; and finally, a sense of logos—an organized presentation of the content, in the text itself, including the language the writer chooses and the reasons and facts he or she provides to support his or her overall purpose.

Purpose

Every piece of writing has a purpose. If you are writing for yourself in a journal, then your purpose is self-expression. Otherwise, the general writing purposes include writing to inform, writing to persuade, and writing to entertain. While these three purposes certainly overlap in many pieces of writing, it is possible to identify a selection for its primary purpose. For example, you may be writing an essay that informs readers about the meaning of an experience you have had or that presents an analysis of a theme in an essay. In contrast, you might be writing a paper to persuade your readers to get involved in an organization on campus or to take a particular stand on a community issue. If you want to entertain your readers, you might even write a satire about relationship that could be both entertaining and persuasive.

More specifically, many college professors give their students assignments that direct them to a purpose. For example, your writing professor might ask you to write an analytical response to a reading selection, a comparison of two different points of view on a controversial issue, or a research essay on a given topic. Always study your instructor's prompts that are designed to guide your purpose. Remember, too, that your instructor expects you to determine a more specific purpose within the framework of his or her assignment. In some cases you will be given a very open-ended assignment such as to write a four-page paper with sources on a topic that interests you. Finding your purpose in this writing situation will involve identifying a topic, narrowing the topic, and then deciding what point of view you want to present. Asking yourself questions about what you want to write, accumulating information and examples, and developing theories that explain the meaning of the information you have gathered will help you to clarify your purpose. Even as you write and rewrite your essay, you will be refining your purpose.

Audience

Thinking about your audience will also help you to limit and shape your writing, although it is important to remember that good writing generally begins with ideas and values that the writer can honestly stand behind. If you are writing in response to an assignment for a college course, your audience will be your classmates and your instructor. If you do writing for your community, you will have a wider range of possible audiences such as business people, community members, politicians, or health professionals. For example, if you were asked to write about an upcoming neighborhood musical event, and you were told the audience was local business people who might potentially donate money for the event, you would immediately have an idea about what parts of the event you wanted to discuss, and you also would have a sense about what kind of tone and vocabulary you should use. You would cover the event differently if you were writing for friends in your neighborhood who were avid fans of the musical group.

Before you begin to write, ask yourself the following questions to help yourself become more consciously aware of how to shape your ideas into a context that reflects your understanding of your audience's knowledge and interest in your topic. These kinds of questions will help you arrive at what Aristotle called the "pathos" of good writing.

Audience Checklist

How large and diverse is my audience?

How might my audience's age; gender; culture; and economic, political, and social background shape their values?

In what ways is my audience different from and similar to me?

Will my audience already be interested in my topic? How could learning about my topic benefit my audience?

What would be the best way to approach my topic? Through a story, an explanation, an argument? Would humor be appropriate?

What background information will my audience need in order to understand the complex concepts in my paper?

What do I need to learn more about my audience to understand how to reach out to them and to develop an effective strategy for presenting my topic?

What personal and relevant experiences can I include that could help my readers to better understand my topic?

The Writer

The rhetorical triangle: Visualizing the relationship of the audience, the purpose, and the writer is often expressed by rhetoricians and writing teachers as a rhetorical triangle with each angle at 60 degrees. One angle is the audience, one the purpose, and one the writer. These are the three major influences on creating a persuasive piece of writing, and they must be in balance for the work to be successful.

As the writer of any paper, you need to come to understand how you want to express yourself to persuade your readers. You need to find your writer's voice in the context of your rhetorical situation.

Building Your Self-Confidence As a Writer

While the strategies for developing successful writing can be clearly stated, many writers still struggle to express themselves. One major reason for this struggle has been identified as writer's block. People who experience writer's block may find writing frustrating and may fear that they will fail to express what they really want to say or that they have nothing to say. Do you ever experience writer's block? Trying to understand what worries or frustrates you about writing can help you to control your fears about producing an essay. At the same time, you must avoid being self-critical or comparing yourself negatively to another writer, especially when you are just starting to write out your ideas. Building self-confidence in your ability to write might just be the most important first step in facing your writer's block and moving on to develop your skills and voice as a writer.

Visualizing your internal critic   If you are committed to building your self-confidence and improving your writing, you will need to discard negative assumptions that you have about your potential as a writer. Many writers have described and discussed the impact of their internal critics on their writing process. Contemporary novelist Gail Godwin offers some excellent advice about how to keep an internal critic, "the nagging voice of negative social judgment and of self-doubt that thwarts so many writers." She symbolizes her critic as "The Watcher at the Gate" and tells us,

> Get to know your Watcher. He's yours. Do a drawing of him (or her). Pin it to the wall of your study and turn it gently to the wall when necessary. Let your Watcher feel needed. Watchers are excellent critics after inspiration has been captured; they are dependable, sharp-eyed readers of things already set down. Keep your Watcher in shape and he'll have less time to keep from shaping you. If he's really ruining your whole working day, sit down, as Jung did with his personal demons, and write him a letter. On a very bad day I once wrote my Watcher a letter. 'Dear Watcher,' I wrote, 'What is it you're so afraid I'll do?' Then I held his pen for him, and he replied instantly with a candor that has kept me from truly despising him, 'Fail,' he wrote back.

Do you have a "watcher at the gate"? Try taking Gail Godwin's advice. Visualize your internal critic. How old is this person? What does he or she look like? What kind of attitude does your internal critic project? Try to draw a picture of your internal critic and write him or her a letter. Does your internal critic have any qualities of other people in your life? What will be most challenging about talking back to the critic within you?

Nurturing Your Muse   Each of us also has a "muse," defined as any of the nine sister goddesses in Greek mythology presiding over song and poetry and the arts and sciences or as a source of inspiration, especially a guiding genius. Each of us has a voice within us that can express our creativity and inspiration. What can you do to nurture the muse within you? The closer you get to your "muse," the more of a sense of "ethos" you will be able to project in your writing—that sense of trustworthiness that is likely to make your readers listen to what you have to say. You will also find that once you can get in touch with your own creativity, your ideas and writing will flow more easily.

We have designed the worksheet that follows to help you to recognize your strengths as a writer and to reacquaint yourself with your muse.

Your Writer's Profile

Do you have original ideas and insights? What are some of your core values? Do you enjoy writing?

Do you try to express yourself honestly and clearly?

Are you a good storyteller?

Are you creative?

Can you be persuasive?

Do you like to do research and find useful evidence?

Are you good at making accurate observations?

Can you explain ideas or events clearly?

Do you have strong analytical skills?

Are you logical?

Do you value what you write?

Writing As a Process

Writers and writing teachers acknowledge the concept of writing as a process and break down the different stages that a writer can anticipate working through on the way to clarifying his or her ideas. The stages in the writing process include prewriting, drafting, revising, and editing for style. At the prewriting stage, you work at generating ideas for your topic; in the drafting stage, you try to get the main ideas for your paper down in words. The revising stage involves developing, clarifying, and refining your ideas; in the editing stage, you check over the mechanics, grammar, and style of your paper. These stages often overlap, and each writer will have a unique way of personalizing his or her writing process.

Prewriting Strategies

People who like to be creative usually enjoy this stage of the writing process, while those who have trouble getting started writing will benefit from experimenting with the strategies that are described next. Journal keeping, freewriting, invisible writing, brainstorming, and clustering are all effective prewriting techniques that will help you to discover ideas that you can develop in your writing. Prewriting can also make the writing of later drafts easier because you will have already done some of the thinking for your essay.

Journal keeping Daily writing in a notebook or journal will help you to develop a record of your thoughts and feelings. You might want to start a journal for your writing course in which you record your responses and questions about each of the selections that you have been assigned to read in *Community Matters.* Alternatively, you might want to keep a journal of responses to the most interesting of the Conversation Starters that follow each selection. Select a special notebook for your journal and make a regular time to write. This practice will help to activate your engagement in writing and to build your self-confidence.

Freewriting   A freewriting can start with any idea and usually lasts from 5 to 15 minutes. During these brief writing sessions, it is important to continue to write and not to censor any idea or feeling that comes to your mind. If you seem to run out of thoughts, just write, "I have no more to say" or anything that comes into your mind. After 10 minutes of freewriting, read what you have produced and try to sum up the central idea or feeling of the piece. Then proceed to another freewriting, using the summary statement as a new starting point. Writers often do several freewrites before they finally decide how to focus their thoughts.

Invisible writing   With invisible writing, the writer creates "invisible" words, or words that can't be seen while the writer is working. You can create invisible writing by typing on your computer with the computer screen dimmed. While you are freewriting or invisible writing, do not consciously pay attention to punctuation, grammatical, or spelling errors of any kind; concentrate instead on getting your ideas and feelings down in words.

Brainstorming   Brainstorming, which can be done effectively in groups or individually, involves writing a list of all the words, phrases, ideas, descriptions, thoughts, and questions that come to your mind in response to a topic or an issue. As in freewriting and invisible writing, do not stop to censor, judge, or correct any idea or feeling. The process itself will bring up new ideas and associations. Ideas will build on one another, leading to thoughts that are original and fresh, while creating a list will help you to see relationships between ideas that may have previously seemed unrelated. When your list is complete, go back to find patterns of thought or main ideas that you have uncovered. Bracketing or circling related ideas and details may help you to form an organizational plan for your essay.

Clustering   Clustering or mapping closely reflects the way in which the mind functions in making nonlinear connections between ideas. Combined with brainstorming or freewriting, clustering can also help you to perceive clearer relationships between ideas. Start your cluster by placing the topic to be explored in the center of the page. Draw a circle around it, and then draw lines out from your central circle in different directions to connect it with other circles containing additional ideas, phrases, or clues to experiences. The words in these circles will naturally develop their own offshoots as new associations emerge from your mind. The pattern being created by the clustering process continually changes in complex ways because each new idea may relate to all the ideas already recorded. As in freewriting or invisible writing, clustering should be done without stopping. Once the cluster seems completed, write for a few minutes about what you have discovered through your clustering. Finishing a cluster and a related freewrite can help you to understand how you want to focus your topic and help you to organize relationships between ideas, examples, and details.

Drafting

Writing a draft has been compared to meeting someone for the first time. Just as it takes time to get to know a person, you also have to get to know your thoughts as you express them in your own written words and read them on a piece of paper or a computer screen. You will need to figure out what you want to say as you go along, to be responsive to your own words. Like developing a friendship, drafting is a creative and sometimes unpredictable process that really demands that you be flexible.

You may have been taught the traditional thesis support method of developing an essay. In outline form, this type of essay begins with an introductory paragraph that invites the reader into the topic and ends with the essay's thesis statement. The following body paragraphs each support a main idea and are developed through evidence and example. The final paragraph then presents conclusions about your topic.

In contrast, some writers like to start drafting without an outline. In discovery drafting, a writer just begins writing about his or her concept for a paper. While trying the discovery approach, you may find that you have stated the thesis in the second or third or even the concluding paragraph. When this occurs, as it often does, don't be concerned. You will just need to work with that thesis as a part of the opening paragraph in the next draft of your essay. Once you accept that you will discover meaning in your writing through drafting and redrafting, you can work to shape an essay that has an organic coherent unity and intuitive strength.

Don't censor your ideas   Whether you write from an outline or prefer the discovery approach to finding your purpose, your voice, and a thesis, you must concentrate deeply as you write. Do not stop to edit or censor your ideas. Simply try to keep your thoughts flowing during the time you've set aside for composing the first draft. If you can focus and concentrate as you draft, your mind will be able to bring together the many insights that came to you while you were thinking about your topic and gathering the materials. Drafting will help you to discover new relationships and new ideas.

Step back after your first draft   Once you have finished getting all of your thoughts down for the first draft, put your paper aside and take a break. You will need time away from your paper to develop some perspective on what you are trying to express. While you are relaxing or working on another activity, your creative self will have the chance to renew itself;

your unconscious mind may solve a problem that you are having with your writing. Your rational mind will have time to think about what you've already said and what you may still want to say.

Revising

As in drafting, it is best to revise in stages. When you look over your first draft, it might strike you as messy and confusing. If in a moment of frustration you feel like trashing it, don't! First drafts are typically messy. Read over your draft slowly to get a sense of how effectively the ideas work together. While much of the writing in your first draft will be strong, relevant, and focused on your purpose and for your audience, you may need to cross out sections that wander from your paper's subject or passages where you seem to be repeating yourself, including irrelevant information, or expressing yourself awkwardly.

Developing your ideas Sometimes writing helps us discover a new idea or ideas. Now you may also need to develop the new ideas that emerged as you wrote your draft. Be sure to develop your new ideas with strong support. Check that all of your main ideas are carefully developed with relevant evidence and examples.

Outlining your first draft After you have read over your first draft and thought about the changes that you want to make, create an outline of your paper that includes your thesis, main ideas, and supporting evidence and examples. Writing this outline will help you to check if you really are staying focused on the thesis and if you are making your ideas and organization clear for your readers. You may have to make changes: additions and deletions or transitions and rearrangements. Working at this point with a more formal outline can help you to clarify and tighten the structure of your paper.

Considering the essay as a whole Check that your paper has a clear and focused sense of purpose and audience and that your thesis is clearly stated. Then check that each paragraph has a main idea that is supported through evidence and examples. Next make sure that your transitions and logic are clear: that your reader understands why and how you are moving from one main idea to the next main idea, from one paragraph to the next. Finally, ask yourself if your introduction is engaging and if your conclusion ties the ideas together and keeps your reader thinking.

A special note on writing your introduction While it is certainly sensible to think that you should begin at the beginning, and of course you must, don't let yourself get blocked there, trying to compose a perfect introduction before continuing on. Know that many professional writers and student writers delete their opening paragraph after finishing their first or second draft because writing a good first paragraph requires that the writer have a clear sense of purpose. Many writers need to write more than one draft before clarifying their purpose. As an experiment you might try writing several introductions. This may help you to figure out your purpose and relieve the pressure and awkwardness of beginning. One of these experimental first paragraphs might even work as a conclusion.

Looking closely at your paragraphs   Now it is time to think more specifically about the form and structure of your paragraphs. Each paragraph signifies a turn or shift of ideas in your paper. Your paragraphs will probably arrive at a certain average length, depending on the overall length of your essay. While strong central ideas and organizational strategies will help to give your paragraphs a sense of larger purpose and a general feeling of unity, transitional expressions and the repetition of key words, images, and expressions will alert your readers to how your thinking is developing, both from sentence to sentence and from paragraph to paragraph. Transitional expressions include "for example," "in contrast to," "as a result," "the next step," "however," "therefore," and "nevertheless." Transitions need not include these words but must connect the concepts of the two adjacent sentences or paragraphs.

Editing for Style

Editing in the early stages of your writing process can be distracting and discouraging. Editing is best left for last. Remember that editing is not just a matter of correctness—editing for style is also an essential part of the "logos" and "ethos" of your paper, as well as a crucial aspect of "pathos," the impression your essay makes on the audience.

Punctuation   While punctuation is a matter of learning the correct rules for commas, semicolons, apostrophes, and parentheses, punctuation is a reflection of your voice and style. A period, for instance, expresses finality, a complete ending. If you want to imply that ideas are related or that one thought continues on, parallel to or simultaneous with another, you might use a comma with a coordinating conjunction to join two sentences: "We waited all night for his answer, and as we waited we glanced nervously at the telephone every few minutes." Conversely, joining ideas together with a semicolon implies a relationship between sentences that is less final than a period but more formal than that provided by a comma: "We waited nervously for hours; however, the mayor did not return our call." Refer to a punctuation handbook or an online punctuation web site if you need to review the rules of punctuation. Think about how you can use punctuation marks in various ways to help you express your ideas and to develop your own writing style.

Thinking about words   When you revise the individual words and phrases of your text, you are working with language in its most basic form. Again, many students are concerned about correctness in their use of language: correct meaning, spelling, and appropriate "level" of diction for audience and occasion. All of these matters are important aspects of revision and proofreading, but also remember that language is what brings your writing to life. Try to find words that will help to make your paper engaging and lively. Try experimenting with word choices, or refer to a thesaurus and a dictionary for help. Think about the type of diction that would be best understood and appreciated by your particular audience. If your intended audience is a group of students, for instance, the level of formality of diction would be different from the choices you would make if you were writing for your professor.

The Class As a Writing Community

Begin to think about your writing classroom as a community. The students in your class are a natural audience for your writing. Through responding to one another's writing, you will learn how to express and clarify the purpose of your writing. *Community Matters* assumes that the writing classroom is a place where democracy should prevail, a place where all opinions should be considered. While this assumption is idealistic, we believe that it is worth striving toward.

A writing group functions best when members can trust one another to be informative, honest, and supportive. You can begin to develop that trust as you listen to and learn from how the others in your writing group respond to what you write and, in turn, as you respond to what they write. In the first weeks of your class, simply sharing your writing with the members of your writing group will help you to develop your self-confidence. In time you will come to value your peer sharing sessions and to welcome the responses and suggestions that your classmates have for you.

An analogy between dancing and writing may be helpful here. Writing, like dancing, is an expressive and persuasive art form created for an audience. Every writing student, like every dancer, must learn to overcome some of his or her feelings of self-consciousness and/or performance anxiety. While dancers often practice together, as do musical groups like rock bands or symphony orchestras, writing students are probably less familiar with the notion of working as a community of readers and writers. Still, when you are learning to write, *community does matter.* Having a group that you practice with, like the friends one might have in a dance class or in a musical group, will help you express and shape what you may know inside yourself but may have some trouble expressing and communicating in written words. As you learn to listen and to trust your writing group's responses to your writing, you can learn how to write more clearly and effectively. You also will learn when not to listen because some responses will be at odds with your purpose and intent. Nevertheless, this is also a crucial part of becoming a writer. Professional writers usually read critiques of their work and need to think about when the responses are useful and when they are not. You can disagree with someone's interpretation of your work without making it a personal issue.

Once the members of your writing group feel comfortable sharing essays with one another, you can move on to develop specific criteria for responding to one another's writing. Analyzing and evaluating the content and style of student writing is a more traditional approach to collaborative learning in a writing group. In doing such an analysis, remember what we said earlier about the importance of being supportive, of listening, and of the difficulty arriving at a group consensus due to the uniqueness and subjectivity of every reader's responses to readings. Again remember that the primary goal of analyzing and evaluating student drafts is improvement and not perfection. In almost every case you will be reading works in progress, drafts that will benefit from supportive and constructive advice. You can use the following worksheet on your own or with the students in your writing group. Working through multiple drafts of your papers will help you to improve your writing.

Guidelines for Peer Writing Groups

Impression and Initial Response

What were you thinking and feeling when you read or heard the paper for the first time?

Did the paper interest, inform, persuade, or inspire you?

What is your overall response to this paper?

Subject, Purpose, and Audience

What is the paper about?

Is the paper focused on its topic?

What is the paper's purpose?

Who is the audience for the paper?

Content

What is the paper's thesis?

What are the main supporting ideas?

Is each supporting idea developed through evidence and examples?

Organization

What organizational strategies are used: description, comparison, narration, cause and effect, argument, definition, textual analysis?

Are the ideas developed in a logical sequence?

What is the overall order of ideas (from simple to complex, time sequence, spatial sequence, order of importance)?

How does the writer move from paragraph to paragraph and from idea to idea?

Does the writer use helpful transitions?

Voice, Tone, and Stance

Does the writer project a sense of commitment to his or her ideas? How and where?

Does the writer try to engage your interest in the paper? How and where?

What is the writer's attitude and tone toward his or her material?

Style and Language

How would you describe the word choice in the paper: objective, general, specific and detailed, formal, informal, expressive, poetic, jargon, slang?

How would you describe the sentence structures: simple, short, long, varied, emphatic?

Does the writer use images: similes, metaphors, or analogies?

Are ideas expressed concisely? Can you identify passages that seem wordy? Are ideas repeated?

Overall Impressions

What did you like most about the paper?

What are the paper's primary strengths?

What support and advice do you have for the writer?

Developing your own writing process   Finished writing has been shaped in stages. This is one practical truth that you can always return to as you continue to strengthen your abilities as a writer. The ease and clarity of good writing always reflects the hard work that went into creating a sense of forceful, fluid, or elegant expression. Developing a writing process will help you acknowledge and apply what you are learning about how you write and will help you to integrate the insights of your conscious and unconscious mind. Keeping a writing process journal will help you to develop a writing ritual that suits your personality and work style. Each piece that you write will present different challenges. Try experimenting with your writing process when that feels comfortable and think about how you answer the questions listed on the next page.

Writing Process Journal: Questions to Ask Yourself

What was the relationship between the thinking you did for your essay and the way you wrote your essay?

Did you experience writer's block? When? Why?

What aspects of writing are most difficult for you?

Did you begin with an outline? Did you just start writing?

How much time did you give yourself to revise your essay before it was due?

If you read your paper to other students in your class or to friends, why was that helpful?

How many times did you revise your draft? What strategies did you use in each revision?

What did you learn about your skills as a writer from completing this essay? How will you approach writing your next essay differently?

After completing each essay we suggest that you write a one-page summary that describes your particular writing process as well as your insights about your learning process. Your instructor may want you to include this summary with the final draft of your essay.

The student example by Melissa Burns, "The Best Seat in the House," is followed by a description and analysis of her writing process.

Melissa Burns   Burns 1

Melissa Burns wrote "The Best Seat in the House" the summer before her sophomore year at college. While Melissa enjoys writing, she has declared a double major in economics and psychology. Volunteering and helping other students is important to Melissa. She is a peer academic advisor to six freshmen, volunteers to work with teen women who are interested in developing their understanding of how to become entrepreneurs, and is in charge of selecting and inviting speakers to share their views on timely issues related to the theme of her "global affairs" dorm.

"The Best Seat in the House"

On my dormitory bookshelf sits a beautiful medium-oak box, approximately six inches long by three inches wide and high. Its four sides, each with two triangular end-

Burns 2

pieces, are masterfully flush; they fit together so as to unfold completely into a flattened, moss green felt-lined surface, like scales on a dinosaur. Well-placed brass hinges and tight fittings guarantee a smooth alignment when the box is latched shut. The top panel was stamped with a hot-iron oval and just barely reads "PATENTED 1889 FEBRUARY." I have been told that my grandfather, Poppy, constructed this treasure from a kit. My mother, a young girl at the time, remembers her father meticulously gluing the velvet upholstery fabric, now faded and fraying, to the box's interior. For decades, it sat undisturbed on Poppy's dresser, the keeper of his rarely worn cufflinks. When Poppy passed away, my grandmother handed the box to my mother, who subsequently placed it into my hands. It is a memory of the grandfather I never knew, a man who loved me with all his heart. Today, this distinguished and cherished oak box is known as the "reed graveyard." It is the place where good bassoon reeds go to die. Poppy was a master craftsman, a WWII statistical officer in Italy, a peacemaker, a member of a bombardier squadron in the European Theater, a looker, a fighter pilot, a gentleman, a joke-teller. He traveled the globe, swam Lake Erie from Buffalo to Toronto, and constructed ornate and precision grandfather clocks, among countless other works of art. Poppy fixed all things broken—electrical appliances, furniture, hearts. He was a gentle German giant: six foot four and slender, with an olive complexion and dark but graying hair. He wore a wicked grin, as if to forewarn all whom he met of his mischievous pranks, funny sayings, and unique brand of sarcasm. My grandfather awoke one freezing morning, concerned that the razor-sharp icicles dangling from the awning of his Amherst, New York, home might injure his family and friends. Instead, it was Poppy himself who succumbed to nature's wrath. While diligently chipping away at the deadly spikes, he suffered a massive coronary heart attack, dying immediately and painlessly. There were no good-byes. Poppy left my physical world on January 10, 1986, just four days after his seventy-second birthday. I was two and a half years old.

My mother shows me countless photographs of her father and me. At times, I truly believe that I can conjure the contours of his long, hollowed face and cheeks, or his warm embrace, as we snuggled in a lawn chair in the tall green grass of summertime in upstate New York. On other occasions, I realize that I possess no actual recollection of Poppy; I've simply deceived myself into believing false, picture-induced memories, all the while praying to God that I should someday reunite with my grandfather. Poppy is gone from the earth, but not from my soul. I embrace him through stories, maxims, and possessions. Over the years, I have learned to take comfort in his status as my Guardian Angel, protecting and sheltering me from the atrocities of this world. Matt, my older brother and only sibling, bears an eerily striking resemblance to Poppy—he shares the height, the charm, the gait, and most of all, that devilish, cockeyed smile. Growing up, however, it was I who captured my grandfather's precious attention. Poppy was well known to occupy our living room rocking chair, listening anxiously for the soft cries signaling that I had awoken from an afternoon nap. He would race upstairs, sweep me from my crib, and hold me soothingly against his broad chest. That was our special time together, my only grandfather and me.

When I was in a playful, alert mood, Poppy would lay me down on the family room floor and conduct a series of "tests." Very much the mathematician, calculating the release of bombs and their ensuing catastrophic destruction, Poppy transformed his wartime accuracy into tender, delicate, and methodical child rearing. He concealed my toys behind his back—Would I perceive their continued existence? He raided the kitchen for pots and pans and walked circles around the room, clanging them loudly in different locations while watching my tiny head move frantically from side to side. I have a vivid mental image of a photograph in which Poppy has placed colorful plastic rings around my arms to gauge my strength. Poppy's premature testing was often dismissed as playtime nonsense by the rest of the family, yet he was seriously equipping his only granddaughter with the resources necessary to grow up strong, healthy, autonomous, resourceful, smart, and intuitive. Poppy was preparing my two-year-old self for a life of terrific struggles and achievements, failures and triumphs. He took great pride in his beautiful baby granddaughter, but he never felt the satisfaction or the joy of witnessing her metamorphosis into a little girl, a teenager, and now, a woman—a woman with a talent of which Poppy was entirely unaware.

Burns 4

I began to play the bassoon—an extremely difficult and intricate double reed instrument, the lowest in the woodwind family—at the unprecedented age of ten. My decision to play this instrument was prompted by words of encouragement from family friends who recognized my musical aptitude for the piano, as well as the great orchestral demand for young bassoonists. As I now realize, this musical decision was to become perhaps the most consequential, life-altering choice of my entire life. My bassoon journeys have carried me from Williams College to New York City to Germany to Prague, and most recently, to Stanford University. Through my musical sojourn, I have experienced the world's most amazing sights and sounds while interacting with extraordinarily talented, brilliant, kindhearted members of society.

My story begins with a stroke of luck. I established contact with a renowned bassoon performer and instructor named Stephen Walt, a Williams College teacher in high demand, who had never before considered working with a beginning pupil. Instantaneously, I could tell that our personalities were well-suited, and the rest, as they say, is history: he became my one and only bassoon coach for the seven years I studied bassoon until moving to California. Mr. Walt is an inspiration, a musical virtuoso, and the most warm, encouraging, all-the-while demanding instructor I can possibly imagine. My success as a musician is due in great part to his absolute dedication and guidance. Every other weekend, my father drove me from Niskayuna, New York, to Williamstown, Massachusetts. Mr. Walt's lessons were worth every second of the hour-and-twenty-minute car ride along often slippery, snow-covered mountain roads.

As my years of dedication and hours of practice slowly accumulated, I steadily increased my skill level, becoming a proficient high school bassoonist. The summer before my sophomore year, I auditioned for, and gained acceptance to, one of America's premier youth orchestras, the Empire State Youth Orchestra. I was initially intimidated by the phenomenally talented musicians surrounding me in the orchestra; before long, however, lengthy bus rides together, nights spent in hotels in foreign countries, and a sense of mutual admiration, created an atmosphere in which these musicians became several of my closest lifelong friends. I will never forget the day our revered and beloved conductor,

Francisco Noya, secured his imposing stance on the podium before us and announced in a thick Venezuelan accent, "Are you prepared to work extremely hard? 'Jes or no? 'Dis year, we play Carnegie Hall." I momentarily lost my grip on reality. Life for an orchestral musician does not reach a zenith more meaningful, more overwhelming, or more spectacular than the opportunity to perform at *Carnegie Hall.*

For months, the notion of my orchestra's concert at Carnegie Hall interrupted my every waking thought. When I wasn't practicing the musical selections, my hands rehearsed complicated fingering passages, I imagined the sights and the sounds of the hall, and I stared at my monthly planner, scratching off each slowly passing day. One such day a week or so before the performance, I sat in my practice chair in the den trying to relax my aching mouth muscles, and I turned to my right; there perched the reed graveyard. Every single reed over the years, painstakingly handcrafted from raw cane by Mr. Walt, inevitably found its way to the graveyard when it was worn-down, broken, cracked, weak, decomposing, overused, unreliable, or simply resigned. I unfolded Poppy's box to examine its contents: hundreds of reeds, varying slightly in size, shape, cane discoloration, and string color—red, green, blue, even multihued—stuffed the box's interior. As I carefully lifted the reeds and let them sift through my fingers, each one evoked memories of a particular concert, practice session, summer camp, quintet, lesson, rehearsal, or pit orchestra. To this day, every tiny wooden relic, unique, beautiful, and delicate, tells a different, unforgettable story. The reed graveyard, I realized, is a metaphor for Poppy's undying love; it is representative of his personal contribution to my achievements. My greatest accomplishments, I now understood, were housed in this creation, crafted by his strong but gentle hands. My embouchure feeling revived, I closed the precious box, placed it on the shelf beside me, and resumed my practice.

My dream, from the moment that I began my avocation as a musician, was now materializing. I was standing in the wings of Carnegie Hall, placing my black patent leather shoes where all "the greats" had placed theirs. I peered around the velvet curtain, trembling slightly and sweating profusely. Scanning the sea of faces for a few seconds, I finally located my large cohort of immediate family and close friends. I found them sitting in the upper left-

Burns 6

hand balcony in a private box protruding far from the wall. Matt, rather appropriately, was directly in front and practically falling over the railing, grinning with a true pride that I had never seen before and have not seen since. Poppy, I'm quite certain, was witnessing the entire scene from above. He undoubtedly had the best seat in the house. As Poppy's presence filled the air above my head, he beamed his joy through Matt, the surrogate physical representation for a grandfather who would have loved, more than anyone else, to hug and hold his granddaughter on that emotional afternoon.

From the time I found my seat on the stage until the concert was over, my memories are blurred. I have been told that the show ran its entirety without a single hitch; I, for one, was too nervous, excited, ecstatic, and satisfied, to have known what transpired. Thankfully, my musical bodily functions—lungs, heart, fingers, and muscles—took over for a severely wandering mind. I simply cannot describe the fantastic, awe-inspiring, all-encompassing feeling of earning and achieving one's greatest goal.

I regained mental composure after the last note of our program finished resonating in Carnegie Hall. My attention was called immediately to my support group, cheering and clapping above the roar. Beneath it all was the underlying essence of my grandfather's love. I breathed a sigh of relief, took my bows, and, bassoon clutched close to my heart, walked off the stage of the world-renowned Carnegie Hall. What happens to the dreamer when her dream becomes a reality? Is a new dream born? I currently attend Stanford University in northern California, a place I consider to be an ideal launching pad for the discovery of fresh and thrilling ambitions. I am searching for my calling, yet again.

As for Poppy, he resides in the heavens, continuing to protect his baby granddaughter as she matures, strong, free, and independent. Late that night of the concert, when I arrived at my home in Niskayuna, I walked into the den and cradled the reed graveyard in my hands. I opened Poppy's box and placed the most absolutely perfect reed I had ever known inside, where it would retire among the masses that had come before. I latched the box shut, as I positioned it in its resting place on the shelf, thus signifying the end to one marvelous chapter of my life. With Poppy at the helm of my cockpit, I flew off in search of uncharted horizons.

Melissa's Writing Process Reflection

Before I could begin to structure my narrative, entitled "The Best Seat in the House," I needed the reed box in my presence, to cradle and unfold in my hands. This source of inspiration was urgent and essential. I phoned my Mom in New York and asked her to gingerly ship the box, or the "reed grave-yard" as I call it, to my college address in California. After all, I had originally decided to leave it at home, knowing full well that the antics in a rowdy dormitory can create an unsafe environment for a cherished, fragile possession.

Once the reed graveyard arrived, I again called home to conduct formal interviews with family members, namely, my mother and grandmother. I was hoping to procure those missing links—the tidbits of information about Poppy's life and our relationship that added flavor and richness to my story. Rather than carry about this process in a casual fashion, I gave my interviewees a clear understanding of my objectives for the interviews. I recommended that they be seated, relaxed, and reflective. Then I asked them questions and jotted detailed notes and quotes.

Next, I thought about the various themes that had emerged during the interviews and in the time I had spent mulling over my private thoughts. I carefully wove the ideas together, attempting not to over- or underemphasize any concept in particular. The piece revolves around, but is certainly not limited to, the following motifs: Poppy's character, his achievements, and his influence on my life; the role of music in my personal development; the accomplishment of my grandest dream; the importance of a loving, supportive family; and the reed graveyard as a metaphor for everything I have just described.

When I sat down at the computer to write, I placed many items before me: the notes I had taken from my interviews, hand-scrawled sentence fragments on scraps of lined paper, old photographs, a program from my Carnegie Hall concert, my Fox 220 bassoon, and, of course, the reed graveyard itself. As a writing habit, I immerse myself in anything that might spark a creative remembrance or thought. Although to others my desk looks like a mess, to me it is truly an organized chaos.

This piece was intended to be a rather short narrative, and I wrote the bulk of it in one afternoon, typing away with little concern for proper grammar, diction, etc. Many athletes, artists, and scholars describe this state of mind as being in "the zone." Once you're there, you don't leave until you've finished. I realized that the small details could wait for later, but the passion, the love, the dream—those elements of the story must flow, uninterrupted by trivial thoughts about how and where to place proper punctuation.

The narrative was overhauled in a lengthy revision process in which I read and reread the paper, start to finish, at least ten times. I am as slow to revise as I am quick to type entire pages of text. By the last revision, I was changing only a single word or sentence each time I perused the entire document. Yet, I now consider those final touches to be just as important as, for example, the decision to omit an entire paragraph. I have always been a perfectionist, and my writing process is no exception to the rule.

Before I submitted my work to Professor Ford, I took the wonderful opportunity to read it aloud to my mother and grandmother. (Reading a document aloud, whether to an audience or to oneself, is an excellent technique. In simply proofreading, my eyes will often glaze across a poorly worded sentence and leave it unchanged; however, when I force myself to speak the words, thus breathing real life into them, there is simply no escaping my own inferior writing.) I wanted input on the piece from those who knew Poppy and me best. My family members provided excellent suggestions and advice, which I promptly incorporated into the final draft.

Lastly, I was left with the unenviable task of choosing a title. Summing up one's personal memoir in a handful of words or a catchy phrase is no simple chore. Many of my initial titles left me feeling that I had failed to capture the essence of the work and the overlapping of numerous motifs. In one last skimming of my narrative, I found exactly what I was searching for; like Poppy himself, the title had simply been there all along.

Writing Strategies

Writers use a variety of strategies to achieve their purposes. The individual writing strategies explained are often used in combination, as you will see in many of the selections included in this reader. We also suggest that you study the annotated student essay by Heidi Meltzer, "Hats Off to Helpers," that follows the list of writing strategies provided below as guidelines. You can also return to Melissa's essay and work with your writing group to identify the different writing strategies that she uses.

Description

Description focuses primarily on the five senses: touch, taste, smell, sight, and sound. When we need to describe a person, place, thing, or even something so seemingly imprecise as an emotion, we can use specific, carefully chosen words to create a series of images, or sensory clusters of detail, which, taken together, convey to our readers an original description of our experiences.

Narration

While we begin to define the world by describing our sensations and experiences, we often tell stories to help explain a fact, feeling, issue, event, idea, or transformation. Storytelling also allows us to reflect on the values of our culture: to define ourselves and our feelings about people. The basic ingredients of a story include plot, character, setting or a sense of place, point of view, and theme. In creating narratives within your essay, you may find that it is not necessary to develop all of the basic narrative ingredients in such great depth as a short-story writer might. Narratives can be used by writers in a variety of ways. Sometimes writers develop an entire essay around a single extended narrative using the drama of their tale to evoke feelings and thoughts.

Example

When your purpose for writing becomes more directed to making points and explaining issues than to conveying and reflecting on experiences, the stories you use will be more concentrated and directed. They will be more like examples than narratives and can serve as a support for a main idea in the essay. Examples are invaluable for helping your readers to understand abstract ideas or complex processes that you are trying to explain. They provide evidence, add clarity, engage the reader's interest, and can help to persuade skeptical readers. Always select an example that is both vivid and representative. You can use an example anywhere in a paper. In the body an example will serve primarily as a strategy for developing main ideas, while in the opening paragraph an example may grab the reader's attention or introduce an issue in a clear and specific context.

Process Analysis

We think about processes all the time. They can be as simple as explaining how to cook a meal or as complex as explaining the theory of evolution. Process analysis is a useful strategy when you want to understand and clarify for others how an event has been shaped or how something operates. In writing a process paragraph or essay, even about a task that you think you have mastered, you may develop insights into your thinking process. For example, you may discover that there are steps in a process that you had previously completed "unconsciously," that you didn't articulate to yourself precisely or formally. To test this idea, try writing directions for a friend who has never visited your community to a place you like to go: your health club, a coffee shop, a record store, the local mall, or a club. Developing an ability to describe a sequence of actions as they need to be carried out by another person will help you to better understand and improve your communication skills. Remember to always anticipate questions that your audience might have and include responses to those questions in your process explanation.

Definition

A definition clarifies the precise meaning of a word by distinguishing it from several similar words. In every type of writing you will need to make careful distinctions among your thoughts, feelings, and the words you use to convey them. Definition analysis will help you to clarify your position and values and to explore your own thoughts and feelings before presenting them in writing.

Most common words have several shades of meaning and association; key terms that you are using can be defined in a variety of ways. If the word you are using is associated with a complex idea, or if you are writing for an audience that expects formal precision, you may want to begin with a formal definition. Formal definition involves classification in that we clarify the word's meaning by placing it within a larger class or group. It also involves contrast in that we differentiate it from other members of the larger group by using details and qualifying language: for example, "Love is an intense emotion involving great concern for and commitment to the person or object of the feeling." Although looking at dictionary meanings is essential, it also is helpful to define a term in relation to your own feelings and values. To clarify your personal understanding of a word, try clustering or brainstorming to explore the associations that you have with it.

Comparison and Contrast

Your mind may organize life experiences through making comparisons. To clarify and better understand different but related issues, you can compare and contrast, exploring the relationships between subjects that, despite apparent distinctions, have qualities in common. While making comparisons is a natural part of our thinking processes, comparative writing requires a balanced structure that is less fluid and more complex than the comparative associations you make all the time in your everyday life. When writing a standard comparison essay, after choosing two subjects to compare and contrast (e.g., two films, two books, two teachers), you will need to decide on three different issues that will focus your comparison and contrast. Make sure that your thesis makes a point about the two items being compared and about why you are using comparison as a strategy.

In preparing an outline for a comparison paper, consider which of the two major types of organization you want to use: the point-by-point approach or the subject-by-subject approach. As the names suggest, you structure the point-by-point paper around points of similarity or difference, whereas in subject-by-subject comparing, you make your points about your two subjects in separate sections of your paper, discussing the two subjects together once again in your conclusion. Either method can work, although the point-by-point method helps you to see the contrasts between the two subjects more immediately.

Classification

Classification analysis can help you make sense of a complex subject that consists of a number of individual items by grouping related items into named classes. You can use classification systems in your writing in many different ways as you develop an essay. It is an essential part of a formal definition, as you must place a subject within a class or group before proceeding to define it thoroughly. In an introduction you can use classification to provide an overview of a broad topic before focusing in on the subject you are planning to develop. We constantly use classification in our daily lives. Do you ever use classification when reorganizing your books, your types of appointments or errands, your clothes, or your CD collection?

Cause and Effect

Finding connections that exist between one event and another event, understanding how one event led to or produced another event, and speculating about the consequences of earlier events—all involve causal reasoning. People naturally search for solutions to legal, physical, financial, political, and social problems, wanting to be able to explain why something occurred and how they can improve the situation. Always try to observe carefully and consider all possible causes, not simply the obvious and immediate ones, and then provide adequate evidence, of both a factual and a logical nature, for the conclusions that you draw. While you may understand the causes involved quite clearly, perceiving these connections for yourself is not enough; your writing needs to explain for your reader the causal relationships that you made in order to arrive at your conclusions.

Annotated Example of Writing Strategies

Heidi Metzler's "Hats Off to Helpers," written for a college writing class that emphasized community writing, has been anthologized in a volume of service learning essays entitled *Small Miracles,* published by Chandler Community College in Chandler, Arizona.

Heidi Metzler   Metzler 1

Hats Off to Helpers!

attention-grabbing sentence citing authority

    "Blessed are those who can give without remembering and take without forgetting," writes Elisabeth Bibesco in a "daily thoughts" calendar I display on my bathroom vanity. What a great thought to start and end each day with! I had a very challenging situation two years ago that prepared me to give my time to a volunteer organization, Parents Anonymous, for which I now facilitate classes once each week for their "Nurturing Program."

narrative

    In 1994, I moved to Arizona and was trying to start my daycare business, and I wasn't financially capable of being

example

choosy about the ages and attitudes of the children I would take. One of the first women I met in my neighborhood was just beginning her recovery path from alcoholism and

---

Metzler 2

needed help watching her three untamed and hyperactive children. Another neighbor sent me two children, one of whom had hyperactive problems. Another neighbor sent me three children; the hyperactive one earned them an eviction. At one point, I felt more like a health nurse administering their medication than a daycare provider. Since then, I have spent some time trying to learn more about attention deficit disorder and providing loving advice to others who don't understand how to parent these difficult children.

In February 1997, I had the unique opportunity to choose Parents Anonymous as an organization to do my service learning project at CGCC (Chandler Gilbert Community College). This was an excellent opportunity to see families seeking guidance for parenting skills while I worked on my research involving the challenges of parenthood.

Before I ever had a chance to work with parents or children, I attended two training sessions and submitted references and fingerprints. I felt flattered to be chosen by an organization that cares so much about the message they teach AND the welfare of the people they teach. I was given the title "team leader" and assigned to duties of setting up the snacks and beverages for the evening, checking the classrooms, and being available to co-facilitate any classes with absent instructors. The "Nurturing Program" provides classes with corresponding curriculum for children ages 5–12 and also provides nursery care for children ages 0–4. We had the opportunity to involve ourselves with one family in a difficult situation. They live in a one-bedroom trailer; the mother (approximate age 35) is currently learning to read; they live with a grandparent and four very needy, hyperactive children, all of whom have special learning needs. By the fourth week of the program, the instructors were complaining about having to deal with these particular children and were frustrated with not being able to follow their normal curriculum. I had observed all the children's classes and was aware which of their children were the most incapable of cooperating in a standard classroom setting, so I suggested that we pull those children out and hold a customized class for their learning capabilities. Some of the instructors thought it was too generous to give them individual attention, and so you can guess which person got volunteered for that job!

Timothy and Sharon are two beautiful and bright children. I was not aware that Sharon could not talk—she's eight

example

comparison

narrative

definition

narrative

Metzler 3

narrative examples

years old. Timothy is constantly hitting and climbing—he's six years old. I invited my ten-year-old daughter to come to class with me, so she could help guide me with games that were fun to play. Now every week, we start our class period

process analysis

with a game that I know they will enjoy, and while they are sitting still and talking (which they both know how to do), I start my praise for how well they are doing at their game. After we've had a chance to warm up a little, I start talking to them about the subject matter that is in the curriculum and just use it in normal conversation. I allow the kids to demonstrate their new subject knowledge on the marker board, and we talk about how they feel about the things they are learning. This is something I call "stand-up learning."

comparison

These children, like the ones who tore my house apart two years ago, are simply not capable of sitting down and holding their attention; however, they are just as deserving

summary of main points

of being told "Good job," "You did wonderful!" and "That is so cool." With a clear understanding of what our purpose is as an organization, what the specific needs of the children are, and what lengths I was willing to go to, I feel that I've possibly been a good role model for future volunteers, and hopefully a good example for the children. I am more convinced every day that there is no standard for "normal," and that common sense and consistent dedication are the keys to raising great children. I hope that my own children grow to be the children-lovers, and that if they have special needs in social settings, that someone will see clearly to provide the means to that goal. I loved my volunteer expe-

concluding sentence looking to the future

rience and plan to work with Parents Anonymous. I feel it is a joy to work with kids and hope that it molds me for my career goals in secondary education.

Argument

The main purpose of a piece of writing is often persuasion. Although you can use a variety of strategies and argument patterns to convince your audience, traditional argument begins by defining a problem or issue and then taking a position on that issue. In this form of argument the advocate proceeds to develop a clear thesis and to demonstrate its validity through a series of convincing logical arguments, factual supports, and references to authority. One basic strategy for writing an argument essay is to end the first paragraph of your essay with a thesis statement that puts the opponent's point of view in the dependent clause and your point of view in the independent clause. The second paragraph would then acknowledge your opponent's point of view and begin to refute it. Subsequent paragraphs then will argue your point of view. The value and advantage in this model is that you must acknowledge and consider your opponent's point of view in the opening of your essay. Many of us want to write argument essays without mentioning the opponent's point of view, but this approach is less effective since the people you want to persuade are those who disagree with you. Without acknowledging their point of view, you may not get them to even listen to your point of view, let alone persuade them.

Working to understand these "opposite" positions does not necessarily imply that you totally accept them, or that you abandon your own ideas and viewpoint. What it does suggest is that you are beginning to consider the possibilities of strong arguments, positions, and value systems that are different from your own, and that you are making a real attempt to integrate these positions into your thinking.

Before you begin to write an argument, try to establish a dialogue with your imaginary audience. Try to determine the interests and values of your audience. Creating a clear "mental image" of your audience is essential before appropriate arguments can be selected. (You might want to refer to the "Audience Checklist" on p. 19–20.) Once you have a clear image of the audience in mind, approach your readers directly and respectfully. Make your audience's concerns an integral part of your arguments; do not try to manipulate or dazzle them with your facts and figures. Instead, establish a common ground with your audience, stating the positions you hold in common with them while designating areas of mutual disagreement or possible compromise. This approach will remind you to keep your audience's point of view in mind and will facilitate meaningful communication.

Defining key terms   It is essential to define your key terms. Definitions support clear communication and help develop rapport in an argument. People feel more comfortable in a discussion when they understand what key terms refer to and mean.

Evaluating "facts"   If you have taken a statistics course or read articles in journals, you already know that facts and statistics can be interpreted in a variety of ways. In reading the factual studies that will form an important part of the support in any argument paper, you need to consider a number of questions. Have the results of the social scientists or psychologists you are studying been confirmed by other researchers? Are the data current? Were they collected by qualified researchers using thorough and objective methods? Are they expressed in clear and unambiguous language? These and other questions should be asked about your sources of information so that you can create a sound factual base for the arguments you use in your paper.

In doing research for your argument, you might read through a variety of web sites to get an idea of some of the strong sentiments that different groups have about your issue—but don't rely on these partisan, advocacy sites to provide objective information. On the other hand, you do need to mention both widely believed facts and popular misconceptions that may oppose the argument you are making. While remaining respectful of your audience's values, you will need to show them how some of these beliefs are not based on factual evidence, how others are not relevant, and concede that some are relevant and either can be dealt with by your proposed argument, or cannot but that you are arguing about the practical limits of the situation at hand. Present your factual supports clearly; avoid overstating your conclusions in absolute, unqualified terms or generalizing from limited data.

Feelings in argument   Emotions play such a significant role in our lives that any argument that tried to be altogether rational, pretending that emotional concerns are unimportant and that only "facts" count, would be unrealistic and uninteresting. Emotions, both your own and those of your audience, are a central concern in argument. Although you need to present your ideas in ways that won't offend your readers, feelings are often a central issue in the argument itself. Remember that on subjects as emotionally charged as abortion, it may be difficult to offer new arguments or to change readers' minds. Indeed, some teachers may insist that you do not try to make an argument when there is not a common ground between the audience and the writer. If you want to try to establish a common ground, however, it would be impossible to discuss a subject such as abortion without acknowledging your own feelings and those of the audience relative to issues as emotionally involving as the life of a fetus. In this case, sharing such feelings will help to create an open and trusting relationship with your audience.

However, an important distinction must be made between acknowledging feelings and exploiting them to manipulate your readers. Often, strong arguments are based on emotions, which can be exaggerated in an attempt to strengthen a position and may cause you to overlook important issues. Avoid language that could ignite the emotional climate in a discussion. Bringing in irrelevant appeals for pity or fear can obscure the real issues involved in a discussion. Try to use language that is objective or neutral in describing the positions and ideas taken by your opposition. By doing so, you are more likely to keep the confidence of readers who might otherwise be offended by an adversarial position and manipulative language.

Causal logical fallacies   People create connections between events or personal issues about which they feel strongly, often rushing their thinking process to a hasty conclusion. One of the most common causal errors, **the post hoc fallacy** ("after this, therefore because of this"), mistakenly attempts to create a causal connection between unrelated events that follow each other closely in time. But a sequence in time is not at all the same thing as a causal sequence. In fact, much "magical" or superstitious thinking is based on faulty causal analysis of sequences in time. For instance, people may carry a burden of guilt because of accidental sequential parallels between their inner thoughts and outer events, such as a dream of the death of a loved one and a subsequent death or accident.

Another common causal thinking and writing problem is **causal over-simplification.** A person who argues that one thing caused something to happen, when in fact a number of different elements worked together to produce a major effect or outcome, is thinking illogically. An example of oversimplification would be if a local community leader argued that students' poor math scores were soley the result of incompetent teachers. When trying to apply a broad theory to explain many individual cases, thinkers often become involved in causal oversimplification. Asking about other possible causal relations not covered by a causal thesis will help you to test the soundness of your analysis.

The **"slippery slope" fallacy** is also of particular relevance to the issues explored in this text. In the slippery slope fallacy, a reasoned analysis of causes and effects is replaced by a reaction of fear, in which a person might argue that if one seemingly insignificant event is allowed to happen, there will be serious consequences. Of course, in some cases this may be true: If one isn't careful about sexually transmitted diseases, there is the possibility that a person may get AIDS and eventually die. In most cases, however, theorizing about dreadful future events can become a way of validating irrational fears or providing an excuse for maintaining the status quo. Recognizing the slippery slope fallacies both in others' thinking and within one's own thinking can help you to free yourself from irrational fears and develop better critical thinking skills.

Good causal reasoning can lead you closer to understanding and developing theories and explanations for the multiple causes and effects of the issues and events you encounter in your reading and in your community. With an awareness of the complexities of causal thinking, you will be able to think and to write more critically, clearly, and persuasively.

Guidelines for Formulating an Argument

Develop a dialogue in journal form that explores the different positions on your issue.

Investigate an issue that can be explored thoroughly in the number of pages that you have been asked to write.

Identify your audience using the checklist in this chapter; try to acknowledge the assumptions and needs of your audience.

Define key terms.

Include a balanced range of sources from facts and statistics to authority, to personal experience and example.

Be honest and direct in your treatment of the emotional aspects of an issue.

Avoid logical fallacies.

Annotated example of argument essay

Hazel Clarke wrote "Volunteering," her first-year composition course at Foothill College in northern California.

Hazel Clarke   Clarke 1

Volunteering

personal example

    In the seventh grade, my class heard a presentation about volunteering and service to the community and the world. I can vividly recall listening intently to the soft voice of a young lady speaking about her experience working with the Peace Corps. I remember thinking how wonderful the lady was, and how I was going to join the Corps myself when I was older. I thought I could really make a difference; however, the years passed by, and so did my innocent dream. In fact, I haven't remembered this experience until now, as I write this essay. I look back and long for the determination and will I once had as a kid to help those in need; yet my priorities have changed, and I have to admit that joining the Peace Corps, a goal once so high on my list, no longer exists as my life ambition.

examples

    Although I haven't gone to other countries to help people, in high school I participated in a number of service-related activities. Many of these projects were required for classes I was taking, but there have been a number of outings to soup kitchens and to Agnews State Hospital that I volunteered to go on. What I discovered was that most of the time there aren't enough people available to help the needy. It annoys me when I hear people say what a great job these volunteers are doing and how they are so helpful to the community. I feel as though those who pat volunteers on the shoulder should go out and do something themselves for people in need.

argument thesis

refutation

    People say they can't volunteer because of their tight schedules; work, kids, school, or after-school activities all seem to conflict with lending a hand, and serving food to the homeless or visiting the elderly is just too time-consuming. These excuses are just that: excuses. If you really want to help out your community, you can find the time. In many cases, people are afraid of what they don't know. Everyone expects other people to feed the hungry and help the sick,

Clarke 2

but each person needs to begin with himself or herself. It is the responsibility of the individual to stop watching others and start acting, and it all begins with letting go of the fear of becoming involved.

example

An example of a group that has made a strong commitment to volunteering is the Truck of Love, a group of adults and teens who pack their minimum essentials and drive to Tijuana, Mexico, to continue their service to poor families every month or so. This group is led by Pete and Sue Fullerton, who joined the organization twenty-seven years ago. This group of giving people not only make trips to Mexico to help build houses and educate children, but also travel to reservations in Arizona. Sue, who also works in the Campus Ministry Department at St. Francis High School, is a prime example of just how all of us should strive to be: "If everyone in the world helped just one person, life would be so much better," Sue states. She has seen firsthand the power that just one person can have, and believes that the ability to create a loving and caring environment is within each one of us.

citing authority

causal reasoning

People seem to be afraid of the poverty-stricken because they don't appear to be like us. They lead entirely different lifestyles, whether it be living on the streets with an alley as their home, or sleeping in a dirty, thatch-roofed room with no glass windows. This is a huge part of our fear of becoming involved in the lives of the underprivileged. Sue has seen and known people such as these, and she says a remarkably interesting and sensible thing: "People are all the same, anywhere you go. It's just circumstances that makes us seem different." Once we learn to see others as part of us, we can begin to break the barrier of fear, and we can grasp the strength that each of us has to help those in need. Some form of tragedy has befallen every one of us at one time, yet we are still here today. We had the capability of picking ourselves up and standing up again, so taking the step as individuals to begin to serve the community should be easy. If you can look deep within yourself to realize how strong you are alone, then it should be obvious as to how great you can be with others by your side.

citing authority

causal solution

persuasive appeal

In his inaugural address in 1963, JFK stated that he felt that the power and strength each individual has is tremendous: "For man holds in his mortal hands the power to

citing authority

Clarke 3

abolish all forms of human poverty, and all forms of human life"(89). We can go either way: We can help our community, or we can choose to ignore our call to service and leave the responsibility for others. However, only one route will give our lives a sense of fulfillment, and only that route will make our world stronger, healthier, and more productive. We can destroy life not by committing murder, but by simply standing back, being passive, watching the hunger and the poverty, and then turning the other way.

In her essay "Christmas at Home," P. W. Alexander describes her lifelong commitment to helping the needy: "I work at the homeless shelter and I stand in the serving line and ladle soup and gravy. I shake hands with people who don't bathe and I have on occasion hugged people with dried vomit on their clothing. . . . If you ask me why I do it, I can only say, because I have so much" (101). P. W. Alexander describes a vivid, almost grotesque picture of what she deals with in helping the homeless. I can admit that I have witnessed people in states such as these, but honestly, after a while you get used to the bad odors, the dirty faces, and the crusted clothes. You begin to see the needy for what they actually are: people like you and me. When I began volunteering, I was afraid of the outward differences, of what I did not know and could not understand. Now I am grateful I had to go to help in a soup kitchen as a class project, because I honestly don't think I could have voluntarily offered my services without any support from others. However, I do believe that if I was not required to go, yet if I knew that I was not alone in being afraid about taking on the experience, I would have gone to help anyway. I hope that today there is enough support so that individuals can take the first step toward learning how to help the community.

In certain situations, we tend to surprise ourselves with the actions we take; yet when we come to realize that we can handle the unexpected, life becomes more worthwhile. In the book and movie, *The Power of One*, the protagonist, P. K., takes it upon himself to help his community by teaching black people how to read. This was controversial and dangerous, and he was threatened not to continue with the lessons, but he remained strong and held his ground because, as Truck of Love's Sue Fullerton says, "Education is a huge key for people in

causal reasoning

persuasive appeal

citing authority

concession

contrast

solution

literary example

Clarke 4

poverty." P. K. believed he was doing the right thing, and this was a great help to the community. He pushed aside his fears and let his determination rule. This is exactly

rhetorical question

what each individual needs to do. Otherwise, what is the point of living and taking from a community, when you give nothing in return?

We are blessed with the fact that we are able to learn every day and that no one can stop us; nevertheless, we need to pass on our knowledge so that others can benefit from it. We need to take the time out of our busy lives to help those who need food, shelter, education, and love. Just as John F. Kennedy said, we have the power within us to change the world. We have the strength to overcome the fears and doubts, as did P. K. The compassion for other human beings lies within everyone, and the stereotypes can be broken. P. W. Alexander broke her stereotypes and became able at last to see all types of people for what they really are, not for what they appear to be. Life can be so ful-filling and meaningful if we just take time out from every-

rebuttal & clarification of position

day schedules to help others. No one is asking us to take a vow of poverty or to pack up all our belongings and move to India to work with the Peace Corps; however, a visit to a retirement home would make a lot of people smile, while a helping hand at a homeless shelter would bring a bit of comfort to those who are in need. It won't happen by just thinking about it and letting someone else do the work. Let-ting go of our fears and facing reality and the unfamiliar can be a rewarding experience if we just take the chance. When asked what would be the one thing she would tell others about doing community service, Sue smiled and said just a few simple words that will always stick in my mind when-

persuasive quotation

ever I have doubts about helping those in need: "Don't be afraid to say yes." There are endless possibilities and oppor-tunities when we open up our hearts and help someone

clincher sentence

else. All a person has to do is to begin by saying, "Yes!"

RELEVANT WEB SITES

ENGLISH USAGE, STYLE AND COMPOSITION <http://www.bartleby.com/usage/>

A collection of reference works at Bartleby.com, including *American Heritage,* Strunk and White, Fowler's *King's English.*

WRITERS WRITE <http://www.writerswrite.com/>

A writer's guide to online publications, weekly writing and publishing news, message boards, and job listings.

REJECTION COLLECTION <http://www.rejectioncollection.com/>

An online collection of rejection letters submitted by artists and writers.

POETS AND WRITERS ONLINE <http://www.pw.org/>

An online publication for creative writers, including articles, advice, forums, and contest listings.

Research Writing

3

Researching a topic for a writing project can be a creative learning experience filled with new and worthwhile challenges. It is always best to research a topic that interests you because your curiosity can serve as a motivation. In every case, writing your paper will involve exploring your topic from different perspectives and reflecting on written as well as oral sources of information. You may even be researching and writing for a community audience such as a local newspaper or a nonprofit organization. As you absorb new information and points of view while completing your research, you will be able to develop a more informed and substantial perspective on your topic.

Guidelines for Writing a Research Paper

A good research paper evolves from a mind that is fully engaged. Completing a research paper requires discipline to follow the stages in the process; insight to evaluate, interpret, and integrate a range of evidence as well as different points of view; and creativity to shape a paper that engages its audience and presents evidence and logic that will persuade its readers. The following guidelines will help you to research and write your paper.

Choose a General Subject

Finding a topic for your paper is the first step. You may need to explore several topic areas before finally deciding on the one that interests you most. To help you get started, we have included many research writing topics on issues related to community in the thematic chapters of this text. A question that you have about your life and the world might also lead you to an issue that you want to understand more deeply. In defining your topic area, consider whether you can develop a paper on this chosen topic in the number of pages that you have been assigned to write. If your topic is too broad, you may not be able to present a thorough and focused perspective.

Begin a Research Notebook

One way of keeping yourself on a productive schedule for doing research is to follow a timetable that allocates a sufficient amount of time for each stage of the research and writing process. Take as much time as is available to work through the stages involved in the research process given the deadlines of your local community organization and/or your writing instructor. Keep a research notebook (on your computer) with a projected schedule for the major stages of your project and a log of your sources: those that you have found and those that you still need to find. As you work through your project, you may find that you need to revise your original schedule, but keep your final goals in mind as you move ahead. Also keep a record of any questions that you have about your topic or about how to proceed with your research. You can make an appointment to discuss these questions with your writing instructor.

Compile a Working Bibliography

A working bibliography reflects a general search of sources that are available on your topic. Keep a record of all the bibliographic information that documents your sources, including their call number and location in the library, author, title, volume, publisher, place of publication, date of publication, and relevant pages. If you are using Internet sources, keep a record of the URLs. Also write a one- or two-sentence summary of each source and why or how it will be relevant to your thesis or serve as background information. All of this information can be kept either on separate cards for easy rearranging or in electronic files on your computer.

Research Your Topic Thoroughly

Thorough research will involve locating library and Internet sources, doing field research such as survey-based questionnaires or interviews, and writing out relevant personal experiences. Begin at your college library. Librarians regularly offer students introductions to their collections. At this introduction, you will learn about the procedures for finding sources in the library as well as online. You will want to use primary sources, which directly convey the information that you need, as well as secondary sources, which report on, evaluate, and/or interpret primary sources.

Field Research: Interviews and Case Histories

Many authorities who are sources of information on your topic can be discovered in your immediate community: leaders of groups and organizations, professors or administrators at your college, older persons who have seen a neighborhood change or have witnessed many different political administrations, a community political leader or even average citizens and consumers whose opinions can become the basis of general statements and conclusions about public sentiment on current issues.

Your field research can bring a new and lively dimension to your project, helping you to understand your topic and its relationship to daily life more fully. Two widely used forms of field research are the interview and the case history. Because fieldwork may be new to you, we have included worksheets with student examples that will help you to gather and organize materials for a case history and an interview.

Case History Worksheet

The following questions will help to prepare you for conducting and writing up your case history:

Have you established a clear purpose for your case history or narrative?

Have you gathered enough details for your case history, using techniques such as freewriting, brainstorming, and reviewing on-site observations collected in your journal?

If your narrative is based on your own observations, have you gone back to observe again, using your journal to record more detail?

Do you need to gather research from the library or the Internet to support your observations and narration?

As you rewrite, have you been as specific as you can be, or do you need to use a dictionary to replace vague words with more specific and descriptive terms? Have you replaced abstract verbs, nouns, and adjectives with more concrete ones? Have you captured concrete images?

As you continue to write and revise your paper, have you taken out details and incidents that seem to slow down your narrative, that don't relate to or help explain the main point of your article or essay?

Have you tried using some dialogue? Dialogue often brings a narrative to life, but it is best to use dialogue sparingly. Try to include just a few key lines from the people involved that will help to establish their characters or the nature of the conflict among them.

As you rewrite, are you developing clear, logical connections between all the events mentioned in the narrative so that it will be easy for your reader to follow?

We have included the following essay by Amy Gilliam, which presents a case history written for the Ecumenical Hunger Program's newsletter. The Ecumenical Hunger Program (EHP) provides emergency food, clothing, furniture, and other assistance to people experiencing emergency hardship in Palo Alto, East Palo Alto, and Menlo Park, California. Recognizing that hunger is but one of many problems that low-income families face, EHP is committed both to responding to immediate need and to helping families address the root causes of their situation. EHP provides an average of 1,500 people every month with an emergency supply of groceries. While alleviating immediate need remains a major force of EHP's work, EHP also assists families in moving toward greater independence and self-sufficiency by working with families to locate resources for jobs, housing, health care, and education and by acting as an advocate with other social service agencies.

Amy Gilliam   Gilliam 1

"Give of Yourself"

"Good afternoon, EHP," I said. There was an uncomfortable pause, and then the female voice at the other end of the line began hesitantly in Spanish. My Spanish background being quite limited, I thought it only fair to warn her, "Yo hablo un poco Espanol. . . ." I could sense her relief upon hearing her native language as she began again, this time faster and more fluidly. I was completely lost. "Un momento por favor," I said desperately, frantically scanning the office for a potential translator.

This was my first afternoon to volunteer at the Ecumenical Hunger Program, and the director, Nevida, had asked if I wouldn't mind answering the phone. No problem, I thought. I did not know what I was in for. One of my fellow volunteers, Lorraine, was packing food boxes in the back while Heather, who lived in my dorm, had been in the clothes closet distributing clothes to the needy families. Basically, those who volunteer at the Ecumenical Hunger Program do whatever needs to be done on any particular day. We were all glad to help in any way we could but felt self-conscious about making mistakes, untrained as we were. Despite these blunders, "the volunteers at EHP are indispensable," according to Lisa, the coordinator.

In fact, Lisa herself, an energetic black woman in her early twenties, started out as a volunteer at EHP under the wing of her mother, the director. This service-oriented family began at the Red Cross, where Nevida worked and Lisa volunteered as a young girl. "I have always wanted to help people," Lisa explained. So when her mother moved on to EHP in 1978, Lisa went along. Yet Lisa was not hired by EHP as "the daughter of Nevida." Instead, in 1982, she was offered a job in her own right when her mother took a leave of absence.

Gilliam 2

The project has many goals and functions, including the provision of emergency goods, clothing, and furniture to individuals and families in need, and the coordination of local resources to locate housing, jobs, educational opportunities, counseling, and health care for these people. Yet sometimes, Lisa explained, these "emergency" situations become recurring ones. "Some families come in here year after year," Lisa said. "In fact, I have been seeing one family for five years now." Due to the problem of illegal immigration, many large Hispanic families encounter economic problems at the end of each month. The cycle is a vicious one, Lisa told me, because these people are only able to obtain jobs that offer minimum wage and pay in cash. In addition, they must support the many children who are often found in Hispanic Catholic families. Lisa observed, "Oftentimes, a woman will come in with a new baby each year."

Thus, some families become more or less dependent on the help of EHP at the end of the month due to circumstances that are beyond their control. In extreme cases, EHP will provide cash to supplement rent payments, but the staff at EHP tries to veer away from this practice and to stick with more "therapeutic" measures. They explore all avenues for reducing this dependency, such as maintaining a job referral service. EHP remains in close contact with many local businesses that keep the program in touch with their job opportunities. Also, the EHP staff has often attempted to bring large families together in cooperation. This method allows for one parent to assume responsibility for child care while the others seek employment. The extra wage earner can often help tide the families over.

Unfortunately, not all of these clients have quite as valid reasons for their need. That is why keeping records on them is so important at EHP. Lisa explained the necessity of the formal request for food supplementation. She pointed out that it does not probe the personal life of the applicant but simply asks for statistics such as income and family size. Lisa's concern was that the program not be thought of as "a free handout." The only time EHP confronts problems of this sort is when drugs are involved. Because the local community harbors a frighteningly large population of drug users, the staff at EHP takes measures of caution to be certain that their emergency help with food and clothing is not taken advantage of. This happens when the individual receiving aid uses any money available for drug purchases, while depending on the program for necessities. That is why records are kept on the clients, applications are required, and interviews are utilized. If drug addiction is suspected, Lisa explained, the staff will not turn the individual away but instead will take the person into the EHP kitchen and make him or her a meal. This practice satisfies the person's immediate need yet does not allow the individual to become dependent on the organization as a source of food.

I could tell that the drug problem truly disturbed Lisa because of its effects on the children of the community. Her concern for these children was made quite evident throughout the interview as she described not only how some go hungry even after receiving help (because of their parents' addiction), but also how they are raised in an atmosphere that perpetuates the same problems. "I have been here long enough to see the children of clients become clients themselves," Lisa observed sadly. The way EHP tries to remedy this situation is to concentrate on these underprivileged children. In the future, the staff is planning an after-school program where the children can participate in planned activities and be provided with food. "What they really need is for someone to care for them and love them. It has probably been a long time since they heard the words. 'I love you.'" One could tell from the look on Lisa's face that she wished she could do this for each and every one of them. It saddened me to hear Lisa's story about the teachers who would call from school to complain that some of the children in their classes were hungry. "By the way the children tore into their food at lunch, the teachers believed that the kids hadn't eaten since the day before," Lisa said.

Upon hearing this, one wonders, "what can I do to help these children and their families?" Of course, food, clothing, and furniture donations are always appreciated at EHP. Yet hands-on assistance has a more lasting effect. Volunteers help out with the work, but more importantly, they contribute a little of themselves to the program. A volunteer working in the clothing closet has those extra few minutes to pay attention to the child whose mother is juggling her other children, while sorting through the clothes. Thus, when considering what one can do to help, one should remember that the gift of time can be the most precious one.

Amy's Project Evaluation

1. I decided to work on the Ecumenical Hunger Program for my real writing project because I had volunteered there in the fall and the staff there had struck me as being dedicated and sincere. Therefore, I called the director (a number of times because they are extremely busy there) and was eventually set up with an interview with her daughter, Lisa. The interview proved to be very helpful and gave me quite a bit of information about the program. I was considering also interviewing a client family but ran into so many problems trying to set it up with the staff at EHP that I changed my mind and decided to draw upon my own experiences as a volunteer at EHP. My assignment was to write a case history article for the EHP newsletter.

2. I found this project quite interesting because I was faced with the prospect of writing for an audience I had never considered writing for before. As opposed to writing for a teacher, instructor, or student peers in an "academic" setting, I was communicating to the public on a different level. I found myself using less complicated vocabulary and sentence structure and (upon suggestion) attempting to be more concise than I am accustomed to.

3. As I mentioned earlier, I had quite a bit of trouble contacting the public service organization and its staff. They are extremely busy there, so I completely understand their level of disorganization, yet I would not suggest depending on them for a real writing project. Often I had trouble catching my contact person at the office.

Interview Worksheet

The questions on this worksheet will help you to prepare yourself for your interview, develop background information on the person you are going to interview, organize your ideas, conduct the interview, and write up your ideas. The materials generated by your interview may be integrated into your research paper, inspire you to do more research, and serve as background information for your paper. Perhaps your teacher will ask you to write an interview essay like the one we have following the worksheet.

How and why did you select the person you are interviewing?

How do you plan to conduct the interview? Will you ask the interviewee if you can tape your discussion? Do you plan to take notes during the interview?

What has the interviewee written or accomplished? Be sure to be prepared to ask your interviewee about his or her most recent and most important work.

What are the age, gender, education, social, cultural, and family background of the interviewee? How might the person's background influence his or her point of view on the topic of the interview?

What were your expectations before the interview? What did you hope to learn? Contrast your expectations of the interviewee's responses to his or her actual responses.

Where did the interview lead you? Did it bring up new issues? Did it help you understand a part of your subject that you had found difficult or confusing?

If you are going to write an article, remember to include some direct quotations from the interview or summary. Note this information.

Did the interviewee suggest any solutions to the issue? Did the interview change your mind about any aspect of the issue that you are researching?

Did the interview encourage you to do more research? What type? What do you want to learn about your topic now?

How do you plan to incorporate the information gathered in this interview into the paper or article that you are writing?

Interviews take many forms. We have included two different student approaches to writing the interview essay. After reading them, think about the strengths of each.

Donald Matsuda   Matsuda 1

Student Donald Matsuda developed the following essay after interviewing his grandmother about her experiences in the internment camps during World War II.

Bachan's Story

Until recently, one of the lesser known episodes in the history of the United States was the forced exclusion and detention during World War II of over 120,000 Japanese American civilians who resided on the West Coast. These civilians were denied their constitutional rights, forced by armed military guards to abandon their homes and jobs, and herded into internment camps, which had all the trappings of prisons. Although unfairly stigmatized by accusations of disloyalty to America, the Japanese could not find the voice within themselves to tell others, often even their own children, about what happened to them during the devastating and humiliating years of wartime incarceration. As I began to learn about this tragic event that forever altered the lives of my ancestors, I was motivated to discover how and why these Japanese Americans were taken from their homes in the spring of 1942 and incarcerated in concentration camps. In order to gain a personal and intimate view of the internment camp experience, I decided to conduct a candid interview with my grandmother, or bachan, Alice Watanabe, a proud and loyal United States citizen who survived three years of internment at Tule Lake Relocation Camp in California. I felt that Bachan Watanabe would be able to provide some vital information and valuable insight into the living conditions of the camps and her experience as a Japanese American in postwar America.

My grandmother was born in Marysville, California, on May 9, 1924. Her parents were *issei,* Japanese Americans who were born on the mainland of Japan and subsequently immigrated to the United States. They settled in Marysville, California, where they owned a grocery store and many acres of farmland. Bachan Watanabe vividly recalled how wonderful life was in their close-knit town of Marysville, but when I asked her if she recalled the day of the Pearl Harbor attack, her response reflected a more serious tone. With a look of apprehension and great sadness, she began to tell her painful story of internment in America: "I do remember Pearl Harbor day. It was a December Sunday and I was at church with our neighbors, the Tanakas, preparing for the upcoming Christmas service. The sanctuary doors were suddenly flung open and our minister hurried in and shouted, 'Pearl Harbor has just been bombed. We are at war with Japan.' We sat there and looked at one another fearing the worst, yet not knowing what to fear." As my grandmother continued her emotional account, I began to comprehend the devastating impact that both fear and an uncertain future had had on the Japanese Americans who were caught between their ancestral ties and their loyalty to their new country.

As a *nisei*, a Japanese American who was born in the United States, my grandmother faced an uncertain fate following the shock of the Pearl Harbor attack; unfortunately, her worst fears were confirmed as exclusion orders began to appear on telephone poles throughout the Japanese community, signaling the beginning of a government-ordered evacuation. Bachan Watanabe painfully recalled the early stages of the incarceration during which her family was given forty-eight hours notice to dispose of all of their property, including their store and countless acres of farmland, prior to vacating the West Coast. They were allowed to take only what they could carry, and were immediately placed under detention in what the U.S. government euphemistically called Assembly Centers—temporary camps that were hastily converted racetracks where entire families were housed in horse stalls. Although the living conditions in the Assembly Centers were unbearable, my grandmother's tearful recollection served as a powerful testament to the even more devastating shock of being betrayed by her own country. As she clearly expressed, "Here I was a loyal American citizen who was being labeled as a traitor to America simply because of my ancestry—it was an alienating, humiliating, and embarrassing experience."

According to my grandmother, she and most other Japanese Americans did not remain in the Assembly Centers for more than a few weeks before being tagged, like luggage, and transported to more permanent relocation centers, which were to serve as their "home" for the next two to three years. While I had read about the sordid living conditions in these barbed wire compounds, it was quite overwhelming to hear the many details that my grandmother so vividly recollected and related to me.

In particular, when I asked her to describe her first impressions of the relocation camp, she paused for a moment before responding, as if her memories of the actual internment were too painful for her to recall. However, she continued: "We were loaded onto buses with all the windows blacked out, and a blanket was placed behind the side door so we could not see where they were taking us. When we finally reached our destination, I was shocked to see that the sites were not prepared for human habitation—the toilets consisted of one level board with holes just inches apart with no partitions, and the 'apartments' each family were assigned to were, in reality, six by nineteen foot makeshift barracks surrounded by scrubby sagebrush, dirt, and barbed wire."

In addition to these unbearable living conditions, my grandmother noted that she and the other internees were crowded into long lines three times a day to eat starchy, unsavory meals, and that they were forced to work long hours, earning no more than $12 a month. What I found most disheartening about her account was the devastating impact that the internment camps had on the once orderly and spirited lives of the Japanese Americans. She sadly recounted, "Our dignity was destroyed. We were over-

Matsuda 4

whelmed with despair, for our families were torn apart, and our hopes and dreams for the future were shattered."

Considering the trauma that Japanese Americans were forced to endure during the internment, I found it quite remarkable that they did not develop any feelings of bitterness or anger toward the Americans for imprisoning them solely because of their ancestry. In fact, my grandmother proudly recalled that her brother, Leonard, was one of over 33,000 Japanese Americans who fulfilled their obligation and loyalty as United States citizens by serving in the armed forces. "They literally gave their lives and limbs to prove their loyalty," she explained, "and, as a result, military observers agreed that the Japanese American battalion was the most decorated unit in United States military history." Since many of the internees helped America win the war against Japan, there was clearly no need for the government to continue its incarceration of Japanese Americans. Consequently, the evacuation order had been canceled, and the government had begun to close the internment camps.

Expecting the postwar period to have been a liberating experience for the internees, I asked my grandmother how her life had changed after being released from camp. She immediately appeared dispirited as she indicated that the years following the internment were more difficult than the incarceration itself. "In many respects, this was the hardest part of the internment because my family had no home to go back to—we had lost our store and all of our farmland. We also faced considerable discrimination in housing and employment, and everywhere we went, we were met with hostile signs that read: 'No Japs Allowed,' 'No Japs Welcome.'" Not surprisingly, however, she and the other Japanese American internees did not allow the pain and shock of postwar discrimination to affect their efforts to rebuild their lives. Instead, they accepted the grave injustice that was done to their race and found the courage to withstand the shame of being treated as traitors in their own country.

After painfully reliving the details of wartime incarceration, my grandmother described her feelings about this relatively unknown period in both our family's history and the history of America: "I do not hold any feelings of bitterness because of the internment. While it was a humiliating and shameful event in my life as a United States citizen, I feel that I have worked very hard to overcome any disadvantages

Matsuda 5

that I have faced, and have successfully proven myself as a loyal, diligent, and respectful American." Bachan Watanabe's reflections on her internment experience are strikingly representative of the responses of most Japanese American internees, who have made their unique mark and have responded admirably to the challenges that they faced and endured amid strong postwar racism. The Japanese values of hard work, education, and survival, which were instilled by their traditional *issei* parents, have enabled them to rebound from the devastation of the incarceration and to succeed economically in America.

The internment of Japanese Americans is undoubtedly a tragic chapter in the history of America. However, it is also a courageous story of a group of United States citizens who would not let racism and incarceration affect their dedication and loyalty to their country. After hearing my grandmother's emotional account of her experience in an American concentration camp, I better understand what a devastating impact the internment had on persons of Japanese ancestry—psychologically, emotionally, and physically. I was overwhelmed by the reality that a group of American citizens could so easily become innocent victims of a racist policy that ignored all the protections of individual rights, which are fundamental principles of constitutional government. Indeed, the exclusion and internment of Japanese Americans during World War II was an injustice felt at the deepest personal level by those who experienced it, but for all Americans, it remains a betrayal of the tenets upon which this nation was founded—a grave violation of liberty that will hopefully never again be repeated.

Some teachers ask their students to write an interview or an interview essay, which can take a variety of forms. The following interview was written for Professor Ford's "Community Matters" course. The form and content of Vanya's essay developed from her personal experiences, her reading and discussion experiences in her writing class, and her interview with Pat Fobair, Director of Social Work at the Patient Resource Center at the Stanford Hospital. We hope that the following interview essay will inspire you to write one of your own that integrates personal and classroom experiences, readings from your text, and the interview that you prepare for and conduct.

Ivanka (Vanya) Choumanova   Choumanova 1

The Healing Power of Listening

As the daughter of a breast cancer survivor, I am familiar with the effects cancer imposes on family members. However, I yearned to better understand the emotions victims experience, the ways families deal with this terrifying disease, as well as the benefits of participating in a support group. In search of these answers, I interviewed Pat Fobair, the head social worker of the Patient Resource Center at the Stanford Hospital. Pat greeted me with a smile as I stepped into her office. She carried herself graciously and asked me how I felt, but even this commonplace question resonated with warmth.

In the oncology ward I had visited beforehand, the patients were staring blankly at the white floors only to avoid revealing their preoccupations; a child was screaming desperately; a woman was weeping. A nurse was quietly humming a sorrowful tune as she continued pushing a handicapped elderly woman in a wheelchair. At first, the hospital seemed like a frightening revelation of patients' illnesses and pain. Even though most of the women in the Patient Resource Center were terminally ill cancer patients, Pat's presence and silent comfort made all of us feel much more at ease than we would have felt outside, in the oncology ward.

Soon, Pat began sharing her life stories with me. Born in 1935, she is the oldest of five children. While the responsibilities of being the oldest made her reluctant to have children of her own, her patients and coworkers have become her family. Pat enjoyed helping others from an early age, and after reading an inspirational story in *The Ladies' Home Journal,* she decided to devote her life to caring for others. As a social worker, she has reached out to hundreds of patients in the fight against cancer.

Pat first discovered the power of group discussions after joining the Encounter Group Movement, an organization designed to encourage college students to speak openly about diversity. "It was a liberating process," she remarked, "and through these groups I could share my experiences with others. I became familiar with new perspectives. What I learned from others was priceless." Years later, as a social worker at a hospital in San Francisco, Pat realized that many patients wanted to talk although their treatments had finished. The staff, however, was too busy to listen. Pat Fobair couldn't say good-bye to her patients, knowing that they desperately needed to share their feelings. So she stepped in and started listening.

Until this day, Pat listens. She leads four groups every week and also does research on breast cancer. The support groups include six to ten people, and the only rule is confidentiality. As Pat Fobair explained, "The therapy groups are not just for the recently diagnosed patients. There are four stages of cancer—discovery, treatment, recovery, and progression—and patients need to speak about their emotions at every stage." One of Pat's most inspirational cases is a woman in her early thirties who had Hodgkin's disease and was frustrated with the estranged relationship she had with her parents following her diagnosis. After participating in a support group for two years, she conquered the fear of speaking to her parents about her illness. As part of her triumph, she persuaded her parents to attend a weekend workshop, an event that brought an end to their alienation.

In addition to healing patients, Pat is a cancer patient herself. She was diagnosed with breast cancer in 1987 and underwent two surgeries and chemotherapy. After speaking about the various cancer treatments, Pat quietly remarked, "Group therapy is especially important and necessary for cancer victims. Sickness is frightening, but by engaging themselves in group therapy, patients are able to alleviate their turmoil and anxieties." Pat Fobair also shared her feelings on breast cancer both as a patient and as a social worker. "I've learned that a positive lymph node does not mean death," she said humbly. "Still, breast cancer is a community issue, a public health problem similar to cholera and malaria. We must work together to fight cancer, to find a cure."

From my own experiences, I knew it was important to ask Pat how the family can best deal with cancer when a family member becomes ill. "Cancer often leads to disruption in family dynamics and communications. Every mother and wife has a vital role, and if she gets sick," Pat remarked, " the entire family is affected." Pat mentioned that some of her patients are husbands, who often remain depressed long after their wives are cured. Other cancer

Choumanova 3

patients attend the support group meetings to share their thoughts on the dying process. Pat's approach, however, is not to simply comfort them. She lets them express their fears and acknowledges their emotional turbulence. Pat avoids talking to her patients excessively; instead, she listens. While she doesn't have the magical power of curing, Pat most certainly has the healing power of listening. She selflessly believes, "People help themselves. I just create an atmosphere which allows for that."

As we were ending the interview, Pat suggested that I attend a breast cancer support group to better understand what she had been experiencing during the many years of her service. I began volunteering at a breast cancer clinic, where I helped organize support group meetings. The patients shared their life stories with an incredible sense of honesty and openness. We were strangers, but only an hour later, we knew each other's deeply hidden fears, fears that had never been spoken out loud.

Surgery, radiation therapy, and medication were all provided for my mother's cure, but was she healed? Had anyone like Pat listened to her? Or was the only acknowledgment of her illness a nurse's sorrowful tune? From the interview and my volunteer experience with support groups, I have grasped how caring it is to listen to others. And I, like every family member of a cancer victim, needed to do that. I need to listen to my mom.

Web Research

Information available on the web is virtually limitless, providing a wealth of resources for research while presenting a seemingly endless task of sorting through that information. For this reason, it is essential to clarify the purpose of your research and begin your web search with a plan. Before turning on your computer and beginning your online search, decide what information you have and what information you are looking for. While there is an abundance of interesting information on the Internet, only a small percentage of that information will apply to your research.

Searching the Web

You can begin your research on the web by using a search engine such as Yahoo!, Google, or AltaVista. All of these search engines will ask you to provide "keywords" to guide your research. Depending on what your keywords reveal about your research topic, your search results will be more or less specific. For example, if you are interested in learning about community and you type in the word "community" as your keyword, you are likely to generate several thousand results to your search. Sorting through this information would certainly be overwhelming—possible perhaps, but not very efficient. However, if you narrow your search to indicate a specific community by providing additional information to your keywords search, your results will be more specific and much more useful.

In addition to being specific about the community you are interested in, try to be specific about what you are trying to learn about that community. For example, if you wanted to learn more about the environmental issues facing the community discussed in Kimi Eisele's essay, "The Other Side of the Wires," you would want to read the article carefully and summarize the key issues discussed, making note of any references to specific organizations and any terms used that were unfamiliar. Appropriate keywords for "The Other Side of the Wires" could include "U.S. Mexican Border," "Environmental Protection Agency," and "Superfund site."

Once you have decided on a series of words and phrases to be the designated keywords, you will have to make some strategic choices about how to apply this information to your search. The more constraints you add to your search, the more specific your results will be. The simplest search will include a single word or phrase. When searching for a phrase, enclose it in parentheses to indicate the relationship between the words; otherwise, for example, the computer will look for Environment and Protection and Agency, a search that would provide thousands of irrelevant results. A more complex search would include a series of words and phrases and will require the use of parentheses and linking words such as *and, or,* and *not* to clarify your search request.

Evaluating web resources One of the benefits of conducting your research on the Internet is that you are gaining access to a broader range and variety of information than is available at your college library. Information on the web may have been produced by private citizens, commercial agencies, government entities, nonprofit organizations, and educational institutions. With this wealth of information, it is important to maintain a critical perspective when reviewing online resources. A number of suffixes used by American web sites can give you fundamental insight into what you are reading as well as the source of the information. Some of the most common suffixes include:

.com	commercial site
.edu	educational site
.gov	government site
.mil	military site
.net	news and other network sites
.org	nonprofit organization site

Online resources are not subject to the same standards of fairness and accuracy; statistics may not always be valid or reliable; the editing and review process of web sites may not be as thorough as those that traditional publications receive. As a result, you as the reader have an increased responsibility to understand the context in which the resource was created and the audience that the resource was intended to inform. You can begin by asking the traditional reporter's questions about the web sites: who, what, where, when, why, and how.

Who is the author of the site? Is the author identified? Is the author a legitimate authority on the topic of the web site? Is the author affiliated with a reputable organization?

What information does the site present? Is the coverage of the material superficial or thorough? Can the facts, statistics, and opinions be traced to a legitimate source or verified? Is there advertising on the site that might make the presentation of information biased? If you can tell that the site is popular through the hit counter, why do you think people visit it?

Where does the information come from? What does the domain name tell you? Has the source appeared in print?

When was the site created? Is the site updated frequently?

Why is the information presented? What is the site's purpose: to inform, to persuade, to entertain, to sell a product?

How is the information presented? Is the site well designed so that you can easily access and understand the information embedded through its format?

You can also consider the **TASALS** method developed by Anson and Schwegler, authors of the *Longman Handbook*, which offers a more wholistic approach for evaluating an electronic community.

Evaluating Online Sources

Topic: On what subject(s) does the site focus? Do contributors belong to any organization or share any other kind of affiliation?

Attitude: Does the site have a clear point of view or set of values? Do contributors have similar perspectives or values?

Strategies: Does the site use particular writing or visual strategies? Does the design of the site have a particular style or emphasis?

Authority: Does the site try to be authoritative, giving support for claims it makes or information it provides? Do contributors reason carefully and offer evidence, or do they give unsupported opinions and supposed "facts"?

Links: Is the site linked to similar sites? Do postings refer to related online documents, lists, or resources?

Summarize: On the basis of your answers to these questions, summarize the qualities of this electronic community.

Throughout *Community Matters,* we encourage you to follow up on the reading selections by doing additional web research on a specific organization, on a topic as it affects your community, and on the keywords in a selection to encourage you to better understand the ideas covered. Learning to do web research requires you to be creative and resourceful and to think critically about the authority and validity of each site that you encounter. Web research will help you to learn through experience and reflection.

Evaluating Your Resources

You will need to evaluate the authority of your sources. The following checklist for evaluating sources will provide you with guidelines, but no one can predict with certainty the types or ranges of sources that you will need to interpret and integrate into your paper. As a researcher, you will be following guidelines and learning through experience.

Evaluating Sources Checklist

Why does the article engage your interest?

What approach does the author take: Is the article primarily factual? Narrative? Descriptive? Theoretical? Is it based on a study or an interview? Does it argue for a point of view or a particular value system? Does it evaluate or critique the ideas of others?

Is the factual evidence sound and convincing?

Does the author rely on authoritative and current sources?

Do the author's reasons follow logically? Do the reasons and facts support the thesis and conclusion?

Is the author an authority on your subject, or does he or she have a limited indepth knowledge of the subject?

Is the author sincere and ethical or does he or she seem manipulative? Does the author have a vested interest or a hidden agenda?

Is the language concrete, objective, and precise? Is it emotional? Argumentative? Full of jargon or generalizations?

Do you agree or disagree with the author's point of view? Even if you disagree with the author's point of view, does the article bring up significant issues that need to be considered when writing a reasoned and fair analysis of your topic?

How do you think you will use the article in your research paper? If you use it directly, how will you cite the source on your Works Cited page? If you don't use the source directly, how has it helped you formulate ideas for your paper?

Taking Notes on Your Sources

As you develop your own point of view, it is essential to maintain an accurate record and presentation of the ideas of experts on the subject you are exploring. To give your own perspective a weight of authority while introducing a lively set of divergent voices in response to the issues you are examining, include appropriate summaries, paraphrases, and quotations in your paper.

When you take notes and write in response to your sources, you are in effect conducting a dialogue with the "experts" you have chosen to quote, to summarize, and to paraphrase for your research paper. This dialogue with sources can help you to develop your paper with a "real" voice, a point of view of its own. Remember too that good, professional research writing does not sound strained, dry, or pieced together because the writers have carefully considered, evaluated, and interpreted the point of view and information reflected in the sources they are working with, and then they have integrated the expert opinions into their own perspective.

Paraphrasing

In taking notes for your research paper, you may need to paraphrase source material. Paraphrasing involves putting materials from your original sources into your own words. If you use any original language from the source, set those words off in quotation marks. When using paraphrasing in your note-taking, make sure that you write at the top of your page, computer file, or note card the exact source of the paraphrased passage, including the author's name, name of article or book, and the page from which the material was taken. You will need to include this information in the body of your paper and on your Works Cited page.

Summarizing

Effective use of summary can reduce a longer article or even an entire book to a brief passage ready to be included in your research paper. Summaries are frequently used in research writing to present a concise account of crucial ideas and data. The summary can be used either as a way to emphasize the main idea or thesis of an entire article or book or as a way to shorten longer passages that really don't need close direct analysis because they function mainly as background or they bring authority to the text. (Again, remember to always keep a record of your sources to include in the final draft of your paper.)

Quotations

Although much of your research material can probably be incorporated into your paper in the form of paraphrases and summaries, in some cases a writer will have stated his or her position so eloquently or succinctly that you will want to incorporate the language of the original source directly into your paper. Particularly if the author you quote is a respected authority on the subject you are writing about, strategic quoting will strengthen your argument. However, don't overuse quotations, as they can break up the flow of your own voice in the paper. Usually a sentence or even a phrase will be enough to give the flavor of the reasoning and language of the original source.

Comment on quoted material either before or after its inclusion, and try to blend such quoted material smoothly with your own sentences so that the quotation seems like an integral part of your argument and style even though it is set off clearly with quotation marks.

If you use a quotation that is longer than three lines, it should be set off from the body of your text, and it should be introduced. A research paper that is interrupted by many lengthy "block" quotations may begin to seem like a collage or collection of notes from the ideas of others.

Avoiding Plagiarism

You can avoid plagiarism by following the advice on paraphrasing, summarizing, and quoting that we have presented. Do not use the ideas or words of others without giving them credit in the body of your paper. Direct quotes, summaries, and paraphrases must all be accompanied by a parenthetical source information note. (For the MLA or APA citation style, refer to an appropriate handbook or check an online style web site. We suggest the *Columbia Guide to Online Style,* which provides guidelines for both the MLA and APA formats: <http://www.columbia.edu/cu/cup/cgos/idx_basic.html>.

Developing a Working Thesis

After you have completed all the research for your paper, you will need to develop a working thesis. Don't allow yourself to feel constrained by your initial topic. It is natural for a research paper topic to evolve as you do your research. Your working thesis should reflect what you have learned about your topic. The paper can take many forms, such as presenting a problem and posing a solution, explaining a new method or approach, analyzing the reasons for a form of behavior, refuting a misconception, showing causes of a trend or phenomenon, or persuading an audience to change an opinion or an aspect of a lifestyle. Consider the thesis and the outline that you create at this stage as "in progress." Continue to revise your outline as you actually draft the paper.

Developing an Outline

Organize your note cards or computer files into an outline that supports your tentative thesis. Review and apply the organizational strategies that we have discussed in the three opening chapters of this text as you develop this outline.

Writing a First Draft

You can begin by thinking of writing your first draft as an activity that will help you to clarify the information and ideas you have gathered, and to understand what it is about your question and topic that most interests you, that you want to explore further.

Because we are sometimes our own severest critics, when you are writing the first draft, it is important to write as much of your paper as you possibly can from your outline and note cards in one writing session. Try to let your paper develop an energy and flow of its own; don't worry about details of style; and try to keep your "internal critic" quiet. If the paper is long, write it in whole sections. While this draft does not have to be formally documented, it should indicate references to your sources.

Sharing Your First Draft

Sharing your research paper with your writing group will allow you to find out if you have realized your intended purpose. We suggest that you share your research paper with at least two other students in your class. Completing the following worksheet before discussing a peer's research paper will help you to analyze and evaluate his or her paper and to prepare a thoughtful and helpful response.

Research Paper Checklist

Thesis

Is the thesis limited, clearly stated, and placed appropriately to guide the reader into the paper's point of view or argument?

Did the paper's topic engage your interest?

Audience and Purpose

Is there a clear purpose and audience for the paper?

Would the language, information, and examples presented be of interest to the designated audience?

Development, Support, and Examples

Is the main point of each paragraph clear?

Are paragraphs well developed?

Is the evidence balanced with facts and examples? Do they support the writer's main points?

Which of the examples are most useful and convincing? Which of the examples could be developed or clarified?

Argumentation

Does the writer consider the opponent's point of view in the process of making his or her own argument?

Is the overall framework of the paper logical and systematic, reflecting a hierarchy of importance and a clear sequence of thought?

What makes the paper especially persuasive?

Did you identify any logical fallacies?

Use of Sources

Does the writer use sufficient and varied source references?

Are there particular points in the paper that could be more carefully supported?

Which points are especially well supported?

Are the sources well integrated into the writer's point of view?

Is research material stated primarily through the writer's voice or does it feel just "pasted in" rather than evaluated or interpreted?

Are quotations frequent enough to lend authority, yet not so numerous and lengthy that they break up the text?

Are sources correctly cited and documented?

Voice and Language

Does the paper sound like the student's own writing voice or like an "imitation" authority?

Is the language use consistent and appropriate, or does the language seem too technical, pretentious, or jargon-like?

Mechanics

Is the sentence structure clear, readable, and lively?

Are quotations well integrated with the author's own syntax?

Did you find faulty pronoun reference, lack of parallel structure, mistakes in subject–verb agreement, dangling modifiers, or voice shifts?

Are the spelling, punctuation, and capitalization correct?

Overall Response

What is your overall impression of the draft?

What are its greatest strengths?

What suggestions do you have for improving the paper? Be as specific and helpful as you can.

Preparing Your Final Draft

After reading and discussing your peers' evaluations of your paper, you will want to have a final conference with your instructor. Then you will know what must be done to finish your paper. Most students find that they need to sharpen their thesis, develop their evidence, and refine their style, directing it more clearly to its purpose or particular audience. You may want to go back to the library to do some more research. You will also need to document all sources in your paper, including quotations, paraphrases, summaries, and statistics. Body sources and the final Works Cited page will need to follow the MLA or APA style of documentation. MLA and APA style guidelines are available online and as handbooks.

The following research paper was written by Elizabeth Derse, whose class text was *Community Matters.*

Elizabeth Derse   Derse 1

The Standardized Test and Its Implications in the
American Classroom

In the United States today, our culture places inequitable value on the measuring of intelligence. The addiction our society embraces over the rating of mentality

---

prevails in every aspect of American life, and comparisons between intellects can be made within minutes in such form as IQ tests taken over the Internet. The problem, however, extends far beyond the adult desire to feel intellectually superior to other people their age; the root of such social disorder begins when we are in grade school, when parents and teachers attempt to rate children according to standardized tests. Indeed, it appears that the measurement of intelligence has become a cultural norm, and children are, at an early age, subject to this American need to label and rate mental capabilities. This year alone, the Educational Testing Service will administer standardized tests to over nine million children in the United States, with the intent of assessing and grading each individual's ability to learn. This, I believe, is completely unacceptable, for the tests not only lack an objective ability to predict a child's will to succeed, but also appear biased toward those children who possess the forms of intelligence that are inappropriately overvalued by society.

Over the past few years, a hot debate has swept through United States classrooms concerning the standardized test and its connection to any reasonable evaluation of a child's intelligence. Many who support such tests argue that they are necessary not only for individual assessment, but also for the logical measurement of a school's effectiveness and a child's motivation to succeed. As Thomas Kellaghan notes in *The Effects of Standardized Testing,* "for teachers and counselors tests are a source of information about students, individually and in groups, that can be helpful in teaching and in student guidance. They can also be of assistance to administrators as well as teachers in monitoring the educational programs of schools and in evaluating the effectiveness of new curricula, instructional methods, and teaching methods" (2). Finally, many argue that standardized tests can be seen as a source of motivation for students, parents, and teachers who wish to improve their previous scores.

However, it seems that while the intentions of the standardized tests appear honorable, the fact remains that they fail to meet the objectives originally established. For example, the tests are meant to assess a child's knowledge in school and his or her individual ability to succeed in the classroom. Yet, the testing in schools focuses on what Kel-

Derse 3

laghan calls "norm-referenced standardized tests," which he defines as tests whose results are fixed according to procedure, materials, and scoring (4). The outcomes of the tests are then compared to the "average" performance of the children in that age group. Kellaghan notes, "This is seen as unsatisfactory because the score provides no information about what a student has learned in a particular subject area, only how he or she stands relative to other students" (4). It is possible, for example, that a child can do well on a multiple-choice test simply because he or she is a lucky guesser. Therefore, many standardized tests provide no information about how much a student has learned or how effective the educational system is; rather, they reflect only where a student should stand based on cultural norms.

While many of the controversies concerning standardized tests date back to the 1980s, most modern critics complain that the tests themselves are inherently biased and poorly written. For example, children who come from underprivileged families or minority groups tend, on average, to score 15 to 20 % lower than those who belong to middle-class families or to more predominant races (Murray 234). The results of such tests, critics argue, cannot be trusted, for they are discriminatory in structure and do not accurately reflect what a child knows. For instance, many placement tests contain portions that require a child to read a passage and then to answer questions regarding the chosen selection. However, the content of the reading itself might be better understood with prior knowledge that is naturally available to students (such as upper-class white children) who have been fortunate in their exposure to privileges such as travel or the arts (235). Therefore, many standardized tests might not assess a child's ability to learn or an educator's ability to teach, for low scores might be a mere reflection of those aspects of a child's life that are beyond his or her control.

Moreover, because "assessment in education is not a value-neutral enterprise," many classrooms across America have seen a change in the curriculum in an attempt to raise test scores nationwide, as Doug Archbald observes in *Beyond Standardized Testing* (1). As teachers set aside traditional curricula and replace them with material that might appear on a district or nationwide test, they are forced to exclude knowledge that could be necessary for a child's growth. Teachers have felt increasing pressure to present their students with material that is included in a standardized test, for higher scores reflect American values. Furthermore, because assessment is not "value-neutral," the standard curriculum in American schools might not be what Archbald calls an "accurate estimate of worthwhile knowledge" (1). Among other criticisms, traditional tests have been faulted for neglecting the kinds of competence expressed in authentic, 'real life' situations beyond school" (vi). Indeed, it appears that many teachers must neglect the traditional needs of children as they give way to "less meaningful forms of mastery" (vi).

Additionally, many critics argue that standardized tests are not only ineffective but also can be emotionally damaging to the children who take them. As Archbald notes, "We endorse outcomes, such as high test scores, without scrutinizing the tasks on which they are based" (1). Indeed, it seems that the tests, while they are meant to objectively examine what a child has learned in the classroom, may in fact only compare one pupil to another. While this may appear effective for the standardized tests that aim to place children in the appropriate classroom environment, the fact remains that the tests might not, as Archbald argues, reflect a child's true intelligence. It appears that the tests, if understood and utilized properly, might encourage young students to increase their learning or their effort in school. However, according to Kellaghan, most tests adversely affect an individual's self-esteem, particularly when an individual scores "below" the average child (9). As Thomas Hoerr once observed, "Intelligence has come to be represented by a two or three digit number," and therefore problems may arise when a teacher alters his or her perception of a student according to the results of a standardized test (7). Such labeling could result in "suppressing a child's learning" (Kellaghan 14), or, worse yet, cause the child to believe that he or she is below the norm and therefore below the socially acceptable level of intelligence.

Perhaps my problem with standardized tests stems from the fact that they attempt to precisely evaluate a child's intelligence and ability to learn, which is a feat that

Derse 5

I do not believe is possible. Tests such as the "Gifted and Talented" (G/T) examinations venture, as early as grade school, to place children in classes according to their intellect and supposed ability to succeed in school. While I believe that this integration into "Gifted" classrooms is an important step toward advanced education in younger children, it is not possible to rank a child's intelligence through a quiz that in reality only partially defines a child's abilities. If the cutoff to a G/T program, for example, is an IQ of 130, a child who has an IQ of 129 should not be excluded from the program because of a one-point difference. This one-point difference, although trivial on paper, could distinguish one child from another and exclude an equally deserving child from an advanced learning program.

The issue of intelligence has long been debated and is, perhaps, the most valuable evidence of the day concerning the need to eliminate standardized tests from American classrooms. In 1983, Howard Gardner took the first step toward recognizing several different forms of intelligence in a world that distinctly acknowledges two forms mental capabilities. His theory of "multiple intelligences," although still unrecognized in many places, has gained acceptance in a series of studies concerning child development. Gardner suggests in *Frames of Mind* that there are seven different types of intelligence; and, while the American educational system recognizes only two, all deserve equal respect and priority in our society (346). Currently, argues Gardner, our culture accepts only the mathematical and linguistic intelligences as a valuable and productive form of mental capacity: Success in school is assessed by a child's ability to solve math problems and read or write (347). However, there are five virtually unrecognized forms that, in order to properly accommodate an individual child's needs, must be integrated into our educational system. They are, by no order of importance, the bodily kinesthetic, musical, spatial, interpersonal, and intrapersonal intelligences.

Gardner believes that American society, in implementing standardized testing, has further engrained the idea of a "one-dimensional view of how to assess people's minds" in an already intelligence-biased world (356). He suggests that because people in the real world make different contributions to society based on their own natural skills and talents, it is unfair to base a child's success in school on a test that fails to measure a variety of intelligences. Gardner notes, "I believe that we should get away altogether from tests and correlations among tests, and look instead at more naturalistic sources of information about how peoples around the world develop skills important to their life" (360). Indeed, I believe it is necessary to recognize all intelligences in a school setting, for only then will American culture make the effort accept that there may be different ways to "assess people's minds."

In his pamphlet *Implementing Multiple Intelligences,* Thomas Hoerr, a teacher at New City School in St. Louis who has been involved in multiple intelligence assessment, asserts that the qualities necessary to achieve success in school are far different from those needed to achieve success in life (23). Thus, society has placed too much emphasis on the mathematical and linguistic intelligences when there are many other human skills that deserve equal recognition. While many gifts are essential for successful integration into society, it is, unfortunately, this unitary view of intelligence that is examined through standardized tests. As Hoerr notes, "In many schools, success comes in the form of knowing 'stuff'—possessing information without understanding, following directions without question, and working alone" (15). However, while those students who comply with these criteria excel in school, there is doubt as to whether the socially acceptable forms of intelligence truly reveal whether a student will succeed in life. In such a way, Hoerr accepts Gardner's view of multiple intelligences, for in the world outside the classroom, "we use our various intelligences to gain and to share information" (14). Thus, Hoerr denounces the standardized test in its entirety, for he believes that the material through which children are examined poorly measures an individual's ability to succeed in life (15). He believes that, while society values the mathematical and linguistic intelligences, it is necessary to extend beyond our current cultural norms to encourage and benefit all children equally, including those whose tal-

Derse 7

ents are strongly associated with the other five forms. It is my opinion, therefore, that schools should model the human skills needed to succeed beyond the classroom setting, such as working together, resourcefulness, and interpersonal development.

Several recent studies have proven that teachers, in assessing a pupil's mental capacity, automatically search for these different uses of intelligence before recommending them for higher learning. In looking at extended G/T programs, for example, it has been found that many teachers may establish that a certain child is "gifted" in the spatial intelligence due to excellence of work or an altered learning style in the classroom. However, because the standardized tests that formally assess such a child are faulty in structure, they do not examine these multiple intelligences. Even though the teacher may have acknowledged a gifted ability, the tests merely assess the mathematical and linguistic intelligences; consequently, such a child might be excluded from the G/T program entirely when, in reality, he or she deserved to advance. Therefore, Louisa Melton, a teacher at Oakland Elementary School and a longtime journalist, observed that those students who excel in the classroom may not pass a test simply because it was biased toward the socially acceptable intelligences, despite the fact that the teacher strongly believed the child was "gifted" (Melton 16).

It has been argued, however, that Gardner's MI theory has a distinctly egalitarian theme. One must be cautious in assessing the differences between intelligences and the differences between the average student and the exceptionally gifted. It is possible, for instance, to mistakenly label a child who has strong spatial intelligence to be a child who is "gifted" in spatial abilities (Melton 14). Thus, if used improperly, MI theory could potentially close the gap between the gifted student and the average student. For, the point remains that American culture desires to rate and label young children; therefore, a distinction must be made between the difference in intelligence and the degree to which a child is gifted (14).

It is unlikely that, despite the controversy over the use of standardized tests, our society will eliminate such tests from our schools completely. For it appears that assessment is necessary in modern culture despite the fact that not all children possess the same gifts or qualities that are currently recognized by the educational system. It is important, therefore, not only to implement Gardner's MI theory in classrooms across the nation, but also (if our current educators move to keep standardized tests on the curriculum) to alter the tests according to the many different forms of intelligence that our children possess. As Gardner notes in *Frames of Mind,* "it is not a question of how smart the student is, it is a question of how the student is smart" (356). Should the examinations be changed to assess the talents of all students, the tests would more accurately reflect a child's abilities and therefore mimic the "real-world" situations that are currently not addressed in American classrooms.

Louisa Melton argues in *Improving K–8 Reading Using Multiple Intelligences* that many changes that can be made within the traditional curriculum to accommodate those children who are currently overlooked because they are not strongly associated with the mathematical or linguistic intelligences (19). Consequently, if we initiate a change in the learning structure of our classrooms, a change in the way standardized tests are given will ultimately follow. Melton notes, "MI theory is relatively easy for even young children to grasp. Thus, in addition to presenting a way for teachers to think about teaching, it also offers a way for students to reflect on their own learning" (30). Indeed, it appears that in order for our culture to accept a view of multiple intelligences, we must first integrate the theory into the classrooms of our young children. Only when understanding of different mental abilities is acknowledged can we make the effort to restructure the current testing system.

Like Melton, Thomas Hoerr highlights several ways that MI theory can be adapted in classrooms, resulting in an advanced curriculum and an ultimate change in the way we view education. Hoerr argues that the only way to improve our current educational system is to "incorporate a variety of intelligences so that all students have an opportunity to learn through their strengths" (26). For example, he offers several insights as to how certain teachers have already integrated the MI theory into their curriculum. One

Derse 9

teacher at New City School in St. Louis, Missouri, offers her students a new and creative chance to learn how to spell. In teaching the word *families,* for instance, she takes the kids outside to play "rag-tag," and when a child is tagged, "he or she must correctly spell a word from the 'ag' word family in order to be set free to pursue another child" (28). Similarly, another primary school teacher introduces MI into the classroom by playing leapfrog along a number line to teach numbers to the students. In both cases, such integration of the bodily kinesthetic intelligence into the standard curriculum allows the children to express themselves in new and exciting ways.

Additionally, by incorporating MI into the classroom at an early age, teachers are enhancing the social awareness of the fact that there are several different ways to teach and assess a child's mind. While the children are unaware that this new teaching style differs from the traditional curriculum, they are learning "real-life" skills that will be essential to their future success. In fact, I believe that if all schools were to stress the importance of teaching through the use of MI, we could appropriately balance the necessary learning in the classroom with the knowledge needed to make the world after school a better place. Increased awareness on behalf of the children concerning MI will ultimately increase the awareness of our culture as a whole.

Standardized tests are the result of societal values and stem from the inappropriate cultural desire to rate and assess intelligence even at an early age. Unfortunately, it appears unlikely that our school system will ever be entirely rid of such tests, for many believe that they are an effective way to assess a child. However, it is possible to change the way the exams are taken. It is my hope that with the integration of MI into the American classroom, greater social awareness of the theory and its implications will result. If such a revolutionary cultural advancement is made, I believe that similar changes can be made on standardized tests to coincide with these changing societal values. Currently, the tests represent an unfair, biased, and intolerant component of our culture; changes must be made to ensure a more favorable future for *all* American children.

Derse 10

Works Cited

Archbald, Doug A. <u>Beyond Standardized Testing: Assessing Authentic Academic Achievement in the Secondary School.</u> Reston, VA: National Association of Secondary School Principals, 1988.

Gardner, Howard. <u>Frames of Mind.</u> 10th ed. New York: Basic Books, 1993.

Hoerr, Thomas R. "Implementing Multiple Intelligences: The New City School Experience." <u>Fastback</u> 107. Ed. Donovan Walling. Bloomington, IN: Phi Delta Kappa Educational Foundation, 1996. 1–53.

Kellaghan, Thomas. <u>The Effects of Standardized Testing.</u> Hingham, MA: Kluwer Nijhoff Publishing, 1982.

Melton, Louisa. "Improving K–8 Reading Using Multiple Intelligences." <u>Fastback</u> 411. Ed. Donovan Walling. Bloomington, IN: Phi Delta Kappa Educational Foundation, 1997. 1–41.

Murray, David W. "The War Against Testing." <u>Commentary</u> 106 (1998): 34–37.

RELEVANT WEB SITES

BIOGRAPHY.COM <http://www.biography.com>

This web site is based on the A&E Biography series and includes biographies of over 25,000 personalities.

ENCYCLOPEDIA.COM <http://www.encyclopedia.com/>

This web site includes over 14,000 articles searchable by keyword or phrase.

THE QUOTATIONS ARCHIVE <http://www.aphids.com/quotes/index.shtml>

This online resource contains a searchable database of general purpose quotations organized by subject, author, and keywords.

CYBER TIMES NAVIGATOR
<http://www.nytimes.com/library/tech/reference /cynavi.html>

The New York Times guide to the Internet with links to search engines, databases, and online publications.

Writing About the Community: Resources

4

In a writing course that focuses on the topic of community, you may actually be working on projects that ask you to go out of the classroom and into your surrounding community—whether it is your campus community or beyond the campus into the place where you live or work. Working with community groups and institutions can be challenging, but also immensely rewarding. This chapter offers hands-on resources: guidelines, worksheets, web links to local and national service learning sites that will help you with your community projects. Throughout *Community Matters* we have included examples of many kinds of action projects developed by students and professionals for community organizations and institutions. In this chapter we include community projects that our students have completed. We hope that these examples will inspire you and help you to understand the many possibilities for learning through active participation and reflection about community projects.

Guide to Worksheets and Examples

You will encounter new opportunities and challenges when working with the community. As in any collaborative endeavor, it is valuable to think about your goals and objectives and then to identify the tools and resources that will help you to successfully meet those goals. The worksheets that follow will help you to plan, execute, evaluate, and reflect upon what you have learned about your learning process, your writing skills, and community through completing a community project.

PART ONE
Getting Acquainted with Your Community

Community Mapping

Creating a community map will help you to become familiar with the available resources in the community where you are doing a community action project or with your college campus if your are not doing a community action project. Note the community's physical and socioeconomic characteristics, and the community's resources, needs, and expectations. Indicate patterns you observe as you walk through the community and talk with residents. Use any medium to record your findings, including videotaping, photographs, drawings, or writing.

What resources exist within the community? Interview members of the community to obtain this information. *How do members of the community respond to your inquiries?* Record your observations about the physical characteristics of the community. *How much of the community is residential, business, or industrial? Does the community feel urban, suburban, or rural? Is there a sense of community pride? What evidence did you find to support this? How did you feel being in the community?* Present your observations and your understanding of the community in the form of a map using both visual and written materials.

STUDENT EXAMPLE

Michael Garcia

Community Matters

When mapping out the Stanford University campus, I look to the landmarks that are important to my Stanford community. These landmarks allow me to find my way around. First of all, rather than using a conventional compass, I use a "Stanford community" compass, which allows me to place landmarks according to my individual perception of the campus. Lagunita is placed at the top of the map because it is the most important aspect of my community. This is where I eat, sleep, and find most of my best friends. White Plaza is at the center of the map because I use it as a center point for finding my way around. Also, through White Plaza, I am able to stay in contact with my community back home (post office), meet with friends for a good lunch (Tressidder), and buy books that are essential to my academic community. My perception of the campus places Memorial Church and the Quad to the right of White Plaza. This landmark is essential to my church community and academic community. To the left is Hoover Tower. This is not necessarily an important community landmark, but one that allows me to find my bearing of other community landmarks. The track and Arrillaga Sports Complex are located at the bottom of the map because it is the base of my Stanford Community. Through these five landmarks, I am able to find any location on campus. Rather than using individual roads to find my way around, I use the routes that connect my community landmarks. On the map, the items that look like roads are, in fact, these routes and may consist of more than one road. The little arrows indicate what and who I am able to find, once I am at the landmarks.

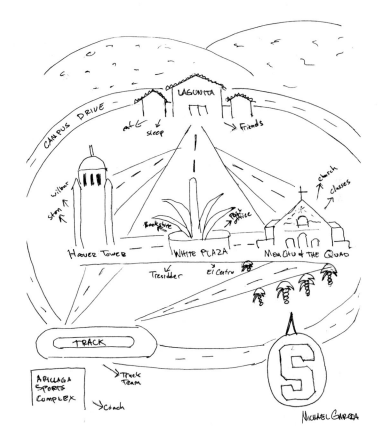

Critical Thinking about the Community

- Do you think of yourself as part of a community? What is your role in that community?

- In what ways is the community in which you live different from the community that you are writing about? How have these differences impacted your thinking and writing about the community?

- How do you think of yourself with respect to the community you are writing about? What is your role? Are you part of the community?

- Record any incidents that occur while you are writing about the community that are inspiring or provide you with new insights.

- Record any incidents that occur while you are writing about the community that you find confusing or disturbing.

- What have you learned about how to communicate with the community you are writing about? With your own community? What strategies have you learned that will help you in the future?

Collage Activity

Thinking critically about the community will help you to better understand your community experience, the experience of the community you will be working with, and the potential for collaboration and mutual learning. We would like you to create a collage that expresses what community means in the context of your daily life and values. Use any materials that seem appropriate to create your collage. On the back of your collage, write one paragraph that explains your artistic and content choices. Write a second paragraph that compares and contrasts your map and collage. In a final paragraph, draw conclusions about what you learned about your community and your own values from the two activities. Following is a collage by student writer Matt Leva, with the first part of his written explanation below.

There are a few things I associate with my Stanford Community. All of these compound my endless fatigued state. I feel the burden of books and work pressing down on me. I find myself feeling absent-minded and forgetful. The combination of baseball, ping pong, and computer, coupled with inefficient time management, has dug a nice hole for me. I need someone to help pull me out. But then again, maybe it's just a matter of Adaptation.

Part Two
Defining and Working Through the Project

Community Writing: Site Placement Worksheet

Name of Proposal_____

Student Name_____

Course Title_____

Instructor_____

Names of any peer group members

1._____   2._____

3._____   4._____

Agency representative and contact telephone:

Topic for community assignment:

Goals and objectives:

Community Writing: Journal Worksheet

What information and resources do you bring to this project?

What interests you about this writing project?

What selections in *Community Matters* will help you to think about your topic? What relationships do you see between your writing topic and these selections?

Record your questions, concerns, and insights as you work through your writing project.

What have you learned about the community through completing this project?

Community Writing: Collaboration Guidelines

College writing and much writing in the working world is collaborative—people work together both to initiate and generate materials and to compose and revise them. These guidelines may prove useful for collaboration projects.

- However groups are formed—by putting together people who sit near each other in class, through assignment to projects, or through common interests in a topic—get the names, telephone numbers, and addresses of others in your group right away.

- Share your schedules; write down times and days when everyone has free time or can make free time; check on evenings and weekends as well, but remember that if you work with community groups, some are open only traditional office hours, weekdays 8 a.m. to 5 p.m.

- Find out if someone in the group has a car. If you work with a community group off campus, figure out how you will get there: walking, bicycle, public transportation, or private car.

- If possible, assign a coordinator who will get in touch with everyone for work sessions, whether they take place in the community to gather information or on campus at the library for a writing or research session.

Community Writing: Evaluation Worksheet

Define community. Has your definition changed as a result of your experience writing for the community?

Did your experience help you to better understand any of the readings in *Community Matters?* Which ones? In what ways?

What did you learn about writing? How did your writing change?

If you were asked to establish criteria for grading this project, how would you decide on your criteria? What would indicators of success be within your grading system (writing, research, participation, collaboration, ability to meet deadlines, etc.). Assign a grade to yourself and include an explanation.

What suggestions do you have for your instructor or your community partners?

Assuming that your work will be carried on by the community through another student or volunteer, write a letter of introduction about the project, including background information, advice, and possible challenges.

A Model of A Community Writing Project

We have included the *Reach Out Newsletter* brochure as a model of community service writing projects.

Model Community Service Writing Project: Reach Out Newsletter

About the Assignment

The Community Service Writing Project for Reach Out[1] was completed by students in a first-year composition class that focused on the social issues theme "Writing for Change." Thematic issues in the students' reader included education and community, health and community, and nature and community. The placement for the education theme was at Reach Out, a program that helps high school students whose parents did not attend college to make a positive transition into college. The students in this eleven-week composition course were required to write four essays and complete one collaborative community service writing project, or they could have chosen to write five essays and not participate in a service-learning project. Fifteen of the eighteen students in the course decided to work on community service projects. Six of the students chose to help produce the Reach Out newsletter.

Reach Out is a program designed to provide a variety of academic support service to low-income and/or first-generation, college-bound students. The program's goals are to motivate students to attend college, to improve their academic preparation, and to demystify the process of preparing for and applying to college. During the academic year, Reach Out students receive tutoring and college counseling and participate in academic and career workshops on Saturdays throughout the semester.

Students were asked to write articles for the newsletter. Regular features include profiles of students, profiles of tutors, and program updates. Each of the six students kept a journal that included a record of their work on the project and what they were learning as they worked on their project.

"An Introduction to The Reach Out Project"

by Ann Sheehy

Performing community service had been important to me throughout high school, and I wanted to continue to make it a priority in college. The following is a summary of my CSW experience. On the first day of the

Continued

---

[1] The names of the program, the program participants, and the program director have all been changed to protect their privacy.

Continued

course, each of my classmates and I got to choose a public service organization to work with. I chose Reach Out, a federally funded program that provides a variety of academic support service to low-income and/or first-generation, college-bound students. Its purpose is to motivate and aid these high school students who might otherwise not attend college or even graduate from high school. In our program, eligible high school students from the local school district are matched with college tutors. Each Saturday, these tutors and tutee pairs meet for three hours to study high school coursework, review for standardized tests, work on college applications, and basically create an outlet for support and friendship. During the 1992–1993 school year in our local program, 75 such pairs existed. Of those 75, 22 were with high school seniors of whom 100 percent will graduate in June and go on to a two- or four-year university.

After selecting my placement, I got to work immediately. First, on the advice of my professor, I began to keep a journal of my community service experience. Then my group and I met with the woman in charge of the program who explained our project. We learned that we would each be writing a short article on an individually assigned topic. Each article would be submitted to the Reach Out newsletter, which was to be distributed throughout the school district, around the campus, to the U.S. Department of Education in Washington, and to other private sponsors. Its purpose was to help create an awareness of what Reach Out is and to stimulate some financial support from the surrounding community.

Before we left the director's office, she gave us a brief history of the organization, some more specifics of our project, and the names of some additional people to contact to get more information. At this point, we were to gather information from these sources, write a draft of our article, and meet back with the director two weeks later on an individual basis. This process of gathering and revising was repeated (for me, three times!) until the final paper was produced.

Journal

by Rich Crowe

Oct. 20
I called my director at 4:45 p.m. and he was not available. I left a message that I called and said that I would attempt to call him back tomorrow.

Oct. 21
I called the director at 6:30 p.m. and the office was closed. I left a message on his answering machine for him to return my phone call with my phone number.

Continued

Continued

Oct. 23

I attempted to contact the director by phone at 12:45 p.m. and again he was not in. I left another message asking for him to return my call with my phone number.

Oct. 23

The director returned my call at 2:00 p.m. and I told him that I wanted to write for the Reach Out newsletter. He told me that I needed to contact the newsletter's office.

The newsletter's editor was going to be out of town until Tuesday. The director said that he would give her the message to call me when she gets back into the office. He also said that if she does not call me by Wednesday, I should contact her.

Oct. 30

I called Reach Out at 1:30 p.m. and asked to speak with Susan, the editor. She was not available at that time, so I left a message for her to call me with my phone number. I am now beginning to get impatient, since I would like to get the necessary information to begin my writing project.

Nov. 1

I called Susan at 1:00 p.m. and she was not in. I left another message for her to return my phone call.

Nov. 3

I phoned Reach Out at 11:45 a.m. and Susan was not available. I again left a message for her to call me back. I have talked to other students in our newsletter group, and they also have had difficulties contacting Susan.

Nov. 4

I called Susan at 10:00 a.m. and she was not in. I again asked for her to return my call as soon as possible. It is apparent that Susan is difficult to get hold of. I have now tried calling her at numerous different times of day, but it has not seemed to work. I will continue calling and hopefully she will call me back.

Nov. 6

I phoned Susan at 9:30 a.m. and she was there. She asked me to meet with her at 10:00 a.m., so I did. At the meeting she explained to me what the Reach Out program is all about. She told me that all of last year's students are now going to college. She then gave me three choices to write about for the newsletter. They were:

1. Writing a profile of the senior class.
2. Writing profiles of the teen counselors.
3. Writing about Reach Out alumni.

Continued

Continued

I chose to write about the alumni. I chose to write about Maria, who is in her second year at the University of California at Santa Barbara. It is my job to interview her by telephone and write a short piece on her. I need a rough draft by Friday at 9:00 a.m., which is my next meeting with Susan. She also recommended that I focus the article on how well high school prepared Maria for college.

Nov. 8

I interviewed Maria by phone. I took notes of the conversation in shorthand in a notebook. I should be able to write my article from these notes, but I told Maria that I might need more information later and she said that it would be fine if I called back again. I thanked her for her time, and that was my first ever interview.

Nov. 13

I met with Susan at 9:00 a.m. and gave her a copy of my rough draft. She seemed to like it. She liked the points I made and the quotes I used to support them. Susan asked me to include one or two more sentences on being away from home and any advice for parents that Maria might have. I agreed that this would make the article better, and I said that I would call Maria back to ask her the questions. That was the only change that Susan wanted me to make in the article. I am to bring in a copy of my final draft on Tuesday or Friday of next week along with my computer disk, which they will take the article from to set up the newsletter. I feel like I've actually written something worthwhile. I enjoy this type of writing much more than writing essays.

Nov. 14

I called Maria at 12:45 p.m. and she was not in. She does not have an answering machine, so I will call back later.

I tried again at 3:30, but no one was home at that time either. At 8:30 p.m. I again tried and got in touch with Maria. I asked her the questions I needed to complete the article and told her how it was coming along. She seemed happy and asked me to tell Susan that she would like a copy of the finished newsletter.

Nov. 20

I went to the Reach Out office at 10:00 a.m. and dropped off my article and my computer disk. I thanked them all for their time and they thanked me for writing the article. That was the end of my writing project.

Continued

Continued
"Reach Out"

by Kathleen B. Chandler

One Saturday, I had the opportunity to meet some of the high school seniors in the Reach Out program. When I arrived at the center, they were writing essays for college applications; when I left a few hours later, they were just on their way to individual three-hour study sessions with the tutors.

For three to five years these high school seniors have been spending their Saturdays and summers doing schoolwork. Sound crazy? No. They're smart. Focused. Dedicated. Hardworking. Determined . . . and totally inspirational.

Heather is a young woman with a plan for her future. She explained that she plans to be an elementary or junior high school counselor and eventually open her own practice. Currently, she is one of the vice principal's student assistants, and she works as a peer counselor to help kids at her school keep on track and stay in school by talking to them, calling them daily, and making sure they go to class and do their homework. In talking with Heather, it is clear that her gentle but commanding voice would make her a good counselor. Heather has been in Reach Out since the summer of her eighth grade year and says that it has "helped me out tremendously." She says that it is like an alternative to school, where you know all the kids and have counselors whenever you need them.

Dana goes to Woodside High School now, but she and her family have lived in many parts of the world. She was born in what is now Ho Chi Minh City, Vietnam. When she was four years old, she and her family moved to Indonesia, and one year later, they came to the United States. She has a great talent for languages and can speak Vietnamese, Chinese, and English, and she is learning Spanish in school. Dana wants to major in business administration in college. She wants a job where she can travel to other places and meet different people. Reach Out has helped Dana a lot, even though at times she says she's been exhausted from all the work. "They keep nagging you!" Now as she looks forward to college, Dana is happy she had the emotional and academic support from Reach Out. "I feel really comfortable with these people."

Alberto found out about Reach Out when a representative came to his junior high school. Meeting new people is one of the great things about this program for Alberto. And, like nearly all of the people I interviewed, his favorite part of being in Reach Out has been the summer school program. Every year since he was accepted into Reach Out, he has lived with his fellow students in the dorms for six weeks during the summer. He has taken a

Continued

Continued

variety of classes ranging from math to ethnic studies. But Alberto's real love is music. One day he'd like to work as a DJ or a technician or "just anything" at a radio station.

Rosa wants to be a civil engineer. In eighth grade her class went on a tour of the city and talked to the mayor, maintenance workers, and a civil engineer. The engineer told her about a housing project that was about to be built on an old dump site. The project was eventually built, but Rosa says that even though it looks nice, she wouldn't like to live there. Now she is determined to do better. At her school, she takes part in a group called Math, Engineering, and Science Achievement (MESA). She has been in Reach Out for four years and says, "It's really good to come every Saturday and see the friends I haven't seen all week."

When I asked Patty if she was glad to have been involved in Reach Out for the past five years, she replied with a definite, "Oh yeah." She was soft-spoken and friendly, and said that Reach Out has helped her get good grades in high school. Reach Out tutors and counselors have answered her many questions, academic and beyond, about high school, college, and job opportunities. Patty speaks Spanish and English, studies French in high school, and is thinking about continuing her French studies in college. However, like most high school seniors and college freshmen, she hasn't decided in which field she might like to major in college.

"Reach Out is a great program," according to Jane, and she would recommend it to any high school student wanting to go to college. Jane goes to Kennedy High School and insists that she wouldn't be thinking about college if she hadn't gotten involved in Reach Out, although she adds that her mom has helped her a lot as well because she "pushes me all the time." Today, women in the police force are still not all that common, but Jane plans to beat the statistics. Her lifelong goal is to become a police officer.

Pilár is a high-energy young woman who is very involved in her high school and her church. She goes to a private school, where she is one of only seven Latinos. As a cofounder of her high school's multicultural awareness club, she is part of a support group for minority students and their parents. The group provides tutoring and counseling and helps recruit minority students to the school. She also is part of a church group that goes on retreats with high school kids who are having problems at home or in school. Pilár plans to work hard and take advantage of the opportunities that a college can offer by majoring in human biology or premed. She also wants to try something new and take a Mexican dance class (ballet folklorico).

These are only a few of the students of the 1992 Reach Out senior class. With just this small taste of the character of the students involved in Reach Out, I was taken by the energy and determination these high school students have. With the amount of time and energy Reach Out students put

Continued

Continued

into their high school studies, it's no wonder that the program has a 100 percent college entrance rate.

"Southern California College Trip"

by Jayme Plunkett

On October 20, 1992, eighteen Reach Out seniors and two staff members set out on a trip that covered nearly seventeen hours of driving, ten hours of tours and discussions, and five different cities . . . all in a matter of four days. Why? Their goal was to visit five southern California colleges, giving the students some firsthand experience of what each individual campus is like.

After leaving their host college, their first stop was the University of California at Santa Barbara (UCSB). From there, it was on to California State University at Long Beach (CSULB), San Diego State University (SDSU), the University of San Diego (USD), and Pomona College. At each school, the students received a tour of the campus and were given a chance to ask questions.

The tour allows each student to gain his or her own perspectives about each college by talking with current college students and being able to see the campus itself, instead of just glancing through a college catalog. Jane, a third-year Reach Out student and a senior from Kennedy High School, said the tour influenced her decision to apply to one of the colleges that the group visited. Prior to her visit, she had no intention of applying to any southern California schools.

The southern California college tour is an excellent idea and offers students a great opportunity to learn firsthand what prospective college students are like and whether the atmosphere is what they are looking for as a part of their college experience. It is the best alternative to college catalogs.

"Alumni Advice"

by Rich Crowe

Maria C., a Stanford Reach Out alumna, has some advice for high school students. Maria is now in her second year of college at the University of California at Santa Barbara. She attended Sequoia High School for four years and was in the Reach Out program for the last three.

Continued

Continued

Maria started high school in the ESL program since her native language was Spanish. As a result of her language difficulties, she was placed in the low-level math classes in which she did not belong. Maria worked hard on her English skills and got A's in her math classes before she realized that she could get involved in her own education and change to more challenging classes. She transferred into the more difficult math courses that helped her to be better prepared for college, where she plans to major in accounting. If Maria had not changed her classes, she may never have been in the position to major in accounting.

Stories like this one cause Maria to think that high schools could do a better job of preparing students for college. "High schools should be geared toward preparing students for college," says Maria. "Nowadays, a high school education is not enough. The high school needs to prepare you for a college education." This is where the Reach Out program comes in. The program helps high school students prepare for college. Maria's advice for high school students is to stay in the Reach Out program and not to fear college. She says, "Do not be afraid of the large college classrooms, the entrance exams, or the applications. Stay in the program, and you'll be all right." Being away from home is another concern of many high school students. Maria made new friends at college by joining the STEP program (similar to the Bridge program), which she recommends. By making many friends she says, "you won't become as lonely or as homesick." Maria also recommends that "parents support their children's leaving home for college since it helps them become more mature adults." The moral of the story is to get involved in the education process that can start by joining Reach Out, and to see it through to a college education as Maria has.

"Point Incentive System"

by Ann Sheehy

Free movie passes, $100 GAP gift certificates, Santa Cruz boardwalk passes?

It's really easy through the Reach Out Point System! Initiated last year, the system was designed to monitor the extra incentive to work hard. Everything from telephone calls between tutor pairs to actual attendance at Saturday sessions is recorded, and points are then awarded accordingly. Each tutor pair can earn a total of 30 points a week—ten for tutor/tutee communication and 20 for each Saturday morning session. Tutor coordinators may even award bonus points for perfect attendance, going to meetings, and other supplemental activities that teach students to be more accountable for their actions. The tutor pairs with the most points at the end of the year win incredible prizes!

Continued

Continued

But does the Point System work? According to Heather O., the students involved feel that they have been more motivated and excited since the program started. Heather, last year's second-place winner and four-year Reach Out student, thought that the program increased motivation for those students who may not have kept in close contact with their tutor otherwise. The prizes, she said, are "an extra boost!" And this year, that boost is even greater—with the cooperation of many local businesses, even *more* great prizes will be offered!

So, lift your expectations and meet the challenges of the Reach Out Point System—what do you have to lose when there's so much to gain?

"Reach Out Through Academic-Year Programs"

by Kwan Ping Chua

Hey you! Now that I have your attention, do you know why high school students from East Palo Alto come to Stanford on Saturdays? Is it to watch the football game between the Cardinals and the Stags from UC Berkeley or is to catch the Stanford women's volleyball team in action? Of course not! They come to Stanford to "Reach Out."

Reach Out is a national academic program targeted at high school students who are first-generation, college-bound or who come from low-income families. The program's goal is to help these high school students academically and to prepare them for college. Seventy students are currently participating in the program and more than 90 percent of these students will eventually enter college.

Reach Out achieves its aim by organizing and coordinating various academic and counseling programs. The most important one is the Academic-Year Program, which has an intensive academic focus all year-round. This program is designed to assess the individual student's academic needs, to assist the student's progress in class, and to provide the student with necessary information concerning the college application process.

The program is divided into different sections to meet the specific needs of different classes of students. Freshmen are enrolled in the Study Skills class while sophomores are enrolled in the College Exploration class. The purpose of the Study Skills class is to help ninth graders make the transition into high school. The purpose of the College Exploration class is to expose sophomores to the many different college systems and to help them to select high school classes on the basis of college requirements for admission. Juniors are enrolled in an intensive test preparation class that emphasizes verbal drills, as many of the students are not native speakers of

Continued

Continued

English. A typical lesson includes doing comprehension exercises and learning new words to help expand the student's vocabulary.

In their senior year, Reach Out students have many opportunities to talk with the project director about their thoughts of going to college and any other questions or concerns they might have concerning college life, which usually includes sharing their apprehension about going away from home to college, as well as selecting colleges and majors. Seniors also receive help in completing the cumbersome college applications, financial aid applications, and housing forms. A crash course in writing is also organized for the seniors to help prepare them for college application essays. Furthermore, seniors are counseled about what college to attend after they have received responses from the various admissions offices.

Another way Reach Out assists the students academically is to conduct tutoring sessions every Saturday from 12 p.m. to 3 p.m. Each student has an individual tutor to help him or her with the subjects in which he or she needs help. The tutors are Stanford students who volunteer three hours every Saturday for an entire academic year. The tutors also serve as mentors and counselors to the students. In addition, exciting field trips to various college campuses and places of social, cultural, and recreational value are planned for the students regularly.

Rosa, a senior at Sequoia, has been with Reach Out since her freshman year in high school, when her brother introduced her to the program. She is receiving tutoring in English and math that she finds "very useful." The tutoring sessions also help her "not to get behind in class." As a senior in high school, she finds the SAT prep class especially beneficial as it provides her with practice tests and testing strategies. Rosa believes that Reach Out is a "worthwhile program" and she is "very glad to join it."

Reach Out has helped hundreds of first-generation, college-bound, high school students perform better academically and thus has increased their chances to enter college. If you are also a first-generation, college-bound, student in need of advice about college and help with schoolwork, get an application now and complete it today.

The following student evaluation will help you to understand the learning process, the challenges, and the rewards of this particular community service writing project:

"Evaluating the Reach Out Project"

by Kwan Ping Chua

When I requested a freshman English track with a community service writing program, I hoped to be involved in some community work besides writing for the various organizations. I was very excited when I learned that

Continued

Continued

I had been placed in such a track, and I looked forward to volunteering my time to do some community service. On the third week of class, my professor showed us the list of agencies that were participating in the CSW program. I decided to get involved in Reach Out, a federally funded program that helps first-generation, college-bound, high school students, because I was interested in working with teenagers. However, I was disappointed when I went for my first meeting with the assistant director of the program. I found out that I would be writing an article for their newsletter and would not be actually participating in any community work. Nevertheless, I was still enthusiastic about writing the article as that would be my first time writing for a real audience instead of writing only for my class instructor.

My first meeting with the project director went smoothly. She showed me a list of topics to write about for the newsletter; I chose the Academic-Year Program as I was interested in the ways that Reach Out had been helping the students. I was feeling very excited at the prospect of my article appearing in a newsletter. We decided to meet later in the week to discuss more about my assignment. Meanwhile, she gave me a copy of the latest newsletter and some brochures to read. Reading the articles in the newsletter was especially helpful; I developed insight into the style and tone to use when writing the article. I realized that most of the articles were written in an enthusiastic tone that portrayed Reach Out as a program filled with fun and excitement. Furthermore, reading the articles kindled a burning desire within me to start writing immediately. Unfortunately, I had to wait a few days for my second meeting with Susan to get more information.

My second meeting with Susan was also a successful one. We had an interesting conversation, as well as an informal interview. She gave me a lot of information on the Academic-Year Program to help me get started with my article. In addition, she suggested that I contact one of the participants in the program in order to get a different perspective on the program. I got the contact number of Rosa, a senior from Sequoia High School, whom I planned to call that night.

After the meeting, I rushed back to my room to write the article. However, writing the article was not as easy as I thought it would be. I was unaccustomed to writing for a real audience, and it was difficult starting the article. Only after reading through the articles in the previous newsletters did I manage to write the introduction. I tried to convey enthusiasm to the readers through the use of short sentences; furthermore, I tried to use simple language as English is not the native language of most of the readers of Reach Out's newsletter. My writing process was slow and tedious, as I had to stop constantly to think of ways to make the article more interesting.

Besides the difficulty in writing the article, I was frustrated with Susan when she did not turn up for the third meeting. I tried calling her many times after that but she was always not around. It was after a week that I

Continued

Continued

managed to get her. Unfortunately, we could not agree on a time to meet. Finally, I decided to leave my first draft in her office for her to go over. During the week, I tried calling Susan to find out if she had finished looking through my draft but I was always unsuccessful. Just before Thanksgiving, I managed to contact her and she promised to give me back my draft before the Thanksgiving break. I completed my article over the Thanksgiving break and I gave it to Susan on the first day of December. She seemed to be impressed with it and even commented that it would appear on the front page of the newsletter. Although I was really excited about that, I was more relieved that the project was completed as it was both time-consuming and frustrating to work with Reach Out.

Looking back at my involvement in the project, I realized that although I was not actively involved in community work, writing an article for Reach Out's newsletter has enabled me to understand the work that goes on behind the scenes in a community service organization. I began to understand that it was often not Susan's fault when she couldn't make time for an appointment; most of the time, she was too busy or her attention was needed in some other more urgent matters. Besides coordinating the program, she has to write proposals to improve the program, advise the students when they have difficulties, and bring the students for field trips to various universities in California. I began to sympathize with her.

Perhaps the greatest joy in participating in the community service writing program is to know that Susan, along with her staff, really appreciated my time and my effort to help lighten their loads. It is comforting to know that the article will be published in the newsletter and will serve as another way of reaching out to those students who are in need of academic help and advice but are unaware of Reach Out's program. I believe that I have benefited more from the community service project than I have contributed to Reach Out. It has been a learning experience working on "a real-world project," writing for real audiences, and interacting with other people who have different viewpoints. I certainly look forward to another quarter of involvement in the community service writing program.

"Closing Advice: Student to Student"

by Ann Sheehy

When I was done, I had a chance to reflect on my community service writing experience. Performing community service almost always produces a feeling of well-being—helping to write the Reach Out newsletter was no exception. I share the following tips, based on my experience, that I think will help you to meet the challenges of your service-learning experience:

Continued

Continued

1. Always keep in mind the audience who will be reading your writing.

I had always written essays to be read and graded by a professor, but with my CSW project, I had to grasp the attention of parents, students, and teachers in the Sequoia school district, as well as the Stanford community. Although it is hard to write for a different audience, this aspect of the project helped me develop and expand my writing skills.

2. Keep a journal

I recorded every phone call, appointment, frustration, and excitement I experienced through the course of my project. This not only helped me to stay organized, but also helped me to evaluate my experience after I had finished.

3. Realize that a community service writing project is more difficult than an ordinary essay.

When writing a research paper, it is easy to open a book to find information whenever you need to. With CSW, you may call an important information source only to find that they are out of town for the week! Missed meetings, numerous phone calls, and multiple revisions are all inherent in this type of writing project. Try your best not to get discouraged.

4. Start early!

5. Most importantly, keep in mind that your work is valuable.

My experience with Reach Out taught me so much about what actually goes on "behind the scenes" at community service organizations. I saw how much work, dedication, and determination goes into making a public service organization run smoothly, and how much of that burden is laid on a disproportionately small number of people. This made me realize that yes, Reach Out really *did* need our help, as we were helping, in however small a way, to lighten the organization's enormous workload. This realization helped make the frustrating times a little easier.

Our group was glad we had the opportunity to work together on the newsletter. As classmate Jeremy Taylor summarized, "This project gave purpose to my writing and introduced me to something new and challenging."

"Agency's Evaluation"

by Armand Merced

I just wanted to go on record in praise of the experience Reach Out has had with the real writers. I participate in the program because I enjoy working with the students and strongly believe that students are provided

Continued

Continued

with an educational experience unlike that in an average undergraduate course. I must also admit that Reach Out really benefits from the writing assistance the students provide.

I usually assign newsletter articles that consist of student profiles, program descriptions, staff interviews, and general press releases about up-to-the-minute events. I give real writers options: I allow them to choose the article they want to pursue. I love sitting with them and playing the editor looking for various angles to the same story. Quite frankly, it's fun!

My approach is simple: Real writers call and I set up a meeting with them as a group. I provide them with an overview of the program, its mission, participants, and successes. This usually hooks them. They then select their topics and make an individual appointment with me to discuss the specifics of their assignments. If a real writer's assignment is to interview a Reach Out student, I will issue a phone number and invite the writer to a tutoring session or Saturday college where he or she can meet with the person. I also make it a point to meet with each real writer prior to first and final draft deadlines to review his or her work and answer program–related or technical questions.

One of the reasons that Reach Out might be so popular as a community sponsor is that the students not only learn about the writing process, voice, and audience, but also see in flesh and blood the subjects they are writing about. That is to say, Reach Out consists of individuals working collectively in various components of the program toward a common goal: to prepare and motivate low-income, high school students for college. And each real writer, as part of a collective, is researching and writing about one piece of this large puzzle that is then given shape in the form of a newsletter. This, I believe, motivates a real writer to write for Reach Out.

I would love to answer any questions you have about community service writing and Reach Out. Feel free to call me at anytime.

Sincerely,

Armand
Program Director

"Instructor's Evaluation"

by Marjorie Ford

The Reach Out placement has always been one that I can depend on. Because the office is on campus and I have worked with the directors in previous quarters, I had a good sense of what types of writing they would

Continued

Continued

expect from students and how they would work with them. I think the directors do an excellent job of setting up a positive collaborative relationship among the students. I believe that having established a relationship with an agency before sending students to work at that agency can be a crucial factor in a project's success. While new placements are certainly worth undertaking, they do involve more time and more risk.

The six students who worked on this newsletter were motivated to learn more about the lives of the high school students and share their new insights in the articles they wrote for the Reach Out newsletter. The students matured through the process of working together and with the agency. In addition, all of the students felt challenged by having to write for a new audience. They shaped their writing with their audience's backgrounds and interests in mind. Their world views were broadened by finding out more about the Reach Out program and the students who participate in the program. Most of all, the students realized that what they were doing was genuinely appreciated and useful to the overworked staff at Reach Out. Many of these students went on to volunteer at other nonprofit organizations on and off campus.

Community Writing: Reflection Worksheet

Did you learn new strategies for communicating with an audience as a result of this writing assignment? Discuss these strategies.

Did the reading and writing that you completed for your class help you to understand the issues in the community? In what ways?

Through completing this writing assignment, what did you learn about yourself—your personal values, your cultural values, your gender assumptions, your expectations, and your responsibilities?

What did you learn about working collaboratively? What insights have you developed about the value of discussing experiences, ideas, and strategies as part of your writing process? If you produced a collaboratively written piece, what did you learn from this particular aspect of the project?

Compare and contrast your community writing project with your previous writing experiences? Did your understanding of how you learn change through completing this writing project?

Would you choose to be involved in a similar type of project in the future? Explain your decision.

Community Action Projects with Reflections

Ivanka (Vanya) Choumanova   Choumanova 1

Habitat for Humanity: The Gift of Hope

Two months after immigrating to the United States from Bulgaria, my family moved into a small brick apartment in Westchester County, New York. The worn-out floor, the gray, dingy couch spread in the midst of our living room, and the leaky pipes in the apartment added to the turmoil of our cultural adjustments. We were ashamed of our new home. I knew that by living in America we had made a sacrifice, but I had never pictured us living in such an impoverished home. I had never imagined that my family would be struggling for survival. My mother was fired from her first job at the bakery, and my father remained unemployed as he couldn't speak English. Soon we realized that we should return to Bulgaria. After all, America was not the dream we had envisioned.

We were pleasantly surprised when our neighbor gave us a brochure advertising Habitat for Humanity, a nonprofit organization, whose mission is to provide decent, affordable housing for low-income families. My mom continued holding that small piece of "hope" in her hands, as she exclaimed in her thick Bulgarian accent, "We can build our house, our new house! The community will help us!" We were thrilled about having the opportunity to build our first home in America. In addition, we were promising candidates: We were willing to work in partnership with Habitat and pay the no-interest mortgage.

Then unexpectedly, both of my parents were offered full-time positions. Instead of participating in Habitat, we decided to save money and buy a house. This way, we could give the chance to be involved with Habitat to another struggling family. Because my family chose not to become involved in the project, I never experienced the satisfaction of building our own home. Nonetheless, the belief in Habitat for Humanity uplifted my family's spirits: it gave us faith that we could survive in America. Habitat for Humanity bestowed upon us the much-needed verification that compassionate people in our community would support us if we needed their help.

Choumanova 2

Those first weeks in the United States when my family was given hope by the opportunity to work with Habitat has led me to want to further understand the organization, how it functions, and what types of families it serves. Founded in 1976 by Millard and Linda Fuller, Habitat for Humanity International (HFHI) provides decent shelter for hardworking families deserving a home. Habitat has built "more than 100,000 houses around the world, including 30,000 houses in the United States." The houses are affordable because they are sold at no profit. Corporations, individuals, and faith groups often provide financial support. HFHI, however, is not a give-away program. In addition to a down payment and the monthly mortgage payments, home owners must invest hundreds of hours of their own labor into building their homes. By lowering the down payment and providing a down payment subsidy to home buyers, Habitat makes homes more affordable. Furthermore, the home owners' monthly mortgage payments are used to build additional Habitat houses, so the new home owners are engaged in helping others who desperately need a home.

Habitat welcomes all volunteers to build affordable houses in partnership with those in need of adequate shelter. Home owner families are chosen according to their need and their willingness to work in partnership with Habitat. HFHI is also currently involved in the fund-raising campaign "More than houses: rebuilding our communities." The campaign aids families affected by disasters and rebuilds their security. HFHI recognizes that decent, permanent housing remains a necessity long after relief organizations complete their work.

Although two thirds of the population of the United States own homes, thousands of families cannot afford mortgage payments and struggle paying their rent. As housing costs continue to skyrocket, decent housing remains out of reach for many working families. As a result, the gap is growing between those who live in a stable environment and are part of a mainstream society and those who live in isolation and poverty. The efforts of Habitat for Humanity are examples of how the gap between these two communities can be closed. Unfortunately, this problem is growing faster than the collective efforts of Habitat and other organizations addressing housing needs.

Choumanova 3

So, how is it possible for a single organization to assist families all around the world? Habitat for Humanity's work is accomplished at the community level by affiliates—independent, locally run, nonprofit organizations. Each affiliate coordinates aspects of home building in the area by fund-raising and selecting both the building sites and the partner families. There are more than 1,900 active affiliates in 79 countries. Hundreds of volunteers perform community service for each of the affiliates, and Habitat volunteers are universally known as "angels with tool belts."

I had the chance to speak to two such "angels," who are students at Stanford University and volunteer at a building site in nearby Redwood City. Jenny, a freshman at Stanford, spent last Saturday painting a house. "I want to help the homeless," she remarks, "and I love to build houses just because I can see the visual product of what I am helping out with. It might sound selfish, but I also feel a personal satisfaction after being altruistic." Rachel, who is also a new member of Stanford's Habitat for Humanity, likes another aspect of the organization: "We built a community so quickly this last Saturday," she comments, "and the people I met were amazing. Fifty years from now I can go to Redwood City, and the house we worked on will still be there. We built a home today."

After my research and interviewing some of the volunteers, I really wanted to encourage my "Community Matters" writing class to participate in Habitat. Each tile we glued firmly to the floor and each piece of sheetrock we nailed into the walls brought a family's dream closer to becoming a reality. We were building the foundations of a community, a community of hardworking, deserving families, who until now did not have a home. But we also established another community, one that consisted of ten students, all wanting to help others.

Thousands of people are in need of decent homes just like my family was four years ago. The truth is that all of us can help and bring hope to a family in need of a safe home. One Saturday you could volunteer at a local Habitat for Humanity site. Do not let the opportunity to become a part of such a meaningful community slip away. Spread your wings and become an "angel with a tool belt."

Melissa Burns   Burns 1

Our Class Project: Habitat for Humanity

Repetitive motions ran mindlessly through my head and body: Grab a nail. Place it near the penciled line on the sheetrock. BANG! Grab a nail. Place it near the penciled line on the sheetrock. BANG! Grab a nail. Place it near the penciled line on the sheetrock. BANG! Finally, I had finished one narrow wall. Now it was time to measure and cut the next piece of sheetrock, only to repeat the grueling process. Every hour or so I would break from my work, walk toward a tiny window, and lower my face mask to take a deep breath of fresh air. I wiped the beads of sweat from my upper lip with a once dark T-shirt that was now completely whitened from hazardous drywall filings, as though I had weathered a New York blizzard. Besides lunch, however, break times were short and infrequent. I was determined, along with my friends Tiffany Castillo and Peter Finlayson, to complete our assignment before we left the Redwood City, California, "Peninsula Habitat for Humanity" construction site on the afternoon of March 9, 2002.

"Habitat for Humanity" is a renowned humanitarian organization that provides quality housing to thousands of struggling families every year. Although most people are familiar with this volunteer organization, relatively few have actually found the time and the opportunity to contribute to its cause. Several members of my writing class, called "Community Matters," took the initiative to arrange a group volunteer session with a "Habitat for Humanity" site in a poor, neighboring community.

I had expected to build a small apartment, from foundation to finishing touches, in a matter of hours; apparently, the notion of constructing an entire home within one day is a common misconception about "Habitat for Humanity." Instead, when Peter's car pulled into the work site, we saw a miniature village of connected townhouses, each in a different state of construction. One of the complexes was completely finished, while others required only the final steps: carpet installation, cleaning, and painting. Several hundred feet away, another cluster of townhouses had just taken root, with only the wiring and basic framework completed.

I was amazed at the turnout of volunteers. By nine o'clock, more than sixty people had assembled around a main tent. The majority of the helpers represented various religious and student groups, while a handful had no particular affiliation. (These individuals appeared to be "regulars" who knew the ropes.) We were all quickly briefed on safety procedures and then split into teams based on our personal work preferences. Tiffany, Peter, and I opted to install sheets of drywall. Others went in separate directions to lay carpet, clean and vacuum, plant flowers, fill potholes in the street, and move heavy wheelbarrows filled with construction debris.

Once inside the home where we would spend the next eight hours, the head "Habitat for Humanity" volunteers instructed us about correct sheetrock procedures. After this "crash course," we were left on our own. Thankfully, Tiffany had construction experience. In fact, she had helped her father build their family home. She assumed the leadership role in our small group and delegated tasks, such as hammering, filing, and measuring. Although Tiffany was directing us, this was a true team effort. When I had trouble pounding nails into tight corners (as was often the case), Peter came to my assistance. On several occasions, the collective strength of the three of us was required to fit the drywall into place. Halfway through the day, when I accidentally stepped on a piece of sheetrock that Tiffany had already measured and cut, snapping it into two jagged pieces, Tiffany laughed it off. While we worked, we joked about our whitened appearances and our previous construction experience, or lack thereof. We even had the opportunity to work with Bill, an older, heavyset, and mentally challenged man who helped us measure the drywall while providing much-needed conversational relief.

Looking back on the time I spent at "Peninsula Habitat for Humanity," I am reminded of the trust, friendship, and feeling of community that our team established. That day, sixty very diverse individuals joined together to improve the welfare of those who had been less fortunate. In the process, I shared an amazing time with my close friends, met new people, and observed the inherent goodness in the members of our society. This activity represented a stark contrast to the evil, the terror, and the war that we witnessed on the daily news in the wake of September 11. I walked away from "Habitat for Humanity" covered with dust, dripping in sweat, and aching all over. Inside, however, I felt satisfied and spiritually renewed. I believe that human beings, who occasionally choose to commit atrocities, are exceedingly more capable of showing intense love and compassion for their fellow man. Every so often, we need to be reminded about the strengths of our inner characters, and the ability in each and every one of us to make a small difference in the world.

Relevant Web Sites

American Association for Higher Education (AAHE)
Service Learning Project <http://www.org/service/srv-lrn.html>

This web site describes publications and conferences sponsored by AAHE related to service learning, as well as related service learning links.

Campus Compact <http://www.compact.org>

Campus Compact is a national alliance of colleges and universities interested in promoting service and leadership at their institutions. The web site includes syllabi of courses with service dimensions, full text of and order forms for its publications, and job postings related to service and higher education.

Campus Outreach Opportunity League (COOL)
<http://www.cool2serve.org>

COOL is dedicated to the education and empowerment of college students to strengthen the nation through community service. The web site's "frequently asked questions" describe the function and nature of COOL, describe COOL's program "Into the Streets," and introduce its publications and other materials available for purchase.

National Society for Experiential Education (NSEE)
<http://www.nsee.org>

NSEE is a national resource center that promotes experienced-based approaches to teaching and learning.

Raise Your Voice <http://www.actionforchange.org>

Campus Compact's Raise Your Voice Campaign is a national effort to engage students in public life through support for student voices, service, and engagement in the democracy.

A Sense of Place

5

Community volunteers participate in building a home for Habitat for Humanity

When we think about community, many of us remember popular images in movies, sitcoms, and reality television. We may think about coffee-houses and clubs, backyard barbecues, and house parties. In contrast, television news tells us something different about the places where we live. Violence, distrust, and tragedy are also a part of daily lives and, ultimately, form some of our senses of place and our understandings of community.

Our communities are always in a state of transition, and any change may demand new ways of understanding and communicating. While our houses look the same, television, telephones, faxes, and e-mail have turned our homes into information hubs from which we can communicate with the world. As virtual communication thrives, more traditional forms of communication remain a necessity. The issues we confront in our daily lives are indicators of problems that persist within our modern world: population growth, shifting economic trends, environmental degradation, and racial intolerance. The selections in "A Sense of Place" address the complexities, ambiguities, and contradictions we encounter in the communities where we live.

The readings in the first section, "Memories of Place, Identity, and Community," explore the relationships between individuals and the places that have influenced their experiences and values. These selections ask us to think about our memories of place as a way of understanding who we are, where we come from, and how we interact within a community. By remembering the places that have made an impression on us, we often recall the people who have shared those spaces with us—family, friends, neighbors, teachers—all members of our community. In the first selection, "My Grandmother's House," Mary Gordon returns to her childhood home in search of the "connections between where we live and who we are, between how we experience place and how we become ourselves." The intersections between her memories and observations become the foundation of her self-understanding and her life as a writer. The next selection, Sandra Cisneros's "Monkey Garden," offers a window into the changing world of adolescents. In the privacy of a small neighborhood garden, a community of friends confront the expectations and disappointments of friendship and love while also moving closer to understanding their need for independent values and separate identities. In "Baghdad Cafe," Jason Florio, a New York photographer, is drawn to the diversity of the Muslim world, where he connects with a strong cultural tradition rooted in words. Our sense of place is shaped by the ways in which we connect with our memories, our traditions, and our beliefs. What are the connections between the places where you have lived and who you are? What traditions and daily rituals characterize your community experience?

Place-based communities are informed by the collective experience of many individuals, where the power of community can be both positive and negative. The readings in the second section, "Political and Natural Challenges," explore a variety of ways that change takes place within communities. In "A Moral Place," Tracy Kidder reveals the complexity that lies beneath the surface of a seemingly peaceful New England town where the democratic process is undermined by social pressures and cultural expectations. The next selection, "The Invisible Riot," describes a community struggling to prosper in the face of growing economic instability. This community's solidarity, expressed in public riots, wide-scale looting, and destruction of property, is a testimony to the dangerous and destructive power of community. In the final selection, "Total Eclipse," Annie Dillard travels to a small town to witness a natural happening, and through her shared experience with a group of strangers she is able to process and make sense of the experience.

What systems support your community experience? Do you participate in the decision-making process within your community? Are your individual beliefs represented in the community? Through community organizations and public forums we can work together to meet the demands of change; we can make a difference in our communities. A deeper understanding of our connection to community provides a foundation for effecting change within our communities. The selections in "Activists Rebuilding Communities" profile different ways that individuals and members of a group—artists, researchers, and environmentalists—have found ways to express their commitment to change through their participation in a community. In "The Art of Change," Sue Halpern profiles Jane Golden, director of the Mural Arts Program, has helped to improve the landscape of Philadelphia by involving over 10,000 kids and a roster of 300 artists in beautification projects throughout the city. Kimi Eisele has brought national attention to the impoverished lives of children in Mexican border communities. Former President Jimmy Carter and his wife Roslyn work in partnership with Habitat for Humanity International in the global effort to alleviate homelessness.

Has someone in your community inspired you? What has he or she contributed to your community? Would you like to participate in an action-based project in your community? As you read through the selections in "A Sense of Place," we hope that you will also think about the people who have influenced you and the places that have helped to define your experiences. Through a better understanding of the issues that confront and shape our communities we can develop a sense of how to make our world a better place to live.

Mary Gordon (b. 1949)

My Grandmother's House

Mary Gordon was raised on Long Island, New York. She received a B.A. from Barnard College (1971) and a M.A. from Syracuse University (1973). Gordon has worked as a college teacher and has written many novels, short stories, and essays including Final Payments *(1978),* The Company of Women *(1981),* Men and Angels *(1985),* The Other Side *(1989), and* Seeing Through Places *(2000). In her essay "My Grandmother's House," included in* Seeing Through Places, *Gordon explores her Catholic upbringing through the places, both physical and emotional, that have shaped her identity.*

Some days I would be left at my grandmother's house. I never knew why. Usually, I could ask my father anything, but I couldn't ask him that, why I was being left at my grandmother's, because I knew it was a privilege to be in that house, and no one, even my father would understand my reluctance. It was only a partial reluctance anyway, and I believed then that I had no business communicating anything I only partially understood.

Entering the house, I was plunged into an atmosphere of bafflement. The words, the manners, all the things, were foreign to me. The foreignness almost seemed literal; often I didn't understand what the people in my grandmother's house were saying, and often what I said was not understood.

What do I mean by understand? There were names for things that I found unfamiliar: "commode" for toilet, "box" for the area of the floor where the dog was made to lie, "pantry" for a series of shelves on one of the kitchen walls. My mother used these words easily, but she didn't use them to describe anything in our house. Or our apartment, what my father and I called home but what was to her something else. Something serious and untemporary. Something that generated no names proper to itself. In her mother's house, my mother knew that everything had been named long ago, once and for all.

I had trouble placing my grandmother's house. I knew it had nothing to do with America. Or postwar life. And yet it stood at the center of the lives of all her children and her children's children. It expressed an era—historical, perhaps, wholly imaginary, that we grandchildren only vaguely understood. We knew that it had ended long before we were born; it seemed to have touched upon our parents' early childhood, but we weren't sure. There were twenty-one grandchildren who visited my grandmother's house regularly. Of her nine children, only two had settled more than ten miles away from her. We all lived on Long Island, in towns that bordered Queens and took their identity more from "the city" than "the island." My grandmother had lived in the same house since 1920, when the area was farmland; she despised the people who had moved there from Brooklyn or the Bronx after the war. She condemned new houses and the objects in them.

5   Each object in her house belonged to the Old World. Nothing was easy; everything required maintenance of a complicated and specialized sort. Nothing was disposable, replaceable. There were no errors of taste because there were no other imaginable choices. I was not unhappy there; each object's rightness of placement made me feel honored to be among them. Yet I was always guilty among those things, as if they knew I preferred what was in my glamorous aunt's house. She lived in the next town from my grandmother's; her husband owned a liquor store and made more money than anyone we knew. My aunt and uncle bought things easily, unlike the rest of the family, and so the house was full of new or newish objects: the plastic holders for playing cards, like shells or fans, the nut dishes in the shape of peanuts, the corn dishes in the shape of ears of corn, the hair dryer like a rocket, the makeup mirror framed by light-bulbs, the bottles of nail polish, the ice bucket, the cocktail shaker, the deep freeze. And the house was stocked with pleasurable things to eat, drink, sit on, listen to, lean against, watch, sleep in, ride, or wear. I knew these pleasures to be inferior, but I sank into them each time, stealing their luxury and fearing for my soul, as I half feared for my aunt's, which I couldn't imagine to be the same, interested as she was in having a good time.

My grandmother had no interest in having a good time—that is, in doing anything that would result only in pleasure—and her house proclaimed this, as it proclaimed everything about her. Her house was her body, and like her body, was honorable, daunting, reassuring, defended, castigating, harsh, embellished, dark. I can't imagine how she lived, that is to say how she didn't die of the endless labor her life entailed. Nine children. It's easy either to romanticize her or utterly to push her aside.

Although I wasn't happy there, I did, somehow, like her house. Her garden had old-fashioned flowers, bright colored, a little wild; marigold, cosmos, foxglove, phlox. Older varieties of roses, whose petals seemed thinner than those of more recent types, more susceptible, as my soft flesh was more susceptible than those of the adults around me, to insect bites that made it horrible to the eye. I liked her garden even better than my aunt's, where the greens were deeper than the greens of any leaves of grass I'd seen anywhere else. I linked dark greenness to prosperity, as if my uncle had invested in that greenness so that we would all be more secure. My grandmother's house had no connection to prosperity; it had righteousness instead.

CONVERSATION STARTER

Discuss your feelings about visiting the home of a grandparent, relative, or family friend when you were young. When you go back to visit, do you feel the same way as you did then?

READING MATTERS

1. Gordon asks the question, "What do I mean by understand?" How does this question frame the narrative? Does Gordon find understanding?
2. Gordon contrasts her grandmother's house with her aunt's house, yet she barely mentions her own home. What does this tell us about Gordon and her sense of place?
3. What do you think the grandmother's house represents? How is it different from the aunt's house?
4. Gordon writes of her grandmother's house, "Although I wasn't happy there, I did, somehow, like her house." What does this tell us about Gordon's relationship with her family?

WRITING MATTERS

1. Gordon writes, "Her house was her body, and like her body, was honorable, daunting, reassuring, defended, castigating, harsh, embellished, dark. . . ." Write an essay that captures your feelings about your home. Use your memory and descriptive imagery to express your sense of place.
2. Gordon writes that her grandmother's house "stood at the center of the lives of all her children and her children's children." Given Gordon's attitude about the house, what do you think this statement tells us about her relationship with her family community? Write an essay that explores your response.
3. Interview a family member, neighbor, or an elder friend about a place that has significance in your life. After conducting the interview, revisit this place. Write an essay that brings together your perspective and the perspective you gained from the interview.

RELEVANT WEB SITES

AN INTERVIEW WITH MARY GORDON
<http://www.columbia.edu/cu/record/archives/vol23/vol23_iss18/22.html>

Learn more about Mary Gordon through this interview, which explores her roles as teacher and writer.

Sandra Cisneros (b. 1954)

The Monkey Garden

Sandra Cisneros grew up in a large family that traveled frequently between Chicago and Mexico. She graduated from Loyola University with a B.A. in English (1976) and went on to earn an M.F.A. from the University of Iowa's Writing Workshop (1978). While Cisneros has taught at all levels, she now works full-time on her writing. Her publications include My Wicked Wicked Ways *(1987),* Woman Hollering Creek and Other Stories *(1991),* Loose Women *(1996) and most recently* Caranelo *(2002). In the following selection, "The Monkey Garden" from* The House on Mango Street *(1983), we learn about how a young girl's sense of place is intimately connected with her coming of age.*

The monkey doesn't live there anymore. The monkey moved—to Kentucky—and took his people with him. And I was glad because I couldn't listen anymore to his wild screaming at night, the twangy yakkety-yak of the people who owned him. The green metal cage, the porcelain table top, the family that spoke like guitars. Monkey, family, table. All gone.

And it was then we took over the garden we had been afraid to go into when the monkey screamed and showed its yellow teeth.

There were sunflowers big as flowers on Mars and thick cockscombs bleeding the deep red fringe of theater curtains. There were dizzy bees and bow-tied fruit flies turning somersaults and humming in the air. Sweet sweet peach trees. Thorn roses and thistle and pears. Weeds like so many squinty-eyed stars and brush that made your ankles itch and itch until you washed with soap and water. There were big green apples hard as knees. And everywhere the sleepy smell of rotting wood, damp earth and dusty hollyhocks thick and perfumy like the blue-blond hair of the dead.

Yellow spiders ran when we turned rocks over and pale worms blind and afraid of light rolled over in their sleep. Poke a stick in the sandy soil and a few blue-skinned beetles would appear, an avenue of aunts, so many crusty lady bugs. This was a garden, a wonderful thing to look at in the spring. But bit by bit, after the monkey left, the garden began to take over itself. Flowers stopped obeying the little bricks that kept them from growing beyond their paths. Weeds mixed in. Dead cars appeared overnight like mushrooms. First one and then another and then a pale blue pickup with the front windshield missing. Before you knew it, the monkey garden became filled with sleepy cars.

5   Things had a way of disappearing in the garden, as if the garden itself ate them, or, as if with its old-man memory, it put them away and forgot them. Nenny found a dollar and a dead mouse between two rocks in the stone wall where the morning glories climbed, and once when we were playing hide-and-seek, Eddie Vargas laid his head beneath a hibiscus tree and fell asleep there like a Rip Van Winkle until somebody remembered he was in the game and went back to look for him.

This, I suppose, was the reason why we went there. Far away from where our mothers could find us. We and a few old dogs who lived inside the empty cars. We made a clubhouse once on the back of that old blue pickup. And besides, we liked to jump from the roof of one car to another and pretend they were giant mushrooms.

Somebody started the lie that the monkey garden had been there before anything. We liked to think the garden could hide things for a thousand years. There beneath the roots of soggy flowers were the bones of murdered pirates and dinosaurs, the eye of a unicorn turned to coal.

This is where I wanted to die and where I tried one day but not even the monkey would have me. It was the last day I would go there.

Who was it that said I was getting too old to play the games? Who was it I didn't listen to? I only remember that when the others ran, I wanted to run too, up and down and through the monkey garden, fast as the boys, not like Sally who screamed if she got her stockings muddy.

10   I said, Sally, come on, but she wouldn't. She stayed by the curb talking to Tito and his friends. Play with the kids if you want, she said, I'm staying here. She could be stuck-up like that if she wanted to, so I just left.

It was her own fault too. When I got back Sally was pretending to be mad . . . something about the boys having stolen her keys. Please give them back to me, she said punching the nearest one with a soft fist. They were laughing. She was too. It was a joke I didn't get.

I wanted to go back with the other kids who were still jumping on cars, still chasing each other through the garden, but Sally had her own game.

One of the boys invented the rules. One of Tito's friends said you can't get the keys back unless you kiss us and Sally pretended to be mad at first but she said yes. It was that simple.

I don't know why, but something inside me wanted to throw a stick. Something wanted to say no when I watched Sally going into the garden with Tito's buddies all grinning. It was just a kiss, that's all. A kiss for each one. So what, she said.

15   Only how come I felt angry inside. Like something wasn't right. Sally went behind that old blue pickup to kiss the boys and get her keys back, and I ran up three flights of stairs to where Tito lived. His mother was ironing shirts. She was sprinkling water on them from an empty pop bottle and smoking a cigarette.

Your son and his friends stole Sally's keys and now they won't give them back unless she kisses them and right now they're making her kiss them, I said all out of breath from the three flights of stairs.

Those kids, she said, not looking up from her ironing.

That's all?

What do you want me to do, she said, call the cops? And kept on ironing.

20   I looked at her a long time, but couldn't think of anything to say, and ran back down the three flights to the garden where Sally needed to be saved. I took three big sticks and a brick and figured this was enough.

But when I got there Sally said go home. Those boys said leave us alone. I felt stupid with my brick. They all looked at me as if *I* was the one that was crazy and made me feel ashamed.

And then I don't know why but I had to run away. I had to hide myself at the other end of the garden, in the jungle part, under a tree that wouldn't mind if I lay down and cried a long time. I closed my eyes like tight stars so that I wouldn't, but I did. My face felt hot. Everything inside hiccuped.

I read somewhere in India there are priests who can will their heart to stop beating. I wanted to will my blood to stop, my heart to quit its pumping. I wanted to be dead, to turn into the rain, my eyes melt into the ground like two black snails. I wished and wished. I closed my eyes and willed it, but when I got up my dress was green and I had a headache.

I looked at my feet in their white socks and ugly round shoes. They seemed far away. They didn't seem to be my feet anymore. And the garden that had been such a good place to play didn't seem mine either.

CONVERSATION STARTER

Have you ever had your own personal "Monkey Garden?" Describe this place and what made it special for you.

READING MATTERS

1. Why were the narrator and her friends previously afraid to enter the monkey garden? Why does the garden appeal to them?
2. Read the description of the garden before and after "it began to take over itself." Why does it begin to take over itself? What is the significance of the screaming monkey, the dense natural growth and decay, and the "sleepy cars"?
3. Why does the narrator want "to be dead . . . to melt into the ground"?
4. Why does the narrator think that Sally needs to be "saved" from Tito's games? What does the narrator learn from her community in the "Monkey Garden"?

WRITING MATTERS

1. Write an essay that discusses the themes of community in the story.
2. In what ways is this a coming-of-age story? Write an essay in response to this question. Refer to the text and to your own experience.
3. Using the narrator's point of view, write a sequel to "The Monkey Garden." How has the narrator's view of the garden, of her childhood friends, of her community, and of herself changed?

RELEVANT WEB SITES

LAS MUJERES: SANDRA CISNEROS <http://www.lasmujeres.com/sandracisneros/>

Las Mujeres provides profiles of notable Latin women who have contributed to the culture in diverse ways. The web site provides a biography of Sandra

Cisneros as well as a description of her literary goals, highlights of her books, and links to interviews with the author.

THE OFFICIAL WEB SITE OF SANDRA CISNEROS
<http://www.sandracisneros.com/home.html>

In this official web site for Sandra Cisneros, the author shares some of her favorite possessions, poems, and stories.

Jason Florio (b. 1972)

Baghdad Café

Jason Florio is a London-born, New York–based photographer. His work has appeared in The New Yorker, Newsweek, *and* Talk *magazine, and has been acquired by the Brooklyn Museum of Art. He has been most drawn to the diversity of the Muslim world and has concentrated his work there for the past six years. The following selection was written just before the recent U.S.-led invasion of Iraq.*

Throughout the Islamic world, Friday is known as the day for Juma prayer. But for the literati that fill the benches and rest their short Turkish coffees on the small wobbly tables at the Sh'ah Bander Café, Friday is dedicated to the written word. By 9:30 a.m the café is full with betweeded middle-aged men. If stripped of their nagila pipes and shai Iraqi teas, they would more resemble characters from an Evelyn Waugh novel than stereotypical Arabs, their pin-stripes, Yorkshire caps, and dapper ties reminiscent of 1920s England.

The Caribbean-colored walls of the café reflect the nobility of the word-smiths who sit beneath them, crammed as they are with black-and-white photographs of what seems to be a rather sophisticated time in Baghdad's past. Antique frames are stuffed with yellowed pictures of Iraq's first king, Faisal Abdul Aziz, as both boy and man, hand-colored prints of a Baghdad street riot during British times, and endless faces from an era that knew no weapons of mass destruction.

Outside, on Mutanabi Street, booksellers hustle dust-covered volumes for however many dinar might change hands. The street, named for a legendary poet who thought himself a prophet, is the historic heart of Baghdad's book district. Sh'ah Bander, in fact, is located in a former printing press. It's no surprise that such literary interests persist in the region that produced the Epic of Gilgamesh. This, after all, is present-day Mesopotamia.

Throughout the Al-Mutanabi district, the restaurants are full, the fruit stands are fully stocked, and the red double-decker buses rolling by seem oddly familiar. There are no armed militiamen at intersections. No tanks grinding up the asphalt on Sharia Raschid. But through the carbon monoxide haze one sees the shattered underbelly of a country crippled by twelve years of economic sanctions, two self-destructive wars with its neighbors in the past fourteen years, and an oppressive, self-serving dictatorship.

5   The Sh'ah Bander and other nearby cafés are a haven from the sanctions that have left many intellectuals driving taxis for dinar instead of pounding the keys of Crown typewriters. There is little money in Baghdad at all, even less for the purchase of words, but their passion for writing has not been dissuaded by lack of financial remuneration. "We don't need a full stomach, but we do need to read and write" says Wajeeh Abbas, who writes for next to nothing for the weekly magazine al-Itihad. A few of the writers who gather here have been awarded small stipends from the government, but they have yet to receive any payments.

It seems that the oppression and economic struggles have given these writers an even stronger desire to produce. Many poems reflect their suffering, but others still relish romantic ideals. "We are human not iron" retorts Abdulati el Rashed of the al-Jumhuriah newspaper. The current trend among many of the poets is to write in what they call a European style, without rhyme. But some still prefer the more traditional Arab colloquial form known as she'ar shabi. Whatever the style, the writers at the Sh'ah Bander call their passion for writing "a form of madness."

Although many of these men have begrudgingly sold off their book collections to traders on al-Mutanabi, they feel the need to look forward, not back—a reflection of Iraqi life outside the walls of Sh'ah Bander, where a city waits in limbo. The people have nothing more to do than go through the daily motions of normality. In the shadow of impending chaos, the café is filled with a sense of not just preserving less troubled times, but of continuing a strong cultural tradition rooted in words.

"This is my homeland / It's my home and grave / And last place" writes poet Amer Abdil Ameer, "Who'll carry its bags but me?"

CONVERSATION STARTER

Describe a place, real or imagined, where you would feel comfortable writing and expressing your ideas.

READING MATTERS

1. Describe the patrons of the Baghdad Café. How does the fact that women are absent from the café impact the community? How does it impact your experience as a reader?
2. Describe the physical characteristics of the café. Do you think the setting has an impact on the writers? What evidence supports your opinion?
3. Why does the author feel it is important to keep writing "In the shadow of impending chaos"? What impact does writing have on the men in the café?
4. Why do the writers at the Sh'ah Bander call their passion for writing "a form of madness"?

WRITING MATTERS

1. Write a research paper comparing and contrasting Baghdad before and after the Gulf War. Use the Internet and the media as resources. How have these changes impacted the writers at the café? How would life for the writers be different today?
2. After reading this selection, what value do you think writing can bring to a community? What role do writers have in shaping the response to the conflict in Iraq?
3. Select a local café to observe and write about your findings. Discuss the setting, the people, and the atmosphere. Is there a community that exists at the café? How is it similar or different from the community at the Sh'ah Bander café?

RELEVANT WEB SITES

JASON FLORIO PHOTOGRAPHY <http://www.floriophoto.com>

This is the official Jason Florio web site featuring his photographs from Afghanistan, Southeast Asia, Africa, London, and New York.

ORION MAGAZINE
<http://www.orionmagazine.org/pages/om/03-3om/Florio.html>

View this article online along with additional photographs from Sh'ah Bander.

Political and Natural Challenges

Tracy Kidder (b. 1945)

A Moral Place

Tracy Kidder earned an A.B. from Harvard University (1967) and an M.F.A. from the University of Iowa (1974). Kidder has worked as a contributing editor for the Atlantic Monthly *and has written numerous nonfiction books including* The Road to Yuba City *(1974),* The Soul of a New Machine *(1981),* House *(1985),* Among Schoolchildren *(1989),* Old Friends *(1993), and most recently* Mountains Beyond Mountains: Healing the World *(2003). He has received many literary honors including the Pulitzer Prize, the National Book Award, and the Robert F. Kennedy Award. In the following selection from* Hometown *(1999), Kidder explores the complex social and economic forces that undermine the democratic process of a seemingly peaceful community.*

In the days before it had a town clock, Northampton paid a citizen to sound a trumpet, calling all to Sunday Meeting. Attendance was required. Proper Sabbath behavior was enforced by tithing-men, each one of whom was also charged with checking on the morals of a dozen families. They carried black canes tipped with brass as symbols of their office. In Northampton nowadays, local ordinances policed a great deal of what went on outdoors, such as skateboarding and street music, and the tobacco control coordinator prowled around with a camera, looking for violations of the ban against smoking in restaurants. Even downtown, for all its flamboyance, had a serious air. Off and on, little groups stood in front of Memorial Hall, protesting international arms dealing and whatever war was current. Battles against homelessness, racism, domestic abuse, the burning of black churches in the South, were carried on from pamphlet-laden tables in Pulaski Park, and in lectures and discussion groups inside the Unitarian Society and the First Church. In spite of the nightly masquerades and all the luxuries for sale, Northampton was a moral place.

On a billboard out by the Interstate, an ad for a Main Street shop read, STUFF YOU WANT; below that someone had written, in artfully drippy red paint, WHILE OUR GHETTOS BLEED. That message had lingered for months. The fading graffito on the back wall of Thorne's Marketplace—GENTRIFICATION IS WAR, FIGHT BACK—had remained undisturbed for years. On Main Street, inside the shop that caters to recreational runners, a middle-aged customer tells the clerk that he must be fitted to only one brand of sneaker. "It's the only kind that isn't made by sweatshop labor in China," he explains. In a dress and accessories shop a block away, a woman gazes longingly at a pair of shoes—black with a gold-colored adornment like a snaffle bit on top. Then she turns away. Of course, she could afford the shoes, she tells her husband that night. But she doesn't actually *need* them, and there are so many problems in the world—starving children, threatened species, political prisoners—that she can't help but think the money would be better spent elsewhere. Besides, she says, smiling sheepishly, she's afraid she'd feel pretentious wearing fancy shoes in Northampton. People who dyed their hair green were more comfortable here, it seemed, than people who bought leather pumps.

Downtown had a tone, and the tone had a history. It probably stretched back to the Puritans' sumptuary laws, which were intended to keep average citizens from aping the rich. There were exceptions, of course, but anecdotes from the town's annals suggest that by the time of the Revolution the rich of Northampton were endeavoring not to look too different from everyone else. In the early 1800s a resident recorded in his diary a story he'd heard, an object lesson on this theme: In 1775 or thereabouts, a young tradesman came to seek his fortune in Northampton. He carried letters of introduction to the town's leading men. First he visited the famous soldier Seth Pomeroy, hero of the French and Indian Wars, soon to fight, at the age of sixty-five, at the battle of Bunker Hill. "But to his surprise found Col. Pomeroy clothed with a leather apron and arms naked, busy at the Anvil. . . ." Then he called on a Major Hawley. He found him living in an old, plain house, sitting in a ratty old armchair.

> The young man had doubts whether this man could be the famous Major Hawley and received the affirmative reply that his name was Hawley—the young man presented his letter of introduction and soon found the Great Man and that Greatness did not consist in splendid buildings or courtly dress and was taught the useful lesson of not Judging a man by his outward dress.

Timothy Dwight, the president of Yale, visited Northampton in the early 1800s and noticed a peculiarity about the town's three hundred homes. "A considerable number of the house are ordinary, many are good, and not a small proportion are handsome," he wrote. But the handsome ones weren't situated together. The rich hadn't settled down in exclusive neighborhoods, the way Dwight seemed to think they should. The handsome houses were "so scattered on the different streets as to make much less impression on the eye than even inferior buildings in many other places."

5   During the 1980s Northampton had indulged in a spree, extravagant by local standards, with money and real estate. But the boom had ended now. Many of the bon vivants of the eighties had moved away, been indicted, or simply calmed down. And the wealthy had generally become retiring again. Gossip had punished ostentation in the past. It still did today. The rich

were especially vulnerable, because they were greatly outnumbered. For years the town's median income had stood below the Massachusetts average, and as of the 1990 federal census, only seventy-nine households, fewer than one percent, considerably less than the national average, had incomes of $150,000 or more. Wealthy people here tended to live on remote hilltops, far away from inquiring eyes, or else discreetly, in houses with plain exteriors but interiors that contained kitchens good enough for restaurants, and private libraries, and art collections of great worth. The wealthy of Northampton drove good cars but not the very best. They didn't have live-in servants, though some maintained the equivalents of staffs, in caterers, cleaners, gardeners. One tier below, there was a much larger prosperous class, the upper middle by local standards—academics, business owners, various professionals. Many people had given up a little something to live here, forsaking their chances to maximize profits.

As long as they avoided ostentation, people could be wealthy in Northampton and still be called "progressive." In fact, the combination was likely. One way to achieve it was to open one's house to fund-raisers for a worthy cause. Mayor Ford once remarked, "It does seem to me that the rich here are quite benign." Of course, she was a beneficiary of fund-raisers, but she had a point. In Northampton inequality was more muted than in many American places.

Not that unanimity prevailed. A while ago the progressive forces had gone too far for some, and now the town was fighting over a proposed local statute, called the Domestic Partnership Ordinance, a gay rights initiative of sorts.

In other places, this kind of argument usually came mixed with practical questions about municipal finance and economic fairness, about discrimination in the workplace and freedom from harassment. Not in Northampton. The ordinance would allow an unmarried couple, whether heterosexual or homosexual, to license themselves as domestic partners at city hall for a ten-dollar fee. In return, one partner would have the right to view the school records of the other partner's child, with the partner's written permission. But anyone could do that already. One domestic partner would also have the right to visit the other in any city-owned jail or hospital. But Northampton didn't own a hospital, and the only jail under its control was the lockup at the police station, which didn't allow visitors of any sort. So the ordinance would grant rights that either didn't exist or that everyone already possessed. It wouldn't cost the town a penny. Maybe in other places the DPO wouldn't have seemed worth arguing about. But it had any number of symbolic meanings here. It set the town up for an election of great purity, an election about principle alone.

"This has always been a tolerant community," some natives liked to say. But not all that long ago, in the 1950s, the police had arrested a Smith College professor named Newton Arvin, winner of the National Book Award for a biography of Melville. His crime was possessing pictures of scantily clad young men. Exposed as a homosexual, and too weak to resist pressure from police, Arvin snitched on some of his best gay friends, was retired from Smith, and checked himself into the state mental hospital.

10   Gay-bashing in Northampton seems to have grown, along with the numbers of openly gay residents, until the early 1980s, when Judge Ryan, then the district attorney, prosecuted a man for making harassing phone calls to a local lesbian. Ordinarily the culprit would have gotten a stern warning, but the people who spoke for gay residents had been demanding action. Ryan pressed to have the man be given jail time. The judge remembered that case with mixed feelings. "He was just some poor slob and we made an example of him. But it seemed to work."

A place often gets known for one of its parts. In tabloids as far away as England, Northampton was now described as overrun by lesbians, teeming with weird and florid sexuality. The city census didn't ask the citizens what kind of sex they preferred, but a careful, between-the-lines analysis by the city planner suggested that lesbians constituted only one of many sizable minorities in town. Perhaps they only seemed more numerous than retired persons, because here they felt safe enough to come out of hiding. Several churches now performed gay marriages and the *Gazette* carried the announcements alongside traditional ones. Lesbians had become some of the city's sturdiest burghers. They ran thriving businesses. They served on civic boards. Three of the city's cops were openly gay, after all, and so were two city councillors. The first cop to come out had found FAGGOT written on his locker, but that was years ago, and if some people on the force still didn't like the idea of gay colleagues, they knew better than to say so. The First Church, scion of the Puritan church, had, after a little struggle, officially declared itself to be "open and affirming"—that is, to people of all sexual persuasions.

Nowadays so many people in Northampton, both gay and straight, referred to their significant others as "my partner" that you might have thought it was almost entirely a town of lawyers. So when the council proposed the Domestic Partnership Ordinance, it hadn't seemed likely to arouse much opposition. But an organization called Northampton for Traditional Values hastily assembled, and in no time at all they collected three thousand signatures, forcing the ordinance onto the ballot.

Tommy O'Connor watched from a little distance. He thought the DPO gave gay people here a way of sort of getting married, a state that he approved of. "It'd be kind of nice for them," he said. What he didn't like about the ordinance was its licensing of unmarried heterosexuals—another assault, he felt, on the sanctity of marriage. And what he disliked much more was that this seemed like an attempt to rub new lifestyles in old-timers' faces. This wasn't a simple argument between newcomers and natives, between Noho and Hamp, but elections make an issue two-sided. He felt that newcomers were trying to declare that they'd taken over. He lived across the border now. He didn't have a vote. If he had, he'd have voted against the ordinance.

The opposition, Northampton for Traditional Values, declined grand public debate. In lieu of real public discourse, lawn signs sprouted up all over town and the papers printed hundreds of letters to the editor. The backers of the DPO said, among many other things, that the DPO would represent a start, one small stand against the scorn and persecution that gay people had forever suffered. They said their cause was civil rights. Nonsense, said the opposition. The ordinance didn't ask for tolerance, which gay people here already had, but for official recognition, corporate approval, of gay and out-of-wedlock cohabitation. It asked the town to vote for lifestyles that many people here could tolerate but not in good conscience affirm. That seemed to be the essence of the argument at its most decorous. Both sides, of course, uttered meaner thoughts behind closed doors.

15   The camps held strategy sessions. They conducted phone-banking. The proponents even did some sophisticated polling. They raised far more money than the opposition, and no wonder. They had better fund-raisers: name tags, cocktails, and elevating surroundings. At one pro-DPO fund-raiser, cocktails ended with the bright sound of a bell, and the host, standing on a rug that looked like a work of art, said to the crowd, "This Tibetan bell can be heard for miles, and sometimes even in the kitchen." Short, inspiring speeches followed.

On election day, people who listened to National Public Radio the rest of the year tuned into the 1400 Team. You could hear Ron Hall's voice coming out of car windows and through doorways all morning. It rained that afternoon. Campaigners stood their ground, lining streets outside the polling places, holding up their competing signs: VOTE NO ON 1 and VALUE ALL FAMILIES. Many actually looked cheerful.

"This is democracy," said one sign-holder, as waterfalls of rain spilled off his hat.

"As good as it gets," said another.

For the first time in Northampton's history, the votes were counted electronically, so the results came in much earlier than ever before. Against most expectations, Northampton for Traditional Values had prevailed—but by a margin so narrow that the contest looked like a dead heat.

20   Two religious services followed the vote. The winners held theirs on election night in the World War II Club, a smoky bar on Conz Street. When the returns were announced, someone cried, "It's a miracle. Hallelujah!" A group of about thirty gathered in a circle, holding hands, bowing their heads, while Father Honan of St. Mary's said a prayer. "We had a cause worth fighting for," he said afterward. Then the father raised up a glass, thanking the electorate and, presumably, God.

The losers put on a more elaborate service. They called it "A Healing Ceremony." It was held two weeks after the election, in the grand hall of the Unitarian church—by far the loveliest in a town full of churches. It has a vaulted ceiling, as tall as the Sistine Chapel's. It looks like a religious place without religion's somber side. The place is warm and bright and airy. The pews are comfortable, the architecture neoclassical, with authentic Tiffany windows fifteen feet tall and Corinthian columns. The place seems designed less for worship than for thought.

A photographic exhibit of gay and lesbian families hung on the walls, and the crowd—the majority female—filled up every pew. Victoria Safford, the Unitarian's pastor, the local rabbi, three different Christian ministers—Congregational, Episcopal, Methodist—and several lay speakers mounted the high pulpit in turn and offered consolation. As they spoke, sounds of sniffling, now and then of weeping, came from the congregation. The hall was full of handkerchiefs. But one lesbian couple was giggling softly, and whispering loud enough to attract the attention of someone nearby.

"Shhh. You shouldn't laugh in church."

"She's a recovering Catholic."

25   They giggled a little more and then composed their faces. They at least seemed to have emerged from grief. Perhaps the music helped. First the assembly sang a Unitarian hymn, one that doesn't mention God, called "We Sing Now Together":

> We sing of community in the making
>
> In every far continent, region and land

Then Andrea Ayvazian, for many years a lecturer on racism, now a seminary student, and the owner of one of the town's finest voices, stood near the Steinway and sang a more modern sort of song. Her lovely, deep voice filled the hall. She gestured with her arms, pulling the congregation with her, sing-along style. She could have worked a crowd in Las Vegas, but the song belonged in New Northampton. It was entitled, "How Could Anyone?" It began, "How could anyone ever tell you you are anything less than beautiful?" Andrea wore an enormous smile. "Sing with me," she called, and after another verse or two, she asked, "Is it too low for you?"

It was not. The congregation had the hang of it by then, but Andrea's voice could still be heard, shining among the rest. "How could anyone fail to notice your loving is a miracle," she sang. "Now get angry!" She showed them how. *"Don't* let *anyone ever* tell you you are *anything* less than beautiful. *Don't* let *anyone ever* tell you you are less than whole." She called for "one more *don't"* and then let her voice begin to fall. Still filling up the nave, it fell toward the vocal embodiment of great calm after a storm: "How could anyone ever tell you you are less than beautiful. . . ."

Of course, in a democracy, if one group of people asks the electorate questions such as "Do you agree with us?" and "Do you like us?" they ought to be prepared to hear them answer, "No." But it would be a while before some women in Northampton stopped bursting into tears and a while before many others could look at fellow citizens without wondering, "Which way did you vote?"

Liberalism had seemed to be in season here. It had seemed like the political philosophy against which all others had to struggle, or else shut up. But now it looked as if Northampton's current residents stay almost equally divided in their strong opinions about their town, about how people ought to conduct their private lives inside it, about the way Northampton defined tolerance, about who owned the place. Was the town destined to remain forever split in two camps, forever scowling at each other? Only if less than half of a town can be said to define it. As usual, a majority of the adult population hadn't even bothered to vote.

CONVERSATION STARTER

Describe a political event in your community that provoked conflict. How did the event provide an opportunity for public debate and education?

READING MATTERS

1. Why does Kidder entitle the selection, "A Moral Place"? How does he feel about the town of Northampton? Refer to specific evidence within the selection to illustrate your main ideas.
2. What does Kidder mean when he says, "the ordinance would grant rights that either didn't exist or that everyone already possessed"?
3. What role does Northampton's history play in shaping the dominant values in the community?
4. "It looked as if Northampton's current residents stood almost equally divided in their strong opinions about their town, about how people ought to conduct their private lives inside it, about the way Northampton defined tolerance, about who owned the place." Given the outcome of the Domestic Partnership Ordinance, do you consider Northampton a "healthy" community? Explain your opinion.

WRITING MATTERS

1. Write an editorial on a community issue. Approach the topic as an opportunity to provide information to your community.
2. Write an essay about the controversy around the Domestic Partnership Ordinance in Northampton. How did politics, history, and social status shape the outcome of the vote? Research the issue through the Internet or at your college library.
3. Kidder concludes the selection by pointing out that "as usual, a majority of the adult population hadn't even bothered to vote." Research the statistics on voter registration in your community and then write an editorial to your local newspaper that raises public awareness about this issue.

RELEVANT WEB SITES

CITY OF NORTHAMPTON <http://www.city.northampton.ma.us/>

This is the official web site of the City of Northampton, which provides information about local resources and community events.

HOW TO REGISTER AND VOTE IN THE UNITED STATES
<http://www.registervote.com/>

This web site is nonpartisan and is designed to assist individuals in registering to vote in any of the 50 states.

Mike Davis (b. 1946)

The Invisible Riot

Mike Davis is a native of southern California. He has worked as a meat cutter, a long-distance truck driver, and a professor at the Southern California Institute of Architecture. He was a fellow at the Getty Institute and was awarded a MacArthur Fellowship. He is the author of Prisoners of the American Dream *and* City of Quartz *(1990). The following selection, "The Invisible Riot" from* The Ecology of Fear *(1998), examines the political and social climate that surrounded the 1992 Los Angeles riots.*

If, as some contend, the Los Angeles riots were a class rebellion, then this neighborhood is a rebel-held territory.

—Los Angeles Times (1992)

Friday, 5 May 1992. The armored personnel carrier squats on the corner like *un gran sapo feo*—a "big ugly toad"—according to nine-year-old Emerio. His parents talk anxiously, almost in a whisper, about the *desparecidos:* Raul from Tepic, big Mario, the younger Flores girl, and the cousin from Ahuachapan. Like all Salvadorans, they know about those who "disappear"; they remember the headless corpses and the man whose tongue had been pulled through the hole in his throat like a necktie. That is why they came here—to zip code 90057, Los Angeles, California.

Their neighborhood, on the edge of MacArthur Park, is part of the large halo of older, high-density housing surrounding the scanscape of the fortified core. These tenement districts perform the classic functions of Burgess's "zone in transition": providing urban ports of entry for the city's poorest and most recent immigrants—in this case from Mexico, Guatemala, and El Salvador rather than Ireland and Bohemia—who work in Downtown hotels and garment factories. But the normally bustling streets are now eerily quiet. Emerio's parents are counting their friends and neighbors, Salvadoran and Mexican, who are suddenly gone.

Some are in the county jail on Bauchet Street, little more than brown grains of sand lost among the 17,000 other alleged *saqueadores* (looters) and *incendarios* (arsonists) detained after the most violent American civil disturbance since enraged Irish immigrants burned Manhattan in 1863. Those without papers are already back in Tijuana, broke and disconsolate, cut off from their families and new lives. Violating city policy, the police fed hundreds of hapless undocumented *saqueadores* to the INS for deportation before the ACLU or immigrant rights groups had even realized that they had been arrested.

For many days the television talked only of the "South Central riot," "Black rage," and the "Crips and Bloods." Truly, the Rodney King case was a watershed in national race relations, a test of the very meaning of the citizenship for which African-Americans have struggled for four hundred years. It was also the fuse on an explosive accumulation of local grievances among young blacks, ranging from Chief Gates's infamous mass detentions ("Operation Hammer") to the murder of 15-year-old Latasha Harlins by a Korean grocer in 1991. But the 1992 upheaval was far more complex than the 1965 Watts rebellion, although some issues, especially police abuse, remained the same. While most of the news media remained trapped in the black-and-white world of 1965, the second Los Angeles riot burst emphatically into technicolor.

5   Emerio's parents know that thousands of their neighbors from the MacArthur Park district, as well as from the adjoining Mid-Wilshire area and the Hollywood flatlands—together constituting Los Angeles's Mid-City district—also looted, burned, violated curfew, and went to jail. Despite the tabloid media's obsession with black violence, only 36 percent of the riot arrestees were African-American, while 52 percent has Spanish surnames and 10 percent were white. Moreover, the greatest density of riot-related "incidents" occurred north of the Santa Monica Freeway in predominantly Latino and Asian areas. Indeed, nearly as many suspects were booked by the LAPD's Ramparts station, which polices Emerio's neighborhood, as by all four stations which make up the department's South Bureau in South Central Los Angeles. Even the Hollywood station made twice as many arrests as the 77th Street station, which patrolled the supposed riot epicenter—where the truck driver Reginald Denny was nearly beaten to death—at the intersection of Florence and Normandie Avenues.

This invisible Mid-City riot, conflated by most news reports with events in majority-black areas, was driven primarily by empty bellies and broken dreams, not by outrage over the acquittal of the cops who beat Rodney King. It was the culmination of a decade of declining economic opportunity and rising poverty followed by two years of recession that tripled unemployment in Los Angeles's immigrant neighborhoods. Academic studies since the riot have shown that Mexican and Central American immigrants arriving after 1980 had less hope than their predecessors of finding stable, entry-level positions in a regional economy that had become supersaturated with unskilled labor. "Massively growing numbers of Mexican immigrants," according to UCLA sociologist Vilma Ortiz, "have been packed into a relatively narrow tier of occupations." Already by 1980, starting wages for new arrivals had fallen by 13 percent compared to 1970, and in the decade that followed, the portion of the Los Angeles population falling below the poverty line grew by a full percentage point or more each year.

Then, 1990: cutbacks in defense spending and the bursting of the Japanese financial bubble (source of massive "super-yen" investments in Los Angeles real estate during the 1980s) converged to plunge the Southern California economy into its worst recession since 1938. An incredible 27 percent of national job loss was concentrated in the Los Angeles metropolitan region. In Los Angeles County this translated into a catastrophic 30 percent decline in manufacturing employment that savaged light industry, where Mexican immigrants make up the majority of workers, as well as aerospace and military electronics. The impact of the recession, moreover, was intensified by simultaneous cutbacks in AFDC and medical benefits as well as deep slashes in local school budgets. Tens of thousands of families lost their tenuous economic footholds, while the number of children living in poverty increased by a third during the course of the recession.

For anyone who cared to pay attention there were dramatic social storm warnings in the months before the spring 1992 riots. Indeed, no image revealed the mixed origins of the upheaval more clearly than the photograph published in the *Los Angeles Times* three days before Christmas 1991. It showed part of the throng of 20,000 women and children, predominantly recent Latino immigrants, waiting outside skid row's Fred Jordan Mission for the handout of a chicken, a dozen corn tortillas, three small toys, and a blanket. According to the *Times*, "Eight blocks were cordoned off around 5th Street and Towne Avenue to accommodate the crush of people. Some in the five-hour line said they were willing to brave the gritty streets for what one woman described as her 'only possibility' for a Christmas dinner." Human distress on so broad a scale had not been photographed in California since the famous depression-era documentaries of Margaret Bourke-White and Dorothea Lange.

10 Nineteen-thirties-type misery was no surprise, however, to food bank volunteers, who had been warning city officials about the ominous decline in emergency food resources, or to public health workers, who were reporting classic symptoms of malnutrition—anemia and stunted growth—in nearly a quarter of the poor children passing through a county screening program. Other visible barometers of the crisis included the rapidly growing colonies of unemployed busboys, gardeners, and construction laborers living on the desolate flanks of Crown Hill across from Downtown or in the concrete bed of the Los Angeles River, where the homeless are forced to use sewage outflow for bathing and cooking.

Emerio's parents and their neighbors spoke of a gathering sense of desperation in early 1992, a perception of a future already looted of opportunity. The riot arrived like a magic dispensation. In Mid-City neighborhoods people were initially shocked by the violence, then mesmerized by the televised images of black and Latino crowds in South Central Los Angeles helping themselves to mountains of desirable goods without interference from the police. On the second day of unrest, 30 April, the authorities blundered twice: first by suspending school and releasing the kids into the street, second by announcing that the National Guard was on the way to help enforce a dusk-to-dawn curfew.

Thousands immediately interpreted this as a last call to participate in the general redistribution of wealth in progress. Looting exploded through the majority-immigrant neighborhoods of Mid-City as well as Echo Park, Van Nuys, and Huntington Park. Although arsonists struck wantonly and almost at random, the looting crowds were governed by a visible moral economy. As one middle-aged lady explained to me, "Stealing is a sin, but this is more like a television game show where everyone wins." In contrast to the looters on Hollywood Boulevard who stole Madonna's underwear from Frederick's, the masses of Mid-City concentrated on the prosaic necessities of life like cockroach spray and Pampers.

A veteran fifth-grade teacher in the area explained to me the attitudes of the hardworking and otherwise law-abiding families who were swept up in the looting.

> I teach at a new school which is a block west of Olympic and Hoover. My students and I watched from our classroom window as a video store burned. Later, my wife, who teaches at Hoover Street School, and I watched on television as stores near our schools were looted by parents and students whom we recognized.
>
> Since most of the liquor stores and markets in this area greatly overcharge the customers for poor quality merchandise, there is great resentment. My students told me that when some of them saw Viva Market, on Hoover and Olympic, being looted as they watched television, their parents immediately left the apartment only to return an hour later with food and other items. They didn't see this as a "riot," just an opportunity to get even with the "exploiters."
>
> There was no coordination or planning by the people north of the Santa Monica Freeway, other than that provided by the roadmap shown on television. . . . I do not think that Korean stores were attacked for exclusively ethnic reasons. If Korean-owned liquor stores were burned, Korean travel agencies and beauty-shops were not touched. The uprising was directed against the police and rip-off merchants in general. It was driven by economic desperation and class resentment, not race.

The official reaction to this postmodern bread riot was the biggest multiagency law enforcement operation in history. For weeks afterward, elite LAPD Metro Squad units, supported by the National Guard, swept through the tenements in search of stolen goods, while Border Patrolmen from as far away as Texas trawled the streets for undocumented residents. Meanwhile, thousands of *saqueadores,* many of them pathetic scavengers captured in the charred ruins the day after the looting, languished for weeks in the county jail, unable to meet absurdly high bails. One man, apprehended with a packet of sunflower seeds and two cartons of milk, was held on $15,000 bond. Some curfew violators received 30-day jail sentences, despite the fact that they were either homeless or spoke no English. Angry suburban politicians, meanwhile, outbid one another with demands to deport immigrants and strip their U.S.-born children of citizenship.

15   The riot also accelerated the flight of capital and jobs from the Wilshire corridor, just west of MacArthur Park, that forms the high-rise commercial spine of the Mid-City area. Known as "Los Angeles's Champs Elysées," this two-mile segment of Wilshire Boulevard once boasted such icons as the

Ambassador Hotel, I. Magnin, Perino's, the Brown Derby, and Bullock's Wilshire. Insurance companies, corporate law offices, and county agencies formerly consumed millions of square feet of circa 1950s modernist office space. The economic decline of the area began in the mid-1970s when leading tenants began to relocate to newer properties on the booming west side. Office workers and professionals who lived in apartment complexes north and south of Wilshire soon followed, as did restaurants, department stores, and hotels. The residential vacuum was filled by thousands of Mexican and El Salvadoran immigrants, while Korean small businesses brought back retail vitality. But the hemorrhage of white-collar jobs and sales taxes was permanent.

During the riots, looters did $10 million damage to Bullock's, the last of the Wilshire landmarks to remain open—it promptly closed its doors for good. In less than a year, home prices in the nearby exclusive enclave of Hancock Park had fallen by a staggering $200,000. As remaining corporate tenants bolted for the west side, desperate landlords tried to give away premium office space at $1 per square foot but found few takers. In the year before the riot, there had been much speculation in the business press that large Korean investors might be induced to resurrect what was already being called colloquially the "Wilshire ruins." However, the destruction or looting of nearly two thousand Korean family businesses during the riot scotched that possibility for the foreseeable future. As a result, Los Angeles has added a unique category to Burgess's urban ecology: the modern high-rise ghost town.

CONVERSATION STARTER

Discuss your knowledge of the 1992 Los Angeles riots.

READING MATTERS

1. "For anyone who cared to pay attention there were dramatic social storm warnings in the months before the Spring 1992 riots." What warnings does Davis refer to?
2. Davis writes, "The riot arrived like a magic dispensation." Interpret the meaning of this simile.
3. Compare and contrast the communities depicted by Davis and Kidder. What conclusions can you draw from your comparison?
4. "Stealing is a sin, but this is more like a television game show where everyone wins." Explain this resident's perspective based on what you learned from community accounts of the riots.

WRITING MATTERS

1. Davis argues that the 1992 upheaval was far more complex than the 1965 Watts rebellion. Research the Watts rebellion and write an essay that supports or refutes this thesis.

2. Interview friends and family about their memories of the 1992 Los Angeles riots. Write an essay that presents what you have learned and that offers an interpretation of the impact of the riots.
3. Research an economic, social, or political issue in your community. Write an essay for a local paper that addresses a debate in your community on this issue.

RELEVANT WEB SITES

CITY OF LOS ANGELES <www.ci.la.ca.us>

This official web site of the City of Los Angeles provides links to government departments and citywide projects, and information about destination points throughout the city.

LOS ANGELES POLICE DEPARTMENT <www.lapdonline.org>

The official web site of the Los Angeles Police Department provides information on the area it presides over, which encompasses 467 square miles and 18 community areas representing over 3.4 million residents.

Annie Dillard (b. 1945)

Total Eclipse

Annie Dillard, poet, essayist, and naturalist, was raised in Pittsburgh. She received an M.A. from Hollins College in Virginia (1968). Dillard has worked as an editor and college teacher, and has written many essays and books, including Pilgrim at Tinker Creek *(1974), for which she received a Pulitzer Prize. The autobiography of her early years is entitled* An American Childhood *(1987). Other well-known works include* Holy the Firm *(1978),* Teaching a Stone To Talk *(1982),* Writing Life *(1989),* The Living: A Novel *(1992),* Mornings Like These: Found Poems *(1995), and* For the Time Being *(1999). In the selection that follows, "Total Eclipse," included in* Teaching a Stone To Talk, *Dillard sees past the darkness to capture the mysterious and enduring power of the sun and the spirit.*

It has been like dying, that sliding down the mountain pass. It had been like the death of someone, irrational, that sliding down the mountain pass and into the region of dread. It was just like slipping into fever, or falling down that hole in sleep from which you wake yourself whimpering. We had crossed the mountains that day, and now we were in a strange place—a hotel in central Washington, in a town near Yakima. The eclipse we had traveled here to see would occur early the next morning.

I lay in bed. My husband, Gary, was reading beside me. I lay in bed and looked at the painting on the hotel room wall. It was a print of a detailed and lifelike painting of a smiling clown's head, made out of vegetables. It was a painting of the sort which you do not intend to look at, and which, alas, you never forget. Some tasteless fate presses it upon you; it becomes part of the complex interior junk you carry with you wherever you go. Two years have passed since the total eclipse of which I write. During those years I have forgotten, I assume, a great many things I wanted to remember—but I have not forgotten that clown painting or its lunatic setting in the old hotel.

The clown was bald. Actually, he wore a clown's tight rubber wig, painted white; this stretched over the top of his skull, which was a cabbage. His hair was bunches of baby carrots. Inset in his white clown makeup, and in his cabbage skull, were his small and laughing human eyes. The clown's glance was like the glance of Rembrandt in some of the self-portraits: lively, knowing, deep, and loving. The crinkled shadows around his eyes were string beans. His eyebrows were parsley. Each of his ears was a broad bean. His thin, joyful lips were red chili peppers; between his lips were wet rows of human teeth and a suggestion of a real tongue. The clown print was framed in gilt and glassed.

To put ourselves in the path of the total eclipse, that day we had driven five hours inland from the Washington coast, where we lived. When we tried to cross the Cascades range, an avalanche had blocked the pass.

5   A slope's worth of snow blocked the road; traffic backed up. Had the avalanche buried any cars that morning? We could not learn. This highway was the only winter over the mountains. We waited as highway crews bulldozed a passage through the avalanche. With two-by-fours and walls of plyboard, they erected a one-way, roofed tunnel through the avalanche. We drove through the avalanche tunnel, crossed the pass, and descended several thousand feet into central Washington and the broad Yakima valley, about which we knew only that it was orchard country. As we lost altitude, the snows disappeared; our ears popped; the trees changed, and in the trees were strange birds. I watched the landscape innocently, like a fool, like a diver in the rapture of the deep who plays on the bottom while his air runs out.

The hotel lobby was a dark, derelict room, narrow as a corridor, and seemingly without air. We waited on a couch while the manager vanished upstairs to do something unknown to our room. Beside us on an overstuffed chair, absolutely motionless, was a platinum-blond woman in her forties wearing a black silk dress and a strand of pearls. Her long legs were crossed; she supported her head on her fist. At the dim far end of the room, their backs toward us, sat six bald old men in their shirtsleeves, around a loud television. Two of them seemed asleep. They were drunks. "Number six!" cried the man on television, "Number six!"

On the broad lobby desk, lighted and bubbling, was a ten-gallon aquarium containing one large fish; the fish tilted up and down in its water. Against the long opposite wall sang a live canary in its cage. Beneath the cage, among spilled millet seeds on the carpet, were a decorated child's sand bucket and matching sand shovel.

Now the alarm was set for six. I lay awake remembering an article I had read downstairs in the lobby, in an engineering magazine. The article was about gold mining.

In South Africa, in India, and in South Dakota, the gold mines extend so deeply into the earth's crust that they are hot. The rock walls burn the miners' hands. The companies have to air-condition the mines; if the air conditioners break, the miners die. The elevators in the mine shafts run very slowly, down, and up, so the miners' ears will not pop in their skulls. When the miners return to the surface, their faces are deathly pale.

10   Early the next morning we checked out. It was February 26, 1979, a Monday morning. We would drive out of town, find a hilltop, watch the eclipse, and then drive back over the mountains and home to the coast. How familiar things are here; how adept we are; how smoothly and professionally we check out! I had forgotten the clown's smiling head and the hotel lobby as if they had never existed. Gary put the car in gear and off we went, as off we have gone to a hundred other adventures.

It was before dawn when we found a highway out of town and drove into the unfamiliar countryside. By the growing light we could see a band of cirrostratus clouds in the sky. Later the rising sun would clear these clouds before the eclipse began. We drove at random until we came to a range of unfenced hills. We pulled off the highway, bundled up, and climbed one of these hills.

II

The hill was five hundred feet high. Long winter-killed grass covered it, as high as our knees. We climbed and rested, sweating in the cold; we passed clumps of bundled people on the hillside who were setting up telescopes and fiddling with cameras. The top of the hill stuck up in the middle of the sky. We tightened our scarves and looked around.

East of us rose another hill like ours. Between the hills, far below, was the highway which threaded south into the valley. This was the Yakima valley; I had never seen it before. It is justly famous for its beauty, like every planted valley. It extended south into the horizon, a distant dream of a valley, a Shangri-la. All its hundreds of low, golden slopes bore orchards. Among the orchards were towns, and roads, and plowed and fallow fields. Through the valley wandered a thin, shining river; from the river extended fine, frozen irrigation ditches. Distance blurred and blued the sight, so that the whole valley looked like a thickness or sediment at the bottom of the sky. Directly behind us was more sky, and empty lowlands blued by distance, and Mount Adams. Mount Adams was an enormous, snow-covered volcanic cone rising flat, like so much scenery.

Now the sun was up. We could not see it; but the sky behind the band of clouds was yellow, and, far down the valley, some hillside orchards had lighted up. More people were parking near the highway and climbing the hills. It was the West. All of us rugged individualists were wearing knit caps and blue nylon parkas. People were climbing the nearby hills and setting up shop in clumps among the dead grasses. It looked as though we had all gathered on hilltops to pray for the world on its last day. It looked as though we had all crawled out of spaceships and were preparing to assault the valley below. It looked as though we were scattered on hilltops at dawn to sacrifice virgins, make rain, set stone stelae in a ring. There was no place out of the wind. The straw grasses banged our legs.

15   Up in the sky where we stood this air was lusterless yellow. To the west the sky was blue. Now the sun cleared the clouds. We cast rough shadows on the blowing grass; freezing, we waved our arms. Near the sun, the sky was bright and colorless. There was nothing to see.

It began with no ado. It was odd that such a well-advertised public event should have no starting gun, no overture, no introductory speaker. I should have known right then that I was out of my depth. Without pause or preamble, silent as orbits, a piece of the sun went away. We looked at it through welders' goggles. A piece of the sun was missing; in its place we saw empty sky.

I had seen a partial eclipse in 1970. A partial eclipse is very interesting. It bears almost no relation to a total eclipse. Seeing a partial eclipse bears the same relation to seeing a total eclipse as kissing a man does to marrying him, or as flying in an airplane does to falling out of an airplane. Although the one experience precedes the other, it in no way prepares you for it. During a partial eclipse the sky does not darken—not even when 94 percent of the sun is hidden. Nor does the sun, seen colorless through protective devices, seem terribly strange. We have all seen a sliver of light in the sky; we have all seen the crescent moon by day. However, during a partial eclipse the air does indeed get cold, precisely as if someone were standing between you and the fire. And blackbirds do fly back to their roosts. I had seen a partial eclipse before, and here was another.

What you see in an eclipse is entirely different from what you know. It is especially different for those of us whose grasp of astronomy is so frail that, given a flashlight, a grapefruit, two oranges, and fifteen years, we still could not figure out which way to set the clocks for Daylight Saving Time. Usually it is a bit of a trick to keep your knowledge from blinding you. But during an eclipse it is easy. What you see is much more convincing than any wild-eyed theory you may know.

You may read that the moon has something to do with eclipses. I have never seen the moon yet. You do not see the moon. So near the sun, it is as completely invisible as the stars are by day. What you see before your eyes is the sun going through phases. It gets narrower and narrower, as the waning moon does, and, like the ordinary moon, it travels alone in the simple sky. The sky is of course background. It does not appear to eat the sun; it is far behind the sun. The sun simply shaves away; gradually, you see less sun and more sky.

20   The sky's blue was deepening, but there was no darkness. The sun was a wide crescent, like a segment of tangerine. The wind freshened and blew

steadily over the hill. The eastern hill across the highway grew dusky and sharp. The towns and orchards in the valley to the south were dissolving into the blue light. Only the thin river held a trickle of sun.

Now the sky to the west deepened to indigo, a color never seen. A dark sky usually loses color. This was a saturated, deep indigo, up in the air. Stuck up into that unworldly sky was the cone of Mount Adams, and the alpenglow was upon it. The alpenglow is that red light of sunset which holds out on snowy mountaintops long after the valleys and tablelands are dimmed. "Look at Mount Adams," I said, and that was the last sane moment I remember.

I turned back to the sun. It was going. The sun was going, and the world was wrong. The grasses were wrong; they were platinum. Their every detail of stem, head, and blade shone lightless and artificially distinct as an art photographer's platinum print. This color has never been seen on earth. The hues were metallic; their finish was matte. The hillside was a nineteenth-century tinted photograph from which the tints had faded. All the people you see in the photograph, distinct and detailed as their faces look, are now dead. The sky was navy blue. My hands were silver. All the distant hills' grasses were finespun metal which the wind laid down. I was watching a faded color print of a movie filmed in the Middle Ages; I was standing in it, by some mistake. I was standing in a movie of hillside grasses filmed in the Middle Ages. I missed my own century, the people I knew, and the real light of day.

I looked at Gary. He was in the film. Everything was lost. He was a platinum print, a dead artist's version of life. I saw on his skull the darkness of night mixed with the colors of day. My mind was going out; my eyes were receding the way galaxies recede to the rim of space. Gary was light-years away, gesturing inside a circle of darkness, down the wrong end of a telescope. He smiled as if he saw me; the stringy crinkles around his eyes moved. The sight of him, familiar and wrong, was something I was remembering from centuries hence, from the other side of death: yes, *that* is the way he used to look, when we were living. When it was our generation's turn to be alive. I could not hear him; the wind was too loud. Behind him the sun was going. We had all started down a chute of time. At first it was pleasant; now there was no stopping it. Gary was chuting away across space, moving and talking and catching my eye, chuting down the long corridor of separation. The skin on his face moved like thin bronze plating that would peel.

The grass at our feet was wild barley. It was the wild einkorn wheat which grew on the hilly flanks of the Zagros Mountains, above the Euphrates valley, above the valley of the river we called *River*. We harvested the grass with stone sickles, I remember. We found the grasses on the hillsides; we built our shelter beside them and cut them down. That is how he used to look then, that one, moving and living and catching my eye, with the sky so dark behind him, and the wind blowing. God save our life.

25   From all the hills came screams. A piece of sky beside the crescent sun was detaching. It was a loosened circle of evening sky, suddenly lighted from the back. It was an abrupt black body out of nowhere; it was a flat disk; it was almost over the sun. That is when there were screams. At once this disk of sky slid over the sun like a lid. The sky snapped over the sun like a lens cover. The hatch in the brain slammed. Abruptly it was dark night, on the land and in the sky. In the night sky was a tiny ring of light. The hole where the sun belongs is very small. A thin ring of light marked its place. There was no sound. The eyes dried, the arteries drained, the lungs hushed. There was no world. We were the world's dead people rotating and orbiting around and around, embedded in the planet's crust, while the earth rolled down. Our minds were light-years distant, forgetful of almost everything. Only an extraordinary act of will could recall to us our former, living selves and our contexts in matter and time. We had, it seems, loved the planet and loved our lives, but could no longer remember the way of them. We got the light wrong. In the sky was something that should not be there. In the black sky was a ring of light. It was a thin ring, an old, thin silver wedding band, an old, worn ring. It was an old wedding band in the sky, or a morsel of bone. There were stars. It was all over.

III

It is now that the temptation is strongest to leave these regions. We have seen enough; let's go. Why burn our hands any more than we have to? But two years have passed; the price of gold has risen. I return to the same buried alluvial beds and pick through the strata again.

I saw, early in the morning, the sun diminish against a backdrop of sky. I saw a circular piece of that sky appear, suddenly detached, blackened, and backlighted; from nowhere it came and overlapped the sun. It did not look like the moon. It was enormous and black. If I had not read that it was the moon, I could have seen the sight a hundred times and never thought of the moon once. (If, however, I had not read that it was the moon—if, like most of the world's people throughout time, I had simply glanced up and seen this thing—then I doubtless would not have speculated much, but would have, like the Emperor Louis of Bavaria in 840, simply died of fright on the spot.) It did not look like a dragon, although it looked more like a dragon than the moon. It looked like a lens cover, or the lid of a pot. It materialized out of thin air—black, and flat, and sliding, outlined in flame.

Seeing this black body was like seeing a mushroom cloud. The heart screeched. The meaning of the sight overwhelmed its fascination. It obliterated meaning itself. If you were to glance out one day and see a row of mushroom clouds rising on the horizon, you would know at once that what you were seeing, remarkable as it was, was intrinsically not worth remarking. No use running to tell anyone. Significant as it was, it did not matter a whit. For what is significance? It is significance for people. No people, no significance. This is all I have to tell you.

In the deeps are the violence and terror of which psychology has warned us. But if you ride these monsters deeper down, if you drop with them farther over the world's rim, you find what our sciences cannot locate or name, the substrate, the ocean or matrix or ether which buoys the rest, which gives goodness its power for good, and evil its power for evil, the unified field: our complex and inexplicable caring for each other, and for our life together here. This is given. It is not learned.

30 The world which lay under darkness and stillness following the closing of the lid was not the world we know. The event was over. Its devastation lay round about us. The clamoring mind and heart stilled, almost indifferent, certainly disembodied, frail, and exhausted. The hills were hushed, obliterated. Up in the sky, like a crater from some distant cataclysm, was a hollow ring.

You have seen photographs of the sun taken during a total eclipse. The corona fills the print. All of those photographs were taken through telescopes. The lenses of telescopes and cameras can no more cover the breadth and scale of the visual array than language can cover the breadth and simultaneity of internal experience. Lenses enlarge the sight, omit its context, and make of it a pretty and sensible picture, like something on a Christmas card. I assure you, if you send any shepherds a Christmas card on which is printed a three-by-three photograph of the angel of the Lord, the glory of the Lord, and a multitude of the heavenly host, they will not be sore afraid. More fearsome things can come in envelopes. More moving photographs than those of the sun's corona can appear in magazines. But I pray you will never see anything more awful in the sky.

You see the wide world swaddled in darkness; you see a vast breadth of hilly land, and an enormous, distant, blackened valley; you see towns' lights, a river's path, and blurred portions of your hat and scarf; you see your husband's face looking like an early black-and-white film; and you see a sprawl of black sky and blue sky together, with unfamiliar stars in it, some barely visible bands of cloud, and over there, a small white ring. The ring is as small as one goose in a flock of migrating geese—if you happen to notice a flock of migrating geese. It is one 360th part of the visible sky. The sun we see is less than half the diameter of a dime held at arm's length.

The Crab Nebula, in the constellation Taurus, looks, through binoculars, like a smoke ring. It is a star in the process of exploding. Light from its explosion first reached the earth in 1054; it was a supernova then, and so bright it shone in the daytime. Now it is not so bright, but it is still exploding. It expands at the rate of seventy million miles a day. It is interesting to look through binoculars at something expanding seventy million miles a day. It does not budge. Its apparent size does not increase. Photographs of the Crab Nebula taken fifteen years ago seem identical to photographs of it taken yesterday. Some lichens are similar. Botanists have measured some ordinary lichens twice, at fifty-year intervals, without detecting any growth at all. And yet their cells divide; they live.

The small ring of light was like these things—like a ridiculous lichen up in the sky, like a perfectly still explosion 4,200 light-years away: it was interesting, and lovely, and in witless motion, and it had nothing to do with anything.

35 It had nothing to do with anything. The sun was too small, and too cold, and too far away, to keep the world alive. The white ring was not enough. It was feeble and worthless. It was as useless as a memory; it was as off kilter and hollow and wretched as a memory.

When you try your hardest to recall someone's face, or the look of a place, you see in your mind's eye some vague and terrible sight such as this. It is dark; it is insubstantial; it is all wrong.

The white ring and the saturated darkness made the earth and the sky look as they must look in the memories of the careless dead. What I saw, what I seemed to be standing in, was all the wrecked light that the memories of the dead could shed upon the living world. We had all died in our boots on the hilltops of Yakima, and were alone in eternity. Empty space stoppered our eyes and mouths; we cared for nothing. We remembered our living days wrong. With great effort we had remembered some sort of circular light in the sky—but only the outline. Oh, and then the orchard trees withered, the ground froze, the glaciers slid down the valleys and overlapped the towns. If there had ever been people on the earth, nobody knew it. The dead had forgotten those they had loved. The dead were parted one from the other and could no longer remember the faces and lands they had loved in the light. They seemed to stand on darkened hilltops, looking down.

IV

We teach our children one thing only, as we were taught: to wake up. We teach our children to look alive there, to join by words and activities the life of human culture on the planet's crust. As adults we are almost all adept to waking up. We have so mastered the transition we have forgotten we ever learned it. Yet it is a transition we make a hundred times a day, as, like so many will-less dolphins, we plunge and surface, lapse and emerge. We live half our waking lives and all of our sleeping lives in some private, useless, and insensible waters we never mention or recall. Useless, I say. Valueless, I might add—until someone hauls their wealth up to the surface and into the wide-awake city, in a form that people can use.

I do not know how we got to the restaurant. Like Roethke, "I take my waking slow." Gradually I seemed more or less alive, and already forgetful. It was now almost nine in the morning. It was the day of a solar eclipse in central Washington, and a fine adventure for everyone. The sky was clear; there was a fresh breeze out of the north.

40 The restaurant was a roadside place with tables and booths. The other eclipse-watchers were there. From our booths we could see their cars' Cali-

fornia license plates, their University of Washington parking stickers. Inside the restaurant we were all eating eggs or waffles; people were fairly shouting and exchanging enthusiasm, like fans after a World Series game. Did you see . . . ? Did you see . . . ? Then somebody said something which knocked me for a loop.

A college student, a boy in a blue parka who carried a Hasselblad, said to us, "Did you see that little white ring? It looked like a Life Saver. It looked like a Life Saver up in the sky."

And so it did. The boy spoke well. He was a walking alarm clock. I myself had at that time no access to such a word. He could write a sentence, and I could not. I grabbed that Life Saver and rode it to the surface. And I had to laugh. I had been dumbstruck on the Euphrates River, I had been dead and gone and grieving, all over the sight of something which, if you claw your way up to that level, you would grant looked very much like a Life Saver. It was good to be back among people so clever; it was good to have all the world's words at the mind's disposal, so the mind could begin its task. All those things for which we have no words are lost. The mind— the culture—has two little tools, grammar and lexicon: a decorated sand bucket and a matching shovel. With these we bluster about the continents and do all the world's work. With these we try to save our very lives.

There are a few more things to tell from this level, the level of the restaurant. One is an old joke about breakfast. "It can never be satisfied, the mind, never." Wallace Stevens wrote that, and in the long run he was right. The mind wants to live forever, or to learn a very good reason why not. The mind wants the world to return its love, or its awareness; the mind wants to know all the world, and all eternity, and God. The mind's sidekick, however, will settle for two eggs over easy.

The dear, stupid body is as easily satisfied as a spaniel. And, incredibly the simple spaniel can lure the brawling mind to its dish. It is everlastingly funny that the proud, metaphysically ambitious, clamoring mind will hush if you give it an egg.

45   Further: while the mind reels in the deep space, while the mind grieves or fears or exults, the workaday senses, in ignorance or idiocy, like so many computer terminals printing out market prices while the world blows up, still transcribe their little data and transmit them to the warehouse in the skull. Later, under the tranquilizing influence of fried eggs, the mind can sort through this data. The restaurant was a halfway house, a decompression chamber. There I remembered a few things more.

The deepest, and most terrifying, was this: I have said that I heard screams. (I have since read that screaming, with hysteria, is a common reaction even to expected total eclipses.) People on all the hillsides, including, I think, myself, screamed when the black body of the moon detached from the sky and rolled over the sun. But something else was happening at the same instant, and it was this, I believe, which made us scream.

The second before the sun went out we saw a wall of dark shadow come speeding at us. We no sooner saw it than it was upon us, like thunder. It roared up the valley. It slammed our hill and knocked us out. It was the monstrous swift shadow cone of the moon. I have since read that this wave of shadow moves 1,800 miles an hour. Language can give no sense of this sort of speed—1,800 miles an hour. It was 195 miles wide. No end was in sight—you saw only the edge. It rolled at you across the land at 1,800 miles an hour, hauling darkness like plague behind it. Seeing it, and knowing it was coming straight for you, was like feeling a slug of anesthetic shoot up your arm. If you think very fast, you may have time to think, "Soon it will hit my brain." You can feel the deadness race up you arm; you can feel the appalling, inhuman speed of your own blood. We saw the wall of shadow coming, and screamed before it hit.

This was the universe about which we have read so much and never before felt: the universe as a clockwork of loose spheres flung at stupefying, unauthorized speeds. How could anything moving so fast not crash, not veer from its orbit amok like a car out of control on a turn?

Less than two minutes later, when the sun emerged, the trailing edge of the shadow cone sped away. It coursed down our hill and raced eastward over the plain, faster than the eye could believe; it swept over the plain and dropped over the planet's rim in a twinkling. It had clobbered us, and now it roared away. We blinked in the light. It was as though an enormous, loping god in the sky had reached down and slapped the earth's face.

50 Something else, something more ordinary, came back to me along about the third cup of coffee. During the moments of totality, it was so dark that drivers on the highway below turned on their cars' headlights. We could see the highways' route as a strand of lights. It was bumper-to-bumper down there. It was eight-fifteen in the morning, Monday morning, and people were driving into Yakima to work. That it was dark as night, and eerie as hell, an hour after dawn, apparently meant that in order to *see* to drive to work, people had to use their headlights. Four or five cars pulled off the road. The rest, in a line at least five miles long, drove to town. The highway ran between hills; the people could not have seen any of the eclipsed sun at all. Yakima will have another total eclipse in 2086. Perhaps, in 2086, businesses will give their employees an hour off.

From the restaurant we drove back to the coast. The highway crossing the Cascades range was open. We drove over the mountain like old pros. We joined our places on the planet's thin crust; it held. For the time being, we were home free.

Early that morning at six, when we had checked out, the six bald men were sitting on folding chairs in the dim hotel lobby. The television was on. Most of them were awake. You might drown in your own spittle, God knows, at any time; you might wake up dead in a small hotel, a cabbage head watching TV while snows pile up in the passes, watching TV while the chili peppers smile and the moon passes over the sun and nothing changes and nothing is learned because you have lost your bucket and shovel and no longer care. What if you regain the surface and open your sack and find, instead of treasure, a beast which jumps at you? Or you may not come back at all. The winches may jam, the scaffolding buckle, the air conditioning collapse. You may glance up one day and see by your head-lamp the canary keeled over in its cage. You may reach into a cranny for pearls and touch a moray eel. You yank on your rope; it is too late.

Apparently people share a sense of these hazards, for when the total eclipse ended, an odd thing happened.

When the sun appeared as a blinding bead on the ring's side, the eclipse was over. The black lens cover appeared again, backlighted, and slid away. At once the yellow light made the sky blue again; the black lid dissolved and vanished. The real world began there. I remember now: we all hurried away. We were born and bored at a stroke. We rushed down the hill. We found our car; we saw the other people streaming down the hillsides; we joined the highway traffic and drove away.

55   We never looked back. It was a general vamoose, and an odd one, for when we left the hill, the sun was still partially eclipsed—a sight rare enough, and one which, in itself, we would probably have driven five hours to see. But enough is enough. One turns at last even from glory itself with a sigh of relief. From the depths of mystery, and even from the heights of splendor, we bounce back and hurry for the latitudes of home.

CONVERSATION STARTER

Discuss a memory of a profound natural event that you experienced. Were you alone or with others during the event?

READING MATTERS

1. How does Dillard feel about the image of the "lifelike painting of the smiling clown's head, made out of vegetables" in her hotel room? How does she use this image as a contrast point for her thoughts about the meaning of the total eclipse?

2. Why does Dillard say that in the case of the total eclipse, "What you see is more convincing than any wild-eyed theory you may know"? Did you experience the eclipse vicariously as you were reading Dillard's account?

3. How does Dillard's image of herself "standing in a movie of the hill-side grasses filmed in the Middle Ages" help to capture her sense of dislocation during the eclipse? Why does she feel that she is dead? How does Dillard develop a relationship between the natural world and the spiritual world in her account?

4. Why are the people who are witnessing the eclipse screaming? How does Dillard process the overwhelming experience of the total eclipse? (Refer to specific images in the text as you answer this question.) In what ways do the people with whom Dillard witnesses the eclipse help her to make sense of it?

Writing Matters

1. Compare and contrast a solitary experience you had in nature to one that you experienced with your community. What conclusions about the natural world can you draw from these experiences?
2. Write about a profound natural event that you experienced with family, neighbors, friends, or even strangers. Discuss the impact the event had on you. Did you feel that the experience was a spiritual one? How did the event affect your sense of the importance of community?
3. Write an essay that first presents Dillard's interpretation of the total eclipse's meaning. Refer to specific passages in her text to support your main ideas. Then discuss your response to Dillard's presentation of the meaning of the total eclipse.

Relevant Web Sites

Annie Dillard <http://www.well.com/user/elliotts/smse_dillard.html>

Read the essay "The Mysticism of Annie Dillard's Pilgrim at Tinker Creek," by Sandra Elliott, at this URL and also find out about the life and works of Annie Dillard. The article focuses on the writer as a modern-day mystic and on her ideas about our relationship with the divine.

The Ecotheology of Annie Dillard: A Study in Ambivalence
<http://www.crosscurrents.org/dillard.html>

Visit the "Cross Currents" web site from the Association of Religion and Intellectual Life and read Pamela A. Smith's article, "The Ecotheology of Annie Dillard: A Study in Ambivalence." In this essay you will learn about Annie Dillard's unique brand of "ecotheology" and her resistance to any labels at all.

Activists Rebuilding Communities

Sue Halpern

The Art of Change

Sue Halpern is the author of Four Wings and a Prayer: Caught in the Mystery of the Monarch Butterfly, *and* Migrations to Solitude, *both published by Vintage books. She divides her time between the Adirondack Mountains of New York State, and the Green Mountains of Vermont.*

Jane Golden is driving by a corner of North Philadelphia that most people, given the chance, would leave as fast as they could. Golden, however, is riding the brake: She can't go slow enough. "Over there!" she calls. Over there is a bleak row of tumbledown, three-story buildings that would seem uninhabitable but for the people walking in and out of them. Yet Golden, who directs the city's Mural Arts Program, the most prolific mural project in the country, sees the place differently.

"Isn't that a terrific wall!" she exclaims. The wall is aged brick and runs the length of the building. It used to be attached to the row house next door, but that building is long gone, as are many in this neighborhood, and in its place is a vacant, trash-strewn lot.

"We could do a lot with that wall," says Golden, an artist herself. She turns the corner. On another stretch of brick, the mural program has painted a three-story tribute to Rachel Bagby and Lloyd Logan, two community leaders, their faces serious and forceful and of a size usually seen on billboards, selling something. (Here they are selling, too: commitment and neighborhood pride.) Half a block later, on the back side of the Jones Memorial Baptist Church, is a panorama of city life, the city life of this very street, in fact, of boys riding bikes, and men and women going about their business as seen through the windows of tenements, and these words from Proverbs 15:3 wrapped around it all like a stole: "The eyes of the Lord are in every place beholding the evil and the good."

Golden pulls up to a stoplight. The likeness of the late musician Grover Washington Jr., who lived here for much of his life, reaches 60 feet skyward, playing a saxophone 20 feet tall. Golden's own creation, Peace Wall, a multicultural wheel of clasped hands, is in another neighborhood, maybe 100 murals away, maybe more. At last count, there were more than 2,100 murals in Philadelphia, and the number is growing steadily.

5   "The murals are all over the city," Golden says, "though the majority are in neighborhoods that are the most neglected. People want to have beauty in their lives."

Much of North and West Philadelphia has fallen into ruin in recent decades, their neighborhoods scarred by more than 15,000 vacant lots and abandoned buildings. The residents who remain look to the murals for visual relief from the stark, denatured environments in which they live. There is the intricate mosaic of Salvador Gonzalez's *Butterflies of the Caribbean* on Susquehanna Street, and Ras Malik's agricultural triptych *Seasons*, whose perfect rows of ripe Big Boys are the backdrop, in summer, to real vines growing real tomatoes in a community garden tended by the residents of Howard and Master Streets. And there are waterfalls, lots of waterfalls, on walls all over town.

"One mural I was painting, the people there said, 'Put in a waterfall,'" says Ana Uribe, a muralist from Colombia who had already put waterfalls into a number of the murals she has painted in Philadelphia, where she now lives. "I didn't want to. But they were insistent. They said they wanted the flowing water to show how things were going to be cleaned up and get better. They didn't want to look at any more sadness. They said they already knew how bad things were and didn't need to be reminded."

Over on Norris Street, in North Philadelphia, block captain Ruth Birchett and her neighbors took a different approach. Though they, too, already knew how bad things were, they saw their mural as a kind of totem that could speak the truth of their lives, and change it.

"There used to be 50 houses on this street," says Birchett, a 49-year-old African American woman with a youthful face, surveying a block that is defined, now, by what is missing. "There was an ice cream parlor and a bakery, a cleaners and a pharmacy." Now there is no commerce at all, at least none that requires a storefront. A homeless shelter anchors one end of the street. Around the corner at the other end is a homemade shrine to the three young people who have been shot here so far this year. "We have lost so very much," Birchett says. "This is a government-forsaken neighborhood."

10   The Norris Street project was painted in the summer of 2000, after Birchett submitted an application to the Mural Arts Program demonstrating the neighborhood's support for a mural and its commitment to maintaining it. Competition was tough; the project receives 200 applications a year and only has the resources—from city and private funds—to paint about 75.

"The Mural Arts Program will not do a mural unless they know they can work directly with people in the neighborhood," Birchett says, recounting the numerous planning meetings between residents and the mural artist, Cavin Jones, himself a resident of North Philadelphia, who was chosen by Golden and her staff from a roster of 300 artists. As with all of the city's murals, the residents and the artist designed the mural jointly.

"The artist paints the picture," says Ariel Bierbaum, who serves as the project's director of community murals, "but the community paints the vision."

In 1984, when Golden was hired to paint murals in Philadelphia, it was part of an official effort to stem the proliferation of graffiti in the city. Under her direction, young people—most of them graffiti artists themselves, teenagers who had never dipped a brush in watercolors or seen even the outside of an art museum—were enlisted and paid to put in "scrub time" and to learn how to paint murals. Golden introduced them to professional artists, to poetry, to fine arts. She and her small staff started after-school art programs and summer mural-painting programs and apprenticeship programs. More than 10,000 kids have participated so far, many of them year after year, through junior high and high school, internships, apprenticeships, and jobs.

Beautification projects have been going on for decades in inner cities across America, often with striking results. But it is still remarkable, even to an artist and activist like Golden, how democracy can be advanced in real and tangible ways simply by putting paintings on the sides of buildings in communities that reflect the very failure of democracy. "I always thought murals made art accessible to people, and they do," Golden says. "But I've witnessed how they create real neighborhood change, too."

15   Golden is standing with Ruth Birchett in front of the mural on Norris Street when she says this, both women tipping back their heads to take it all in. Covering the entire side of the last house on the block, the mural shows an elderly black couple looking down on the younger generations— on an anguished woman bemoaning the senseless violence in the neighborhood and on an unwed teenage mother cradling a baby. Traditional African symbols decorate the center of the towering canvas, as do a rainbow and a pair of clasped hands, each meant to convey its own message of hope tempered by love and remembrance. Still, the eye is drawn to the outline of a crack pipe that hovers in the picture like a ghost—a symbol, surely, but something more as well.

"The main economy here is the drug economy, which is why the crack pipe is in the picture," Birchett explains. "The only people who had trouble with it were the 'entrepreneurs.'"

And this, it turns out, was a good thing. After the mural was painted, drug dealers no longer felt comfortable hanging out at Norris and 19th. They are still in the neighborhood, but with more and more murals dominating blocks like Ruth Birchett's, the dealers have less and less room to maneuver. Invariably, once a mural goes up, it becomes a catalyst for other kinds of neighborhood improvements. Gardens are planted and tended, picnics are held there, people venture out of their homes, neighborhoods are reclaimed, communities are reconstituted.

As if on cue, a woman about half Birchett's age approaches the block captain and points to the strip of dirt between the mural and the sidewalk. It is barren, not counting soda bottles and plastic bags and shards of glass and brick.

"We have to do something about this," the woman says, toeing the soil. Birchett agrees.

20   They begin to make a plan: to get wood chips, to plant bulbs, to enlist volunteers. They agree to meet out here on the weekend with rakes and hoes and friends, and the woman moves on.

"We're all community organizers now," Birchett says, watching her go.

CONVERSATION STARTER

Discuss a mural that has made an impression on you. How did it change your community experience? What impact did it appear to have on the neighborhood?

READING MATTERS

1. Why does Halpern believe that the murals offer a vision of hope? Do other members of the community share this view? Is there evidence that this is true?
2. Why does the Mural Arts Program focus on neglected neighborhoods? What impact do the murals have on the neighborhood?
3. Describe the relationship that exists between the neighborhood and the Mural Arts Program. What impact does this relationship have on the success of the Mural Arts Program? What impact does it have on the neighborhood?
4. According to Golden, how is democracy being advanced "by putting paintings on the side of buildings"? Refer to specific examples from the text.

WRITING MATTERS

1. Visit the Mural Arts Program web site. Select a mural that inspires you and write an essay about your reaction to the piece. Do you think your reaction to the mural would change significantly if you were to see it in the context of the neighborhood? Why?
2. Make a map of your community indicating murals, public sculptures, memorials, public squares, or other public amenities that create a unique sense of place. Write about what you learned though this project. Were you surprised by what you discovered? Present your findings to your classmates.
3. Visit a mural in a community where you have lived or visited. Interview the residents about their opinion of the mural. Write about your findings.

RELEVANT WEB SITES

THE MURAL ARTS PROGRAM <http://www.muralarts.org>

Since its inception in 1984, the Mural Arts Program has completed more murals than any other public art program in the nation—more than 2,300 indoor and outdoor murals throughout Philadelphia. This effort has brought art to the cityscape, turning graffiti-scarred walls into scenic views, portraits of community heroes, and abstract creations.

THE PHILADELPHIA DEPARTMENT OF RECREATION MURAL ARTS PROGRAM (MAP) <http://www.gophila.com/murals/body.htm>

The official web site of the Philadelphia Department of Recreation Mural Arts Program (MAP) includes an online gallery of mural art along with directions for self-guided tours through the city of Philadelphia.

Kimi Eisele

The Other Side of the Wires

Kimi Eisele is the founding editor of You Are Here: The Journal of Creative Geography, *housed in the Department of Geography at the University of Arizona. She continues to learn about history and geography from young people on both sides of the border from her home in Tucson. This is Kimi Eisele's first publication.*

Colonia Solidaridad spills over the southeastern hills of Nogales, Sonora, as if by accident. In the Sonoran Desert upland, once covered by blue oak, mesquite, yucca, and grasslands, plastic bags float through the air and diapers tumble down slopes. Houses of block, wood, cardboard, and aluminum teeter up the hillsides. Eroding gravel roads snake in between them, flanked by walls of tires. This is a neighborhood in a Mexican city at the edge of the United States.

In July, when the rainy season starts, downpours carve arroyos into the streets. Debris flows like a river. Some of it is visible: soda bottles, orange rinds, a high-heeled shoe, the pink plastic leg of a baby doll. Other things—pathogenic bacteria, protozoa, gastrointestinal helminthes and enteric viruses—blend into the stream and quietly multiply.

By August *la laguna*, the lagoon, stretches across an intersection and laps at the front porch of the flimsy house where ten-year-old María Fernanda lives with her parents. Her neighbors, three young boys, stand at its edge to send egg cartons afloat and see whose hurled rock can make the biggest splash.

I first meet María Fernanda during the summer of 1998, shortly after I begin fieldwork for a master's degree in geography. For nearly a year, I make regular trips to Colonia Solidaridad to understand the everyday geography of children who live there. It is a geography complicated by big words like urbanization, industrialization, and globalization, which over the past three decades have reshaped local landscapes all along this border. I want to know how these words play out in real life, to discover whether or not the

Photograph of her home in Colonia Solidaridad taken by María Fernanda, age 10.

flows of capital, goods, and labor across international boundaries create openings through which these children can leap forward, or fissures through which they fall.

5   The transformation of the borderlands began in earnest long before any of these children were born. Since the mid-1960s, when the Mexican government initiated an industrialization program to revive its northern economy, U.S. and other foreign-owned companies have located assembly plants called *maquiladoras* on the Mexican side of the border, paying taxes only on the value added to goods through manufacture. In Nogales, Sonora—just one of the loci for the ever-expanding borderwide industry— more than eighty maquiladoras now employ about twenty percent of the population. In them, laborers assemble, among other things, automatic lawn sprinklers, suitcases, television remote controls, garage door openers, microchips, trombones, hospital supplies, auto parts, and computers for the world market.

    When María Fernanda was six, her family moved to Nogales from the state of Sinaloa so her parents could find steady work. Hers is a common story. From 1950 to 1980, the population of the Mexican border states nearly tripled. In those same years, Nogales's population grew to almost five and one half times that of its twin city to the north, Nogales, Arizona, estimated then at nearly 16,000. The 1990 Mexican census reported 105,873 residents. Some claim it's now three times that.

The municipal government has been unable to keep up with infrastructure demands. A severe housing shortage has left many new residents to fend for themselves, building homes out of what they can afford in squatter settlements that lack running water, sewage systems, and sometimes even electricity. Colonia Solidaridad is one such neighborhood.

Early on, I decide I do not want to be yet another researcher who whizzes in, documents people's lives, and disappears into the halls of academia. Perhaps it is the teacher in me: I want to involve children in my investigation. To do this, I offer a series of workshops in Solidaridad's school, in which I ask children (eight to twelve years old, sometimes younger) to photograph, draw pictures, make maps, and talk to me about where they live.

I am also looking for a more hopeful narrative about life on the U.S.–Mexico border. Within one year, I read dozens of stories in Tucson newspapers about underground drug tunnels, nameless Mexicans found dead in the desert, cardboard houses that catch fire and burn to the ground. *The New York Times* can run a handful of stories a month on the border; none of them report anything good.

10   I do not contest these stories. I just get tired of them.

The first time I give these children cameras, a ten-year old girl takes a photograph of her friend, Lucero, standing at the edge of the accidental lake that has formed at the intersection of two streets. Lucero wears a white dress, the kind young girls wear for their first communion, and a bewildered look. "That's contaminated water," says Yesenia, an eleven-year-old who likes to ask questions and catches on to things quickly. "Nothing but infection there. When the big puddle forms, lots of us get sick from the flies."

In another photo a young boy wades through the water. Yesenia, the oldest of five, remarks that it is the duty of older children to teach their younger siblings about how dangerous this water is. Though the children are not exactly sure what's in it, they make good guesses. There is no running water in Solidaridad, no plumbing, no sewage system. Some households have ceramic toilets but no way to flush them. The rest have dug holes in the ground, but not deep enough.

On and off for several weeks I am a guest in one family's house. I sleep on a lopsided couch in the bedroom where ten-year-old Josué and his three younger sisters share the top of a full-sized bunk bed. Josué's parents sleep on the bottom. In the bathroom, where buckets hold water used to flush down waste, I discover tiny black worms. I scoop up a bowlful of water from the bucket and watch as the worms flow into the toilet. My stomach churns.

In Solidaridad water comes from a *pipa*, a three-hundred-gallon tank on the back of a truck. When the pipa passes by, Josué's mother calls out to its driver. He pulls a long hose from the tank and throws it over the wall of a concrete cistern that Josué's father has built next to the house. The same thing happens at María Fernanda's house, though her family doesn't have a cistern, just three metal drums they got from the maquiladoras. I look in one of them and see debris floating on the surface. These drums probably once held toxic chemicals. María Fernanda's mother knows this. "We only drink from this one," she explains, pointing to a yellow plastic barrel.

15   Eventually I realize that the worms I see inching their way through the water in Josué's bathroom are mosquito larvae. Though a hazard in their own right, these larvae seem minor compared to the other things that have been found in this city's water. In 1987 the Arizona Department of Environmental Quality named the Nogales Wash, the main waterway through Ambos Nogales (both Nogaleses), a state Superfund site. Mexican studies throughout the 1990s found the wash and several wells heavily contaminated with bacteria and volatile organochlorate compounds, hazardous pollutants used by border industries. In wells downstream from several maquiladoras, the same studies found levels of perchloroethylene (PCE), an industrial and dry-cleaning solvent known to cause cancer in laboratory animals; vinyl chloride, a human cancer agent; nitrates, which impair the ability of infants to absorb oxygen; and disease-causing coliform bacteria.

When I ask them about Solidaridad's environmental problems, the children do not list any of these chemicals. Instead, they say "garbage" over and over. The nearest trash dump is visible from the schoolyard. Standing there, I make out the irregular form of quotidian wastepapers, tires, plastic bags, and scrap metal, oozing over a barren hillside into a ravine.

One morning we turn the fifth-grade classroom into a barrio museum. The task, I explain, is to collect things that represent this particular place. The children scatter about the neighborhood and return with a strange collection. A pair of scuffed white high-heeled shoes, one hard tortilla, a bottle cap, flowers, a mango pit, a plastic soda bottle, a popsicle stick, oak leaves, a juice can, a sock, a potato chips bag, a cookie box, a prickly pear pad, and a dry tamale husk. The items fill five desks and the children crowd around to look. They tie yellow labels to their objects, recording where each was found. We make categories—clothing, agricultural products, processed foods, plants, refuse—and arrange the objects accordingly. On a large piece of butcher paper I write where the objects were found. On this day, trash becomes a lesson in local geography.

Most other days, trash is just trash—stinky, dirty, ugly, dangerous. Every now and then I remind them to pick up their empty juice cartons, candy wrappers, lollipop sticks. But then I wonder: What is the use of putting trash in a can when there is no collection service to haul it away? This place is teeming with contradictions.

Another day I show a photograph of a group of children playing Ring-Around-the-Rosie on a barren plot in Ciudad Juárez, the Chihuahuan border city of 1.5 million. Behind them rise two concrete towers of the Asarco copper smelting plant just across the border in El Paso, Texas. A wisp of white smoke curls out of one tower into the sky. Alejandro says he'd like to be in the photo to play with the other kids. "I like the factory," he says. "I can help there."

20   Ten-year-old Sarahi says she has seen a scene like this at the factory where her mother works. Her older sister Lidia, twelve, says she doesn't like the factory because it contaminates. Others chime in. "Factories here pollute," Sarahi agrees.

"Yeah, they throw garbage," says Leticia, but adds she'd still want to work there.

There is plenty to deplore about the kind of industrialization that has extended across the U.S.–Mexico borderlands. In his book about the maquiladora industry, *The Terror of the Machine*, sociologist Devon Peña writes,

> The road to free trade . . . leads to an environmental wasteland wrought by capitalist maldevelopment. To a world deficient in biological and cultural diversity. This is a place in the heart of darkness. It is a free-trade netherworld, lethally contaminated by toxic wastes and the garbage of self-indulgent lifestyles. This is a world born of a ruthless, globe-trotting search for material wealth violently extracted from nature, women, worker, and colony . . . this is a concrete, steel, and barbed wire world, an antihabitat.

There are times when Peña's apocalyptic vision doesn't seem so far off the mark. When I read reports about the kind of contaminants that might be seeping into these children's bodies. When the rain rushes down the hillside taking with it half the road, food scraps, dead dogs, grocery bags, loose shoes, and fecal matter. When the wind rattles the aluminum walls of one family's house so hard I think we all might get pulled up into the sky. When I see the skeleton of a new factory and imagine a line of young workers snaking its way to the door. When I drive home to Tucson through the desert and pass a string of bright green golf courses watered daily by automatic lawn sprinklers. When I push a button to turn on the television from across the room and see glossy commercials for household cleaners, reclining chairs, miracle hair growth formulas, investment brokers, and "emerging" Third World markets.

The word *antihabitat* fits nicely.

25   In the office of civil protection in downtown Nogales, a large map outlines the city's "high risk zones" for flooding and landslides with big red circles. One of the circles covers the zigzag of streets in Solidaridad. Part of the neighborhood is designated as a refuge, where people would go if the walls of water pushed through the canyons and flooded the neighborhood. I recognize the area as the school, a series of cement-block buildings perched on a hill, where I have spent most of my time asking children to tell me, in all sorts of ways, about how they perceive their surroundings.

When classes are in session, these children learn no specific information about where they live. The desert is depicted as a vast, Sahara-like expanse of sand, and maquiladoras are described, parenthetically, as "foreign businesses that establish in Mexico to take advantage of our cheap labor." There is no mention of industrial waste, squatter settlements, occupational hazards, or contaminated water along the two-thousand-mile border. These children do not learn the statistics that I learn about young people and environmental health on the border. They do not know, for example, that during the first six months of 1992, according to a report in *The Arizona Daily Star*, four babies in Nogales were born with part of their brains missing. That in the three years prior, more than seventeen babies were born with the same condition, believed to be related to contamination from toxic chemicals. They do not know that, according to the Pan American Health Organization, in 1987 and 1988—the years some of them were born—the life expectancy for residents of Mexican border states was five years less than that for residents of U.S. border states. That in those years children on the Mexican side died from intestinal infections, respiratory diseases, and nutritional deficiencies, diseases that did not even appear among the leading causes of death for children on the U.S. side.

Yet these children's textbooks do include chapters about caring for the environment. The arguments spin around reforestation and the ozone layer and about doing your part to protect the big blue planet. They conveniently illustrate that nature is global not local, "out there" not "here." In this narrative, things like the maquiladora industry are easily justified. In a city with no nature, no nature can be destroyed.

Still, children learn to take up the cause. The words spill out of Yesenia's mouth. "In school they teach us about the environment, that I should take care of it, I should protect it. But even though I want to take care of it the rest of the people don't. I would like to give to the whole colonia, so that they could help me, but you see, I can't. How I would like for everyone to have the same thoughts as me."

Yesenia, in all of her optimism, persuades the director of the school to put up signs in the schoolyard that say, "Take care of the plants." It's important, she thinks, to protect the strip of feeble young palms, flowerless rose bushes, and dusty marigolds from feet and candy wrappers. Later she gathers her neighbors together one morning to collect trash. She is resilient the way children are supposed to be.

30   One afternoon a handful of children and I make the journey to a stretch of green just beyond the neighborhood limits, less than a fifteen-minute walk from school. At the end of the road, we pull apart two strands of barbed wire and crawl through to the other side. Tall grasses spread out thinly over the hills, and a floor of rocks fills the spaces in between. There are flowers here, globemallow and daisies, oak and mesquite trees, a few horses. We pretend not to notice a spattering of trash—plastic bags and used toilet paper. We face south, where a succession of green hills reach out for miles in front of us.

Yesenia's younger brothers, the twins, run ahead then quickly descend into a narrow gorge. Just seven, they know how to ham it up. They pose tirelessly for photographs, then run, jump, pretend to fall, and feign dead. One of them spends most of the day's excursion crawling on his belly, saying, "Water, water," as if lost in the desert. Then he flips over on his back, lets his tongue flop out of his mouth, and lies still for long moments. He opens one eye to see if I'm looking. When he finally gets up, he jumps high into the air and skips to catch up with me. "In the desert there's no water," he says. "Good thing we live in the city. We don't have that problem."

"What are we seeing?" Suzi asks. "Grasshoppers! Two grasshoppers making love."

Yesenia begins to pick up rocks. She marvels at each one and stuffs those she judges as pretty into her backpack. "Yesenia, why do you collect rocks?" Suzi asks.

"Ah, because they're very pretty and white and they shine and they're part of nature."

35 Suzi says she likes this place, "because it's very clean, there are horses, and beautiful plants. For the fresh air, the trees. You don't have to do anything here. I also like it because you can see everything from up here."

"More than anything the rocks, the flowers, nature, everything, everything!" Yesenia shouts with her arms in the air.

"I like it here because there are colored grasshoppers," Suzi says. "Does this grasshopper have a girlfriend? Look, it has blue feet. Lucky are those that wear sneakers."

Josué is the only one who thinks to take his camera into the hills. He takes pictures of horses, kids in the grass, the reach of landscape, and almost a dozen photos of plain blue sky.

In renderings of the place they'd like to live in, some of these children draw pastures of green, forests, horses, beaches, swimming pools, and large houses surrounded by flowers and trees. When I ask them what they like most about their own neighborhood, they mention the view of these hills or the patches of green they find in front of their own or neighbors' houses—prickly pear cacti, an occasional mesquite tree, sometimes geraniums or zinnias.

40 Beyond the two strands of barbed wire at the end of the road, my notions about the importance of separate "natural" spaces, distinct from the cluttered geography of urban life, get turned upside down. For most of my life, I have believed that open space cultivates a sense of adventure, wonder, resiliency. That because there are cities—dirty, paved over, dangerous—there also need to be separate, healthy wild spaces—clean, unpaved, and safe. I base my prescription on what the wilderness has done for me: allowed me to experience the "non-urban"; reminded me that I am not the only kind of creature that inhabits the space of the world; opened me up to beauty, change, possibility. My own forays into the woods, canyons, and rivers have allowed me to return home rejuvenated and inspired. But the home that has always awaited me has never looked anything like the home these children return to when they squeeze back through the barbed wires and slide down gravel streets into houses made of cardboard.

In Solidaridad, the distinction between the natural and the nonnatural gets tangled. I recognize that it is made too easily in one small moment. When one of the twins declares that water is not a "problem" in his city, he separates the expanse of desert from the place where he lives. In this, the division of "nature" from "urban" seems more perilous than redeeming.

I remind myself of what Cindi Katz, a geographer who has studied the consequences of globalization on children in places as distant as Sudan and New York City, argues about the disappearing spaces of childhood. What children need, Katz argues, is not necessarily nature or wilderness, but rather, "at the minimum an environment that provides them health and well-being; safety; physical, emotional, and intellectual development; and future." Requisites that "depend on adequate food, shelter, health care, sanitation, social services and protection from environmental pollution and hazards."

In Solidaridad, I learn to not be overly romantic about green space and open air. I cannot confidently claim these hills as the Eden that will cancel out what cannot truly be erased.

Sometime in February my friend Jeff and I take a picnic lunch to Solidaridad. With a truckload of kids, we drive up the highest hill in the neighborhood. Carrying a cooler full of food, we slip between the barbed wires and traipse to the other side of the hill to where earlier in the fall a small stream cut through the canyon.

45   After lunch most of the children follow Jeff up the next hill. Others descend into the arroyo to dig for water. I stay behind for a moment of quiet. I can still hear the kids' voices on the other side of the canyon. I squint through the trees and see them reach the summit. Below, the others dig ferociously—a deep hole into damp earth—then take turns standing in it.

When these children laugh and run and jump and sing in this space, I can sense their joy, their freedom. The way their parents talk to me about opportunity might convince me that things are better now than they were before—there is steady work, school, the skeleton of a home. But when I stand at the top of this hill and look into the folds of the neighborhood below, it is clear to me that capital accumulation and profit, economic growth and progress, both depend upon and create uneven geographies. On the border, as elsewhere, global economic restructuring and its guises of "development" are advantaged by invisibility. Those who run the companies and profit from inexpensive labor and unregulated operations do not have to see the consequences of their actions. In Nogales, the inability of the city to provide basic services, lax enforcement of environmental laws in maquiladoras, suppressed wages, nonexistent labor unions, and a national countryside seized by multinational agribusiness, illustrate the inconsistency of global capitalism—what it provides to some it does not provide to others. Despite the rhetoric of opportunity, this place lacks the requisites of a healthy future.

From here, too, I recognize even my own cultural optimism and economic advantage. That the ideas I have carried with me from the other side of the border have made me want to find easy solutions, have made me want to tell a different story about this place. But things here are not that simple. How do fields and flowers, carefully rendered in crayon, hold up against a chaotic backdrop of warehouse factories, insufficient paychecks, overflowing sewage, and inadequate housing?

I want to forget that a city grinds down daily on the space just over the hill behind us. But I know that this boundary is permeable, like all borders I have come to know. They do not ultimately contain what they are made to contain—habitats, economies, ideas, toxins, people. Most certainly this city will spill across these wires. But it is possible that as long as it remains, this place in the hills will also flow into these children's lives. That from here they too, will learn to see the complete view—the sweep of mountains, the piles of litter, trees, the rise of houses, mysterious puddles, grasshoppers, and the flow of industry across the city. That here, at the edge of two converging habitats, they will learn to discover, dream, and adapt.

Conversation Starter

Discuss the differences between natural areas and nonnatural areas in your community.

Reading Matters

1. What are some of the contradictions Eisele encounters in the daily life of Colonia Solidaridad? Discuss specific examples from the text.
2. Describe the children of Colonia Solidaridad. What does Eisele learn from them?
3. What does Eisele find on "the other side of the wire"?
4. How does the author feel about her role as a researcher? What has she learned?

Writing Matters

1. Using the fifth-grade class's "museum exercise" as a model, collect objects that represent your community. Record your objects, including where they were found and what they reveal about your community. Write an essay for your class that will help them to understand more about the local geography.
2. The Nogales Wash, the main waterway through Ambos Bogales was named a state Superfund site. What does this mean? Write an essay that defines this term. Use the Relevant Web Sites section to begin your research.
3. Write an essay that explores the distinctions between "nature" and "urban" settings in your community. Where do you encounter nature? What constitutes a "natural area"?

Relevant Web Sites

SCERP: Southwest Center for Environmental Research and Policy
<http://www.scerp.org>

This web site highlights the efforts of SCERP, in partnership with many stake-holders along the U.S.-Mexico border including the U.S. EPA and the Border Trade Alliance, to develop solutions to the environmental problems that affect the 10 million people who live in the region.

Environmental Protection Agency US–Mexico Border Program
<http://www.epa.gov/usmexicoborder>

This web site provides information about the Environmental Protection Agency U.S.–Mexico Border Program. The site focuses on the federal, state, and local government programs that protect the environment and the public health in the U.S.–Mexico border region.

Habitat for Humanity and The Jimmy Carter Work Project

Habitat for Humanity International is a nonprofit, ecumenical Christian housing ministry dedicated to eliminating substandard housing and making decent shelter a matter of conscience and action. Habitat has built more than 150,000 houses worldwide. Volunteers work with future homeowners to build or renovate houses, which are then sold to partner families at no profit, with no interest charged on the mortgage. The money from the sale of each house goes into a revolving Fund for Humanity, to support future building projects.

Jimmy Carter's involvement with Habitat for Humanity International began in 1984 when the former president led a work group to New York City to help renovate a six-story building with 19 families in need of decent, affordable shelter. That experience planted the seed, and the Jimmy Carter Work Project has been an internationally recognized event of HFHI ever since. Each year, Jimmy and Roslynn Carter give a week of their time—along with their building skills—to build homes and raise awareness of the critical need for affordable housing. The JCWP is held at a different location each year and attracts volunteers from around the world. "We have become small players in an exciting global effort to alleviate the curse of homelessness," Carter said. "With our many new friends, we have worked to raise funds, to publicize the good work of Habitat, to recruit other volunteers, to visit overseas projects and even build a few houses."

The 2002 JCWP (http://www.habitat.org/jcwp/2002) took place in Africa. One thousand houses were built in 18 countries, with the final 100 houses constructed in a five-day build in Durban, South Africa. The following diary entries were written by Leigh Powell, a Habitat for Humanity writer and editor on special assignment for the Jimmy Carter Work Project.

Diary of House 949

DAY ONE

International volunteers poured out of their hotels along the Durban beachfront and loaded onto waiting buses. A short drive across town delivered them to the build site, where 100 foundations lay ready for the Jimmy Carter Work Project 2002.

Excited volunteers ate breakfast together and were greeted by Harry Goodall, vice president of Habitat's Africa/Middle East area. Then Millard Fuller, Habitat's founder and president, led the morning devotions. "Let us love one another," Millard charged the volunteers. "Let us get to know the homeowners and love them and let them love us."

With that, the volunteers set off in high spirits to find their house assignments for the first day of building. I was assigned to House 949 and walked down the hill toward the house as the sun rose over Durban.

House 949 sits back from the road on the left. I strolled over and met David, the house leader, and the other crew members assigned to assist Richard Zondi build his new home.

5   Mark, Anna, and I began laying blocks on the long wall. Joanne and Birgit jumped in on the opposite wall. Ashley and Clive joined Dudzilie Theresa in bringing fresh "mud" (mortar) from the "mud pit" to our walls while Richard's brother-in-law, Maviti, started setting the windows.

Everyone had a job, and I think we were all surprised when lunch came so quickly. We grabbed our brown-bag lunches off the lunch delivery truck, ate and went right back into the building. The afternoon was a rigorous one of block lifting, block laying, and mortar mixing. But it was also an afternoon of jokes and conversation, as we all stopped being strangers from around the globe and started being a team, started being friends.

We finished late, but we met our goals for Day One. We worked until after dark laying the last row of bricks at the top of the house, tidying up our masonry work, and preparing the site for Day Two.

Tired and already a little sore, we slowly climbed the hill toward the dinner tents, checking out the other crews' progress, congratulating ourselves on a good day's work, and wishing each other a good night's sleep before returning to work the next day.

Day Two

The crew of House 949 was unanimous: We went to bed early last night! But I have to say how proud I am of myself—I'm not even sore—and everyone was again in high spirits as we met at the house to begin the day's building a little before 7:30 a.m. this morning. We began by scraping the excess mortar from the walls we completed late yesterday (they weren't too bad, considering we finished in the dark!), and then split into different teams to start today's work.

10 David, our house leader, led several of the guys in setting the trusses and getting the roof ready for tiling. Max and Birgit worked on getting the ceiling supports ready inside. The rest of us decided to tackle the house's paint job.

We weren't using just any old paint; we used "stipplecrete." Stipplecrete is actually a concrete mixture that spreads on like paint—only much, much thicker—and dries with a look much like adobe. It has to be mixed from a powder, which comes packaged in 40-kilo bags. My American mind isn't sure exactly how much 40 kilos is in pounds, but I know I shouldn't try to lift a bag of stipplecrete by myself. If I had any doubts about that, Maviti cleared them up as he took the bag away from me (right before I dropped it) and said, "We did not want you to come to South Africa to kill yourself!"

After Maviti poured the bag into a wheelbarrow for me, I was able to measure out the water and mix the stipplecrete. And more stipplecrete. And still more stipplecrete. I think I made about 12 wheelbarrows full to complete the painting of the house, inside and out.

This went on throughout the morning and well into the afternoon. After the painting was done (and might I add that our crew was one of the very first to have their whole house painted?), we cleaned up the brushes and paint pails before they became stipplecreted, too. That's when the hose decided to lose its nozzle, soaking me, Anna, Dudzilie Theresa, Maviti, and Ashley in the process. Thank goodness winters (it is the beginning of winter here) in Durban are warm.

Meanwhile, the roofing had continued and was nearly ready for the tiles, so we formed a brigade to pass the tiles from their pile on the ground up to the scaffolding for easier access. As the sun went down, we were laying the first of our tiles. Sure, some of the other houses were a little ahead of us today, roofing-wise, but we're not too far behind at all.

15 Besides, you should see how great our stipplecrete looks.

DAY THREE

Remember when I said I wasn't sore yesterday? Wow, talk about speaking too soon! I'm glad our stipplecrete looks so good, because mixing it has totally taken out my right shoulder.

I am very stiff today—but that's OK, because the house is coming together well. Today we got the roof tiles laid, started installing the "blueboard" that will insulate the house, raised the walls inside, installed the interior doors, and put the first coat of paint on the windowpanes and door frames. It was a full day!

Richard Zondi, the homeowner, works quietly, but he's wholeheartedly dedicated to getting his new house built. Toward the end of lunch, most of us were sitting around sipping our drinks, chatting, and sharing family pictures with one another. Richard was already back on the roof, placing more tiles. I can't even imagine what this opportunity means to him and his family. It's thinking about the improvement in the lives of Richard and 99 other families that keeps me going through the tiredness.

Before we left the site this evening, we were at the point to be able to take down all but one side of the scaffolding. Birgit exclaimed, "It looks much more like a house now, doesn't it?" She's right—now that there's a roof and no scaffolding, you can see just how close we are to making Richard's dream a reality.

DAY FOUR

20 It wasn't as chilly this morning as it has been, or maybe I'm getting used to the idea that it's actually winter here, and it's going to be a little cool before the sun comes up. I know it's silly, but I never really thought about there being a winter in Africa.

Today we did mostly inside work. We put the second coat of paint on all the windowpanes and doors, and then we continued putting up the ceiling and walls. Anne told me a couple of days ago that she and her husband had been on a lot of Habitat builds, but last year's JCWP in South Korea was the first and only time she had done construction (she'd always helped with the food services on builds previously). Today, though, you wouldn't have known she hadn't always done construction—she jumped right in on the installation of "RhinoBoard" for the walls, just like a pro!

One of the most exciting things today was when President Carter stopped by our house. He's been hard at work on his own house all week, but this morning he came by and asked if he could help us install our front porch awning. I was busy in the back scraping extra paint from the glass on the windows, so I didn't even know he was there till Joanne stuck her head into the bedroom and exclaimed, "Jimmy Carter is building our front porch!" I think Howard, Mark, and David helped him with it, but I'm not sure; exciting as it is to see President Carter, I think most people agree that it's more important to keep working and get things finished than it is to gawk during the build.

Later in the morning several house teams got to pose for a picture with President and Mrs. Carter and Millard and Linda Fuller. President Carter's grandson Jason delivered a message in Zulu to the crowd (I wonder what he said; I'll have to ask Theresa tomorrow) and received rousing applause. After the picture, President Carter presented Bibles to all of the homeowners present. I was walking back to the house with Richard, homeowner of house #949, as he read the inscriptions Millard and President Carter had written in the front, and he said, "I'm going to read this every night."

We all wrote down our addresses and/or e-mail addresses for one another this afternoon, and I'm going to make copies for everyone tonight at the hotel so we can keep in touch. Max has taken more than 100 digital pictures so far, and he's definitely going to have to e-mail some of them to me or post them on his web site or something. Plus I know that Clive, a native of Durban, wants an American flag, so maybe I'll mail him one when I get back to the States. In any case, I think we'd all like to keep in touch.

25   A crew of volunteers stayed late to spackle and hang drywall throughout the site tonight after dark (we have the electricity working in the house now, too!). In the morning, we should be ready to paint the interior, finish the installation of the plumbing fixtures, landscape—and dedicate the house in the afternoon!

Day Five

Today was a long, busy, and emotional day. There was a definite sense of pressure this morning, as the house had to be finished. There was a lot of spackling, caulking, painting, landscaping, and cleanup to be done. The sense of teamwork that has been building all week was plain to see.

Most everyone grabbed brushes and worked on painting throughout the early afternoon. Clive, Ashley, Birgit, and Maviti took care of the landscaping—leveling the yard, planting trees and making a little bench and a front porch from some extra concrete blocks. With paint on the walls and the yard in shape, it was amazing how quickly this house started looking like a "home."

Though everyone worked diligently, we took several breaks to make sure we had each other's correct addresses. A couple of the guys brought T-shirts and permanent markers so we could all sign our names (a great idea to remember for my next JCWP). We also wrote messages to Richard and his family on the back of the sign that had been standing in the yard in front of a mere foundation five days earlier.

Happily, Richard's wife, Phindile, was able to take Friday off from work to be at the site. It was fun to watch her excitement as she helped wrap up the construction of her new house.

30   A little after 4 p.m., David called us all together in front of the house for the dedication. Howard led us in prayer and read a chapter from the Bible about building your house—and your life—on a rock, a firm foundation. David congratulated and thanked us for being a great crew, and then Richard, the homeowner, spoke briefly. Then he made his way around the group, shaking hands and hugging us, saying "God bless you."

Phindile followed, hugging us and crying. I can't speak for everyone else, but that's also when I started crying, and I saw a few other folks wiping their eyes, too. Is it possible to be unmoved by such a display of joy?

When Phindile's parents arrived, her mother, Noreen, sang a blessing in each room of the house. Hearing her call of "Amen" mingling with the other sounds of song, praise, and laughter across the build site, as others dedicated their homes, was enough to bring tears to my eyes again.

After the tears, it was time to celebrate with the rest of the house crews, homeowners, and staff. Everyone gathered for the closing ceremony, followed by a "braai"—a South African barbecue "with all the fixin's" (as we'd say in my home state of Tennessee).

It was bittersweet to board the bus and leave the site for the last time. A little part of myself lives in that neighborhood; a little part of everyone who volunteered there this week lives there. It is a community built of blocks and mortar, stipplecrete and tile, spackle and paint—but it is ultimately a community built of love in its purest form.

35   God bless Richard, Phindile, and their daughters. God bless all 100 families who have a new house of their own. God bless all of the people who made the 2002 Jimmy Carter Work Project possible.

Conversation Starter

Discuss the housing market in your community. Do you think housing is affordable?

Reading Matters

1. What motivates a HFHI volunteer to get involved? How does HFHI and the JCWP attract volunteers from around the world?
2. How does Jimmy Carter's involvement with HFHI support the mission of the project? Is his role different from that of the other volunteers?
3. How does HFHI change the communities they serve? What role do volunteers have in the community? What is the role of HFHI and their volunteers when the project is complete?
4. What strategies make HFHI successful? How is this strategy replicated throughout the world? Why is the JCWP held at different locations each year?

Writing Matters

1. Visit the Habitat for Humanity web site (http://www.habitat.org) and learn about a specific project. Write a summary of your research and share it with your class.

2. Research your local community to find out about options for afford-able housing. What resources are available? What type of information were you able to collect? Did your findings surprise you? Write about your experience.
3. Volunteer to support a local branch of Habitat for Humanity or another nonprofit agency supporting issues of affordable housing or neighbor-hood beautification. Write about your experience.

Relevant Web Sites

Habitat for Humanity International <http://www.habitat.org>

The official web site for Habitat for Humanity International provides high-lights and stories from projects around the world, profiles of volunteers, information about how to get involved, and links to local affiliates.

The Carter Center <http://www.cartercenter.org>

The official web site for The Carter Center, a nonprofit public policy center founded by Jimmy and Roslynn Carter to fight disease, hunger, and poverty.

Writing About a Sense of Place

1. Draw a map of your community. Distinguish between natural and urban areas, new and old development, private and public spaces. Write a short introduction to your map and then present it to your classmates.
2. Write an essay that explores what you have learned about resolving conflict and supporting effective strategies for change within a community. In presenting your discussion, refer to specific examples in this chapter.

3. Research a community project that relates to one of the chapter's themes. Give an overview of the project and its impact on the community. Compare and contrast the strategies for change used by each community organization.

4. Write an essay that reflects on the different ways that memory affects an individual's sense of place.

5. Reflect on what you have learned about shared community experiences. Write an analysis of a community event that shaped your sense of place.

6. Develop an outreach plan for an existing community organization's web site using links, e-mail, and news groups to encourage participation.

7. Write a personal account of your participation with a local community organization that could be used to promote the program and demonstrate community support. Or, contribute to the community organization by writing a newsletter article, a brochure, or press release.

8. Write a short story or a poem that focuses on one of the themes explored in this chapter.

9. Describe the importance of place in one of your favorite films. What are the places being depicted? How do these sites affect your reaction to the film?

10. Write an essay for your class that introduces your hometown. Use visual information including maps, pictures, historical documents, or objects that have symbolic meaning for you. Try to help your class to see, understand, and appreciate your hometown as you do.

6 Family

Each weekend the YA/YA artists' UpHill Gallery and Studios opens its doors for drop-in family programming. Children and their guardians are invited to work with artists using a wide variety of media.

The American family is in a state of crisis. Psychologists, religious leaders, politicians, corporate executives, technology moguls, actors, poets, and musicians, all in their own way address this crisis. We see the effects of the breakdown of the American family in our daily lives. We know children whose parents are divorced, children who come to empty homes after school, teens who have children, single mothers who work two jobs to support their family. Our purpose in writing this chapter has been to ask you to think about how the institution of the American family can adapt to the changing realities of modern-day life and continue to function as a primary community. Can you imagine yourself as a parent? If you do have children, how do their lives reflect changing American values?

Our first understanding of how community groups function develops within the circle of our family. Family traditions and relationships help to shape an individual's character and his or her sense of community rituals and values. The first section of this chapter, "Memories of the Traditional Family," presents a variety of first-person narratives that reflect on the role and impact of family traditions. We open the chapter with "No Name Woman," from Maxine Hong Kingston's classic memoir, *The Woman Warrior*. The narrator in the selection explores the intense impact that her outcast aunt's suicide has had on three generations of her family. Hers is a tale of protest against a male-dominated community that denigrates women to a second-class status within the family and the community. This story will spark insights and reflection about how much has changed—What is the balance of power between men and women within the American family today? The next selection from Regina Louise's first memoir, *Somebody's Someone*, speaks to us in a direct personal voice about the life of a child who is shuffled through a system of group and foster homes after being abandoned by her mother. The selection we have chosen, "The Sins of the Mother," shares the author's struggles. With her courage and fortitude, Louise becomes a successful businesswomen, but more importantly she has written the story of her life; speaking in her own voice from her own experience, she makes the life of a black foster child more poignant and painful than we would like to think is a reality in our country. On a more positive note, this section of the chapter ends with a spiritual awakening: In "The Way to Rainy Mountain," N. Scott Momaday travels to his grandmother's burial site, where he reconnects with the legacy of his tribal community. We realize how he has been deeply shaped by the ways traditions and beliefs of his Native American family.

The struggles of working mothers, the impact of the divorce culture, and the value of children in American culture are topics explored in the section "Complexities of Family Life Today." We begin with Tillie Olsen's short story, "I Stand Here Ironing," a personal account of a working mother's concerns about the impact of having had to work and raise her daughter at the same time. In "Somebody's Baby," fiction and essay writer Barbara Kingsolver, writing about a year she spent in southern Spain, draws our attention to the rejecting way that children are often treated in American culture. Her "only genuine culture shock [in Spain] reverberated from this earthquake of a fact: People there like children." The next selection explores the ways that the divorce culture has irrevocably changed the American family. In an excerpt from her new book, Judith Wallerstein, a leading authority on divorce, provides us with many reasons and strong evidence to make us understand the consequences of the divorce culture. She also offers us advice on how to reshape the family community, in hopes of it once again being a viable institution.

While the complexities of modern family life may often seem overwhelming, many people and organizations work toward solutions to specific community problems. The chapter section "Community Projects that Support Children and Families" highlights four successful community projects that have helped children, parents, and families. In "A Family Legacy," Marian Wright Edelman, the first Black woman to pass the bar in Mississippi and the founder of the Children's Defense Fund to help underprivileged children, offers a positive perspective on the enduring power of love and family tradition. Her family valued education, the role of the family as a part of the extended church community, and the importance of service. In "How To YA/YA in Your Neighborhood," our next selection, community activist Claudia Barker describes a nonprofit organization based in New Orleans, which began as a community center that taught art to high school students after school. This community of young artists became a type of extended family, touring the world and gaining international recognition. Our final selection, Cleve Jones's "The Vision Quilt," details the vision for the AIDS quilt, which began within the Castro District community in San Francisco as a way of creating a sense of remembrance for people who died of AIDS and came eventually to include remembrances by families, lovers, others, and survivors all over the country. The project's success has been stunning; the AIDS quilt has grown over the years and has been on tour all over the world. We have included Cleve's vision and three of the accompanying letters to remind us of how the quilt project has helped survivors to work through their grief and build a support community.

In many different ways, through laws and community organizations, through medical advice support networks, through changing expectations in family communities, the definition and institution of marriage and family are clearly undergoing the process of revision and revitalization. All the selections in this chapter speak of the power of tradition while acknowledging the inevitability of change. Think for a moment about how your generation has been shaped by family traditions and how you have started to reinterpret these traditions. Traditional and nontraditional families embody significant attributes of community. Children growing up in the new millennium will create different types of families. Hopefully they will take what was best about their childhoods and help to reenvision the family community as a viable top priority. Our children and a faith in human goodness are our greatest resources.

Memories of the Traditional Family

Maxine Hong Kingston (b. 1940)

No Name Woman

Maxine Hong Kingston was born and raised in Stockton, California. She earned a B.A. in English from the University of California at Berkeley (1962). She married and taught high school in the Bay Area until l967, when she moved to Hawaii and taught English as a Second Language for 10 years at a private high school on Oahu. She currently lives with her husband in Oakland, California, and teaches in the English Department at the University of California at Berkeley.

Highly acclaimed for her "postmodernist memoirs" in The Woman Warrior: Memories of a Childhood Among Ghosts *(1976),* China Men *(1980), and* The Fifth Book of Peace *(2003), Maxine Hong Kingston is one of the most influential Asian-American authors of the twentieth century. Her essay collections include* Hawaii One Summer: 1978 *(1980) and* Through the Black Curtain *(1987). Her first novel was* Tripmaster Monkey: His Fake Book *(1989). The following selection from* The Woman Warrior *is based on one of the stories Maxine Hong Kingston heard from her mother when she reached adolescence. Deeply affected by her mother's stories about her aunt's suicide in a traditional Chinese village, Kingston reflects on how customs within a traditional community can be used to justify brutality and sexism.*

"You must not tell anyone," my mother said, "what I am about to tell you. In China your father had a sister who killed herself. She jumped into the family well. We say that your father has all brothers because it is as if she had never been born.

"In 1924 just a few days after our village celebrated seventeen hurry-up weddings—to make sure that every young man who went 'out on the road' would responsibly come home—your father and his brothers and your grandfather and his brothers and your aunt's new husband sailed for America, the Gold Mountain. It was you grandfather's last trip. Those lucky enough to get contracts waved good-bye from the decks. They fed and guarded the stowaways and helped them off in Cuba, New York, Bali, Hawaii. 'We'll meet in California next year,' they said. All of them sent money home.

"I remember looking at your aunt one day when she and I were dressing; I had not noticed before that she had such a protruding melon of a stomach. But I did not think, 'She's pregnant,' until she began to look like other pregnant women, her shirt pulling and the white tops of her black pants showing. She could not have been pregnant, you see, because her husband had been gone for years. No one said anything. We did not discuss it. In early summer she was ready to have the child, long after the time when it could have been possible.

"The village had also been counting. On the night the baby was to be born the villagers raided our house. Some were crying. Like a great saw, teeth strung with lights, files of people walked zigzag across our land, tearing the rice. Their lanterns doubled in the disturbed black water, which drained away through the broken bunds. As the villagers closed in, we could see that some of them, probably men and women we knew well, wore white masks. The people with long hair hung it over their faces. Women with short hair made it stand up on end. Some had tied white bands around their foreheads, arms, and legs.

5   "At first they threw mud and rocks at the house. Then they threw eggs and began slaughtering our stock. We could hear the animals scream their deaths—the roosters, the pigs, a last great roar from the ox. Familiar wild heads flared in our night windows; the villagers encircled us. Some of the faces stopped to peer at us, their eyes rushing like searchlights. The hands flattened against the panes, framed heads, and left red prints.

"The villagers broke in the front and the back doors at the same time, even though we had not locked the doors against them. Their knives dripped with the blood of our animals. They smeared blood on the doors and walls. One woman swung a chicken, whose throat she had slit, splattering blood in red arcs about her. We stood together in the middle of our house, in the family hall with the pictures and tables of the ancestors around us, and looked straight ahead.

"At that time the house had only two wings. When the men came back, we would build two more to enclose our courtyard and a third one to begin a second courtyard. The villagers pushed through both wings, even your grandparents' rooms, to find your aunt's, which was also mine until the men returned. From this room a new wing for one of the young families would grow. They ripped up her clothes and shoes and broke her combs, grinding them underfoot. They tore her work from the loom. They scattered the cooking fire and rolled the new weaving in it. We could hear them in the kitchen breaking our bowls and banging the pots. They overturned the great waist-high earthenware jugs; duck eggs, pickled fruits, vegetables burst out and mixed in acrid torrents. The old woman from the next field swept a broom through the air and loosed the spirits-of-the-broom over our heads. 'Pig.' 'Ghost.' 'Pig,' they sobbed and scolded while they ruined our house.

"When they left, they took sugar and oranges to bless themselves. They cut pieces from the dead animals. Some of them took bowls that were not broken and clothes that were not torn. Afterward we swept up the rice and sewed it back into sacks. But the smells from the spilled preserves lasted. Your aunt gave birth in the pigsty that night. The next morning when I went up for the water, I found her and the baby plugging up the family well.

"Don't let your father know that I told you. He denies her. Now that you have started to menstruate, what happened to her could happen to you.

Don't humiliate us. You wouldn't like to be forgotten as if you had never been born. The villagers are watchful."

10   Whenever she had to warn us about life, my mother told stories that ran like this one, a story to grow up on. She tested our strength to establish realities. Those in the emigrant generations who could not reassert brute survival died young and far from home. Those of us in the first American generations have had to figure out how the invisible world the emigrants built around our childhoods fit in solid America.

The emigrants confused the gods by diverting their curses, misleading them with crooked streets and false names. They must try to confuse their offspring as well, who, I suppose, threaten them in similar ways—always trying to get things straight, always trying to name the unspeakable. The Chinese I know hide their names; sojourners take new names when their lives change and guard their real names with silence.

Chinese-Americans, when you try to understand what things in you are Chinese, how do you separate what is peculiar to childhood, to poverty, insanities, one family, your mother who marked your growing with stories, from what is Chinese? What is Chinese tradition and what is the movies?

If I want to learn what clothes my aunt wore, whether flashy or ordinary, I would have to begin, "Remember Father's drowned-in-the-well sister?" I cannot ask that. My mother has told me once and for all the useful parts. She will add nothing unless powered by Necessity, a riverbank that guides her life. She plants vegetable gardens rather than lawns; she carries the odd-shaped tomatoes home from the fields and eats food left for the gods.

Whenever we did frivolous things, we used up energy; we flew high kites. We children came up off the ground over the melting cones our parents brought home from work and the American movie on New Year's Day—*Oh, You Beautiful Doll* with Betty Grable one year, and *She Wore a Yellow Ribbon* with John Wayne another year. After the one carnival ride each, we paid in guilt; our tired father counted his change on the dark walk home.

15   Adultery is extravagance. Could people who hatch their own chicks and eat the embryos and the heads for delicacies and boil the feet in vinegar for party food, leaving only the gravel, eating even the gizzard lining—could such people engender a prodigal aunt? To be a woman, to have a daughter in starvation time was a waste enough. My aunt could not have been the lone romantic who gave up everything for sex. Women in the old China did not choose. Some man had commanded her to lie with him and be his secret evil. I wonder whether he masked himself when he joined the raid on her family.

Perhaps she encountered him in the fields or on the mountain where the daughters-in-law collected fuel. Or perhaps he first noticed her in the marketplace. He was not a stranger because the village housed no strangers. She had to have dealings with him other than sex. Perhaps he worked an adjoining field, or he sold her the cloth for the dress she sewed and wore.

His demand must have surprised, then terrified her. She obeyed him; she always did as she was told.

When the family found a young man in the next village to be her husband, she stood tractably beside the best rooster, his proxy, and promised before they met that she would be his forever. She was lucky that he was her age and she would be the first wife, an advantage secure now. The night she first saw him, he had sex with her. Then he left for America. She had almost forgotten what he looked like. When she tried to envision him, she only saw the black and white face in the group photograph the men had taken before leaving.

The other man was not, after all, much different from her husband. They both gave orders: she followed. "If you tell your family, I'll beat you. I'll kill you. Be here again next week." No one talked sex, ever. And she might have separated the rapes from the rest of living if only she did not have to buy her oil from him or gather wood in the same forest. I want her fear to have lasted just as long as rape lasted so that the fear could have been contained. No drawn-out fear. But women at sex hazarded birth and hence lifetimes. The fear did not stop but permeated everywhere. She told the man, "I think I'm pregnant." He organized the raid against her.

On nights when my mother and father talked about their life back home, sometimes they mentioned an "outcast table" whose business they still seemed to be settling, their voices tight. In a commensal tradition, where food is precious, the powerful older people made wrongdoers eat alone. Instead of letting them start separate new lives like the Japanese, who could become samurais and geishas, the Chinese family, faces averted but eyes glowering sideways, hung on to the offenders and fed them leftovers. My aunt must have lived in the same house as my parents and eaten at an outcast table. My mother spoke about the raid as if she had seen it, when she and my aunt, a daughter-in-law to a different household, should not have been living together at all. Daughters-in-law lived with their husbands' parents, not their own; a synonym for marriage in Chinese is "taking a daughter-in-law." Her husband's parents could have sold her, mortgaged her, stoned her. But they had sent her back to her own mother and father, a mysterious act of hinting at disgraces not told me. Perhaps they had thrown her out to deflect the avengers.

20   She was the only daughter; her four brothers went with her father, husband, and uncles "out on the road" and for some years became western men. When the goods were divided among the family, three of the brothers took land, and the youngest, my father, chose an education. After my grandparents gave their daughter away to her husband's family, they had dispensed all the adventure and all the property. They expected her alone to keep the traditional ways, which her brothers, now among the barbarians, could fumble without detection. The heavy, deep-rooted women were to maintain the past against the flood, safe for returning. But the rare urge west had fixed upon our family, and so my aunt crossed boundaries not delineated in space.

The work of preservation demands that the feelings playing about in one's guts not be turned into action. Just watch their passing like cherry blossoms. But perhaps my aunt, my forerunner, caught in a slow life, let dreams grow and fade and after some months or years went toward what persisted. Fear at the enormities of the forbidden kept her desires delicate, wire and bone. She looked at a man because she liked the way the hair was tucked behind his ears, or she liked the question-mark line of a long torso curving at the shoulder and straight at the hip. For warm eyes or a soft voice or a slow walk—that's all—a few hairs, a line, a brightness, a sound, a pace, she gave up family. She offered us up for a charm that vanished with tiredness, a pigtail that didn't toss when the wind died. Why, the wrong lighting could erase the dearest thing about him.

It could very well have been, however, that my aunt did not take subtle enjoyment of her friend, but, a wild woman, kept rollicking company. Imagining her free with sex doesn't fit, though. I don't know any women like that, or men either. Unless I see her life branching into mine, she gives me no ancestral help.

To sustain her being in love, she often worked at herself in the mirror, guessing at the colors and shapes that would interest him, changing them frequently in order to hit on the right combination. She wanted him to look back.

On a farm near the sea, a woman who tended her appearance reaped a reputation for eccentricity. All the married women blunt-cut their hair in flaps about their ears or pulled it back in tight buns. No nonsense. Neither style blew easily into heart-catching tangles. And at their weddings they displayed themselves in their long hair for the last time. "It brushed the backs of my knees," my mother tells me. "It was braided, and even so, it brushed the backs of my knees."

25   At the mirror my aunt combed individuality into her bob. A bun could have been contrived to escape into black streamers blowing in the wind or in quiet wisps about her face, but only the older women in our picture album wear buns. She brushed her hair back from her forehead, tucking the flaps behind her ears. She looped a piece of thread, knotted into a circle between her index fingers and thumbs, and ran the double strand across her forehead. When she closed her fingers as if she were making a pair of shadow geese bite, the string twisted together catching the little hairs. Then she pulled the thread away from her skin, ripping the hairs out neatly, her eyes watering from the needles of pain. Opening her fingers, she cleaned the thread, then rolled it along her hairline and the tops of her eyebrows. My mother did the same to me and my sisters and herself. I used to believe that the expression "caught by the short hairs" meant a captive held with a depilatory string. It especially hurt at the temples, but my mother said we were lucky we didn't have to have our feet bound when we were seven. Sisters used to sit on their beds and cry together, she said, as their mothers or their slave removed the bandages for a few minutes each night and let the blood gush back into their veins. I hope that the man

my aunt loved appreciated a smooth brow, that he wasn't just a tits-and-ass man.

Once my aunt found a freckle on her chin, at a spot that the almanac said predestined her for unhappiness. She dug it out with a hot needle and washed the wound with peroxide.

More attention to her looks than these pullings of hairs and pickings at spots would have caused gossip among the villagers. They owned work clothes and good clothes, and they wore good clothes for feasting the new seasons. But since a woman combing her hair hexes beginnings, my aunt rarely found an occasion to look her best. Women looked like the great sea snails—the corded wood, babies, and laundry they carried were the whorls on their backs. The Chinese did not admire a bent back; goddesses and warriors stood straight. Still there must have been a marvelous freeing of beauty when a worker laid down her burden and stretched and arched.

Such commonplace loveliness, however, was not enough for my aunt. She dreamed of a lover for the fifteen days of New Year's, the time for families to exchanged visits, money, and food. She plied her secret comb. And sure enough she cursed the year, the family, the village, and herself.

Even as her hair lured her imminent lover, many other men looked at her. Uncles, cousins, nephews, brothers would have looked, too, had they been home between journeys. Perhaps they had already been restraining their curiosity, and they left, fearful that their glances, like a field of nesting birds, might be startled and caught. Poverty hurt, and that was their first reason for leaving. But another, final reason for leaving the crowded house was the never-said.

30   She may have been unusually beloved, the precious only daughter, spoiled and mirror-gazing because of the affection the family lavished on her. When her husband left, they welcomed the chance to take her back from the in-laws; she could live like the little daughter for just a while longer. There are stories that my grandfather was different from other people, "crazy ever since the little Jap bayoneted him in the head." He used to put his naked penis on the dinner table, laughing. And one day he brought home a baby girl, wrapped up inside his brown western-style greatcoat. He had traded one of his sons, probably my father, the youngest, for her. My grandmother made him trade back. When he finally got a daughter of his own, he doted on her. They must have all loved her, except perhaps my father, the only brother who never went back to China, having once been traded for a girl.

Brothers and sisters, newly men and women, had to efface their sexual color and present plain miens. Disturbing hair and eyes, a smile like no other, threatened the ideal of five generations living under one roof. To focus blurs, people shouted face to face and yelled from room to room. The immigrants I know have loud voices, unmodulated to American tones even after years away from the village where they called their friendships out across the fields. I have not been able to stop my mother's screams in public libraries or over telephones. Walking erect (knees straight, toes pointed forward, not pigeon-toed, which is Chinese-feminine) and speaking in an inaudible voice, I have tried to turn myself American-feminine. Chinese communication was loud, public. Only sick people had to whisper. But at the dinner table, where the family members came nearest one another, no one could talk, not the outcasts nor any eaters. Every word that falls from the mouth is a coin lost. Silently they gave and accepted food with both hands. A preoccupied child who took his bowl with one hand got a sideways glare. A complete moment of total attention is due everyone alike. Children and lovers have no singularity here, but my aunt used a secret voice, a separate attentiveness.

She kept the man's name to herself throughout her labor and dying; she did not accuse him that he be punished with her. To save her inseminator's name she gave silent birth.

He may have been somebody in her own household, but intercourse with a man outside the family would have been no less abhorrent. All the village were kinsmen, and the titles shouted in loud country voices never let kinship be forgotten. Any man within visiting distance would have been neutralized as a lover—"brother," "younger brother," "older brother"—115 relationship titles. Parents researched birth charts probably not so much to assure good fortune as to circumvent incest in a population that has but one hundred surnames. Everybody has eight million relatives. How useless then sexual mannerisms, how dangerous.

As if it came from an atavism deeper than fear, I used to add "brother" silently to boys' names. It hexed the boys, who would or would not ask me to dance, and made them less scary and as familiar and deserving of benevolence as girls.

35   But, of course, I hexed myself also—no dates. I should have stood up, both arms waving, and shouted out across libraries, "Hey, you! Love me back." I had no idea, though, how to make attraction selective, how to control its direction and magnitude. If I made myself American-pretty so that the five or six Chinese boys in the class fell in love with me, everyone else—the Caucasian, Negro, and Japanese boys—would too. Sisterliness, dignified and honorable, made much more sense.

Attraction eludes control so stubbornly that whole societies designed to organize relationships among people cannot keep order, not even when they bind people to one another from childhood and raise them together. Among the very poor and the wealthy, brothers married their adopted sisters, like doves. Our family allowed some romance, paying adult brides' prices and providing dowries so that their sons and daughters could marry strangers. Marriage promises to turn strangers into friendly relatives—a nation of siblings.

In the village structure, spirits shimmered among the live creatures, balanced and held in equilibrium by time and land. But one human being flaring up into violence could open up a black hole, a maelstrom that pulled in the sky. The frightened villagers, who depended on one another to maintain the real, went to my aunt to show her a personal, physical representation of the break she made in the "roundness." Misallying couples snapped off the future, which was to be embodied in true offspring. The villagers punished her for acting as if she could have a private life, secret and apart from them.

If my aunt had betrayed the family at a time of large grain yields and peace, when many boys were born, and wings were being built on many houses, perhaps she might have escaped such severe punishment. But the men—hungry, greedy, tired of planting in dry soil, cuckolded—had been forced to leave the village in order to send food-money home. There were ghost plagues, bandit plagues, wars with the Japanese, floods. My Chinese brother and sister had died of an unknown sickness. Adultery, perhaps only a mistake during good times, became a crime when the village needed food.

The round moon cakes and round doorways, the round tables of graduated size that fit one roundness inside another, round windows and rice bowls—these talismans had lost their power to warn this family of the law: a family must be whole, faithfully keeping the descent line by having sons to feed the old and the dead who in turn look after the family. The villagers came to show my aunt and lover-in-hiding a broken house. The villagers were speeding up the circling of events because she was too shortsighted to see that her infidelity had already harmed the village, that waves of consequences would return unpredictably, sometimes in disguise, as now, to hurt her. This roundess had to be made coin-sized so that she would see its circumference: punish her at the birth of her baby. Awaken her to the inexorable. People who refused fatalism because they could invent small resources insisted on culpability. Deny accidents and wrest fault from the stars.

40   After the villagers left, their lanterns now scattering in various directions toward home, the family broke their silence and cursed her. "Aiaa, we're going to die. Death is coming. Death is coming. Look what you've done. You've killed us. Ghost! Dead Ghost! Ghost! You've never been born." She ran out into the fields, far enough from the house so that she could no longer hear their voices, and pressed herself against the earth, her own land no more. When she felt the birth coming, she thought that she had been hurt. Her body seized together. "They've hurt me too much," she thought. "This is gall, and it will kill me." With forehead and knees against the earth, her body convulsed and then relaxed. She turned on her back, lay on the ground. The black well of sky and stars went out and out forever; her body and her complexity seemed to disappear. She was one of the stars, a bright dot in blackness, without home, without a companion, in eternal cold and silence. An agoraphobia rose in her, speeding higher and higher, bigger and bigger; she would not be able to contain it; there would be no end to fear.

Flayed, unprotected against space, she felt pain return, focusing her body. This pain chilled her—a cold, steady kind of surface pain. Inside, spasmodically, the other pain, the pain of the child, heated her. For hours she lay on the ground, alternately body and space. Sometimes a vision of normal comfort obliterated reality: she saw the family in the evening gambling at the dinner table, the young people massaging their elders' backs. She saw them congratulating one another, high joy on the mornings the rice shoots came up. When these pictures burst, the stars drew yet further apart. Black space opened.

She got to her feet to fight better and remembered that old-fashioned women gave birth in their pigsties to fool the jealous, pain-dealing gods, who do not snatch piglets. Before the next spasms could stop her, she ran to the pigsty, each step a rushing out into emptiness. She climbed over the fence and knelt in the dirt. It was good to have a fence enclosing her, a tribal person alone.

Laboring, this woman who had carried her child as a foreign growth that sickened her every day, expelled it at last. She reached down to touch the hot, wet, moving mass, surely smaller than anything human, and could feel that it was human after all—fingers, toes, nails, nose. She pulled it up on to her belly, and it lay curled there, butt in the air, feet precisely tucked one under the other. She opened her loose shirt and buttoned the child inside. After resting, it squirmed and thrashed and she pushed it up to her breast. It turned its head this way and that until it found her nipple. There, it made little snuffling noises. She clenched her teeth at its preciousness, lovely as a young calf, a piglet, a little dog.

She may have gone to the pigsty as a last act of responsibility: she would protect this child as she had protected its father. It would look after her soul, leaving supplies on her grave. But how would this tiny child without family find her grave when there would be no marker for her anywhere, neither in the earth nor the family hall? No one would give her a family hall name. She had taken the child with her into the wastes. At its birth the two of them had felt the same raw pain of separation, a wound that only the family pressing tight could close. A child with no descent line would not soften her life but only trail after her, ghostlike, begging her to give it purpose. At dawn the villagers on their way to the fields would stand around the fence and look.

45   Full of milk, the little ghost slept. When it awoke, she hardened her breasts against the milk that crying loosens. Toward morning she picked up the baby and walked to the well.

Carrying the baby to the well shows loving. Otherwise abandon it. Turn its face into the mud. Mothers who love their children take them along. It was probably a girl; there is some hope of forgiveness for boys.

"Don't tell anyone you had an aunt. Your father does not want to hear her name. She has never been born." I have believed that sex was unspeakable and words so strong and fathers so frail that "aunt" would do my father mysterious harm. I have thought that my family, having settled among immigrants who had also been their neighbors in the ancestral land, needed to clean their name, and a wrong word would incite the kinspeople even here. But there is more to this silence: they want me to participate in her punishment. And I have.

In the twenty years since I heard this story I have not asked for details nor said my aunt's name; I do not know it. People who comfort the dead can also chase after them to hurt them further—a reverse ancestor worship. The real punishment was not the raid swiftly inflicted by the villagers, but the family's deliberately forgetting her. Her betrayal so maddened them, they saw to it that she would suffer forever, even after death. Always hungry, always needing, she would have to beg food from other ghosts, snatch and steal it from those whose living descendants give them gifts. She would have to fight the ghosts massed at crossroads for the buns a few thoughtful citizens leave to decoy her away from village and home so that the ancestral spirits could feast unharassed. At peace, they could act like gods, not ghosts, their descent lines providing them with paper suits and dresses, spirit money, paper houses, paper automobiles, chicken, meat, and rice into eternity—essences delivered up in smoke and flames, steam and incense rising from each rice bowl. In an attempt to make the Chinese care for people outside the family, Chairman Mao encourages us now to give our paper replicas to the spirits of outstanding soldiers and workers, no matter whose ancestors they may be. My aunt remains forever hungry. Goods are not distributed evenly among the dead.

My aunt haunts me—her ghost drawn to me because now, after fifty years of neglect, I alone devote pages of paper to her, though not origamied into house and clothes. I do not think she always means me well. I am telling on her, and she was a spite suicide, drowning herself in the drinking water. The Chinese are always very frightened of the drowned one, whose weeping ghost, wet hair hanging and skin bloated, waits silently by the water to pull down a substitute.

Conversation Starter

Discuss a conflict in your family between a member of the older generation and the younger generation. Has the conflict been resolved? How?

Reading Matters

1. Why does the narrator tell her aunt's story? What role does her aunt's ghost play in the narrative?
2. Why does the narrator suggest several reasons for the aunt's pregnancy and suicide? Which of the explanations makes most sense to you? Compare and contrast your reaction to the No Name Woman's suicide and the narrator's response to it.
3. What did you learn about the values that supported family life in Chinese villages? For example, why did they value roundness? Why were women considered less valuable than men? Did reading about this family that may have been very different from your own help you to think about your own family from a new perspective?
4. Maxine Hong Kingston is extremely descriptive in this essay, as seen in the raid against the family whose daughter is pregnant. What impact does Kingston's very concrete and richly detailed style have on your response to the memoir? Discuss and analyze several images that you find powerful.

WRITING MATTERS

1. Write an essay that presents your interpretation of the story's meaning. Use details from the story as support for your interpretation. Does this story have meaning for you as a member of a family community and as an individual? Explain.
2. Write about gender roles that your grandparents or parents accepted but that you have rebelled against. Why did you reject their values? What role has your family community played in shaping your values? How has this generation gap influenced the functioning of your family?
3. Interview a family member or members to learn more about a story or myth that shaped your family's values and sense of identity. You might even want to do some research into that time period to help put your relative's story into historical perspective. Write the story for your classmates. Include what you have learned and why you think the story is relevant today.

RELEVANT WEB SITES

MAXINE HONG KINGSTON
<http://voices.cla.umn.edu/authors/MaxineHongKingston.html>

At this informative web site on Maxine Hong Kingston you will find extensive biographical writings on the Chinese-American author. Links to other web sites are also included.

THE ASIAN AMERICAN EXPERIENCE
<http://www.lib.uci.edu/rrsc/asiamer.html>

Created by the University of California at Irvine, this web site provides service links to various URLs devoted to understanding the Asian-American experience and Asian culture.

Regina Louise

Sins of the Mother

Now a successful businesswoman, Regina Louise's first memoir is Somebody's Someone *(2003). Her life story begins after being abandoned by her mother at birth and placed in foster care and institutions. With a lyrical and sometimes painful honesty, Regina Louise speaks to us telling of how she ran away and was then shuffled through a legal system of foster care that was hardly better than her first home. Her struggle to survive is poignant and shows the courage and resilience of a child determined to make a life for herself that is worth living. The excerpt that follows is the first chapter of her memoir.*

If somebody was to ask me how I came to be here, I swear b'fore God that I wouldn't know what to say to 'em. My whole life, I always wanted to be able to hear stories 'bout how I came into the world a wanted and special child. But the folks I lived with told stories 'bout my mama that wasn't meant for children's ears. Truth be told, seemed like nobody could even dig up a idea of how I got inside my mama, let alone what happened afterwards. Since no one was gonna tell me what I wanted to hear, I let myself believe that God had gave me a mouth and mind of my own to do what I seen fit, and I set about 'maginin' what my beginnings would've been like. That way, if folks was to ask me 'bout myself, I'd have an answer ready for 'em.

There she'd be, my mama, sittin' in her hospital room in a rocking chair, arms wide open to collect me—her head leaning to the side as she smiled and reached out. I'd be folded up in a soft pink blanket that smelled like flowers from God's backyard. After the nurse laid me in my mama's arms, she'd drag her breath in and know that everything was the way it was s'posed to be. Then for the fun of it, my mama would pull my li'l arm out to see whose hands I'd got. Maybe they'd be stubby and fat like Uncle So-and-so's? Or even lean and long like Great-grandmama Whatchamacallit. And somehow, knowing that she was thinking 'bout me, I'd reach out and bind my little fingers round her one and know we belonged to each another. We'd feel just like the white families do on them TV shows I watched. 'Cause finally, there I'd be, the one my mama'd been waiting her whole life for—a li'l girl to call her own.

In no time at all, she'd name me. Not just any ole ugly name, like Lula Mae or Donna Janine. No, it'd be one that had been hanging round her mind, waiting for me to come so she could finally give it a rightful resting place. After that, she'd unwrap me like a present and count all my fingers and toes to make certain they was all there. Then the nurse would call my daddy and he'd come, and drive us all home. We'd live happily ever after. And that would be the end.

If anybody was to ask me, that's what I'd tell 'em.

5   Truth was, from as far back as folks could recollect, me and my sister Doretha lived off and on in a foster home with a woman named Johnnie Jean Thornhill. We called her Big Mama since using her first name was out the question if you was under a hundred. And the times when we wasn't with Johnnie Jean, we'd be trying to get back together with our mama, Ruby, whose only talent—accordin' to the grown folks—was running round town drunk and cussing up a storm while trying to take up with other women's husbands. This meant that those few visits we did have always got cut short and Big Mama'd have to come and pick me and Sister up from wherever my mama would've left us. Nobody would tell me this stuff to my face—I had to play like I was 'sleep most of the times to hear the whispers of the grown folks.

When I did ask somebody 'bout the exact reason my mama left, and how it came down, everybody got deaf and dumb all a sudden like that girl Helen Keller that I read 'bout so I had to play possum real good and just sit and listen. I finally got the answer and then some. I learned that Doretha had come some five years b'fore I was even thought of. They say that

Ruby's not wantin' Sister started way b'fore Doretha was even born. It was all on account of Ruby being thirteen with nobody to claim what was laying in her belly, and since Big Mama could get money for taking in a pregnant girl, she convinced Ruby to stay on. And once Sister was born, Big Mama took to her like she was her very own. Apparently, five years later, nobody was stepping up to claim her second child either—that would've been me, Regina Louise—but I never got that far to hear how I came.

If you let Doretha tell it, she didn't even know I was her sister till she was almost nine and me four. But that was almost seven years ago, and I couldn't recall knowing her any different. And the part 'bout Ruby being her mama was something she never talked on. And if you did, it was sho' to put her in a bad way. I learned quick how to stay on Sister's good side. If the truth was to *really* be told, I never even knowed Ruby was gone till she called one day and said she was on her way to get me and my sister. But she never showed up.

The first time Ruby didn't come wasn't so bad. I just told myself that she hadn't been to the house in such a long time that she prob'ly forgot the address and was still driving round looking for it. But the many times after that, when she'd promise and still didn't come, there'd be a achin' in the middle of my bosom anytime I'd hear her name talked 'bout.

If anybody bothered to ask me, I'd tell 'em that the worst thing 'bout a mama leaving her children was that there ain't nobody to take up for 'em if trouble seemed to find 'em. And at Big Mama's, folks sho' needed taking up for.

10   Careful not to disturb the raggedy screen door that barely kept the man-eatin' mosquitas from tearin' our asses up, I leant my body into the frame and stared up at the sky. I could tell by the way the clouds moved that God was gonna start cryin' soon. I wondered who had pissed the angels off this time. The white lady from the Church of the Nazarene told me that whenever somebody committed a cruel act against one of God's children, their guardian angel would run and tell him, and he would cry for their pain—that's where raindrops come from. The white lady said that when the clouds changed quickly from fluffy white to smoky gray, well that's when the angelic messengers was runnin' 'cross the heavens. And when every breath you take holds the promise of his tears mixin' with the dirt, it was guaranteed to be a grand event. Thunder! Lightnin'! And sometimes if the crime was unforgivable, he might just throw golf balls made of ice at 'em. I know one thing: I felt sorry for whoever it was this time, but I sho' was glad it wasn't me.

That screen door was what sep'rated where we lived from the other folks who also lived on our land. See, there was two houses plus a silver Airstream trailer on our one property. Me and Sister lived with Big Mama and her husband Daddy Lent in one house. Since our house was so small, Sister and I shared a room. That made two rooms left: one for Big Mama and Daddy Lent, and the last one for none other than Lula Mae Bledsoe—the dangerous one.

The other house was for Big Mama's real daughter Aint Bobbie and her four children plus one. The plus one was a nobodies' child named Donna Janine—who Aint Bobbie took care of even though she wasn't hers. As for the trailer—it was used for the overflow of visitors that we would sometimes have.

I 'magined that living with Big Mama wouldn't have been so bad if it wasn't for ole Lula Mae—she was Big Mama's oldest ex-foster child, who'd moved out and back in. And on account of her Christian ways, Johnnie Jean couldn't turn nobody away who was in need. That means Lula Mae was part of the family again—right along with her two kids, Ella and Sherry, who didn't have no daddy to speak of. You should've seen how spiteful that ole Lula was to folks. Talking 'bout people behind they backs and in front of they faces for that matter. She acted like everybody in the whole world had jumped her from behind and left her for dead, and she'd be damned if they was gonna get away with it. Many times the things I overheard her saying 'bout me, my mama, and a lot of other folks wasn't fit for the ears of a junk-yard dog on its last leg. I even heard the grown folks say Lula was more ornery than a tick full of turpentine. Big Mama said that Lula Mae was meaner than she could ever be, and that was a good thing. That way Lula could do all of Big Mama's dirty work and not get in the way with Big Mama making it into heaven.

If you didn't do what Lula Mae asked faster than she could get the words out her mouth, she'd be on you like flies to a pile of shit. All I could say was that, even though her kids might've had they mama living right with 'em, she was no real mama to them—that's why right now, I had her baby strewn 'cross my side. She'd been with me since I finished up my chores this morning, If anybody'd bothered to ask, I would've much rather been rolling down the river with Huckleberry Finn and Jim the slave. But instead I had to be the child's keeper. Secretly I didn't mind being with the baby that much—I just sometimes rather be round Huckleberry.

15   Ever since my teacher Miss Schenkel loaned me *The Adventures of Huckleberry Finn*, I would 'scape to his world every chance I got. I read that book so many times I lost count somewhere round ten. Over and over Miss Schenkel would ask me to return the book back to her, and each time I'd tell her I'd misplaced it. I got to telling her that so much, she just told me to keep it. And I did. The truth was I always kept the book hiding in the underside of my pillowcase. I put it there very night after reading it, just in case Huckleberry and Jim would think to come and get me so we could ride down the Mississippi on they raft.

My mind returned to me as I pushed Huckleberry to the side. The sweat had slid down the back of my legs and polled its way to the bottom of my feet. We needed some shade. Holdin' baby Ella on my hipbone, I decided that we should 'go outside to the front yard and wait for the rain to break through. There was so much heat hanging in the air I thought I'd lose my mind. As I stepped outside onto the dirt in my flip-flops and tried to breathe in the muggy air, I felt like I was being smothered with a wet blanket. But I didn't let the stickiness bother me too much, on account that Big Mama'd said it's what makes the women of the South stay younger-lookin' longer.

Outside we sat down under a big oak tree, on a pallet somebody'd left out, so its branches could shade our skin from the heat of the too-hot sun. I placed the baby tween my legs and licked the dust from the pacifier that was pinned to her bib—then I put it in her mouth. Within no time Ella's dark Karo syrup–colored eyes was rollin' into the back other head—till she fell off to sleep.

Since right after she was born, Ella was like my own child. She was with me almost all the time. Ofttimes, seemed like I was the only one who wanted to get next to the baby other than her mamma. You see, Ella was born clubfooted, which mean that her feet was turned backwards from the ankle. She had to wear special shoes that was screwed on to a curved metal bar—they was meant to force her feet forward. As long as the brace was on, her little ankles looked fine, but when them shoes was off, you didn't know which direction her toes was heading. Since the braces made her twice as heavy, nobody wanted to tote her round when she wore 'em. Everybody else complained 'bout how they back hurt and how uncomfortable holding Ella was. Not me—no siree. I never whined. I'd pick that child up and sling her 'bout my side, and we'd be on our way.

Instead of being with her child, most of the time, Lula Mae could be found watching her soaps and yelling at me to take her baby and git.

20   I tried not to argue with Lula. Instead, every chance I got I aimed to get her to like me, but the harder I worked, it just seemed to make her more and more ill-tempered, which meant that she was either apt to cuss me out or find a reason to go upside my head with whatever she could get her hands on. Sometimes it was a rosebush switch with the stickers left on it, and other times it might be an extension cord pulled from a old iron or maybe even one of those orange Hot Wheel track pieces. But the worst of all of 'em was the Green Monster: the cut-off green water hose. And when the beatin's wasn't 'nough, she'd haul off and start cussing—saying things like, "Yo' mama ain't shit, and if you don't watch out you gonna be just like her. And all I know is I bet' not ketch you even looking at a boy with yo' fast-ass self."

I hated how Lula always had something to say 'bout me being "hot" or "fast." I never understood why I always had to hear that kind of mess, when I hardly had nothin' to do with boys, except for maybe Huck—and since he lived somewhere in Mississippi he didn't count. So other than him, I wasn't studying boys in no kinda way. Deep inside, I kind of figured out the reason I was called those names was 'cause of my mama and the reputation she'd made for herself by chasing after other married men and leaving us for other folks to look after. I finally came to figure that where I come from, it wasn't a matter of whether or not you yourself was guilty of what you was being accused of, but that what your mama did could hang over your head like heavy, dark clouds on a sunshiny day. I guessed when she left us my mama didn't figure that Lula Mae was gonna be the one to look out for me and Sister, on account that Big Mama was getting old and was more concerned with having a spot in heaven than takin' care of young girls.

Seeing how low-down my mama maybe was, I tried real hard to make it easier for Lula by helping her with Ella. Most times, unless I was doing my schoolwork, or reading, Lula didn't even have to ask me, 'cause I kinda figured that the less Lula had to take care of kids, the less right she'd have to be hateful. I started out by going to the baby if she cried out at night. The walls of the house were so thin you could almost hear everything throughout the entire property. I'd even change her diaper and warm a bottle for her if she was hungry. Since combing hair was one of my favorite things to do, I had no qualms 'bout caring for Ella's. It was easy to comb her hair 'cause Ella and her sister Sherry had what black folks called "real good" hair, not like mine. Theirs was soft to the touch, and each curl would wrap itself round your finger like a Slinky round your wrist. I would just section her jet-black tiny curls into plaits rubbed with Alberto VO5, so she wouldn't get tangles. I wanted baby Ella to be hardly any trouble a'tall to her mama. I guess I was hoping that somehow I could make what my mama did go away from Lula's mind. But it made no difference to Lula if I was good or bad. She must've just looked at me and seen Ruby, and I figured it was reason enough to keep her plain old ornery and plumped full of hate. There was very few things that scared me, but Lula Mae's nasty temper'mint and God was at the top of the list. The only thing that could top them was being beat with that Green Monster hose, and told not to cry when the whooping was done.

'Cross the yard from where me and the baby was sitting, I seen Donna Janine, the nobodies' child, standing on the curb talking to some high-yellow-skinned boy. I don't know what she thought she was doing, 'cause she knowed that talking to boys was off-limits on account we already had 'nough mouths to feed. From far away, the boy looked like he could've been kin to her, but I knowed better: she had no peoples in these parts. According to the whispers, Donna Janine was a product of a inna-racial thing, and her white mama couldn't take her home for fear that her own peoples would kill her for sleeping with a Negro and then bringing some half-breed baby round 'em. So, Donna Janine was left with the rest of us. For years, folks in Austin who didn't want they kids could drop 'em off at Johnnie Jean Thornhill's. And for a small price, she would take anybody in. I heard she even had insurance policies on everbody she took care of just in case they was to drop dead. Again, it was 'cause of her Christian background that she couldn't let folks go hungry or without. I know this to be true first-hand since she'd taken in my mama Ruby b'fore me. That's right, I was living in the same foster home my mama'd lived in, which maybe shoulda made it feel more like home to me, but since my mama wasn't with me, it didn't feel much like a home a'tall.

Big Mama's motto was, "If you play, you should pay," and that was that. A lot of folks must've agreed with her, 'cause over the years there sho' was a lot of kids that came and went.

25   Accordin' to the grown folks, there was only one thing that Donna Janine's mama forgot to tell Big Mama when she dropped her child off: the fact that she was crazier than a bedbug. Donna Janine had that look in her eyes like them folks who you ain't s'posed to point and stare at 'cause they different than you—the kind that came to school early on them yellow buses. The only difference was, she could talk and walk like most other folks round her, and she didn't have stringy spit runnin' from her mouth. I'd heard that the way she became mentally off was 'cause she got jumped in the girls' locker room at her school by a gang of heathen girls on account of her talkin' trash. I heard tell that they cracked her skull open with a combination lock and watched some of her brain slip out. My sister told me that some folks had found Donna Janine in the back of a Laundromat, curled up in one of them baskets and returned her to her mama, then they told her 'bout Big Mama. However she got that way, Donna Janine turned out to be somebody not to mess with. There was something way off in her.

Every now and again when she got overly upset or caught off guard, she would fall out wide on the floor and go wet on herself, while her eyes would turn so all you could see was the whites of 'em. A coupla times Big Mama'd yell at me to try and hold her tongue still with a Popsicle stick, to keep her from biting her ole tongue off. All you had to do is see that mess one time, and you knowed better than to bother Donna Janine.

But that girl hurt more'n herself. Not only could she tell bald-faced lies longer than Lake Travis, but she could steal you blind faster than you could smell a roadrunner's fart. All us kids learned quick not to say anything round her, 'cause if we did, she'd take what you'd say and turn it into the most outlandish concoction anybody'd ever heard. And since the grown folks was 'fraid she'd snap into one of them fits where somebody was gonna have to clean up her piss, they just believed whatever she told 'em.

I'd found out the hard way 'bout Donna Janine's thieving ways. One day, after spending the better part of my morning digging round the neighborhood for empty soda-water bottles, I decided to go and turn my findin's in at the 7-Eleven corner store. I wanted some Little Debbie nickel cakes more than anything, and it was for certain that I'd make 'nough money for two cakes, being that they only cost a nickel. I wanted one oatmeal cake with white icing and the other would be vanilla with pink filling. I could already see myself nibbling round the thin smooth edges of the cookie first, then making my way to the thick center. I'd also figured there may be change left for a coupla pieces of banana taffy candy. After getting my bottles all bagged up in two old pillowcases, I headed for the dirt trail that led from our house directly to the front of the store. I don't think I got four good steps down the driveway b'fore Donna Janine shows up out of nowhere and invited herself along. I guessed I didn't mind, seeing how she was willing to help me carry the Coke and Pepsi bottles, as long as she didn't think she was getting some of my money.

Once we was in the store, I got my thirty cents and bought the nickel cakes and the other candy I wanted and still had change left over. I was 'bout to go outside and wait for Donna Janine until her whistle made me look up and see her. She was motioning with her hand for me to come on over to where she was standing—the too-expensive candy aisle.

30   "Come here, Gina. Let me show you how to get any kind of candy you want wit'out having to spend your hard-found money," Donna Janine whispered to me, while at the same time shoving a big ole candy bar down the front of my panties.

"Ain't what we doing s'posed to be against the Bible?" I asked.

"Looka here girl, that's why God created thieves. He made it so that all the li'l folks who was meant to have they share could get it. God wouldn't want for some to have and others to not, so take this and walk out the door. I'll meet cha on the other side."

"Wait a minute now." I asked, real confused. "Won't God punish me for stealing?"

"Hell nah! My mama told me that as long as I was under twelve years old, then God didn't bother keeping track of all the things I did. But, she said that after twelve that was a different story, 'cause then you was a grown-up. And since you is still eleven, and I'm sixteen, you have some time left to do good by those who don't have."

35   Well by the way she put it, it did seem like I had heard something 'bout that "being twelve" thing b'fore. And since her mama had told her it was okay, I let her talk me into taking that Milky Way candy bar.

I pushed the king-size thing deeper b'tween my legs and headed straight for the front door. As my feet turned in and almost tripped me up every step I took, you could hear the paper crackle. But I kept going. I could feel the candy seesaw against my thighs as it poked out, making me look like a boy with wet swim trunks on. When the store clerk looked up at me, I knowed I was caught, and as I waited for him to move 'round to my side of the counter, I peed all over the candy bar. He made me pay for it by turning in my other goodies and my spare change.

"Don't ever let me see you face round here no more," he said. "If I do, I'll tell you peoples."

I promised he'd never see me again; then I ran out that store for home like a hunted-down jackrabbit. Along the way I seen a Almond Joy wrapper that wasn't there b'fore. I knowed that to be Donna Janine's favorite candy, but Donna Janine was nowhere to be found. By the time I reached our house, Big Mama was waiting on me with a rosebush switch in her hand. No questions was asked—she whooped me like there was no tomorrow, and told me that every time she thought about my stealing, she'd beat me again. I learned that day to leave that crazy Donna Janine alone.

Baby Ella must have been teething, 'cause she was rubbing her gums with the grass she kept pulling up. Seemed like the more I tried to take it from her, the more she fought to get it back. "Stop girl!" I whispered to her, hoping she could understand me. "Stop! 'Fore your mama think I feed you blades of grass. Heaven only knows what kinda trouble that would lead to." After a small tug of war, the baby gave in and started sucking on her pacifier again.

40   Sittin' under the tree, all I could think on was what fun me and Big Mama was gonna have that night at the town carnival, which was in the grocery store parking lot. The carnival came every year, and since I was a tiny girl, I loved nothing more than hoping it was my turn to go. Big Mama only took one child to the carnival every year. This time it was my turn. Last year she took my older sister, and Donna Janine had had her turn the year b'fore that.

Hallelujah! I had waited a long while for it to be my turn to go. I was gonna pretend that it was the county fair, like the one that Huckleberry and Tom would go to. Maybe the Widow Douglas would be there with all her pies and cakes and fixin's. And maybe they would have a corn-on-the-cob eating contest or bobbin' for apples. Maybe if I was lucky, I could enter and win a watermelon seed–spitting contest. Lord knowed I could already taste the shiny, red, hard, candy apple crunchin b'tween my teeth. While my mind was wanting to take me to the carnival, I sensed that Donna Janine wasn't so glad about me going. She had come up to me after Big Mama'd told us that I'd be goin' and called me a "titty sucker" and said that she hoped I'd choke b'fore I had a chance to go. I tried my best not to worry 'bout what that fool girl said.

So I was sitting on the pallet, trying to put everything right in my thinking, when Donna Janine called to me.

"Hey, Regina, bring the baby over so my friend can see her." One thing 'bout Ella, besides her feet problem, is she was the prettiest black baby this side of the Rio Grande. The grown folks said that if the Gerber baby food folks ever needed a new face, Ella was the one for the job, with her good curly hair and dimpled cheeks. Folks always wanted to grind they first finger into the dimpled part of her cheek and pinch her fat face. I cain't say that she liked that too much, but other'n that, she was a pretty smiley chile.

Seeing nothing wrong with a simple look, I strolled over to where her and the fella was standing. B'fore I could say a word, the high-yellow-skinned boy took Ella out of my hands and started throwing her up in the air, back and forth like she was some kind of rag doll or something. I could see that she liked that 'bout as much as having her cheeks pinched. So, after she started hollering bloody murder, I took her away from the boy and pulled her close to me like I'd seen Buffy do with Miss Beasley on "Family Affair."

45   "Sssh, it's all right, hush up now," I whispered in Ella's ear as I rocked her from side to side.

Just as I was 'bout to give Mr. Stupid a piece of my mind, the rain came pouring down. Oh how I loved it; I'd been waiting all day for God's tears to come and cool us off! I could hear that ole Lula yelling through the open window, asking what the matter was with Ella. Not wanting to miss God's tears, I just called out that she was fine. I was having such a good time, swaying the baby in my arms and playfully quieting her down, I never seen Donna Janine leave. Instead I was holding my mouth open, trying to get all the water in it I could. Within no time our hot bodies was cooler, and the baby was holding on to me real tight and she was finally quiet. We wasn't having fun five minutes b'fore Donna Janine showed up out of nowhere, saying, "Lula Mae wants you right now. You's gonna get it and get it good!" Then she snatched Ella out of my hands, hard and serious-like, scaring the daylights out the baby and making her cry again. I had no idea what that fool girl was taking 'bout, but I sure was going to find out.

As I turned and headed for the house I could see that the screen door to Big Mama's house was partly open, and that Lula was standing in the middle of it with her hands on her hips. My heartbeat got louder the closer I came to the porch. I didn't know what the trouble could be. I hadn't done nothing. But there was Lula, seeming like she was just waiting for me to get closer so she could pounce on me, like a rattlesnake waits on a rat. Making each step more important than the last, I minded the cracks—I wanted to be careful to protect my mama's back. Somehow I figured if I tried to help her, she might be able to rescue me too someday.

By the time I got to the porch I was moving at a snail's pace. I tried to distract myself by snapping my fingers to the beat of my heart, but the wetness on my hands made 'em slide oft each other, creating a dull thumping sound. When I looked up from my hands, there was Lula Mae, standing right in front of me, holding the door open with her big ugly foot. Her face was so twisted in knots she looked like one of them old dried-apple dolls. And her mouth was pinched up like the hind part of a polecat. Her hair was plaited so tight from the roots that it curled and flipped at the ends, making her look like a black Pippi Longstocking.

"Where my baby at?" her lips asked me, 'cause her teeth never moved.

50 "Ova there." I pointed a palsied finger, aiming towards the curb of the street, where Donna Janine stood holdin' Ella.

"Come a l'il closer; I cain't hear ya, heifah," Lula told me.

With all the strength I had, I lifted my foot to the next step. The sound of my heart was drowning out all else, even my eyesight somehow.

"Donna Janine said you was playing in the street wit' my baby."

"Nah! That's a lie," I screamed. "She's lying again. I cain't stand her." I shoulda knowed better than to keep tryin' to talk Lula Mae down. It only meant that she'd pitch a bigger fit and I'd be hit harder. But I couldn't stop screaming, "She's lying again!" I could feel it in my belly that I was in for a whoopin'. But this time it was gonna be different.

55 The last time Lula beat on me I made a pact with God. I told him that the next time she hit me for no reason it meant that she was wanting to kill

me, and that I would take it as his way of letting me know I should run away. I promised him, and unlike my mama, I'd planned on keeping my word.

"Didn't you hear me the first time I told you to come closer, heifah? Don't make me have to fell you twice and snatch your smart-mouth self up them steps."

I was scared. She was gonna get me. I could tell by the way her eyes moved tightly together, pullin' her forehead towards her nose. And when her nostrils grew wide 'nough to see her brains, I knowed I was in for it.

But this time, I wasn't gonna pay no mind to her. Something came over my mind, and I turned to run. I put all I had into that first pump, but b'fore my other foot hit the ground, Lula was on me like white on rice. Her fingers was buried deep in the rubber bands that held my ponytails together. As she drug me into the house, I swear 'fore God that I heard and felt my hair pull away from the scalp—it reminded me of what weeds being pulled out the ground sounded like. B'fore I could try and say or do anything else, she had yanked me into the bathroom and locked the door. I slammed my face against the commode as I tried to break loose. I was tossing and turning, trying hard to get free of her grip.

"Let me go!" I screamed. I didn't do nothing; Donna Janine is lying!" I was only making the situation worse, but I didn't care anymore. Lula's hold on me tightened.

60 "Shut yo' stupid ass up," she yelled at me. Out of nowhere, the Green Monster appeared, ready to do Lula's business.

Lula raised that rubber monster above her head, holding on to the little gold nozzle to make sure she had her grip. Just as I reached for the door, I could hear the water hose gaining speed as it whistled through the air and slammed onto my skin, like snake whip. *Whoosh, whoosh, thwack.* "You *little bitch, you ain't shit!" Thwack-whoosh-thwack.*

"*How you gonna stand in the middle of the street wit' my baby?*" *WhooshWhoosh Thwack.* "*You just like you whorish-ass mama.*" *Thwack thwack thwack.*

"*You ain't good for shit!*"

"Please stop. . . . I didn't do nothing to you, why you hittin' on me?" *Snap!* Please! Don't hit me no more." *Whoosh-thwack.*

65 "*I'm tired of fuckin' looking at you.*" *Thwack. . . .*

"*Even if yo' mama don't want yo' ass, that don't mean I don't want my baby.*"

I tried to grab hold of the water hose. . . . I felt Lula was gonna kill me, but I couldn't get away. I was grabbing for the hose to try to stop her.

"*Oh, you bad now, you gonna grab it from me.*" *SlamSlam!* She kept on hitting me. I knew for sure that was a sign from God. . . . I knew it was time for me to go. "*All's you good for is to ask too many goddamned questions and get yo ass whooped.*" *Slam!* "*I wish Big Mama had left you where she found you, right in that ho' bag motel where yo' triflin' mama left you!*"

She was lyin' 'bout my mama now. Her words hurt pretty bad, but not as bad as the Green Monster.

70   "Lula! Pleeeasse don't hit me no more!"

"Who you talking to? You talkin' to me?"

The look in her eyes told me she had no plans to stop hittin' on me. That garden hose kept flying through the air to bite my flesh. *Thwack!* I could see that hate running through her veins. Somewhere in the distance, I heard Big Mama coming. She was yelling at Lula to stop!

"Lula Mae Bledsoe, you let that chile go, you hear. That' *nough. . . . She cain't take no mo'."*

There was a loud knocking on the door. "Leave her be!" More banging, then Lula got another lick offa me.

75   *"You ain't shit now, and you ain't never gonna be shit either! And just like yo' mama, you gonna have kids by the time you thirteen! All you ever gonna know is how to lay up with some man and have babies you don't want!" Whack!*

Lula got her last lick, sealing in her wicked spell of evil sayin's and hateful doins. The door flew open as Big Mama pushed it in. She fell on top of Lula. I took the first chance I got, gathered myself up, jumped over their bodies, and ran. I ran like hell! Past Big Mama, through the screen door, and over them juniper bushes lining the front porch! All the while asking the question, "Now that I gotta live up to my word, God, where do I go?" I didn't care. I kept on runnin'.

I kept on running 'cause my life depended on it. My body was so numb I could'n' feel the gashes in my arms and legs where the Green Monster had left its bite, or the stinging in my body from the skin being gone—pieces of me was left stuck to the hose, but I didn't feel nothing. Lula wouldn't have to worry 'bout ever seeing me again. 'Cause as God was my witness I wasn't never going back there!

Over my back, I could hear Big Mama's voice. She was screaming at me, "Gina, Gina, where's you going—is you coming back in time for the carnival tonight?"

I didn't know where I was going. I hated the carnival and never wanted to go again. I couldn't stop to answer her. All I knowed was I had to keep moving. I looked over my shoulder and waved her on.

80   "When you coming on back?" I heard her asking me again. "When you coming back, Gina?"

There wasn't no words to answer her with. I kept telling myself to run. Just keep on running. It was all I could do.

CONVERSATION STARTER

Imagine what it would be like to grow up as a foster child. If you did grow up in foster care, describe one of your most vivid memories.

READING MATTERS

1.   Contrast what Regina actually knows about her real mother and father and how she imagines her birth. In what sense is her imagination a positive force, a force that helps her to survive? How does Regina's

sense of language engage you in her struggle to find a family that will really love her?

2. Why does Ruby, Regina's mother, leave her and her older sister? Why does Regina need her real mother at Big Mama's? Why and how is Regina blamed for her mother's unwillingness to accept responsibility for her?

3. Why is Lulu Mae the biggest troublemaker at Big Mama's? Why does Regina never think of Big Mama as her mother? How does reading about the adventures of Huckleberry Finn help Regina when she has to take care of Lulu Mae and Baby Ella? Describe the relationship between Regina and Lulu Mae, between Regina and Big Mama. What does Regina learn from enduring and surviving these relationships?

4. Explain the source and consequences of Donna Janine's behavior and relationship to Regina. Why is Gina beaten? How does she escape from Big Mama's house?

Writing Matters

1. Write a discussion and response to Gina's experience at Big Mama's. Select a particular incident or two to analyze and reflect upon. Compare your life as a child to Gina's. What would you have done if you were in her situation? Was the situation at Big Mama's typical or atypical of foster care? You may have to do some research to answer this question.

2. Do research on the Internet or in the library, and go out to observe and interview caretakers and children in foster care. Write a paper for your class and a local paper that explains the specific issues related to foster care in your community. While sharing what your have learned, also make suggestions for making the lives of children in foster care in your community better.

3. Do research on your state's funding and policies regarding foster care. Write an essay that reports on the situations that foster children are likely to face. Then write about what you think the government needs to do to improve the living conditions of children in foster care in your state.

Relevant Web Sites

Regina Louise <http://www.reginalouise.com>

Regina Louise's personal web site includes a short biography as well as links to other sites that feature information on foster care and child advocacy.

Casey Family Programs <http://www.caseyfamilyprograms.org>

The Casey Family Programs web site provides information about services for children and youth, with foster care as its core. Casey services include adoption, guardianship, kinship care (being cared for by extended family), and family reunification (reuniting children with birth families). Casey is also committed to helping youth in foster care make a successful transition to adulthood.

N. Scott Momaday (b. 1934)

The Way to Rainy Mountain

N. Scott Momaday came from different Native American tribes; his father was Kiowa and his mother was part Cherokee. Momaday grew up on his family's reservation in Oklahoma and later moved to New Mexico, where his parents worked among the Jemez Indians in the state's high canyon and mountain country. He earned a B.A. from the University of New Mexico (1958) and a Ph.D. in English at Stanford University (1963). Momaday taught at a number of universities, including the University of California at Santa Barbara and at Berkeley, as well as at Stanford. Since 1982, he has been a professor of English at the University of Arizona. His first novel, House Made of Dawn *(1968), was awarded the Pulitzer Prize for fiction. In the selection from* The Way to Rainy Mountain *(1969) that follows, Momaday develops a compelling symbol of his tribe's historical and spiritual community through the image of the mountain where his grandmother was buried.*

A single knoll rises out of the plain in Oklahoma, north and west of the Wichita Range. For my people, the Kiowas, it is an old landmark, and they gave it the name Rainy Mountain. The hardest weather in the world is there. Winter brings blizzards, hot tornadic winds arise in the spring, and in summer the prairie is an anvil's edge. The grass runs brittle and brown, and it cracks beneath your feet. There are green belts along the rivers and creeks, linear groves of hickory and pecan, willow and witch hazel. At a distance in July or August the steaming foliage seems almost to writhe in fire. Great green and yellow grasshoppers are everywhere in the tall grass, popping up like corn to sting the flesh, and tortoises crawl about on the red earth, going nowhere in plenty of time. Loneliness is an aspect of the land. All things in the plain are isolated; there is no confusion of objects in the eye, but *one* hill or *one* tree or *one* man. To look upon that landscape in the early morning, with the sun at your back, is to lose the sense of proportion. Your imagination comes to life, and this, you think, is where Creation was begun.

I returned to Rainy Mountain in July. My grandmother had died in the spring, and I wanted to be at her grave. She had lived to be very old and at last infirm. Her only living daughter was with her when she died, and I was told that in death her face was that of a child.

I like to think of her as a child. When she was born, the Kiowas were living the last great moment of their history. For more than a hundred years they had controlled the open range from the Smoky Hill River to the Red, from the headwaters of the Canadian to the fork of the Arkansas and Cimarron. In alliance with the Comanches, they had ruled the whole of the southern Plains. War was their sacred business, and they were among the finest horsemen the world has ever known. But warfare for the Kiowas was preeminently a matter of disposition rather than of survival, and they never understood the grim, unrelenting advance of the U.S. Cavalry. When at last, divided and ill-provisioned, they were driven onto the Staked Plains in the cold rains of autumn, they fell into panic. In Palo Duro Canyon they abandoned their crucial stores to pillage and had nothing then but their lives. In order to save themselves, they surrendered to the soldiers at Fort Sill and were imprisoned in the old stone corral that now stands as a military museum. My grandmother was spared the humiliation of those high gray walls by eight or ten years, but she must have known from birth the affliction of defeat, the dark brooding of old warriors.

Her name was Aho, and she belonged to the last culture to evolve in North America. Her forebears came down from the high country in western Montana nearly three centuries ago. They were a mountain people, a mysterious tribe of hunters whose language has never been positively classified in any major group. In the late seventeenth century they began a long migration to the south and east. It was a journey toward the dawn, and it led to a golden age. Along the way the Kiowas were befriended by the Crows, who gave them the culture and religion of the Plains. They acquired horses, and their ancient nomadic spirit was suddenly free of the ground. They acquired Tai-me, the sacred Sun Dance doll, from that moment the object and symbol of their worship, and so shared in the divinity of the sun. Not least, they acquired the sense of destiny, therefore courage and pride. When they entered upon the southern Plains they had been transformed. No longer were they slaves to the simple necessity of survival; they were a lordly and dangerous society of fighters and thieves, hunters and priests of the sun. According to their origin myth, they entered the world through a hollow log. From one point of view, their migration was the fruit of an old prophecy, for indeed they emerged from a sunless world.

5   Although my grandmother lived out her long life in the shadow of Rainy Mountain, the immense landscape of the continental interior lay like memory in her blood. She could tell of the Crows, whom she had never seen, and of the Black Hills, where she had never been. I wanted to see in reality what she had seen more perfectly in the mind's eye, and traveled fifteen hundred miles to begin my pilgrimage.

Yellowstone, it seemed to me, was the top of the world, a region of deep lakes and dark timber, canyons and waterfalls. But, beautiful as it is, one might have the sense of confinement there. The skyline in all directions is close at hand, the high wall of the woods and deep cleavages of shade. There is a perfect freedom in the mountains, but it belongs to the eagle and the elk, the badger and the bear. The Kiowas reckoned their stature by the distance they could see, and they were bent and blind in the wilderness.

Descending eastward, the highland meadows are a stairway to the plain. In July the inland slope of the Rockies is luxuriant with flax and buckwheat, stonecrop and larkspur. The earth unfolds and the limit of the land recedes. Clusters of trees, and animals grazing far in the distance, cause the vision to reach away and wonder to build upon the mind. The sun follows a longer course in the day, and the sky is immense beyond all comparison. The great billowing clouds that sail upon it are the shadows that move upon the grain like water, dividing light. Farther down, in the land of the Crows and Blackfeet, the plain is yellow. Sweet clover takes hold of the hills and bends upon itself to cover and seal the soil. There the Kiowas paused on their way; they had come to the place where they must change their lives. The sun is at home on the plains. Precisely there does it have the certain character of a god. When the Kiowas came to the land of the Crows, they could see the dark lees of the hills at dawn across the Bighorn River, the profusion of light on the grain shelves, the oldest deity ranging after the solstices. Not yet would they veer southward to the caldron of the land that lay below; they must wean their blood from the northern winter and hold the mountains a while longer in their view. They bore Tai-me in procession to the east.

A dark mist lay over the Black Hills, and the land was like iron. At the top of a ridge I caught sight of Devil's Tower upthrust against the gray sky as if in the birth of time the core of the earth had broken through its crust and the motion of the world was begun. There are things in nature that engender an awful quiet in the heart of man; Devil's Tower is one of them. Two centuries ago, because they could not do otherwise, the Kiowas made a legend at the base of the rock. My grandmother said:

> Eight children were at play, seven sisters and their brother. Suddenly the boy was struck dumb; he trembled and began to run upon his hands and feet. His fingers became claws, and his body was covered with fur. Directly there was a bear where the boy had been. The sisters were terrified; they ran, and the bear after them. They came to the stump of a great tree, and the tree spoke to them. It bade them climb upon it, and as they did so it began to rise into the air. The bear came to kill them, but they were just beyond its reach. It reared against the tree and scored the bark all around with its claws. The seven sisters were borne into the sky, and they became the stars of the Big Dipper.

From that moment, and so long as the legend lives, the Kiowas have kinsmen in the night sky. Whatever they were in the mountains, they could be no more. However, tenuous their well-being, however much they had suffered and would suffer again, they had found a way out of the wilderness.

My grandmother had a reverence for the sun, a holy regard that now is all but gone out of mankind. There was a wariness in her, and an ancient awe. She was a Christian in her later years, but she had come a long way about, and she never forgot her birthright. As a child she had been to the Sun Dances; she had taken part in those annual rites, and by them she had learned the restoration of her people in the presence of Tai-me. She was about seven when the last Kiowa Sun Dance was held in 1887 on the Washita River above Rainy Mountain Creek. The buffalo were gone. In order to consummate the ancient sacrifice—to impale the head of a buffalo bull upon the medicine tree—a delegation of old men journeyed into Texas, there to beg and barter for an animal from the Goodnight herd. She was ten when the Kiowas came together for the last time as a living Sun Dance culture. They could find no buffalo; they had to hang an old hide from the sacred tree. Before the dance could begin, a company of soldiers rode out from Fort Sill under orders to disperse the tribe. Forbidden without cause the essential act of their faith, having seen the wild herds slaughtered and left to rot upon the ground, the Kiowas backed away forever from the medicine tree. That was July 20, 1890, at the great bend of the Washita. My grandmother was there. Without bitterness, and for as long as she lived, she bore a vision of deicide.

10   Now that I can have her only in memory, I see my grandmother in the several postures that were peculiar to her: standing at the wood stove on a winter morning and turning meat in a great iron skillet; sitting at the south window, bent above her beadwork, and afterwards, when her vision failed, looking down for a long time into the fold of her hands; going out upon a cane, very slowly as she did when the weight of age came upon her; praying. I remember her most often at prayer. She made long, rambling prayers out of suffering and hope, having seen many things. I was never sure that I had the right to hear, so exclusive were they of all mere custom and company. The last time I saw her she prayed standing by the side of her bed at night, naked to the waist, the light of a kerosene lamp moving upon her dark skin. Her long, black hair, always drawn and braided in the day, lay upon her shoulders and against her breasts like a shawl. I do not speak Kiowa, and I never understood her prayers, but there was something inherently sad in the sound, some merest hesitation upon the syllables of sorrow. She began in a high and descending pitch, exhausting her breath to silence; then again and again—and always the same intensity of effort, of something that is, and is not, like urgency in the human voice. Transported so in the dancing light among the shadows of her room, she seemed beyond the reach of time. But that was illusion; I think I knew then that I should not see her again.

Houses are like sentinels in the plain, old keepers of the weather watch. There, in a very little while, wood takes on the appearance of great age. All colors wear soon away in the wind and rain, and then the wood is burned gray and the grain appears and the nails turn red with rust. The window-panes are black and opaque; you imagine there is nothing within, and indeed there are many ghosts, bones given up to the land. They stand here and there against the sky, and you approach them for a longer time than you expect. They belong in the distance; it is their domain.

Once there was a lot of sound in my grandmother's house, a lot of coming and going, feasting and talk. The summers there were full of excitement and reunion. The Kiowas are a summer people; they abide the cold and keep to themselves, but when the season turns and the land becomes warm and vital they cannot hold still; an old love of going returns upon them. The aged visitors who came to my grandmother's house when I was a child were made of lean and leather, and they bore themselves upright. They wore great back hats and bright ample shirts that shook in the wind. They rubbed fat upon their hair and wound their braids with strips of colored cloth. Some of them painted their faces and carried the scars of old and cherished enmities. They were an old council of warlords, come to remind and be reminded of who they were. Their wives and daughters served them well. The women might indulge themselves; gossip was at once the mark and compensation of their servitude. They made loud and elaborate talk among themselves, full of jest and gesture, fright and false alarm. They went abroad in fringed and flowered shawls, bright beadwork and German silver. They were at home in the kitchen, and they prepared meals that were banquets.

There were frequent prayer meetings, and great nocturnal feasts. When I was a child I played with my cousins outside, where the lamplight fell upon the ground and the singing of the old people rose up around us and carried away into the darkness. There were a lot of good things to eat, a lot of laughter and surprise. And afterwards, when the quiet returned, I lay down with my grandmother and could hear the frogs away by the river and feel the motion of the air.

Now there is a funeral silence in the rooms, the endless wake of some final word. The walls have closed in upon my grandmother's house. When I returned to it in mourning, I saw for the first time in my life how small it was. It was late at night, and there was a white moon, nearly full. I sat for a long time on the stone steps by the kitchen door. From there I could see out across the land; I could see the long row of trees by the creek, the low light upon the rolling plains, and the stars of the Big Dipper. Once I looked at the moon and caught sight of a strange thing. A cricket had perched upon the handrail, only a few inches away from me. My line of vision was such that the creature filled the moon like a fossil. It had gone there, I thought, to live and die, for there, of all places, was its small definition made whole and eternal. A warm wind rose up and purled like the longing within me.

15   The next morning I awoke at dawn and went out on the dirt road to Rainy Mountain. It was already hot, and the grasshoppers began to fill the air. Still, it was early in the morning, and the birds sang out of the shadows. The long yellow grass on the mountain shone in the bright light, and a scissortail hied above the land. There, where it ought to be, at the end of a long and legendary way, was my grandmother's grave. Here and there on the dark stones were ancestral names. Looking back once, I saw the mountain and came away.

CONVERSATION STARTER

Describe your favorite place in nature. Does this place symbolize the legacy of your community? How?

READING MATTERS

1. Discuss several of the metaphors and similes in the first paragraph that you think are especially vivid. What is the effect of Momaday's describing Rainy Mountain before letting his reader know that he is going there to visit his grandmother's grave?
2. "Whatever they were in the mountains, they could be no more." How do the Kiowas maintain their legacy of spiritual power, community, and destiny in the face of conflict and change?

3. How does Momaday recreate the legacy of the Kiowa tribe through the portrait of his grandmother's life? How are the natural world, the Native American community, and immortality linked through the symbol of Rainy Mountain?
4. Compare and contrast Momaday's and Gordon's descriptions in Chapter 5. How does the description of place in each selection help us to understand the writer's relationship with his or her grandmother?

Writing Matters

1. Write about a natural place where you feel connected with your community. If appropriate, submit your essay to a local paper to encourage others to visit and share your appreciation and respect for this natural setting.
2. Discuss a relationship you have with a person in your family who has influenced or inspired you through describing the place that symbolizes your connection.
3. Like Momaday, write about a journey to a place of family and community significance. After narrating the journey, discuss what you learned on your trip about your heritage, the importance of the landscape to your community, and yourself.

Relevant Web Sites

N. Scott Momaday
<http://www.english.uiuc.edu/maps/poets/m_r/momaday/momaday.htm>

This web site is devoted to understanding the life and works of authors of modern American poetry. Explore information on Momaday and his Native American culture.

Native American Authors <http://www.ipl.org/ref/native/aboutus.html>

The Native American Authors web site was created for the Internet Public Library by five graduate students at the University of Michigan to help people around the world learn about and celebrate the achievements, lives, and works of these important writers.

Complexities of Family Life Today

Tillie Olsen (b. 1912)

I Stand Here Ironing

Tillie Olsen was born in Nebraska to parents who were socialists and political refugees of the 1905 Russian Revolution. She left high school in eleventh grade to work and help support her family. Married twice, she raised four children with Jack Olsen and continued the family tradition of labor organizing. The family moved from the Midwest in the 1930s and settled in San Francisco, where she currently lives.

Olsen had difficulty finding time to write when her children were young. Encouraged by her daughter to attend San Francisco State University, she went on to receive a fellowship in creative writing at Stanford University (1956–1957) and a Ford Foundation Grant for her writing in 1959. Olsen won the O'Henry Prize in 1961 for her short story "Tell Me a Riddle," which became the title of her most highly acclaimed collection of four stories that includes "I Stand Here Ironing," the selection that follows. Olsen edited Silences *(1978), a collection that explores how the work situations and family obligations in women's lives affect their creativity. She has won many awards and has been a writer in residence at a number of universities including Massachusetts Institute of Technology (1973–1974), University of Massachusetts, Boston (1986), and Kenyon College (1987).*

I stand here ironing, and what you asked me moves tormented back and forth with the iron.

"I wish you would manage the time to come in and talk with me about your daughter. I'm sure you can help me understand her. She's a youngster who needs help and whom I'm deeply interested in helping."

"Who needs help." Even if I came, what good would it do? You think because I am her mother I have a key, or that in some way you could use me as a key? She has lived for nineteen years. There is all that life that has happened outside of me, beyond me.

And when is there time to remember, to sift, to weigh, to estimate, to total? I will start and there will be an interruption and I will have to gather it all together again. Or I will become engulfed with all I did or did not do, with what should have been and what cannot be helped.

5   She was a beautiful baby. The first and only one of our five that was beautiful at birth. You do not guess how new and uneasy her tenancy in her now-loveliness. You did not know her all those years she was thought homely, or see her poring over her baby pictures, making me tell her over

and over how beautiful she had been—and would be, I would tell her—and was now, to the seeing eye. But the seeing eyes were few or non-existent. Including mine.

I nursed her. They feel that's important nowadays. I nursed all the children, but with her, with all the fierce rigidity of first motherhood, I did like the books then said. Though her cries battered me to trembling and my breasts ached with swollenness, I waited till the clock decreed.

Why do I put that first? I do not even know if it matters, or if it explains anything.

She was a beautiful baby. She blew shining bubbles of sound. She loved motion, loved light, loved color and music and textures. She would lie on the floor in her blue overalls patting the surface so hard in ecstasy her hands and feet would blur. She was a miracle to me, but when she was eight months old I had to leave her daytimes with the woman downstairs to whom she was no miracle at all, for I worked or looked for work and for Emily's father, who "could no longer endure" (he wrote in his good-bye note) "sharing want with us."

I was nineteen. It was the pre-relief, pre-WPA world of the depression. I would start running as soon as I got off the streetcar, running up the stairs, the place smelling sour, and awake or asleep to startle awake, when she saw me she would break into a clogged weeping that could not be comforted, a weeping I can hear yet.

10   After a while I found a job hashing at night so I could be with her days, and it was better. But it came to where I had to bring her to his family and leave her.

It took a long time to raise the money for her fare back. Then she got chicken pox and I had to wait longer. When she finally came, I hardly knew her, walking quick and nervous like her father, looking like her father, thin, and dressed in a shoddy red that yellowed her skin and glared at the pockmarks. All the baby loveliness gone.

She was two. Old enough for nursery school they said, and I did not know then what I know now—the fatigue of the long day, and the lacerations of group life in the nurseries that are only parking places for children.

Except that it would have made no difference if I had known. It was the only place there was. It was the only way we could be together, the only way I could hold a job.

And even without knowing, I knew. I knew the teacher that was evil because all these years it has curdled into my memory, the little boy hunched in the corner, her rasp, "why aren't you outside, because Alvin hits you? that's no reason, go out, scaredy." I knew Emily hated it even if she did not clutch and implore "don't go Mommy" like the other children, mornings.

15   She always had a reason why she should stay home. Momma, you look sick, Momma. I feel sick. Momma, the teachers aren't there today, they're sick. Momma, we can't go, there was a fire there last night. Momma, it's a holiday today, no school, they told me.

But never a direct protest, never rebellion. I think of our others in their three-, four-year-oldness—the explosions, the tempers, the denunciations, the demands—and I feel suddenly ill. I put the iron down. What in me demanded that goodness in her? And what was the cost, the cost to her of such goodness?

The old man living in the back once said in his gentle way: "You should smile at Emily more when you look at her." What *was* in my face when I looked at her? I loved her. There were all the acts of love.

It was only with the others I remembered what he said, and it was the face of joy, and not of care or tightness or worry I turned to them—too late for Emily. She does not smile easily, let alone almost always as her brothers and sisters do. Her face is closed and somber, but when she wants, how fluid. You must have seen it in her pantomimes, you spoke of her rare gift for comedy on the stage that rouses a laughter out of the audience so dear they applaud and applaud and do not want to let her go.

Where does it come from, that comedy? There was none of it in her when she came back to me that second time, and I had had to send her away again. She had a new daddy now to learn to love, and I think perhaps it was a better time.

20   Except when we left her alone nights, telling ourselves she was old enough.

"Can't you go some other time, Mommy, like tomorrow?" she would ask. "Will it be just a little while you'll be gone? Do you promise?"

The time we came back, the front door open, the clock on the floor in the hall. She rigid awake. "It wasn't just a little while. I didn't cry. Three times I called you, just three times, and then I ran downstairs to open the door so you could come faster. The clock talked loud. I threw it away, it scared me what it talked."

She said the clock talked loud again that night I went to the hospital to have Susan. She was delirious with the fever that comes before red measles, but she was fully conscious all the week I was gone and the week after we were home when she could not come near the new baby or me.

She did not get well. She stayed skeleton thin, not wanting to eat, and night after night she had nightmares. She would call for me, and I would rouse from exhaustion to sleepily call back: "You're all right, darling, go to sleep, it's just a dream," and if she still called, in a sterner voice, "now go to sleep, Emily, there's nothing to hurt you." Twice, only twice, when I had to get up for Susan anyhow, I went in to sit with her.

25   Now when it is too late (as if she would let me hold and comfort her like I do the others) I get up and go to her at once at her moan or restless stirring. "Are you awake, Emily? Can I get you something?" And the answer is always the same: "No, I'm all right, go back to sleep, Mother."

They persuaded me at the clinic to send her away to a convalescent home in the country where "she can have the kind of food and care you can't manage for her, and you'll be free to concentrate on the new baby." They still send children to that place. I see pictures on the society page of sleek young women planning affairs to raise money for it, or dancing at the affairs, or decorating Easter eggs or filling Christmas stockings for the children.

They never have a picture of the children so I do not know if the girls still wear those gigantic red bows and the ravaged looks on the every other Sunday when parents can come to visit "unless otherwise notified"—as we were notified the first six weeks.

Oh it is a handsome place, green lawns and tall trees and fluted flower beds. High up on the balconies of each cottage the children stand, the girls in their red bows and white dresses, the boys in white suits and giant red ties. The parents stand below shrieking up to be heard and the children shriek down to be heard, and between them the invisible wall "Not To Be Contaminated by Parental Germs or Physical Affection."

There was a tiny girl who always stood hand in hand with Emily. Her parents never came. One visit she was gone. "They moved her to Rose College," Emily shouted in explanation. "They don't like you to love anybody here."

30   She wrote once a week, the labored writing of a seven-year-old. "I am fine. How is the baby. If I write my letter nicely I will have a star. Love." There never was a star. We wrote every other day, letters she could never hold or keep but only hear read—once. "We simply do not have room for children to keep any personal possessions," they patiently explained when we pieced one Sunday's shrieking together to plead how much it would mean to Emily, who loved so to keep things, to be allowed to keep her letters and cards.

Each visit she looked frailer. "She isn't eating," they told us.

(They had runny eggs for breakfast or mush with lumps, Emily said later, I'd hold it in my mouth and not swallow. Nothing ever tasted good, just when they had chicken.)

It took us eight months to get her released home, and only the fact that she gained back so little of her seven lost pounds convinced the social worker.

I used to try to hold and love her after she came back, but her body would stay stiff, and after a while she'd push away. She ate little. Food sickened her, and I think much of life too. Oh she had physical lightness and brightness, twinkling by on skates, bouncing like a ball up and down up and down over the jump rope, skimming over the hill; but these were momentary.

35   She fretted about her appearance, thin and dark and foreign-looking at a time when every little girl was supposed to look or thought she should look a chubby blonde replica of Shirley Temple. The doorbell sometimes rang for her, but no one seemed to come and play in the house or be a best friend. Maybe because we moved so much.

There was a boy she loved painfully through two school semesters. Months later she told me how she had taken pennies from my purse to buy him candy. "Licorice was his favorite and I brought him some every day, but he still liked Jennifer better'n me. Why, Mommy?" The kind of question for which there is no answer.

School was a worry to her. She was not glib or quick in a world where glibness and quickness were easily confused with ability to learn. To her overworked and exasperated teachers she was an overconscientious "slow learner" who kept trying to catch up and was absent entirely too often.

I let her be absent, though sometimes the illness was imaginary. How different from my now-strictness about attendance with the others. I wasn't working. We had a new baby, I was home anyhow. Sometimes, after Susan grew old enough, I would keep her home from school, too, to have them all together.

Mostly Emily had asthma, and her breathing, harsh and labored, would fill the house with a curiously tranquil sound. I would bring the two old dresser mirrors and her boxes of collections to her bed. She would select beads and single earrings, bottle tops and shells, dried flowers and pebbles, old postcards and scraps, all sorts of oddments; then she and Susan would play Kingdom, setting up landscapes and furniture, peopling them with action.

40 Those were the only times of peaceful companionship between her and Susan. I have edged away from it, that poisonous feeling between them, that terrible balancing of hurts and needs I had to do between the two, and did so badly, those earlier years.

Oh there are conflicts between the others too, each one human, needing, demanding, hurting, taking—but only between Emily and Susan, no, Emily toward Susan that corroding resentment. It seems so obvious on the surface, yet it is not obvious. Susan, the second child, Susan, golden- and curly-haired and chubby, quick and articulate and assured, everything in appearance and manner Emily was not; Susan, not able to resist Emily's precious things, losing or sometimes clumsily breaking them; Susan telling jokes and riddles to company for applause while Emily sat silent (to say to me later; that was *my* riddle, Mother, I told it to Susan); Susan, who for all the five years' difference in age was just a year behind Emily in developing physically.

I am glad for that slow physical development that widened the difference between her and her contemporaries, though she suffered over it. She was too vulnerable for that terrible world of youthful competition, of preening and parading, of constant measuring of yourself against every other, of envy, "If I had that copper hair," "If I had that skin. . . ." She tormented herself enough about not looking like the others, there was enough of the unsureness, the having to be conscious of words before you speak, the constant caring—what are they thinking of me? without having it all magnified by the merciless physical drives.

Ronnie is calling. He is wet and I change him. It is rare there is such a cry now. That time of motherhood is almost behind me when the ear is not one's own but must always be racked and listening for the child cry, the child call. We sit for a while and I hold him, looking out over the city spread in charcoal with its soft aisles of light. "*Shoogily,*" he breathes and curls closer. I carry him back to bed, asleep. *Shoogily.* A funny word, a family word, inherited from Emily, invented by her to say: *comfort.*

In this and other ways she leaves her seal, I say aloud. And startle at my saying it. What do I mean? What did I start to gather together, to try and make coherent? I was at the terrible, growing years. War years. I do not remember them well. I was working, there were four smaller ones now, there was not time for her. She had to help be a mother, and housekeeper, and shopper. She had to set her seal. Mornings of crisis and near hysteria trying to get lunches packed, hair combed, coats and shoes found, everyone to school or Child Care on time, the baby ready for transportation. And always the paper scribbled on by a smaller one, the book looked at by Susan then mislaid, the homework not done. Running out to that huge school where she was one, she was lost, she was a drop; suffering over the unpreparedness, stammering and unsure in her classes.

45 There was so little time left at night after the kids were bedded down. She would struggle over books, always eating (it was in those years she developed her enormous appetite that is legendary in our family) and I would be ironing, or preparing food for the next day, or writing V-mail to Bill, or tending the baby. Sometimes, to make me laugh, or out of her despair, she would imitate happenings or types at school.

I think I said once: "Why don't you do something like this in the school amateur show?" One morning she phoned me at work, hardly understandable through the weeping: "Mother, I did it. I won, I won; they gave me first prize; they clapped and clapped and wouldn't let me go."

Now suddenly she was Somebody, and as imprisoned in her difference as she had been in anonymity.

She began to be asked to perform at other high schools, even in colleges, then at city and statewide affairs. The first one we went to, I only recognized her that first moment when thin, shy, she almost drowned herself into the curtains. Then: Was this Emily? The control, the command, the convulsing and deadly clowning, the spell, then the roaring, stamping audience, unwilling to let this rare and precious laughter out of their lives.

Afterwards: You ought to do something about her with a gift like that— but without money or knowing how, what does one do? We have left it all to her, and the gift has as often eddied inside, clogged and clotted, as been used and growing.

50 She is coming. She runs up the stairs two at a time with her light graceful step, and I know she is happy tonight. Whatever it was that occasioned your call did not happen today.

"Aren't you ever going to finish the ironing, Mother? Whistler painted his mother in a rocker. I'd have to paint mine standing over an ironing board." This in one of her communicative nights and she tells me everything and nothing as she fixes herself a plate of food out of the icebox.

She is so lovely. Why did you want me to come in at all? Why were you concerned? She will find her way.

She starts up the stairs to bed. "Don't get me up with the rest in the morning." "But I thought you were having midterms." "Oh, those," she comes back in, kisses me, and says quite lightly, "in a couple of years when we'll all be atom-dead they won't matter a bit."

55 She has said it before. She *believes* it. But because I have been dredging the past, and all that compounds a human being is so heavy and meaningful in me, I cannot endure it tonight.

I will never total it all. I will never come in to say: She was a child seldom smiled at. Her father left me before she was a year old. I had to work her first six years when there was work, or I sent her home and to his relatives. There were years she had care she hated. She was dark and thin and foreign-looking in a world where the prestige went to blondeness and curly hair and dimples, she was slow where glibness was prized. She was a child of anxious, no proud, love. We were poor and could not afford for her the soil of easy growth. I was a young mother, I was a distracted mother. There were the other children pushing up, demanding. Her younger sister seemed all that she was not. There were years she did not want me to touch her. She kept too much in herself, her life was such she had to keep too much in herself. My wisdom came too late. She has much to her and probably nothing will come of it. She is a child of her age, of depression, of war, of fear.

Let her be. So all that is in her will not bloom—but in how many does it? There is still enough left to live by. Only help her to know—help make it so there is cause for her to know—that she is more than this dress on the ironing board, helpless before the iron.

Conversation Starter

How would you characterize a good mother, a good father, and a good parent?

Reading Matters

1. The narrator's monologue is initiated as a response to a note from her daughter's high school counselor who thinks that Emily "needs help." Does the narrator believe that the school community can help Emily? How have other social service organizations impacted Emily's life and the narrator's sense of her own parenting skills? Do you think that Emily does need help? Do you think the counselor can help Emily?
2. What does the tone of the narrator's monologue tell you about how she feels about her daughter Emily and herself as a mother? What does the narrator value and hope to pass on to her daughter? Does she believe that she has been a good mother? Do you think that she has been a good mother? Why do you think that Emily has become a comedian?
3. Why does Olsen open and close her story with an image of the mother sifting through the experiences of her daughter's life while standing and ironing? What symbolism does the iron come to have in the story?
4. How do working-class family values differ from middle-class family values? How are the narrator's life and Emily's life changed by their changing social class?

WRITING MATTERS

1. Retell this story from Emily's point of view, trying to bring out some of her feelings about her life in school and her mother's work.

2. This story raises the question of whether social services agencies can be helpful to parents who need assistance providing for their children. Do you think they can? You can respond from a personal perspective, or you might decide to profile several social service organizations for families in your community. Discuss how and why these agencies are succeeding or why they have been unsuccessful.

3. Write an essay that presents an extended definition of a good mother, a good father, or a good parent. Refer to your own experiences, materials that you have read about parenting, or perhaps films that explore issues related to parenting. Or, write an essay that compares and contrasts different perspectives about what makes a good father and a good mother.

RELEVANT WEB SITES

NEBRASKA CENTER FOR WRITERS
<http://mockingbird.creighton.edu/ncw/olsen.htm>

This web site from the Nebraska Center for Writers at Creighton University features extensive information on Tillie Olsen, a Nebraska natives. The site features a biography, an interview, critics' reviews, as well as a bibliography of her work.

THE INTERNATIONAL NON-PROFIT SINGLE MOMS AND DADS ORGANIZATION
<http://www.singlemoms.org>

This web site is dedicated to providing resources, support, and information to single mothers, single fathers, and single parents. It includes resources on family law, professional counseling, and discussion forums.

Barbara Kingsolver (b. 1955)

Somebody's Baby

Barbara Kingsolver grew up in eastern Kentucky in an area that featured both opulent horse farms and impoverished coal fields. Kingsolver always loved storytelling and wrote as a child. Because of the practical rural environment of her youth, she never thought that she would grow up to become a writer. Kingsolver attended college in Indiana at De Paul University. She majored in biology and went on to complete her M.S. degree at the University of Tucson in biology and ecology. During her college years and while she was living abroad, Kingsolver wrote to support herself. After her marriage in 1985, she settled in Tucson; during her pregnancy the following year, she began to write full-time. All of her novels have an autobiographical base. She writes about the worlds she grew up in and knows best. Her works include Homeland and Other Stories *(1989),* Animal Dreams

(1990), The Bean Trees *(1998),* The Poisonwood Bible *(1998), which was nominated for the Pulitzer Prize,* Pigs in Heaven *(1999), and* Prodigal Summer *(2000). In 2000 Kingsolver was awarded the National Humanities Medal, our nation's highest honor for service through the arts. The selection that follows from* High Tide in Tucson: Essays from Now or Never *(1995) reflects upon how significant a nation's attitudes toward children and family can be.*

As I walked out the street entrance to my newly rented apartment, a guy in maroon high-tops and a skateboard haircut approached, making kissing noises and saying, "Hi, gorgeous." Three weeks earlier, I would have assessed the degree of malice and made ready to run or tell him to bug off, depending. But now, instead, I smiled, and so did my four-year-old daughter, because after dozens of similar encounters I understood he didn't mean me but *her.*

This was not the United States.

For most of the year my daughter was four we lived in Spain, in the warm southern province of the Canary Islands. I struggled with dinner at midnight and the subjunctive tense, but my only genuine culture shock reverberated from this earthquake of a fact: people there like kids.

They don't just say so, they *do.* Widows in black, buttoned-down CEOs, purple-sneakered teenagers, the butcher, the baker, all would stop on the street to have little chats with my daughter. Routinely, taxi drivers leaned out the window to shout *"Hola, guapa!"* My daughter, who must have felt my conditioned flinch, would look up at me wide-eyed and explain patiently, "I *like* it that people think I'm pretty." With a mother's keen myopia I would tell you, absolutely, my daughter is beautiful enough to stop traffic. But in the city of Santa Cruz, I have to confess, so was every other person under the height of one meter. Not just those who conceded to be seen and not heard. Whenever Camille grew cranky in a restaurant (and really, what do you expect at midnight?) the waiters flirted and brought her little presents, and nearby diners looked on with that sweet, wistful gleam of eye that I'd thought diners reserved for the dessert tray. What I discovered in Spain was a culture that held children to be its meringues and éclairs. My own culture, it seemed to me in retrospect, tended to regard children as a sort of toxic-waste product: a necessary evil, maybe, but if it's not our own we don't want to see it or hear it or, God help us, smell it.

5   If you don't have children, you think I'm exaggerating. But if you've changed a diaper in the last decade you know exactly the toxic-waste glare I mean. In the U.S. I have been told in restaurants: "We come here to get *away* from kids." (This for no infraction on my daughter's part that I could discern, other than being visible.) On an airplane I heard a man tell a beleaguered woman whose infant was bawling (as I would, to clear my aching ears, if I couldn't manage chewing gum): "If you can't keep that thing quiet, you should keep it at home."

Air travel, like natural disasters, throws strangers together in unnaturally intimate circumstances. (Think how well you can get to know the bald spot of the guy reclining in front of you.) Consequently airplanes can be a splendid cultural magnifying glass. On my family's voyage from New York to Madrid we weren't assigned seats together. I shamelessly begged my neighbor—a forty-something New Yorker traveling alone—if she would take my husband's aisle seat in another row so our airweary and plainly miserable daughter could stretch out across her parents' laps. My fellow traveler snapped, "No, I have to have the window seat, just like you *had* to have that baby."

As simply as that, a child with needs (and ears) became an inconvenient *thing*, for which I was entirely to blame. The remark left me stunned and, as always happens when someone speaks rudely to me, momentarily guilty: yes, she must be right, conceiving this child was a rash, lunatic moment of selfishness, and now I had better be prepared to pay the price.

In the U.S.A., where it's said that anyone can grow up to be President, we parents are left pretty much on our own when it comes to the Presidents-in-training. Our social programs for children are the hands-down worst in the industrialized world, but apparently that is just what we want as a nation. It took a move to another country to make me realize how thoroughly I had accepted my nation's creed of every family for itself. Whenever my daughter crash-landed in the playground, I was startled at first to see a sanguine, Spanish-speaking stranger pick her up and dust her off. And if a shrieking bundle landed at *my* feet, I'd furtively look around for the next of kin. But I quickly came to see this detachment as perverse when applied to children, and am wondering how it ever caught on in the first place.

My grandfathers on both sides lived in households that were called upon, after tragedy struck close to home, to take in orphaned children and raise them without a thought. In an era of shortage, this was commonplace. But one generation later that kind of semipermeable household had vanished, at least among the white middle class. It's a horrifying thought, but predictable enough, that the worth of children in America is tied to their dollar value. Children used to be field hands, household help, even miners and factory workers—extensions of a family's productive potential and so, in a sense, the property of an extended family. But *precious* property, valued and coveted. Since the advent of child-labor laws, children have come to hold an increasingly negative position in the economy. They're spoken of as a responsibility, a legal liability, an encumbrance—or, if their unwed mothers are on welfare, a mistake that should not be rewarded. The political shuffle seems to be about making sure they cost us as little as possible, and that their own parents foot the bill. Virtually every program that benefits children in this country, from *Sesame Street* to free school lunches, has been cut back in the last decade—in many cases, cut to nothing. If it takes a village to raise a child, our kids are knocking on a lot of doors where nobody seems to be home.

10   Taking parental responsibility to extremes, some policymakers in the U.S. have seriously debated the possibility of requiring a license for parenting. I'm dismayed by the notion of licensing an individual adult to raise an

individual child, because it implies parenting is a private enterprise, like selling liquor or driving a cab (though less lucrative). I'm also dismayed by what it suggests about innate fitness or nonfitness to rear children. Who would devise such a test? And how could it harbor anything but deep class biases? Like driving, parenting is a skill you learn by doing. You keep an eye out for oncoming disasters, and know when to stop and ask for directions. The skills you have going into it are hardly the point.

The first time I tried for my driver's license, I flunked. I was sixteen and rigid with panic. I rolled backward precariously while starting on a hill; I misidentified in writing the shape of a railroad crossing sign; as a final disqualifying indignity, my VW beetle—borrowed from my brother and apparently as appalled as I—went blind in the left blinker and mute in the horn. But nowadays, when it's time for a renewal, I breeze through the driver's test without thinking, usually on my way to some other errand. That test I failed twenty years ago was no prediction of my ultimate competence as a driver, anymore than my doll-care practices (I liked tying them to the back of my bike, by the hair) were predictive of my parenting skills (heavens be praised). Who really understands what it takes to raise kids? that is, until after the diaper changes, the sibling rivalries, the stitches, the tantrums, the first day of school, the overpriced-sneakers standoff, the first date, the safe-sex lecture, and the senior prom have all been negotiated and put away in the scrapbook?

While there are better and worse circumstances from which to launch offspring onto the planet, it's impossible to anticipate just who will fail. One of the most committed, creative parents I know plunged into her role through the trapdoor of teen pregnancy; she has made her son the center of her life, constructed a large impromptu family of reliable friends and neighbors, and absorbed knowledge like a plant taking sun. Conversely, some of the most strained, inattentive parents I know are well-heeled professionals, self-sufficient but chronically pressed for time. Life takes surprising turns. The one sure thing is that no parent, ever, has turned out to be perfectly wise and exhaustively provident, 1,440 minutes a day, for 18 years. It takes help. Children are not commodities but an incipient world. They thrive best when their upbringing is the collective joy and responsibility of families, neighborhoods, communities, and nations.

It's not hard to figure out what's good for kids, but amid the noise of an increasingly antichild political climate, it can be hard to remember just to go ahead and do it: for example, to vote to raise your school district's budget, even though you'll pay higher taxes. (If you're earning enough to pay taxes at all, I promise, the school needs those few bucks more than you do.) To support legislators who care more about afterschool programs, affordable health care, and libraries than about military budgets and the Dow Jones industrial average. To volunteer time and skills at your neighborhood school and also the school across town. To decide to notice, rather than ignore it, when a neighbor is losing it with her kids, and offer to baby-sit twice a week. This is not interference. Getting between a ball player and a ball is interference. The ball is inanimate.

Presuming children to be their parents' sole property and responsibility is, among other things, a handy way of declaring problem children to be someone else's problem, or fault, or failure. It's a dangerous remedy; it doesn't change the fact that somebody else's kids will ultimately be in your face demanding *now* with interest what they didn't get when they were smaller and had simpler needs. Maybe in-your-face means breaking and entering, or maybe it means a Savings and Loan scam. Children deprived—of love, money, attention, or moral guidance—grow up to have large and powerful needs.

15   Always there will be babies made in some quarters whose parents can't quite take care of them. Reproduction is the most invincible of all human goals; like every other species, we're only here because our ancestors spent millions of years refining their act as efficient, dedicated breeders. If we hope for only sane, thoughtful people to have children, we can wish while we're at it for an end to cavities and mildew. But unlike many other species we are social, insightful, and capable of anticipating our future. We can see, if we care to look, that the way we treat children—*all* of them, not just our own, and especially those in great need—defines the shape of the world we'll wake up in tomorrow. The most remarkable feature of human culture is its capacity to reach beyond the self and encompass the collective good.

It's an inspiring thought. But in mortal fact, here in the U.S. we are blazing a bold downhill path from the high ground of "human collective," toward the tight little den of "self." The last time we voted on a school-budget override in Tucson, the newspaper printed scores of letters from readers incensed by the very possibility: "I don't have kids," a typical letter writer declared, "so why should I have to pay to educate other people's offspring?" The budget increase was voted down, the school district progressed from deficient to desperate, and I longed to ask that miserly nonfather just *whose* offspring he expects to doctor the maladies of his old age.

If we intend to cleave like stubborn barnacles to our great American ethic of every nuclear family for itself, then each of us had better raise and educate offspring enough to give us each day, in our old age, our daily bread. If we don't wish to live by bread alone, we'll need not only a farmer and a cook in the family but also a home repair specialist, an auto mechanic, an accountant, an import-export broker, a forest ranger, a therapist, and engineer, a musician, a poet, a tailor, a doctor, and at least three shifts of nurses. If that seems impractical, then we can accept other people's kids into our lives, starting now.

It's not so difficult. Most of the rest of the world has got this in hand. Just about any country you can name spends a larger percentage of its assets on its kids than we do. Virtually all industrialized nations have better schools and child-care policies. And while the U.S. grabs headlines by saving the occasional baby with heroic medical experiments, world health reports (from UNESCO, USAID, and other sources) show that a great many other parts of the world have lower infant mortality rates than we do—not just the conspicuously prosperous nations like Japan and Germany, but others, like Greece, Cuba, Portugal, Slovenia—simply because they attend better to all their mothers and children. Cuba, running on a budget that would hardly keep New York City's lights on, has better immunization programs and a higher literacy rate. During the long, grim haul of a thirty-year economic blockade, during which the United States had managed to starve Cuba to a ghost of its hopes, that island's child-first priorities have never altered.

Here in the land of plenty a child dies from poverty every fifty-three minutes, and TV talk shows exhibit teenagers who pierce their flesh with safety pins and rip off their parents every way they know how. All these punks started out as somebody's baby. How on earth, we'd like to know, did they learn to be so isolated and selfish?

20   My second afternoon in Spain, standing in a crowded bus, as we ricocheted around a corner and my daughter reached starfishwise for stability, a man in a black beret stood up and gently helped her into his seat. In his weightless bearing I caught sight of the decades-old child, treasured by the manifold mothers of his neighborhood, growing up the way leavened dough rises surely to the kindness of bread.

I thought then of the woman on the airplane, who was obviously within her rights to put her own comfort first, but whose withheld generosity gave my daughter what amounted to a sleepless, kicking, squirming, miserable journey. As always happens when someone has spoken to me rudely, I knew exactly what I should have said: Be careful what you give children, for sooner or later you are sure to get it back.

CONVERSATION STARTER

Do you think that the vast majority of children in America are highly valued, well taken care of, and respected? Explain your point of view.

READING MATTERS

1. How does the brief example in the opening paragraph help to show the contrast between how children are valued in Spain and in the United States? Is this an appropriate and persuasive way to begin the essay considering Kingsolver's thesis? Why do you think she uses the title "Somebody's Baby"? To what might it refer?
2. What effective examples and metaphors does Kingsolver develop to reflect the American attitude toward children? What is ironic, as Kingsolver points out, about the American attitude toward children?
3. Why is Kingsolver opposed to the publicly debated issue of requiring a license for parenting? Why does she think it would reflect a class bias? Do you agree with her? Does Kingsolver believe that is it is possible to know how to raise a child before having one? Why does she believe that values are more important when raising children than a "particular styles"? Do you agree with her? Explain.

4. What solutions does Kingsolver propose? Why does she look to small communities and social and political institutions to correct the current tendency "to regard children as a toxic waste product"? Do you agree with her analysis and solutions?

WRITING MATTERS

1. Write an argument in which you agree or disagree with Kingsolver's assessment of the way children in the United Stated are treated. Support your ideas with research that you do and examples from your own experiences and observations.
2. Schools are clearly a part of the problem of raising children in our society. After doing research about the funding for teachers, administrators, and supplies for schools in your area, write a proposal for changing the existing conditions and a defense of your proposal.
3. Do some research into attitudes toward raising and educating children in a European country and an Asian country. Then contrast the way that Americans raise and educate their children. Write a paper that suggests ways that we can draw from the information of other countries (in particular the two you researched) and improve the lives of children and youth in the United States.

RELEVANT WEB SITES

BARBARA KINGSOLVER <http://www.kingsolver.com>

Barbara Kingsolver's personal web site includes a short biography as well as a complete bibliography, an audio library, and resources for discussion.

THE NEWS HOURS—INTERVIEW WITH BARBARA KINGSOLVER
<http://www.pbs.org/newshour/gergen/kingsolver.html>

Read a transcript of an interview with Barbara Kingsolver conducted by David Gergen in which they discuss issues including family, community, and the natural world.

Judith Wallerstein

The Legacy of Divorce

In 1980 Judith Wallerstein established the Center for the Family in Transition, which has become a nationally acclaimed center for research, education, and counseling for families going through separation, divorce, and remarriage. Judith Wallerstein has taught and lectured all over the world to attorneys, judges, pediatricians, educators, and mental health professionals. From 1966 to 1992, Dr. Wallerstein was a senior lecturer in the School of Social Welfare at the University of California at Berkeley.

Wallerstein's most recent book looks at the lives of the young people in her original California Children of Divorce study, now in their adult years, and completes their stories. In The Unexpected

Legacy of Divorce: A 25-Year Landmark Study (2000), Wallerstein describes the feelings, expecta-
tions, and memories of their parents' divorce that these children carry into adulthood, especially in
their own relationships—love, marriage, cohabitation, divorce, and becoming parents themselves.
In the following selection, excerpted from her latest book, Wallerstein also offers advice on how to
reverse some of the negative effects of the divorce culture.

"What's done to children, they will do to society."

Karl A. Menninger

Around the time I was finishing this book, a very important judge on
the family law bench in a large state I shall not name invited me to come
see him. I was eager to meet with him because I wanted to discuss some
ideas I have for educating parents under court auspices that go beyond the
simple advice "don't fight." After we had talked for a half an hour or so,
the judge leaned back in his chair and said he'd like my opinion about
something important. He had just attended several scientific lectures in
which researchers argued that children are shaped more by genes than by
family environment. Case in point, studies of identical twins reared separately show that in adulthood such twins often like the same foods and
clothing styles, belong to the same political parties, and even bestow
identical names on their dogs. The judge looked perplexed. "Do you think
that could mean divorce is in the genes?" he asked in all seriousness.
"And if that's so, does it matter what a court decides when parents
divorce?"

I was taken aback. Here was a key figure in the lives of thousands of
children asking me whether what he and his colleagues do or say on the
bench makes any difference. He seemed relieved by the notion that maybe
his actions are insignificant.

I told him that I personally doubt the existence of a "divorce gene." If
such a biological trait had arisen in evolution, it would be of very recent
vintage. But, I added, "What the court does matters enormously. You
have the power to protect children from being hurt or to increase their
suffering."

Now it was his turn to be taken aback. "You think we've increased
children's suffering?"

5   "Yes, Your Honor, I do. With all respect, I have to say that the court
along with the rest of society has increased the suffering of children."

"How so?" he asked.

We spent another half hour talking about how the courts, parents, attorneys, mental health workers—indeed most adults—have been reluctant to
pay genuine attention to children during and after divorce. He listened
respectfully to me but I must say I left the judge's chambers that day in a
state of shock that soon turned to gloom. How can we be so utterly lost and
confused that a leading judge would accept the notion of a "divorce gene"
to explain our predicament? If he's confused about his role, what about the
rest of us? What is it about the impact of divorce on our society and our
children that's so hard to understand and accept?

Having spent the last thirty years of my life traveling here and abroad talking to professional, legal, and mental health groups plus working with thousands of parents and children in divorced families, it's clear that we've created a new kind of society never before seen in human culture. Silently and unconsciously, we have created a culture of divorce. It's hard to grasp what it means when we say that first marriages stand a 45 percent chance of breaking up and that second marriages have a 60 percent chance of ending in divorce. What are the consequences for all of us when 25 percent of people today between the ages of eighteen and forty-four have parents who divorced? What does it mean to a society when people wonder aloud if the family is about to disappear? What can we do when we learn that married couples with children represent a mere 26 percent of households in the 1990s and that the most common living arrangement nowadays is a household of unmarried people with no children? These numbers are terrifying. But like all massive social change, what's happening is affecting us in ways that we have yet to understand.

For people like me who work with divorcing families all the time, these abstract numbers have real faces. I can relate to the millions of children and adults who suffer with loneliness and to all the teenagers who say, "I don't want a life like either of my parents." I can empathize with the countless young men and women who despair of ever finding a lasting relationship and who, with a brave toss of the head, say, "Hey, if you don't get married then you can't get divorced." It's only later, or sometimes when they think I'm not listening, that they add softly, "but I don't want to grow old alone." I am especially worried about how our divorce culture has changed childhood itself. A million new children a year are added to our march of marital failure. As they explain so eloquently, they lose the carefree play of childhood as well as the comforting arms and lap of a loving parent who is always rushing off because life in the postdivorce family is so incredibly difficult to manage. We must take very seriously the complaint of children like Karen who declare, "The day my parents divorced is the day my childhood ended."

10   Many years ago the psychoanalyst Erik Erikson taught us that childhood and society are vitally connected. But we have not yet come to terms with the changes ushered in by our divorce culture. Childhood is different, adolescence is different, and adulthood is different. Without our noticing, we have created a new class of young children who take care of themselves, along with a whole generation of overburdened parents who have no time to enjoy the pleasures of parenting. So much has happened so fast, we cannot hold it all in our minds. It's simply overwhelming.

But we must not forget a very important other side to all these changes. Because of our divorce culture, adults today have a greater sense of freedom. The importance of sex and play in adult life is widely accepted. We are not locked into our early mistakes and forced to stay in wretched, lifelong relationships. The change in women—their very identity and freer role in society—is part of our divorce culture. Indeed, two-thirds of divorces are initiated by women despite the high price they pay in economic and parenting burdens afterward. People want and expect a lot more out of marriage than did earlier generations. Although the divorce rate in second and third marriages is sky-high, many second marriages are much happier than the ones left behind. Children and adults are able to escape violence, abuse, and misery to create a better life. Clearly there is no road back.

The sobering truth is that we have created a new kind of society that offers greater freedom and more opportunities for many adults, but this welcome change carries a serious hidden cost. Many people, adults and children alike, are in fact not better off. We have created new kinds of families in which relationships are fragile and often unreliable. Children today receive far less nurturance, protection, and parenting than was their lot a few decades ago. Long-term marriages come apart at still surprising rates. And many in the older generation who started the divorce revolution find themselves estranged from their adult children. Is this the price we must pay for needed change? Can't we do better?

I'd like to say that we're at a crossroads but I'm afraid I can't be that optimistic. We can choose a new route only if we agree on where we are and where we want to be in the future. The outlook is cloudy. For every person who wants to sound an alarm, there's another who says don't worry. For everyone concerned about the economic and emotional deprivations inherited by children of divorce there are those who argue that those kids were "in trouble before" and that divorce is irrelevant, no big deal. People want to feel good about their choices. Doubtless many do. In actual fact, after most divorces, one member of the former couple feels much better while the other feels no better or even worse. Yet at any dinner party you will still hear the same myths: Divorce is a temporary crisis. So many children have experienced their parents' divorce that kids nowadays don't worry so much. It's easier. They almost expect it. It's a rite of passage. If I feel better, so will my children. And so on. As always, children are voiceless or unheard.

But family scholars who have not always seen eye to eye are converging on a number of findings that fly in the face of our cherished myths. We agree that the effects of divorce are long-term. We know that the family is in trouble. We have a consensus that children raised in divorced or remarried families are less well adjusted as adults than those raised in intact families.

15   The life histories of this first generation to grow up in a divorce culture tell us truths we dare not ignore. Their message is poignant, clear, and contrary to what so many want to believe. They have taught me the following:

From the viewpoint of the children, and counter to what happens to their parents, divorce is a cumulative experience. Its impact increases over time and rises to a crescendo in adulthood. At each developmental stage divorce is experienced anew in different ways. In adulthood it affects personality, the ability to trust, expectations about relationships, and ability to cope with change.

The first upheaval occurs at the breakup. Children are frightened and angry, terrified of being abandoned by both parents, and they feel responsible for the divorce. Most children are taken by surprise; few are relieved. As adults, they remember with sorrow and anger how little support they got from their parents when it happened. They recall how they were expected to adjust overnight to a terrifying number of changes that confounded them. Even children who had seen or heard violence at home made no connection between that violence and the decision to divorce. The children concluded early on, silently and sadly, that family relationships are fragile and that the tie between a man and woman can break capriciously without warning. They worried ever after that parent-child relationships are also unreliable and can break at any time. These early experiences colored their later expectations.

As the postdivorce family took shape, their world increasingly resembled what they feared most. Home was a lonely place. The household was in disarray for years. Many children were forced to move, leaving behind familiar schools, close friends, and other supports. What they remember vividly as adults is the loss of the intact family and the safety net it provided, the difficulty of having two parents in two homes, and how going back and forth cut badly into playtime and friendships. Parents were busy with work, preoccupied with rebuilding their social lives. Both moms and dads had a lot less time to spend with their children and were less responsive to their children's needs or wishes. Little children especially felt that they had lost both parents and were unable to care for themselves. Children soon learned that the divorced family has porous walls that include new lovers, live-in partners, and stepparents. Not one of these relationships was easy for anyone. The mother's parenting was often cut into by the very heavy burdens of single parenthood and then by the demands of remarriage and stepchildren.

Relationships with fathers were heavily influenced by live-in lovers or stepmothers in second and third marriages. Some second wives were interested in the children while others wanted no part of them. Some fathers were able to maintain their love and interest in their children but few had time for two or sometimes three families. In some families both parents gradually stabilized their lives within happy remarriages or well-functioning, emotionally gratifying single parenthood. But these people were never a majority in any of my work.

20   Meanwhile, children who were able to draw support from school, sports teams, parents, stepparents, grandparents, teachers, or their own inner strengths, interests, and talents did better than those who could not muster such resources. By necessity, many of these so-called resilient children forfeited their own childhoods as they took responsibility for themselves; their troubled, overworked parents; and their siblings. Children who needed more than minimal parenting because they were little or have special vulnerabilities and problems with change were soon overwhelmed with sorrow and anger at their parents. Years later, when contemplating having their own children, most children in this study said hotly, "I never want a child of mine to experience a childhood like I had."

As the children told us, adolescence begins early in divorced homes and, compared with that of youngsters raised in intact families, is more likely to include more early sexual experiences for girls and higher alcohol and drug use for girls and boys. Adolescence is more prolonged in divorced families and extends well into the years of early adulthood. Throughout these years children of divorce worry about following in their parents' footsteps and struggle with a sinking sense that they, too, will fail in their relationships.

But it's in adulthood that children of divorce suffer the most. The impact of divorce hits them most cruelly as they go in search of love, sexual intimacy, and commitment. Their lack of inner images of a man and a woman in a stable relationship and their memories of their parents' failure to sustain the marriage badly hobbles their search, leading them to heartbreak and even despair. They cried, "No one taught me." They complain bitterly that they feel unprepared for adult relationships and that they have never seen a "man and woman on the same beam," that they have no good models on which to build their hopes. And indeed they have a very hard time formulating even simple ideas about the kind of person they're looking for. Many end up with unsuitable or very troubled partners in relationships that were doomed from the start.

The contrast between them and children from good intact homes, as both go in search of love and commitment, is striking. Children raised in extremely unhappy or violent intact homes face misery in childhood and tragic challenges in adulthood. But because their parents generally aren't interested in getting a divorce, divorce does not become part of their legacy. Adults in their twenties from reasonably good or even moderately unhappy intact families had a fine understanding of the demands and sacrifices required in a close relationship. They had memories of how their parents struggled and overcame difference, how they cooperated in a crisis. They developed a general idea about the kind of person they wanted to marry. Most important, they did not expect to fail. The two groups differed after marriage as well. Those from intact families found the example of their parents' enduring marriage very reassuring when they inevitably ran into marital problems. But in coping with the normal stresses in a marriage, adults from divorced families were at a grave disadvantage. Anxiety about relationships was at the bedrock of their personalities and endured even in very happy marriages. Their fears of disaster and sudden loss rose when they felt content. And their fear of abandonment, betrayal, and rejection mounted when they found themselves having to disagree with someone they loved. After all, marriage is a slippery slope and their parents fell off it. All had trouble dealing with differences or even moderate conflict in their close relationships. Typically their first response was panic, often followed by flight. They had a lot to undo and a lot to learn in a very short time.

Those who had two parents who rebuilt happy lives after divorce and included children in their orbits had a much easier time as adults. Those who had committed single parents also benefited from that parent's attention and responsiveness. But the more frequent response in adulthood was continuing anger at parents, more often at fathers, whom the children regarded as having been selfish and faithless.

25   Others felt deep compassion and pity toward mothers or fathers who failed to rebuild their lives after divorce. The ties between daughters and their mothers were especially close but at a cost. Some young women found it very difficult to separate from their moms and to lead their own lives. With some notable exceptions, fathers in divorced families were less likely to enjoy close bonds with their adult children, especially their sons. This stood in marked contrast to fathers and sons from intact families, who tended to grow closer as the years went by.

Fortunately for many children of divorce, their fears of loss and betrayal can be conquered by the time they reach their late twenties and thirties. But what a struggle that takes, what courage and persistence. Those who succeed overcome their difficulties the hard way—by learning from their own failed relationships and gradually rejecting the models they were raised with to create what they want from a love relationship. Those lucky enough to have found a loving partner are able to interrupt their self-destructive course with a lasting love affair or marriage.

In other realms of adult life—financial and security, for instance—some children were able to overcome difficulties through unexpected help from fathers who had vanished long before. Still others benefit from the constancy of parents or grandparents. Many men and women raised in divorced families establish successful careers. Their workplace performance is largely unaffected by the divorce. But no matter what their success in the world, they retain some serious residues—fear of loss, fear of change, and fear that disaster will strike, especially when things are going well. They're still terrified by the mundane differences and inevitable conflicts found in every close relationship.

I'm heartened by the hard-won success of these adults. But at the same time, I can't forget those who've failed to straighten out their lives. I'm especially troubled by how many divorced or remained in wretched marriages. Of those who have children and who are now divorced, many, to my dismay, are not protecting their children in ways we might expect. They go on to repeat the same mistakes their own parents made, perpetuating problems that have plagued them all their lives. I'm also concerned about many who, by their mid- and late thirties, are neither married nor cohabiting and who are leading lonely lives. They're afraid of getting involved in a relationship that they think is doomed to fail. After a divorce or breakup, they're afraid to try again. And I'm struck by continuing anger at parents and flat-out statements by many of these young adults that they have no intention of helping their moms and especially their dads or stepparents in old age. This may change. But if it doesn't, we'll be facing another unanticipated consequence of our divorce culture. Who will take care of an older generation estranged from its children?

What We Can and Cannot Do

Our efforts to improve our divorce culture have been spotty and the resources committed to the task are pitifully small. The courts have given the lion's share of attention to the 10 to 15 percent of families that continue to fight bitterly. Caught between upholding the rights of parents and protecting the interests of children, they have tilted heavily toward parents. Such parents allegedly speak in the name of the child just as those who fight bloody holy wars allegedly speak in the name of religion. Thus, as I explained to the judge with whom I began this chapter, our court system has unintentionally contributed to the suffering of children. At the same time, most parents receive little guidance. Some courts offer educational lectures to families at the time of the breakup, but the emphasis is on preventing further litigation. Such courses are typically evaluated according to how much they reduce subsequent litigation and not on how they might improve parenting. Curricula to educate teachers, school personnel, pediatricians, and other professionals about child and parenting issues in divorce are rare. Few university or medical school programs in psychiatry, psychology, social work, or law include courses on how to understand or help children and parents after separation, divorce, and remarriage. This lack of training persists despite that fact that a disproportionate number of children and adolescents from divorced homes are admitted as patients for psychological treatment at clinics and family agencies. In many social agencies, close to three-quarters of the children in treatment are from divorced families. Some school districts have organized groups for children whose parents are divorcing. And some communities have established groups to help divorcing parents talk about their children's problems. A few centers such as ours have developed programs to help families cope with high conflict and domestic violence. But such efforts are not widespread. As a society, we have not set up services to help people relieve the stresses of divorce. We continue to foster the myth that divorce is a transient crisis and that as soon as adults restabilize their lives, the children will recover fully. When will the truth sink in?

30   Let's suppose for a moment that we had a consensus in our society. Suppose we could agree that we want to maintain the advantages of divorce but that we need to protect our children and help parents mute the long-term effects of divorce on future generations. Imagine we were willing to roll up our sleeves and really commit the enormous resources of our society toward supplementing the knowledge we have. Suppose we gave as much time, energy, and resources to protecting children as we give to protecting the environment. What might we try?

I would begin with an effort to strengthen marriage. Obviously, restoring confidence in marriage won't work if we naively call for a return to marriage as it used to be. To improve marriage, we need to fully understand the nature of contemporary man-woman relationships. We need to appreciate the difficulties modern couples confront in balancing work and family, separateness and togetherness, conflict and cooperation. It's no accident that 80 percent of divorces occur in the first nine years of marriage. These new families should be our target.

What threats to marriage can we change? First, there's a serious imbalance between the demands of the workplace and the needs of family life. The corporate world rarely considers the impact of its policies on parents and children. Some companies recognize that parents need time to spend with their children but they don't understand that the workplace exerts a major influence on the quality and stability of marriage. Heavy work schedules and job insecurity erode married life. Families with young children especially postpone intimate talk, sex, and friendship. These are the ties that replenish a marriage. When the boss calls, we go to the office. When the baby cries, we pick up the child. But when a marriage is starving, we expect it to bumble along. Most Western European countries provide paid family leave. What about us? Why do we persist in offering unpaid leave and pretend that it addresses the young family's problem? One additional solution might be social security and tax benefits for a parent who wants to stay home and care for young children. That alone would lighten the burden on many marriages. Other suggestions for reducing the stresses on young families include more flex time, greater opportunities for part-time work, assurances that people who take family leave will not lose their place on the corporate ladder, tax advantages for families, and many other ideas that have been on the table for years. Public policy cannot create good marriages. But it can buffer some of the stresses people face, especially in those early, vulnerable years when couples need time to establish intimacy, a satisfying sex life, and a friendship that will hold them together through the inevitable challenges that lie ahead. Ultimately, if we're really interested in improving marriage so that people have time for each other and their children, we need to realign our priorities away from the business world and toward family life.

We might also try to help the legions of young adults who complain bitterly that they're unprepared for marriage. Having been raised in divorced or very troubled homes, they have no idea how to choose a partner or what to do to build a relationship. They regard their parents' divorce as a terrible failure and worry that they're doomed to follow in the same footsteps. Many adults stay in unhappy marriages just to avoid divorce. We don't know if we can help them with educational methods because we haven't tried. Our experience is too limited and our experimental models nonexistent. But when so many young people have never seen a good marriage, we have a moral obligation to try to intervene preventively. Most programs that give marital advice are aimed at engaged couples who belong to churches and synagogues. These are very good beginnings that should be expanded. But many offer too little and arrive too late to bring about changes in any individual's values or knowledge. Nor is the excitement that precedes a wedding the best time for reflection on how to choose a lifetime partner or what makes a marriage work. Academic courses on marriage mostly look at families from the lofty perch of the family scholar and not from the perspective of children of divorce who feel "no one ever taught me."

In my opinion, a better time to begin helping these youngsters is during mid-adolescence, when attitudes toward oneself and relationships with the opposite sex are beginning to gel. Adolescence is the time when worries about sex, love, betrayal, and morality take center stage. Education for and about relationships should begin at that time, since if we do it right, we'll have their full attention. It could be based in the health centers that have been established in many schools throughout the country. Churches and synagogues and social agencies might provide another launching place. Ideally, adolescents in a well-functioning society should have the opportunity to think and talk about a wide range of relationships, issues, and conflicts confronting them. As an opening gambit, think about asking the deceptively simple question: "How do you choose a friend?" A group of teenagers considering this problem could be drawn to the important question of how to choose a lover and life partner—and even more important, how not to choose one. Specific topics such as differences between boys and girls, cultural subgroups, and how people resolve tensions would follow based on the teenagers' interests and their willingness to discuss real issues. Colleges could also offer continuing and advanced courses on an expanded range of subjects, including many problems that young men and women now struggle with alone.

35   We are on the threshold of learning what we can and cannot do for these young people. Still one wonders, can an educational intervention replace the learning that occurs naturally over many years within the family? How do we create a corps of teachers who are qualified to lead meaningful courses on relationships? By this I mean courses that are true to life, honest, and respectful of students. I worry about the adult tendency to lecture or sermonize. In a society where the family has become a political issue, I'm concerned about attacks from the left and the right, about the many people who would attack such interventions the way they've attacked the Harry Potter books. Mostly I'm concerned about finding a constituency of adults who would rally behind an idea that has so many pitfalls. But I'm also convinced that doing nothing—leaving young people alone in their struggles—is more dangerous. We should not give up without a try.

CONVERSATION STARTER

Discuss the positive and negative effects of divorce on the American family.

READING MATTERS

1. Wallerstein asks: "What is it about the impact of divorce on our society and our children that's so hard to understand and accept?" What is your answer?
2. What are the positive effects of the divorce culture?
3. Why does Wallerstein believe that the most negative impact of the divorce culture has been on children? Do you agree or disagree with her? Explain.

4. What advice does Wallerstein offer to children? To parents? To our society? Which of her suggestions seem most important? Why?

WRITING MATTERS

1. Despite Wallerstein's negative conclusions about the impact of the divorce culture, she still believes that marriage as an institution has a chance to endure. Write an essay that supports or refutes Wallerstein's position on marriage. Refer to specific evidence in the selection as you discuss your own point of view.
2. Writing from your own experiences with your family, at school, and with friends, as well as your interpretation of relevant myths in our popular culture, discuss the most significant causes and effects of divorce.
3. Write a paper that profiles an organization in your community that helps families that are undergoing divorce. What recurring issues do staff members at these organizations try to resolve? How effective has the organization been? Alternatively, volunteer to help at an agency that helps families who have experienced divorce. Write a paper that presents some background on the agency and your role as a helper there. Then discuss what you have learned from your experiences.

RELEVANT WEB SITES

DIVORCE NET <http://www.divorcenet.com>

Divorce Net features a state-by-state resource center, interactive bulletin board, and information on related family law issues.

FACTS FOR FAMILIES <http://www.aacap.org/info_families/index.htm>

The Facts For Families web site includes 51 fact sheets with information on many crucial issues such as children and divorce, TV violence, learning disabilities, AIDS, and sexual abuse. The web site is presented by the America Academy of Child and Adolescent Psychiatry.

Community Projects that Support Children and Families

Marian Wright Edelman (b. 1939)

A Family Legacy

Marian Wright Edelman was raised in South Carolina in the family of a Baptist minister who expected his children to serve the community. Edelman said, "Working for the community was as much a part of our existence as eating and sleeping and church."

Education was a priority in her family, and after graduating from high school, Edelman attended the University of Paris and the University of Geneva. She went on to complete her B.A. at Spelman College (1960). After finishing Yale University Law School (1963), Edelman became the first Black woman lawyer in Mississippi and directed the NAACP Legal Defense and Educational Fund office in Jackson, Mississippi. In 1968, Edelman moved to Washington, D.C., to help with the Poor People's March that Martin Luther King Jr. began organizing before his death. She was the founding president of the Children's Defense Fund (1973) and served as chair on the Spelman College Board of Trustees (1976–1987). Always an activist for civil rights and civil liberties, Edelman has received many honorary degrees and awards including the Albert Schweitzer Humanitarian Prize and the Heinz Award; she has also been a MacArthur Foundation Prize Fellow. Edelman's most widely read books include Children Out of School in America *(1974);* Families in Peril: An Agenda for Social Change *(1987);* The Measure of Our Success: A Letter to My Children and Yours *(1992), from which the selection that follows is excerpted; and* Lanterns: A Memoir of Mentor *(1999). In the following selection, this children's rights advocate discusses the ethics and values of family, church, school, and community to conclude that "service is the rent we pay for living."*

South Carolina is my home state and I am the aunt, granddaughter, daughter, and sister of Baptist ministers. Service was as essential a part of my upbringing as eating and sleeping and going to school. The church was a hub of Black children's social existence, and caring Black adults were buffers against the segregated and hostile outside world that told us we weren't important. But our parents said it wasn't so, our teachers said it wasn't so, and our preachers said it wasn't so. The message of my racially segregated childhood was clear: let no man or woman look down on you, and look down on no man or woman.

We couldn't play in public playgrounds or sit at drugstore lunch counters and order a Coke, so Daddy built a playground and canteen behind the church. In fact, whenever he saw a need, he tried to respond. There were no

Black homes for the aged in Bennettsville, so he began one across the street for which he and Mama and we children cooked and served and cleaned. And we children learned that it was our responsibility to take care of elderly family members and neighbors, and that everyone was our neighbor. My mother carried on the home after Daddy died, and my brother Julian has carried it on to this day behind our church since our mother's death in 1984.

Finding another child in my room or a pair of my shoes gone was far from unusual, and twelve foster children followed my sister and me and three brothers as we left home.

Child-rearing and parental work were inseparable. I went everywhere with my parents and was under the watchful eye of members of the congregation and community who were my extended parents. They kept me when my parents went out of town, they reported on and chided me when I strayed from the straight and narrow of community expectations, and they basked in and supported my achievements when I did well. Doing well, they made clear, meant high academic achievement, playing piano in Sunday school or singing or participating in other church activities, being helpful to somebody, displaying good manners (which is nothing more than consideration toward others), and reading. My sister Olive reminded me recently that the only time our father would not give us a chore ("Can't you find something constructive to do?" was his most common refrain) was when we were reading. So we all read a lot! We learned early what our parents and extended community "parents" valued. Children were taught—not by sermonizing, but by personal example—that nothing was too lowly to do. I remember a debate my parents had when I was eight or nine as to whether I was too young to go with my older brother, Harry, to help clean the bed and bedsores of a very sick, poor woman. I went and learned just how much the smallest helping hands and kindness can mean to a person in need.

5   The ugly external voices of my small-town, segregated childhood (as a very young child I remember standing and hearing former South Carolina Senator James Byrnes railing on the local courthouse lawn about how Black children would never go to school with whites) were tempered by the internal voices of parental and community expectation and pride. My father and I waited anxiously for the *Brown v. Board of Education* decision in 1954. We talked about it and what it would mean for my future and for the future of millions of other Black children. He died the week before *Brown* was decided. But I and other children lucky enough to have caring and courageous parents and other adult role models were able, in later years, to walk through the new and heavy doors that *Brown* slowly and painfully opened—doors that some are trying to close again today.

The adults in our churches and community made children feel valued and important. They took time and paid attention to us. They struggled to find ways to keep us busy. And while life was often hard and resources scarce, we always knew who we were and that the measure of our worth was inside our heads and hearts, and not outside in our possessions or on our backs. We were told that the world had a lot of problems; that Black people had an extra lot of problems, but that we were able and obligated to struggle and change them; that being poor was no excuse for not achieving; and that extra intellectual and material gifts brought with them the privilege and responsibility of sharing with others less fortunate. In sum, we learned that service is the rent we pay for living. It is the very purpose of life and not something you do in your spare time.

When my mother died, an old white man in my hometown of Bennettsville asked me what I do. In a flash I realized that in my work at the Children's Defense Fund I do exactly what my parents did—just on a different scale. My brother preached a wonderful sermon at Mama's funeral, but the best tribute was the presence in the back pew of the town drunk, whom an observer said he could not remember coming to church in many years.

The legacies that parents and church and teachers left to my generation of Black children were priceless but not material: a living faith reflected in daily service, the discipline of hard work and stick-to-it-ness, and a capacity to struggle in the face of adversity. Giving up and "burnout" were not part of the language of my elders—you got up every morning and you did what you had to do and you got up every time you fell down and tried as many times as you had to get it done right. They had grit. They valued family life, family rituals, and tried to be and to expose us to good role models. Role models were of two kinds: those who achieved in the outside world (like Marian Anderson, my namesake) and those who didn't have a whole lot of education or fancy clothes but who taught us by the special grace of their lives the message of Christ and Tolstoy and Gandhi and Heschel and Dorothy Day and Romero and King that the Kingdom of God was within—in what you are, not what you have. I still hope I can be half as good as Black church and community elders like Miz Lucy McQueen, Miz Tee Kelly, and Miz Kate Winston, extraordinary women who were kind and patient and loving with children and others and who, when I went to Spelman College, sent me shoeboxes with chicken and biscuits and greasy dollar bills.

It never occurred to any Wright child that we were not going to college or were not expected to share what we learned and earned with the less fortunate. I was forty years old before I figured out, thanks to my brother Harry's superior insight, that my Daddy often responded to our requests for money by saying he didn't have any change because he *really* didn't have any rather than because he had nothing smaller than a twenty dollar bill.

10   I was fourteen years old the night my Daddy died. He had holes in his shoes but two children out of college, one in college, another in divinity school, and a vision he was able to convey to me as he lay dying in an ambulance that I, a young Black girl, could be and do anything; that race and gender are shadows; and that character, self-discipline, determination, attitude, and service are the substance of life.

I have always believed that I could help change the world because I have been lucky to have adults around me who did—in small and large ways. Most were people of simple grace who understood what Walker Percy wrote: You can get all As and still flunk life.

Life was not easy back in the 1940s and 1950s in rural South Carolina for many parents and grandparents. We buried children who died from poverty (and I can't stand it that we still do). Little Johnny Harrington, three houses down from my church parsonage, stepped on and died from a nail because his grandmother had no doctor to advise her, nor the money to pay for health care. (Half of all low-income urban children under two are still not fully immunized against preventable childhood diseases like tetanus and polio and measles.) My classmate, Henry Munnerlyn, broke his neck when he jumped off the bridge into the town creek because only white children were allowed in the public swimming pool. I later heard that the creek where Blacks swam and fished was the hospital sewage outlet. (Today thousands of Black children in our cities and rural areas are losing their lives to cocaine and heroin and alcohol and gang violence because they don't have enough constructive outlets.) The migrant family who collided with a truck on the highway near my home and the ambulance driver who refused to take them to the hospital because they were Black still live in my mind every time I hear about babies who die or are handicapped from birth when they are turned away from hospitals in emergencies or their mothers are turned away in labor because they have no health insurance and cannot pay pre-admission deposits to enter a hospital. I and my brothers and sister might have lost hope—as so many young people today have lost hope—except for the stable, caring, attentive adults in our family, school, congregation, civic and political life who struggled with and for us against the obstacles we faced and provided us positive alternatives and the sense of possibility we needed.

At Spelman College in Atlanta, I found my Daddy and Mama's values about taking responsibility for your own learning and growth reinforced in the daily (except Saturday) chapel service. Daily chapel attendance was compulsory and enforced by the threat of points taken off one's earned grade average as a result of truancy. For all my rebellion then, I remember now far more from the chapel speakers who came to talk to us about life and the purpose of education than from any class. And during my tenure as chairwoman of Spelman's board, I advocated reinstitution of some compulsory assemblies (monthly, not daily!) so our young women would have to hear what we adults think is important.

Many of my mentors and role models, such as Dr. Benjamin Mays, then president of Morehouse College, Whitney Young, dean of the School of Social Work at Atlanta University and later National Urban League head, M. Carl Holman, a professor at Clark College, later head of the National Urban Coalition, Dr. Howard Thurman, dean of the Chapel at Boston University, and Dr. King, all conveyed the same message as they spoke in Sisters Chapel at Spelman: education is for improving the lives of others and for leaving your community and world better than you found it. Other important influences during my Spelman years—Ella Baker, Septima Clark, Howard Zinn, Charles E. Merrill, Jr., and Samuel Dubois Cook—stretched my vision of the future and of one person's ability to help shape it. I'm still trying to live up to their teachings and to the examples of the extraordinary ordinary people whom I had the privilege to serve and learn from after law school during my civil rights sojourn in Mississippi between 1963 and 1968.

15   Fannie Lou Hamer, Amzie Moore, Winston and Dovie Hudson, Mae Bertha Carter, school desegregation and voting rights pioneers in Mississippi, and Unita Blackwell, who rose from sharecropper to mayor of rural Mayersville, Mississippi—and countless courageous men and women who gave their voices and homes and lives to get the right to vote and to secure for their children a better life than they had—guide and inspire me still. Those largely unknown and usually unlettered people of courage and commitment, along with my parents, remind me each day to keep trying and to let my little light shine, as Mrs. Hamer sang and did through her inspiring life. In a D.C. neighborhood church, I recently saw a banner that reminded me "there is not enough darkness in the world to snuff out the light of even one small candle."

I have always felt extraordinarily blessed to live in the times I have. As a child and as an adult—as a Black woman—I have had to struggle to understand the world around me. Most Americans remember Dr. King as a great leader. I do too. But I also remember him as someone able to admit how often he was afraid and unsure about his next step. But faith prevailed over fear and uncertainty and fatigue and depression. It was his human vulnerability and his ability to rise above it that I most remember. In this he was not different from many Black adults whose credo has been to make "a way out of no way."

The Children's Defense Fund was conceived in the cauldron of Mississippi's summer project of 1964 and in the Head Start battles of 1965, where both the great need for and limits of local action were apparent. As a private civil rights lawyer, I learned that I could have only limited, albeit important, impact on meeting epidemic family and child needs in that poor state without coherent national policy and investment strategies to complement community empowerment strategies. I also learned that critical civil and political rights would not mean much to a hungry, homeless, illiterate child and family if they lacked the social and economic means to exercise them. And so children—my own and other people's—became the passion of my personal and professional life. For it is they who are God's presence, promise, and hope for humankind.

It is the responsibility of every adult—especially parents, educators, and religious leaders—to make sure that children hear what we have learned from the lessons of life and to hear over and over that we love them and that they are not alone. Daddy used to say that in school we got our lessons from our teachers first and then got examined on how well we had learned them. In life the consequences often come first and the lessons afterward. In today's era of AIDS and drugs and violence and too-early and unsafe sex, the consequences can be deadly or last a lifetime. So parental communication, guidance, and example are more crucial than ever.

Too many young people—of all colors, and all walks of life—are growing up today unable to handle life in hard places, without hope, without adequate attention, and without steady internal compasses to navigate the morally polluted seas they must face on the journey to adulthood.

20   As a result, we are on the verge of losing two generations of Black children and youths to drugs, violence, too-early parenthood, poor health and education, unemployment, family disintegration—and to the spiritual and physical poverty that both breeds and is bred by them. Millions of Latino, Native American, and other minority children face similar threats. And millions of white children of all classes, like too many minority children, are drowning in the meaninglessness of a culture that rewards greed and guile and tells them life is about getting rather than giving.

I believe that we have lost our sense of what is important as a people in a world that is reinventing itself at an unprecedented pace both technologically and politically. My generation learned that to accomplish anything, we had to get off the dime. Our children today must learn to get off the paradigm, over and over, and to be flexible, quick, and smart about it.

Children and young adults—all of us—face dazzling international changes and challenges and extraordinary social and economic upheavals. One single decade's profligacy has changed our nation from a lender to a debtor. Our aging population and future work force depend on a shrinking pool of young workers, a majority of whom will be female, minority, or both. Our culturally diverse child and worker population confronts increasing racial and gender intolerance fueled by recession and greed. Our education system is drowning in the wake of the new and flexible skills required in a postindustrial economy. The nurturance of children is at risk as extended families disappear, both parents work, and more children rely on a single parent. A cacophony of cultural messages bombard our children about what they must buy and how they must act to be "with it"—with a nearly deafening silence from too many homes and too-few moral leaders and positive role models in either our private or public lives. Meanwhile, time and economic pressures mount and are unrelieved by extended family networks or family-friendly private sector and public policies.

Despite these social and cultural tidal waves, I believe there are some enduring spiritual, family, community, and national values and lessons that we need to rediscover in this last decade of this last century in this millennium. I agree with Archibald MacLeish that "there is only one thing more powerful than learning from experience and that is not learning from experience."

CONVERSATION STARTER

Did your family encourage you to help at a place of worship or to do other forms of volunteer work in your community? Describe such an experience.

READING MATTERS

1. What did Edelman learn growing up in a racially segregated community in South Carolina in the late 1940s and early 1950s? Contrast your family's values with Edelman's family's values. For example, was there a particular religious or secular community that provided support for you and your family when you were growing up? Did your family value education?

2. Do some research into the 1954 *Brown v. Board of Education* decision. Then explain why it represented a milestone in Edelman's life and the lives of other Black citizens who wanted to have the opportunity to get a good education.
3. What kinds of role models did Edelman have as a child and as an adult? Why were these mentors important to her?
4. Edelman discusses her role in the establishment and success of the Children's Defense Fund. Research the programs that the Children's Defense Fund supports and then explain why this role supports her assertion: "I do exactly what my parents did—just on a different scale."

WRITING MATTERS

1. Edelman believes that "Service is the rent we pay for living. It is the very purpose of life and not something you do in your spare time." Write an essay that discusses why you agree or disagree with her point of view. Refer to your own experiences, Edelman's text, and the ideas of other writers in this chapter to support your point of view.
2. Write about a volunteer or service learning experience that you have had and reflect on what you learned from your experience.
3. Write a research paper that highlights the accomplishments and impact of a community leader who has inspired you.

RELEVANT WEB SITES

THE CHILDREN'S DEFENSE FUND <http://www.childrensdefensefund.org>

The official web site of the Children's Defense Fund (CDF) provides a biography of Marian Wright Edelman's public life and an overview of the program and services available through CDF in support of children.

THE HISTORY MAKERS
<http://www.thehistorymakers.com/biography/biography.asp?bioindex=127&category=civicMakers>

The History Makers is a national nonprofit educational institution committed to preserving, developing, and providing easy access to an internationally recognized, archival collection of thousands of African-American video oral histories and photo archives including Marian Wright Edelman.

Claudia Barker

How to Ya/Ya in Your Neighborhood

Young Aspirations/Young Artists (YA/YA), Inc., a New Orleans nonprofit arts organization, was started in 1988 by painter Jana Napoli. The organization serves students after school and functions as an art school and a community center. The YA/YAs became nationally known through an art exhibit at Lincoln Center in New York that featured their painted chairs, and for creating

582 unique slipcovers for the United Nations General Assembly Room in honor of the UN's fiftieth anniversary. The YA/YAs have traveled in Europe, Japan, and throughout the United States. They have been featured in almost a hundred publications, including Life, Vogue, Fortune, *the* New York Times, *and* New York Magazine.

In the following selection, excerpted from YA/YA! Young New Orleans Artists and Their Storytelling Chairs, *Claudia Barker, who served as the organization's director from l990 to 1995, frames the YA/YAs as a community that functions like a family.*

I think the basic thing that happened with YA/YA is that it started and we became a family before we became an institution, even though the family seems a lot more interesting than the institution. But we actually got to know each other as individuals, as a family, and we grew. We argued, we cried, we lived, we had dinner, we grew.

> *—Darryl White, addressing the National Council on the Arts, August 5, 1994*

In many ways YA/YA resembles a family more than it does an art gallery, school, or community center. Although, as in a gallery, there is a space to display artwork, and as in a school, students gather there regularly—afternoons and weekends—to receive a specific kind of training, YA/YA feels and functions more like a household than an institution. First, there are young people who share the common bond of creativity. Among these young people there are various generations, starting with the very first YA/YA Guild members and continuing across the spectrum to the newest recruits. Various staff members resemble parental figures, big sisters and brothers and even a grandmother or two. Older YA/YAs serve as mentors for younger ones. There are even little kids in the environment sometimes—staff members' children and YA/YAs' little brothers and sisters—running around the space, crayons in hand, ready to join in the fun.

In addition to the people and their personalities, there is another strong familial link: the YA/YA art. The work created by the first YA/YA Guild members started a tradition, a tangible incarnation of the YA/YA spirit and style, that turns up in the work of subsequent "generations" of YA/YAs. Not only does the work have a certain "look," but in some instances younger YA/YAs actually incorporate images by and of the older YA/YAs into their own work, weaving the thread of YA/YA's history into the fabric of their own personal creativity.

September 21, 1994. The YA/YAs are hard at work on their pieces for the upcoming Art for Arts' Sake show, to be held this year at the newly expanded Louisiana Children's Museum. At least three thousand people will see the work, most of them on opening night, which is less than two weeks away. We all stop for a few minutes during our regular Wednesday meeting to do a critique of the works in progress—in this case miniature houses, each with one open side, featuring doll-sized YA/YA furniture and fabric.

The minihouse by Monica Scott, a fourth-generation Guild member, generates much discussion. Monica has transformed her house into an art school. She has carefully crafted draftsmen's tables from what appear to be small spiral notebooks turned horizontally, painted bright jewel tones, and set on pedestals in the shape of the numerals one, two, and three. The effect is strikingly original: a whimsical Dr. Seuss-like tableau that sits waiting for tiny students to come and occupy it.

5   The interior and exterior walls of the little schoolhouse, however, are not so original. Monica has chosen to interpret them literally, pasting pictures cut from magazines on the walls to represent the posters that might adorn a typical art-school studio. A lively discussion begins about whether it is appropriate for Monica to use published images, which are essentially the work of another artist, in her design. Ms. Neske suggests that the only way to do so is to alter the images in some way. Apprentice Eddie Washington says that she could paint mustaches on them all like Marcel Duchamp. Everyone laughs. Monica agrees to rethink her piece in order to make the walls as interesting as the furnishings.

A couple of days later we look at Monica's house. She has taken most of the "posters" off of the walls and replaced them with hand-made items. But that isn't all. Monica covered the outside of the house—its sides, back, and roof—with drawings of various YA/YAs in poses taken from photographs. She has drawn some of the portraits with a thick black paintbrush, then whitewashed over them and superimposed, with a fine black pen, other portraits, some full-length and detailed. The thick figures look like ghosts inhabiting the walls of the house. The penned figures are sophisticated caricatures, drawn by someone who knows her subjects' mannerisms and style of dress. Former YA/YA Lionel Milton appears in his signature horned-rimmed glasses and loose baggy pants. A lanky figure slouches against the side of the house. The backwards baseball cap tells us it is Eric Russell.

Monica has managed to paint the essence of the YA/YA "family" and the many layers of the YA/YA experience: successive generations of YA/YAs *one on top of the other,* a colorful environment for learning, the YA/YAs' images and their strong spirits literally etched into the walls of the place. That's how it *is.*

Family Dynamics

Of course, as in any family, things aren't always smooth. YA/YA has its ups and downs, and since the place isn't very hierarchical, there tends to be a good deal more conversation about them than one would find in most business environments. Over the course of its history, YA/YA has evolved from an unorganized hodgepodge of curious high-school students receiving intense one-on-one training from Jana to a much larger program trying to serve both high-school and college students through the application of a long list of byzantine rules and regulations, and most recently to a third incarnation that combines the best of the two extremes. Getting there, however, hasn't always been easy.

June 1993. YA/YA is closed for two weeks. Clif St. Germain, a friend and educational consultant, has told the staff that we are crazy for opening our doors six days a week with virtually no break from January to December. We breathe a collective sigh of relief and tell the YA/YAs to take a holiday, we are going to sit down and plan the year. We convene daily afternoon marathon sessions, each devoted to a different topic, ranging from the schedule of shows and trips to more basic issues such as "What's the purpose of the program?" and "Who do we really want to serve?

10   Madeleine Neske sees YA/YA's focus as most appropriately directed toward her Rabouin students. She says, "I have a personal commitment to everybody I'm working with. I can't separate myself from them being my students. I'm very possessive of all of my students. Those are my *kids.* I want them to succeed, and I have a lot of students who are not getting the benefits of YA/YA." But Jana and some of the other staff members feel a huge responsibility to the YA/YAs who have graduated and gone on to college. "We haven't done anything if we don't help them get through college and get jobs," Jana says. Madeleine is doing her job, being an advocate for the younger YA/YAs, trying to get the others to understand that the organization has limited resources—staff time, studio space—that should be divided equitably. We try a compromise, limiting the amount of time the college YA/YAs may spend at the studio when the young YA/YAs are there. Still the issue persists, causing tension among staff from time to time.

It's not only the adults, however, who create friction in the environment. The older YA/YAs have been known to vent their frustrations on the younger ones, too. Just as in a family, the older guys are watching the adults; the younger guys are watching the older guys.

Carlos Neville explains how the older YA/YAs felt about the first group of new students: "We had been there for a long time without no one else coming in, nobody even seeming interested. It was like our organization, this is for us, we had made our deal. So when some other kids came in . . . I was just like, Who are they? I had never even learned y'all's names for a whole year. We felt we owned it."

Such resentment looks and sounds and feels a lot like how only children feel when a little brother or sister comes along. Reactions run the gamut from elation ("Now I have somebody to play with, somebody to blame!") to mischief ("Let's see what happens when I set his clothes on fire!"). Of course, as in a family, there are genuine feelings of love and affection once some rapport has been established. And when that is combined with some skill, real mentoring relationships develop. Older students pass on their talents, their good tricks, their shortcuts, their experience to the younger ones. The training cycle turns, stopping every once in awhile to let someone off, pick up someone new. Students become teachers. Younger ones not only listen to what the older ones say, but also watch what they do. Just like adults, the older ones become role models *whether they want to be or not!*

"As everybody grows up, things change," says Chris Paratore. New YA/YAs suddenly begin to know how to paint. They're not new anymore. Then the really new ones come in, not knowing much of anything. For a few months. Then they create something that makes us all stand there in amazement. Then they leave a paint can open and waste thirty dollars' worth of paint. Rondell Crier says, "You should expect when new people come in to . . . act crazy. You should expect it already and try to find out how you gonna handle it."

15   Handling it is a process, not an event.

"What works is that kids need time, and no matter how stupid you are, if you give it to them it works."

—*Jana Napoli, 1994*

As in a family, time is the key: working with young people day after day, with them knowing you are going to be there, at least when you say you will be there. This is what works. Young people desperately need continuity from adults to feel safe and secure. If we adults show youngsters what it *looks* like to be on time, to be where you say you will be, to give them what you have promised them, they will learn how to be responsible adults. If we promise them a piece of ourselves every day at four o'clock and we only manage to show up two days out of the week at four o'clock, we give them the message that they aren't important to us. We also show them that adults don't keep promises, that promises don't mean anything. We teach them irresponsibility. Like trust, continuity doesn't come quickly. Youngsters are right to be wary of adults who promise them the world and don't deliver. Darryl White sums it up for the National Council: "Being in high school, so often we've had a lot of people approach our class, and they would come in and say, 'We want to work with you. We want to do so much with you,' and then like, 'We'll meet you tomorrow.' Come tomorrow, no one's there. But Jana actually didn't do that."

She showed up. Plain and simple. You want to work with youngsters? You show up. And if you have some special skill to offer them, you give them that with your heart and your head and everything that you can remember about how you learned what you know.

In Jana's case, what she knew was painting. "I kept drawing pictures. I wouldn't use words. I'd draw against them and say, 'Is this what you mean?' That way they can defend themselves. Whatever images they keep putting back in, that's what you know is important to them."

Darlene Francis talks about how best to teach: "You shouldn't try to make a person change, because you don't know what's inside their heads and what's inside their heart, their conscious or subconscious. Whatever it is they're trying to do, you should just let them do it and try to help them on the technique, making sure that it doesn't look tacky."

20   You don't have to know how to paint to help youngsters, to make a difference in their lives. What adults have to give can be anything. It can be help with homework. It can be help filling out a financial-aid form for college. It can be an afternoon snack. It can be teaching someone how to use a bandsaw or write a letter. Sometimes it is just sitting there, doing your own work, but knowing that the students know that you are there for them and that you will be there for them until they finish their work.

Carlos Neville says, "I always did mention to people who came in and asked about how they could do it, I say, "If anybody in the community has access to an old factory or building and have some type of skill and they're

retired, that they can offer to the kids . . . ." This is what YA/YA did. This is
how to YA/YA.

Jana agrees. "If you do great at something—a welder, a plumber—and
you do beautiful work, whatever it is that you love, then you can share it
with someone and they've got something to learn. I *love* my profession. I
love painting. I have ultimate respect for making images. I think it's important, the pictures you make. I felt that they should be honest. Images are
important. And people look at them in here and they pick all kinds of stuff
out of them. That's important to me. You have to be confident in the profession you are trying to share."

That is the reason that YA/YA adopted the concept of the guild, in
which more experienced craftsmen share their expertise with younger
apprentices in order to create a product that they can sell to make a living.

In working with young people, it is vital that the adults who are "in
charge" be of sound mind and spirit. We do not say this lightly. Whatever
your problems, if you do not recognize them and consciously work to
resolve them you will pass them on to the next generation. This is as true
at YA/YA as it is in a family. So those of us who work with young people
must be extremely vigilant—hyperaware, in fact—of our fears, our short-
comings, our resentments, and our flaws. We must work to fix them in a
diligent and methodical manner. Otherwise they become ingrained in our
"offspring," who then pass them on to the *next* poor, unsuspecting group of
youngsters.

THE VALUE OF STRUCTURE

25 Wednesday, September 21, 1994. Meeting with the YA/YAs about final
arrangements for the show that opens in ten days. "You have to have your
pieces finished by next Tuesday," I say, "so that they can be varnished and
can dry before we install the show on Friday. Okay? Everybody understand
that?" One of the YA/YAs says, "What's the real deadline?" "What do you
mean?" I ask. "I mean, you know how you all always say the deadline is
this day, and then everybody just keeps working right up until the last
minute and you all let 'em do that. So what's the real deadline? I mean,
when do we *really* have to have it finished or else it can't be in the show?"

We're busted. We know in our hearts that what this person is saying is
absolutely true. We have institutionalized a laissez-faire attitude about
deadlines so much that no one respects them anymore. Clearly it's the
adults' fault. In an effort to be "nice," to go the extra mile for the YA/YAs,
to be as flexible as we possibly can, we have managed to teach them that
deadlines aren't real, aren't important, aren't to be respected. Although we
may have had the best of intentions, we have done the young people a dis-
service. The same thing happens when we fail to suspend or expel someone
who breaks a cardinal rule (such as the need to be enrolled in school to participate in YA/YA.) The organization takes a labored breath, and a grimace
creeps across its collective face. We think we are just bending over backwards to hold on to someone. The others think we are playing favorites.

What we have learned from this is that we must make reasonable rules and then enforce them without exception. It's hard because sometimes we are itching to see a young person succeed and are seduced into believing that if only we give him or her the benefit of the doubt, or a little extra time or special dispensation, then maybe, just maybe, he or she will come through, finish the project, graduate from high school, live a happy life. What we have found instead is that breaking our own rules leads others to disrespect them. We put ourselves in the position of enabling students to circumvent the system, which gives them a false view of life. It ultimately causes a kind of helplessness in them, an inability to deal with the demands of doing business, even a false sense of entitlement.

Of course, sometimes the system works against young people. Rondell Crier: "They got teachers that the students say, 'You're not teaching me good enough.' So they might say, 'Well, you just ain't trying hard enough.' But some people just teach wrong. They teach and nobody in class learns and everybody be failing and, I guess, then they start passing who they want to pass and failing who they want to fail and you can't do nothing about it. Even if you knew all of it before you got in his class, it's still, the way they teach, you just don't pass. But you can't do nothing about it because your voice is not heard."

Is it right that young people's voices are not heard? And perhaps an even more important question: Is their lack of access and power working to anyone's advantage? Or is it just an example of one group trying to keep another down? Remember: historically, oppressors have been people who, above all else, feared losing control.

30   June 1994. The YA/YA staff and alumni (college YA/YAs) are sitting around a big table talking about how best to make the most difficult decisions—for example, which students get to go on trips and compete for the most lucrative jobs. Staff has always made those decisions and always been criticized for them. "Just once," one of us says, "I would like for you guys to see how it feels, how hard it is, to decide who deserves to go on a trip." Someone hits on a brilliant solution: turn this responsibility over to a committee made up of both YA/YAs and staff. Give that committee all the information it needs, such as YA/YAs' records of participation and grades. Have that committee meet regularly to decide these tough questions, and make the committee's judgment final. Heads nod. Seems workable, doesn't it? The YA/YA Committee is born.

This may not seem earthshaking, but to the staff and young people of YA/YA it is the first step in grooming the YA/YAs to take ultimate responsibility for the organization. And that is as it should be.

Making Them Investors

Fall, 1993. YA/YA begins employing some of the YA/YAs as interns. Courtney Clark serves the office as administrative intern, and Chris Paratore works in Print YA/YA as production intern. The YA/YAs perform so well in their jobs that YA/YA decides to hire several more interns, with turnover each semester to give others a chance to compete for the positions. An internship is both a part-time paying job and an honor. It is prestigious to be a YA/YA intern. Competition is stiff and the positions usually go to hard workers who bring a positive attitude along with an excellent portfolio of artwork.

After nearly eight years of doing YA/YA, we keep coming back to the same conclusions: that the YA/YA organization should belong to the young people it serves, and that it is the adults' responsibility to make sure they are given the tools they will need to run it. Part of what they will need to run it is experience, which comes from having the chance to make decisions and implement them—which means the adults have to step back and allow young people to do this.

So we let go. We relinquish control a little. And we give some to the young people so that they may learn to use it. Perhaps most important, we create a means by which the YA/YAs will have direct input into the major decisions that they most care about. They learn respect for one another and for the process of decision making. They learn about compromise. They lean how hard it is to be fair all the time. YA/YA benefits greatly from their insight and their hard work. A new generation of young adults begins to make the decisions about the face of the organization—literally, which faces represent YA/YA on jobs and on the road. It is an important moment in our organization's development, perhaps even more important than the YA/YAs realize.

35   This step is hard for us, as it would be for any concerned parent, teacher, or adult working with students. What if they take the organization that we have worked so hard to create and they fail? What if they make mistakes? So what! We did!

June 1992. On the road in Europe with the YA/YAs. I am trip manager, ticket purchaser, banker. I spend most days counting money, writing things down, making lists, trying to keep a dozen YA/YAs in one place and safe. I lead the way to the train station, stare at a map, go to the ticket counter, try to make myself understood. I ask directions or buy tickets for everyone, then return to the group and say, "This way!" and start walking.

Sometime during the trip, one of the YA/YAs complains: "Why you always taking off and we have to follow you? I mean you just disappear and then come back and we all just standing there!" I think about this. I realize how these very capable people must feel when I do not give them the opportunity to help make the travel arrangements or find out which way to go or hold on to the passports or keep the receipts. I literally deny them the opportunity of learning how to travel. They feel disenfranchised. Powerless. Helpless. I learn a great lesson and do things differently next time.

Unless we allow them to take power, how else will they learn what it means to grow up? Jana tells the members of the National Council on the Arts, "We fought like cats and dogs, and the kids refused absolutely to grow up unless I did it first." Everyone laughs. But she is telling the truth.

"Just because you body grows older doesn't mean you're actually an adult."

        —Darryl White, addressing the National Council on the Arts, 1994

Most of us don't grow up until we are approaching middle age. Think about it. When did you first feel grown-up? When you graduated from college? Got a job? Got married? Had children? Or was it one Saturday morning when you woke up and knew exactly what you wanted to do and went and did it. Being grown-up is a feeling that comes when our adolescence—that time in our lives between puberty and maturity—ends. It's often accompanied by nostalgia, which most always comes out of a sense of loss.

40   Adolescence is scary. It is filled with possibilities, the new awakening of our sexuality, and the beginning of big questions about ourselves. Consequently it is also a time of much turmoil, fear, and rage. Adolescents look at what adults promised them, their images from childhood, compare those pictures with the real world, and get angry. They rail against authority and denounce hypocrisy. That's their *job.*

So-called adults see this and are reminded of our own adolescence. Our response to these big scary pictures is often to slink quietly out of the room and complain that our children are incomprehensible. People who are of adult age chronologically but who have not resolved their adolescent feelings—in other words, most of us—are petrified of dealing with youngsters. We are literally "irresponsible"—unable to respond—when challenged by young people, whether it be about the state of the world adults have made or the reason for a particular rule. We hear things like "That's just the way it is" or "Because I said so" coming out of our mouths, and we remember our parents saying that and cannot believe we are saying the same thing. But we don't know what else to do. We don't have the answers. Our parents weren't grown-up either.

The only solution is to allow youngsters to take some control over their own destinies, to let them push the big buttons that will ultimately catapult them out of adolescence and into responsible adulthood. Training for adulthood involves allowing young people the opportunity to make decisions, make mistakes, and take consequences. Like training for the space program, it is demanding, it is risky, and it occasionally involves being turned upside-down.

The Struggle of Growing

May 5, 1993. Staff gets a letter signed by several of the YA/YAs. It starts off, "What does the term 'at risk' mean? In our opinion, it describes someone or thing that is a danger to their society. YA/YA has fed off of this term, 'at risk,' and has failed to justify their reasons for doing so. To say you use the term 'at risk' because we are all 'at risk' and any one of us could get killed today is both a cop-out and a lame excuse. Yes, it's true that society at large isn't safe, but you can't generalize a group of high school kids in order to get grants. It's immoral, and very demoralizing. Basically it's conforming to white society's prejudices about minorities. They want us to be 'at risk' because it keeps us 'at risk' mentally. If you keep telling someone, you're a nothing, you'll never be as good as you think you are, people start to believe it."

Strong words from a bunch of "adolescents." The letter gives us pause. We have given the YA/YAs the power to speak out, and they speak loudly and clearly. In addition to anger over the use of "at risk," the letter states the YA/YAs' desire to suspend the weekly group-counseling sessions that YA/YA requires they attend and criticizes the staff for failing to have YA/YAs and their parents ratify the newly created YA/YA Charter.

45   The experience is an empowering one for the YA/YAs. Gradually we begin hearing more from them—about the way they are portrayed in the press, about their frustrations with the adults who run YA/YA, and about the way they see themselves and the organization. As the young people grow up, they demand that the organization change to accommodate them. Staff resolves not to use the term *at risk* to describe the people who participate in the YA/YA program.

As the organization changes and grows, it attracts more and different people—ones who think of YA/YA as an institution that they are bound and determined to join. The earliest YA/YAs came because they were curious and wanted to do artwork; the people who now compete to join YA/YA do so because it is a prestigious extracurricular activity that will afford them many opportunities. The first YA/YAs were pioneers who cut a trail for everyone else. Their success made YA/YA the desirable place it is for everyone who comes after them.

Apprentice Caprica Joseph says she was determined to make her way into YA/YA, even though she is younger than most of the students YA/YA normally takes. "I said, 'Oh, no! They not lettin' in no ninth graders!' And I said, 'Oh yeah? I'm gonna get in.'" So she starts coming to YA/YA every day after school and volunteering for jobs and projects. She paints YA/YA desk ornaments. She paints her first baby chair. It sells to some tourists before she even has a chance to photograph it. She makes herself known in the organization, she takes to everybody, she watches what the older YA/YAs do, and she paints and paints. She becomes a part of the YA/YA family.

And the family grows up. We watch the YA/YAs handle themselves and their clients, and we begin to see young professionals. We remember how they used to be and we make comparisons and we smile at the leaps and bounds a young person makes in a few short years.

DOING BUSINESS, GAINING PERSPECTIVE

November 1993. The YA/YAs have been commissioned by a company called Bishop Partners in New York to make 150 miniature chairs, in six different designs. The company chooses two designs by Edwin Riley and one each by Chris Paratore, Tarrie Alexis, Darlene Francis, and Shazell Johnson. Rondell Crier gets the job of art director. He runs the project, deals with the client, gets the wood cut to make the chairs, puts them together, and makes sure everybody does his or her work in a timely manner.

50   It is, however, the job from hell. It is like a giant cuckoo clock with hundreds of moving pieces that must click into place in order for it to work

properly. Nothing clicks. Everybody is trying hard, but the YA/YAs don't have any idea how complicated a job it is or how long it will take. Almost everyone is late submitting designs—and time is a problem because the older YA/YAs are rushing to get the job finished during their holiday break from school and the client is anxious for delivery. Rondell is trying to keep on top of five designers to design and then paint the chairs. The work is uneven and some of it has to be redone. Rondell not only has to order special small boxes to package each little chair, but also has to go and get the boxes and assemble them. Mrs. Dennis, YA/YA's operations coordinator, gets stuck staying half the night to get the pieces boxed and shipped on time. The client isn't happy with the quality of some of them, which come back and have to be repainted. The job drags on and on. It is the first job that the YA/YAs really manage on their own, and they learn great lessons in doing it.

A year later Susan Bishop calls again. For the tenth anniversary of her business, she wants to commission a poster that features one of the little chairs, shown from a variety of angles, above her company's name. This time the YA/YAs are ready. Shazell and Rondell talk to Ms. Bishop to determine exactly what she wants, how much she is willing to pay for it, and when she needs it. They negotiate the terms of the job and collaborate with the other YA/YAs on the poster design. Together they create a tight design that the client approves, and they provide finished artwork that sings, and they do it on time. The client is happy.

The YA/YAs are happy, too. They feel good because they get repeat business from an important client who took the time to engage in their learning process during the first job. Ms. Bishop is willing to deal directly with the YA/YAs and holds them accountable for the quality of their work. Working with her enhances their professionalism, helps them along their path of self-sufficiency. After the job is done, they are a little closer to grown-up. And they are aware of the difference between how they handled the job a year ago and how they handle it now. They gain perspective.

And they become colleagues. From collaborations like this one the YA/YAs learn who possesses which skills, who can be depended upon to do which piece of a job. Now, when one YA/YA gets a commission, especially a commercial art job, he or she often calls upon another YA/YA—or former YA/YA—to help.

GAINING PERSPECTIVE

October 1994. Eric Russell and Carlos Neville visit Ms. Neske's commercial-art class at Rabouin High School. Everything is chaos. Too many students are trying to draw and paint in a small space, they are laughing loud and ribbing each other and not paying real attention to the assignment. Madeleine is doing her best to keep order in a crazy, creative environment full of boisterous sixteen-year-olds. Afterward she asks Eric and Carlos if they have any suggestions about how she could handle the class better. "Nope," Eric says, smiling and shaking his head. "No recommendations?" she asks her alumni. "Nope," Eric repeats, and looks right at her. "There's not a thing you can do. It's just their age."

THE VERY BIG PICTURE

55 When we really look at what we are doing at YA/YA, at how much what we are doing affects people's lives, we are overwhelmed. The time, attention, and money, the pieces of ourselves that all of us—staff and students—invest in this YA/YA "monster" (as former staff member Lyndon Barrois once called it) are enormous. It is by no means "just a job" for any of us who work here. It is by no means "just an extracurricular activity" for any of the young people who come here every day.

Doing YA/YA is a commitment, pure and simple. By investing so much of ourselves and so much of other people's money in YA/YA, we are making a contract to be good stewards. The responsibility is a shared one. Both students and staff are stating, every single day, that what we are doing is important and that we will strive to do our very best with what we have been given. And we have been given so much. Money from generous people, the space, both physical and emotional, in which to grow. YA/YA is a kind of laboratory in which we all come together to perform a noble experiment with one anothers' lives. Can we really make a difference, a long-term difference, in how we live with one another? Can we really affect the *quality* of one anothers' lives?

The answer is yes, or else we wouldn't be doing this. Jana tells the YA/YAs: "Think about it. Try to work hard. Get out there and do your best because it's a lot of money and some other kid could be eating off this plate." Participating in the experiment is a big responsibility. It means being far more serious than the average adolescent *or adult* tends to be about doing one's job. It means being responsible. And it is doubly hard because the more press attention and opportunities come YA/YA's way, the bigger the stakes and the more we have to lose. And if we lose it, we lose it for everyone—not just for the young people we currently serve, but for all those who might have come after them, and for every young person around the nation and world who might have benefited from YA/YA's success. If we lose it, if we don't meet the highest standards of performance, then we make right all those people who look at YA/YA and say, "Those are just kids! Who do they think they are?" We give credence to every naysayer, every detractor, every person who gains something by denigrating what the YA/YAs have worked so hard to do.

So our message in the YA/YA laboratory, to ourselves and to the students, is to use resources wisely—whether it is in the form of your own time, someone else's time, or the contents of a brand new paint can—or you may not get any more.

There is another kind of stewardship that is vital to YA/YA and is paramount in any endeavor whose focus is on young people. It goes beyond banking and bookkeeping, it is far more important than being written up in

the newspaper, and it transcends the daily rules by which we run the organization. It is the careful stewardship of young people's souls. Sound awesome? It is.

60   When a youngster chooses to participate in something like YA/YA, it is
as if he were walking carefully down a hallway, heart and soul held lightly
in cupped hands, offering the best pieces of himself to relative strangers
waiting at the other end. It is a risky business, particularly if that young
person is asked to reach down into the depths of his experience and pull out
images that mean something to him, draw them on a piece of paper, and
then share them with others. The amount of trust involved is enormous.
Therefore, the way we receive those images, the level of respect we give
them and the person who made them, is critical. We adults must value the
creativity and the spirit of young people and guard it from harm. It is the
job of adults to serve as advocates for the young people who entrust us with
themselves. This means not competing with them and not envying their
success—or trying to own it—even if we help them achieve it.

Adults, who presumably see a bigger picture than youngsters, must act
as catalysts, as gadflies—goading, pushing, often annoying young people
into action. Sharon Riley, mother of YA/YA Guild member Edwin Riley,
witnessed Jana Napoli's tactics. She describes them to a group of the students: "She was a thorn in your side just like you were a thorn in hers. She
got you to clean up and she got you to do this and that. And you showed the
people on the outside, 'I am worthy to be here.' And you showed the people
on the inside, 'I am worthy to be here.' And that's why it works."

Another reason it works is because as the YA/YAs grow up, they venture
out of the organization. Trips to other cities, schools, and organizations
allow the students to experience other environments. Internships in other
places allow them to work in new frames of reference. The students know
the value of this. Rondell Crier, who has had internships in Washington and
Chicago, advocates encouraging students to leave the nest. "Y'all see somebody staying at YA/YA—push them! When they get old enough, shove them
away! Go see around before they trap themselves and then when they get
older they like, 'God, I wish I could have been . . . ' Who knows, maybe they
might leave, maybe they might like it. Maybe they might come back on
their own. Let them." He also says, "All kids need a life. You have to have
fun—a fun life."

THE MODEL: TAKE WHAT YOU LIKE AND LEAVE THE REST

If we have learned anything through the YA/YA experience about working
with talented youngsters, it is that whatever works should be shared.
YA/YA can offer the world a model of how to take young people from one
level to another. The point of sharing what YA/YA has done, whether it be
in training sessions in other cities or through this book, is not to say, "Look
how great we are," but rather to say, "Look how many mistakes we made
and we still managed to do something extraordinary! Don't be afraid to try!"

Bill Strickland, a National Council on the Arts member and founder of the highly successful Manchester Craftsmen's Guild in Pittsburgh, suggests that YA/YA may have something to offer: "I think that you should be replicated in every community, in every child's life in this country, without a doubt. The kind of thing that you're representing here today in its elegance and its simplicity is precisely the path of hope that our nation's youth have lost."

65   National Council member Wendy Luers comments on the importance of investing in individuals, in the Jana Napolis of the world, who have the vision and the passion to make an experiment like YA/YA a success: "We can't clone you, but we should try to define what the 'you' is."

It is a tall order. The "you" must include the artistic vision, the space, the money, the interested young people, and the generosity of many individuals. But perhaps most important, the "you" must include the passion and, as Cheryl Bowmer, NEA site visitor, calls it, the "single-mindedness" that drives Jana Napoli and people like her who want to work with youth. Therein lies the magic that makes any "noble experiment" a success. This driving force is also what will make each "experiment" unique.

There can be no other YA/YA. But there can be any number of successful efforts in which caring adults work with youngsters to nurture their creativity and teach them to make a living. It might be through writing, or through performance, or through some specialized craft or skill. The key element is having adults who know how to do something well, love what they do, and have the desire to share it with younger people. If you really have this, then everything else—the space, the money, the young people, even the product—falls into place.

CONVERSATION STARTER

If you have participated in a collaborative art project such as a theater production, an art show, or a dance performance, share the reasons why you valued this experience.

READING MATTERS

1. How does the YA/YA community function like a family? Why does Monica's house capture the essence of the YA/YA family?
2. How do the "parents" (founders and teachers) of YA/YA teach their students? Why did they become a Guild?
3. Why do the YA/YA adults give their students some of their challenging financial, artistic, and planning responsibilities? What, for example, did the YA/YAs learn from their European road trip in 1992? What did they learn from the experience of making 150 mini-chairs for the Bishop Partners firm in New York?
4. In what ways is a sense of stewardship essential to the YA/YA community? Why is risk crucial to the growth and success of the YA/YA project? What other values are fundamental to the YA/YA's success?

Writing Matters

1. Write a paper for your class or for publication in a local community paper that profiles a nonprofit organization that helps families.
2. Do some research into the YA/YA project. Focus on an aspect of its mission and success that you find especially interesting. Write a paper for your class that presents a profile of the project.
3. Develop some of your insights from the Conversation Starter discussion into an essay.

Relevant Web Sites

Louisiana Division of the Arts <http:/www.crt.state.la.us/arts>

The Louisiana Division of the Arts web site provides a guide to the art programs in Louisiana and highlights many of the different Youth Aspirations/ Young Artists projects.

National Endowment for the Arts <http:/www.artsendow.gov>

This official web site of the National Endowment for the Arts allows you to search all the projects that they support including the Youth Aspirations/ Young Artists.

Cleve Jones

The NAMES Project: "The Vision Quilt"

In June of 1987, a small group of close friends met in a San Francisco storefront to begin a project that would document the lives of many people who had died of AIDS. Cleve Jones and Mike Smith, the project's leaders, wanted to create a memorial for those who had died of AIDS and to help people understand the devastating impact of the disease. The AIDS Memorial Quilt, the resulting memorial, is a powerful visual reminder of the AIDS epidemic. More than 42,000 individual 3- by 6-foot memorial panels, each one commemorating the life of someone who has died of complications related to AIDS, have been sewn together by friends, lovers, and family members. The NAMES Project Foundation coordinates displays of the Quilt worldwide.

A Vision of the Quilt

After eight months on Maui I was back in the Castro. I had no job, no money, and was sleeping on a friend's couch (Jim Foster had taken me in). But I had a plan. I'd written a speech that I hoped would reignite the will to fight. I would give my speech at the candlelight march commemorating the day Harvey Milk and George Moscone had been shot. After that, who knows? I never really worried about career and fortune in those days. I was surviving, and that seemed quite a lot.

It's hard to communicate how awful it was in the fall of 1985. I'd left town out of my own fear and frustration. And somehow that sabbatical had been recuperative. Physically I felt fine. The shingles had left with only lingering tingles. And I'd gotten myself out of the coke and drinking routine thanks in part to Randy Shilts, an old friend from the Haight-Ashbury days. He, alone among my friends, had encouraged me to go to an AA meeting. It was hard as hell to attend those first meetings. Then, slowly, I broke the pattern and eventually learned to sleep without numbing myself with drink.

But there was something different in the San Francisco I returned to. Everyone seemed exhausted, almost fatalistic about AIDS. I understood that, certainly; but I also detected signs of hope within the despair. For one, the media had caught on to what was happening. Randy, who'd been a staff writer for the *Advocate,* was hired full-time by the *Chronicle* to write weekly AIDS columns, and he was extremely dogged in his attempts to puncture all the myths. There was a piece on the fallacy of AIDS being transmitted by mosquito bites, by tainted water, by waiters handling dinner plates. He went into AIDS wards and interviewed the nursing staff and doctors, and the truth was coming out.

Other newspapers followed his lead, and the public began to learn, if not always to accept, that this disease was not divine retribution. And other "points of light" flared up. Bobbi Campbell and his lover sat smiling on the cover of *Newsweek* in an article on the new disease—appearing shockingly alive and productive. There were respected physicians speaking out against the panic. These were all important achievements, but still it was just so much whistling in the dark. We desperately needed an immediate fix, and it wasn't even on the horizon.

5   Seven years before, on the night of Harvey Milk's murder, I swore to myself that he would not be forgotten and began organizing a candlelight march to mark the day of his and Mayor Moscone's deaths. It had become a ritual, with thousands attending every year. A few days prior to the 1985 march, my friend Joseph Durant and I were working the Castro handing out leaflets reminding people of the candlelight memorial. We stopped to get a slice at Marcello's Pizza and I picked up a *Chronicle.* The front-page heading was chilling: "1,000 San Franciscans Dead of AIDS." I'd known most of them from my work with the KS Foundation. Virtually every single one of them had lived within a ten-block radius of where we were standing at Castro and Market. When I walked up Eighteenth Street from Church to Eureka, I knew the ugly stories behind so many windows. Gregory died behind those blue curtains. Jimmy was diagnosed up that staircase in that office behind the venetian blinds. There was the house Alex got kicked out of when the landlord found an empty bottle of AZT in his trash can: "I'm sorry, we just can't take any chances." I wasn't losing just friends, but also all the familiar faces of the neighborhood—the bus drivers, clerks, and mailmen, all the people we know in casual yet familiar ways. The entire Castro was populated by ghosts.

And yet, as I looked around the Castro with its charming hodge-podge of candy-colored Victorians, there were guys walking hand in hand, girls kissing each other hello, being successfully, freely, openly who they were. So much had been accomplished since the closeted days when the community met furtively in a back-alley culture. The Castro was a city within the city, an oasis and harbor for thousands who lived there and millions of gay men and lesbian women around the world for whom it symbolized freedom. And now, in what should have been its prime, it was withering.

Angrily, I turned to Joseph: "I wish we had a bulldozer, and if we could just level these buildings, raze Castro. . . . If this was just a graveyard with a thousand corpses lying in the sun, then people would look at it and they would understand and if they were human beings they'd have to respond." And Joseph, always the acid realist, told me I was the last optimist left standing: "Nobody cares, Cleve. This thing doesn't touch them at all."

November 27, 1985, the night of the memorial march, was cold and gray. As we waited for people to gather, Joseph and I handed out stacks of poster board and Magic Markers, and through the bullhorn I asked everyone to write down the name of a friend who'd been killed by AIDS. People were a little reluctant at first, but by the time the march began we had a few hundred placards. Most of the marchers just wrote first names, Tom or Bill or George; some of the signs said "My brother" or "My lover," and a few had the complete names—first, middle, and last—in bold block letters.

That Thanksgiving night we marched as we had for six years down Market Street to city hall, a sea of candles lighting up the night. One of the marchers asked me who else would be speaking this year and I said, "No one else. Just me. People are tired of long programs anyway." I was an angry, arrogant son of a bitch. The candles we'd been carrying were stumps by the time we'd gathered at Harvey Milk Memorial Plaza at city hall.

10 ". . . We are here tonight to commemorate the deaths of Supervisor Harvey Milk and Mayor George Moscone, victims of an assassin's bullets seven years ago this very day . . . " I talked of Harvey and how even back then he was not really our first martyr, that we'd lost many people to murder and suicide and alcohol and AIDS. "Yes, Harvey was our first collective martyr, but now we have many more martyrs and now our numbers are diminished and many of us have been condemned to an early and painful death. But we are the lesbian women and gay men of San Francisco, and although we are again surrounded by uncertainty and despair, we are survivors and we shall survive again and the dream that was shared by Harvey Milk and George Moscone will go forward . . . "

Then we moved down Market to the old federal building. At that time it housed the offices of Health and Human Services—not such an effective rallying point as city hall, but perfect for our next demonstration, one that turned out to have more impact than I ever imagined. Earlier in the day, Bill Paul, a professor at San Francisco State University, and I had hidden extension ladders and rolls of tape in the shrubbery around the building's base. As the federal building came into view, I ended the chanting ("Stop AIDS now! Stop AIDS now!") and explained through the bullhorn that we were going to plaster the facade with posters inscribed with our dead. And that's what happened. The crowd surged forward, the ladders were set in place, and we crawled up three stories, covering the entire wall with a poster-board memorial.

It was a strange image. Just this uneven patchwork of white squares, each with handwritten names, some in script and some in block letters, all individual. We stared and read the names, recognizing too many. Staring upward, people remarked: "I went to school with him" . . . "I didn't know he was dead" . . . "I used to dance with him every Sunday at the I-Beam" . . . "We're from the same hometown" . . . "Is that our Bob?"

There was a deep yearning not only to find a way to grieve individually and together but also to find a voice that could be heard beyond our community, beyond our town. Standing in the drizzle, watching as the posters absorbed the rain and fluttered down to the pavement, I said to myself, *It looks like a quilt.* As I said the word *quilt,* I was flooded with memories of home and family and the warmth of a quilt when it was cold on a winter night.

And as I scanned the patchwork, I saw it—as if a Technicolor slide had fallen into place. Where before there had been a flaking gray wall, now there was a vivid picture and I could see quite clearly the National Mall, and the dome of Congress and a quilt spread out before it—a vision of incredible clarity.

15   I was gripped by the same terror and excitement that I'd felt standing before other large works commemorating other large issues. Not long ago I'd seen Christo's running fence in Sonoma County. It was a beautiful and moving sight, and I was struck by the grandeur of those vast expanses of shimmering opalescent fabric zigzagging up and down the golden hills. How it billowed in the breeze with the light playing off it, like a string of azure tall ships sailing on a golden sea. And there was the memory of Judy Chicago's *The Dinner Party.* This was a long table, maybe one hundred feet in length, with each place setting designed by a different artist. Both Christo and Judy Chicago had taken commonplace items, sheets drying on a line in his case, plates and utensils in hers, and by enlarging them had made the homely a dramatic, powerfully moving statement. It seemed an apt synthesis: individual quilts, collected together, could have the same immense impact.

When I told my friends what I'd seen, they were silent at first, and as I tried to explain it, they were dubious: "Cleve, don't you realize the logistics of doing something like that? Think of the difficulty of organizing thousands of queers!" But I knew there were plenty of angry queers with sewing machines. I wouldn't be working alone, I told my friends. Everyone understands the idea of a quilt. "But it's gruesome," they said.

That stopped me. Was a memorial morbid? Perhaps it was. And yet there is also a healing element to memorials. I thought of the Vietnam Veterans Memorial wall. I did not expect to be moved by it. I was influenced by the Quakers, who are suspicious of war memorials, which they believe tend to glorify war rather than speak to the horror of it. But I was overwhelmed by the simplicity of it, of that black mirrorlike wall and the power it had to draw people from all across America to find a beloved's name and touch it and see their face reflected in the polished marble and leave mementos.

So I thought about all these things and also about how quilting is viewed as a particularly American folk art. There was the quilting bee with its picture of generations working together, and the idea that quilts recapture history in bits of worn clothing, curtains, jackets—protective cloth. That it was women who did the sewing was an important element. At the time, HIV was seen as the product of aggressive gay male sexuality, and it seemed that the homey image and familial associations of a warm quilt would counter that.

The idea made so much sense on so many different levels. It was clear to me that the only way we could beat this was by acting together as a nation. Though gays and lesbians were winning political recognition in urban centers, without legitimate ties to the larger culture we'd always be marginalized. If we could somehow bridge that gap of age-old prejudice, there was hope that we could beat the disease by using a quilt as a symbol of solidarity, of family and community; there was hope that we could make a movement that would welcome people—men and women, gay or straight, of every age, race, faith, and background.

20   To this day, critics ignore one of the most powerful aspects of the Quilt. Any Quilt display, no matter how small or large, is filled with evidence of love—the love between gay men and the love we share with our lesbian sisters as well as love of family, father for son, mother for son, among siblings. Alongside this love, the individual quilts are filled with stories of homophobia and how we have triumphed over it. There's deep and abiding pain in letters attached to the quilts from parents bemoaning the fact that they didn't accept their dead son. And there's implacable anger in the bloodsplashed quilts blaming President Reagan for ignoring the killing plague. All these messages are part of a memorial that knows no boundaries. We go to elementary schools, high schools, the Bible Belt of the Deep South, rural America, Catholic churches, synagogues, and wherever we unfold this fabric we tell the story of people who've died of AIDS.

That night, standing with those few men and women in the damp and dark, I saw a way out for all of us, a method surmounting our fears and coming together in a collective memorial of our experience: all the sadness, rage, and anger; all the hope, all the dreams, the ambitions, the tragedy.

Eleven years later, this picture in my mind's eye became reality. But that night in November 1985 it was just an idea, and on the 8 Market bus up to the Castro, my friend Joseph Durant and Gilbert Baker and Joseph Canalli were unimpressed. Reagan will never let you do it, they said. Straight families won't join any cause with a bunch of San Francisco queers. It was late, they were tired. An AIDS quilt was a sweet idea, but it was morbid, corny, impossibly complicated. Give it up. But I was on fire with the vision. The idea made so much sense, in so many ways—the irony and truth of it. I couldn't get it out of my head.

Names Project

The Names Project produced a book that contains letters from people who made quilt squares for the AIDS memorial quilt. We have included three of these letters in the pages that follow.

Paul Rohrer taught social studies at Edison Junior High School in Council Bluffs, Iowa, in 1969. He began teaching there the year after I had gone on to high school. However, he had my sister in his class and I frequently had afterschool conversations with him and my English teacher, Beth Reeves, when I visited there. This was during the Vietnam era and I was in a period of moral, ethical, political and personal searching. Though sexuality was not discussed, I was not surprised when I saw him at a gay bar in Omaha, Nebraska, during the summer I came out (1974). This was very important to me. I was not certain that I could be gay and still be everything else that I had come to know about myself. Paul was an example of a man with enormous personal integrity who was gay. My last conversation with him was when he visited St. Paul in 1984. We talked about the process that brought us from adult/child, teacher/student to being together as two equal adults. He died of AIDS in the winter of 1986.

Keith Gann

AIDS QUILT: LETTER ONE

Keith Gann planned to make a difference in the world. He grew up in a working-class, fundamentalist Christian family of nine. Hunting and fishing were the things that boys did in his Iowa town. Keith, however, became an avid newspaper reader, a straight-A student, president of the student council and editor of the high school yearbook. He had his own ideas of what education should be. In high school, he formed an alternative study group in which members read Native American legends and explored gestalt therapy.

Keith owed much of his strong-minded, independent streak to the nurturing and encouragement provided by a few role models including Paul Rohrer. Paul's influence helped Keith, 33, decide to take on his life's work as a social worker, caring for mentally retarded adults and working for Child Protective Services in St. Paul, Minnesota.

Not long after hearing about Paul's death, Keith found that he, too, had AIDS. Keith entered the hospital with pneumocystis pneumonia in January 1987, having been diagnosed a year previously with ARC. He had lost a lot of weight and was scared. The same day he called home to tell his family that he had AIDS, his sister-in-law had a baby boy and they were celebrating the birth of this new child. His youngest brother was about to be married in February, so Keith's mother suggested that they put off telling the rest of the family about his diagnosis until after the wedding.

Keith discouraged his mother and sister from visiting him in the hospital because it has always been important to him that he look good in front of his family. Now it became urgent for him to speak with his family. "In the summer, I realized that I wanted to let them into my life more," he says. "I decided that I had to take the lead in order for them to get to know me again and to get to know what it's like for me living with this disease, and what it might be like for them."

5   In August, Keith went home to talk to his parents. He knew that they had not mentioned his AIDS diagnosis to anybody. He wanted to say to them, "Your secrecy makes me feel that you are ashamed of me. You are ashamed that I have AIDS and that I am gay. There is no time left for shame."

In trying to come up with a loving, creative way to broach the subject of his illness and his probable early death—something that they were not ready to deal with—Keith brought a project home. He had decided to make a quilt panel for his teacher, Paul Rohrer. "The idea was to make visiting my family a bit easier," Keith explains. "Sometimes they get bored, and this would give us something to do. It might open the door for us to talk about my having AIDS. Because Paul was from Council Bluffs, I thought it would bring it closer to home."

As it turned out, the Ganns were fully engaged with canning and other harvest activities. "I really do understand that when the crops are in, you have to can, so I didn't take it personally," Keith says, laughing. "But I was disappointed. Bringing Paul's panel home didn't really accomplish what I had set out to do."

Nevertheless, Keith recruited other helpers. He asked his high school girlfriend, Cathy, and her mother to work on Paul's panel. Working in the basement at the home of Cathy's parents, they sewed into the night—four in the morning, to be exact, although Cathy's mom went to bed at about one. When Keith was first diagnosed, Cathy checked out a videotape about AIDS from the library for Keith's parents. She hoped it would help prepare them for what was ahead.

Keith wanted Paul's panel to salute the strength he had learned from the older man. "He had shown me some solid values, integrity, and concern about justice in the world," says Keith. "I had this fear that coming out as a gay man would just be glitter and glitz. Knowing Paul helped me realize that my sexuality would be one part of my life and would fit with everything else."

10   After a conversation with a reporter, Keith asked his mother if she would mind his story being included in an article about The Quilt.

"What if people turned against us?" she asked.

"Possibly one of your friends will see my name or face and associate me with AIDS or being gay," Keith told his mother. "If that happens, I'm really sorry if they treat you badly. But it's not your fault or my fault—it's their fault. I need to do this—speak out about AIDS—this is for us!"

"Go ahead. You'll do what you want to do anyway," she replied, reminding Keith of the way she used to respond when he nagged her as a kid.

In fact, Keith decided to make a television commercial educating the public about safe sex, and he's editing a newsletter for people affected by AIDS called *PW Alive!*

15   Despite his scrupulous presentation as he laid out his need for total acceptance, his mother could not support him enthusiastically. Keith

thought that she'd never understand until one day she explained a private anecdote from her own life. Ever since her children were little, she had sewn pillows, stuffed animals, quilts and clothes for them. She told him that she will always continue to make things despite her debilitating arthritis because she wants her children to have something to remember her by. "I suddenly felt kind of naked," says Keith. "It's one thing being able to look at the possibility of my own death, but to hear that expressed so openly by my mother caught me off guard. She did understand what I was talking about after all. The connection was so strong and so clear—how each of us are facing mortality—each other's and our own."

Although Keith's illness wasn't mentioned at his brother's wedding, everyone sensed that this could be their last time together. Relatives kept snapping photographs of Keith, and he knew exactly what was going on. This event had to be perfect. It was, after all, the first Gann wedding where there was no major family fight. When he was first diagnosed, Keith's greatest fear was that his brothers and sisters would not want him to be around their children. One of the joys of his trips home is the time he spends with his nieces and nephews.

"I'm letting my family know more than ever before who I am," says Keith. "The reality is that I do respect all of them, and myself, and have worked real hard to come to a place where I can be myself and maintain a relationship with them."

AIDS QUILT: LETTER TWO

Arla Ellsworth thought she had a typical suburban marriage. John, her husband of 22 years, was a lawyer and vice-president of a church-oriented insurance group in Washington, D.C. He traveled frequently, but that, too, was typical. Sometimes she wished that there was more "togetherness" in their marriage, but then, so did all her friends.

Arla's perception of her world turned upside down on June 10, 1986, when the family doctor called to inform her that her husband was dying of AIDS. They had just spent ten days vacationing together in Hawaii. John hadn't told her that he was sick. Five days after their return he was hospitalized, and Arla learned for the first time that he had AIDS meningitis. Six months later he was dead.

20   Arla wanted to believe that John contracted AIDS from a blood transfusion, but she knew very well that he had never had one. "First there was this numbness," she says. "I didn't want it to penetrate. I didn't want to know that John was gay. I couldn't deal with the stigma and the betrayal. But I knew that I was going to have to face it. I tried, I didn't know too much then, to talk to John about the fact that I realized that he was bisexual." John responded with denials that he had AIDS. He also denied that he had sex with men.

John was in the hospital for six weeks, and Arla visited him every day. Their children visited, too. Arla told the children, a son in college and a daughter in high school, that their father had AIDS. Nevertheless, John's denials persisted. "John didn't want to talk," Arla remembers. "The kids didn't want to talk. I didn't know what to do. Nobody wanted to talk. It was like a nightmare."

Arla didn't know how to care for John when he came home from the hospital. "Do you need to wear gloves and gown up like the nurses do?" she wondered. She didn't know if she could sit on the bed. "I needed to know more than how much Clorox and water you mixed to clean things," she says. "I needed to know how to relate day to day."

While John was still in the hospital, Arla attended her first AIDS Support Group meeting where she met Randy Reichart, a 24-year-old art student with pneumocystis. "Randy was blond and fair and hardly had to shave," Arla remembers. She was the only woman in the room, as well as the only straight person. "I went to strangers—people I thought that I'd never rub shoulders with—for support," she says.

Arla invited Randy, his brother Allen and Allen's lover Didier for dinner soon after John got out of the hospital. "John and Randy were the only people we—the kids and me—knew who had AIDS," says Arla. "To all be sitting at the table in our backyard, breaking bread together, was the closest we, as a family of four, got to acknowledging that John had AIDS. This would be the most open we could be about it. Randy asked John how he got AIDS, and once again John replied that he wasn't sure that he actually had AIDS."

25   After John died in November 1986, Arla still felt hurt and betrayed. Sometimes she questioned how much he really loved her. Because John refused to deal with his prognosis, Arla had to attend to all the papers in his estate after he died. She found letters confirming his gay life. "I was always pushing for more intimacy," she says. "He had led me to believe that I was enough," she recalls. "Now I know for a fact that I could never be enough." What kept going through her mind over and over again was, "If he cared about me at all, how could he have put me at risk? He never did anything to protect me. Of all the people in my life, how could this person, my husband, be dangerous to me?" Arla has since tested negative for HIV antibodies.

In her mind, Arla knew that she wanted to forgive John, but she couldn't bring herself to think about their good times together. "Will my heart always be a rock?" she wondered. "When will I be able to feel again?"

Allen Reichart encouraged her to make a commemorative panel for John to be included in The NAMES Project quilt. Arla's 17-year-old daughter didn't want her father's name on the quilt. "It would make me uncomfortable," she admits. "I don't want people to be nasty to me and my friends." So in black glitter, in the space where the name should be, she simply wrote "Love you Dad."

Making the quilt helped Arla remember some of the happy times with John again. The shoelaces she sewed into it are for hiking and the green around the heart is for Christmas, two of John's great loves. She also attached a bit of the purple fabric from Randy Reichart's memorial panel around the heart. Their 21-year-old son, a business major, ironed on the decals, and Arla's mother helped put the panel together.

A full year after John's death, Arla went to the cemetery. She lay on his grave, wanting to be close to him, and cried. "I'm no longer crying because I'm mad at what you have done to me," she said. "I'm crying out of love and forgiveness. What a lonely life you must have had, John, not really knowing who you were.

30   "It's almost Christmas. I can't believe that you are not here to cut down our tree and stop for coffee, just as we always do. Christmas together, making love in front of the fireplace. I want to be near you. I want to be with you. I want you back.

"Now I feel like other people, mourning someone I loved so much," says Arla. "Now I can say, 'I love you for you, whoever you were. I love you for all you gave to my life.' There was pain for me that John was dishonest, but then I think of the joy that John had from having children. I wouldn't want to deprive him of that. I was married to him and I've got these two beautiful kids.

"I had a driving need to stay with people with AIDS and people who are gay. The men in my support group helped me get acquainted with a side of John I didn't know—the giving, caring side of the gay personality. I'm lucky that there are men who have been willing to open themselves to me.

"I never thought that I'd be in the minority with a bunch of gay people," Arla says. "I wanted to find out about AIDS, but I have learned so much more. Some nights I can't sleep. Thoughts about the inhumanity of our society are racing through my mind. I've been a guest in the homes of gay people. I've gone to their parties. I'd grown to love them. It's ridiculous that I'm O.K. in this society and they are not."

AIDS Quilt: Letter Three

A man delivers a sky-blue panel with a pink triangle emblazoned on a swatch of black fabric for his lover. The name "Michael" is written on one side, but on the other side where his last name should appear, there is a gaping hole. His surname was cut out, literally, by his parents, when Michael's lover showed them the memorial he had made for their son.

35   AIDS has brought out the best in some Americans—an outpouring of compassion in response to tragic reality. But society also makes outcasts of people suffering with AIDS. All too often, people with AIDS are shunned by their friends, alienated from their families and abandoned by the world. Families like the Rays of Arcadia, Florida, have been hounded out of their hometown after the neighbors discovered that the Rays' three hemophiliac sons were carrying the AIDS virus.

"I realize that this is The NAMES Project, but I must ask you one favor—please keep my friend anonymous," a woman writes. "I want to respect the privacy of the living. His parents and brother would be completely undone if they knew about this memorial. They maintain that he died of meningitis, not AIDS."

Meningitis, cancer, pneumonia, a rare blood disease—so many continue to maintain that their loved one did not die of AIDS. The disease is still an embarrassment to some, who attempt to conceal the truth through the falsification of death certificates. Press spokesmen for Liberace, conservative fundraiser Terry Dolan, and clothing designer Perry Ellis tried to cover up their AIDS diagnoses. Lawyer Roy Cohn claimed he had a liver disease, the director-choreographer Michael Bennett had heart problems. Meanwhile, the families of people who have died of AIDS continue to live with their secret. A sister writes: "Jimmy was very handsome, but I haven't sent you his picture because my mom still has so much to deal with on this. She can't tell all her friends the truth."

Letters like this one arrive regularly at The NAMES Project, not for shame but for fear. "Three children were burnt out of their home," says one fearful mother. "I live in a small town," says another. "The neighbors are already suspicious." One mother nursed her son at home for two years, yet she had the local newspaper list cancer as the cause of his death in his obituary. Another mother, who writes, "My darling son was special! His specialness might be the very reason he was with us for such a short time— 27 years. God needed him more than we did. I am so very proud that he was my son," didn't put her son's full name on the panel, respecting his wishes to keep his diagnosis a secret. As each panel-maker writes the name on a quilt, they are fighting that secrecy—a battle some gay people know well, having lived portions of their lives closeted. Many lovers grieve alone, worried that they may lose their jobs or their insurance if it becomes public knowledge that their partner died of AIDS. One man has been challenged with a lawsuit and a threat to run him out of town by his lover's family after they saw his panel in a newspaper article.

"Out of all those people who loved Ric and attended his funeral, only a handful knew that he died of AIDS," writes his lover, Paul Hill, from Dallas, Texas. "Being gay and having lived a lie, it was no problem lying about death as well. My lover who died of pneumocystis quickly became a roommate who died of viral pneumonia. This sham angers me now, but during that period of vulnerability which occurs immediately after a great loss, one can be talked into just about anything. This scenario repeats itself many times a day all over the United States. There are just too many people who don't realize that this awful disease already has touched their lives."

CONVERSATION STARTER

Share your knowledge about the AIDS quilt with your classmates. Have you ever seen it on display? If you have, share your response to it.

READING MATTERS

1. Why was November 27, 1985, chosen for the AIDS memorial march? What strategic planning and preparation did Cleve Jones make for the launching of the quilt?
2. Why was the situation in the Castro depressing in 1985? What progress has been made since? What forms of support has Cleve Jones had?

3. What was the impact of plastering the façade of the old federal building on Market Street with a patchwork of white squares, each memorializing the death of a loved one to AIDS? Consider the impact on Cleve Jones, on the crowd that night, on the movement to find cures for AIDS.
4. Why is a quilt an appropriate symbol for the struggle against AIDS? Why does Cleve Jones believe that the quilt is a symbol of love?

WRITING MATTERS

1. Do some research into the AIDS quilt and the NAMES Project, and then write a paper that presents a history of the project's impact and successes. Alternatively, design a web site that features the journey of the AIDS quilt. If possible, share your work with an appropriate local community organization.
2. After studying the quilt pieces and the stories that we have included, write a personal essay that discusses some of the insights that you have about the impact of AIDS on families in this country. You may want to read more about the AIDS quilt before writing your essay.
3. Write an essay that is focused on how the NAMES Project presents a positive model for a community organization.

RELEVANT WEB SITES

THE AIDS MEMORIAL QUILT <http://www.AIDSQUILT.org>

The official web site of the AIDS Memorial Quilt provides a history of the quilt, pictures of the quilt squares, and interactive information that will help you to contribute a quilt square.

HEALTH ACTION AIDS CAMPAIGN'S GLOBAL AIDS ACTION QUILT
<http://www.phrusa.org/campaigns/aids/quilt/overview.html>

This site provides information about the Health Action AIDS Campaign's Global AIDS Action Quilt. The project was inspired by the success of the internationally reknowned NAMES Project AIDS Quilt and is intended to create a symbolic visual display of health professionals' call to action against global AIDS. Across the United States, representatives from medical, nursing, and public health schools and associations are creating quilt panels.

Writing About Family

1. Create a family tree. Include family photographs, documents, recipes, letters, or drawings to communicate your family's history. Write an introduction to your family tree and analyze the issues reflected by your family tree. Write and reflect on why it is important to have a sense of your family legacy. Then present your family tree and essay to your classmates. See if they have insights that you had not thought about yet.

2. Write an essay that discusses the different ways that communities serve as extended families. Refer to the relevant selections in this chapter, research, and personal experiences to support your main ideas.

3. Write an essay that examines the links between family and culture. Select one culture to focus on or do a comparison and contrast between two cultures. Support your perspective through research, reference to selections in this chapter, and personal experience when relevant.

4. Write an essay that suggests ways that modern family life is changing to accommodate the needs of nontraditional families. Refer to research, relevant selections in this chapter, and personal experience when relevant.

5. Volunteer to work at a community organization that helps families. Write a profile of the organization for a local newspaper or help the organization by writing a press release, an article for their newsletter, a brochure, or publicity flyer. Alternatively, create a web site or brochure that provides information about a service that supports families, either traditional or nontraditional, within your community. For example, you might want to create a web site or brochure for working mothers, one for teens who need information on health issues, one for children whose parents have divorced, or one for recent immigrants who may be having difficulty adjusting to life in your community. Include a reflection of what you have learned from your experiences as a conclusion to your project.

6. Watch a film that explores issues related to traditional or nontraditional family life. Then write an individual or collaborative essay about the film that discusses how family and community issues are presented and what relevance the film has for your generation. Films about family and community to consider but certainly not the only ones available include *The Joy Luck Club, Mississippi Masala, The Cider House Rules, Avalon, The Wedding Banquet, The Prince*

of Tides, Life is Beautiful, Losing Isaiah, Erin Brockovich, Bend It Like Beckham, or *Chocolat.*

7. Write a short story, memoir, or a poem that focuses on one of the themes explored in this chapter.

8. As a class activity, bring in brochures and/or newsletters from local community organizations. After discussing the format and content of the brochures, design one for a local community group at your school or in your neighborhood.

9. Write an essay in which you define the term *family.* Do you consider families to be communities? Discuss the family's primary roles today.

10. Write an essay that expresses the different meanings of love. Show how some of the expressions of love are related to families while others are not. Refer to the articles in this chapter and your own experiences when relevant.

Education

"My Precious Water, I Kiss You." Parkpoom Poompana, age 15. 1996 Grand Prize Winner, River of Words Contest. © River of Words.

Education is a topic that provokes strong opinions from politicians, business people, educators, parents, and citizens. As a nation, our values, social patterns, and economic well-being are tied to the success of our educational institutions. While we all have a stake in developing and supporting effective strategies for education, there is no consensus about how to improve the quality of education in the United States. Every community has a different set of interests, needs, expectations, and strategies for reaching their educational goals. The selections in this chapter introduce you to both traditional and innovative approaches to educating people of all ages and from all walks of life.

The readings in "Reflecting on Educational Experiences" document some of the many concerns that confront educators, parents, teachers, and students from a number of different communities. In the first selection, "Ordinary Resurrections," Jonathan Kozol returns to the community that has been the subject of his research on educational inequalities. This time he enters the community as a citizen to experience his former research subjects as friends and teachers with their own stories of strength, compassion, and hope. The next selection, "The First Day," presents a fictional account of a parent's expectations and hopes for her daughter to be admitted to a "better" school district. In "Postcards from the Edge," Professor Jane Tompkins discusses her experiences as a teacher in a classroom where her students are expected to help guide their own learning process. Reflect on your own experience in school. Do you think that you have received a good education? What factors influenced the quality of your education? Has your perspective on education changed now that you are in college?

The readings in "Economic, Political, and Technological Issues in School" profile some of the diverse approaches to solving educational problems in today's schools and colleges. In the first selection, Deborah Meier argues against the national educational movement to standardize the curriculum for all school-age children; she believes that curriculum standards need to be developed locally by educators and parents if classrooms are to function as democratic communities. In "Multiple Intelligences," Howard Gardner argues that IQ tests are an inadequate way to assess the many forms through which people express their intelligence. "Digital Divide," by Bolt and Crawford, discusses why the shift from the traditional model of education to a technology-driven curriculum has emerged without a national plan, leaving many educators with questions about the effectiveness of this investment and concerns about the equity in the allocation of resources across the system. This section's selections give us a range of ideas about how to prioritize our educational goals.

Amid the national debate over standards, technology, and equity, there are local solutions that rely on human resources, alternative strategies for education, and collaboration between schools and their communities. The readings in "Education Outside of the Classroom" demonstrate the value of rooting educational strategies in the community and giving educators and students the opportunity to benefit from community partnerships. The essay by Michael Schudson, "How People Learn to Be Civic" explores the roots of a civic education and the informal lessons that students learn in school and in the community. Former Poet Laureate Robert Hass and Pamela Michael demonstrate the power of collaboration by bringing together the Library of Congress and the International River Network to sponsor an art and poetry contest for children. In "Jazz Gives Teens New Footing," a concerned citizen applies his expertise as a dance teacher to help incarcerated youth at a local prison find an outlet for their feelings and build confidence through weekly dance classes. In the final selection, "Teach for America," Wendy Kopp shares her experience as founder of Teach for America in 1990, bringing 5,000 AmeriCorps members to the most disadvantaged schools in the country to serve as teachers.

The educational challenges that face school administrators, educational researchers, politicians, teachers, and students are more complex than ever. We are at an educational crossroads. If we want our children to be prepared to find jobs and develop fulfilling relationships in the new millennium, we must think critically about how to best educate our children; we must participate actively in shaping and supporting legislation and educational programs that will help us to develop a much higher standard of education in schools and communities all over the United States.

Jonathan Kozol (b. 1936)

Ordinary Resurrections

Jonathan Kozol was born in Boston to a traditional middle-class Jewish family. Kozol's father was a neurologist and psychiatrist, and his mother was a social worker. Kozol attended Harvard and later Oxford as a Rhodes Scholar, and then lived in the poor neighborhoods of Paris for several years while he worked on a novel. After returning to the United States, he heard about three young civil rights workers who had been murdered by the Ku Klux Klan and, deeply affected by the news, began working as a teacher in a freedom school that had been set up in a Black church in a low-income, predominantly Black area in Roxbury, just south of Boston. Kozol's first book, Death at an Early Age: The Destruction of the Hearts and Minds of Negro Children in the Boston Public Schools *(1967), a devastating chronicle of children he met during his first year of teaching, won the National Book Award.* Rachel and Her Children *(1988), a study of homeless families, won the Robert F. Kennedy Book Award.* Amazing Grace *(1995) appeared on the* New York Times *best-seller list for several months, and* Savage Inequalities: Children in America's Schools *(1992) was both a New England Book Award and National Book Critics Circle Award finalist. In the following selection, excerpted from* Ordinary Resurrections: Children in the Years of Hope *(2000), Kozol departs from his previous work by writing from the children's point of view, thereby creating a personal and hopeful vision of the future.*

Students from colleges not far from New York City come to St. Ann's Church from time to time to get to know the children. More young women do this than young men, perhaps because their consciousness of gender issues renders them more empathetic to the women of the neighborhood, perhaps too because some of them hope to become teachers.

Many of these politically engaged young women comment later on the strength of character and courage they perceive in women at the church. Sometimes, though, they comment also on the feelings of discouragement and resignation that they sense during their conversations. Then, fearful of assuming too much from a single meeting, they may ask if these are my impressions too.

I find it hard to answer. I'm reminded of how risky it can be to think you know what even people who appear to like you and confide in you may actually feel. I've made my share of errors by assuming too much on the basis of the conversations that I've had with people who befriend me.

Still, some impressions do sustain themselves over the course of years. Even with caution, I think it is accurate to say that many of the older people in Mott Haven who have talked with me at length feel *contradictory* emotions—and, at times, a roller-coaster of emotions—in regard to the conditions of their lives and prospects for their neighborhood. Episodes of resignation and discouragement are common; but so too are periods of hope inspired by specific signs of progress such as housing reconstruction, and parental activism, and reductions in the rate of homicide. Then, however, there are times of terrible frustration when these hopes are disappointed or when promised transformations of a neighborhood turn out to be primarily cosmetic, or selective in the economic groups they benefit.

5   Some of the grounds for optimism seem well-founded. New housing units, some of them attractive and surrounded by small lawns and metal railings, have been going up for several years in areas that had been devastated by abandonment and arson in preceding decades. HIV infection in young women remains high—the HIV infection rate for older adolescent females in Mott Haven is, according to physicians here, the highest in the nation—but pediatric HIV has been declining since new perinatal treatments were developed. Homicide is down, as is the use of crack cocaine; but heroin remains pervasive. The mass arrests of hundreds of young men have made some neighborhoods much safer but have also left too many families without fathers, sons, and brothers.

The press refers to the more positive developments in language borrowed from theology. "Miracle" and "resurrection" are two of the terms employed sometimes to draw attention to the hopeful aspects of the story. Words such as "rebirth" and "renaissance" are often used as well. The inclination to disown an old cliché about an inner-city neighborhood—the "ravaged" and "despairing" South Bronx of the past—only to invent a new one—the "restored" and "flourishing" and "optimistic" South Bronx of the present—is a constant risk to which the press is not immune. Like all clichés, the old one never told more than a part of the full story. (There were always people in the South Bronx who led normal and rewarding lives, attended school, held jobs, stayed free from drugs, in even the most troubled periods of time.) The new one is somewhat simplistic too. (Even amidst blocks of new or renovated houses, safer streets and better-tended parks, there still are far too many children losing years of life in separate and unequal schools that are abominations of apparently eternalized apartheid, and too many children who go hungry, and too many who cannot breathe freely.)

Still, there are genuine improvements in some areas, above all in aesthetics, some in private commerce, many in housing, several in pediatric care, and some, although by far too few, in secondary education. It is, in all, a complicated and diverse scenario that warrants neither a reflexive optimism nor the morbid and reiterated incantations of despair. Between these twin polarities, most people that I'm close to in the neighborhood do what they can to steer a sane and life-affirming course.

When it comes to education, though, most of the parents of the children that I know don't buy their affirmation cheaply. Those whose children go to P.S. 30 tend to like the school, and with good reason, I believe; but, when they look ahead into the middle schools and high schools of the area, they recognize the outer limits of the opportunities that this society is giving to their children. They also know the limits of the opportunities that *they* can offer to their children; and they know these aren't the same as what another class of people in another section of the city are providing for their children. So they look at their sons and daughters with this secret piece of knowledge. They know how destinies are formed out of particulars.

A few of the mothers of the children here work as domestics in the homes of wealthy people in Manhattan. Others have done so in the past, as have a number of grandmothers. Usually they've come to know the children of these families fairly well and, in this way, have gained a close-up sense of what their lives are like. They learn about particular ingredients of life that cultivate entitlement and graciousness and opportunity and also leave these children with the likable capacity for understated recognitions of their own advantage. They aren't inert submissive stones. They see and *understand* these things. They wish that they could give some of the same things to *their* children.

10   Many people in Mott Haven do a lot of work to make sure they are well-informed about conditions in their children's public schools. Some also know a great deal more about the schools that serve the children of the privileged than many of the privileged themselves may recognize. They know that "business math" is not the same as calculus and that "job-readiness instruction" is not European history or English literature. They know that children of rich people do not often spend semesters of their teenage years in classes where they learn to type an application for an entry-level clerical position; they know these wealthy children are too busy learning composition skills and polishing their French pronunciation and receiving preparation for the SATs. They come to understand the processes by which a texture of entitlement is stitched together for some children while it is denied to others. They also understand that, as the years go by, some of these children will appear to have deserved one kind of role in life, and some another.

One of the mothers at St. Ann's once said to me, "My daughter should have gone to Brown. If she had had the opportunities you had in school, she would have gone there. I didn't want her to get stuck at a big public university. I wanted something special because I thought *she* was special."

I asked her how she'd come to know about Brown University. Only a few of the parents in the neighborhood had ever mentioned colleges like Brown, or even New York University, Columbia, Cornell, or other private colleges in New York State. People spoke of community colleges at times, occasionally of Lehman College or John Jay. Brown came out of a different kingdom of familiarity and expectation.

I apologized for asking this, because I was afraid she'd find it patronizing; but she said she understood exactly why I asked. "I know. . . . It seems like something that I wouldn't know about. People around here aren't supposed to be familiar with some places; but some of us are. I know what Brown is like. It's small. It's nice. It's not impersonal. My daughter's smart, and naturally polite. She would have fitted in. They would have liked her there."

She said her daughter got into a branch of New York's City University, in which she had been doing reasonably well. But something about Brown University had lingered in her mind as an idea—"a hankering," she said—a yearning, a regret, that she could not shake off.

15   I asked if she resented that I'd had an opportunity she never had and which she could not give her daughter. She knew I'd gone to Harvard and that Mother Martha went to Radcliffe. I used to sense at times the slightest hint of an ambivalence or holding back when she was talking with the pastor. I knew she liked her and was close to her; but I had also seen these moments when she seemed to step away into a kind of "distancing," a knowledgeable look, a recognition, that was not as sharp-edged as resentment but suggested it somehow.

"We all know certain things," she said. "We know the way things are."

I was glad she wasn't too polite to cut right through my hesitation. I was trying to be careful. She did not want me to be careful. She wanted us to have a real talk, not "an inter-racial dialogue."

Her name was Eleanor Jackson. She died a few months after we had gotten to be friends. I still remember the place we were, the color of the sky and time of day, the food that we were eating—she had a chicken sandwich without mayonnaise, I had a hamburger—on the afternoon we had that talk. I remember too the deep, deep note of unaccepted anger and of unassimilated sadness in her voice when she had said, "We know the way things are." You cannot begin to address this kind of sadness by polite, evasive conversation, or by small gestures of philanthropy, or by incantatory repetition of encoded words. You cannot talk about "a renaissance of hope" when Eleanor is telling you of broken dreams.

Eleanor's assumption that I'd had advantages unknown to her or to her daughter was well-justified. My father brought me to the Dean of Admissions at Harvard College when I was eighteen. I wanted to go to Princeton. The dean, who was my father's friend and classmate, talked me into Harvard and assured me that I didn't need to bother filing other applications. Brown would have been a third or fourth choice for most of the boys who went to school with me. To Eleanor, it was a dream deferred forever.

20   Eleanor was a descendant of one of the presidents of the United States. Her grandmother's grandmother was a seamstress and a slave and, she believed, the mistress of John Tyler. On a genealogy chart she handed me the next time that we met, her great-grandmother's name was listed in this way: "Mary Emma Susan Tyler Jones—born in Charles City, Va., on December 25, 1841, died in 1930 at age 89." Mary Emma's mother, Eleanor told me, made the shirt that President Tyler wore to his inauguration.

Sitting in a coffee shop two blocks from St. Ann's Church one afternoon, she showed me sepia-colored photographs of her ancestors and described their lives in slavery, and later in the segregated South after emancipation, then here in the segregated Bronx. Irony and wistfulness suffused her gloss on our undemocratic nation's history.

"President Carter's daughter went to Brown," she said in passing. "I thought my daughter ought to go there too."

Maybe, I thought later, it was this association that had led her first to think of Brown. Maybe she'd heard of it from someone in the neighborhood, a counselor at her daughter's school perhaps, or one of the women in Manhattan she had worked for as a maid. Whatever the seed that planted this idea, it had remained with her for all these years. Something about Brown University had seemed appropriate to her for the descendant of a president.

Eleanor's death was sudden; it was wholly unexpected and, to this day, it does not seem real. In the spring of the year we'd gotten together several times for lunch, and once for a long walk. She suffered from asthma, but she'd had it for at least a decade and had learned to joke about the miseries it caused her, even when she had a serious attack. She had a gift for turning miseries to satires, often at her own expense, sometimes at mine. She flirted outrageously with eligible men and told me she regarded me as "wholly eligible" and said she knew men "better than you might expect" because she had been in the prostitution business for ten years before we met. She said she wished that she had stayed in it "a few years more" so that she could have paid for private college for her daughter.

25   She developed a peculiar skin disease in August of that year. No one at the church was told the name of the disease, but it disfigured her and turned her face into a mass of reddish welts and open sores. I was not in New York City then, but Mother Martha told me she was rushed into intensive care and was in terrible discomfort but, at first, in no apparent danger. Then, suddenly, she told me simply, "Eleanor has died. The funeral will be tomorrow."

I asked the cause of death but, for some reason, it remained unknown to people at the church. I never found out why she died. I never found out why she had become a prostitute instead of keeping on as a domestic worker, which is how she'd earned her living when she first got out of school, or why she stopped being a prostitute, or why she had been drawn into the congregation at St. Ann's, or why religion had become important in her life in recent years.

I ought to know some of these things because we talked so many times and she was not at all reserved in what she would agree to talk about. I know a good deal, for example, of her high school years because she spoke of this when she was telling me about the hopes she later nourished for her daughter. She told me she had graduated from Jane Addams High School, which was one of the more integrated high schools in the Bronx when she was growing up. "There were still white students at the high school then," she said, "but it was segregated by curriculum. Only the white girls took the college courses." Black girls, she believed, had been discouraged from enrolling in these courses.

"I told my counselor, 'I want to go to college.' Well, I can't explain the way she looked at me, but it was like the kids would say it now, 'Yeah, right! You want to go to college!' So I got this message very clearly. What you have to understand is that they didn't even talk to you about the kinds of courses you and Mother Martha would have taken. They didn't *plan* for you to go to college and they didn't lead you to expect that it was something *you* should plan on either. They led you to expect to clean the houses of the girls who went to college."

I asked what would have happened if a student had enough determination to reject the counselor's advice.

30   "You could insist," she said. "Some students did. But it was like a hand went up. 'Don't waste my time, or yours, because we both know where you're going.'" She lifted her hand like a policeman stopping traffic. "'Talk to the hand because the mind is busy.'"

We were at Blimpie's, at one of the tables in the back, the time we had that conversation. It was in mid-afternoon. She was wearing a red imitation-leather jacket. She said she wasn't hungry, but she had hot chocolate. I had a cup of coffee. We were nibbling on macadamia cookies.

I asked her if she thought the counselors at school did things like this with real awareness. "I mean—that they didn't *want* you to succeed?"

"No. That's not quite it," she said. "You could 'succeed,' but in the way they *meant* you to succeed. You could succeed in learning what they thought that you were capable of learning, but no more than that. I guess they didn't think that I was capable of college."

Her mother, she told me, died when she was nine years old. She was brought up by a cousin who was kind to her—"she bought me patent-leather shoes for first communion"—but was "not aggressive like a mother, not the type to go up to the principal and fight for you and back you up."

35   I told her of schools I visit in which dozens of black and Hispanic women have been channeled into classes like hairdressing that don't give the credits they would need to go to four-year colleges but are viewed by educators, and sometimes by students too, as sensible accommodations to diminished possibilities. She nodded quickly and immediately followed up by saying, "Thank you!" She said this often when I mentioned something that corroborated an opinion she had held but didn't think I would believe.

Once I asked her, "What did you think your teachers and your counselors believed that they were doing with your life—or thought *you* should be doing?"

"Truthfully? I think they felt that I could do domestic work, or help out in a hospital, or something of that sort, or maybe be a secretary, possibly a nurse," although she also said she didn't think they had reflected on it long enough to call it an "intention" or an "expectation." This, she said, was why she tried so hard to give her daughter opportunities that she herself had been denied. I think she felt she'd won a partial victory. If her daughter could have gone to Brown, I know she would have felt the victory was more complete.

She used to tell me funny stories about people she'd encountered when she was, as she had put it, "working on my feet" around Times Square and, later, on Brook Avenue. During the latter period, she said that she had fallen into using crack cocaine. "Get your Crackerjacks right here!" she said, remembering the advertising pitch of dealers up on Cypress Avenue, who sold, she said, a brand of crack that came in a short vial with a yellow top and was so powerful "you'd think the radio was talking to you even if you hadn't turned it on."

She told me also that she liked having a woman priest "because I tell her things I wouldn't dare say to a man." When I asked, "Like what?" she laughed and said, "Like, if the man you sleep with couldn't satisfy your needs? You wouldn't dare to say that to a priest that was a man. He might take off his collar and say, 'I have a solution to that problem!'"

40 She must have been well over 45 years old, but she seemed younger. She had a sensual-looking body, mocking eyes, and orange-colored hair. I remember the elastic bands that held her asthma pump against her wallet because it was almost always on her lap or on the seat right next to her at church.

In a letter I got from her in mid-July, she enclosed a photo of her cat. "Here's a picture of my baby, two years old," she wrote. She also included a cassette of gospel music she recorded for me.

"When we were at Blimpie's last time I was going to order a club sandwich, but I was too shy," she wrote in the same letter. "That isn't like me. Is it?" Then she said, "Next time I'll tell you when I'm hungry." She gave me her telephone number, which had just been changed, and said that she was always home by nine.

For all the wickedness that she enjoyed imputing to herself, I know she took a mischievous delight in being with the younger children at St. Ann's. "I never would have been a good schoolteacher," she once said, "because I love them most when they're most devilish."

I know the children liked her too. Elio was often sitting with her at a table in the corner of the afterschool when she was there. She used to say he was her "boyfriend." She was one of the good people who, for many years, had been out on their own and then had found a sense of safety at St. Ann's. A lot of women of about her age seem to find safety there, and a release from loneliness.

45 An Episcopal priest named Robert Morris speaks about the commonplace and frequently unnoticed ways that people rise above their loneliness and fear as "ordinary resurrections." He points out that the origin of "resurrection" is the Greek word *anastasis*, which, he notes, means "standing up again," and, as he puts it unpretentiously, "We all lie down. We all rise up. We do this every day." The same word, as he notes, is used in Scripture: "I am the resurrection and the life." But, in an afternote directed possibly at fellow members of the clergy, he observes, "The Resurrection does not wait for Easter."

I think of his words when I remember Eleanor. She was a good friend for a person who allowed himself to get discouraged but had never found the kinds of resurrections that are made of steel and stone and slogans utterly convincing. Sometimes, at the end of a long conversation over coffee as we said goodbye to one another, she would say, "God bless." But life itself, lived with a sense of fun, defiance, and courageous humor even at the most upsetting times, is the enduring blessing that she left behind to those who miss her and remember her.

She liked to talk about her cat, whose name was Sasha. I know his name because she wrote it underneath his photograph. I can't remember her daughter's name and I'm not even sure she ever told me. I know she had a grandson, though, because I was at church for his baptism.

She often helped to read parts of the services on Sundays. She was a member of the vestry and took pride in her position. The suddenness of her death has made it harder to accept that she is gone. Some of the younger children asked about her for a long time after she had died. "When is Miss Eleanor coming back?" one of the little ones would ask. It was a while before they understood that she would not return.

CONVERSATION STARTER

Discuss the opportunities you have had as a result of your education.

READING MATTERS

1. Why did Eleanor regret that her daughter never went to Brown? What did Brown represent to Eleanor?
2. How do residents of Mott Haven learn about educational opportunities outside their community?
3. How do the differences in their social class and race impact the relationship between Jonathan and Eleanor?
4. How does Eleanor's death affect Jonathan?

WRITING MATTERS

1. Write about an "ordinary resurrection" that you have experienced or witnessed.
2. Research Jonathan Kozol's career as a social scientist. Write an essay in which you discuss Kozol's ideas about educational inequalities and how they have changed or evolved.
3. Do you think Jonathan is part of the Mott Haven community? Write an essay supporting your opinion. Is he a teacher? Is he a student? What is his role? Why is his point of view significant?

RELEVANT WEB SITES

AN INTERVIEW WITH JONATHAN KOZOL
<http://www.education-world.com/a_issues/issues164.shtml>

Learn more about Jonathan Kozol by reading this interview with "Education World" in which he discusses his book *Ordinary Resurrections* and life in the urban United States.

CAMPAIGN FOR AMERICA'S FUTURE <http://www.ourfuture.org>

The official web site for the Campaign for America's Future founded by national leaders, including Reverend Jesse Jackson, Patricia Ireland, Jonathan Kozol, Robert Reich, Betty Friedan, and William Julius Wilson. The site provides information about issues and actions related to a new vision of an economy and a future that works for all of us.

Edward P. Jones (b. 1950)

The First Day

Edward P. Jones was born and raised in Washington, D.C., where he attended public schools. He graduated from Holy Cross College and did graduate work in fiction writing at the University of Virginia under a Henry Hoyns Fellowship. He also received a fellowship from the National Endowment of the Arts in 1986. The short story that follows, "The First Day," is included in his first book, Lost in the City (1992).

On an otherwise unremarkable September morning, long before I learned to be ashamed of my mother, she takes my hand and we set off down New Jersey Avenue to begin my very first day of school. I am wearing a checkered-like blue-and-green cotton dress, and scattered about these colors are bits of yellow and white and brown. My mother has uncharacteristically spent nearly an hour on my hair that morning, plaiting and replaiting so that now my scalp tingles. Whenever I turn my head quickly, my nose fills with the faint smell of Dixie Peach hair grease. The smell is somehow a soothing one now and I will reach for it time and time again before the morning ends. All the plaits, each with a blue barrette near the tip and each twisted into an uncommon sturdiness, will last until I go to bed that night, something that has never happened before. My stomach is full of milk and oatmeal sweetened with brown sugar. Like everything else I have on, my pale green slip and underwear are new, the underwear having come three to a plastic package with a little girl on the front who appears to be dancing. Behind my ears, my mother, to stop my whining, has dabbed the stingiest bit of her gardenia perfume, the last present my father gave her before he disappeared into memory. Because I cannot smell it, I have only her word that the perfume is there. I am also wearing yellow socks trimmed with thin lines of black and white around the tops. My shoes are my greatest joy, black patent-leather miracles, and when one is nicked at the toe later that morning in class, my heart will break.

I am carrying a pencil, a pencil sharpener, and a small ten-cent tablet with a black-and-white speckled cover. My mother does not believe that a girl in kindergarten needs such things, so I am taking them only because of my insistent whining and because they are presented from our neighbors, Mary Keith and Blondelle Harris. Miss Mary and Miss Blondelle are watching my two younger sisters until my mother returns. The women are as precious to me as my mother and sisters. Out playing one day, I have overheard an older child, speaking to another child, call Miss Mary and Miss Blondelle a word that is brand new to me. This is my mother: When I say the word in fun to one of my sisters, my mother slaps me across the mouth and the word is lost for years and years.

All the way down New Jersey Avenue, the sidewalks are teeming with children. In my neighborhood, I have many friends, but I see none of them as my mother and I walk. We cross New York Avenue, we cross Pierce Street, and we cross L and K, and still I see no one who knows my name. At I Street, between New Jersey Avenue and Third Street, we enter Seaton Elementary School, a timeworn, sad-faced building across the street from my mother's church, Mt. Carmel Baptist.

Just inside the front door, women out of the advertisements in *Ebony* are greeting other parents and children. The woman who greets us has pearls thick as jumbo marbles that come down almost to her navel, and she acts as if she had known me all my life, touching my shoulder, cupping her hand under my chin. She is enveloped in a perfume that I only know is not gardenia. When, in answer to her question, my mother tells her that we live at 1277 New Jersey Avenue, the woman first seems to be picturing in her head where we live. Then she shakes her head and says that we are at the wrong school, that we should be at Walker-Jones.

5   My mother shakes her head vigorously. "I want her to go here," my mother says. "If I'da wanted her someplace else, I'da took her there." The woman continues to act as if she has known me all my life, but she tells my mother that we live beyond the area that Seaton serves. My mother is not convinced and for several more minutes she questions the woman about why I cannot attend Seaton. For as many Sundays as I can remember, perhaps even Sundays when I was in her womb, my mother has pointed across I Street to Seaton as we come and go to Mt. Carmel. "You gonna go there and learn about the whole world." But one of the guardians of that place is saying no, and no again. I am learning this about my mother: The higher up on the scale of respectability a person is—and teachers are rather high up in her eyes—the less she is liable to let them push her around. But finally, I see in her eyes the closing gate, and she takes my hand and we leave the building. On the steps, she stops as people move past us on either side.

"Mama, I can't go to school?"

She says nothing at first, then takes my hand again and we are down the steps quickly and nearing New Jersey Avenue before I can blink. This is my mother: She says, "One monkey don't stop no show."

Walker-Jones is a larger, new school and I immediately like it because of that. But it is not across the street from my mother's church, her rock, one of her connections to God, and I sense her doubts as she absently rubs her thumb over the back of her hand. We find our way to the crowded auditorium where gray metal chairs are set up in the middle of the room. Along the wall to the left are tables and other chairs. Every chair seems occupied by a child or adult. Somewhere in the room a child is crying, a cry that rises above the buzz-talk of so many people. Strewn about the floor are dozens and dozens of pieces of white paper, and people are walking over them without any thought of picking them up. And seeing this lack of concern, I am all of a sudden afraid.

"Is this where they register for school?" my mother asks a woman at one of the tables.

10   The woman looks up slowly as if she has heard this question once too often. She nods. She is tiny, almost as small as the girl standing beside her. The woman's hair is set in a mass of curlers and all of those curlers are made of paper money, here a dollar bill, there a five-dollar bill. The girl's hair is arrayed in curls, but some of them are beginning to droop and this makes me happy. On the table beside the woman's pocketbook is a large notebook, worthy of someone in high school, and looking at me looking at the notebook, the girl places her hand possessively on it. In her other hand she holds several pencils with thick crowns of additional erasers.

"These the forms you gotta use?" my mother asks the woman picking up a few pieces of the paper from the table. "Is this what you have to fill out?"

The woman tells her yes, but that she need fill out only one.

"I see," my mother says, looking about the room. Then: "Would you help me with this form? That is, if you don't mind."

The woman asks my mother what she means.

15   "This form. Would you mind helpin' me fill it out?"

The woman still seems not to understand.

"I can't read it. I don't know how to read or write, and I'm askin' you to help me." My mother looks at me, then looks away. I know almost all of her looks, but this one is brand new to me. "Would you help me, then?"

The woman says "Why sure," and suddenly she appears happier, so much more satisfied with everything. She finishes the form for her daughter and my mother and I step aside to wait for her. We find two chairs nearby and sit. My mother is now diseased, according to the girl's eyes, and until the moment her mother takes her and the form to the front of the auditorium, the girl never stops looking at my mother. I stare back at her. "Don't stare," my mother says to me. "You know better than that."

Another woman out of the *Ebony* ads takes the woman's child away. Now, the woman said upon returning, let's see what we can do for you two.

20   My mother answers the questions the woman reads off the form. They start with my last name, and then on to the first and middle names. This is school, I think. This is going to school. My mother slowly enunciates each word of my name. This is my mother: As the questions go on, she takes from her pocketbook document after document, as if they will support my right to attend school, as if she has been saving them up for just this moment.

Indeed, she takes out more papers than I have ever seen her do in other places: my birth certificate, my baptismal record, a doctor's letter concerning my bout with chicken pox, rent receipts, records of immunization, a letter about our public assistance payments, even her marriage license—every single paper that has anything even remotely to do with my five-year-old life. Few of the papers are needed here, but it does not matter and my mother continues to pull out the documents with the purposefulness of a magician pulling out a long string of scarves. She has learned that money is the beginning and end of everything in this world, and when the woman finishes, my mother offers her fifty cents, and the woman accepts it without hesitation. My mother and I are just about the last parent and child in the room.

My mother presents the form to a woman sitting in front of the stage, and the woman looks at it and writes something on a white card, which she gives to my mother. Before long, the woman who has taken the girl with the drooping curls appears from behind us, speaks to the sitting woman, and introduces herself to my mother and me. She's to be my teacher, she tells my mother. My mother stares.

We go into the hall, where my mother kneels down to me. Her lips are quivering. "I'll be back to pick you up at twelve o'clock. I don't want you to go nowhere. You just wait right here. And listen to every word she say." I touch her lips and press them together. It is an old, old game between us. She puts my hand down at my side, which is not part of the game. She stands and looks a second at the teacher, then she turns and walks away. I see where she has darned one of her socks the night before. Her shoes make loud sounds in the hall. She passes through the doors and I can still hear the loud sounds of her shoes. And even when the teacher turns me toward the classrooms and I hear what must be the singing and talking of all the children in the world, I can still hear my mother's footsteps above it all.

CONVERSATION STARTER

Discuss what you remember about your first day of school, or discuss your first memories of school.

READING MATTERS

1. What obstacles do the narrator and her mother have to overcome in order for the daughter to attend school?
2. How are the narrator and her mother supported by their community?
3. Why does the narrator's mother take her daughter to the "wrong" school?
4. How does the importance of appearances shape the narrator's sense of belonging?

WRITING MATTERS

1. Building on the Conversation Starter, write an essay about your first day of school or your first memories of school.

2. Research and write an essay about two different neighboring communities and the education they provide. What role does funding play in providing quality education? What resources within the community support and strengthen the schools?
3. Interview people within your community about the opportunities they had at school. Write an essay that discusses what you learned. What conclusions can you draw about the range of educational opportunities that are available to different communities?

RELEVANT WEB SITES

FIRST DAY FOUNDATION <http://www.firstday.org>

This web site from the First Day Foundation provides information about the First Day of School America campaign, a grassroots movement that brings together schools, families, and communities in celebration of education. The site provides information about fun, practical, effective way to get parents involved in their children's education starting on Day One of each school year.

NATIONAL ASSOCIATION OF NEIGHBORHOOD SCHOOLS

<http://www.nans.org>

This web site from the National Association of Neighborhood Schools provides resources for a united effort to promote neighborhood schools that facilitate parental participation, community pride and support, safety, and proper use of education dollars.

Jane Tompkins (b. 1940)

Postcards from the Edge

Jane Tompkins, English professor, author, and lecturer, received her Ph.D. from Yale (1966). She has taught at several schools and currently teaches at Duke. Tompkins edited Reader-Response Criticism: From Formalism to Poststructuralism *(1980), and is the author of* Sensational Designs: The Cultural Work of American Fiction, 1790–1870 *(1985),* West of Everything: The Inner Life of Westerners *(1992), and* A Life in School: What the Teacher Learned *(1996). She gives lectures and workshops around the country on making the classroom a more humane environment. In the next selection, excerpted from* A Life in School: What the Teacher Learned, *Tompkins reflects back on her own life in the classroom to discover both what she learned and what remains to be learned. Tompkins presents her thoughts as a series of postcards that might be posted on a faculty bulletin board.*

• 1 •

Dear Fellow Teachers,

What do you do when silence breaks out in your class, the times when you suddenly forget everything you were going to say, or you ask a question no one answers, and you sit there wishing you were dead, blush rising from the throat, face hot, throat clenched?

Last semester when I tried to hand authority over to my students, we had many such moments. Often we just sat there looking at each other. I nearly died, and so did they.

Yet living through those silences taught me something. They had a bonding effect, like living through a war. As a result of this experience I've come to think pain and embarrassment are not the worst things for a class. At least the moments are real. At least everyone feels intensely. At least everyone is *there*.

What do you think?

Jane

·2·

Poem Postcard

No monuments record the bravery of teachers,
Or tell our conquered fears,
There is no Tomb of the Unknown Teacher,
No surgery for our scars.

All our injuries are internal.
No one counts the pain,
Least of all the teachers.
We go sightless on.

To teach is to be battered,
Scrutinized, and drained,
Day after day. We know this.
Still, it is never said.

What it is to be up there
Exposed to the hostile gaze
Will never be told by teachers—
The knowledge is too much.

·3·

DEAR ALL-WISE, IMAGINED MENTOR,

My class had suffered together. Its members had gotten to know each other. People had taken risks. Something like authenticity has begun to mark the level of exchange. But whenever we tried to talk about literature, authenticity would fly out the window. Our talk seemed forced, desultory.

One day, to break the ice (again), we played Pictionary, a game like charades, only you draw instead of acting. We screamed, we jumped up and down, laughed, were intensely quiet. There was total concentration, participation, self-forgetfulness.

Then we switched gears. For the last twenty minutes people read aloud their assignments—what they thought Holden Caulfield did after the end of *Catcher in the Rye.* Silence descended; it was the living and the dead. This happened over and over. It was as if, given the opportunity to choose between literature and life, or rather, between literature and each other, we chose each other. The class never did learn how to discuss a literary text, though we fell into a habit of reading poetry aloud from time to time.

What could we have done to avoid this quandary?

Should it have been avoided?

Wondering, in Durham

• **4** •

[To Parker Palmer, a leader in higher education reform and author of *To Know as We Are Known: A Spirituality of Education*]

Dear Parker,

When I began paying attention to students, I stopped caring about knowledge. Knowledge, for me, became something "over there—Behind the Shelf," as in the line from the Dickinson poem:

I cannot live with You—
It would be Life—
And Life is over there—
Behind the Shelf

If knowledge is "over there—Behind the Shelf," life is right in front of me in the classroom, in the faces and bodies of the students. *They* are life, and I want us to share our lives, make something together, for as long as the course lasts, and let that be enough.

I think the thing I'm aiming for is a sense of the classroom as sacramental. The class experience itself becomes the end and aim of education. Not something learned that you can take away from the class, not a skill, or even a perspective on the world, but an experience worth having as it goes by, moment by moment. I'm really looking for somebody to give me permission to think these things. Will you do it?

Love,
Jane

• **5** •

Dear Students,

When I pay attention to the subject matter in class, instead of to you, I get excited, think of an idea that just *has* to be said, blurt it out, and, more often than not, kill something. As in the Dickinson poem

My life had stood
A loaded gun
In corners

when I speak the report is so loud it deafens. No one can hear anything but what I've said. Discussion dies. It seems it's either you or me, my authority or your power to speak. What do I do that shuts people up? Or is this a false dilemma? Help!

Sincerely,
Jane

•6•

To I Don't Know Who:

Sometimes the feelings I have toward my students are romantic. It's like being in love. You know how when you're in love or have a crush on somebody, you're always looking forward to the next meeting with desire and trepidation—will he or she be glad to see me? Will he or she be late? not come at all? Will she or he think I'm smart? good-looking? a nice person? It's the roller-coaster of love—up one day and down the next—no two classes the same. How soon will we be going steady? Will our love be true? Do you love me like I love you?
　　Am I the only person who feels this way about teaching?

Wondering, in Durham

•7•

[This postcard is addressed to the registrar at Duke University, whose name is Harry Demik.]

Dear Mr. Demik,

Last semester I stopped giving letter grades in my courses and got into trouble with your office. There were mix-ups regarding both classes, rules against what I was doing, but things got straightened out, and I didn't have to give grades.
　　Grades, of course, are judgments. Judgments rendered by One Who Knows. The way I teach now, judgment seems inappropriate—judgment of the students by the instructor, or of the instructor by the students, or even of the whole course by all its members. I offered these courses Pass/Fail for a reason: you can't grade a person's soul.
　　Of course, toward the end of the semester, as the pressure from their other courses mounts, the students in my courses slack off, and then I feel put out. I have no solution for this problem.

Jane Tompkins

· 8 ·

To Whom It May Concern:

I cleared a pile of newspapers from the kitchen table in order to write this postcard, but on top of the pile a section on hunger and homelessness caught my eye. There were terrible statistics, such as forty thousand children die in the world every day from starvation. The lead sentence in one article read: "The longest journey a person can take is the twelve inches from the head to the heart."

Who is helping our students to make this journey?

Wondering, in Durham

· 9 ·

Nightmare Postcard

Dear Professor Tompkins,

I've read your article, and I think you're fooling yourself. You're cheating your students under the guise of liberating them. These students need guidance; they need a model. They need to hear books discussed boldly, rigorously, with discipline, and in a spirit of inquiry. They're only eighteen or nineteen; they don't know how to be intellectuals. It's your job to show them, and you're not doing it. You ought to be fired.

Disgusted

· 10 ·

Dear Disgusted,

You may be right. But twisting in my seat, looking away in an agony of frustration, staring down at the desk, and taking deep breaths, I've learned to curb my impulse to correct the students, to show them the way, because when I do it shuts them up. Allowed to meander to its furthest most insignificant trickle, ending in a long moment of emptiness, or allowed to reach a pinnacle of disorderly, excited hilarity and confusion, a class discussion can give birth to the moment that changes the destiny of the course. The student too afraid to speak up at any other time may step into that moment of silence; or the giddiness of the atmosphere may produce an insight, a wild metaphorical leap of the imagination on someone's part that crystallizes everything. Then there's the silence that attends the recognition of an important event. To me that precarious path is more precious than all the modelling in the world. Besides, they get that from their other professors.

Jane Tompkins

· 11 ·

Dear Jane,

Come on, now. You know this guy is onto something, but you're afraid to admit it. You just can't stand preparing for class anymore, so you get the students to do it. You can't stand the responsibility of making discussions work, so you opt out. You hand responsibility over to the students as a way of pretending to teach while really doing something else. Why not just quit?

Your Conscience

· 12 ·

To My Internalized Critic:

A class doesn't get to know itself until it has been let go. People's personalities won't be visible, their feelings and opinions won't surface, unless the teacher gets out of the way on a regular basis. You have to be willing to give up your authority, and the sense of identity and prestige that come with it, for the students to be able to feel their own authority. To get out of the students' way, the teacher has to learn how to get out of her own way. To not let her ego call the shots all the time. This is incredibly difficult. But I think it is a true path for a teacher.

Jane

· 13 ·

Dear C.,

Do you remember once we were having a telephone conversation about how busy we were? You were worrying about how you were ever going to finish the critical biography you'd been working like a dog on for years, we'd been talking about our families, when suddenly you burst out with: "I don't know what I would do. If my parents should die I wouldn't have time."

I'll never forget that moment, or the sound of your voice.

Jane

· 14 ·

Dear Friends,

I would have written you a letter instead of a postcard, but I didn't have time.
I wanted to tell you about what's happening in my life, but I didn't have time.
I would have invited you to dinner, but I didn't have time.

I would have done more reading before writing this paper, but I didn't have time.

We never got to cover the end of the novel because we ran out of time.

I would have read your article more carefully, but I didn't have time.

I didn't have time to read your article.

I wanted to call you, but I was afraid it would take too much time.

In haste,
Jane

·15·

Dear Fellow Teachers:

In the classroom we say over and over that there's not enough time to do what we really want. But it's a lie. Listen to Mary Rose O'Reilley's reflection on this:

> Sister Teresa was past her prime, getting eccentric. She was supposed to teach us Art History from Prehistory to the Present. We spent weeks on primitive cave painting, then stalled on Giotto. Day after day, we sat in a dark classroom, looking at the confusion of spears and torches in "The Kiss of Judas"—until we knew it. Knew it. Later, lurking morosely in the positivist pews of Johns Hopkins University, where I read the Gospel of John in first year Greek, it was Giotto that rose before my eyes. That confusion of spears, and that alone, opened the Greek text to me. Now I knew two things.
>
> This nun having done her work, art stops short for me in the early fourteenth century. Somewhere, filed in some Platonic syllabus, lie Raphael's fat madonnas, but they are not for me: I do not know them. I suppose that is a loss. But I know two things.

So you see, whether or not you have enough time depends on what your conception of learning is.

Jane

·16·

Dear Colleagues:

Here's a joke I remember from junior high school, or maybe it was college. A woman went to the doctor and said, "Doctor, I have this enormous desire to eat pancakes. I just can't get enough of them. What can I do?" "Well," said the doctor, "That doesn't sound too serious. How many pancakes are we talking about?" "Oh," said the woman, "at home I have sixteen chests full."

When it comes to knowledge, we are like that woman. At home we have sixteen chests full, and we're dying to get our hands on sixteen more. But since even one cold pancake is too many, why are we doing this?

Jane

·17·

[This postcard is to John Orr, my meditation teacher.]

Dear John,

I've begun to realize lately that I read as a reflex, to stuff my mind. It's too painful to remain conscious for very long at a time, attention free; even a fraction of the day is too much. So I read or write, talk or listen, watch TV, do a task that requires some degree of concentration; that way I can avoid the unpleasantness of open attention. Mainly it's reading I use to stanch the flow of unwanted mental events.

Love,
Jane

·18·

[This postcard was written to the Ford Foundation Scholars at Eckerd College in St. Petersburg, Florida.]:

Dear Ford Foundation Scholars:

In the Political Correctness wars, where we fight over whether to teach *The Color Purple*, or what the First Amendment really means, we forget the weather. People's feelings get hurt; resentments build.

A friend of mine whose marriage was breaking up told me that how you deal with the problems that come up in a relationship is more important than what the problems are. It's the same in intellectual life. But we, your professors, do not know how to conduct ourselves when there is real conflict, inside the classroom or out. We fumble around. Sometimes we tear each other apart, or, afraid of doing that, we avoid speaking. I for one could use some instruction in how to disagree fruitfully. And in how to listen constructively to an opponent. I wish your generation would learn these skills and then teach them to us.

Hopefully,
Jane Tompkins

· 19 ·

Dear Teachers,

In school it's students not books that are the important things. And the students are growing. And like other growing things, they need the right atmosphere to grow in. The atmosphere is what determines whether or not they will flourish. Of this atmosphere, books are only one part. What about the rest?

Do students get the sunshine of love and attention from their instructors? Do they receive the rain of affection and intimate exchange from one another? Do they have time and space to grow in?

J.T.

· 20 ·

[To Myself (from the future)]

Dear Jane,

Try not to worry so much about teaching. As you become more at peace with yourself, your classroom will become more peaceful. What is important is to carry your students in your heart, as you have begun to do.

Your inner guide

Conversation Starter

Discuss a teacher who inspired you or challenged your perspective.

Reading Matters

1. What are Tompkins's expectations of herself? What are her expectations of her colleagues? What expectations does she have of her students?
2. Tompkins reflects on her experience through a series of postcards rather than in an essay or another form. How does the form affect the message? Why do you think Tompkins chose this form?
3. Which of Tompkins's postcards did you find most interesting? Why?
4. What aspects of community exist in Tompkins's classroom?

Writing Matters

1. What do you think about Tompkins's approach to teaching? Write an essay supporting your position.
2. Following Tompkins's model, write a series of postcards to your fellow students expressing your hopes, expectations, and frustrations about your life as a student.

3. How would you describe your experience in classroom situations? Write an essay that captures what you see as your role in a classroom community. What would you like to change about the way that you participate in the classroom?

Relevant Web Sites

Educational Resources Information Center <http://www.ericsp.org/>

A clearinghouse on teaching and teacher education with a large database of articles and resources.

Teachers Net <http://www.teachers.net>

This web site brings together hundreds of thousands of educators in an environment specially designed to foster peer support and development.

Economic, Political, and Technological Issues in School

Deborah Meier (b. 1931)

Educating a Democracy

Deborah Meier started teaching kindergarten in public schools in Chicago and has spent more than three decades working in public education as a teacher, writer, and public advocate. She was the founder and teacher-director of a network of highly successful public elementary and secondary schools in East Harlem and the founder-principal of Central Park East Secondary School. The schools she has helped create serve predominantly low-income African-American and Latino students and are nationally considered exemplars of reform. Meier is currently the vicechair of the Coalition of Essential Schools, the principal of Boston's Mission Hill Elementary School, and the author of The Power of Their Ideas *(1996),* Central Park East *(1999),* Lessons From a Small School in Harlem *(2001) and* In Schools We Trust *(2002). In the following selection, excerpted from* Will Standards Save Public Education? *(2000), Meier offers a clear perspective on the effects of standardized tests.*

In the past two years, the number of students expelled from elementary and secondary schools in Chicago has nearly doubled. Expelled kids get sent to something called "safe schools," run by for-profit organizations. When a reporter asked Chicago officials why the number of spaces in the for-profit academies was far smaller than the number of expelled students, the reported was reassured. Not to worry. They don't all show up. Meanwhile, the city is writing new categories and new zero-tolerance policies to push reform along. Chicago is the home of get-tough reform, and all these changes have been made in the name of upgrading "standards." The results? Test scores over the past three years have risen, we are told, by 3.4 percent in Chicago. That's a few more right answers on a standardized test, maybe.

Back in my home state of Massachusetts, the town of Lynnfield announced that it was time to end METCO, a program that for twenty years brought minority children into nearly all-white, middle-class, suburban communities. The board members explained to the press that the program wasn't helping the Lynnfield schools raise their "standards"—that is, their scores on the new tough state tests. Sometimes equity and excellence just don't mix well. So sorry.*

The stories of Chicago and Lynnfield capture a dark side of the "standards-based reform" movement in American education: the politically popular movement to devise national or state-mandated standards for what all kids should know, and high-stakes tests and sanctions to make sure they all know it. The stories show how the appeal to standards can mask and make way for other agendas: punishing kids, privatizing public education, giving up on equity.

I know how advocates of the movement to standardize standards will respond: "Good reform ideas can always be misused. Our proposals are designed to help kids, save public education, and ensure equity."

5   I disagree. Even in the hands of sincere allies of children, equity, and public education, the current push for far greater standardization than we've ever previously attempted is fundamentally misguided. It will not help to develop young minds, contribute to a robust democratic life, or aid the most vulnerable of our fellow citizens. By shifting the locus of authority to outside bodies, it undermines the capacity of schools to instruct by example in the qualities of mind that schools in a democracy should be fostering in kids—responsibility for one's own ideas, tolerance for the ideas of others, and a capacity to negotiate differences. Standardization instead turns teachers and parents into the local instruments of externally imposed expert judgment. It thus decreases the chances that young people will grow up in the midst of adults who are making hard decisions and exercising mature judgment in the face of disagreements. And it squeezes out those schools and educators that seek to show alternate possibilities, explore other paths.

The standardization movement is not based on a simple mistake. It rests on deep assumptions about the goals of education and the proper exercise of authority in the making of decisions—assumptions we ought to reject in favor of a different vision of a healthy democratic society. Drawing on my experience in schools in New York City and Boston, I will show that this alternative vision isn't utopian, even if it might be messy—as democracy is always messy.

STANDARDS-BASED REFORM

Standards-based reform systems vary enormously in their details. But they are generally organized around a set of four interconnected mechanisms: first, an official document (sometimes called a framework) designed by experts in various fields that describes what kids should know and be able to do at given grade levels in different subjects; second, classroom curricula—

---

*Eventually, Lynnfield backed off and decided to keep METCO but impose more stringent standards on METCO students than on others—a decision that prompted METCO to cut off its relationship with Lynnfield.

commercial textbooks and scripted programs—that are expected to convey that agreed-upon knowledge; third, a set of assessment tools (tests) to measure whether children have achieved the goals specified in the framework; and fourth, a scheme of rewards and penalties directed at schools and school systems, but ultimately at individual kids, who fail to meet the standards as measured by the tests. Cutoff points are set at various politically feasible points—in some states they are pegged so that nearly 90 percent of the students fail, whereas other states fail less than 10 percent. School administrators (and possibly teachers) are fired if schools fail to reach particular goals after a given period of time, and kids are held back in a grade, sent to summer school, and finally refused diplomas if they don't meet the cutoff scores.

Massachusetts, for instance, has recently devised tests in English, mathematics, history, and science (to be followed by other subjects over time) covering the state's mandated frameworks. The tests are given in grades four, eight, and ten. Beginning in 2003, students will need to pass the grade-ten tests to get a Massachusetts high school diploma; moreover, the tests are intended to serve as the sole criterion for rating schools, for admission to public colleges, and for as many other rewards and sanctions as busy state officials can devise.

The Massachusetts tests are not typical; each state has its own variant. The Massachusetts tests are unusually long (fifteen to twenty hours), and cover a startling amount of territory. For fourth graders the history and social studies portions allow the test makers to ask questions about anything that happened between prehistoric times and A.D. 500 in "the world" and in the United States until 1865. While world history expands in the upper grades, a student can get a high school diploma without ever studying U.S. history after 1865. The science and math portions are equally an inch deep and a mile wide. And the selections and questions on the reading tests were initially designed with full knowledge (and intent) that if scores did not immediately improve 80 percent of all fourth graders would fail, even though Massachusetts fourth graders rank near the top in most national reading assessments.

10   But the specifics of the tests are not the central issue. Even if they were replaced by saner instruments, they would still embody a fundamentally misguided approach to school reform. To see just how they are misguided, we need first to ask about their rationale. Why are these tests being imposed?

WHY STANDARDS?

Six basic assumptions underlie the current state and national standard-setting and testing programs now off the ground in forty-nine of fifty states (all but Iowa):

1. *Goals:* It is possible and desirable to agree on a single definition of what constitutes a well-educated eighteen-year-old and demand

that every school be held to the same definition. We have, it is argued, gotten by without such an agreement at a great cost—witness the decline of public education—in comparison with other nations with tight national systems.

2. *Authority:* The task of defining "well-educated" is best left to experts—educators, political officials, leaders from industry and the major academic disciplines—operating within a system of political checks and balances. That each state's definition at the present time varies so widely suggests the eventual need for a single national standard.

3. *Assessment:* With a single definition in place, it will be possible to measure and compare individuals and schools across communities—local, state, national, international. To this end, curricular norms for specific ages and grades should be translated into objective tests that provide a system of uniform scores for all public, and if possible private, schools and districts. Such scores should permit public comparisons between and among students, schools, districts, and states at any point in time.

15 4. *Enforcement:* Sanctions, too, need to be standardized, that is, removed from local self-interested parties, including parents, teachers, and local boards. Only a more centralized and distant system can resist the pressures from people closest to the child—the very people who have become accustomed to low standards.

5. *Equity:* Expert-designed standards, imposed through tests, are the best way to achieve educational equity. While a uniform national system would work best if all students had relatively equal resources, equity requires introducing such a system as rapidly as possible regardless of disparities. It is especially important for schools with scarcer resources to focus their work, concentrating on the essentials. Standardization and remotely controlled sanctions thus offer the best chance precisely for underfunded communities and schools, and for less well educated and less powerful families.

6. *Effective Learning:* Clear-cut expectations, accompanied by automatic rewards and punishments, will produce greater effort, and effort—whether induced by the desire for rewards, fear of punishment, or shame—is the key to learning. When teachers as well as students know what constitutes failure, and also know the consequences of failure, a rational system of rewards and punishments becomes an effective tool. Automatic penalties work for schooling

much as they do for crime; consistency and certainty are the keys. For that reason compassion requires us to stand firm, even in the face of pain and failure in the early years.

A Crisis?

The current standards-based reform movement took off in 1983 in response to the widely held view that America was at extreme economic risk, largely because of bad schools. The battle cry, called out first in *A Nation at Risk*, launched an attack on dumb teachers, uncaring mothers, social promotion, and general academic permissiveness. Teachers and a new group labeled "educationists" were declared the main enemy, which undermined their credibility, and set the stage for cutting them and their concerns out of the cure. According to critics, American education needed to be reimagined, made more rigorous, and, above all, brought under the control of experts who, unlike educators and parents, understood the new demands of our economy and culture. The cure might curtail the work of some star teachers and star schools, and it might lead, as the education chief of Massachusetts recently noted, to a lot of crying fourth graders. But the gravity of the long-range risks to the nation demanded strong medicine.

Two claims were thus made: that our once-great public system was no longer performing well, and that its weaknesses were undermining America's economy.

20   Most critics have long agreed that the data in support of the claim about school decline are at best weak (see Richard Rothstein's 1998 book, *The Way We Were?*). As a result, the debate shifted, although the average media story hardly noticed, to an acknowledgment that even if there wasn't a decline in school achievement, the demands of the new international economy required reinventing our schools anyway. Whether the crisis was real or imagined, change was required. But efforts to induce changes in teaching and learning met with widespread resistance from many different quarters: from citizens, parents, teachers, and local officials. Some schools changed dramatically, and some changed bits and pieces, but the timetable was far too slow for the reformers. The constituents who originally coalesced around *A Nation at Risk* began to argue that the fault lay either in the nature of public schooling itself or in the excesses of local empowerment. The cure would have to combine more competition from the private or semiprivate sector and more rigorous control by external experts who understood the demands of our economy and had the clout to impose change. This latter viewpoint has dominated the standards-based reform movement.

Unfortunately, a sense of reality has been lost in these shifting terms of debate. Now, fifteen years (more or less) after analysts discovered the great crisis of American education, the American economy is soaring, the productivity of our workforce is probably tops in the world, and our system of advanced education is the envy of the world. In elementary school literacy (where critics claim that sentimental pedagogues have for decades failed to teach children how to read), the United States still ranks second or third, topped only by one or another of the Scandinavian countries. While we rank lower in math and science tests, we continue to lead the world in technology and inventiveness. If the earlier argument was right and economics prowess requires good schooling, then teachers in America ought to be congratulated, and someone should be embarrassed by the false alarm. Instead, the idea that schools are a disaster, and that fixing them fast is vital to our economy, has become something of a truism. It remains the excuse for all reform efforts, and for carrying them out on the scale and pace proposed.

Educators from the progressive tradition are often accused of "experimenting" on kids. But never in the history of the nation have progressives proposed an experiment so drastic, vast, and potentially serious in its real-life impact on millions of young people. If the consequences are other than those its supporters hope for, the harm to the nation's educational system and the youngsters involved—maybe even to our economy—will be large and hard to undo.

THE REAL CRISIS

The coalition of experts who produced *A Nation at Risk* were wrong when they announced the failure of American public education and its critical role in our economic decline. Constructive debate about reform should begin by acknowledging this misjudgment. It should then also acknowledge the even bigger crisis that schools have played a major part in deepening, if not actually creating, and could play a big part in curing. This crisis requires quite a different set of responses, often in direct conflict with standardization.

An understanding of this other crisis begins by noting that we have the lowest voter turnout by far of any modern industrial country; we are exceptional for the absence of responsible care for our most vulnerable citizens (we spend less on child welfare—baby care, medical care, family leave—than almost every foreign counterpart); we don't come close to other advanced industrial countries in income equity; and our high rate of (and investment in) incarceration places us in a class by ourselves. All of these, of course, affect some citizens far more than others: and the heaviest burdens fall on the poor, the young, and people of color.

25   These social and political indicators are suggestive of a crisis in human relationships. Virtually all discussions, right or left, about what's wrong in our otherwise successful society acknowledge the absence of any sense of responsibility for one's community and of decency in personal relationships. An important cause of this subtler crisis, I submit, is that the closer our youth come to adulthood the less they belong to communities that include responsible adults, and the more stuck they are in peer-only subcultures.

We've created two parallel cultures, and it's no wonder the ones on the other side live and act seemingly footloose and fancy-free but in truth often lost, confused, and knit together for temporary self-protection. The consequences are critical for all our youngsters, but obviously more severe—often disastrous—for those less identified with the larger culture of success.

Many changes in our society aided and abetted the shifts that have produced this alienation. But one important change has been in the nature of schooling. Our schools have grown too distant, too big, too standardized, too uniform, too divorced from their communities, too alienating of young from old and old from young. Few youngsters and few teachers have an opportunity to know each other by more than name (if that); and schools are organized such that "knowing each other" is nearly impossible. In these settings it's hard to teach young people how to be responsible to others, or to concern themselves with their community. At best they develop loyalties to the members of their immediate circle of friends (and perhaps their own nuclear family). Even when teens take jobs their fellow workers and their customers are likely to be peers. Apprenticeship as a way to learn to be an adult is disappearing. The public and its schools, the "real" world and the schoolhouse, young people and adults, have become disconnected, and until they are reconnected no list of particular bits of knowledge will be of much use.

In my youth there were over 200,000 school boards. Today there are fewer than 20,000 and the average school, which in my youth had only a few hundred students, now holds thousands. At this writing, Miami and Los Angeles are in the process of building the two largest high schools ever. The largest districts and the largest and most anonymous schools are again those that serve our least-advantaged children.

Because of the disconnection between the public and its schools, the power to protect or support them now lies increasingly in the hands of public or private bodies that have no immediate stake in the daily life of the students. CEOs, federal and state legislators, university experts, presidential think tanks, make more and more of the daily decisions about schools. For example, the details of the school day and year are determined by state legislators—often down to minutes per day for each subject taught, and whether Johnny gets promoted from third to fourth grade. The school's budget depends on it. Site-based school councils are increasingly the "in" thing, just as the scope of their responsibility narrows.

Public schools, after a romance with local power, beginning in the late 1960s and ending in the early 1990s, are increasingly organized as interchangeable units of a larger state organism, each expected to conform to the intelligence of some central agency or expert authority. The locus of authority in young people's lives has shifted away from the adults kids know well and who know the kids well—at a cost. Home schooling or private schooling seems more and more the natural next step for those with the means and the desire to remain in authority.

30   Our school troubles are not primarily the result of too easy course work or too much tolerance for violence. The big trouble lies instead in the company our children keep—or, more precisely, don't keep. They no longer keep company with us, the grown-ups they are about to become. And the grown-ups they do encounter seem less and less worthy of their respect. What kid, after all, wants to be seen emulating people he's been told are too dumb to exercise power, and are simply implementing the commands of the real experts?

ALTERNATIVE ASSUMPTIONS

Just as the conventional policy assumptions emerge naturally from a falsely diagnosed crisis, so does the crisis I have sketched suggest an alternative set of assumptions.

1. *Goals:* In a democracy, there are multiple, legitimate definitions of "a good education" and "well-educated," and it is desirable to acknowledge that plurality. Openly differing viewpoints constitute a healthy tension in a democratic, pluralistic society. Even where a mainstream view (consensus) exists, alternate views that challenge the consensus are critical to the society's health. Young people need to be exposed to competing views, and to adults debating choices about what's most important. As John Stuart Mill said, "It is not the mind of heretics that are deteriorated most, by the ban placed on all inquiry which does not end in the orthodox conclusions. The greatest harm is done to those who are not heretics, and whose whole mental development is cramped, and their reason cowed, by the fear of heresy."

2. *Authority:* In fundamental questions of education, experts should be subservient to citizens. Experts and laymen alike have an essential role in shaping both ends and means, the what and the how. While it is wise to involve experts from both business and the academy, they provide only one set of opinions, and are themselves rarely of a single mind. Moreover, it is educationally important for young people to be in the company of adults—teachers, family members, and other adults in their own communities—powerful enough to decide important things. They need to witness the exercise of judgment, the weighing of means and ends by people they can imagine becoming; and they need to see how responsible adults handle disagreement. If we think the adults in children's lives are, in Jefferson's words, "not enlightened enough to exercise their control with a wholesome discretion, the remedy is not to take it from them, but to inform their discretion by education."

3. *Assessment:* Standardized tests are too simple and simpleminded for high-stakes assessment of children and schools. Important decisions regarding kids and teachers should always be based on multi-

ple sources of evidence that seem appropriate and credible to those most concerned. These are old testing truisms, backed even by the testing industry, which has never claimed the level of omniscience many standards advocates assume of it. The state should require only the forms of assessment be public, constitutionally sound, and subject to a variety of "second opinions" by experts representing other interested parties. Where states feel obliged to set norms—for example, in granting state diplomas or access to state universities— these should be flexible, allowing schools maximum autonomy to demonstrate the ways they have reached such norms through other forms of assessment.

35   **4.** *Enforcement:* Sanctions should remain in the hands of the local community, to be determined by people who know the particulars of each child and each situation. The power of both business and the academy are already substantial; their access to the means of persuasion (television, the press, and so forth) and their power to determine access to jobs and higher education already impinge on the freedom of local communities. Families and their communities should not be required to make decisions about their own students and their own work based on such external measures. It is sufficient that they are obliged to take them into account in their deliberations about their children's future options.

5. *Equity:* A fairer distribution of resources is the principal means for achieving educational equity. The primary national responsibility is to narrow the resource gap between the most and least advantaged, both between 9 A.M. and 3 P.M. and during the other five sixths of their waking lives when rich and poor students are also learning—but very different things. To this end publicly accessible comparisons of educational achievement should always include information regarding the relative resources that the families of students, schools, and communities bring to the schooling enterprise.

6. *Effective Learning:* Improved learning is best achieved by improving teaching and learning relationships, by enlisting the energies of both teachers and learners. The kinds of learning required of citizens cannot be accomplished by standardized and centrally imposed systems of learning, even if we desired it for other reasons. Human learning, to be efficient, effective, and long-lasting, requires the engagement of learners on their own behalf, and rests on the relationships that develop between schools and their communities, between teachers and their students, and between the individual learner and what is to be learned.

No "scientific" argument can conclusively determine whether this set of assumptions or the set sketched earlier is true. Although some research suggests that human learning is less efficient when motivated by rewards and punishments, and that fear is a poor motivator, I doubt that further research will settle the issue. But because of the crisis of human relationships, I urge that we consider the contrary claims rather more seriously than we have. We may even find that in the absence of strong human relationships rigorous intellectual training in the most fundamental academic subjects cannot flourish. In a world shaped by powerful centralized media, restoring a greater balance of power between local communities and central authorities, between institutions subject to democratic control and those beyond their control, may be vastly more important than educational reformers bent on increased centralization acknowledge.

An Alternative Model

Suppose, then, we think about school reform in light of these alternative assumptions. What practical model of schools and learning do they support? In brief, our hope lies in schools that are more personal, compelling, and attractive than the Internet or TV, where youngsters can keep company with interesting and powerful adults who are in turn in alliance with the students' families and local institutions. We need to surround kids with adults who know and care for our children, who have opinions and are accustomed to expressing them publicly, and who know how to reach reasonable collective decisions in the face of disagreement. That means increasing local decision making, and simultaneously decreasing the size and bureaucratic complexity of schools. Correspondingly, the worst thing we can do is to turn teachers and schools into the vehicles for implementing externally imposed standards.

40   Is such an alternative practical? Are the assumptions behind it mere sentiment?

At the Mission Hill in Boston, one of ten new Boston public schools initiated by the Boston Public Schools and the Boston Teachers Union, we designed a school to support such alternative practices. The families who come to Mission Hill are chosen by lottery and represent a cross section of Boston's population. We intentionally keep the school small with fewer than two hundred students ages five to thirteen—so that the adults can meet regularly, take responsibility for each other's work, and confer and argue over how best to get things right. Parents join the staff not only for formal governance meetings, but for monthly informal suppers, conversations, good times. Our oldest kids, the eighth graders, will graduate only when they can show us all that they meet our graduation standards, which are the result of lots of parent, staff, and community dialogue over several years.

All our students study—once when they are little, once when they are older—a schoolwide interdisciplinary curriculum. Last fall they all became experts on Boston and Mission Hill, learning its history (and their own), geography, architecture, distinct neighborhoods, and figures of importance.

Last winter they all re-created ancient Egypt at 67 Allegheny Street. This coming winter they will re-create ancient China. Each spring they dig into a science-focused curriculum theme. The common curriculum allowed us, for example, to afford professional and amateur Egyptologists, who joined us from time to time as lively witnesses to a lifelong passion. We have a big central corridor that serves as our public mall, where kids paint murals and mix together to read and talk across ages. High school youngsters who share the building with us read with little ones, take them on trips, and generally model what it can mean to be a more responsible and well-educated person.

We invented our own standards, not out of whole cloth but with an eye to what the world out there expects and what we deem valuable and important. And we assess them through the work the kids do and the commentary of others about that work. Our standards are intended to deepen and broaden young people's habits of mind, their craftsmanship, and their work habits. Other schools may select quite a different way of describing and exhibiting their standards. But they too need to consciously construct their standards in ways that give schooling purpose and coherence, and then commit themselves to achieving them. And the kids need to understand the standards and their rationale. They must see school as not just a place to get a certificate, but a place that lives by the same standards it sets for them. Thus the Mission Hill school not only sets standards but has considerable freedom and flexibility with regard to how it spends its public funds and organizes its time to attain them. All ten pilot schools offer examples of different ways this might play out, ways that could be replicated in all Boston schools.

Standard setting and assessment are not once-and-for-all issues. We reexamine our school constantly to see that it remains a place that engages all of us in tough but interesting learning tasks, nourishes and encourages the development of reasonable and judicious trust, and nurtures a passion for making sense of things and the skills needed to do so. We expect disagreements—sometimes painful ones. We know that even well-intentioned, reasonable people cross swords over deeply held beliefs. And we know, too, that these differences can be sources of valuable education when the school itself can negotiate the needed compromises.

What is impressive at Mission Hill, at the other pilot schools, at the Central Park East School in New York's East Harlem, where I worked for twenty-five years, and the thousands of other small schools like them, is that over time the kids buy in. These schools receive the same per capita public funding as other schools receive, are subject to city and state testing, and must obey the same basic health, safety, and civil rights regulations. But because these schools are small, the families and faculties are together by choice, and all concerned can exercise substantial power over staffing, scheduling, curriculum, and assessment, the schools' cultural norms and expectations are very different than those of most other public schools.

45   The evidence suggests that most youngsters have a sufficiently deep hunger for the relationships these schools offer them—among kids and

between adults and kids—that they choose school over the alternative cultures on the Net, tube, and street. Over 90 percent of Central Park East's very typical students stuck it out, graduated, and went on to college. And most persevered through higher education. Did they ever rebel, get mad at us, reassert their contrary values and adolescent preferences? Of course. Did we fail with some? Yes. But it turns out that the hunger for grown-up connections is strong enough to make a difference if we give it a chance. Studies launched in New York between 1975 and 1995 conducted on the other similar schools show the same pattern of success.

Standards, yes. Absolutely. But as Thedore Sizer, who put the idea of standards on the school map in the early 1980s, also told us then: we need standards held by real people who matter in the lives of our young. School, family, and community must forge their own, in dialogue with and in response to the larger world of which they are a part. There will always be tensions; but if the decisive, authoritative voice always comes from anonymous outsiders, then kids cannot learn what it takes to develop their own voice.

I know this "can be" because I've been there. The flowering of so many new public schools of choice over the past two decades proves that under widely different circumstances, very different kinds of leadership and different auspices, a powerful alternative to externally imposed standards is available.

And I also know the powerful reasons why it "can't be"—because I've witnessed firsthand the resistance even to allowing others to follow suit, much less encouraging or mandating them to do so. The resistance comes not simply from bad bureaucrats or fearful unions (the usual bogeymen), but from legislators and mayors and voters, from citizens who think that if an institution is public it has to be all things to all constituents (characterless and mediocre by definition), and from various elites who see teachers and private citizens as too dumb to engage in making important decisions. That's a heady list of resisters.

50   But small self-governing schools of choice, operating with considerable flexibility and freedom, also resonate with large numbers of people, including many of those who are gathering around charter schools, and even some supporters of privatization and home schooling. They too come from a wide political spectrum and could be mobilized.

ACCOUNTABILITY

And yet doubts about accountability will linger. In a world of smaller, more autonomous schools not responsible to centralized standardization, how will we know who is doing a good job and who isn't? How can we prevent schools from claiming they're doing just fine, and having those claims believed, when they may not be true? Are we simply forced to trust them, with no independent evidence?

What lies behind these worries? For those who buy into the conventional assumptions, anything but top-down standardization seems pointless. But for those whose concern is more practical, there are some straightforward and practical answers to the issue of accountability that do not require standardization.

To begin with, I am not advocating the elimination of all systems for taking account of how schools and students are doing. In any case, that is hardly a danger.

Americans invented the modern, standardized, norm-referenced test. Our students have been taking more tests more often than any nation on the face of the earth, and schools and districts have been going public with test scores starting almost from the moment children enter school. For the third- or fourth-grade level (long before any of our international counterparts bother to test children) we have test data for virtually all schools, by race, class, and gender. We know exactly how many kids did better or worse in every subcategory. We have test data for almost every grade thereafter in reading and math, and to some degree in all other subjects. This has been the case for nearly half a century. Large numbers of our eighteen-year-olds now take standardized college entry tests (SATs and ACTs). In addition, the national government now offers us its own tests—the NAEP—which are given to an uncontaminated sample of students from across the United States and now reported by grade and state. And all of the above is very public.

55   In addition, public schools have been required to produce statements attesting to their financial integrity—how they spend their money—at least as rigorously as any business enterprise. They are held accountable for regularly reporting who works for them and what their salaries are. In most systems there are tightly prescribed rules and regulations; schools are obliged to fill out innumerable forms regarding almost every aspect of their work: how many kids are receiving special education, how many incidents of violence, how many suspensions, how many graduates, what grades students have received, how many hours and minutes they study each and every subject, and the credentials of their faculties. This information, and much more, is public. And the hiring and firing of superintendents has become a very common phenomenon.

In a nation in which textbooks are the primary vehicle for distributing knowledge in schools, a few major textbook publishers, because of a few major state textbook laws, dominate the field, offering most teachers and schools (and students) very standardized accounts of what is to be learned, and when and how to deliver this knowledge. Moreover, most textbooks have always come armed with their own end-of-chapter tests, increasingly designed to look like the real thing; indeed, test makers also are the publishers of many of the major standardized tests.

In short, we have been awash in accountability and standardization for a very long time, but we are missing precisely the qualities that the last big wave of reform was intended to respond to: teachers, kids, and families who know each other or each other's work and take responsibility for it; we are missing communities built around their own articulated and public standards and ready to show them off to others.

The schools I have worked in and support have shown how much more powerful accountability becomes when one takes this latter path. The work produced by Central Park East students, for example, is collected regularly in portfolios, and it is examined (and in the case of high school students, judged) by tough internal and external reviewers, in a process that closely resembles a doctoral oral exam. The standards by which a student is evaluated are easily accessible to families, clear to kids, and capable of being judged by other parties. In addition schools such as this undergo schoolwide external assessments that take into account the quality of their curriculum, instruction, staff development, and culture as well as the impact of the school on students' future success (in college, work, and so forth).

Are the approaches designed by Central Park East or Mission Hill the best way? That's probably the wrong question. We never intended to suggest that everyone should follow our system. It would be nice if it were easier for others to adopt our approach; it would be even better if it were easier—in fact required—for others to adopt alternatives to it, including the use of standardized tests if they so choose. My argument is for more local control, not for one true way.

60   I opt for more local control not because I think the larger society has no common interests at stake in how we educate all children, or because local people are smarter or intrinsically more honorable. The interests of wider publics are important in my way of thinking. I know that pressure exists at Mission Hill to not accept or push out students who are difficult to educate, who will make us look worse on any test, or whose families are a nuisance. It's a good thing that others are watching us to prevent such exclusion.

But the United States is now hardly in danger of too much localized power. (The only local powers we seem to be interested in expanding are those that allow us to resegregate our schools by race or gender.) What is missing is balance—some power in the hands of those whose agenda is first and foremost the feelings of particular kids, their particular families, their perceived local values and needs. Without this balance by knowledge that holding David over in third grade will not produce the desired effects is useless knowledge. So is my knowledge of different ways to reach him through literature or history. This absence of local power is bad for David's education and bad for democracy. A backseat driver may be more expert than the actual driver, but there are limits to what can be accomplished from the rear seat.

In short, the argument is not about the need for standards or accountability, but what kind serves us best. I believe standardization will make it harder to hold people accountable and harder to develop sound and useful standards. The intellectual demands of the twenty-first century, as well as the demands of democratic life, are best met by preserving plural definitions of a good education, local decision making, and respect for ordinary human judgments.

EDUCATION AND DEMOCRACY

If we are to make use of what we knew in Dewey's day (and know even better today) about how the human species best learns, we will have to start by throwing away the dystopia of the ant colony, the smoothly functioning (and quietly humming) factory where everything goes according to plan, and replace it with a messy, often rambunctious, community, with its multiple demands and complicated trade-offs. The new schools that might better serve democracy and the economy will have to be capable of constantly remaking themselves and still provide for sufficient stability, routine, ritual, and shared ethos. Impossible? Of course. So these schools will veer too far one way or the other at different times in their history, will learn from each other, shift focus, and find a new balance. There will always be a party of order and a party of messiness.

If schools are not all required to follow all the same fads, maybe they will learn something from their separate experiments. And that will help to nurture the two indispensable traits of a democratic society: a high degree of tolerance for others, indeed genuine empathy for them, as well as a high degree of tolerance for uncertainty, ambiguity, and puzzlement, indeed enjoyment of them.

65   A vibrant and nurturing community, with clear and regular guideposts—its own set of understandings, its people with a commitment to one another that feels something rather like love and affection—can sustain such rapid change without losing its humanity. Such a community must relish its disagreements, its oddballs, its misfits. Not quite families, but closer to our definition of family than of factory, such schools will make high demands on their members and have a sustaining and relentless sense of purpose and coherence, but will be ready also to always (at least sometimes) even reconsider their own core beliefs. Their members will come home exhausted, but not burned out.

Everything that moves us toward these qualities will be good for the ideal of democracy. A democracy in which less than half its members see themselves as "making enough difference" to bother to vote in any election is surely endangered—far more endangered, at risk, than our economy. It's for the loss of belief in the capacity to influence the world, not our economic ups and downs, that we educators should accept some responsibility. What I have learned from thirty years in small powerful schools is that it is here above all that schools can make a difference, can alter the odds.

We can't beat the statistical advantage on the next round of tests that being advantaged has over being disadvantaged; we can, however, substantially affect the gap between rich and poor where it will count, in the long haul of life. Even there it's hard to see how schools by themselves can eliminate the gap, but we can stop enlarging it. The factory-like schools we invented a century ago to handle the masses were bound to enlarge the gap. But trained mindlessness at least fit the world of work so many young people were destined for. We seem now to be reinventing a twenty-first-century version of the factory-like school—for the mindworkers of tomorrow.

It is a matter of choice; such a future does not roll in on the wheels of inevitability. We have the resources, the knowledge, and plenty of living examples of the many different kinds of schools that might serve our needs better. All we need is a little more patient confidence in the good sense of "the people"—in short, a little more commitment to democracy.

CONVERSATION STARTER

Discuss your learning style. What motivates you to learn? Do you think tests are an effective motivation for learning? If you were a teacher, how would you motivate your students to learn?

READING MATTERS

1. What assumptions support the standardization movement?
2. According to Meier, why is the relationship between schools and community essential to the reform of our educational system?
3. How are educational standards defined in Meier's schools? How does this differ from the standards she argues against?
4. Meier argues against standards. Is her argument effective? What are the strengths and/or weaknesses of her argument?

WRITING MATTERS

1. Write an essay in response to Meier's argument. Do you support or oppose the standards movement?
2. What skills will be important in the new economy? What role will education play in shaping people for the workplace? Write an essay that reflects your point of view.
3. Write an educational plan for the school you currently attend that would support your vision of a well-educated student.

RELEVANT WEB SITES

U.S. DEPARTMENT OF EDUCATION <http://www.ed.gov>

The official web site of the U.S. Department of Education provides information about current educational headlines and debates, research and statistics, and links to relevant web sites.

THE CHALLENGE OF STANDARDS
<http://www.pbs.org/wgbh/pages/frontline/shows/schools/standards/>

This PBS web site provides links to relevant historical documents, articles, and organizations addressing the challenge of educational standards in our schools.

Howard Gardner (b. 1943)

Multiple Intelligences

Howard Gardner is best known for his theory of multiple intelligences and for his individualized and humanistic approach to education: "My feeling is that assessment can be much broader, much more humane than it is now, and that psychologists should spend less time ranking people and more time trying to help them." Gardner, the author of 15 books on learning and the mind, has been involved in school reform since 1983, when his theory of multiple intelligences was first presented in Frames of Mind. *A professor of education and adjunct professor of psychology at Harvard, Howard Gardner is the codirector of Project Zero, a research group in human cognition that has a special focus on the arts and community. His most widely read books include* The Mind's New Science *(1985),* The Unschooled Mind *(1991),* Leading Minds: An Anatomy of Leadership *(1996),* Creativity and Development Counterpoints *(2003) and* Changing Minds *(2004). The selection that follows is excerpted from* Frames of Mind.

Allow me to transport all of us to the Paris of 1900—La Belle Epoque—when the city fathers of Paris approached a psychologist named Alfred Binet with an unusual request: Could he devise some kind of a measure that would predict which youngsters would succeed and which would fail in the primary grades of Paris schools? As everybody knows, Binet succeeded. In short order, his discovery came to be called the "intelligence test"; his measure, the "IQ." Like other Parisian fashions, the IQ soon made its way to the United States, where it enjoyed a modest success until World War I. Then, it was used to test over one million American recruits, and it had truly arrived. From that day on, the IQ test has looked like psychology's biggest success—a genuinely useful scientific tool.

What is the vision that led to the excitement about IQ? At least in the West, people had always relied on intuitive assessments of how smart other people were. Now intelligence seemed to be quantifiable. You could measure someone's actual or potential height, and now, it seemed, you could also measure someone's actual or potential intelligence. We had one dimension of mental ability along which we could array everyone.

The search for the perfect measure of intelligence has proceeded apace. Here, for example, are some quotations from an ad for a widely used test:

> Need an individual test which quickly provides a stable and reliable estimate of intelligence in four or five minutes per form? Has three forms? Does not depend on verbal production or subjective scoring? Can be used with the severely handicapped (even paralyzed) if they can signal yes or no? Handles two-year-olds and superior adults with the same short series of items and the same format? Only $16.00 complete.

Now, that's quite a claim. The American psychologist Arthur Jensen suggests that we could look at reaction time to assess intelligence: a set of lights go on; how quickly can the subject react? The British psychologist

Hans Eysenck suggests that investigators of intelligence should look directly at brain waves.

There are also, of course, more sophisticated versions of the IQ test. One of them is called the Scholastic Aptitude Test (SAT). It purports to be a similar kind of measure, and if you add up a person's verbal and math scores, as is often done, you can rate him or her along a single intellectual dimension. Programs for the gifted, for example, often use that kind of measure; if your IQ is in excess of 130, you're admitted to the program.

5   I want to suggest that along this one-dimensional view of how to assess people's minds comes a corresponding view of school, which I will call the "uniform view." In the uniform school, there is a core curriculum, a set of facts that everybody should know, and very few electives. The better students, perhaps those with higher IQs, are allowed to take courses that call upon critical reading, calculation, and thinking skills. In the "uniform school," there are regular assessments using paper and pencil instruments, of the IQ or SAT variety. They yield reliable rankings of people; the best and the brightest get into the better colleges, and perhaps—but only perhaps— they will also get better rankings in life. There is no question but that this approach works well for certain people—schools such as Harvard are eloquent testimony to that. Since this measurement and selection system is clearly meritocratic in certain respects, it has something to recommend it.

But there is an alternative vision that I would like to present—one based on a radically different view of the mind, and one that yields a very different view of school. It is a pluralistic view of mind, recognizing many different and discrete facets of cognition, acknowledging that people have different cognitive strengths and contrasting cognitive styles. I would also like to introduce the concept of an individual-centered school that takes this multifaceted view of intelligence seriously. This model for a school is based in part on findings from sciences that did not even exist in Binet's time: cognitive science (the study of the mind), and neuroscience (the study of the brain). One such approach I have called my "theory of multiple intelligences." Let me tell you something about its sources, its claims, and its educational implications for a possible school of the future.

Dissatisfaction with the concept of IQ and with unitary views of intelligence is fairly widespread—one thinks, for instance, of the work of L. L. Thurstone, J. P. Guilford, and other critics. From my point of view, however, these criticisms do not suffice. The whole concept has to be challenged; in fact, it has to be replaced.

I believe that we should get away altogether from tests and correlations among tests, and look instead at more naturalistic sources of information about how peoples around the world develop skills important to their way of life. Think, for example, of sailors in the South Seas, who find their way around hundreds, or even thousands, of islands by looking at the constellations of stars in the sky, feeling the way a boat passes over the water, and noticing a few scattered landmarks. A word for intelligence in a society of these sailors would probably refer to that kind of navigational ability.

Think of surgeons and engineers, hunters and fishermen, dancers and choreographers, athletes and athletic coaches, tribal chiefs and sorcerers. All of these different roles need to be taken into account if we accept the way I define intelligence—that is, as the ability to solve problems, or to fashion products, that are valued in one or more cultural or community settings. For the moment I am saying nothing about whether there is one dimension, or more than one dimension, of intelligence; nothing about whether intelligence is inborn or developed. Instead I emphasize the ability to solve problems and to fashion products. In my work I seek the building blocks of the intelligences used by the aforementioned sailors and surgeons and sorcerers.

10   The science in this enterprise, to the extent that it exists, involves trying to discover the *right* description of the intelligences. What is an intelligence? To try to answer this question, I have, with my colleagues, surveyed a wide set of sources which, to my knowledge, have never been considered together before. One source is what we already know concerning the development of different kinds of skills in normal children. Another source, and a very important one, is information on the ways that these abilities break down under conditions of brain damage. When one suffers a stroke or some other kind of brain damage, various abilities can be destroyed, or spared, in isolation from other abilities. This research with brain-damaged patients yields a very powerful kind of evidence, because it seems to reflect the way the nervous system has evolved over the millennia to yield certain discrete kinds of intelligence.

My research group looks at other special populations as well: prodigies, idiot savants, autistic children, children with learning disabilities, all of whom exhibit very jagged cognitive profiles—profiles that are extremely difficult to explain in terms of a unitary view of intelligence. We examine cognition in diverse animal species and in dramatically different cultures. Finally, we consider two kinds of psychological evidence: correlations among psychological tests of the sort yielded by a careful statistical analysis of a test battery; and the results of efforts of skill training. When you train a person in skill A, for example, does that training transfer to skill B? So, for example, does training mathematics enhance one's musical abilities, or vice versa?

Obviously, through looking at all these sources—information on development, on breakdowns, on special populations, and the like—we end up with a cornucopia of information. Optimally, we would perform a statistical factor analysis, feeding all the data into a computer and noting the kinds of factors or intelligences that are extracted. Alas, the kind of material with which I was working didn't exist in a form that is susceptible to computation, and so we had to perform a more subjective factor analysis. In truth, we simply studied the results as best we could, and tried to organize them in a way that made sense to us, and hopefully, to critical readers as well. My resulting list of seven intelligences is a preliminary attempt to organize this mass of information.

I want now to mention briefly the seven intelligences we have located, and to cite one or two examples of each intelligence. Linguistic intelligence is the kind of ability exhibited in its fullest form, perhaps, by poets. Logical-mathematical intelligence, as the name implies, is logical and mathematical ability, as well as scientific ability. Jean Piaget, the great developmental psychologist, thought he was studying *all* intelligence, but I believe he was studying the development of logical-mathematical intelligence. Although I name the linguistic and logical-mathematical intelligences first, it is not because I think they are most important—in fact, I am convinced that all seven of the intelligences have equal priority. In our society, however, we have put linguistic and logical-mathematical intelligences, figuratively speaking, on a pedestal. Much of our testing is based on this high valuation of verbal and mathematical skills. If you do well in language and logic, you should do well in IQ tests and SATs, and you may well get into a prestigious college, but whether you do well once you leave is probably going to depend as much on the extent to which you possess and use the other intelligences, and it is to those that I want to give equal attention.

Spatial intelligence is the ability to form a mental model of a spatial world and to be able to maneuver and operate using that model. Sailors, engineers, surgeons, sculptors, and painters, to name just a few examples, all have highly developed spatial intelligence. Musical intelligence is the fourth category of ability we have identified: Leonard Bernstein had lots of it; Mozart, presumably, had even more. Bodily-kinesthetic intelligence is the ability to solve problems or to fashion products using one's whole body, or parts of the body. Dancers, athletes, surgeons, and craftspeople all exhibit highly developed bodily-kinesthetic intelligence.

15   Finally, I propose two forms of personal intelligence—not well understood, elusive to study, but immensely important. Interpersonal intelligence is the ability to understand other people: what motivates them, how they work, how to work cooperatively with them. Successful salespeople, politicians, teachers, clinicians, and religious leaders are all likely to be individuals with high degrees of interpersonal intelligence. Intrapersonal intelligence, a seventh kind of intelligence, is a correlative ability, turned inward. It is a capacity to form an accurate, veridical model of oneself and to be able to use that model to operate effectively in life.

These, then, are the seven intelligences that we have uncovered and described in our research. This is a preliminary list, as I have said; obviously, each form of intelligence can be subdivided, or the list can be rearranged. The real point here is to make the case for the plurality of the intellect. Also, we believe that individuals may differ in the particular intelligence profiles with which they are born, and that certainly they differ in the profiles they end up with. I think of intelligences as raw, biological potentials, which can be seen in pure form only in individuals who are, in the technical sense, freaks. In almost everybody else the intelligences work together to solve problems, to yield various kinds of cultural endstates—vocations, avocations, and the like.

This is my theory of multiple intelligences in capsule form. In my view, the purpose of school should be to develop intelligences and to help people reach vocational and avocational goals that are appropriate to their particular spectrum of intelligences. People who are helped to do so, I believe, feel more engaged and competent, and therefore more inclined to serve the society in a constructive way.

These thoughts, and the critique of a universalistic view of the mind with which I began, lead to the notion of an individual-centered school, one geared to optimal understanding and development of each student's cognitive profile. This vision stands in direct contrast to that of the uniform school that I described earlier.

The design of my ideal school of the future is based upon two assumptions. The first is that not all people have the same interests and abilities; not all of us learn in the same way. (And we now have the tools to begin to address these individual differences in school.) The second assumption is one that hurts: it is the assumption that nowadays no one person can learn everything there is to learn. We would all like, as Renaissance men and women, to know everything, or at least to believe in the potential of knowing everything, but that ideal clearly is not possible anymore. Choice is therefore inevitable, and one of the things I want to argue is that the choices that we make for ourselves, and for the people who are under our charge, might as well be informed choices. An individual-centered school would be rich in assessment of individual abilities and proclivities. It would seek to match individuals not only to curricular areas, but also to particular ways of teaching those subjects. And after the first few grades, the school would also seek to match individuals with the various kinds of life and work options that are available in their culture.

20   I want to propose a new set of roles for educators that might make this vision a reality. First of all, we might have what I will call "assessment specialists." The job of these people would be to try to understand as sensitively and comprehensively as possible the abilities and interests of the students in a school. It would be very important, however, that the assessment specialists use "intelligence-fair" instruments. We want to be able to look specifically and directly at spatial abilities, at personal abilities, and the like, and not through the usual lenses of the linguistic and logical-mathematical intelligences. Up until now nearly all assessment has depended indirectly on measurement of those abilities; if students are not strong in those two areas, their abilities in other areas may be obscured. Once we begin to try to assess other kinds of intelligences directly, I am confident that particular students will reveal strengths in quite different areas, and the notion of general brightness will disappear or become greatly attenuated.

In addition to the assessment specialist, the school of the future might have the "student-curriculum broker." It would be his or her job to help match students' profiles, goals, and interests to particular curricula and to particular styles of learning. Incidentally, I think that the new interactive technologies offer considerable promise in this area: it will probably be much easier in the future for "brokers" to match individual students to ways of learning that prove comfortable for them.

There should also be, I think, a "school-community broker," who would match students to learning opportunities in the wider community. It would be this person's job to find situations in the community, particularly options not available in the school, for children who exhibit unusual cognitive profiles. I have in mind apprenticeships, mentorships, internships in organizations, "big brothers," "big sisters"—individuals and organizations with whom these students might work to secure a feeling for different kinds of vocational and avocational roles in the society. I am not worried about those occasional youngsters who are good in everything. They're going to do just fine. I'm concerned about those who don't shine in the standardized tests, and who, therefore, tend to be written off as not having gifts of any kind. It seems to me that the school-community broker could spot these youngsters and find placements in the community that provide chances for them to shine.

There is ample room in this vision for teachers, as well, and also for master teachers. In my view, teachers would be freed to do what they are supposed to do, which is to teach their subject matter, in their preferred style of teaching. The job of master teacher would be very demanding. It would involve, first of all, supervising the novice teachers and guiding them; but the master teacher would also seek to ensure that the complex student-assessment-curriculum-community equation is balanced appropriately. If the equation is seriously imbalanced, master teachers would intervene and suggest ways to make things better.

Clearly, what I am describing is a tall order; it might even be called utopian. And there is a major risk to this program, of which I am well aware. That is the risk of premature billeting—of saying, "Well, Johnny is four, he seems to be musical, so we are going to send him to Juilliard and drop everything else." There is, however, nothing inherent in the approach that I have described that demands this early overdetermination—quite the contrary. It seems to me that early identification of strengths can be very helpful in indicating what kinds of experiences children might profit from; but early identification of weaknesses can be equally important. If a weakness is identified early, there is a chance to attend to it before it is too late, and to come up with alternative ways of teaching or of covering an important skill area.

25   We now have the technological and the human resources to implement such an individual-centered school. Achieving it is a question of will, including the will to withstand the current enormous pressures toward uniformity and unidimensional assessments. There are strong pressures now, which you read about every day in the newspapers to compare students, to compare teachers, states, even entire countries, using one dimension or criterion, a kind of crypto-IQ assessment. Clearly, everything I have described

today stands in direct opposition to that particular view of the world. Indeed that is my intent—to provide a ringing indictment of such one-track thinking.

I believe that in our society we suffer from three biases, which I have nicknamed "Westist," "Testist," and "Bestist." "Westist" involved putting certain Western cultural values, which date back to Socrates, on a pedestal. Logical thinking, for example, is important: rationality is important; but they are not the only virtues. "Testist" suggests a bias toward focusing upon those human abilities or approaches that are readily testable. If it can't be tested, it sometimes seems, it is not worth paying attention to. My feeling is that assessment can be much broader, much more humane than it is now, and that psychologists should spend less time ranking people and more time trying to help them.

"Bestist" is a not very veiled reference to a book by David Halberstam called *The Best and the Brightest.* Halberstam referred ironically to figures such as Harvard faculty members who were brought to Washington to help President John F. Kennedy and in the process launched the Vietnam War. I think that any belief that all the answers to a given problem lie in one certain approach, such as logical-mathematical thinking, can be very dangerous. Current views of intellect need to be leavened with other more comprehensive points of view.

It is of the utmost importance that we recognize and nurture all of the varied human intelligences, and all of the combinations of intelligences. We are all so different largely because we have different combinations of intelligences. If we recognize this, I think we will have at least a better chance of dealing appropriately with the many problems that we face in the world. If we can mobilize the spectrum of human abilities, not only will people feel better about themselves and more competent; it is even possible that they will also feel more engaged and better able to join the rest of the world community in working for the broader good. Perhaps if we can mobilize the full range of human intelligences and ally them to an ethical sense, we can help to increase the likelihood of our survival on this planet, and perhaps even contribute to our thriving.

Conversation Starter

Discuss how you evaluate an individual's intelligence.

Reading Matters

1. Do you agree with Gardner's critique of IQ tests? Explain your point of view.
2. What types of argumentative strategies does Gardner use to make his case? Are his strategies effective?
3. What type of research did Gardner conduct before establishing his seven forms of intelligence? Were you convinced by his research and his theory?

4. Why does Gardner connect a one-dimensional view of intelligence to a uniform or core curriculum? Do you agree with him?

WRITING MATTERS

1. Gardner is opposed to the biases in education today as reflected by terms such as "Westist," "Testist," and "Bestist." Do you agree with Gardner's theory of intelligence and how to approach teaching? Write an essay that discusses why you agree or disagree.
2. Write an essay that explains why Gardner believes that his approach to educating people will help to build stronger communities. Then, using support from your own experiences or from the ideas of other educational theorists, develop more evidence for Gardner's claim.
3. Write an essay that supports or refutes Gardner's notion of an individual-centered school, one designed to foster optimal understanding and development of each student's educational potential.

RELEVANT WEB SITES

PROJECT ZERO <http://www.pz.harvard.edu>

Harvard University's Project Zero is dedicated to their mission to understand and enhance learning, thinking, and creativity in the arts, as well as humanistic and scientific disciplines at the individual and institutional levels. This web site highlights the history of Project Zero, provides a description of current research projects, and offers a profile of the principal investigators, including codirector Howard Gardner.

HOWARD GARDNER <http://www.pz.harvard.edu/PIs/HG.htm>

Howard Gardner's personal web site includes a short biography and links to other sites that feature his work, life, and interviews.

David Bolt and Ray Crawford

Digital Divide

David Bolt is a cofounder of Studio Miramar, a San Francisco–based production company. Most recently Bolt created and was the executive producer for Digital Divide, *a four-part documentary series for PBS. David has also held several prominent positions in the field of multimedia production in addition to his role at Studio Miramar: vice-president for educational technology at the California College of Arts and Crafts (1994–1997), production director of the George Lucas Educational Foundation at Skywalker Ranch (1991–1992), executive director of the Bay Area Video Coalition (1986–1991), and production director of the Pacific Educational Network (1984–1986). Bolt has won two CINE Golden Eagles along with numerous awards for his CD-ROM and multimedia programs.*

Ray Crawford is a projects managing editor with a career in technical and educational publishing spanning over two decades. Crawford has contributed to magazines and online journals, and is a member of several scholarly and literary organizations.

The public-school student of 1899 would not have had very much trouble fitting into the classroom of 1979. Despite changes in educational policy and advances in both our understanding of the learning process and knowledge of the world around us, the educational process did not differ notably in that eighty-year span. A knowledgeable educator at the front of the room, books containing the accumulated wisdom to be imparted, and handwritten exercises intended to inculcate the material to be learned were a major part of the experience that spanned generations of students, whatever their socioeconomic background.

A student from 1979, however, might not fit so easily into the classroom world of today. The last twenty years have seen a tremendous leap forward in the use of technology in classrooms, creating a different kind of educational experience for some students—but not, by any means, for all. Access to this technology, around which much of our educational system is becoming based, is equally available to all students, is not handled equally well by all educators, and is not equally useful to everyone in education as it is presently structured.

This is the educational essence of the digital divide.

The arena of education in our nation is being altered by the introduction of computer and connectivity technology—the "wiring" of our schools. As this technology is introduced into the classroom, it can alter the way students are taught. It is important, therefore, to explore some of the fundamental concerns about introducing this technology, as well as its educational applications. There is an increasing disparity between schools and students with and without significant access to this technology, but access to technology itself is only one of many issues involved. In the world of today, more than at any time in the past century, much of a student's educational experience depends on that student's socioeconomic background. It has nothing to do with the student's intelligence, learning ability, or industriousness. Rather, it has to do with whether or not the student has access to technology, access to the information made available by that technology, and access to educators trained in integrating that technology and information into the educational experience.

5   U.S. public education encompasses many different realities, depending upon many variables, including state requirements and curricula, educator licensing requirements, and the funding available to schools. In the area of computer and communications technologies, though, there are some commonalities. The majority of public schools still don't have directly allocated funds for telecommunications and don't have adequate infrastructure to support the technology being touted and dispensed by the computer industry and the government. Of the remaining schools, most do not have adequate

funds for the maintenance and support of the equipment that they have managed to obtain. Even if adequate provision has been made for this (and it rarely is), the seemingly insurmountable obstacle of integrating this mass of equipment into a meaningful curriculum—including the significant teacher training required—still looms large.

Educators nationwide are faced with a set of continuing challenges, including overcrowded classrooms, poorly maintained facilities, uneven support, and insufficient pay scales and benefits packages. Now, in addition to their continuing mandated education requirements, teachers find themselves in the position of having to learn a wide variety of new technology-related skills to meet the social expectations of the Information Age: the use of computers, the use of a variety of software packages on computers, the use of the internet, and elementary troubleshooting techniques to offset the lack of comprehensive technical support. They are also expected to be able to convey this knowledge to their students, a group (like educators) ranging from the technophilic to the technophobic. Elena McFadden, a first grade teacher at Hoover Elementary School in Redwood City, California, is, in many ways, a typical educator trying to do her best with limited resources. "I took the computer class that teachers are required to take for their credentials, and I don't feel I received any training adequate to making me able to teach computers any better than when I walked into the class," Ms. McFadden noted. "You can't buy a bunch of computers and not train teachers to use them, and expect education and learning to go on."

Ms. McFadden is not alone in her views. As Program Director for the Markle Foundation, a private non-profit philanthropy that focuses on emerging technologies, Andrew Blau is one of the nation's preeminent specialists in education technology. While he has seen evidence that access to the technology in America's classrooms has improved, bringing the richest and the poorest schools closer together, he still feels that there are fundamental problems in the way computer technology is being brought into the classroom. "Our research suggests that it's access to trained teachers that makes the most difference in the lives of the kids," he says. "So, while the programs that exist to help poor schools get access to technology do appear to be having some effect, what we're not yet able to address is access to the one thing that seems to make the biggest difference, and that is trained teachers."

Teacher training has always been the central aspect of traditional educational methodologies, and remains so today. What is beginning to change is the way in which educators are taught, utilizing the new technologies that have taken center stage in the educational arena, a process that affords an opportunity for the educational establishment as a whole to engage in self-examination. "One opportunity that the introduction of computers in the classroom offers us," notes Mr. Blau, "is the opportunity to rethink what it is that teachers should be able to do in the classroom. What are we training them? How are we supporting them?"

The downside to this is that, as in many other fields, those instructing the next generation of educators are sometimes among the last to embrace change. Rather than seeing the new technologies as a way to look at the world with new eyes, some post-secondary instructors in education, and educators themselves, view the introduction of these technologies as a threat to their established educational methodologies. It may even be possible that, after putting in all of the time and effort needed to acquire this new skill set, many educators might re-examine their commitment to the teaching profession, precipitating a flight of many of the best and the brightest from the profession.

10 The picture remains bleak. In 1999, the Department of Education published the results of a survey of over thirty-five hundred of the nation's educators that asked about their facility with computer technology. Of those interviewed, only about 20 percent reported that they were "very well prepared" in using computer technology in the classroom, although approximately fourth-fifths of the educators indicated that they had some training in computers and related technology. Only those teachers who had received significant amounts of computer training felt that it helped their ability to use the computer in the classroom. Secretary of Education Richard Riley was not pleased with the survey results, stating that "teacher education and professional development programs are not addressing the realities found in today's classrooms. . . . One-shot workshops . . . carry little relevance to teachers' work in the classroom."

This view was reinforced by a study conducted jointly by the Milken Exchange on Educational Technology and the International Society for Technology in Education (ISTE), showing that most teacher-training programs treat computer technology as an adjunct to the curriculum, and not as a central feature. The study further indicated that teacher-training programs are not showing student educators how to effectively incorporate computer technology into their teaching methodology.

It is not enough to simply drop a bunch of computers into a classroom and walk away. It may not even be enough to completely wire an entire school district, train teachers in the use of the technology, and get students involved in using the computers thus made available. Such research indicates the need for a long, hard look at where educational technology is going. It is important to examine the situation that teachers find themselves in, and to ask whether this isn't another situation of tossing technology at a problem and asking the human factor to make adjustments.

Many of the issues surrounding the role of education in the Information Age were anticipated by former Labor Secretary Robert Reich in his 1991 book *The Work of Nations.* In it he criticized the nation's educational system for failing to provide an environment where general problem-solving and learning skills are taught and learned. He was dismayed by the lack of creativity in teaching and learning and the "simplification of reality" in educational settings, as though life in the real world were a linear series of events, each leading inevitably to the next—"a tour through history or geography or science typically has a fixed route." He attacked the prepackaged nature of lesson plans and textbooks that left no room for exploration, the discovery of greater meanings, or self-expression on the part of students. Speaking at the very beginning of the Information Age, Mr. Reich believed that current educational methodology would leave our children ill-prepared for success in what he styled the "new economy."

In general, none of the Mr. Reich's criticisms have been addressed. Eight years later, many of America's educational institutions are still trying to shoehorn computer technology directly into standardized and outdated curricula. The federal government seems to be proceeding with a program perhaps best characterized as "doing something, even if it's the wrong something" in pressing for the wiring of all of America's public classrooms by the year 2000. They may well achieve this goal, as figures released in late 1998 by the National Center for Education Statistics show that 89 percent of schools were connected to the internet and 51 percent of all classrooms were as well. The figures also indicate that these installations appear to be bridging one aspect of the digital divide. "We're making significant strides to get technology to the place where children learn—the classroom," said Richard Riley. "The 'digital divide' is closing in our nation's schools, but we have to close the continuing divide in our nation's classrooms." Unfortunately, there has been no equally dramatic announcement that a coherent body of thought, in the form of a national plan or even dialogue for using or assessing the effectiveness of these technologies, has been formed—what are we to do with all of that computer and communications technology once it is in place? The repercussions of this titanic head-on collision between the traditional model of education and the useful integration of technology in the classroom will reverberate well into the new millennium.

15   There are still many questions about the role of education in the Information Age, issues pertaining to selection of technology for the schools, proper use of the technology once it's in place, and the proper allocation of funds for computer-related technology. The indicators show that there is a direct correlation between the economic status of a public school and the amount of computer technology and support in that school. While technological support is not the be all and end all of education, it is certainly, as Andrew Blau points out, a head start in the race for the careers of the digital future. "Computers are not a silver bullet for whatever may be ailing public education today," he said. "Computers are tools. And the challenge is to make sure that we don't become slaves to our tools. If we're already wiring America's classrooms, we have a choice: either that we leave it totally to the market resources that each school district has, or we say, 'This is a set of tools that develop and cultivate a set of expertise that we want all kids to have'—that it becomes the new baseline for what it means to have basic educational skills that we want kids to leave high school with."

The major social pitfall of adopting the former option, according to Blau, is that those who initially have a leg up by virtue of their socioeconomic circumstances will have an even greater advantage at the end of their education, including a facility with technology and its vocabulary. As well, they will have a far better understanding of how the Information Age "works," in terms of knowledge about the available opportunities, the mechanism of wealth creation in the new age, and the new sociopolitical interactions being engendered by this technology. This is not a question of newer school texts or better football uniforms. It is literally a social fulcrum point that we as a nation have come to which will determine the face of our society well into the next century.

Blau further indicates the responsibilities that society must take on if we choose a path of equal access to, and equal educational experience, with this new technology: "If we go the other way and we say, 'These are the new tools of opportunity,' then we have a heavy burden. One burden is to make sure that they're used effectively, that they come in the package that will make this a wise investment. And two, that we take those steps that will make sure that we don't increase the gap, that we help the kids who need the help to get access to the tools that will allow them to take advantage of the opportunities they can make for themselves."

Most of us have become convinced that, for better or worse, a person must exhibit a certain level of technological aptitude in order to be of value in the workplace. Facility with computer and connectivity technology is a set of skills that employers look for in potential employees and that institutes of higher education look for in potential students. A lack of proficiency in these skills can be a bar to entry into either of these areas.

It is no longer enough for driven, economically disadvantaged people to spend hours at either a local or school library, teaching themselves what they need to know in order to succeed. In this age, when library economic resources are generally not even back to the level that they were a generation ago, it is ever more difficult for the economically disadvantaged to make use of what resources there are. Those computers that are put into libraries for public access are generally slow, outdated, and overburdened. Software availability is usually limited, decreasing the utility of those machines that are available to young people trying to increase their chances of success in the Information Age.

20   The question is not simply one of socioeconomic status, although this is an important contributing factor. Socioeconomic status contributes in the sense that those people of higher status have the resources to give their children a broader view of the world. One way in which this affects a child's outlook is in enhancing a sense of wonder and discovery that leads to an ability to see, and to seize, opportunities. This is more difficult when the model that a child sees is one of working long hours for little reward, while simultaneously being surrounded by images of the "good life" that seem ever out of reach. Understanding the challenges of being engulfed in this environment makes it easier to see how feelings of hopelessness can occur.

The picture is not all gloom and doom. William Rukeyser, coordinator of Learning in the Real World, a non-profit information clearinghouse with a focus on education technology and its effects on children, has reason to

believe that economically disadvantaged youth who are able to make a connection with technology resources benefit from the exposure. "A couple of
years ago, you very rarely heard evidence or heard opinions questioning the
kind of revealed wisdoms that computers were going to help kids learn,"
he states. "In the last couple of years, we have seen studies by respected
publications, respected newspapers, people involved in the field, saying, 'It
doesn't appear that there is evidence supporting the notion that computers
in all levels of education actually translate into educational performance.'
There are some pieces of evidence, certainly anecdotal evidence, that kids
who are isolated in one way or another, in fact, do get assistance." Mr.
Rukeyser recounts his own experiences with this phenomenon:

> I spent a couple of months on the island of Guam earlier this year. There's
> a perfect example, kids thousands of miles away from the nearest urban
> center, even further from the nearest English-speaking urban center; they
> don't have access to the kind of information sources that the typical North
> American kids do in urban and suburban areas. And so when you have got
> people who are geographically isolated or kids who are isolated by reasons
> of extreme poverty, or kids who have [other problems] we have got some
> pretty convincing anecdotal evidence that they are being helped to learn.
> But just because that is true in those isolated areas, doesn't mean that it's
> true for all the millions of school kids in America.

And indeed for many school kids in America that isn't true. In 1999,
although over half of those school districts that had technical support staff
had at least one full-time person, almost one-third of all districts had no
one at all. This means that even basic full-time support coverage was available in only about one-third of all schools, a level of support that resulted in
less computer access and a less satisfying experience for students. As well,
although more computers exist in schools, teacher access remains low, and
school assistance in this regard remains noncommittal. In 1998, only in
30 percent of school districts did 75 percent or more of the teachers have
computers at home; moreover, district assistance to teachers to purchase
computers existed in only slightly over 15 percent of districts. This lack of
access to computer resources outside of the educational setting inevitably
constrains educators' familiarity and facility with this medium.

More surprisingly, many of the nation's private schools are finding
themselves among the digital have-nots. Overall, only half as many of the
nation's private schools and classrooms had internet access as did public
schools. Additionally, private school educators generally have less training
and are paid less than their public school peers, at a time when the employment need for public school teachers with computer skills, as well as the
ability to integrate computers and connectivity into the learning curriculum, is expanding. Many of the nation's private schools will have to reexamine their policies and physical capabilities in these areas just to keep up
with the public schools.

In light of statistics like these, the digital divide seems even more men-
acing, and the need to close it even more urgent. Yet there are still caveats

to the use of computers and software in the classroom. Ms. Jane Healy, an educator and psychologist with over three decades experience dealing with children's education, and the author of *Failure to Connect: How Computers Affect Our Children's Minds—for Better and Worse,* views with some skepticism the current headlong rush to wire everything, and in so doing completely center education around this new technology. "When you watch kids on computers, you really think they are motivated and we make the assumption from our adult minds that they are motivated to learn," she says. "Of course, why else would they be doing this? Actually I would suggest that what they are motivated to do is use the computer." Ms. Healy believes that, though children may learn as a side effect of using the computer, the computer does not address central issues of a child's development into a healthy, autonomous adult.

25   She states that "in the motivation research it is very clear that the best way to develop a child who is internally motivated, who will be a self-starter as an adult and won't constantly have someone cracking the whip over them, is to have a child who is internally motivated for achievement. And we call this achievement motivation. External stimuli and external rewards tend to reduce and finally maybe even wipe out this kind of achievement motivation." And external stimuli and rewards are exactly those things the computer is best at providing.

While Healy finds it beneficial for computer technology to be implemented within an age-appropriate educational structure, she believes the current trends may be sending the wrong educational messages to children. "So what you have is a child, then, who comes to the computer, expects a reward [and] then goes into the workplace and expects to get rewarded. . . . Somehow we have got this idea in developing software that the way to make kids want to learn is to make it always fun and to make them always feel successful." In this view, internal motivation to attack a problem for the sheer fun of the challenge is eliminated. One could easily envision the grave consequences for a generation of students ill-equipped to confront, accept, and learn from their failures. What needs to be understood by anyone using software (and especially by educators) is that these programs are not all things to all people. Programmers are human just like the rest of us, with their own visions and vices, allegiances and agendas. The software they create will reflect all of these in some way or other.

Ms. Healy has outlined a strategy for integrating computer and connectivity technology into a well-rounded school program. Hers is a policy of inclusion rather than segregation, creating an atmosphere and environment where all the parts of a curricula are seen to be connected, rather than as compartmentalized units that have no interaction. This in itself fosters a new way of thinking—of seeing a larger picture behind any discrete event—and assists in the growth of critical and analytical thinking. A program with good integration of technology with education will seek out new ways of using that technology to enhance the educational atmosphere. An example might be the use of databases in an English class, a combination that would not be apparent to most English teachers. But through the use of database software, it is possible to graphically show, for instance, that William Shakespeare used roughly twice as many different words in his plays as the average person has in their vocabulary, which could then lead to an investigation of word etymologies from Shakespeare's time to the present.

"I think that good teachers are going to get equal or better results," Healy states of her new plan, "but starting in third, fourth grade, then we can start to look for uses of the applications programs. Maybe the word processing. Perhaps we want to start to teach our children how to do keyboarding. Perhaps we do definitely want to teach them to use spreadsheets and databases because those can be mind expanders in a lot of different ways and can be used to teach almost any subject, really."

What purpose, then, does computer and communications technology best serve in the classroom? Is it meant to be a more appealing method of imparting information? Is it meant to be a visual, and virtual, window on the world, showing children the rich diversity of life on our planet, of other cultures and other experiences? Is it meant to be an aid in teaching analytic and problem-solving skills, in educating our youngsters to think for themselves? Is it meant to be a tool to train the next generation of corporate workers?

30   Ideally, of course, it should be all of these, but the complexities of these issues make the creation of a plan for the integration of computers and communications technology into the classroom far from easy. In addition to the computers themselves, which need a certain level of technological sophistication to actually be anything other than expensive paperweights, a school needs to be physically connected to the internet. The computers also need to have the appropriate software to make the connection usable, and a staff trained to use that software and teach its responsible use to students. Likely, political pressures will require that the computers have one or more of the various filtering protocols in place to monitor and circumscribe access of the internet. All of this—and some of these items are recurring expenses—is just for internet access and use, having nothing to do with applications programs for the computers.

What is more, as the first studies on the effect that technology is actually having on student performance are published, some interesting and perhaps surprising results are surfacing. An on-line newsletter of the National Education Goals Panel cited a study done by the Educational Testing Service last year which professed to offer "the first solid evidence of what works and what doesn't when computers are used in the nation's classrooms." It noted that those fourth and eighth grade students who spent more time on computers actually did *worse* on math tests than those who had less time on the computer. The study also indicated that computer technology is most useful when the educators are well-trained on the integration of the technology into an educational plan.

The wiring of America's public schools and classrooms merely scratches the surface of the digital divide. At the end of the day, the U.S.

will have to face a number of issues heretofore ignored, sidetracked, or given only lip service. These issues involve the racial makeup of the U.S. and how we as a people embrace our cultural differences; the vast gulf of socioeconomic differences that exist and how we go about bridging it to present truly equal educational opportunities to all the children of our land; and an intense self-scrutiny of our current educational methodologies.

There is currently an avalanche of computer and communications technology being marketed and sold to states, school districts, and private schools around the country. The factors that contribute to this are as diverse as the segments of the post-industrial society in which they are occurring. Scare tactics in the news media and overblown advertising hype create a climate of fear and anxiety about technology. Creating parental anxiety about whether children will be left behind educationally, economically, and, by implication, socially, appears to be as much a part of their intent as any effort to inform. Subsequent parental pressure on schools to buy computers, peripherals, and software contributes to the huge and at times poorly planned expansion in computer and communications services in the schools, usually without much understanding of the computer's best role in the classroom.

The costs of this grand experiment in American education are many, varied, and uncertain. Currently, the federal government has taken a leading role in creating momentum toward the introduction of computers and communications technology into the nation's classrooms. The President proposed a budget for school technology for the year 2000 of $1.5 billion, almost double the budget for 1999. Some of the additional funds would go towards computer training opportunities for educators in U.S. middle schools, a further acknowledgment of the need for adequately trained teachers. As well, the funding for the 21st Century Learning Centers program, designed to provide computer learning opportunities in an after-school setting for close to two hundred thousand children in forty-six states, would be tripled, from $200 to $600 million. This program provides a place for students to use computers in a safe setting during those hours with a statistically high incidence of teenage violence and substance abuse.

35   Another of the ways in which this massive campaign to wire all public classrooms is being financed is through what is called the "e-rate." Established with bipartisan support in Congress as part of the Telecommunications Act of 1996, the e-rate provides for a 20 to 90 percent discount on telecommunications services, internet access, and internal connections for schools and libraries. Funding for the e-rate program is from long-distance telecommunications provider fees. E-rate funding commitments in 1998 totaled almost $1.7 billion, with about $1.1 billion going to urban schools, $183 million going to rural areas, and the balance to suburban schools. Just over half of the funds will be used to help pay for wiring the schools, and 40 percent will be used to defray the costs of ongoing telecommunications services with the remainder going to related projects. According to FCC documents, thirty-two thousand applicants applied for 1999 e-rate funds,

capped at \$2.25 billion. Even with funding to the cap, FCC chairman William Kennard indicated that the long-distance telecommunications industry would be receiving over half a billion dollars in reductions and restructuring costs, which he indicated should be used to reduce long-distance rates further.

This program was developed to take advantage of the potential of the internet as an educational tool. It is also supposed to redress some of the growing divide between advantaged and disadvantaged schools and school systems, as funds are targeted at the neediest schools in the nation. This program, in concert with other initiatives, seems to be having some effect. While only a handful of classrooms were wired in 1994, the latest figures indicate that most of the nation's public-school classrooms will soon have regular internet access. In this same period, the percentage of schools (as opposed to individual classrooms) that had internet connections at all grew from 35 percent to 78 percent.

The effect of the e-rate contributions on the availability of communications technology in classrooms is abundantly clear. Although the e-rate fund redresses some of the economic issues surrounding connectivity, other issues still remain. Putting a wire in every classroom, or even a computer on every desk, is merely the physical positioning of an already-existing technology, and in many cases, not even the latest iteration of that technology. The standard model is that the hardware technology changes every year and a half, on average, and those changes are of the "bigger, better, faster, more" variety. Is it reasonable to expect that schools, or the average parents for that matter, will be purchasing new computers every two years? Most schools probably don't even purchase new books with that frequency, and books require a lot less overhead in terms of maintenance, support, and training in their use. This merely supports what most Americans know already: unsupported statements about what we need "right now" should be viewed in a larger context.

At the same time, changes in the perception of the academic environment have allowed businesses, through their salespeople and advertising, greater access to (and perhaps influence in) schools than ever before. On the part of the schools themselves, public and private alike, competition for students, acclaim, and funding all play a part in this feverish push to get wired. At worst, public school systems in the United States are treated as little more than another segment of the consumer economy. Have schools become just another marketing target group to have their buying power appealed to? Are these new technologies serving educators and enabling a better and broader education, or are they seen by the business world as a way to train a better "class" of worker?

There is indeed a current trend in education toward schools entering into "partnerships" with businesses, where an educational institution's focus is almost entirely on workplace preparation. The thrust of education for some schools has become centered on strategies for job procurement, providing students as interns to numerous companies as an unpaid labor force, with minimal attention paid to course work not perceived to have a direct bearing on future employment.

40   But this may not be the environment that parents want their children in, or the best education for their children to have. The budgetary reallocations that are being made to fund this massive push to give at least the appearance of every classroom's having computer access are being promoted at the expense of other educational programs. This political and budgetary chicanery may in fact be shortchanging many individual groups of students, and curtailing their activities, in an effort to give the appearance that all students are connected. "What is happening, for example, to good remedial reading programs?" asks Jane Healy. "What is happening to our arts programs, which are being cut? ... This is the most amazing thing to me, that a country could decide to cut arts and humanities budgets to put in technology for children. We are cutting gym programs. We are cutting library resources. A teacher in one of the Western states said, 'our school system could be IBM as far as the technology is concerned. We have everything. But when I want to get reading books for my kids I can't get the budget approved because it has all been spent on the machines.' Now this is foolish and short-sighted."

To Ms. Healy, one of the roots of the problem is that political considerations and economic pressure are being put before children's welfare. "I think that instead of grandstanding on these budgets, we really need to be thinking seriously, 'How can this help? What kind of funding do we need to put in to develop the right kinds of software?' To develop the research that is going to tell us how to use this effectively before we keep just flooding machines into the schools that are, in most cases, frankly being misused."

Given a choice, then, parents certainly need to examine whether cutting programs to put in technology which does not have a demonstrated and documented effectiveness in learning and may, in fact, have a negative effect on children's long-term development, is worth the short-term peace of mind brought by blindly believing that this technology is "the answer." Not that computers don't have an important place in education. As Ms. Healy states, "In good schools, where this is being done well, this [bad allocation] is not happening, because the computers are being used as an adjunct to a very rich, full program. And that is what we might hope that all our children would have an opportunity to experience."

Good schools, of course, start with good teachers, and there are many educators in the United States who have embraced the new computer and communications technologies. Kristi Rennebohm Franz is representative of the educators with whom we hope that our children will come in contact, one of the "next-generation" teachers as comfortable with a keyboard as with a stick of chalk.

Since 1994, Ms. Rennebohm Franz has been a lead teacher with the International Educational and Resource Network (I*EARN), through which she coordinated the Global Art and Water Habitats projects. Her classroom research focuses on literacy and telecommunications, and she is involved in leadership collaborations for educational technology regionally, nationally, and internationally. "The Global Art Project connects visual arts in a wonderful way and shows the different visual art tools that people have in different countries," she said. "The batiks of Thailand, the different ways that the indigenous people in the Zuni pueblo in New Mexico create their art work and the tools that they use to do that. Children can see the richness of the tapestry of cultures that we have in our world through children's art."

45   The Global Art Project—part of a growing trend called "electronic field trips"—works as a collaborative effort, motivated by a diverse group of educators around the country. These educators and their classes are in contact through the internet. One might suggest a group art project revolving around folk tales from around the world. Other educators and their students respond to the proposed project until a group of ten to twelve classes are involved. Students in each of these classes then create an original work of art based on the theme of a folk tale, coupled with an original piece of writing.

After the creative process is finished, some of the artwork is retained at the school that created it and some of it is sent on—by mail, as a graphic file over the internet, or even posted to a website for downloading—to each of the other schools in the group. In this manner, not only are young students exposed to a variety of educational experiences in their own classroom, but they get to share those experiences with others in sometimes distant places, and gain from the experiences of other students and contact with different segments of their own culture or perhaps even other cultures.

Ms. Rennebohm Franz's project, as an integrated form of educating, covers several subject areas and makes the entire experience more meaningful than simply looking at pictures in a book and pointing out a place on a map. "The Global Art Project emphasized the arts, it emphasized the social studies, the multiculturalism of our cultures through the arts and through language, and the multilingual dimensions of our globe," she said. "There's no piece of the curriculum that can't be pulled into it, because you're working with communicating between real people and real places around the world. It's not virtual—it's real."

Critics of these initiatives—and of the introduction of computer and communications technology into educational settings in general—take issue more with the particulars of the presentation than with the information presented. "When I feel the difference between what it means to be playing games, creativity—ideas are bouncing off," said Douglas Goodkin, a music educator at a San Francisco school. "And when I compare that to what it's like to step into a computer lab, I see that all these intelligences are being missed. There isn't a physical involvement, there's not a sensorial involvement, there's not a human social involvement. There's not much." Ms. Rennebohm Franz's experience, however, has been very different: "We discovered very quickly that the opportunity for them [students] to talk to each other—and that's how they describe it—on-line through their written text was providing them incredible motivation to work hard on the writing skills that we were doing in the classroom," she said. "It gave them an extra incentive and motivation to do that when they realized that their writing was going to an audience that they knew. These are all important parts of the writing process."

While there is little debate over the value of the multiculturalism inherent in these projects, there is a feeling among some academics that computers and communications technology introduces a "gee-whiz" aspect to learning that is counterproductive. However, at a time when these same aspects of television, films, and video games make interaction with a visual interface more appealing, and traditional methods of schooling even less of interest to many children, one might think that schools need all the gee-whiz they can get.

50   In March of 1999, President Clinton reaffirmed his administration's commitment to making the benefits of the digital future available to all of the nation's schoolchildren. In his remarks, he said, "Computers, the internet, and educational software can make a real difference in the way teachers teach and students learn. Because of our efforts, children in the most isolated inner city or rural town will have access to the same universe of knowledge as a child in the most affluent suburb. Parents will be able to communicate more frequently with teachers, and keep up with the progress of their child in school. Our children will be 'technologically literate,' and better prepared for the high-tech, high-wage jobs of the future."

Should these predictions come about, through both the equal distribution and installation of hardware and the across-the-board application of knowledge to use these technologies to enhance the educational experience, all of our children can become "technologically literate," and live richer lives as well as be better prepared to enter the workforce of the Information Age. But educational computer and communications technology is still in its infancy and money is being made available without any organized determination as to what to spend it on and whether it should be spent at all on any particular "initiative." As William Rukeyser has said, "In these early years of education technology, it's been the idea, 'Hey we can get a little bit of extra money, maybe we can write a grant and get some money from a foundation, or a company, or from the state or federal government.' And so essentially, this equipment will come in and it will be no cost to us." This reasoning process has likely led to the downfall of a good many well-intentioned initiatives. "What they don't stop to realize," Mr. Rukeyser continues, "is that when you've got what is referred to as the 'boxes and wires' installed in the school, that is just the beginning. You have only begun to pay at that point, so even if you have gotten 80 to 90 percent of the installation taken care of for you, there is still, for an average-size school district, maybe millions, maybe tens of millions of dollars to keep paying out." And not once, but year after year.

Many school districts get into financial difficulties right from the beginning. Mr. Rukeyser cites one study done on the magnitude of the situation.

"The Mackenzie Company, which is a consulting firm in Washington, did a study for the White House, and it estimated that each and every year after computers have been installed in the school, that school district should be prepared to pay at least one-third of the purchase cost, the initial cost, for such things as training, replacement, repairs, upgrades." What this means to an average school district is that, for every one million dollars laid out for initial computer and communications infrastructure purchases, it is going to cost about $350,000 every year thereafter to stay up and running with relatively current equipment and training.

For example, within the last year, the Kentucky State Education Department has been ordered to purchase filtering software for all of its almost twenty-four hundred schools, district offices, and department of education members. This software is intended to capture the locations of educationally desirable websites, and block access to undesirable ones. One of the positive side effects is expected to be that the current 56k internet connections will perform at the same level as T1 lines, since all desktop operations will now go through the servers with the filters. If each school was intended to have a T1 line, this would save each school five to six thousand dollars per year, at an initial cost of only $200,000. Little has been mentioned about upgrades or maintenance costs, or the cost of training. Additionally, there are the potential costs to provide the same software and training to the state's libraries, where children would be able to access the same information as in the schools.

The inability of most schools to accumulate and apply cash reserves of this size for a single program on an annual basis will inevitably lead to a diminishment of the utility of those computers and their infrastructure, which represent perhaps tens of billions of dollars in investment nationwide. However, with the proper planning, training, and the appropriate use of our technological and human resources, the twenty-first century will fulfill the promise of these technologies with benefits that enrich the lives of all of our nation's citizens, not just those who can easily afford the entry fees.

Conversation Starter

Discuss the role that technology has played in shaping your education.

Reading Matters

1. According to Bolt and Crawford, how has the classroom changed from 1979 to the present?
2. What is the digital divide, and why is it a problem in education today?
3. In what ways does technology enhance education? In what ways can technology marginalize learning?
4. What costs are associated with a technological infrastructure? How has the new emphasis on technology affected the school curriculum?

Writing Matters

1. How does your educational experience differ from your parents' experience, your grandparents' experience? Conduct interviews and explain your findings in an essay.
2. Write about the classroom of the future. How will technology change the way we learn?
3. Define technological literacy. Write an essay in which you discuss how technological literacy could best be integrated into the school curriculum.

Relevant Web Sites

Digital Divide <http://www.pbs.org/digitaldivide/>

This is the official web site of the Digital Divide television series and book. The site has information on the role computers play in the classroom and at work, and explores access by gender and race.

Media Literacy Online Project
<http://interact.uoregon.edu/MediaLit/HomePage>

This web site provides information on media literary and education, including international conferences and organizations devoted to media literacy as well as a very large index of articles and resources.

Michael Schudson

How People Learn to Be Civic

Michael Schudson is Professor of Communication at the University of California in San Diego, where he has taught since 1980 and where he has been co-director of the UCSD Civic Collaborative. He holds a Ph.D. from Harvard University in sociology, was a Guggenheim Fellow, and received a MacArthur Foundation "Genius Award." His books include Advertising, the Uneasy Persuasion *(1984),* The Good Citizen: A History of American Civic Life *(1998), and* The Sociology of News *(2003); he also has written for many popular and academic periodicals. The following article appeared in E.J Dionne's collection* United We Serve: National Service and the Future of Citizenship *(2003).*

A sense of citizenship is passed on from one generation to the next not only in formal education or through intentional efforts but indirectly or collaterally in the small details of everyday life. Lecturing in London a few years ago, I illustrated this point with a homely example. I said: Take, for instance, those moments in your own family where you assert your parental authority and declare to your children, Eat Your Vegetables. 'No.' Eat Your Vegetables, Please. 'No.' Eat Your Vegetables Or There Will Be No Dessert. 'No.' Eat Your Vegetables Or Else! And one of those little wise guys retorts, 'You can't make me. It's a free country.'

In the United States, audiences invariably acknowledge this illustration with knowing chuckles or smiles. In London, I looked out at a roomful of blank faces. Not a soul cracked a smile. They had politely puzzled expressions. Only then did it dawn on me. Only then did I realize that no British child in all of history has ever said, "You can't make me, it's a free country." And suddenly I knew that democracy is not just one thing you have more or less of, it comes in an assortment of flavors. Democratic citizenship is not just something one is more or less socialized into; there are different citizenships in different democracies and each of them is renewed in its own subtle fashion.

What I had taken as an invariant expression of children in any democratic society is, in fact, peculiarly American. It is America, not Britain, that conceives of itself self-importantly and extravagantly and naively and tragically and wonderfully as a "free country." America's children pick that up early on. But how? How is it American kids learn to say that it's a free country and British kids learn not to? How do people acquire their sense of civic life and how does that sense become second nature? How do we learn the values we are supposed to learn as members of our national culture? I am not asking how to make people better citizens. Instead, I am asking how people who learn to be citizens learn how to be citizens of the sort they learn how to be. How do they come to know what good citizenship is?

I have no confidence that earnest efforts at teaching U.S. history or turning out the vote or getting more school children to pick up trash on the beach make us good citizens, admirable as these activities may be in their own right.

5   I believe in the values of liberal education but I am not convinced that liberal education does the trick either. Political theorist Richard Flathman writes that the greatest contribution liberal education can make to our common political life is to instill a "disposition . . . wary of politics and government."[1] That is not what you normally hear in circles of educators devoted to civics education. But I was reminded of it in the aftermath of September 11. One of the most noteworthy and, to my mind, admirable features of the American response in the first weeks was that many of our leaders, from the President on down, waved the flag proudly but at the same time cautioned citizens about the dangers of flag-waving. The only precedent I know for this kind of chastened patriotism in other countries is contemporary Germany where the Nazi past envelops even the most timid of patriotic demonstrations with a flood of second thoughts.[2] In the United States, I can think of no prior expression of this kind of proud but muted patriotism, a patriotism tempered by its own self-consciousness.

If citizenship is not learned primarily in school or in get-out-the-vote drives and if college is as likely to induce skepticism about politics as fervent devotion to it, where do people learn their sense of civic obligation? This is a question that civic educators themselves need to think about more clearly, deeply, and historically. What I offer here is a briefly sketched framework for doing so.

A citizen is a person who has full membership in a political community, especially a nation-state. In its common legal usage, citizenship means nationality and its mark would be a passport, a birth certificate, or other citizenship papers. In its political usage, citizenship refers to rights of political participation, and its chief sign is that a person is eligible to vote. In its sociocultural sense, citizenship refers to emotional identification with a nation and its flag, history, and culture. Finally, citizenship has a broad moral meaning, as in the phrase "good citizen." It may refer to a person loyal to the state, and in this sense it is related to patriotism. Even more, it suggests a person

---

[1]Flathman, "Liberal Versus Civic, Republican, Democratic, and Other Vocational Educations" *Political Theory* 24 (February 1996) 4–32 at 26.

[2]See, for instance, Frederick Kempe, *Father/Land: A Personal Search for the New Germany* (New York: G. P. Putnam's, 1999) p. 148.

who is informed about and takes an active role in civic affairs. Although all of these meanings of "citizen" have some relevance to my inquiry here, the broad moral meaning of civic-ness is my primary concern.

"How do people become civic?" is in part the question: how do we come to understand or accept or take for granted what counts as civic? That is, how do people develop a particular sense of the public good, a willingness to participate in its advancement, and a view of what repertoire of acts will engender a better public life? How do we come to understand or accept or take for granted what counts as civic in our own culture? Four different areas need our attention.

First, we become civic if and when the civic penetrates into everyday life. Second, we become civic by what we are called to attend to and what we are called to ignore. Third, we become civic by joining with others in common enterprise. Fourth, we become civic when a civic infrastructure allows, encourages, and supports individual civic engagement. I will say something about each of these points.

EVERYDAY LIFE

First, we become civic when civic activities become a part of everyday life. Think of the recycling bins that, in many communities today, the city or municipality provides so that each household can separate its own recyclables and get them recycled by putting them out at curbside when the city picks up the weekly trash.

10   Think of the Pledge of Allegiance that children say in school. More is learned in this act by ritual repetition than by the actual words. I would be skeptical that school children understand the Pledge of Allegiance. Take the word "indivisible," for instance. Children learn to pronounce it years before they study John C. Calhoun and the doctrine of nullification, or the Lincoln-Douglas debates, or the Civil War. But the presence of the term "indivisible" in the Pledge is incomprehensible without knowing it to be a reference to the Civil War. In the end, however, that is less the point than that the school day is connected in some vague but unifying way to flag and country.

Think about what kind of education happens in the widespread "red ribbon week" of drug education in our public schools. I remember when my daughter, then in first-grade, came home from Drug-Free School Day and told us happily it was Free Drug Day at school. In a personal memoir, essayist Sarah Vowell recalls watching the Mickey Mouse Club on television and singing along with the theme song—but she never quite got the words of it. When the Mouseketeers sang, "forever let us hold our banner high," Sarah thought they were saying, "for every little polar bear to hide."[3] Much more

---

[3]Sarah Vowell, Take the Cannoli: Stories from the New World (New York: Simon & Schuster, 2000).

of education is like that than we would ever want to admit. Still, the ritual of something like saying the Pledge, the activity of it, the collective enterprise of it, leaves a residue.

The activity that enters into ordinary life need not be every day activity. We learn a great deal from ritual moments that come only on rare occasion—like Christmas once a year, or voting every year or two. We do not really know how deeply these activities teach us until we imagine how they might be different. Think about what lessons eighteenth-century Virginians learned when they voted or nineteenth-century Americans, in contrast to us. An eighteenth-century Virginian, that is to say a white male who owned property, went to the polling place, spoke his vote out loud in front of the sheriff and in front of the candidates, and then went over to the candidate he had favored with his vote and shook hands. The whole activity was one of ritually reaffirming a hierarchical social order in which each person knew his place. The whole experience reinforced an understanding of citizenship as appropriate deference to community leaders. There was no campaigning, there were no issues, there were no bombastic speeches, the whole point was to invest responsibility for decision-making in trusted senior members of the community.[4]

The nineteenth century experience of voting taught different civic lessons. In the nineteenth century, political parties controlled the elections. On election day, the parties hired tens of thousands of workers to get out the vote and to stand near the polling place to hand out the "tickets" the parties had printed. The voter approached the polling place, took a ticket from one of these "ticket peddlers" from his own party and went up to the voting station to deposit his ticket in the ballot box. He did not need to look at it. He did not need to mark it in any way. Clearly, he did not have to be literate. He could cast his ballot free of charge, but it would not have been surprising if he received payment for his effort. In New Jersey, as many as one third of the electorate in the 1880s expected payment for voting on election day, usually in an amount between $1 and $3.[5]

What did a vote express? Not a strong conviction that the party offered better public policies; parties tended to be more devoted to distributing offices than to advocating policies. Party was related more to comradeship than to policy, it was more an attachment than a choice, something like a contemporary loyalty to a high school or college and its teams. Voting was not a matter of assent to ideas but a statement of affiliation with people, and the connection of voter to party ticket peddler underscored that. So did the post-election visit to the party's favorite local tavern. Drink, dollars,

---

[4]On this point and the subsequent paragraphs on American political history, I draw directly on my book, *The Good Citizen: A History of American Civic Life* (New York: Free Press, 1998)

[5]John F. Reynolds, *Testing Democracy: Electoral Behavior and Progressive Reform in New Jersey, 1880–1910* (Chapel Hill: University of North Carolina Press, 1988) p. 54. See also Schudson, pp. 144–187.

and drama brought people to the polls, and, more than that, social connection, rarely anything more elevated.

15   Reformers at the end of the 19th century saw little in the parties to recommend them. The Mugwumps sought to make elections "educational" and the Progressives tried to insulate the independent, rational citizen from the distorting enthusiasms of party. It is to them that we owe the ideal of the informed citizen, not to the founding fathers. In the 1880s, political campaigns began to shift from parades to pamphlets, and so put a premium on literacy. In the 1890s, the Australian ballot swept the nation and so for the first time in American history literacy was required to cast a ballot. The novelty of the Australian ballot was that the state took responsibility for printing ballots that listed the candidates from all parties qualifying for the election. This meant that voters received their ballots from state election officials at the polling place, not from party workers en route to the polling place; it meant that the voter had to make a choice of candidates by marking the ballot; and it normally meant that provision was made for the voter to mark the ballot in secret. With this innovation, voting changed from a social and public duty to a private right, from a social obligation to party enforceable by social pressure to a civic obligation or abstract loyalty, enforceable only by private conscience. In the early 1900s, non-partisan municipal elections, presidential primaries, and the initiative and referendum imposed more challenging cognitive tasks on prospective voters than ever before. These changes enshrined "the informed citizenry," incidentally provided a new mechanism and a new rationale for disenfranchising African-Americans and immigrants, and inaugurated an enduring tradition of hand-wringing over popular political ignorance.

Between 1880 and 1910, the most basic understandings of American politics were challenged. Reformers attacked the emotional enthusiasm of political participation, the corruption in campaign financing and campaign practices, and the role of the parties in usurping the direct connection between citizens and their government. They succeeded in inventing the language by which we still judge our politics. It stresses being informed while it dismisses or demeans parties and partisanship. To put this more pointedly, the political party, the single most important agency ever invented for mass political participation, is the institution that current civics talk and current civics education regularly abhor and that is rendered almost invisible in the way we conduct the actual act of voting. Insofar as the way we *do* vote is a set of enduring instructions to us about the way we *should* vote and the way we should think about voting, the civic lesson of election day as we have organized it for the past century recommends contempt for parties and partisanship.

We learn a standard of civic practice by practicing civics. We may not live up to it, but we know, at least implicitly and roughly speaking, what it is, what we are supposed to be held accountable for. We learn it in large part by experience—as political theorist Stephen Elkin writes, "Experience . . . must be the teacher of democratic citizens," and this leads him to an interest in the design of local governments, not the design of school curricula[6]. What we do not know or reflect on is that our present standard is only one of a number of possible standards. We learn it so well we do not even recognize what alternatives it excludes.

STRUCTURES OF ATTENTION

Second, we become civic by what the public will be called to attend to and what it is called to ignore. The media but, even more strenuously, political leaders make the decisions about what will be on the public's agenda. In the weeks after September 11, there were many stories in the media about the stifling of dissent as the country unified behind the President's war on terrorism. Why were we called to attend to this? How did we know, as we read these stories, that stifling dissent is a bad thing? We assuredly were expected to get that point.

Consider an important recent example of citizenship talk: "What you do is as important as anything government does. I ask you to seek a common good beyond your comfort, to defend needed reforms against easy attacks, to serve your nation, beginning with your neighbor. I ask you to be citizens. Citizens, not spectators. Citizens, not subjects. Responsible citizens, building communities of service and a nation of character."

20   At first blush, it is hard to object to the concept of citizenship George W. Bush expressed in these words in his inaugural address. Citizenship, he said, is public-spirited rather than self-centered, neighborly rather than self-seeking, active and participatory rather than passive and spectator-like. And yet, President Bush advanced a subtext here—do not expect too much from your government. "Americans are generous and strong and decent, not because we believe in ourselves but because we hold beliefs beyond ourselves. When this spirit of citizenship is missing, no government program can replace it. When this spirit is present, no wrong can stand against it." Government should not over-reach, government should not over-legislate, government should not over-react. The President favors people who take care of themselves and their neighbors, not those who depend on government for aid and comfort.

Note a second subtext: people are citizens insofar as they do not seek their own comfort, insofar as they serve the nation, and insofar as they hold beliefs beyond themselves. True citizens do not ask, to paraphrase a President from a different party, what the country can do for them but what they can do for the country. There is no place in this vision of citizenship for individuals to sue for their rights or to invoke the law on behalf of their liberties or to initiate actions for damages against tobacco companies or tire

---

[6]Stephen Elkin, "Citizen Competence and the Design of Democratic Institutions" in Stephen L. Elkin and Karol Edward Soltan, eds., *Citizen Competence and Democratic Institutions* (University Park, PA: Pennsylvania State University Press, 1999) p. 394.

manufacturers. There is no acknowledgment that democracy has been enlarged in our lifetimes when individuals have been driven not by a desire to serve but by an effort to overcome indignities they themselves have suffered. This is important. The most important extension of citizenship in this century was produced by the civil rights movement. Not Thomas Jefferson so much as people like Thurgood Marshall and Martin Luther King, Jr. made rights a household term and a household experience; the civil rights movement brought on the extraordinary wave of social movements and rights-centered litigation that has opened doors and windows for African-Americans, women, gays and lesbians, people with disabilities, and many others. Why, then, do we cling rhetorically to a vision of civic education and citizenship that excludes the raw power of self-interested action? Why is citizenship reduced to service rather than linked to justice?

There is also an entirely missing text in President Bush's inaugural: in the idealized world he beckoned his fellow citizens to join, there are citizens, there are neighbors, there are also communities of faith, but there are no parties, and in the good citizen no partisanship; there are no interest groups, and in the good citizen no joining with others in organized self-interest; there are no experts, and in the good citizen no considered judgment about when and how judgment should be delegated. Why are the organizations and individual actors that in fact are the most involved on a day-to-day basis with the operation of government omitted from his account of citizenship?

In times of national crisis, the citizen President Bush envisions is the soldier, who serves country, ignores personal discomfort, and believes in a patriotic ideal. In ordinary times, Bush's ideal is the Rotarian, moved by a sense of neighborliness, Christian charity, and social responsibility, but untouched by any sense of having a personal stake in public justice.

Is this the kind of civic-ness we should be instilling in our children? I don't think so, but that is not my topic here. I am addressing only the question of how people learn to be civic. My point about the President's speech is that it offers one model of civic-ness, not the only model. It is a powerful model, nonetheless, because the President is the country's best placed civic pedagogue. As Justice Felix Frankfurter said, "The Presidency is the most important educational system in the country."[7] The President calls us to attention, and in a particular way, not in the only way.

SHARED ENTERPRISE

25 Third, we become civic by joining with others in common enterprise, common work, common prayer, or common struggle. I will speak about this only briefly because, in this instance, the same President George W. Bush,

---

Cited in Douglas Cater, *The Fourth Branch of Government* (Boston: Houghton Mifflin, 1959) p. 169.

whom I have just criticized, has offered a very shrewd analysis. In his press conference a month after September 11, he observed that his administration before September 11 was planning an initiative to be called "Communities of Character." It was, he said, "designed to help parents develop good character in our children and to strengthen the spirit of citizenship and service in our communities." But, he remarked, "the acts of September 11 have prompted that initiative to occur on its own, in ways far greater than I could have ever imagined." He was right. He cited the cases of Christian and Jewish women who went shopping with Muslim neighbors when the Muslim women were afraid to leave their homes alone. There was, indeed, a rekindling of communal feelings, a reaching out to friends, neighbors, and strangers, and a joining in common enterprises of blood drives, fund raising, prayer services, and community memorials all across the country.

People can feel connections with one another and a sense of public purpose at one remove, through the Internet, or through a novel, a film, or a news story. I do not know anyone who died at the World Trade Centers but, like almost all Americans, I felt intimately linked to what happened there. That lasted, beyond the moment, not because citizens feel an intimate acquaintance with Peter Jennings, Tom Brokaw, and Dan Rather (although they may) but because the information and images the media conveyed in this case touched everyone who has ever visited New York or knows someone there, everyone who has ever traveled by air or who has loved ones who travel by air, everyone who has ever been in a high-rise office building, and the horror and anxiety the news evoked in those millions of people was reaffirmed and reinforced in almost every conversation and in almost every glance from person to person, family member to family member, and co-worker to co-worker in subsequent weeks and months. The experience of September 11 was a national Durkheimian moment, that is, a collective experience where a sense of both power and meaning beyond the personal emerged from face-to-face contact and collective work, collective action embodied, not at a distance.

There is a great deal of attention to that generation, now rapidly aging and dying, that fought World War 2, and it has been lionized in the title of Tom Brokaw's book, as "the greatest generation." Brokaw is not modest about his claims for his parents' generation: "I think this is the greatest generation any society has ever produced."[8] I am not going to quibble over rankings here; surely this generation accomplished a great deal. And, as Robert Putnam has assiduously documented, this same generation continued doggedly civic in voting in large numbers, attending community meetings, getting to know neighbors, maintaining church membership and attendance, exceeding the marks of the generation before them and the generations that followed them.[9] All of this I acknowledge. What I do not

---

[8]Tom Brokaw, *The Greatest Generation* (New York: Random House, 1998).
[9]Robert D. Putnam, *Bowling Alone* (New York: Simon & Schuster, 2000).

accept is the implication that this generation was unusually endowed with moral virtue or community fervor. What it was endowed with was the Great Depression and World War 2, great collective experiences that forged a generational spirit.

This is not to suggest that the experience of World War 2 was a spontaneous emotional upheaval undirected by government leadership and institutional transformation. On the contrary, the Roosevelt administration mobilized the power of the state in the national defense to—literally— enlist the nation in the war effort. If September 11 seems to be a fading memory already for many Americans, it may be because the federal government chose in the end not to take advantage of the emotional effervescence of the moment to call on Americans for sacrifice or service. An opportunity was lost to enlarge national service programs like Americorps—or even to call attention to them.

Civic Infrastructure

Fourth, we cannot become civic if there is not an infrastructure of civicness for people to enroll in. Civic life requires maintenance. It requires staff. It requires investment. It requires access. Democracy does not come cheap. Elections cost money. Effective service programs cost money. Courts cost money. Justice requires dollars.[10] This is not very dramatic stuff. In fact, it is invisible to most of us most of the time. I saw some of it, however, in the 2000 election, as I watched the mounting of the electoral machinery in my home of San Diego, California. Let me just give you a little sense of it.

30   On November 7, in one sixteen hour period, 100 million people broke from their daily routine and voted. It is a mammoth exercise. In California, there were about 100,000 volunteers spending 15 hour days manning the polling places. In San Diego County, running the election cost $3.5 million in taxpayer dollars to produce 552 separate ballots and 552 separate voter information guides mailed out to registered voters to prepare them to act as informed citizens. There were 100 training sessions for 6,000 poll workers at 1,500 polling places, 300 of which had special provision for Spanish-speaking voters and all of which were designed to be accessible for the disabled. This is a massive activity, and a great deal of meaning is still to be found in it, what Walt Whitman called this "ballot-shower from East to West, America's choosing day."

There are 552 different ballots because there are 120 political jurisdictions in San Diego County—hospital districts, water districts, community college districts, school districts, Congressional districts, assembly and state senate districts, etc. There were some 800 candidates on the ballot in

---

[10]See Stephen Holmes and Cass Sunstein, *The Cost of Rights: Why Liberty Depends on Taxes* (New York: W. W. Norton, 1999).

November. Mikel Haas, then the Registrar of Voters, told me: "It's like a watch, there are a whole lot of moving parts. Any one of them can trip you up." The Registrar's core staff of 48 employees was supplemented in the election season by about 300 temporary workers, not to mention the 6,000 poll workers on election day.

Several weeks before the election, I attended what the Registrar's office has entitled "Midnight Madness." On the last day to register to vote in San Diego County, the Registrar's office stays open till midnight for "drive-through" registration. I came by around 8 p.m. to take a look. Cars were lined up for most of a long block and then in a single-file line through half the length of the county building in the dark and the drizzle. The whole area, though, was flood-lit by a set of four flood lights illuminating not only the building and the proceedings outside it but a newly anchored "Uncle Sam" roughly 40 feet high, a vast, cheery, red-white-and-blue inflated Uncle Sam. Registrar of Voters Haas had seen it displayed at a Chevrolet dealer. He had driven by and thought, "I have to have that," and he worked out a rental deal to use the inflatable for Midnight Madness.

There must have been between 15 and 20 Registrar personnel in yellow slickers at Midnight Madness. A number of them were directing traffic. In 3 lines, 3 people handed registration affidavits on clipboards to the driver-voters in their cars, S.U.V.'s, and pick-ups. The drivers were then directed to park while they filled out the form. When completed, they started up their cars again and another yellow-slickered official would come over to the car, take the affidavit, check it to see that it was filled out properly, and then send the new registrant on his or her way.

One senior civil servant I spoke to began her career with court reporting school, then worked in the DA's office, then took the test for the position of Registrar of Voters senior clerk and took the job in 1977 at age 26. In 1980 she left and went to work with one of the vendors who mail the sample ballots. "But I missed it . . . I missed the excitement. " "Not many people leave here. No one will quit." It's not just this office—from email with her counterparts in other counties, "it sounds the same way." There's a lot of stress in the job but people love it. She is married to a political consultant as interested in politics as she is. "When our child was born", she told me, "our birth announcement said "height" and "weight" and "eligible to vote in 2007."

35   Despite the high morale of workers at the registrar's office, not everyone loves every part of it. One of the least popular sections is candidate services, dealing with candidates and would-be candidates as they learn how to file their papers, as they write up their statements for the voter information guides that in California are sent out to all registered voters, as they submit required campaign finance disclosure forms. "The candidates . . . " my informant began, and then rolled her eyes. She talked about the people who walk in and say, "Here's where I live. What can I run for?" "Who are these people?" she asked. When someone want to file who has no chance at all, who has never even turned up at a meeting of the body they're running

for, the personnel in candidate services try to act on behalf of democracy without entering improperly into the process: "We try to politely—well, not talk them out of it, but explain what's involved."

I attended some training sessions for the poll workers, as well as the training session for the trainers. This session was run by Registrar staff plus a motivational speaker. There was strong emphasis on getting people to participate and to have a good time in the training. As one of the trainers said, "adult learning really can be fun, it doesn't have to be toothpicks-in-the-eyelid time."

The training sessions for the poll workers were centered on a "railroad" theme and the trainers were equipped with train engineers' hats, red bandannas, a loud train whistle, and a small flashing light that mimicked the lights at a railroad crossing. The trainers I observed, two vigorous women in their sixties, blew their train whistles together to start the session, and then they sang a song they themselves had written: "We've been working on the election all the live long day,/We've been working on the election, so the voters have their say." Trained to get people talking and involved from the beginning, they asked people to talk among themselves about why they were volunteering their time. After a few minutes they blew the train whistles again and asked people to tell the whole group what they had found out. Some people talked about the free tacos poll workers would get from a local fast food chain, many others spoke of wanting to do their civic duty. Many volunteered election after election and spoke of it as a kind of addiction—"Once you do it, you're hooked."

Multiply these stories of one registrar's office in one county of one state. Multiply it by the seventy California counties, multiply it again by the fifty states, multiply it by the journalists who write about politics, the teachers who teach history and civics, the pre-school teachers and kindergarten teachers who instruct children about sharing, the counselors, clergy, clerks of court and others who are all civics teachers on a full-time basis, and you can see that the possibility of civic-ness for individuals may have less to do with individual virtue than with social investment and collective maintenance.

Civic-ness requires both volunteers and professionals, both ordinary citizens and experts. The kind of populism one finds in universities that is distrustful of expertise, to the point of self-hatred; that prefers participatory democracy over representation or delegation, to the point of having nothing at all to say about the latter; and that prefers John Dewey to Walter Lippmann or, more generally, romantics to realists, to a degree that refuses engagement with the actual messiness of democratic politics, lies somewhere between dreaminess and irresponsibility.

---

[11]Paul Lichtermann, *The Search for Political Community* (Cambridge: Cambridge University Press, 1996).

40   In thinking through the matter of civic education, I look more to structures, contexts, and institutions within which and through which education happens than to specific psychological processes that succeed or fail to attach individuals to the messages about civic engagement they hear. There are multiple meanings of citizenship afloat in the land and practices of civic life have changed more rapidly and more radically than our public rhetoric has yet figured out. Many people still learn to participate in politics through community-based, faith-based experience, as was so often the case with the civil rights movement, but many others today come to politics (as is often the case in the environmentalist movement) through what sociologist Paul Lichterman calls "personalist" motivation.[11] Some opportunities for civic engagement fade—like political party rallies—but others arise without social analysts even noticing—if there is a study of the proliferation of charity runs and charity walks, I have not yet seen it. Or consider the enormous changes in women's lives and the movement toward gender equality in the past fifty years and how the feminization of political and civic life, if you will, has altered civic practices—and should have altered what counts as citizenship and civic engagement. Along with the civil rights movement and the many other rights-oriented struggles that borrowed from it, feminism has extended norms of equality and indignation over injustice into the home, the club, the workplace and other domains once far removed from political consciousness.

Citizens learn citizenship (a) in everyday life and especially in participating in common civic exercises; (b) in structures of attention shaped by political leaders, the media, the schools, and other voices of authority; (c) in experiences of community solidarity that forge attachments to people beyond us (it is a familiar observation that soldiers fight not so much for their flag as for their comrades); and (d) in structures and institutions that are cultivated and cared for by full-time staff whose work is required to make citizenship possible. Meanwhile, the realm of the civic shifts and expands as the legitimate demands of once-excluded groups enter into play and re-shape basic understandings of civic life.

Conversation Starter

Discuss your civic education. Was it formal or informal? Do you feel you have a sense of civic obligation?

Reading Matters

1. According to Schudson, how do pepople learn to be citizens?
2. What is the role of everyday life in a civic education? Refer to specific examples from the text.
3. What is the role of the media in shaping public life?
4. According to Schudson, how is civic life maintained?

WRITING MATTERS

1. Write an essay about an act of patriotism that you have witnessed. How did it confirm or challenge your understanding of "civic-ness"?
2. Develop a definition of citizenship. Identify resources for teaching citizenship to a group of your peers. Include historical documents, web sites, movies, or any other resources that you think are relevant.
3. Write a response to George W. Bush's concept of citizenship: "What you do is as important as anything government does. I ask you to seek a common good beyond your comfort, to defend needed reforms against easy attacks, to serve your nation, beginning with your neighbor. I ask you to be citizens. Citizens, not spectators. Citizens, not subjects. Responsible citizens, building communities of service and a nation of character."

RELEVENT WEB SITES

CIVIC EDUCATION <http://www.civiced.org>

This website for the Center for Civic Education provides resources to promote an enlightened and responsible citizenry committed to democratic principles and actively engaged in the practice of democracy in the United States and other countries.

PRESIDENT GEORGE W. BUSH'S INAUGURAL ADDRESS 2001

<www.whitehouse.gov/news/inaugural-address.html>

The official transcript of President George W. Bush's inaugural address on January 20, 2001.

Introduction: River of Words

River of Words

In December of 1995 the River of Words was launched by a group of activists committed to protecting the environment with the support of Poet Laureate Robert Hass and the Library of Congress. This poetry and art contest invites children in grades K–12 to explore their own watershed, discover its importance in their lives, and express what they learned, felt, and saw in words or images. The program now has an international audience and distributes a curriculum guide on teaching about watersheds, poetry, and art to teachers whose students participate in the annual contest. The River of Words publishes the winners' poems and images.

HISTORY OF THE PROJECT BY PAMELA MICHAEL

For each home ground we need new maps, living maps, stories and poems, photographs and paintings, essays and songs. We need to know where we are so that we may dwell in our place with a full heart.

—Scott Russell Sanders

Children are experts at creating visions of places they've seen only in their imaginations—places made real by the very act of creation. So what happens when you ask those selfsame kids to imagine places that are very real, to find the poetry in water and earth and stone? And what if they are asked not just to explore the simple beauty of a place, but to reveal its environmental wisdom, and find their connection to it?

You get children finding their place in the natural world. You get children who know that water doesn't just come from a tap. You get children who know their "ecological address" as well as they know the name of their street or their town. You get hope.

This is the genesis of *River of Words,* an international poetry and art contest for children in kindergarten through twelfth grade that invites students to explore their own watershed, discover its importance in their lives, and express what they've learned, felt and observed in words and images. The program was sparked by former US Poet Laureate (1995–1997) Robert Hass' commitment to environmental education. His vision was strong enough to inspire a group of hardcore environmental activists—a feisty bunch of dam-fighters at International Rivers Network (IRN), a grassroots group committed to protecting the integrity of watersheds—and a freelance writer like me to leap with both feet into the wonderful world of children's poetry and art.

The jump from activism to art wasn't such a great leap, in fact. River of Words' innovative approach to environmental and arts education was just a different kind of activism, springing from the same roots as most environmental advocacy work—an attempt to reveal the links between people and nature, the physical and the spiritual—then sharing what you've uncovered (networking) with others, and inspiring them to continue the process in their own communities (grassroots organizing).

5   As so often happens, fate and history conspired to create a moment in time when a new idea can find fertile ground and flourish. In 1995 several things happened at precisely the right moment that allowed River of Words to become more just than a catchy phrase—and certainly not a new one—rattling around my head as I awoke one October morning. Half-awake, I somehow knew that River of Words was the name of the yet-to-be-determined project a friend had suggested I come up with to present to the newly-appointed Poet Laureate, whom, she suggested, might be interested in working with a group of activists trying to protect and save the world's rivers. "He's really interested in the environment and education," she'd said. "Come up with an idea and I'll introduce you to him." I had just been hired as a consultant at IRN, and was casting about for ideas to help them further their cause.

Meanwhile, The Academy of American Poets had just announced that they were declaring April as an annual National Poetry Month. Not the cruelest month after all, it seems—April is also the month in which Earth Day falls each year. Rivulets of ideas were beginning to converge—poetry, rivers, education, Earth. But what form was this convergence to take? How would we engage people's attention in the short time before April 1996, the first National Poetry Month? Perhaps River of Words could be a poetry contest. My background in curriculum development and international education led me naturally to addressing children; a poetry contest seemed a good idea. River of Words, yes—we could have an annual environmental poetry contest, I speculated. My initial thought was to have children write about a different theme each year, beginning with rivers, as dictated by my involvement with International Rivers Network, whom I'd hoped would like the idea of sponsoring the contest.

When Robert Hass and I finally met, it was as if we'd been working on the same idea all along. "A contest, yes, I'd thought about that, too," he concurred. "But let's make the theme 'watersheds,' and keep it watersheds. Learning about our own watersheds gets to the essence of how we have to understand our homegrounds, if we're ever to have a hope of managing them effectively. Let's get kids imaginations working from that perspective right from the start." In the next few months, IRN's rabbit warren of offices above a pizza parlor in Berkeley, California was transformed by a flurry of volunteers working to make River of Words a reality.

We quickly realized that our first step was to reach—and teach—the teachers. Having a contest on the theme of watersheds in 1995 (and to some extent even today) meant we'd have to give teachers some background on what a watershed is, why they're important and how students might go about exploring their own watersheds. With the help of poets, scientists, educators, artists and conservationists, a curriculum guide was created and distributed free to teachers across the country, with sections on teaching about watersheds, poetry and art. We encouraged teachers to partner up with other teachers—a science teacher and an English teacher, say—as well as with others in their communities—bird watchers, writers, park rangers, water department employees, photographers, farmers, and so on. Every community, we reasoned, has untapped numbers of folks who might jump at the chance to take kids on a field trip or give a classroom presentation. Most school systems, however, seemed to have no vehicle for engaging such people: one doesn't just knock on the schoolhouse door and say, "I know how to read animal tracks," or "I can identify all our native plants." River of Words, from the start, was as much about building community partnerships as it was about education, nature and the arts.

After creating a curriculum guide, the next step that first year was getting the word out. A list of thousands of arts and environmental organizations was posted on our web site to connect teachers with local resources. A mailing was sent to over 3,000 grassroots watershed-related organizations—creek and river restoration groups, fishing enthusiasts, and so on—encouraging them to contact their local schools and offer to visit the classroom or take kids on field trips and talk about their region's natural and cultural history. We contacted every state arts council in the country and provided them with River of Words (quickly dubbed "ROW") materials, encouraging them to do similar outreach to the schools. Through the American Booksellers Association, we provided bookstore owners with ideas for in-store displays of local poetry and natural history, afternoon children's poetry readings, sidewalk art events, and the like. The idea was to involve as many facets of the community as possible in exploring and learning about that *particular* place—Who lived here long ago? How did they feed themselves? Where does our water come from? Where does our garbage go? What stories, songs, poems, tall tales and art has this place inspired?

10   A mere five months later thousands of entries began to pour into our office from a wide cross-section of America's youth: from public, private and parochial schools representing nearly every state; home-schooling families, after-school programs, 4-H , Girl Scouts, nature centers, youth clubs and libraries. Our favorites of the children's poems and paintings were posted in the mailroom for all to enjoy, alongside the usual office clutter of announcements, flyers, reminders, jokes. Staff meetings began with a newly arrived poem or two.

One unanticipated bonus was the effect of the children's work on the staff of International Rivers Network. Activism is difficult work, filled with long hours of writing and research, legal wrangling, statistical analysis—and often—disappointment and loss. Like most environmental activists struggling to save a species or ecosystem or culture, International River Network's staff had precious little time to actually spend on or near rivers—they were too busy saving them. The humor, love, and tender observations of the children's art and poetry reminded them why their own work was so essential, why it was worth the long hours and low pay; many remarked that they were revitalized by the entries, explaining that the children's work renewed their sense of hope for the future.

We were also heartened by the innovative ways River of Words was being implemented locally around the country. A small town in New Mexico celebrated with a River of Words parade down Main Street, replete with banners made by local children of their artwork. Every shop in town that day had a little basket next to the cash register where you could take a poem or leave a poem. The community also sponsored a river bank clean up and poetry reading, which has become an annual event. In Michigan, a bookstore owner sponsored a River of Words evening at her store for teachers. She invited representatives of all the local groups and agencies she could think of that might have programs or material of use to children and had them meet with teachers to discuss how to utilize their resources. In California, an elementary teacher added a multigenerational aspect to River of Words by having her class visit a senior citizens' home that stood alongside a creek. The students conducted oral history interviews of the elders, many of whom were lifelong residents of the area. They explored the creek together, then returned to their classrooms to write poems and paint. When the seniors received copies of the children's work they were so inspired that they invited the class to return with their families and teacher the following month. To the surprise of the students, the seniors threw a wonderful party for them and read poems they had written in response to the children's work. Many were about the creek, and quite a few included their own childhood memories of the place. Every year, we learn of more and more local events sparked by River of Words—events that build community awareness and support ongoing partnerships in support of education, conservation, and the arts.

Clearly, the children who participate in River of Words each year have gained much, as well. Aside from learning the ecology and value of their watersheds, their imaginations find much to celebrate, honor and nurture. Robert Hass, the contest's mentor, co-founder, and now president of our board of directors, believes that neither poetry nor science alone can make the next generation better stewards of the earth. "We need both things—a living knowledge of the land and a live imagination of it and our place in it—if we are going to preserve it. Good science and a vital art and, in the long run, wisdom."

When Hass was appointed Poet Laureate in 1995 (the first ever from west of the Mississippi), he realized he had an opportunity to bring attention to two issues that were of great importance to him—the environment and literacy. Seizing the moment, he decided to convene an unprecedented gathering at The Library of Congress to celebrate American nature writers, the natural world and community values. The resulting April 1996 event—the largest ever held at The Library—was entitled "Watershed: Writers, Nature & Community." During six landmark days, thousands of representatives of grassroots conservation, restoration and environmental education organizations from around the country shared ideas and strategies with the country's most important nature writers.

15   It was at this seminal gathering (a "watershed" event, if ever there was) that we honored our first River of Words Contest winners. (That the first ROW Awards Ceremony even happened was one of the many "miracles" that have saved us from disaster several times. While caught up in the rush of conceptualizing River of Words that first year, along with the challenge of creating a curriculum guide and reaching the nation's teachers in the space of a few months, our fund raising efforts suffered. The contest was a great success but, to our horror, we had not raised enough money to send the winners to Washington, as we'd promised. Just as we were struggling to find a way out of what was sure to be a public relations, not to mention ethical, nightmare—telling children, no less, that we couldn't make good on their promised prize trip—actor Robin Williams and his wife Marsha stepped in and saved the day with a large donation.)

In the several years since its rocky inception, River of Words has formalized its affiliation with The Library of Congress Center for the Book.

Our annual Award Ceremony for the River of Words' grand prize winners and their families in the Library's Madison Building each April draws an enthusiastic audience of Washington residents, teachers and public officials. The contest now accepts entries from children all over the world and honors an international grand prize winner at the Library ceremony, as well. We publish an annual poetry book of the contest's winning entries, entitled "River of Words: The Natural World as Viewed by Young People." We also conduct teacher training workshops all over the country and have seventeen (and counting!) ROW state coordinators, often housed at state departments of natural resources, or libraries. Many states conduct their own River of Words' contests in conjunction with the larger contest each year, as well, awarding local prizes.

Continuing to utilize the "activist" model on which it was founded, River of Words relies heavily on networking and partnership development. We encourage the leveraging of existing resources and work with many organizations and institutions to provide educational opportunities for students and communities. There is now a Girl Scout "Water Drop" patch, developed in partnership with the US Environmental Protection Agency, for which girls enter the River of Words contest after exploring their watersheds. River of Words poetry and art is reprinted in magazines, books, annual reports and newspapers, and exhibits of the winning art are seen around the world at museums, conferences and other events. In 2001, we took another great leap forward and "spun off" from International Rivers Network, becoming an independent non-profit educational organization.

River of Words participants have given us a unique and encompassing view of our world as seen through the eyes of its children. They have expressed their concerns, dreams, wishes and fears in words and pictures that astound and delight. Now that we know what these children have to say, the question for the rest of us is: what do we have to say to them? Do we know our place in the watery world? Robert Hass again: "There is no reason we cannot give our kids hope, and a sense of pride, and a love of our amazing earth, and a sense of purpose, and we need to begin now. River of Words is the seed of a place to start."

Excerpt from River of Words Teacher's Guide
by Robert Hass

"Oh beautiful for spacious skies," the song goes, "for amber waves of grain, for purple mountain's majesty across the fruited plain." In the future they are going to say of us that, at the end of the twentieth century, we inherited a vast and beautiful and living land, still full of wild mountains and rivers, the remains of great forests, windy desert mesas, bayous and glades and lakes, and a teeming creaturely life, all this endangered and some of it rendered immensely productive by our energy and cleverness and ingenious technologies, and they are going to ask what we did with it.

20   They might come to say that we respected it. That we were a country from the beginning that took its character from our relationship to the immensity and beauty and promise of the land and that, though we exploited it brilliantly, sometimes mercilessly, and often unwisely, we also loved it and that in the end we preserved it and cared for it. That we understood that we were in a relationship of community to the land itself, its watersheds and grasses and trees and elegant quick-eyed life, and that we passed it on, still thriving, to our children.

Or they will say of us that we were clever, energetic, and greedy. That we kept saying how much we loved the land and that we were going to respect it, but we also kept saying that it made good sense to exploit it just a little more before we stop. And we kept cutting down our forests and polluting our rivers and fouling our air just a little more, just a little at a time, until there was not much left.

How is this story going to turn out? The answer to that question lies with our children—the first generation of the twenty-first century. It lies in their own imagination of the land, in their understanding of it and knowledge of it and their feeling for the wild life around them. The idea of *River of Words* is to ask them to educate themselves about the place where they live and to unleash their imaginations. We need both things—a living knowledge of the land and a live imagination of it and our place in it—if we are going to preserve it. Good science and a vital art and, in the long run, wisdom. All this must begin in the classroom, in family conversation, and in family outings. There is no reason we cannot give our kids hope, and a sense of pride, and a love of our amazing earth, and a sense of purpose, and we need to begin now. *River of Words* is the seed of a place to start. Please join us in this effort.

To you students, I would say this: learning your watershed should be an adventure and so should expressing it in poems and art. I hope you'll bring all of your natural energy and imagination to it. It doesn't matter whether you live in the city or the country; water runs through it that supports your life. Your imaginations run through the place where you live like the water does. So I wish you watery minds and earthy minds and airy minds—and fiery minds, and all of us involved with *River of Words* hope you have fun with this project

Tips for Writing Poems by Robert Hass

Two very famous teachers of haiku gave very different advice about writing poetry. Basho, who many think is the greatest of haiku poets, had this to say; "Learn about pines from the pine, and about bamboo from the bamboo." In other words, pay attention. And Buson, another of the great haiku poets, when someone asked him how to improve the spirit of their work, said "Read Chinese poetry."

25   In other words, if you want to write good poems, read good poems. It is an old debate: which comes first, art or experience? What if you have skill

but no heart, or heart but no skill to express it? Luckily, young writers don't have to choose. So here are a few tips:

1. Get something down on paper. Or as the Irish short story writer Frank O'Connor said, "You can't revise nothing." Waiting for inspiration is like waiting to be asked to dance. If inspiration comes, it comes. And it will come more often if you show you are interested.

2. Pay attention to what's around you. If you write nature poems, look at things. If you write poems about people, notice them. There are ways to practice noticing: teach yourself the names of some of the birds in your neighborhood, the trees; learn the names of the stars overhead. Listen to the wind. Look at the way light falls on your street at different times of day.

3. Pay attention to what you're feeling. A lot of poetry has to do not with knowing what you feel, but discovering what you feel. Sometimes, if you notice what you're feeling, a phrase or an image for it will come to you out of nowhere. It will be a place to start and the result may surprise you. It's hard not to present to the world the feeling you think will please other people by having or seeming to have. Poetry ought to be the place where you don't have to do that.

4. Pay attention to your own mind. No thought is too weird for poetry. And everyone has weird thoughts all the time. Some people are just good at not noticing that they have them. Noticing is what makes any kind of art fresh and interesting.

5. Say your poems out loud to yourself until you're pleased with how they sound. Some thoughts are quick, some thoughts are slow and deep. Some skip, some pace slowly. The pleasure of poetry for people who write it a lot is mostly here, whether you write in rhyme with a definite beat, or write in the rhythm of natural speech. The poem isn't finished until it's pleasing to your ear.

6. Read lots of poetry. It will give you ideas about what poetry can do, techniques you can try. And real feeling will put you in touch with real feeling. Someone else's originality will make you feel yours.

RIVER OF WORDS POETRY CONTEST WINNERS

Tyler Mitchell

Age 8
Desert Winds Elementary School

Tucson, Arizona
2003 Grand Prize Winner (Grades K–2)
©River of Words

Wishing Dust

The rain, the trees
the road and my heart
are part of the world.

The windy moonlight
and sunlight
are like wishing dust
that is coming down
on me.

Celia La Luz

Age 15
Lowell High School
San Francisco, California
2003 Grand Prize Winner (Grades 10–12)
©River of Words

Return

Bring me home by moonlight path
Where pale moon stains the ochre earth.
Tell me where to go.
Away from the place where the yellow lanterns glow
Where the insects gather for heat
in the lonely night.
Surround me with trees
where the stubborn houses refuse
to stand
Where the rain breaks delicately
against green leaves
Take me to the place
where the stars do not hide timidly
ashamed of their beauty
Where the smells that rise from the earth
guide me
Guide me home to the forest

Where I can find myself again
hidden in the leaves

CONVERSATION STARTER

Discuss a poem or a piece of art made by a child that inspired you or gave you hope. You might respond to a piece of art that you made as a child.

READING MATTERS

1. What interested you most about the River of Words project? Do you think it would be an interesting project to introduce at a school in your community?
2. What tools did you learn about that would help you to write or teach poetry?
3. How does art help you to connect with nature and your creativity? Draw a picture in nature and then reflect on how this process helped to change your perspective on the subject matter.
4. Why does the River of Words promote the connection between science and art?

WRITING MATTERS

1. Using "Tips for Writing Poems" by Robert Hass, write a poem about a place where you like to be in nature.
2. Identify your ecological address by recording the natural boundaries that define your community. Write an essay that describes your ecological address.
3. Research and write an essay about the ecological, social, and political impacts on your local watershed. Include a discussion on your learning process.

RELEVANT WEB SITES

RIVER OF WORDS <http://www.riverofwords.org>

The River of Words web site provides information about the international environmental and art contest, and includes an online gallery of winning artwork and poetry.

EPA: SURF YOUR WATERSHED <http://www.epa.gov/surf>

This web site is dedicated to the goals of the Environmental Protection Agency and the celebration of its 25 years of progress through the "Adopt Your Watershed" campaign. The site shows how the EPA challenges citizens and organizations to join others working to protect and restore rivers, streams, wetlands, lakes, groundwater, and estuaries.

Introduction: Jazz Gives Teens New Footing

Initiated in California in 1995, Juvie Jazz is a dance program and curriculum for youth incarcerated in Juvenile Hall. Dance classes offer the participants a positive outlet to direct their energy and gain new insights and perspective on their lives. Originally only available at the Santa Clara County Juvenile Hall, the program expanded in 1999 to two children's shelters in Santa Clara County and to San Mateo County's Juvenile Hall.

JAZZ GIVES TEENS NEW FOOTING

It is a crisp, clear winter afternoon and Ehud Krauss, dressed in sweats and cross-training shoes, is standing impatiently in front of the first of several locked metal security doors at the entrance to Juvenile Hall in San Jose, California. As soon as he is buzzed into this jail for convicted juvenile offenders, Krauss begins teasing the probation officers. "Hey, did you have a good weekend?" he jokes as he passes through, suggesting they will be incarcerated along with the inmates for the weekend.

It takes a generous mix of humor, bravado, and unflagging optimism for Krauss to persist in the task he's given himself. He wants no less than to change the lives of hundreds of at-risk and incarcerated teenage boys and girls through dance. "I think these kids have a lot of potential," the Israeli-born Krauss says in heavily Hebrew-accented English. "I do pas de bourrée with them so they learn structure. They drop out of middle school, forget high school. They have no structure. But I make them trust me. With my background, I can relate to these kids. We are climbing the ladder to be a better person through dance."

Krauss can get away with sentiments that might sound naive from anyone else because he is such an anomalous figure in this role. At fifty-three, Krauss still looks like the muscular, competitive Olympic volleyball player he once was and he still moves with an easy grace reflecting his years of training on scholarships at the Martha Graham, Joffrey Ballet, Alvin Ailey, and Luigi schools.

"I'm Israeli and I'm German, so you'd better watch out!" he teases. This afternoon in the high-security B-9 unit, the wing for convicted felons, a dozen boys 13 to 17 years old turn out for Krauss's fast-paced jazz dance class. Participation is voluntary, but usually everyone, and sometimes even a probation officer, joins in.

5   The boys begin by clearing the floor of the room, a drab common eating area smelling of disinfectant and with a cement floor and single row of small, high windows. They shove the tables and chairs to the perimeter, then linger near the portable CD player Krauss sets up, straining to see the recordings he has brought for today's class. Most of these young men graduate to adult jail when they turn 18 to complete sentences that stretch for decades. Yet their high-spirited investment in the moment belies this.

"These guys don't believe they are going to live past 20 or 25," Krauss explains. "From what they see in their communities they expect that drugs, AIDS, or someone is going to kill them before then."

Yet for this one hour, before Krauss moves on to teach the girls of the G–1 unit, the boys are eager, attentive, and fairly nimble as they scramble through his fast-paced warm-up of stretches, slides, skips, and pivoting walks. "OK. Chiquita Banana," he jokes, patting the shaven head of a sad-eyed small boy with gang symbol tattoos on the knuckles of both hands. Now they launch into an ambitious combination of full body springs over one another's prone forms. It's a physically and, in this context, socially risky move but they all dive into it without hesitation, clearing one another with inches to spare and then hopping up for the next move. It is only later that Krauss confides how challenging this action was for most of the boys because its pose suggested one man atop another sexually, a big taboo in the aggressively homophobic culture of "juvie."

Many of the boys are also members of the two leading rival gangs in San Jose, and this adds yet another layer of danger to Krauss's harmonizing ensemble moves. It's easy to think of *West Side Story* as one watches Krauss coax the boys to temporarily put aside their enmity and try a few dance moves together. "It's not cool to ask questions," Krauss explains to a visitor, and so he often has them count out loud when they dance so everyone knows the beat. When they miss a count he teases them. "Count! That's why you go to school, and why else do I pay taxes?" he shouts at them good-naturedly.

The boys' affection for Krauss is readily apparent. He commands respect on their terms as well as his own. Last year, when he was hospitalized with meningitis and unable to attend the annual holiday program, the boys and girls unanimously decided to run the whole show, in his honor, without him. As he moves through the labyrinthine hallways and cell-blocks of Juvenile Hall, Krauss cuts an impressive figure. He's a tough guy by anyone's standards—a former Israeli Army instructor and soldier who, like many of his students, came to English as his second language. He's physically strong and fearless, working in the midst of a room where a half-dozen of his dance students this afternoon are convicted murderers.

"Most of them have nothing to live for," he says. "There are frequent suicide attempts, and once a kid got pissed off and came at me with a chair. They are holding a lot inside. Their brain is all the time in crisis," he continues. "So I always arrive with hundreds of class plans and I find out what went on the night before so I'll know what kind of state the kids will be in and what kind of class they need." Sometimes tensions run so high that Krauss jettisons a regular class and shows dance videos and talks to the kids about how good it can feel, and how beautiful it can look, to really dance fully with one's whole spirit.

10   Krauss is also captivatingly cool when he starts to demonstrate for the kids. There is a panther-like quality to his actions and an ease and surprise

in his gestures. He looks like a guy dancing rather than a rarefied, and for this population, out-of-reach dancer.

Born on a kibbutz in Israel in 1946 to German and Czech immigrant parents, Krauss was, by his own admission, a precocious but difficult child who was easily bored in class. He discovered movement early, first in folk dance on the kibbutz; then in sports; and finally, as a young adult, in modern dance at the Bat-Dor Company School in Tel Aviv.

After touring the U.S. and Canada in the late 1970s as part of a dance duet program with his first wife, Nurit, Krauss settled in the Bay Area to be near the Mountain View studio of his mentor, Richard Gibson. (Krauss now lives in Palo Alto a few blocks from his Zohar Dance Studio with his second wife, Daynee, and their daughter.) By 1979 the first of his outreach programs to the low-income communities of East Palo Alto, Redwood City, East Menlo Park, and San Jose was underway. Krauss says it was seeing a show of the kids from Alvin Ailey's outreach program that was his first inspiration to work with this population.

Krauss's colleagues respond with equal enthusiasm and awe to his blunt manner and remarkable achievement. "It really is him!" says Bill Sommerville, executive director of Philanthropic Ventures, a Bay Area foundation that funds Krauss's work with troubled teens. "He has a commitment, a heart and soul and spirit, and those are essential. Ehud is working in what looks like an impossible situation at Juvenile Hall. These kids have nothing to lose, they've hit bottom," Sommerville said. "Ehud brings them back. It's a high compliment to the field of dance that it can be a tool with such an interesting population. Ehud has shown that maybe dancers sell themselves short. They do have something to give the community in this way and there is a huge demand for it."

Gerald Neary, the affable probation manager of Juvenile Hall, is awed by Krauss as well. "One of the things Ehud is able to work through is that facade incarcerated teens often have. These are all really just kids. You can just go in and watch his class and see dance is working to release tension and build a team with these kids in a way nothing else is."

15   Essentially none of the boys or girls Krauss teaches in Juvenile Hall had ever had a dance class before he started separate boys and girls classes four years ago, supported by funding from the David and Lucile Packard Foundation. Yet once they start it, almost none will miss a class unless they are being disciplined in solitary confinement, or are under observation for a suicide attempt.

John G. (the names of the students have been changed to protect their identities), a 17-year-old boy, has been taking class with Krauss in San Jose Juvenile Hall for two and a half years, and he regards the class as an important crucible for his growing confidence and agreeability.

"At the beginning I didn't like Ehud too much; he didn't have patience and he was grouchy," John said in a telephone interview from Juvenile Hall. "But now I really like the dance class a lot," he continued. "It takes my mind off things and releases all my stress if I am stressed about court. In here, we don't get to jump around. Because we've got to get along with other people when we are dancing, it also helps us do that when we aren't dancing. In class you see that not everyone can learn the same and so you get to know a little about them if you help them with the steps."

Marie T. and Fran E., 15- and 16-year-olds in the Girls Unit at Juvenile Hall, credit the dance classes with giving them confidence, helping them overcome their shyness, and releasing the same kinds of stresses John describes. "My confidence is the biggest surprise I've felt from Ehud's classes," Marie T. says. "He taught us how not to give up if we miss a step. I think this will help me keep my self-control so I'll get off probation this time when I'm finally out."

Fran E. concurs about the positive socializing influence of these dance classes. "There are people in here I don't like, but when I'm dancing with them I forget about it. If you keep in mind how things went with them dancing, then the differences don't seem so important."

20   For John G., the biggest benefit of Krauss's dance experience has been a new model for how to succeed at challenges, particularly academic ones. "In school now I don't give up as easily," he says, referring to the Osborne School with Juvenile Hall. "I'm going to take some college courses and yesterday they gave me this history book that was hard to understand. I wanted to stop, but I stuck with it and in the end I understood it," he said proudly, ascribing his success to Krauss's dance class training in the rewards of perseverance.

"I am interested in why these kids are failing at school," Krauss says. "They are not learning English. They are always on the outside. Through the arts they can learn to succeed at something. I want to show them that dance gives them a better high than drugs." For Alicia H., a 16-year-old now at the Muriel Wright Ranch in Santa Clara, a transitional institution between juvenile jail and a return to society, Krauss's dance classes have provided a new model for getting along with adults. "He treats us like human beings," she says. "I've been in and out of jail since I was 11 and I know now that as long as I keep dancing I have the best chance of not going back to drugs or jail. When I dance I use my imagination, and for a little while I forget where I am."

Krauss's dance classes are demanding, but not intimidating. He overflows with ideas and optimism about the virtues of experience in the arts for the whole gamut of at-risk teens. In addition to his six classes a week for the inmates of Juvenile Hall, he teaches another twenty-two classes a week in youth development centers, juvenile authority ranches, and women's detention centers throughout the Bay Area. "I'd like to see many more dance teachers take two hours a week and go teach dance to these kinds of kids," Krauss says of his dream. "I'd like to teach teachers how we can do this and motivate kids. With art we can give them self-esteem, and self-esteem is the immune system of the soul. It costs $30,000 a year to keep one kid in Juvenile Hall. What if some money were spent on giving them the tools to do something else?"

Before and after class he is warm and personal with the teens, giving a quick hug to one quiet boy as he jokes with another. "You're still here?" he asks. "What, you like the food so much you don't want to leave?" Yet once the class begins the terms of success become toughness, not accessibility. Krauss keeps up a light banter throughout the warm-up, prodding the boys to stay attentive and focused on the task at hand and, most importantly, to drop the heavily coded body language of their gangs and try on the shape of the jazz phrase he is teaching them. "Don't hold your crotch," he keeps reminding four boys in the back row. "Nothing is going to fall off!"

This afternoon the forty-eight girls of G-1 prove a more recalcitrant group. Seated on the gray cement floor of their common area, they chatter softly and tug at their exercise uniform of pink T-shirts and green shorts through Krauss's opening stretches. He halts the class when one girl shouts, "God!" in exasperation. "Don't get religious on me," he jokes. Then he turns serious. "It's nothing to do with God. It's something to do with you."

25   Several weeks later, in late December at Juvenile Probation's Annual Foster Grandparent Holiday Appreciation Program, the dancing boys and girls of B-9 and G-1 sit nervously on a corner section of bleachers in the Juvenile Hall Gym. They all wear new black T-shirts with the words "Juvie Jazz" emblazoned across the front. On cue, they rise and first the girls, and then the boys, go through their dance routine before 400 of their peers from Juvenile Hall. For the boys in particular, self-consciousness rapidly gives way to a swaggering assurance as their bodies find the familiar rhythms and placement of Krauss's phrases.

Dance has become a substitute home for these kids. It is beginning to open them up to themselves. "I believe very hard in art," Krauss says. Watching his Juvie Jazz dancers, art indeed seems the first step toward hope.

Conversation Starter

Discuss an activity that helped you to build confidence and to work as part of a team.

Reading Matters

1. What is the goal of teaching dance to incarcerated teenage boys and girls?
2. Compare and contrast the culture of "juvie" with the culture expressed in Ehud Krauss's dance class.
3. What strategy does Ehud Krauss use to build a sense of community? What cultural traditions or expressions are representative of that community?
4. Is Ehud Krauss a good role model for his students? How does his dance class help students to succeed in school?

WRITING MATTERS

1. Write an essay about an activity that you participated in after school that helped you to succeed in school. How did the skills you learned from that activity help you with your schoolwork?
2. Write a research paper about an organization that supports youth programs. What strategies does the organization use to engage youth? What are the strengths of the program? Why is it effective?
3. Write a research paper about the juvenile detention system in your community. How many juveniles are in the system? How does that figure compare to the number of students in the school system? How many of the inmates are repeat offenders? What resources are in place to support their rehabilitation?

RELEVANT WEB SITE

ZOHAR SCHOOL OF DANCE <http://www.zohardance.org>

This web site profiles the community outreach efforts of the Zohar Dance Company.

Wendy Kopp (b. 1967)

Teach for America

Wendy Kopp founded Teach for America in 1989. Now one of her generation's most recognized social entrepreneurs, Kopp continues to serve as the organization's president. In addition to her role at Teach for America, Kopp is chair of the board of The New Teacher Project, a nonprofit consulting group that helps school districts and states recruit and develop new teachers more effectively. The New Teacher Project is a spin-off of Teach for America that applies Teach for America's knowledge base more broadly in an effort to effect systemic change in the way new teachers are brought into the profession. In 2003, Kopp was appointed to the President's Council on Service and Civic Participation. She has received honorary doctorate degrees from Princeton University, Connecticut College, Drew University, and Smith College. She was the youngest person and the first woman to receive the Woodrow Wilson Award, the highest honor Princeton University confers on undergraduate alumni. She was also recognized in December 1994 as one of Time Magazine's forty most promising leaders under 40. In addition, Wendy has received the Jefferson Award for Public Service, Aetna's Voice of Conscience Award, the Citizen Activist Award from the Gleitsman Foundation, and the Kilby Young Innovator Award.

It was in October of my senior year at Princeton that I realized I needed a plan. What was I going to do after graduation? To this point my life had always been driven toward some academic or extracurricular goal. But now, as I grappled with the biggest decision of my first twenty-one years, I had no idea what I wanted to do. I felt uninspired. I was searching for a place to direct my energy that would give me the kind of significant responsibility that I had enjoyed in various student organizations. I wanted this opportunity right away, not ten or twenty years down the road. More important, I wanted to do something that would make a real difference in the world. I just didn't know what that was.

The issue of my future weighed on me all my waking hours, beginning with my early morning runs. Jogging used to bring me clarity, but now as I ran around the town of Princeton, I felt only more lost. My frustration grew. It became a nagging inner monologue that followed me as I walked across campus between classes or tried to listen to lectures or headed over to Nassau Street, where I would grab lunch and dinner since I'd never found my niche among Princeton's eating clubs. I was in a funk.

This was 1988, and I was a member of the Me Generation. At least that's what the media said. If you believed the pundits, all my generation cared about was making money and leading pampered lives.

It did seem that just about every Princeton senior was applying to a two-year corporate training program, most with investment banks and management consulting firms. Yet something seemed wrong to me about that "Me Generation" label. Most of the people I knew weren't heading to these two-year programs because they were dead set on making money. Most weren't doing so out of a deep interest in business or high finance either. They just couldn't think of anything else to do. I sensed that I was not alone—that there were thousands of other seniors like me who were searching for jobs that would offer them significance and meaning.

5   At the same time that I soul-searched about my future, I found myself increasingly engrossed in another issue: the failures of our public education system. This issue had first captured my attention as a college freshman. My roommate, who had attended public school in the South Bronx, was smart and creative. She was a brilliant poet. Still, she struggled under the academic demands of Princeton.

I had attended public schools in an upper-middle-class community in Dallas. My schools were not typical. For starters, they had money to spare. Lots of it. A $100,000 scoreboard hung above the $3 million football stadium with Astroturf that cost $1 million every three years to replace. The student body was almost completely homogenous, racially as well as socioeconomically. More than 99 percent of the 300 or 400 incoming freshmen would graduate, and about 97 percent would go on to college. Because of the high quality of my schools and the support provided by my family and community, I graduated with an education so solid that I was able to do well at Princeton without locking myself into solitary confinement at Firestone Library.

As I moved through Princeton, I grew increasingly aware of students' unequal access to the kind of educational excellence I had previously taken for granted. I wanted to figure out what could be done about this problem, and so I organized a conference about the issue. At this time I led an organization called the Foundation for Student Communication. Run entirely by

Princeton students, it was designed to bring student leaders and business leaders together to discuss pressing social issues. So in November of my senior year, my colleagues and I gathered together fifty students and business leaders from across the country to propose action plans for improving our education system.

There were many interesting discussions and debates, but one in particular stuck out. In a session about teacher quality, nearly all of the student participants—who had been chosen through a rigorous application process and were certainly among the nation's more talented students—said that they would teach in public schools if it were possible for them to do so. And one speaker maintained that people without education degrees were frequently hired by public schools because there weren't enough education majors interested in teaching in low-income communities.

At one point during a discussion group, after hearing yet another student express interest in teaching, I had a sudden idea: *Why didn't this country have a national teacher corps of recent college graduates who would commit two years to teach in urban and rural public schools?* A teacher corps would provide another option to the two-year corporate training programs and grad schools. It would speak to all of us college seniors who were searching for something meaningful to do with our lives. We would jump at the chance to be part of something that brought thousands of our peers together to address the inequities in our country and to assume immediate and full responsibility for the education of a class of students. I suggested the idea in a discussion group; others responded enthusiastically.

10   The more I thought about it, the more convinced I became that this simple idea was potentially very powerful. If top recent college graduates devoted two years to teaching in public schools, they could have a real impact on the lives of disadvantaged kids. Because they had themselves excelled academically, they would be relentless in their efforts to ensure their students achieved. They would throw themselves into their jobs, working investment-banking hours in classrooms instead of skyscrapers on Wall Street. They would question the way things are and fight to do what was right for children.

Beyond influencing kids' lives directly, a national teacher corps could produce a change in the very consciousness of our country. The corps members' teaching experiences were bound to strengthen their commitment to children in low-income communities and spur their outrage at the circumstances preventing these children from fulfilling their potential. Many corps members would decide to stay in the field of education. And those who would become doctors and lawyers and businesspeople would remain advocates for social change and education reform. They would become school board members. They would become mayors and state legislators, U.S. senators and Supreme Court justices. And they would make better decisions because of their experience teaching in public schools.

Now during my morning runs and campus walks, I would roll the idea of the teacher corps over and over in my head. This could be huge, I thought. This could be the Peace Corps of the 1990s: Thousands would join, and we would fundamentally impact our country.

As I became increasingly excited about the idea of a national teacher corps, I was still trying to figure out a practical answer to my own uninspired job search. Teaching just might be it, I thought. I went to the career services office. They referred me to the teacher preparation office, which helped ten to twenty Princeton students attain teacher licensure each year. It was too late for me to enter this program, but the office pointed me to a file cabinet stuffed with job applications and certification requirements from school districts across the country. The files were a mess of mismatched, multicolored, jargon-filled papers.

15   Overwhelmed by all the information and completely confused about whether I could actually teach without an education degree, I decided to call the New York City public schools directly. I spoke with a former teacher who was working to recruit recent graduates of East Coast colleges to teach in New York. He told me that if I could wait until Labor Day, I would probably get a teaching job. The schools couldn't be sure of their job openings until then. This was a major disappointment. I needed money to live on right after I graduated.

Although this whole experience was initially discouraging, it turned out to be a good thing. In the end, it only made me more convinced of the need for a teacher corps that would recruit as aggressively as the investment banks and management consulting firms that were still swarming all over campus. The teacher corps would make teaching an attractive choice for top grads by surrounding it with an aura of status and selectivity, streamlining the process of applying for teaching positions, and assuring recent graduates a job and a steady income despite districts' inability to hire them until Labor Day.

I became so obsessed by the idea that I decided to try to make it happen. I wrote a letter to President George Bush suggesting that as the "Education President," he should create this new corps. John Kennedy had set up the Peace Corps, I thought. Who better than the President of the United States to create the teacher corps? With high hopes, I mailed off my impassioned letter. It must have slipped into the wrong stack. In return I received a form letter rejecting my application for a job.

At some point in December, I saw that I simply needed a job—a job that would pay my bills after graduation. So I made a weak attempt, applying for a total of five positions—one at an investment bank, two at consulting firms, one at a food products company, and one at a commercial real estate venture.

And I began musing about another possibility. If the President wasn't going to create a teacher corps, maybe I could start one as a nonprofit organization. My experience at the Foundation for Student Communication, where I managed a staff of sixty and sold hundreds of thousands of dollars' worth of magazine advertisements and conference sponsorships, made me think that I just might be able to pull this off. More important, I didn't have the experience to see why it couldn't be done.

Meanwhile, as a senior at Princeton, I was obligated to write a thesis. I had been looking for a topic that would grab me, that would inspire me to spend hours and hours researching and writing. After the education conference, I knew that the teacher corps idea was my answer. Here was something that motivated me personally and that would also satisfy my requirements at the Woodrow Wilson School, Princeton's public policy program.

20 And so, during the spring of my senior year, I withdrew from the world—skipping whatever classes I could and talking to just about no one—in order to research the viability of a national teacher corps. I was certain such a corps must already exist somewhere—it was too obvious!—or that there was some reason it wouldn't work.

I couldn't find one. Just as the conference speaker had told us, even in times of general teacher surplus there is always a shortage of qualified teachers in very low-income areas. Individuals who haven't majored in education are hired to meet the need in underprivileged areas. And although there were a number of initiatives to improve the recruitment of new teachers, there was no national teacher corps. I also researched potential models—the Peace Corps, the teacher corps that had been run by the federal government in the 1960s, and alternative certification programs that existed in certain states to ease people without traditional teacher certification into teaching.

As I wrote my thesis, I became all the more determined to make this idea a reality. Thankfully, the firms to which I was applying for more conventional jobs made my choice easier. I didn't get a single offer. I remember standing at a pay phone at school, hearing the Morgan Stanley recruiter—my last remaining corporate possibility—tell me that they had decided I wasn't the right fit for the firm. I took this rejection personally, but I figured it must have happened for a good reason. The moment I hung up, I made my decision. I would start the teacher corps.

In the end, I produced "A Plan and Argument for the Creation of a National Teacher Corps," which looked at the educational needs in urban and rural areas, the growing idealism and spirit of service among college students, and the interest of the philanthropic sector in improving education. The thesis presented an ambitious plan: In our first year, the corps would inspire thousands of graduating college seniors to apply. We would then select, train, and place five hundred of them as teachers in five or six urban and rural areas across the country. According to the budget calculations I had done, this would cost approximately $2.5 million.

I knew we had to start big. Only a monumental launch would convey the urgency and national importance of our effort. And only that would inspire the nation's most talented graduating seniors—those with the most attractive career options—to forgo other opportunities to be part of this movement. I found support for this plan in my research about the Peace Corps. President Kennedy had appointed Sargent Shriver to develop a proposal for the Peace Corps, and most of Shriver's advisers suggested a cautious beginning. But Shriver knew that a corps that proceeded gradually would never become a symbol of the New Frontier. And so Shriver recommended that Kennedy create the Peace Corps by executive order, that it be launched within weeks, and that several hundred volunteers be placed within the year. Shriver's plan led thousands of idealistic college students to apply, and it ensured the Peace Corps's place as an enduring part of the American landscape. His theory worked for the Peace Corps. I was sure it would work for the teacher corps.

CONVERSATION STARTER

Discuss your opinions about Teach for America and National Service. Have you ever thought about serving in the community? Have you ever thought about teaching?

READING MATTERS

1. What motivated Wendy Kopp to search for an alternative to a "two-year corporate training program"? What kind of influence did her observations about her friends have on her decision? How was her decision influenced by her views of her generation?
2. Why was the idea for Teach for America a success? What facts led Kopp to believe her idea would work? What obstacles did she have to overcome?
3. Why was Kopp interested in the public education system? How did her own education motivate her to get involved? What did she observe about the quality of education among her peers?
4. Why did the author think the idea of a teacher corps would appeal to college graduates? Where did she test this concept? How did her peers respond?

WRITING MATTERS

1. Write a public service announcement encouraging young people to serve as part of the teacher corps. Use the Teach for America web site to learn about the specific requirements.
2. Write an evaluation of your high school education. Develop a list of characteristics that you believe are essential to a successful school and then give your school a grade. Be prepared to present the information to your class.
3. Develop a job description for a teacher. Think about what characteristics make a teacher successful. What are the required skills? Is this a job description that appeals to you? Are you qualified for the job? Write a summary of your findings.

RELEVANT WEB SITES

TEACH FOR AMERICA <http://www.teachforamerica.org>

This is the official web site of Teach for America, a national teacher corps of recent college graduates who commit two years to teach in urban and rural schools. This site provides information about Teach for America, including placement information, applications, and testimonials from alumni.

AMERICORPS <http://www.americorps.org>

This is the official web site of AmeriCorps, a program of the Corporation for National Service. This site provides information about AmeriCorps programs, including job descriptions, applications, and member profiles.

Writing About Education

1. What is the greatest challenge facing educators in their efforts to reform schools? Research a specific issue within this topic and write a paper to share with your classmates.

2. What type of relationships does your university have with the local community? Research local university–community partnerships, and then write a paper that profiles what you have learned. Also present your own ideas for creating more viable university–community partnerships.

3. Write about an experience you have had in your community. Discuss why the experience was educational and how you made an impact on your community.

4. Research the level of computer access at your university. Write an essay that discusses how access to and understanding of technology affects the performance of students at your university.

5. Design a web site or brochure for a nonprofit organization with an educational mission.

6. Write about your first vivid memory of school. How was the experience a formative one? How has the experience continued to impact your attitude about education?

7. Write an essay that defines education. Research the topic on the Internet and refer to relevant readings in this chapter to support your main points.

8. Write an essay about the support systems that you have at your university. Do you receive support from the university? Your family? Your community? What types of support do you receive? What resources are available to you?

9. Research the concept of service-learning as an approach to education. Write an essay that presents a definition of service-learning and that provides examples of how service-learning is being implemented.

10. In your opinion, what is the most promising strategy for education in the new millennium? Write an essay that explores the future design and role of schools in our communities. Include specific examples to support your ideas.

Culture

A Public Display of Mourning for the Victims of 9/11

Culture surrounds us. It is in the billboards we see, the celebrations we share with family and friends, the music we love, even in the ways that we choose to dance. Our cultural experiences shape our perspectives on life, helping us to affirm our individuality. At the same time, through our cultural traditions we express our values and connections to the generations before us and the generations to come. Our cultural traditions can nourish our spirit and help to strengthen our connection to our communities. What are your cultural traditions? How is your connection to your culture or other cultures expressed through your community?

As a result of an increasingly international economy, growing access to the Internet, the ease of long-distance travel, and the increasing number of international business and school exchanges, we have more opportunities to experience cultures that are different from our own. The reading selections in "Encountering New Cultures and Reeexamining Values" present a number of the complex issues in our increasingly multicultural communities. In "Viet-Kieu," Andrew Pham examines the identity issues that Vietnamese Americans face in the United States and when they return to their first home in Vietnam. In the next selection, "The Olympic Games," travel writer Pico Iyer explores the complexities of bringing together athletes and production crews from 160 countries to share in an international celebration. In "Robotic Iguanas," Julia Corbett challenges the reader to think about the consequences of exporting culture in the form of entertainment.

The following section, "New Cultural Rituals " provides insight into the changing face of communities and the ways in which our multicultural environment has led to new forms of communication. In "Should English Be the Law?," Robert D. King explores the issue of English as the official language of the United States. In the next selection, "Virtual Communities," Howard Reingold celebrates the new forms of expression that have emerged with new technologies and the popularity of the Internet. In "We Are What We Eat," Donna Gabaccia presents a historical interpretation of why American eating habits have always marked the boundaries of different cultures within the United States while, at the same time, revealing how these cultures are changing and adapting to reflect new American values. All of these selections suggest that our local, national, and international communities can function as forums for new expressions that are rooted in tradition and enlivened by the emerging climate of multiculturalism and technological innovation.

"Artistic Projects That Reflect Cultural Change" presents examples of ways that community members have struggled to express and preserve their culture's history to inspire and educate other members of their community. In the selection "Write This Down," Jacqueline Tobin explains how she discovered the truth that quilts may have been used to carry encoded messages for slaves, enabling them to escape to the North and freedom. Estella Habel's "Coming Home to Manilatown: Resurrecting the International Hotel" reflects on the coming together of two generations of

Filipino Americans. In the process they build a stronger sense of their own cultural identity through their decision to rebuild the International Hotel. In "Culture Sculpture," Mark Applebaum breaks away from his traditional training as a pianist and invents his own instruments. His fascination with creating new instruments made from assorted junk and found objects leads him to search for a communal standard for his work and ultimately allows him to recognize his place in a cultural discourse already in progress. Michael Shulan's "Here Is New York" reports on a forum for sharing the experience of 9/11 that emerged from a storefront near ground zero and has come to symbolize community healing. Each of the projects profiled in "Artistic Projects That Reflect Cultural Change" shows how a cultural tradition has been transformed and has continued to play a crucial role in the life of the community.

As you read the selections in "Culture," think about your own cultural roots. How do you express your cultural identity within your community? How does your sense of your own culture influence or change your community?

Andrew Pham (b. 1967)

Viet-Kieu

Andrew Pham was born in Vietnam, fled at the age of 10 with his family to California, worked hard, went to UCLA, landed a good technical job at United Airlines—and always carried a letter of resignation in his briefcase. Much to his parents' displeasure, Pham quit his job, set off on bicycle excursions through Mexico, Japan, and, finally, Vietnam. "I have to do something unethnic," he said. "I have to go. Make my pilgrimage." He sold all his possessions to embark on the year-long bicycle journey that took him through the Mexican desert, from Narita to Kyoto in Japan, and 2,357 miles to Saigon. Catfish and Mandala, from which "Viet-Kieu" is excerpted, is a vibrant, picaresque memoir of Pham's bicycle journey that documents an unforgettable search for cultural identity.

The closer I come to Nha Trang the more frequently I see group tours busing to local points of interest. The locals are familiar with the tourist traffic and don't shout *"Oy! Oy!"* at foreigners. The main road loops around a mountain and enters the outskirts of the city from the south side. There is a shortcut, some high school kids point out to me, up the mountain and along the cliff. It's a good sporting ride, they say. I'm about to bag 120 miles today and have no wish to climb a mountain. I come into the city the easy way.

Although the outlying area is a mirror image of all the other dusty little towns, the city center is far more developed than anything I've seen. I limp the battered bike through town, heading toward the water where the locals have told me there is lodging. Shady lanes unroll between banks of sprawling buildings set back behind brick fences. There's a nice flavor here predating the Liberation of '75. I was just a kid then, but I remember Mom being very hip with her bellbottoms and buggy sunglasses. She must have wasted scores of film rolls in Nha Trang, her favorite city. The breeze is fresh, sweet, not salty like Phan Thiet. Out on the beachfront boulevard, I am suddenly in Waikiki! Someone has ripped it out of Hawaii and dropped it in downtown Nha Trang. A colossal skeleton of the Outrigger Hotel is being framed on the beach practically in the surf line. Tall, gleaming towers of glass and steel are already taking residence a stone's throw from the water.

The sandy stretch of beach is jammed with fancy restaurants, bars hopping with modern rock, jazz, and Vietnamese pop. Aromas of grilled food turn heads and sharpen appetites. Along the avenue, fat Europeans and Australians pad about in thong bikinis, sheer sarongs, and Lycra shorts, dropping wads of dollars for seashells, corals, lacquered jewelry boxes, and bad paintings, loot, mementos, evidence.

I take the cheapest room available to a Viet-kieu at a government-run hotel (for some reason, Danes and Germans get lower rates), jump through a cold shower, then get back on my bike to head to the Vietnamese part of Nha Trang, where the food is cheaper and better. I am ravenous. Diarrhea be damned. Tonight I'm going to eat anything I want. After nearly three months of sporadic intestinal troubles, I'm still hoping that my system will acclimatize. I'm Vietnamese after all, and these microorganisms once thrived in my gut as thoroughly as in any Vietnamese here.

I eat dinner at an alley diner, nine tables crammed between two buildings lit with a couple of bare light bulbs. The family running the place says they are happy to have me, although they generally don't like foreigners. Eat too little, drink too little, but talk too much, they complain. Foreigners like to sit and sit and talk. Vietnamese eat and get out. Lounging is done in coffeehouses and beer halls. No problem. I prove to them I'm Vietnamese. I down two large bottles of Chinese beer and gorge myself on a monstrous meal of grilled meat served with a soy-and-pork-fat gravy, wrapping the meat in rice paper, cucumber, mint, pickled daikon, sour carrot, fresh basil, lettuce, chili pepper, cilantro, and rice vermicelli. Then I clear out quickly. I go to a hotel to check on a friend who might be in town. As a tour guide, he is a regular at the hotel. The concierge confirms that my friend Cuong and his tour are in town. I leave him a note and wait for him at an ice-cream parlor down the street.

5   "Hello! Andrew!"

"Cuong!"

I met him a few weeks after I arrived in Saigon. We bummed around the city several times with his girlfriends. I like him. We both agreed to check on each other when in Nha Trang or Vung Tau, both major cities on his itinerary.

He skips across the street, penny-loafing around the dog shit as he dodges motorbikes. Cuong doesn't wear sandals. No more. Not ever again. He told me, You can tell a Vietnamese by the way he wears his sandals. Is the stem firmly held between the toes? Or does the ball of the heel drag beyond the sandal? Do the sandals flap like loose tongues when he walks? Does he know there is mud between his toes? All this from a man who—in his own words—*"dribbled away [his] youth as a roadside petrol-boy selling gasoline out of glass bottles, wiping down motorbikes, hustling for dimes, and playing barefoot soccer in the dirt."*

He smoothes his shirt, fingers the ironed pleats of his gray slacks, straightens his pin-striped blue tie with red polka dots. Then, grinning, he steps closer and pumps my hand enthusiastically. "Calvin," he corrects me.

"I'm sticking with your suggestion: Calvin. It's easier for the foreigners to pronounce." I'd come up with the name at his request. He wanted something that started with a "C" and was short and sharp and American.

10   "You made it! You're not hurt? No?" he says, patting me on the arm and looking me over. "A little thinner and darker, yes. Incredible. You biked all that way? Yes, yes, of course you did."

"You got my message?"

"Of course. May I join you?" he queries, forever the Vietnamese gentleman. I fill him in on all that happened since I last saw him nearly two months ago. When a waitress brings him his chilled Coke—no ice, just like the way foreigners drink their soda—he thanks her. She looks at him, a little startled to hear a Vietnamese man uttering platitudes like Westerners. Calvin has picked up the habit because he finds it more genteel and civilized.

I first made his acquaintance at a sidewalk café. He took me for a Japanese and wanted to practice his English. When I told him I was a Vietnamese from California, he was very uncomfortable using the term Viet-kieu, explaining that people said it with too many connotations. Sometimes, it was just a word, other times an insult or a term of segregation. *"Vietnamese are Vietnamese if they believe they are,"* he had said by way of explanation, and I liked him on the instant.

By Saigon standards, Calvin is a yuppie who came into his own by the most romantic way possible—by the compulsion of a promise made to his mother on her deathbed. One afternoon, when we were touring the outer districts of Saigon on his motorbike, Calvin pointed to a pack of greyhound-lean young men, shirtless, volleying a plastic bird back and forth with their feet. *"That was me. That's how I was until I was twenty-two. Can you believe it? I threw away all my young years, working odd jobs and messing around. I just didn't care."* His mother bequeathed him, her only child, a small sum, which he spent on English classes, not bothering to finish up high school. With what little remained, he bribed his way into a job as a hotel bellhop and worked his way up. He entered a special school for tour guides. After three years of intense training, he makes four hundred dollars a month plus two hundred in tips. Now, twenty-nine, single, and rich even by Saigon standards, he fares better than college grads who are blessed if they can command two hundred dollars a month. His biggest regret: *"I wish my mother could see me now."*

15   Calvin sips his Coke and plucks a pack of Marlboros from his shirt pocket, the American cigarette one of his main props for marking himself one of the upwardly mobile. "I'm down to half a pack a day," he mumbles apologetically, offering me a smoke. I decline. He puts his cigarette down saying: "Dirty, dirty, Vietnamese habit." Calvin keeps a list of "dirty Vietnamese habits" and steels himself against them.

I tell him that Americans used to call cigarettes "white slavers." He considers that for a moment then smirks. *"That has a double meaning for us, doesn't it."* He counts the cigarettes remaining in the pack. *"Last one today,"* he announces. He seems to want my approval so I nod. Vindicated, he ignites the last of his daily nicotine allowance. He sighs the smoke downwind. *"Tell me. Tell me everything about your trip."*

As I recount the events since I last saw him, Calvin grows increasingly excited, digging me more for the details of Vietnam than for the actual mechanics of bike touring. How did the police treat you? Hanoi people are more formal than Southerners, aren't they? You think Uncle Ho's body is a hoax? What's the countryside like? Is it pretty like the Southern country? He flames another cigarette and orders us a round of beer. By our third round, he has chain-smoked into a second pack of Marlboros.

Late in the night, when I am sapped of tales from the road, Calvin, who is beer-fogged, leans back in his chair and asks, *"America is like a dream, isn't it?"*

After all I've seen, I agree. *"Sure."*

20   We contemplate the beer in our glasses. I ask him, *"Do you want to go there?"* I don't know why I ask him this. Maybe, believing that he is my equivalent in Vietnam, I want him to say that he really loves the country and that it is magical, wonderful in ways I have yet to imagine. More powerful, more potent than the West.

Calvin sounds annoyed. *"Of course. Who wouldn't?"* He pauses, taking long, pensive drags on his cigarette. *"But perhaps only to visit. To see, understand—no?"*

"Why?"

"Simple. Here . . . here, I am a king." He leans over the table, shaking the cigarette at me. *"In America you, I mean all you Viet-kieu, are guests. And guests don't have the same rights as hosts."* He sits back, legs crossed at the knees, and throws a proprietary arm over the city. *"At least, here, I am king. I belong. I am better than most Vietnamese."*

"No, we're not guests. We're citizens. Permanent. Ideally we are all equal. Equal rights," I insert lamely, the words, recalled from elementary school history lessons, sounding hollow.

25   *"Right, but do you FEEL like an American? Do you?"*

Yes! Yes! Yes, I do. I really do, I want to shout it in his face. Already the urge leaves a bad taste in my mouth. *"Sometimes, I do. Sometimes, I feel like I am a real American."*

I wish I could tell him. I don't mind forgetting who I am, but I know he wouldn't understand. I don't mind being looked at or treated just like another American, a white American. No, I don't mind at all. I want it. I like it. Yet every so often when I become really good at tricking myself, there is always that inevitable slap that shocks me out of my shell and prompts me to reassess everything.

How could I tell him my shame? How could I tell him about the drive-bys where some red-faced white would stick his head out of his truck, giving me the finger and screaming, "Go home, Chink!" Could I tell him it chilled me to wonder what would happen if my protagonist knew I was Vietnamese? What if his father had died in Vietnam? What if he was a Vietnam vet? Could I tell Calvin about the time my Vietnamese friends and I dined in a posh restaurant in Laguna Beach in Southern California? A white man at the next table, glaring at us, grumbled to his wife, "They took over Santa Ana. And now they're here. This whole state is going to hell." They was us Vietnamese. Santa Ana was now America's Little Saigon.

Could I tell Calvin I was initiated into the American heaven during my first week stateside by eight black kids who pulverized me in the restroom, calling me Viet Cong? No. I grew up fighting blacks, whites, and Chicanos. The whites beat up the blacks. The blacks beat up the Chicanos. And everybody beat up the Chinaman whether or not he was really an ethnic Chinese. These new Vietnamese kids were easy pickings, small, bookish, passive, and not fluent in English.

30   So, we congregate in Little Saigons, we hide out in Chinatowns and Japantowns, blending in. We huddle together, surrounding ourselves with the material wealth of America, and wave our star-spangled banners, shouting: "We're Americans. We love America."

I cannot bring myself to confront my antagonists. Cannot always claim my rights as a naturalized citizen. Cannot, for the same reason, resist the veterans' pleas for money outside grocery stores. Cannot armor myself against the pangs of guilt at every homeless man wearing army fatigues. Sown deep in me is a seed of discomfort. Maybe shame. I see that we Vietnamese Americans don't talk about our history. Although we often pretend to be modest and humble as we preen our successful immigrants stories, we rarely admit even to ourselves the circumstances and the cost of our being here. We elude it all like a petty theft committed ages ago. When convenient, we take it as restitution for what happened to Vietnam.

Calvin senses my discomfort. It is his talent, a marked skill of his trade. He looks away, reaching for yet another cigarette to cover the silence I opened. He asks me the question that Vietnamese throughout Vietnam have tried to broach obliquely: *"Do they look down on Vietnamese in America? Do they hate you?"*

I don't want to dwell on that. Vietnamese believe that white Americans are to Viet-kieu as Viet-kieu are to Vietnamese, each one a level above the next, respectively. And, somehow, this shames me, maybe because I cannot convince myself that it is entirely true or false. I divert the thrust and ask him, *"You are Westernized. You know how different foreigners are from Vietnamese. How do you feel showing them around the country?"*

"I like the work. Many of them are very nice. Curious about our culture. I like the Australians most. Rowdy and lots of trouble, but they respect Vietnamese."

35   *"But don't you see the reactions on their faces when they see our squalor? Don't you hear the things they say about us? Don't tell me you've never heard it."*

He looks uncomfortable, drawing deep from his nicotine stick, sighing the smoke to the stars. Then to his credit and my everlasting respect for him, he says quietly, facing the sky, *"I do. I can't help it but I do. I take them out on the Saigon streets, you know, the poor parts because they ask me. They want pictures. I see them flinch at the beggars, the poverty of Vietnamese. The chicken-shacks we live in."*

A wordless lull falls between us. We're both drunk. I am irritated at having to delve into a subject I avoid, and feeling mean-spirited I have goaded him onto equally disconcerting ground.

"It's very hard being a tour guide. Sometimes I feel like a pimp." He switches into his tour-guide English: "Here, look at this, sir. Yes, ma'am, these are the average Vietnamese. Yes, they are poor. Yes, sir. Here is our national monument. Very big. Very important to Vietnamese. You impressed? No, not so big?" He shrugs, saying, *"I know they've got bigger monuments in their countries. Older, more important. What do our little things mean to them?"*

The silence tells me we are moving too far into no-man's-land. One more cigarette. More beer. Tusking the smoke out of his nostrils, he seems to brace himself, gathering force like a wave, building before cresting white. As his beliefs come barreling out, I know the crushing impact of his words will stay with me, for in them I catch a glimpse of myself and of the true Cuong, the Cuong that came before and is deeper than the suave Calvin facing me. *"Vietnamese aren't ashamed of our own poverty. We're not ashamed of squatting in mud huts and sleeping on rags. There is no shame in being poor. We were born into it just as Westerners are born white. The Westerners are white as we are yellow. There is already a difference between us. Our poverty is minor in the chasm that already exists. A small detail. The real damning thing is the fact that there are Viet-kieu, our own brothers, skin of our skin, blood of our blood, who look better than us, more civilized, more educated, more wealthy, more genteel. Viet-kieu look kingly next to the average Vietnamese. Look at you, look at me. You're wearing old jeans and I'm wearing a suit, but it's obvious who . . . who is superior. Can't you see? We look like monkeys because you make us look like monkeys just by your existence."*

40 *"Is this truly how Vietnamese see us Viet-kieu?"*

"Some call you the lost brothers. Look at you. Living in America has lightened your skin, made you forget your language. You have tasted Western women and you're probably not as attracted to Vietnamese women anymore. You eat nutritious Western food and you are bigger and stronger than us. You know better than to smoke and drink like Vietnamese. You know exercise is good so you don't waste your time sitting in cafés and smoking your hard-earned money away. Someday, your blood will mix so well with Western blood that there will be no difference between you and them. You are already lost to us."

I listened with dismay as his observations fall on me like a sentence, but I can tell in the back of his mind he is saying: And I want to be more like you because that's where the future is. He must suspect I am doubting what he has told me the first time our paths crossed: *"Vietnamese are Vietnamese if they believe they are."*

Calvin and I bid each other good night, each going his own way. He has to resolve a fracas of intoxicated Australians in his charge back at the hotel. In our drunkenness, our conversation crossed forbidden boundaries and we were both depressed. Maybe it is just the beer wearing off. I pedal down to the beach for some sea air. As I coast along the ocean boulevard, a gorgeous girl, unusually tall for a Vietnamese, dressed in the traditional *ao dai* like a college student, tails me on her expensive motorbike, a Honda Dream, the Vietnamese Cadillac. Hello, she says in English. Hello, I smile. She thinks I'm Japanese or Korean. How are you, she asks me. Good, I say—always glad to talk to students eager to practice their English. And you, I say to keep the conversation going, how are you? You are very pretty, she tells me. No, I chuckle, standing now with her on the dark sidewalk, you are pretty. Very pretty. Pretty enough, I fancy silently to myself, for me to fall madly in love with. My heart dances ahead of me with improbable possibilities. Wild schemes streak through my head ratting out ways for me to stay in Nha Trang longer to make her acquaintance. Maybe get a job here. There are so many foreign companies, it should be easy. And on and on. Hopeful. I am smiling.

Then she says, "You go with me?"

45   "Yes, sure. Where? Anywhere! Let's go!"

"You go with me very cheap. You go. Me very cheap, very good. You go with me very cheap. Very, very cheap. I make you happy."

My smile feels waxy. I turn away, looking at the surf rolling on the white sand, the moon pearling us all. She parrots it over and over.

No, yes, maybe, later, I must meet a friend now, see you soon, bye, I blurt for the sake of blurting and I ride away from the tourist boardwalk with my money, my opportunities, my privileges, my life. I look back once and see her glossy cherry lips mouthing those words to me, a red wound in the neon night of Nha Trang.

Conversation Starter

Discuss a time when you were aware of being an outsider in a community.

Reading Matters

1. How did Calvin and Andrew meet? How do both of them feel about the Viet-Kieu? Why do they remain friends?
2. Why does Calvin value his job as a tour guide? Who do you think is happier with his life—Andrew or Calvin?
3. Why isn't Andrew honest with Calvin about how he is treated in the United States? What kind of job does Andrew have?
4. Why does Andrew see the pretty Vietnamese woman's "glossy cherry lips" like "a red wound in the neon night of Nha Trang"?

Writing Matters

1. Write an essay that explores one of the issues raised in the conversation between Andrew and Calvin.
2. Write an essay that discusses some of the problems that a particular immigrant group in your community has had adjusting to American culture.

3. Write an essay that explores the psychological impact of being an immigrant in the United States. Write from your own experiences and/or research the topic.

RELEVANT WEB SITES

VIETNAMESE-AMERICAN.ORG <http://www.vietnamese-american.org>

Vietnamese-American.org is a web site that empowers Vietnamese-Americans through voter registration and education.

FORGING NEW TRADITIONS
<http://www.svcn.com/archives/campbellreporter/12.22.99/pham-9951.html>

Contains Andrew Pham's article, "Forging New Traditions," about his first Christmas in the United States.

Pico Iyer (b. 1957)

The Olympic Games

Pico Iyer was born in England to Indian parents and immigrated to California when he was seven. Iyer returned to England as a young man to attend Eton and then Oxford, where he earned his master's degree in English. Later he completed a second master's degree at Harvard and taught in their English department for two years. Iyer worked for three years (1982–1985) as a staff writer at Time Magazine *before deciding to travel in Asia to develop his understanding of Eastern cultures and philosophy. He has continued to write for* Time *and has written fiction, but he is best known for his travelogues, especially the remarkable* Video Night in Kathmandu and Other Reports from the Not-So-Far East *(1988),* The Lady and the Monk: Four Seasons in Kyoto *(1991), and* Falling Off the Map *(1993). His most recent books include* Abandon *(2003),* Living Faith: Windows into the Sacred Life of India *(2004), and* Sun After Dark *(2004). In the selection that follows, "The Olympic Games," excerpted from* The Global Soul: Jet Lag, Shopping Malls, and the Search for Home *(2000), Iyer explores the emerging international culture and sense of global identity exemplified by the Olympic Games.*

Whenever I wish to get an update on the state of our One World order— how much it is coming together, how much it is falling apart—I try to take myself to an Olympic Games. The image of global harmony the Games consecrate is, of course, a little like a gossamer globe entangled in a crackly cellophane of bureaucracy and bickering, and all the world knows, more and more, how much our official caretakers of purity are tarnished by corruption, as much off the field as on; to attend an Olympiad these days is to sit amongst 100,000 security guards, with teams of Doping Control officers under the stands, while Olympians in the shadows collect illicit payoffs.

Yet for all these reminders of the world outside, the Games do provide as compact and protected a model of our dreams of unity as exists, with hopeful young champions from around the globe coming together in an Olympic Village that is a version of what our global village could be, to lay their talents on the altar of "friendly competition." At their best, the Olympics pay homage to the very sense of "world loyalty" that Whitehead called the essence of religion.

I've been to six Olympiads in the past fifteen years, and at five of them I've been responsible for every sport on offer, and so found myself racing from cycling to three-day event to badminton arenas every day from dawn till after midnight for sixteen days. Every city had its scandals, of course, and no one could soon forget the terrorists of Munich, the bankruptcy of Montreal, yet on every occasion I found myself stilled by the simple, piercing humanity of it all: the sight of Derek Redmond, the British hurdler, hobbling over the finish line with his arms around his father's shoulders, the older man having raced down from the stands as soon as he saw his son pull a hamstring; Iranians trading pins with Iraqis in the sanctified neutral zone of the Olympic Village Plaza; the people of Barcelona streaming out into their spotlit streets, for night after balmy night in 1992, so delighted were they to have their Catalan culture discovered by the world.

The Olympics pose a curious kind of conundrum for people such as me, of course, if only because they affirm affiliation to nation-states in an age that has largely left them behind, mass-producing images of nationalism and universalism without much troubling to distinguish between them. They ask us to applaud the patriotism of others while transcending the patriotism in ourselves, and they draw our attention to the very boundaries that are increasingly beside the point (I, surrounded by cheering fans waving flags, am often reminded how difficult it is for the rootless to root for anyone, and, reluctant to ally myself with a Britain, an India, or an America that I don't think of as home, generally end up cheering the majestically talented Cubans or the perennial good sportsmen from Japan).

5   Still, there's something almost primal—tribal, you could say—about the nationalistic sentiments the Games release, and, in spite of the fifty-foot Gumbies on the skyline, they touch a spark of sweetness that leaps inside us like a flame: forty thousand Japanese stand in thickly falling snow to cheer their ski jumpers to victory, and even Norwegians (or hardened journalists) who've come all the way around the world to pursue their own agendas can't help but smile and say, "Congratulations!" The Games begin with the forces of 197 nations marching out behind flags, strictly segregated and almost military in their color-coordinated uniforms; they conclude, just two weeks later, with all the competitors spilling out onto a central lawn, till you can't tell one team from another. The colors run.

Backstage, away from the scripted tableaux of the cameras, the Games unveil a more human and vulnerable side to international relations, which helps to correct, and sometimes to redeem, the grander shows of global unity. I remember once in Barcelona escaping the ranks of seven hundred TV cameras and the hundreds of thousands forever climbing up Montjuich, past Bob Costas's floodlit throne, to try to catch my breath in the relative calm of the strictly guarded Olympic Village, a utopian global campus complete with its own religious centers, hair salons, nightclubs, movie theaters, daily newspaper, and even mayor. Walking around the stylish new complex, built beside two private beaches, I found myself suddenly surrounded by three very small, very polite, slightly lost-seeming figures. They were archers, from Bhutan, as it transpired, who couldn't quite orient themselves amidst this crush of alienness.

They'd never seen a stadium before, one of the teenagers explained, and they'd never seen a subway. They'd never seen a high-rise building or a working television set, and they'd never seen a boat. I remembered how, in their landlocked home, I'd watched students practice archery between the willow trees behind the Druk Hotel, their arrows whistling through the silent air.

None of them had ever boarded a plane before, one of them went on (in careful English—the Raj having penetrated even those places that television could not reach), and none of them had ever competed before crowds (besides, Olympic rules are so different from Bhutanese that they were all but guaranteed of last place). "I thought Barcelona was going to be peaceful, like Thimbu," one of the young students said. "It's so busy!" The Olympic Village alone was almost the size of their capital.

At that point, the country's first (and only) defense minister interceded to give a more official account of his nation's meeting with the world (he doubled as the Dragon Kingdom's Olympic Committee), and to make the right diplomatic noises; yet what stays with me, many years later, is the image of those guileless, bewildered, excited souls, one day in a hidden kingdom where everyone has to wear medieval clothes and all the buildings are constructed in fourteenth-century style, and the next, in the midst of the greatest planetary show on earth. And then, after two weeks surrounded by exploding flashbulbs, to be back in their forgotten home, where the only concrete mementos they'd have of the surreal episode would be their photographs. Whenever she had a free moment, one of the archers told me, she hurried off to take pictures of the harbor. She'd never seen an ocean before.

10   The figures who oversee our official dreams of harmony—the 115 members of the International Olympic Committee—are often described as presiding over one of the last great empires on earth. Their doyen is the Grand Duke of Luxembourg, and the chief of drug enforcement for all its thirty-one years has been a Belgian prince. It was a count, famously, who assured the world that it was fine to hold the Olympics in Hitler's Berlin (provided a few embarrassing signs were covered up), and the current, increasingly embattled president, Juan Antonio Samaranch (once the sponsor of a Barcelona roller-hockey team), likes to be addressed as "Your Excellency."

Boutros Boutros-Ghali, while head of the United Nations, cited "Olympism" as a "school of democracy"; in fact, its self-elected rulers, officially appointed for life, administer a realm in which their word is final, and senior citizens trump athletes at every turn.

The Olympic Movement is a force that no one should underestimate. It has its own museum, near its headquarters in Lausanne, and it brings out its own glossy magazine; it boasts an honorary degree from the Sorbonne, and recently instituted a prize for Sports Science that, worth $500,000, is the most lucrative such award in the world, other than the Nobel Prize. At Cultural Olympiads, Nobel laureates in literature discuss the future of the soul and at International Youth Camps, children absorb the principles enunciated in a seventy-four page Olympic Charter. The organization even, like every self-respecting government, now has its own front-page scandal, with six different investigations uncovering improprieties.

In recent years, this unofficial empire has expanded dramatically in part through alliances with the two great powers of our global order, multinationals and the media. Thus, eleven of the world's largest companies pay roughly $40 million each for the exclusive right to attach themselves to the Olympic Rings, the Mascot, and the Torch, and U.S. television networks alone sign contracts worth $3.55 billion. The Olympic Rings, its organizers boast, are "the most recognized symbol in the world," and 90 percent of all the people in the world with access to a television—3.5 billion at last count—watch such events as the Opening Ceremonies.

It's tempting to conclude, in fact, that the Olympic Movement is, in its way, more powerful than the UN, especially as it gets to show off its triumphs on the global screen (while the UN has to try to sort out real-world messes behind the scenes, with everyone criticizing it in what has become an ethical Babel). To this day, the IOC has more member states than the United Nations (whose founding it predates by forty-nine years), and all are pledged to an ideal Oversoul that rhymes with our highest, sweetest dreams.

15   Like anyone who attends the Games, I could never help squirming a bit at all the contradictions involved in the marketing of idealism, and a mischievous part of me rejoiced in the Jacobean notion of would-be Olympians trying to bribe the Princess Royal with a fur coat; when Samaranch reminded the world of the Olympic Truce in 1998 (an "ancient concept for the new millennium," as canny Olympic strategists dubbed it), he was conspicuously clad in a Mizuno coat, in a stadium equally conspicuously naked—by Olympic decree—of advertising. The IOC keeps dozens of lawyers on hand to protect the very terms *sacred torch* and *peace festival*; even the slogan "The World Is Welcome Here" is jealously copyrighted Olympic property. When Japanese fans were once seen to wave a banner saying SEIKO, in support of their speed-skating star Seiko Hashimoto, they were told to desist, lest their cheers be interpreted as support for the watch manufacturer that is now an Olympic Gold Sponsor.

Yet always the hope persists that men will be wiser than their institutions, and, in a world where cultures are clashing by the hour, nobody objects to seeing the competition among nations turned into a game; when I was young, I remember largely scoffing at the self-serving claims of Olympic chieftains like Avery Brundage: "The Olympics is perhaps the greatest social force in the world today." Yet these days, even such uninvolved observers as the director of the Institute of American Studies in Beijing, while naming the dominant powers of our "multipole globe," cites not just the classic nation-states but also "such actors as the World Bank, CNN, International Olympic Committee and Exxon."

My own role in all of this, as a longtime member of the "Olympic Family," observes its own rituals, as pronounced as those of any church, and every time I prepare to attend an Olympic Games, I feel as if I'm entering a foreign country (albeit a migrant one founded on the principles of transnationalism).

Well over eighteen months before the Games begin, I apply for what is in effect a visa—a coded credential—and upon arrival in the host city, I am generally greeted by one of the fifty thousand smiling volunteers, who will take me to an Official Accreditation Center. There I am "processed" into a bar-coded entity whose ID will get me through the magnetometers that guard every venue, hotel, and subimage center. To thank me for my troubles, I am given a McDonald's pad, a Media Monster pin from Xerox, a Coca-Cola backpack, and a penguin wearing the IBM logo, so I can serve, in effect, as a walking advertisement for the Worldwide Olympic Partners (whose dream, their ad explains, is of "Creating a World with Principles").

There are often four times more journalists than athletes at the modern Games—fifteen thousand of us in all—and we are stationed in the Main Press Center (or MPC) and its high-tech cousin, the International Broadcasting Center (or IBC). These multistory buildings, constructed more and more according to an international plan, look like monitor-filled airline terminals from which not beings, but words and images, will be beamed around the world. Icons and logos and universally understood pictograms fill their long corridors, and vending machines serve up free drinks (so long as they're made by Coke), Global ATMs belch out banknotes (so long as they're accessed by a Visa card). The MPC has a post office and a travel agency and private offices for seventy different organizations, nearly all of which buzz with local middlemen—or, more often, middlewomen—mediating between the host nation and thousands of foreign bodies (while six thousand "language agents" stand ready to turn Finnish into Korean).

20   For those without a large company at their back, there's a vast Common Work Room lined with rows of telephones and fax machines on which more than six hundred correspondents can send their copy back to Guinea-Bissau or Costa Rica. Around them, giant Panasonic screens broadcast all the action as it happens in twenty-six different venues.

The Olympics today are largely a made-for-TV production, based around the needs of crews from 160 different countries (to the point where South Korea, for example, in 1988, actually instituted daylight saving time just for the duration of the games, so that its high-profile events, already scheduled for the morning, would chime even better with U.S. prime time). More even than the Academy Awards or a Miss Universe contest, the Games are a television producer's dream: every day for sixteen days, they can be relied upon to produce shocks, stirring heroism, and images that shake us to the core (and even villainy touches something universal—the showdown between Tonya Harding and the figure-skating rival she'd attacked, Nancy Kerrigan, was one of the most-watched programs in U.S. television history). And so, as the largest Image Center in the world processes photographs for free (so long as they're Kodak), TV networks spend $7,500 for every dollar they spent in 1960.

And I, for three weeks every two years, move through a parallel universe that looks like a sleeker, on-screen version of our global future. Every day I travel from the MPC to the MTM (Media Transport Mall), by way, often, of IOC offices, on a special network of MTM shuttle buses. There are TVs on all thirty buses, broadcasting the events we're going to; there are TVs in the twenty-four-hour McDonald's outlets in the MPC; there are TVs next to every press seat at the larger venues, with closed-circuit programming of all the other events (Channel 101 plays a "scenic video" of the Olympic Torch burning for eighteen hours every day). Even in the small dormlike rooms in the Media Village (or, as it was nicely called in Nagano, the "Medea" Village), there are TVs in every room so that we can follow the action on BBC or CNN or the special Olympic network. We watch ourselves watching ourselves, with "videos-on-demand."

Perhaps the central event in my own Olympic preparation is a visit or two to the Olympic city a few months before the Games begin (and a few months before the local government tells its citizens to smile at foreigners, its taxi drivers to say "Have a nice day!" and its restaurateurs to stop serving dog: in 1998, in Nagano, even the local professional gangsters observed an official Olympic truce). The cities that compete for the honor of staging the universal road show are, nearly always, somewhat anxious and prideful and prickly places, with something they want to prove to the world. The Olympics provide an almost unique opportunity to address the whole of humanity at once, and to make over one's image at a single stroke: thus, Barcelona, in 1992, was determined to show the world that it belongs not to Spain but to Catalonia (maps appeared on its streets in which Spain did not even appear, and King Juan Carlos himself, while opening the Games, was obliged to speak in Catalan); Seoul, in 1988, aspired to muscle its way into the Executive Club of nations much as its hated rival—and unacknowledged role model—Tokyo had done in 1964; and Atlanta, in 1996, was keen to present itself as the "Next Great International City" (and one day after it won the bid, its paper ran the simple headline WORLD-CLASS!).

Yet what this means, in practice, is that small cities, which are often relatively provincial cities, become the focus for our grandest global expectations, and all our hopes of crossing boundaries converge on a place that is not always accustomed to looking past its own borders. As the cost of staging an Olympics mounts (to $7 billion or more), many of the people they're meant to help rise up against the costly gambles—even placid Stockholm was hit by a series of bombs recently, aimed at disrupting its Olympic bid (while in rival Rome, citizens brought out bilingual pamphlets entitled *Ten*

Good Reasons to Say No to the 2004 Games in Rome). What it also means is that one of the fiercest competitions on display at every Games involves the representatives of second cities handing out favors in an attempt to prove themselves worthy of being a future Olympic host: Bishop Tutu appears to promote the cause of Cape Town, and Istanbul stages a Turkish Blues Night (complete with THE MEETING OF CONTINENTS tote bags), while Athens and Osaka spend $20 million or more on freebies and $1 million lunches and law-abiding Toronto complains about the necessity of bribing.

25   In its desperate attempt to prove itself a major global player (by winning the rights to the 2000 Games), Beijing closed down factories in anticipation of IOC visitations and released some of its famous dissidents (while placing other potential troublemakers in a lunatic asylum). According to the *New York Times* correspondents who won a Pulitzer Prize for their coverage of China, at least one mentally retarded man was beaten to death, lest his untelegenic presence distract visiting Olympians from the banners saying A MORE OPEN CHINA WELCOMES THE 2000 OLYMPICS.

CONVERSATION STARTERS

Discuss your memories of the Olympic Games. How have your attitudes of the games changed over the years?

READING MATTERS

1. Why does Iyer believe that the Olympic Movement is more powerful than the United Nations? Explain why you agree or disagree with him.
2. How many journalists attend the Olympic Games? What role do journalists play in shaping the audience's perception of the games? What role do the media play?
3. Iyer writes, "The Olympics today are largely a made-for-TV production." What evidence does he include to support his assertion? Explain why you agree or disagree with Iyer's point of view.
4. Does Iyer believe that the Olympic Games foster a global community? Explain why you agree or disagree with him.

WRITING MATTERS

1. In what ways do the Olympics reflect the state of "our One World Order"? Write an essay that supports your perspective. Refer to Iyer's essay when relevant.
2. How do you think corporate sponsorship and media coverage have changed the Olympics? Research the history of the Olympics at your college library or on the Internet. Interview friends and family members about their memories, observations, and attitudes about the Olympics. Present your findings and conclusions in an essay.
3. Write a letter to the organizers of the next Olympic Games. Include your observations as a viewer and provide suggestions for improving the upcoming games.

Julia Corbett

Robotic Iguanas

Julia Corbett is associate professor of environmental communication at the University of Utah. She is a former reporter and park ranger. This article originally appeared in Orion, *187 Main Street, Great Barrington, MA 01230. www.oriononline.org.*

On a ledge in a cliff face, a small brown iguana raises his head and says to the chartreuse iguana perched above him, "So, you wanna piece of me or what?" Soon the iguanas, joined by some toucans and macaws, burst into song: "Right here in the jungle mon, that's the life for me." Lights strobe, the toucans flap their wings, and the iguanas bob their robotic heads. On cue, waiters and waitresses join in the singing, waving strips of brightly colored fabric. A toucan shouts, "Hasta la vista baby!" as our waiter leans over and asks, "Who had the shrimp?"

Coming here was my idea. I had returned to Salt Lake City from a summer of outdoor experiences while millions of my fellow humans tuned into "Survivor" and hundreds stood in line at the new Mayan theme restaurant in the suburbs. A combination of stifling late August temperatures, unhealthy levels of smoggy ozone, and thick smoke from dozens of wildfires raging in the West left me feeling lethargic and listless. I called a colleague. "Chris," I said, "as people who teach environmental communication, we really ought to check out this restaurant with the Mayan jungle theme." To my surprise, she didn't hesitate.

Our table is on the third level of the restaurant next to a railing with a good view down to the "stage," a cliff face about two stories high adorned with tropical plants made of plastic. A gentle waterfall pours from the cliff into a large aqua pool. The rocks are molded concrete and the pool reeks of chlorine. Under clear resin, our tabletop bears a colorful design of the

Mayan alphabet and calendar. Down one level to the right is an area with carpeted steps and a large video screen playing cartoons—a sideshow for children not sufficiently captivated by robotic iguanas. High above in the middle of the cliff wall is an office window, light seeping from behind closed blinds.

The house lights—already dim—grow dimmer. On the lower cliff face, steam starts pouring from holes in the rock and two red eyes begin to glow, eventually illuminating a large fiery face in the stone. A deep voice booms, "I am Copac, behold the power. . . . " The message is foreboding and a bit evil, something about heat from the center of the Earth. To break the tension, one of the toucans announces that it is about to get a lot hotter. The waiters and waitresses agree, chiming in with a chorus of, "Feeling hot, hot, hot!"

5   Chris and I laugh; we are seated under an air conditioning vent. By way of contrast, I tell Chris about a Guatemalan jungle I visited, and how even at 3 a.m. lying perfectly still, sweat would trickle from my face into my ears and hair. As the "hot, hot, hot!" number winds down a macaw asks for a cold towel. "I feel Mayan and I'm not even tryin'," it squawks, instructing diners to order another drink.

The owner of the Mayan—a quirky Mormon guy with his own little Intermountain empire of car dealerships, an NBA team, mega movie-theater complexes, and the new theme restaurant—said in a newspaper interview that he took great pains to give his patrons an authentic experience. He sent his architects to Mexico and Central America to ensure that the restaurant could recreate the experience of visiting an ancient Mayan community. They returned with proposals for plastic banyan trees, thatched huts covering computerized cash registers, and chlorinated waterfalls. According to a recent lawsuit, what Salt Lake's Mayan restaurant allegedly recreated was not an ancient Mayan community but a nearly identical Mayan theme restaurant in Denver.

The lights dim again. A disembodied female voice speaks soothingly about standing on sacred ground, hidden in the jungle. Two young men in loin cloths and tall, feathered headdresses emerge on an upper cliff ledge and bang on tall drums, the slap of their hands occasionally out of step with the drumbeat of the amplified soundtrack. An image of a young woman appears on the rock wall, a water goddess of sorts with bright red lipstick. Her name is Tecal. "The spirit of the jaguar calls and I awaken," she says, urging us to return to a lost paradise, to the Earth, to celebrate, rejuvenate, and rebirth. As her speech crescendoes, lightning flashes, thunder booms, and the once-placid waterfall gushes noisily into the pool, spraying the plastic ferns but not the diners beyond. People stop their conversations and turn toward the water.

Chris and I compare notes on our food (her taco salad with iceberg lettuce is unexceptional and my shrimp are tough) and discuss the "flood." She recalls how, in 1983, abundant mountain snowfall and an abrupt spring melt sent City Creek roaring through downtown, past department stores and pawn shops, a muddy torrent of debris and fish slapping against a channel of sandbags. Like many such floods, it was caused by a combination of weather events and failed human attempts to control and divert runoff. Both that flood and the Mayan one, I point out, demonstrate a similar human desire for (and belief in) control of natural elements that by their very nature are largely uncontrollable and highly unpredictable.

The warriors return, wearing only Speedos and asymmetrical facepaint. The crowd has been anticipating this, the most talked-about part of the show. From the highest point on the cliff, the young men alternate fancy dives into the pool, swim around the side of the cliff, and disappear to reappear at the top for another dive.

10   Shortly after the restaurant opened for business, the Salt Lake Tribune did a profile on a diver, who like all the divers was a member of a high school swim team in the valley. The diver they interviewed had emigrated from Guatemala when he was eight, and it was suggested that perhaps he had some Mayan blood in him. The story also mentioned that some restaurant patrons have asked whether the cliff divers are fake like the cliff they jump from and the lagoon they land in.

When I was a naturalist in Olympic National Park, I was frequently asked whether the deer wandering through the parking lot snarfing up Cheetos and sandwich crusts were real. Tourists also asked me what time it would rain in the coastal rainforest, as if there were a button we pressed, or as though, like Old Faithful, we could predict the rain. (Their interest was not so much in the natural patterns of a rainforest but in not getting wet.) Although the gulf between the real and artificial is vast, we have accomplished the illusion of no gulf at all, like silk flowers you must touch to determine whether chlorophyll lies within. We remake and remodel the natural world and its elements into more predictable and controllable versions, our own little theme-park paradise where flowers never fade on the vine and bubbling brooks never run dry.

There is more than humor or sadness in this degree of disconnect; there is danger. We grow increasingly ignorant of the natural original and risk not valuing it—or valuing its replacement more. When Salt Lake's foothills are abloom in early spring with allium, balsamroot, vetch, and sego lilies, most residents are aware only of imported tulips and daffodils. Numerous western cities have gone so far as to codify the imports, making green grass and thirsty flowers not just a cultural imperative but a legal one.

"You wannanother margarita?" asks our waiter.

"Is that what the Mayans drank?" I ask in reply.

15   The skinny young man with spiky platinum hair stares blankly.

"No thank you," I say.

He leaves a small, black notebook on the table and says he'll take it when we are ready.

While paying up, I wonder if my fellow diners believe they are experiencing nature or just some wholesome family entertainment that comes with a mediocre meal. Can someone who knows only censored and stylized depictions of the natural world—Disneyland, PBS, The Nature Company—ever love and understand the wonderfully complex original? Can we care deeply about the jungle or the foothills or an untamed mountain creek if we've never truly known them? The love and compassion I have for the West is rooted in decades of discovery, from brushing against a thousand sagebrush to know its potent perfume and reading the summer sky for signs of late afternoon storms. Such experiences remind me that my control is minuscule, my volition matters little, and the capacity for wonder and entertainment is infinite.

Chris and I contemplate what the Mayan has to teach us. Jungles are colorful, comfortable, and sublime. Ancient gods and goddesses—some benevolent, some not—control the weather. Nature is predictable and friendly. Animals (with human voices) are merely there to amuse us. And you can buy pieces of the jungle in the gift shop to take home. In the end, the Mayan is not so much about nature as it is about a culture that prefers plastic picket fences over wood ones, robotic animals over wild ones, reality TV over real life.

20   The lights on stage grow bright and the birds start jabbering again. One introduces herself as Margarita Macaw; another, Pierre, wears a beret and says he is from Paris. Iguanas Marvin and Harry ask the macaws if they've seen their sunglasses. A bird informs us that "it's always perfect weather" in the jungle. We leave a tip on the table; the entire show is beginning again.

Conversation Starters

Discuss the experience of being at a theme park or a theme restaurant.

Reading Matters

1. What is the author's reaction to the Mayan theme restaurant? What informs her perspective? Why does she go to the theme restaurant?
2. The author cautions that there is danger in "remaking or remodeling the natural world." What does she mean? Do you agree?
3. What does the author learn about culture by dining at the Mayan theme restaurant? How does this impact her perspective about the environment?
4. Why does the author conclude the essay by writing, "the entire show is beginning again"? What significance does this comment have on her message? Is it consistent with her tone throughout the essay?

Writing Matters

1. Learn about the Mayan culture by doing research online or at the library. What aspects of Mayan culture were missing from the representation at the theme restaurant? Write an essay about what you learned.
2. The author poses the question, "Can someone who knows only censored and stylized depictions of the natural world—Disneyland, PBS, The Nature Company—ever love and understand the wonderfully complex original?" Write an essay responding to this question.

3. Write a proposal for a new theme restaurant. The restaurant design should draw on symbols and rituals from your experience. What do you think a restaurant patron would learn about you from eating at your restaurant?

RELEVANT WEB SITES

THE MAYAN THEME RESTAURANT
<http://saltlakecity.about.com/cs/diningbytype/gr/mayan.htm>

Learn more about the Mayan Theme Restaurant by reading a restaurant review that includes a direct link to the restaurant's web site.

NATIONAL PARK SERVICE <http://www.nps.gov/>

The official web site of the National Park Service provides information about the history of the national park service, resources for planning a visit, and educational opportunities available through the park system.

New Cultural Rituals

Robert D. King (b. 1936)

Should English Be the Law?

Robert D. King received an M.S. in mathematics from Georgia Tech and a Ph.D. in German linguistics from the University of Wisconsin in 1965. King is a professor at the University of Texas at Austin, where he has taught since 1965 and served as Chair of the Linguistics Department. He has published numerous scholarly articles in linguistics and a book, Nehru and the Language Politics of India *(1996). Currently he is working on a book about language conflicts in America entitled* Leave Language Alone, Dammit! *In the following essay, written for the* Atlantic Monthly *in 1997, King discusses the "English Only" movement and takes a historical and international perspective on the failure of efforts to establish a single national language or to ban minority languages and dialects.*

We have known race riots, draft riots, labor violence, secession, anti-war protests, and a whiskey rebellion, but one kind of trouble we've never had: a language riot. Language riot? It sounds like a joke. The very idea of language as a political force—as something that might threaten to split a country wide apart—is alien to our way of thinking and to our cultural traditions.

This may be changing. On August 1 of last year [1996] the U.S. House of Representatives approved a bill that would make English the official language of the United States. The vote was 259 to 169, with 223 Republicans and thirty-six Democrats voting in favor and eight Republicans, 160 Democrats, and one independent voting against. The debate was intense, acrid, and partisan. On March 25 of last year the Supreme Court agreed to review a case involving an Arizona law that would require public employees to conduct government business only in English. Arizona is one of several states that have passed "Official English" or "English Only" laws. The appeal to the Supreme Court followed a 6-to-5 ruling, in October of 1995, by a federal appeals court striking down the Arizona law. These events suggest how divisive a public issue language could become in America—even if it has until now scarcely been taken seriously.

Traditionally, the American way has been to make English the national language—but to do so quietly, locally, without fuss. The Constitution is silent on language: the Founding Fathers had no need to legislate that English be the official language of the country. It has always been taken for granted that English *is* the national language, and that one must learn English in order to make it in America. . . .

. . . That tradition began to change in the wake of the anything-goes attitudes and the celebration of cultural differences arising in the 1960s. A 1975 amendment to the Voting Rights Act of 1965 mandated the "bilingual ballot" under certain circumstances, notably when the voters of selected language groups reached five percent or more in a voting district. Bilingual education became a byword of educational thinking during the 1960s. By the 1970s linguists had demonstrated convincingly—at least to other academics—that black English (today called African-American vernacular English or Ebonics) was not "bad" English but a different kind of authentic English with its own rules. Predictably, there have been scattered demands that black English be included in bilingual-education programs.

5   It was against this background that the movement to make English the official language of the country arose. In 1981 Senator S. I. Hayakawa, long a leading critic of bilingual education and bilingual ballots, introduced in the U.S. Senate a constitutional amendment that not only would have made English the official language but would have prohibited federal and state laws and regulations requiring the use of other languages. His English Language Amendment died in the Ninety-seventh Congress. . . .

. . . Many issues intersect in the controversy over Official English: immigration (above all), the rights of minorities (Spanish-speaking minorities in particular), the pros and cons of bilingual education, tolerance, how best to educate the children of immigrants, and the place of cultural diversity in school curricula and in American society in general. The question that lies at the root of most of the uneasiness is this: Is America threatened by the preservation of languages other than English? Will America, if it continues on its traditional path of benign linguistic neglect, go the way of Belgium, Canada, and Sri Lanka—three countries among many whose unity is gravely imperiled by language and ethnic conflicts?

LANGUAGE AND NATIONALITY

. . . The marriage of language and nationalism goes back at least to Romanticism and specifically to Rousseau, who argued in his *Essay on the Origin of Languages* that language must develop before politics is possible and that language originally distinguished nations from one another. A little-remembered aim of the French Revolution—itself the legacy of Rousseau—was to impose a national language on France, where regional languages such as Provençal, Breton, and Basque were still strong competitors against standard French, the French of the Ile de France. As late as 1789, when the Revolution began, half the population of the south of France, which spoke Provençal, did not understand French. A century earlier the playwright Racine said that he had had to resort to Spanish and Italian to make himself understood in the southern French town of Uzès. After the Revolution nationhood itself became aligned with language. . . .

In much of the world, ethnic unity and cultural identification are routinely defined by language. To be Arab is to speak Arabic. Bengali identity is based on language in spite of the division of Bengali-speakers between Hindu India and Muslim Bangladesh. When eastern Pakistan seceded from greater Pakistan in 1971, it named itself Bangladesh: *desa* means "country"; *bangla* means not the Bengali people or the Bengali territory but the Bengali language.

Scratch most nationalist movements and you find a linguistic grievance. The demands for independence of the Baltic states (Latvia, Lithuania, and Estonia) were intimately bound up with fears for the loss of their respective languages and cultures in a sea of Russianness. In Belgium the war between French and Flemish threatens an already weakly fused country. The present atmosphere of Belgium is dark and anxious, costive; the metaphor of divorce is a staple of private and public discourse. The lines of terrorism in Sri Lanka are drawn between Tamil Hindus and Sinhalese Buddhists—and also between the Tamil and Sinhalese languages. Worship of the French language fortifies the movement for an independent Quebec. Whether a united Canada will survive into the twenty-first century is a question too close to call. Much of the anxiety about language in the United States is probably fueled by the "Quebec problem": unlike Belgium, which is a small European country, or Sri Lanka, which is halfway around the world, Canada is our close neighbor.

10   Language is a convenient surrogate for nonlinguistic claims that are often awkward to articulate, for they amount to a demand for more political and economic power. Militant Sikhs in India call for a state of their own: Khalistan ("Land of the Pure" in Punjabi). They frequently couch this as a demand for a linguistic state, which has a certain simplicity about it, a clarity of motive—justice, even, because states in India are normally linguistic states. But the Sikh demands blend religion, economics, language, and retribution for sins both punished and unpunished in a country where old sins cast long shadows.

Language is an explosive issue in the countries of the former Soviet Union. The language conflict in Estonia has been especially bitter. Ethnic Russians make up almost a third of Estonia's population, and most of them do not speak or read Estonian, although Russians have lived in Estonia for more than a generation. Estonia has passed legislation requiring knowledge of the Estonian language as a condition of citizenship. Nationalist groups in independent Lithuania sought restrictions on the use of Polish—again, old sins, long shadows. . . .

. . . Slovakia, relieved now of the need to accommodate to Czech cosmopolitan sensibilities, has passed a law making Slovak its official language. (Czech is to Slovak pretty much as Croatian is to Serbian.) Doctors in state hospitals must speak to patients in Slovak, even if another language would aid diagnosis and treatment. Some 600,000 Slovaks—more than 10 percent of the population—are ethnically Hungarian. Even staff meetings in Hungarian-language schools must be in Slovak. (The government dropped a stipulation that church weddings be conducted in Slovak after heavy opposition from the Roman Catholic Church.) Language inspectors are told to weed out "all sins perpetrated on the regular Slovak language." Tensions between Slovaks and Hungarians, who had been getting along, have begun to arise.

The twentieth century is ending as it began—with trouble in the Balkans and with nationalist tensions flaring up in other parts of the globe. (Toward the end of his life Bismarck predicted that "some damn fool thing in the Balkans" would ignite the next war.) Language isn't always part of the problem. But it usually is.

UNIQUE OTHERNESS

Is there no hope for language tolerance? Some countries manage to maintain their unity in the face of multilingualism. Examples are Finland, with a Swedish minority, and a number of African and Southeast Asian countries. Two others could not be more unlike as countries go: Switzerland and India.

15 German, French, Italian, and Romansh are the languages of Switzerland. The first three can be and are used for official purposes; all four are designated "national" languages. Switzerland is politically almost hyperstable. It has language problems (Romansh is losing ground), but they are not major, and they are never allowed to threaten national unity.

Contrary to public perception, India gets along pretty well with a host of different languages. The Indian constitution officially recognizes nineteen languages, English among them. Hindi is specified in the constitution as the national language of India, but that is a pious postcolonial fiction: outside the Hindi-speaking northern heartland of India, people don't want to learn it. English functions more nearly than Hindi as India's lingua franca.

From 1947, when India obtained its independence from the British, until the 1960s blood ran in the streets and people died because of language. Hindi absolutists wanted to force Hindi on the entire country, which would have split India between north and south and opened up other fracture lines as well. For as long as possible Jawaharlal Nehru, independent India's first Prime Minister, resisted nationalist demands to redraw the capricious state boundaries of British India according to language. By the time he capitulated, the country had gained a precious decade to prove its viability as a union.

Why is it that India preserves its unity with not just two languages to contend with, as Belgium, Canada, and Sri Lanka have, but nineteen? The answer is that India, like Switzerland, has a strong national identity. The two countries share something big and almost mystical that holds each together in a union transcending language. That something I call "unique otherness."

The Swiss have what the political scientist Karl Deutsch called "learned habits, preferences, symbols, memories, and patterns of landholding": customs, cultural traditions, and political institutions that bind them closer to one another than to people of France, Germany, or Italy living just across the border and speaking the same language. There is Switzerland's traditional neutrality, its system of universal military training (the "citizen army"), its consensual allegiance to a strong Swiss franc—and fondue, yodeling, skiing, and mountains. Set against all this, the fact that Switzerland has four languages doesn't even approach the threshold of becoming a threat.

20   As for India, what Vincent Smith, in the *Oxford History of India*, calls its "deep underlying fundamental unity" resides in institutions and beliefs such as caste, cow worship, sacred places, and much more. Consider *dharma, karma,* and *maya,* the three root convictions of Hinduism; India's historical epics; Gandhi; *ahimsa* (nonviolence); vegetarianism; a distinctive cuisine and way of eating; marriage customs; a shared past; and what the Indologist Ainslie Embree calls "Brahmanical ideology." In other words, "We are Indian; we are different." . . .

        . . . We like to believe that to pass a law is to change behavior; but passing laws about language, in a free society, almost never changes attitudes or behavior. Gaelic (Irish) is living out a slow, inexorable decline in Ireland despite enormous government support of every possible kind since Ireland gained its independence from Britain. The Welsh language, in contrast, is alive today in Wales in spite of heavy discrimination during its history. Three out of four people in the northern and western counties of Gwynedd and Dyfed speak Welsh.

        I said earlier that language is a convenient surrogate for other national problems. Official English obviously has a lot to do with concern about immigration, perhaps especially Hispanic immigration. America may be threatened by immigration; I don't know. But America is not threatened by language.

        The usual arguments made by academics against Official English are commonsensical. Who needs a law when, according to the 1990 census, 94 percent of American residents speak English anyway? (Mauro E. Mujica, the chairman of U.S. English, cites a higher figure: 97 percent.) Not many of today's immigrants will see their first language survive into the second generation. This is in fact the common lament of first-generation immigrants: their children are not learning their language and are losing the culture of their parents. Spanish is hardly a threat to English, in spite of isolated (and easily visible) cases such as Miami, New York City, and pockets of the Southwest and southern California. The everyday language of south Texas is Spanish, and yet south Texas is not about to secede from America.

        But empirical, calm arguments don't engage the real issue: language is a symbol, an icon. Nobody who favors a constitutional ban against flag burning will ever be persuaded by the argument that the flag is, after all, just a "piece of cloth." A draft card in the 1960s was never merely a piece of paper. Neither is a marriage license.

25   Language, as one linguist has said, is "not primarily a means of communication but a means of communion." Romanticism exalted language, made it mystical, sublime—a bond of national identity. At the same time,

Romanticism created a monster: it made of language a means for destroying a country.

America has that unique otherness of which I spoke. In spite of all our racial divisions and economic unfairness, we have the frontier tradition, respect for the individual, and opportunity; we have our love affair with the automobile; we have in our history a civil war that freed the slaves and was fought with valor; and we have sports, hot dogs, hamburgers, and milk shakes—things big and small, noble and petty, important and trifling. "We are Americans; we are different."

If I'm wrong, then the great American experiment will fail—not because of language but because it no longer means anything to be an American; because we have forfeited that "willingness of the heart" that F. Scott Fitzgerald wrote was America; because we are no longer joined by Lincoln's "mystic chords of memory."

We are not even close to the danger point. I suggest that we relax and luxuriate in our linguistic richness and our traditional tolerance of language differences. Language does not threaten American unity. Benign neglect is a good policy for any country when it comes to language, and it's a good policy for America.

CONVERSATION STARTERS

Do you believe that language is a bond of national identity? How do you feel about making English the official language in the United States?

READING MATTERS

1. Why does King believe that the debate over official English is rooted in issues around ethnicity and tolerance in America?
2. How did the celebration of cultural traditions in the 1960s influence the use of language in America and ultimately lead to the movement to make English the official language?
3. King presents several arguments made against an official English policy. What are these arguments, and why does he believe that they "don't engage the real issue" of language?
4. How does the American "Frontier Tradition" impact the debate over an official language in the United States? Why does King believe that America's "unique otherness" ensures our survival as a nation, despite language diversity? Do you agree?

WRITING MATTERS

1. King asserts that passing laws about language almost never changes attitudes or behavior. Write an essay supporting or challenging this perspective.
2. "In much of the world, ethnic unity and cultural identification are routinely defined by language." Select an area of the world to research and test the validity of this statement. Your research could include interviews, analysis of movies, advertisements, and other cultural expressions.

3. Rousseau argued that "language must develop before politics is possible and that language originally distinguished nations from one another." Write an essay responding to this theory, considering King's views and your own.

R<small>ELEVANT</small> W<small>EB</small> S<small>ITES</small>

L<small>ANGUAGE</small> P<small>OLICY</small> W<small>EB</small> S<small>ITE</small>
<http://ourworld.compuserve.com/homepages/JWCRAWFORD/new.htm>

This web site focuses on language policy and provides information about English Only laws, bilingual education, English Plus, language rights, and endangered languages.

U.S. E<small>NGLISH</small>, I<small>NC</small>. <http://www.us-english.org/inc/official/>

The U.S. English, Inc. web site is dedicated to preserving the unifying role of the English language in the United States.

Howard Reingold

Virtual Communities

Howard Reingold has been writing about computer technology and its social implications since the early 1980s. He is also a science fiction writer and artist. He has been an editor of online magazines and was the founder of the online community Electronic Minds. His books on computer technology and its impact include The Cognitive Connection: Thought and Language in Man and Machine *(1987),* Virtual Reality *(1991), and* Smart Mobs: The Next Social Revolution *(2002). The selection that follows is excerpted from Reingold's* The Virtual Community: Homesteading on the Electronic Frontier *(1993; 2000).*

Several hundred years ago, large associations of small communities faced an important question: What kind of community is this new political abstraction known as a nation-state? To what degree is this new form of human social organization a step forward from the village life most people have known for centuries? To what degree is it a step backward? Does it grant freedom or restrict it? Does it add to our humanity or subtract from it? Today, with millions of people using the Internet to participate in on-going discussions about everything under the sun, we face a similar question: What kind of community is the virtual community? To what degree is it a step forward or a step backward? Does it grant freedom or restrict it? Does it add to our humanity or subtract from it?

A virtual community is a group of people who may or may not meet one another face to face, and who exchange words and ideas through the mediation of computer bulletin boards and networks. When these exchanges begin to involve interwoven friendships and rivalries and give rise to the real-life marriages, births, and deaths that bond people in any other kind of community, they begin to affect these people's lives in the real world. Like any other community, a virtual community is also a collection of people who adhere to a certain (loose) social contract and who share certain (eclectic) interests. It usually has a geographically local focus and often has a connection to a much wider domain.

The existence of computer-linked communities was predicted twenty years ago by J.C.R. Licklider, who set in motion the research that resulted in the creation of the first such community, the ARPAnet. In an April 1968 article in *International Science and Technology,* Licklider wrote, "What will on-line interactive communities be like? In most fields they will consist of geographically separated members, sometimes grouped in small clusters and sometimes working individually. They will be communities not of common location, but of common interest." My friends and I and millions of others are part of the future that Licklider dreamed about, and we can attest to the truth of his prediction that "life will be happier for the on-line individual because the people with whom one interacts most strongly will be selected more by commonality of interests and goals than by accidents of proximity." But those of us who have spent decades on-line have come to recognize the pitfalls of a communication medium where our minds can meet, but our bodies are left behind, where ideas are honored, but geographic neighborhoods are no longer as important as they were in our grandparents' time.

I visit my virtual communities for the sheer pleasure of communicating with my on-line friends. It is also a practical instrument that I use to scan and gather information on subjects that are of momentary or enduring importance, for child care to neuroscience, from technical questions on telecommunications to arguments on philosophical, political, or spiritual subjects. It's a bit like a neighborhood pub or coffee shop: although I don't have to move from my desk, there's a certain sense of place to it. It's a little like a salon, where I can participate in a hundred ongoing conversations with people who don't care what I look like or sound like, but who do care how I think and communicate. And it's a little like a "group mind," where questions are answered, support is given, and inspiration is provided by people I may never have heard from before and whom I may never meet face to face.

5 Virtual communities have several advantages over the old-fashioned communities of place and profession. Because we cannot see one another, we are unable to form prejudices about others before we read what they have to say. Race, gender, age, national origin, and physical appearance are not apparent unless a person wants to make such characteristics public. People whose physical handicaps make it difficult to form new friendships find that virtual communities treat them as they always wanted to be treated—as transmitters of ideas and feeling beings, not carnal vessels with a certain appearance and way of walking and talking (or not walking and not talking). Don't mistake this filtration of appearances for dehumanization; words on a screen are quite capable of moving one to laughter or tears,

of evoking anger or compassion, of creating a community from a collection of strangers.

During the past fourteen years I have attended three weddings of people who met in virtual communities. I have attended three funerals and stood up and spoke at two of those most solemn community gatherings. I sat by the deathbeds of two people I never would have known if we had not connected through words on the screen. I contributed to scholarship funds for young people whose parents couldn't afford tuition, and I helped pass the hat when members of my virtual community fell on hard times. Although one must always be careful about attributing the characteristics of community to an on-line discussion group, there experiences have convinced me that community is indeed possible through virtual communication, that people can get up from their computers and affect one another's lives in profound ways.

Virtual communities are instruments for connecting people according to shared mutual interests. In traditional kinds of communities, we are accustomed to meeting people, then getting to know them. In virtual communities, you can get to know people and then choose to meet them. In some cases, you can get to know people whom you might never meet on the physical plane. In the traditional community, we search through our pool of neighbors and professional colleagues, of acquaintances and acquaintances of acquaintances, in order to find people who share our values and interests. We then exchange information about one another, share and debate our mutual interests, and sometimes become friends. In a virtual community we can go directly to the place where our particular interests are being discussed, then get acquainted with those who share our passions. You can't simply pick up a phone and ask to be connected with someone who wants to talk about Islamic art or California wine, or someone with a three-year-old daughter or a thirty-year-old Hudson; you can, however, join a computer conference on any of those topics, then open a public or private correspondence with the previously unknown people you find in that conference.

Virtual communities can help their members cope with information overload. One problem created by the information age, especially for students and knowledge workers who spend their time immersed in the infoflow, is that too much information is available with no effective filters for sifting the key data that are useful and interesting to them as individuals. Researchers in the artificial intelligence research community are trying to evolve "software agents" that can seek and sift, filter and find, and save us from the awful feeling we get when it turns out that the specific knowledge we need is buried in fifteen thousand pages of related information. In many virtual communities, people have informal social contracts that allow them to act as software agents for one another. If, in my wanderings through information space, I come across items that don't interest me but that I know one of my group of on-line friends would appreciate, I send him or her a pointer to the key fact or discussion.

This social contract requires us to give something and enables us to receive something. I have to keep my friends in mind and send them pointers instead of throwing my informational discards into the virtual scrap heap. It doesn't take a great deal of energy to do that, since I have to sift that information anyway in order to find the knowledge I seek for my own purposes. And with twenty or a hundred other people who have an eye out for my interests while they explore sectors of the information space that I normally wouldn't frequent, I find that the help I receive far outweighs the energy I expend helping others—a good fit of altruism and self-interest.

10   Virtual communities have several drawbacks in comparison to face-to-face communication, and these disadvantages must be kept in mind if we are to make use of the advantages of these computer-mediated discussion groups. The filtration factor that prevents one person from knowing the race or age of another participant also prevents them from communicating the facial expressions, body language, and tone of voice that constitute the invisible but vital component of most face-to-face communication. Irony, sarcasm, compassion, and other subtle but all-important nuances that aren't conveyed in words alone are lost when all you can see of a person is a set of words on a screen. This lack of communication bandwidth can lead to misunderstandings, and it is one of the reasons that "flames," or heated diatribes that wouldn't crop up often in normal discourse, seem to appear with relative frequency in computer conferences. On-line communication seems to disinhibit people. Those who would be shy in face-to-face discourse can enter the conversation. And those who are polite in face-to-face discourse are tempted to be ruder than they would be to someone in the flesh.

It is easy to deceive people on-line: for nasty people to wear a polite mask and for nice people to pretend to be nasty. We all wear masks in our lives. We all play many roles at home and work and in public. But on-line discourse is nothing *but* masks. We can never be sure about our knowledge of another person when that knowledge is based solely on words on a computer screen.

Other disadvantages stem from the asynchronous and one-to-many nature of on-line communication. When you talk to somebody on the phone, you know they are getting your message right then and there. Electronic mail eliminates telephone tag but adds a degree of uncertainty. When you send someone e-mail, you are never sure when your intended audience will get your message, and when you post a response in a computer conference, you are never sure who is going to get the message. E-mail can become another form of enslavement when you fear being away from your computer because five hundred new messages will be waiting when you return. Another advantage that can turn into a disadvantage is the unpredictability of responses: it is refreshing and fun to find all the unexpected angles and digressions people can come up with in response to a question or statement in a computer conference; it is frustrating when the specific answer you seek is lost in "item drift."

The way to build a virtual community, and to use it effectively, is to spend time to make time. At the beginning, there are unknown commands to learn and new procedures and customs to absorb. This is the steep part of the learning curve, and many people simply give up, because computer conferencing is not as simple as picking up a telephone or addressing a letter. It can be much more rewarding, however, and other people are usually willing to help, which leads to the key advice for building and using a virtual community: don't be afraid to ask questions, and don't hesitate to answer questions. Once you learn your way around, don't be afraid to pose new topics of discussion; plant information seeds and watch discussions grow around them, and see how knowledge emerges from discourse. Use pointers to data or discussions that might interest others—send them and ask for them. Use all the communication tools available to your community: private e-mail for one-to-one communication and for making arrangements to meet people face to face, public computer conferences for one-to-many questions and discussions, and biographies (your own and others) to help you and your community discover what kind of person you are and where your interests lie. Don't forget that telephones and face-to-face meetings are still appropriate ways to cement and extend the friendships you make on-line.

Is a virtual community a degraded community? People have been arguing about the nature of community since the early sociologists discussed the transition from gemeinschaft (community, epitomized by village life) and gesellschaft (society, epitomized by urban and national life). Benedict Anderson pointed out in his book, *Imagined Communities*, that entities such as nation-states are abstractions. Groups of people glue themselves together through shared beliefs in constitutions, national myths and legends, flags, and other symbols. Now we move into an even more abstract realm, mediated by technology. The critic Guy Debord calls this "the Society of the Spectacle," and Jean Baudrillard calls it "hyper-reality." Are the pretty illusions propagated on television and movie screens, and now through personal computers, simply a way of turning human life into a commodity that can be controlled, bought, and sold more easily?

15   Computers contribute to, but did not create, the degree of alienation we find in modern societies. Technologies that have granted us power and freedom have also led to alienation: automobiles led to gridlock and suburbia, elevators led to skyscrapers (how can you have a community when tens of thousands of people work in the same building?), telephones allowed relationships to exist at a distance, air conditioning enabled people to wall in those porches they used to sit on during hot summer evenings. The mass media have turned the political process into a form of entertainment. Issues and candidates are packaged and sold to us like commodities, and we don't have the power to talk back to the television set.

Perhaps the most important characteristic of computer-mediated communication is that it is a many-to-many medium. Unlike few-to-many media (newspapers, books, television, and radio), this is a medium in which many people have access to many others. Every node on the network, every computer plugged into a telephone via a modem, is potentially a printing press, a broadcasting station, and a place of assembly. Of course, we don't read about this aspect of the new medium in newspapers, nor do we see it discussed on television. The mass media concentrate on the spectacular aspects: porno on the Internet and teenage hackers.

The German political philosopher Jürgen Habermas has written about the "public sphere." The public sphere is a part of social life that comes into existence when citizens exchange views on matters of importance to the common good. It is where public opinion can be formed. When people gather to discuss issues of political importance, the public sphere becomes the basis of democracy. Habermas based his work on the role of coffee houses, salons, public societies, and committees of correspondence during the seventeenth and eighteenth centuries, when debates among citizens led to the democratic revolutions in France and America. The advent of the mass media and of the manipulation of public opinion through publicity and advertising led to the commodification and deterioration of the public sphere.

Is many-to-many communication a potential tool for revitalizing the public sphere? Can virtual communities help people reconnect with each other and rebuild the civil society that is essential to the health of democracy? It is too early to know, and too little is known. Before we can make informed judgments about the role of virtual communities in public life, we need to understand how they are affecting the way we think, learn, communicate, and govern. Considering how important these questions are to the future of democratic societies, it is shocking that so little systematic study has been directed at the phenomenon of computer-mediated communication.

Are virtual communities beautiful illusions that lull us into thinking that we are participating in discourse, or are they a step toward a rebirth of the public sphere? I can't think of a more important question to attempt to answer in the closing years of the twentieth century.

CONVERSATION STARTERS

Discuss the role of virtual communities in our culture. Have you participated in online discussion groups? If so, what has been your impression of these "virtual communities"?

READING MATTERS

1. What are the key elements that define a virtual community?
2. According to Reingold, why is life happier for the online individual?
3. What are the drawbacks to virtual communities in comparison to face-to-face communication?
4. Why does Reingold believe that virtual communities are the ultimate expression of democracy? Explain.

WRITING MATTERS

1. Develop your own definition of a virtual community. Write an essay about your process for constructing this definition. What strategies did you use to gather information? Was your definition informed by your personal experience?
2. Respond to Reingold's final question, "Are virtual communities beautiful illusions that lull us into thinking that we are participating in discourse, or are they a step toward rebirth of the public sphere?"
3. Write a story, real or imagined, about an experience in an online community.

RELEVANT WEB SITES

HOWARD REINGOLD <http://www.reingold.com>

The official Howard Reingold web site includes information about the author, excerpts from his books and articles, and access to online networks and resources.

THE BRAINSTORM COMMUNITY <http://www.reingold.com/community.html>

The Brainstorm Community includes a few hundred people around the world who communicate about technology, the future, life online, culture, society, family, creativity, history, books, music, media, health, home, mind, work, and academiaville.

Donna R. Gabaccia (b. 1949)

We Are What We Eat

Donna R. Gabaccia is the Charles H. Stone professor of American history at the University of North Carolina at Charlotte. She is a scholar of American history and immigrant history. Her most recent book, Italy's Many Diasporas, *was published in January 2000. For the academic year 2000–2001 she was on sabbatical while participating as a fellow at the "Global America" seminar at the Harvard University Warren Center. In the selection that follows, excerpted from* We Are What We Eat *(1998), Gabaccia asks us to consider why eating habits symbolize the boundaries of our cultures.*

In 1989, hungry Houstonians learned they could buy "New York deli" without leaving town—at the newly opened Guggenheim's Delicatessen. The restaurateur offering bagels, rugelach, herring, corned beef, and cheese cake at Guggenheim's was Ghulam Bombaywala, an immigrant from Pakistan. Bombaywala had already worked for years in a Houston steakhouse and a local Italian restaurant and had also operated a small chain of Mexican restaurants. Before opening Guggenheim's, Bombaywala went to New York to do his own research, eating in different delis three meals a day for five days. Back in Houston, Bombaywala sought partners, and he borrowed the recipes for Guggenheim's from one of them, a Mrs. Katz. Bombaywala did not seem to know that Germans, not Eastern European Jews, had opened New York's first delicatessens. And needless to say, most Houstonians devouring Guggenheim's New York deli were neither Germans, Eastern Europeans, Jews, nor New Yorkers. But then neither was Bombaywala.

The same year, three transplanted easterners with suspiciously Italian-sounding names—Paul Sorrentino, Rob Geresi, and Vince Vrana—opened their own New York Bagel Shop and Delicatessen in Oklahoma. Bagels packaged by Lender's had been available for years in local frozen food compartments, as were advertisements offering recipes for "pizzels," made of frozen bagels topped with canned tomato sauce. As businessmen looking for a market niche, Sorrentino, Geresi, and Vrana wagered that the most knowledgeable and sophisticated of Oklahoman consumers would enjoy freshly baked "New-York-style" bagels, which were chewier than their frozen counterparts. Like many retailers in the South and West, however, their New York Bagel Shop and Delicatessen offered bagels with sandwich fillings—everything from cream cheese to "California-style" avocado and sprouts.

Meanwhile, in far-off Jerusalem, a New Yorker, Gary Heller, concluded that Israelis too could appreciate bagels, given an opportunity. Importing frozen dough from Manhattan's Upper West Side H & H Bagels (begun in 1972 by the brothers-in-law Heller Toro and Hector Hernandez), Heller did the final baking of his bagels in Israel. He quickly acquired orders from a national supermarket chain and from Dunkin' Donuts, which was about to open its first Tel Aviv franchise. After a long journey from Eastern European bakeries through the multi-ethnic delis of New York and the factories of a modern food industry, the bagel had arrived in the new Jewish homeland.

Heller knew that Americans transplanted to Israel would buy his bagels, but to make a profit, he had to sell 160,000 of them to native consumers, in competition with a local brand under license from Lender's Bagels. As Heller noted, Jews born in Israel (sabras) "think bagels are American, not Jewish." Israelis knew "bagele"—the closest local products—only as hard, salt-covered rounds, unlike Heller's product, or as soft sesame ellipses. And these, ironically, were baked and sold by Arabs.

5   A grumpy cultural observer pauses at this point, well-armed for a diatribe on the annoying confusions of postmodern identities in the 1990s. It is easy to harrumph, as Octavio Paz once did, that "the melting pot is a social ideal that, when applied to culinary art, produces abominations"—bagel pizzas and bagels topped with avocado and sprouts surely qualify. Paz would find a typical American's eating day an equally abominable multi-ethnic smorgasbord. The menu might include a bagel, cream cheese, and cappuccino at breakfast; a soft drink with hamburger and corn chips, or pizza and Greek salad, at lunch; and meat loaf, stir-fried "vegetables orien-

tale" (from the frozen foods section of the supermarket), and apple pie for dinner. Wasn't eating better when delicatessens served sausages to Germans, when Bubbie purchased bagels at a kosher bakery, and when only her Jewish children and grandchildren ate them, uncorrupted by Philadelphia cream cheese? When Houston savored chili from "Tex-Mex" vendors? When only Oklahomans ate their beef and barbecue? And when neither pizza, tacos, nor bagels came from corporate "huts" or "bells," let alone a Dunkin' Donuts in Tel Aviv?

As a historian of American eating habits, I must quickly answer any potentially grumpy critics with a resounding no. The American penchant to experiment with foods, to combine and mix the foods of many cultural traditions into blended gumbos or stews, and to create "smorgasbords" is scarcely new but is rather a recurring theme in our history as eaters.

Consider, for example, the earlier history of the bagel. It is true that in the 1890s in the United States only Jews from Eastern Europe ate bagels. In thousands of nondescript bakeries—including the one founded in New Haven around 1926 by Harry Lender from Lublin, Poland—Jewish bakers sold bagels to Jewish consumers. The bagel was not a central culinary icon for Jewish immigrants; even before Polish and Russian Jews left their ethnic enclaves for ghettoes, their memories exalted gefilte fish and chicken soup prepared by their mothers, but not the humble, hard rolls purchased from the immigrant baker. As eaters, Jewish immigrants were initially far more concerned with the purity of their kosher meat, their challah, and their matzos, and with the satisfactions of their sabbath and holiday meals, than with their morning hard roll. They and their children seemed more interested in learning to use Crisco or eat egg rolls and chicken chow mein than in affirming the bagel as a symbol of Jewish life or as a contribution to American cuisine.

Still, the bagel did become an icon of urban, northeastern eating, a key ingredient of the multi-ethnic mix that in this century became known as "New York deli." The immigrant neighbors of Eastern European Jewish bakers were among the first to discover the bagel and to begin its transformation from a Jewish specialty into an American food. Unconvinced by the turn-of-the-century arguments of home economists that Americanization required them to adopt recipes for codfish and other New-England-inspired-delicacies, consumers from many backgrounds began instead to sample culinary treats, like the bagel, for sale in their own multi-ethnic home cities. In New Haven, by the mid–1940s, for example, the Lenders' bakery employed six family workers, including Harry's sons Murray and Markin, who still lived at home behind the store. Hand-rolling bagels and boiling them before baking, two workers could produce about 120 bagels an hour, enough to allow the Lenders to meet expanding demand from their curious Italian, Irish, and Russian neighbors. The Lenders soon produced 200 dozen bagels daily.

No one knows who first slathered bagels with cream cheese—a product introduced and developed by English Quakers in their settlements in the

Delaware Valley and Philadelphia in the eighteenth century. The blend of old and new, however, proved popular with a wide range of American consumers. With a firm grasp on regional marketing, Harry Lender's sons reorganized the family business in 1962 and decided to seek a national market. They purchased new machines that could produce 400 bagels an hour. The machines eliminated hand-rolling and substituted steaming for boiling. Flash-freezing and packaging in plastic bags for distribution to supermarkets around the country soon followed.

10 When union bagel bakers protested the introduction of the new machines, bagel manufacturers responded by moving production outside the Northeast. Along with the manufacturers of "Jewish" rye bread and other products common to deli display cases, the Lenders had learned "You don't have to be Jewish" to purchase and enjoy Jewish foods. With mass production for a mass market, they learned "You don't have to be Jewish" to produce them, either. In the late 1970s, Lender's was still family-owned and managed, but it employed 300 nonunionized and mainly non-Jewish workers.

In 1984 Kraft purchased Lender's as a corporate companion for its Philadelphia brand cream cheese. All over the country, consumers could now buy a totally standardized, mass-produced bagel under the Lender's label. A bagel, complained Nach Waxman, owner of a New York cookbook store, with "no crust, no character, no nothing." This was a softer bagel, and—like most American breads—sweetened with sugar. Following in the tradition of the long-popular breakfast muffin, bagels emerged from factories in a variety of flavors associated with desserts and breakfast cereals—honey, raisin, blueberry, cinnamon. Sun-dried tomato bagels followed in the 1990s, along with other popular flavors inspired by Mediterranean cuisines. Broney Gadman, a Long Island manufacturer of bagel-steaming equipment, believed that American consumers wanted a bland bagel. They were "used to hamburger rolls, hot dog buns and white bread," he explained. "They prefer a less crusty, less chewy, less tough product—You needed good teeth" to eat hand-rolled and boiled bagels.

Waxman and Gadman made a sharp distinction between mass-produced factory bagels (or cinnamon and sun-dried-tomato bagels) and "the real thing." They preferred authenticity, as defined by their memories of bagels in the Jewish ghettoes of the past. As millions of Americans with no bagel eaters in their family trees snapped up Kraft's Lender's brand, and as sabras came to appreciate American bagels at Dunkin' Donuts in Tel Aviv, Bubbie's descendants, along with a multi-ethnic crowd of well-educated Americans fascinated with traditional ethnic foods, searched elsewhere for their culinary roots and a chewier bagel.

Some of them found authenticity with Bombaywala's renditions of Mrs. Katz's recipes. Others discovered they could buy "real" bagels again from the Lenders. For Murray and Markin Lender chose not to follow their family brand into employment with corporate Kraft. Instead, they opened a suburban restaurant that offered, among other things, a bagel of crust and character, ideal for Nach Waxman. A host of small businessmen like Bom-

baywala and the Lender brothers revived hand-rolling and boiling, sometimes in full view of their customers.

The history of the bagel suggests that Americans' shifting, blended,
multi-ethnic eating habits are signs neither of postmodern decadence, ethnic fragmentation, nor corporate hegemony. If we do not understand how a
bagel could sometimes be Jewish, sometimes be "New York," and sometimes be American, or why it is that Pakistanis now sell bagels to both
Anglos and Tejanos in Houston, it is in part because we have too hastily
assumed that our tendency to cross cultural boundaries in order to eat ethnic foods is a recent development—and a culinary symptom of all that has
gone wrong with contemporary culture.

15   It is not. The bagel tells a different kind of American tale. It highlights
ways that the production, exchange, marketing, and consumption of food
have generated new identities—for foods and eaters alike. Looking at bagels
in this light, we see that they became firmly identified as "Jewish" only as
Jewish bakers began selling them to their multi-ethnic urban neighbors.
When bagels emerged from ghetto stores as a Jewish novelty, bagels with
cream cheese quickly became a staple of the cuisine known as "New York
deli," and was marketed and mass-produced throughout the country under
this new regional identity. When international trade brought bagels to
Israel, they acquired a third identity as "American." And finally, coming
full circle, so to speak, the bagel's Americanization sent purists off in
search of bagels that seemed more authentically "New York Jewish."

If the identity of bagels emerged from an evolving marketplace, can we
say the same of bagel eaters' identities? What, after all, does "what we eat"
tell us about "who we are?" Again, too easily, we assume a recent, sharp
departure into culinary eclecticism or consumerist individualism from the
natural, conservative, and ethnically rigid eating habits of the past. In fact,
eating habits changed and evolved long before the rise of a modern consumer market for food. Human eating habits originate in a paradoxical, and
perhaps universal, tension between a preference for the culinary familiar
and the equally human pursuit of pleasure in the forms of culinary novelty,
creativity, and variety.

Neither the anthropologist nor the man on the street doubts that
humans can be picky eaters, or that humans can exhibit considerable conservatism in their food choices. If you doubt popular wisdom, imagine serving a plate of tripe, corn fungus, or caterpillars at a diner in Garrison
Keillor's Lake Woebegone. Psychologists tell us that food and language are
the cultural traits humans learn first, and the ones that they change with
the greatest reluctance. Humans cannot easily lose their accents when they
learn new languages after the age of about twelve; similarly, the food they
ate as children forever defines familiarity and comfort.

But cultural conservatism, while it cannot be ignored, cannot explain
the history of the bagel, where instead we see evidence of human adaptabil-
ity and curiosity. Cooks know this combination well: they substitute ingredients when necessary, even in well-loved recipes; they "play with their
food" on occasion, just for the pleasure of finding new tastes. When people

of differing foodways come together, whether cooks or merely eaters, they will almost invariably peek into one another's kitchens. They will not like all they find, but they are usually curious and excited to try some of it.

Two closely related histories—of recurring human migrations and of changes in the production and marketing of food—help us to understand why and how American eating habits, and identities, have evolved over time. The migrations sparked by the European empires of the sixteenth and seventeenth centuries mixed the foodways of Spanish and indigenous Americans in today's Southwest and Florida; English, French, Dutch, or German culinary traditions were combined with Indian practices in the Northeast; and African, English, Scotch-Irish, French, and native American eating habits influenced the cuisine of the Southeast. During the long nineteenth century, successive waves of Irish, British, German, Scandinavians, Slavs, Italians, Jews, Chinese, Japanese, and Mexicans changed the face, and the eating patterns, of American farmlands and cities. In the early decades of this century, though restrictive laws lessened immigration from Europe and Asia, internal migrations of southern white and black sharecroppers to Detroit and New York, and of foreclosed "Okies" and "Arkies" to the West, transferred eating habits from one American region to another. And in today's world, again, new immigrants from Asia, the Caribbean, and Latin America bring the smells and tastes of their homeland cuisines to Miami, New York, Minneapolis, and Los Angeles.

20   Four hundred years ago climate and terrain placed harsh restraints on local eaters, reinforcing regional identities, and even today we do not expect Iowans to fish for cod, or eat much of it. The United States remains a nation of many regional environments, and its culinary and ethnic history has been shaped by regionalism, reinforced by territorial expansion from the Atlantic to the Pacific, and then beyond to Alaska and Hawaii. Already in 1550, however, sugar traveled the world because merchants could make huge profits by offering it for sale in nontropical climes. Today, changing technology, the use of fertilizer, and plant and animal breeding have vastly altered any local environment's impact on farming and consuming. Although regional eating habits persist in the United States, they are no longer straightforward reflections of a seaside location or a prairie continental climate.

If our eating is more homogeneous today than in the past, we can thank (or blame) a national marketplace through which the standardized foods of modern food industries have circulated. As farms gave way to "factories in the field," as huge canneries replaced women's domestic labor, and as the corner grocery store gradually gave way to supermarkets, the most ambitious businessmen, regardless of cultural origin, dreamed of capturing regional, and then national, markets by producing a few food items in massive quantities. Corporate food business fostered standardized foods and national connections, while migrations repeatedly introduced new sources of culinary diversity. Migrations also produced new "communities of consumption," which generated small businesses to serve their taste for distinctive foods. Today, food corporations position themselves to compete in a wide variety of market segments defined by ethnicity, gender, age, and income. Yet their most successful competitors are small businessmen like Ghulam Bombaywala and the Lenders, whom many consumers trust to deliver "the real thing."

Commercial food exchanges neither created nor eliminated the fundamental tension between our longing for both familiar and novel foods. While mass production delivered huge quantities of a few standardized, processed foods, expanding markets also linked producers and consumers of diverse backgrounds and tastes, opening opportunities for new blends, new juxtapositions, new borrowing. Food businesses large and small have lured adventurous consumers with novelties while soothing others with traditional foods. American eaters' search for the familiar and the novel became matters of consumer choice, just as producers' and retailers' experiments with both innovation and traditional techniques became marketing strategies.

It is easiest to see how food choices reflect the eater's identity when we focus on culinary conservatism. Humans cling tenaciously to familiar foods because they become associated with nearly every dimension of human social and cultural life. Whether in New Guinea or New Bedsore, humans share particular foods with families and friends; they pursue good health through unique diets; they pass on food lore, and create stories and myths about food's meaning and taste; they celebrate rights of passage and religious beliefs with distinctive dishes. Food thus entwines intimately with much that makes a culture unique, binding taste and satiety to group loyalties. Eating habits both symbolize and mark the boundaries of cultures. Scholars and ordinary people alike have long seen food habits, both positively and negatively, as concrete symbols of human culture and identity. When we want to celebrate, or elevate, our own group, we usually praise its superior cuisine. And when we want to demean one another, often we turn to eating habits; the United States we have labeled Germans as "krauts," Italians as "spaghetti-benders," Frenchmen as "frogs," and British as "limeys."

To understand changing American identities, we must explore also the symbolic power of food to reflect cultural or social affinities in moments of change or transformation. Today, as in the days of the Columbian exchanges, Americans eat what students of linguistics call a "creole," or what cooks describe as a gumbo or a stew. We quite willingly "eat the other"—or at least some parts of some others, some of the time. Eating habits like these suggest tolerance and curiosity, and a willingness to digest, and to make part of one's individual identity, the multi-ethnic dishes Paz deplored. As food consumers, Americans seem as interested in idiosyncratic and individualistic affiliations to the foodways of their neighbors as they are in their own ethnic and regional roots. Ultimately, then, as students of American eating we must not only understand what we eat, and celebrate the many ethnic reflections of who we are, but we must also understand the roots of our multi-ethnic creole foodways, and ask of them, too, "If we are what we eat, who are we?"

CONVERSATION STARTER

Discuss your experiences with eating foods from different cultures.

READING MATTERS

1. Americans combine and mix foods from many cultural traditions into new types of food. Is this a recent development?
2. Why is our eating more homogeneous today than in the past?
3. Were you convinced by the author's claim that America's blended eating habits "are signs neither of postmodern decadence, ethnic fragmentation, nor corporate hegemony"?
4. Why do you think that most people are reluctant to change their eating habits?

WRITING MATTERS

1. Write an essay that discusses the relationships between the foods we eat and our cultural identity.
2. Write an essay about your memories of family meals. What impact did these occasions have on your personality? In what sense were these family meals reflective of your family's values and culture?
3. Share a recipe or a meal with a friend or a group of friends. Write about the experience of selecting and presenting your meal. What adaptations did you make? Do you think that eating foods from different cultures can make us more appreciative and tolerant of other cultures? Explain.

RELEVANT WEB SITE

RECIPE SOURCE <http://www.recipesource.com/>

This web site features recipes primarily identified with an ethnic cuisine and broken down by region and ethnic group.

Artistic Projects That Reflect Cultural Change

Jacqueline Tobin (b. 1950)

Write This Down

Jacqueline Tobin, is a freelance writer and independent scholar, collector and writer of the personal stories of women, is the founder of Storylines, a counseling and education program that teaches women how to write about and tell their own life stories. She received her M.Ed. from the University of Nebraska and is currently an adjunct professor of women's studies at the University of Denver, where she teaches a course on "women's stories." Tobin is also the coauthor of The Tao of Women, an Interpretation of the Tao Te Ching Using the Words and Wisdom of Women *and*

Hidden in Plain View: A Secret Story of Quilts and the Underground Railroad *(1999). In the selection that follows, excerpted from* Hidden in Plain View, *Tobin uncovers a story of how quilts were used on the Underground Railroad to help slaves escape to the North.*

In 1994 I traveled to Charleston, South Carolina, to learn more about the sweet-grass baskets unique to this area and to hear the stories of the African American craftswomen who make them. Charleston is rich in history. A port city, where the Ashley River meets the Cooper to form (as locals like to say) the beginnings of the Atlantic Ocean, Charleston today is a place whose buildings and culture reflect the combined and separate histories of American and African American peoples. It is unique as the location where black slaves first set foot on American soil and once outnumbered the white population four to one.

A walk through the historic district of Charleston is like a walk through the corridors of American Southern history. Here, one is confronted by all the hustle and bustle of the retentions and re-creations of a bygone era. At the heart of historic Charleston is an imposing brick enclosure with open sides, known as the Old Marketplace. It looks very much as it did over one hundred years ago, as it still defines the length of the district. As it was in years gone by, the Marketplace is still the center of commerce for the area. Under the roof of the structure, long wooden tables, laid end-to-end, go on

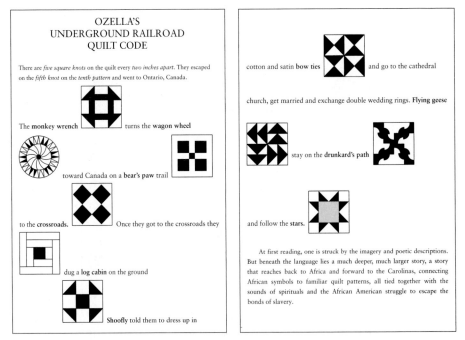

OZELLA'S UNDERGROUND RAILROAD QUILT CODE

There are *five square knots* on the quilt every *two inches apart.* They escaped on the *fifth knot* on the *tenth pattern* and went to Ontario, Canada.

The **monkey wrench** turns the **wagon wheel** toward Canada on a **bear's paw** trail to the **crossroads.** Once they got to the crossroads they dug a **log cabin** on the ground

Shoofly told them to dress up in cotton and satin **bow ties** and go to the cathedral church, get married and exchange double wedding rings. **Flying geese** stay on the **drunkard's path** and follow the **stars.**

At first reading, one is struck by the imagery and poetic descriptions. But beneath the language lies a much deeper, much larger story, a story that reaches back to Africa and forward to the Carolinas, connecting African symbols to familiar quilt patterns, all tied together with the sounds of spirituals and the African American struggle to escape the bonds of slavery.

Ozella's Underground Railroad Quilt Code

for blocks to create two narrow avenues for selling wares. As early as 1841 it was a marketplace for fresh vegetables, fish, meats, and other goods brought to Charleston from the surrounding farms and plantations and other coastal ports and faraway lands; it is still a vendor's market, but with stark contrasts between the old and the new. African American women sit by pails of sweet grass and weave baskets much as their African ancestors did over a hundred years ago. But these craftswomen, many of them descendants of slaves, are now surrounded by merchants of flea market trinkets, Southern memorabilia, and newer, cheaper baskets from China and Thailand.

The smell of the daily ocean catch or freshly slaughtered meats is no longer the predominant early morning smell of the Marketplace. Today the aroma of freshly baked cookies and newly ground coffee beans from the gourmet shops surrounding the area compete for attention. Certain sounds can still be heard; the din of tourists and locals alike crowding the streets and trying to avoid the horses, their hooves providing the percussive rhythm for this city as they clop loudly over original cobblestone streets. Carriages are drawn around the district, past the Custom House and on toward the Battery, where decorative wrought-iron fences accentuate the largess of old historic homes. Taverns and brothels have given way to fern bars and upscale hotels touting Southern hospitality and cuisine. Newly restored, on a lesser traveled street, is the original slave mart, now a historical museum, whose presence jars us into remembering a less civil piece of the history of this Southern port city.

As I walked the aisles of the Marketplace, I found myself standing in front of a stall lined with quilts of all sizes, colors, and patterns. I was drawn in by these piles of quilts, as long-forgotten memories of my grandmother's quilt box, filled with her handmade quilts, were brought to mind. Before I could do much looking or reminiscing, an elderly African American woman, dressed in brightly colored, geometrically patterned African garb, slowly walked up to me from the back of the stall. She motioned me to follow her to the back, where an old metal folding chair sat surrounded by more quilts. "Look," she said. She chose one of the quilts from the pile, unrolled it, and while pointing to it said, "Did you know that quilts were used by slaves to communicate on the Underground Railroad?" The old quilter continued to speak but I could not hear her clearly in the midst of the noise of the Marketplace around us. I wasn't sure why she was telling me, a complete stranger, this unusual story. I listened politely for a short while. When I didn't ask any questions, she stopped talking. I purchased a beautiful, hand-tied quilt and left with her flyer advertising "historic Charleston Marketplace" quilts.

5   I returned home with my quilt and memories of Charleston. I hung my quilt and laid my memories aside. I didn't think too much about my conversation with this quilter until several months later when I came across her flyer again. I remembered the story she had started to tell me and I wondered about it. I had never heard such a story or read about it in any books.

Was there more to the story? The flyer listed the quilter's name and phone number. I decided to call Mrs. Ozella McDaniel Williams and see if she would be willing to tell me more. When she answered the phone, I reminded her of who I was and asked if I might hear more about how quilts were used on the Underground Railroad. She told me curtly to call back the next evening, which I did. At that time she said, "I can't speak to you about this right now." When I tried pressing her, she laughed quietly and whispered into the phone, "Don't worry, you'll get the story when you are ready." And then she hung up.

Ozella had now added an element of intrigue to the already fascinating story. I was hooked. What did she mean by "you'll get the story when you're ready"? I felt I had to explore the story further. If she wouldn't talk, perhaps others would. I began to contact every African American quilter and quilt scholar I could find. I traveled down the Mississippi from St. Louis to New Orleans, stopping to visit quilters and scholars. I toured plantations and slave quarters, looking for clues. Before long, I was speaking to a fairly close-knit circle of people that included art historians, African American quilters, African textile experts, and folklorists. Most of them had heard that quilts had been used as a means of secret communication on the Underground Railroad, but none were exactly sure how. Some referenced particular quilt patterns, some mentioned the stitching, and others cited specific colors. I was not able to find any slave quilts that could verify these stories. Most quilt scholars agreed that few slave quilts had survived the constant strain of excessive use, the poor quality of fabric they had probably been sewn from, and the continual washing in harsh lye soap that would eventually cause them to disintegrate.

As a white person conducting research into African American scholarship, I was hesitant at times to continue. Some people were reluctant to share family stories with me. At one point I suggested that Dr. Raymond Dobard, one of the scholars I was conversing with, continue my research by contacting Ozella himself. I was hoping that she would speak more freely to another African American. Raymond, an art history professor at Howard University, a renowned quilter, and a known expert on African American quilts as they relate to the Underground Railroad, seemed to me to be the perfect person to pursue this research with Ozella. However, when I made my suggestion, Raymond insisted that I was the one with whom Ozella felt comfortable telling the story initially and thus should be the one to pursue it. He told me to be patient and that I would indeed get the story when I was ready. With his encouragement I continued my research.

Three years after first hearing the story, I had come full circle with my research, but there were still missing pieces. I could add nothing new to the information that was already out there. Still lacking was an elaboration of the story connecting quilts and the Underground Railroad. I was hoping for a final link connecting all the quilt stories with details. My intuition told me that Ozella knew more than what she'd already told me. The only way to find out would be to return to Charleston and see if she would speak to me again.

Without contacting her first, I arranged a return visit to Charleston. If Ozella was reluctant to speak, I didn't want to give her any time to think about it and turn me down without my ability to plead my case in person. Besides, I had done my homework, and maybe, I thought, I was now "ready" to receive the story in full. Armed with information and questions, I felt the time was right.

10   Upon my arrival, I took a carriage tour around the historic Charleston district. I wanted to immerse myself once again in the flavor of the Old South before attempting to talk with Ozella. As the carriage passed the Marketplace, I turned to look, my eyes straining to recognize my quilter friend's face. I recognized her immediately, sitting in the same location, amidst her tables of quilts, just as I had seen her three years prior. Today she was dressed all in white. She had on white slacks and a white blouse decorated with a huge lavender flower hand-painted on the front. She wore a large straw hat with a white band that had the same lavender flower painted on it as well.

I completed my carriage ride and walked slowly down the aisles of the Marketplace. I was nervous about meeting her again. Would she remember me? I wondered. What if I had come this far and she still wouldn't speak to me? Or, worse yet, what if she really didn't know anything more than she had already told me? With notebook in hand I took a deep breath and hesitantly approached her. Her back was turned to me as she stood quietly arranging her quilts. I cleared my throat to get her attention. When she turned, I tried to hand her my business card and started to explain who I was and why I was there. With a wave of her hand, brushing my card away, she interrupted me and said, "I don't care who you is. You is people and that is all that matters. Bring over some of those quilts and make a seat for yourself beside me. Get yourself comfortable."

I hesitated, but only briefly. If she was ready to talk, I was ready to listen. I was concerned about sitting on her handmade works of art, but she didn't seem to care. She positioned herself on the metal folding chair, moving quilts to either side of her and around her. I chose several rolled quilts and brought them over in front of her. After placing them on the ground, I sat down in front of her. From this position I was looking directly up into Ozella's face. She pulled her folding chair even closer to me. I became aware that she was now physically creating a space around us, obviously meant only for her and me. After seating herself on the folding chair she leaned down toward me, one hand resting on her knee, her index finger pointing to my notepad. She pushed her straw hat farther back on her head and with her other hand she directed me, "Write this down."

From the moment she said those words until she finished speaking about three hours later, time stood still. The normal chaos of Saturday morning in the Marketplace ceased to exist for us. Nothing and no one entered this space to disturb us. It was as if what she was going to say was for my ears only and that this time and space had been set aside for me to hear it. I felt that fate was honoring this moment. With a faraway look in her eyes, reciting something from memory, Ozella instructed me on what to write, stopping now and then only to ask me to read it back to her.

It took all my journalistic energies to focus on writing the words she spoke and to not get lost in the art of her telling. I was the student; she was the teacher. I was the transcriber; she the storyteller. At that moment, I knew that I was one of only a trusted few people who, down through history, had been told to listen carefully and remember the words she was speaking. Sitting beside this elderly black woman, surrounded by a sea of her handiwork, I felt that she was inviting me to share in her family stories and memories and become a part of an oral tradition that had allowed her culture to survive. I was no longer the journalist in search of a story. My role was to be much different. I felt that Ozella had very purposefully created an atmosphere where I was to receive this information. Surrounding us were only the sounds of her ancestors, family members like her mother and grandmother before her, passing words of information from one woman to another for safekeeping. During this time, I was aware of nothing but her voice and her message and the awesome responsibility she was giving me to write the story down. Seated at the feet of an older woman, I was conscious that we were taking part in a time-honored women's ritual of passing on wisdom from one generation to another. I was aware that we were bridging not only a gap of generations but also one of race. We were transcending age, stereotypes, and boundaries.

Conversation Starter

Discuss a nonverbal form of communication that you have used with a friend, family member, or a member of your community.

Reading Matters

1. Why was the quilt a practical form of communication? Why did so few slave quilts survive?
2. Why did the narrator choose to tell this story with the help of a writing partner? What did each partner bring to the project?
3. What barriers did the narrator encounter in obtaining her research? Do you think her research and evidence are adequate to support her theory of the symbolic language and purpose of slave quilts?
4. What responsibilities was the narrator given when she was asked to "write it down"?

Writing Matters

1. Write about an object of significance to you or your family. What story does it tell? Does it reflect your cultural history?
2. Write an essay about the use of codes in different cultures. In what forms have codes appeared? Why have codes been used?
3. Use code to tell a story. What strategies did you use to simplify your story? What did the use of the code add to the story and its impact?

**ABOARD THE UNDERGROUND RAILROAD: A NATIONAL REGISTER OF
HISTORIC PLACES** <http://www.cr.nps.gov/nr/travel/underground>

The official web site of the National Park Service provides descriptions and
photographs of 46 historic places that are listed in the National Register of
Historic Places and are related to the Underground Railroad, a map of the
most common directions of escape taken on the Underground Railroad, and
maps of the individual states that mark the location of the historic properties.

Estella Habal (b. 1949)

Coming Home to Manilatown: Resurrecting the International Hotel

*Estella Habal was a community activist during the anti-eviction movement of the International
Hotel and now serves on the board of the Manilatown Heritage Foundation. As a mother of four
children and a grandmother of four, she found time to complete a doctoral degree in history, and
she teaches Asian American studies courses in the San Francisco Bay Area.*

*Groundbreaking for the International Hotel low-income senior housing project took place on July 1,
2003, with the building scheduled to be completed in January 2005. When the Manilatown
Museum and Cultural Center is finally completed, it will be, as poet Al Robles puts it, like "coming
home to a fresh crop of rice." Photos of the former tenants will be displayed on each floor of the
new International Hotel, a museum and archive about the struggle and Filipino American will be
established, a performance and exhibition space will be inaugurated, and a large mural will adorn
the facade of the building. The Manilatown Museum and Cultural Center will signify a renewal for
the Filipino community, a place to reap the benefits of a rich history, especially the story of the
"manongs." The rebuilding of the International Hotel has inspired other communities, such as
Stockton, California, to recognize and commemorate their "Filipinotowns." The memory of the IH
tenants and their generation will be preserved, and new generations will come to learn and participate in their history.*

"We won't move!" the crowd of thousands chanted as police on horse-
back clubbed their way to the front door of the International Hotel, the last
remnant of what was once the 10-block Manilatown neighborhood
squeezed between San Francisco's Chinatown and financial district. Finally,
at 3 A.M., after hours of police violence broke through the nonviolent resistance of community activists and elderly tenants, each old Filipino and
Chinese tenant, escorted by a young student or community activist, was
led out the hotel's door. By 7 A.M., the tenants were all evicted, and they
would have all been left homeless except for the work of the young
activists, who had found temporary lodgings for the elderly. Despite the
tears and anguish and despair of that moment on August 4, 1977, there was

From 1920-35 there was a filipino male population of 39,328. Legislation forbid Filipinos to own land or set up businesses. They were to be kept moving, remain transient. They stayed in rooming houses, hotels and labor camps. The International Hotel was one of these. "Manilatown," the Kearny/Jackson Street area of San Francisco, became a permanent settlement, a convenient culture contact. It was the home field workers returned to, where merchant marines lived while in port, where distant relatives and friends could be contacted, where the could enjoy the security of a common culture. Immigration laws enforced the role the International Hotel played as a family, the social protection it provided. The Filipino community in San Francisco existed in groups dictated by economic necessity and blood brotherhood. The International Hotel became a symbol for an entire minority community. About 1954, the International Hotel became significant for yet another reason. Enrico Banduccci, opened his original "Hungry I" nightclub in the basement of the International Hotel where performing artists got there start, such as: Nina Simone, the Smothers Brothers, Lenny Bruce, the Kingston Trio, Dr. Irwin Chory and Bill Cosby, to name a few. In 1977, the tenants of the International Hotel, mostly elderly Filipinos, were evicted. Subsequently because of strong community opposition the site was designated by the Board of Supervisors as a site for low income senior housing.

Jump to...
other MHF pages...

...seeds sown by our elder brothers...
the manongs

MANILATOWN
HERITAGE FOUNDATION

735 Cortland Ave
San Francisco CA 94110-5628
415-206-1080
MHF@manilatown.org

Manilatown Heritage Foundation Web Site

at least one positive result of almost a decade of struggle to prevent the eviction. The older generation of Filipino immigrants, the "manongs," and the youth had bonded; out of the defeat there grew a new sense of common history that forever changed the Filipino American community.

The first generation of Filipinos in San Francisco's Manilatown had planted the seeds of activism in the following generations by fighting to stop the eviction of their home and community. While the anti-eviction battle of the International Hotel lasted from 1968 to 1977, many would have thought the long struggle had ended in complete defeat. But what had seemed to be only a local, San Francisco fight to stop an eviction of a few elderly men had a powerful, national effect within the Filipino American community, helping to galvanize a new sense of identity and purpose. For more than 20 years after the demolition of the hotel, a gapping hole in the ground like a raw wound reminded Filipino Americans of their twin legacies of discrimination and defiance. Today, after more than two decades of activism since the eviction of the tenants of the International Hotel and the destruction of Manilatown, low-income senior housing will be rebuilt in that hole. With the resurrection of a new International Hotel will come a museum, the Manilatown Museum and Cultural Center, to pay tribute to the former tenants and to all the "manongs" (Filipino term of endearment for elder brother or uncle), providing a concrete link of the past to the future generations, the first museum of Filipino America heritage anywhere in the United States.

The **Manilatown Heritage Foundation (MHF)** was founded in 1996 as a nonprofit organization to assist in the development of this museum and cultural center. MHF evolved out of the International Hotel Ad-hoc Advisory Committee formed in 1979 by the city government to ensure that affordable housing would be built on the International Hotel site after the hotel had been demolished that year. MHF's mission seeks to foster and preserve the history of San Francisco's Filipino community and to pay homage to the tenants who fought the battle to save the International Hotel. Through education, exhibits, and live cultural presentations, the Maniliatown Center will provide a venue to display the rich cultural and artistic traditions of the Filipino American community.

Located along Kearny Street on the edge of Chinatown and the financial district, the International Hotel was part of Manilatown, the birthplace of the first Filipino community in San Francisco. From the 1920s to the 1960s, Filipinos congregated on Kearny Street to live and sleep in workingman's quarters, eat in the Filipino and Chinese cafes and restaurants, and relax in the pool halls and barber shops. The International Hotel became a key center for Filipino activity in Manilatown, serving as a way station for the first immigrant wave of Filipinos who came in the 1920s and 1930s. Exploited as a cheap labor force, the early "manongs" were itinerant workers on the agricultural fruit and vegetable farms during the spring and summer in the California central valleys and the Alaskan salmon canneries. During winter, the agricultural off-season, they migrated to the cities and towns to work as culinary helpers, hotel workers, domestic servants or "house boys." Many also stayed close to cities so they could study in the high schools and colleges, though when the Great Depression hit the country, most Filipinos scrapped their plans for an education just to survive.

5   In West Coast cities like San Francisco, Seattle, Los Angeles, and Stockton, Filipinos stayed in cheap rooming houses and residential hotels. Manilatowns sprouted in these cities and towns, usually alongside Chinatowns and tenderloin districts, areas that whites considered undesirable. In San Francisco's Manilatown area, nearly 10,000 Filipinos gathered during the off-season in its heyday of the 1920s and 1930s, with the size of the population expanding and contracting according to the work cycle of the itinerant Filipino worker.

California's antimiscegenation laws and restrictive immigration policies forced many to a "bachelor life" and years of isolation from normal family lives. The average ratio of males to females was 14:1; and in some places it was as high as 35:1. Only when immigration laws were loosened in 1965 did the male to female ratio balance begin to correct itself. Although some were able to marry (usually to Mexicans, African Americans, and

Native Americans), the vast majority of early "manongs" grew old without companionship.

After World War II, many agricultural workers retired to these residential hotels in towns and cities, cheap places where they could afford to pay rent and still manage to send money back to their families in the Philippines. Agricultural life was cruel to them, and many of them lived out the rest of their lives without adequate healthcare. Despite their poverty, they would send part of their wages to the Philippines, helping their families to survive and send their siblings or children to school. Other men, many who had left families in the Philippines to become merchant marines, sailors, longshoremen, and veterans of both World War I and World War II, joined the retired agricultural workers to live in these residential hotels. After World War II, the International Hotel lived up to its name. Other nationalities stayed there as well, men who worked as merchant marines, sailors, and other retired workers. But the "bachelor community" of the Filipinos was the most stable group of tenants, and the "manongs" were also the most vulnerable. They did not have the other resources and commitments as the younger tenants who could uproot themselves more readily. Although they were poor and politically powerless, the "manongs" who stayed the longest evolved into a tight-knit community and the International Hotel became a home and not just a short-term residence. Some had stayed there for more than 50 years by the time the anti-eviction struggle began.

In November 1968, the first notice of eviction came to the tenants of the International Hotel, who immediately organized a picket to call attention to their plight. Their desire was to stay put because this was their home and they had no other place to go. They knew that they could not find a better place for their needs than the International Hotel. A reporter for a San Francisco newspaper told Vincente Robillos' story:

> Eviction notices don't terrorize men like Vincente Robillos, 58, who survived the fall of Corregidor. Today he was equally tenacious in defending his home in the IH, where more than 70 tenants are ignoring the Milton Meyers Real Estate Company's orders to get out as of yesterday. "I like it here," he said, "I plan to stay." . . . Retired in 1960, he returned to Manila with his wife and five children. "There were no good jobs in Manila," he said. Two years ago he returned here and took a room in the International Hotel, the first stop for most Filipino immigrants and a retirement center for older Filipino bachelors who spent their lives in the California harvest cycle. As a hero of Corregidor, and the jungles of Luzon, he took up the best available career opportunity—kitchen helper. He earns about $300 a month plus his Army pension of $147 a month. Of this, he sends $250 a month to his family. . . . His rent is $33 a month.

While Vincente Robillos could live cheaply at the IH and still send most of his earnings to his family in the Philippines, his fight to maintain the hotel was both economic and cultural, a matter of economic survival and family values.

10   Besides, by Chinatown standards for residential hotels, the International Hotel was more pleasant than most. It was more spacious, had lots of light, and although run down, was adequate. After years of friendship and familiarity, the men had developed a community that would watch out for each other. For the elderly, familiar surroundings and convenience was important, while cheap food was readily available in the Chinese and Filipino cafes, restaurants, or grocery stores downstairs or just a block away.

Their notice of eviction fortunately came at the same time that the young generation of the Filipino community was searching for its identity. Youth were looking for answers about their own history and community, and they found their "roots" in the Manilatown community. Filipino history was hidden and "invisible" to the youth, since the schools did not provide the history of minority peoples or the history of colonization of nonwhite peoples in the United States. Many of them, for example, were unaware that the United States had colonized the Philippines in the wake of a Philippine-American War (1899–1902) that had left thousands dead. One legacy of U.S. colonial rule was what is called a "colonial mentality." Filipino immigrants who had been trained by an American school system and American school teachers were taught to believe that they were inferior and Americans were their great benefactors who gave them education and modern civilization. Many parents of the youth chose to ignore their own experiences and history because they wanted to wipe the slate clean, believing that if their children were assimilated into the American way of life that discrimination would not affect them. Parents did not teach them their language and they hoped the children would have no lingering accent. But no matter how much they were assimilated, racism still affected their lives, since Filipinos just did not look like the "real" American, defined as white. Only a search for identity along with a struggle for equality could make a difference.

The key to their quest for identity was involvement in the community. Fortunately, the issue of the International Hotel came at an opportune time. By hearing the life stories of the tenants, as well as by participating in the fight for low-income housing for the poor, the youth discovered their identities in relation to the "manongs" of the past. They uncovered a vibrant labor history previously unknown to them, filled with stories of racial oppression and exploitation, along with courage and resistance, a history that they could be proud of and identify with. For example, at the time that Cesar Chavez and the farm workers union was major news, the youth learned that the first farm-worker leaders who led the grape strike, Larry Itliong and Philip Vera Cruz, were Filipinos.

For the "manongs," the youth provided a newfound strength in a family they had never had. Together, the "manongs" of the International Hotel with Filipino students and youth demanded that their home and community not be torn down in favor of a parking lot. "Manhattanization," or the high-rise expansion of the financial district in downtown San Francisco, had already been underway for more than a decade. Unfortunately, Manilatown was in the way of "progress" and had been chipped away, except for the very last block where the International Hotel stood in 1968. San Francisco city redevelopment razed whole neighborhoods such as the Fillmore district and the South of Market area, moving out thousands of people in its wake, replacing the spaces with high rises, luxury hotels for the tourist industry, and housing for the new white-collar professionals. In the Fillmore district, nearly 5,000 black families had been evicted from their homes, their vibrant community virtually destroyed. Similar plans for the South of Market neighborhood had been slated, even though the elderly in the South of Market, together with community activists, fought back. After protests and negotiations with the city, they were able to gain some concessions with promises of a few thousand units of low-income housing. At the same time, just around the corner from the International Hotel in the Manilatown district, another low-cost residential hotel faced eviction, and when those Filipino tenants were swiftly evicted and found themselves homeless, the lesson was not lost upon the tenants of the International Hotel.

The elderly and the youth observed these events and developed the simple slogan "We Won't Move!" After much wrangling with city officials, they were able to negotiate a two-year lease, with a one-year extension. Although the terms of the lease were onerous, they considered the agreement a victory. The tenants and youth activists had breathing space to renovate the hotel with volunteer labor to create a new space for their home and family.

15   They chanted "We Won't Move!" again when new owners of the International Hotel sent another eviction notice in the fall of 1974. The elderly and youth responded by organizing a coalition of trade union, community, and church groups, and even city officials to support their cause. Support from the city officials collapsed due to heavy pressures from the courts, property forces, and politicians opposing any deals with the tenants that might provide a precedent for affordable housing advocates.

Demonstrators surrounded the building by the thousands, while tenants vowed a nonviolent resistance that galvanized the entire city. The sheriff even went to jail rather than carry out the eviction, finally capitulating on August 4, 1977. In a bloody confrontation, police on horses beat back the human barricade in front of the hotel and hauled out the elderly tenants one by one. The city's promises to provide alternative housing for them after their eviction never came through—because there was nothing better than their home, the International Hotel.

Spanning a decade of anti-eviction battles, tenants and student activists were able to thwart the encroachment of financial development into the last vestige of Manilatown, the International Hotel. While the new owner, Four Seas Investment Corp., demolished the building in 1979, for almost 20 years it was never able to build a garage or any other new building at the old site due to public pressure. Finally, in 1994, Four Seas agreed to sell the land for community use and a $7.6 million grant from the federal Department of Housing and Urban Development (HUD) was awarded to develop the site for low-income housing. The Kearny Street Housing Corporation, a subsidiary nonprofit of the International Hotel Advisory Committee, formed a partnership with the Chinese Community Housing Corporation and St. Mary's Catholic Church. At the new site, St. Mary's parochial school will occupy one side while 104 units of low-income senior housing will occupy the other. The Manilatown Museum and Cultural Center will occupy the ground floor of the senior housing unit.

The International Hotel had become a symbol of activism for both the young and old in the Filipino community, an intergenerational and "family" endeavor. No one realized in 1968 or even in 1977 what significance the International Hotel would have for Filipino Americans. Yet a few isolated, stubborn elderly men joined by energetic young people seeking to right old wrongs engaged in a local, neighborhood development battle that gripped an entire city, provided an example for low-income housing struggles throughout the country, and profoundly affected the character of an entire ethnic community.

When the Manilatown Museum and Cultural Center is finally completed, it will be, as poet Al Robles puts it, like "coming home to a fresh crop of rice." The Manilatown Museum and Cultural Center will signify a renewal for the Filipino community, a place to reap the benefits of a rich history, especially the story of the "manongs." The memory of the IH tenants will be preserved, their photographs put up throughout the new building, and new generations will come to learn and participate in their history.

CONVERSATION STARTER

Discuss an experience you had where you learned something from an elder.

READING MATTERS

1. What positive action followed the August 4, 1977, notice of eviction?
2. What did Filipino youth learn from the "manongs" that they did not learn in school?
3. What strategies did the Filipino community use to save the International Hotel?
4. Why did poet Al Robles compare the completion of the Manilatown Museum and Cultural Center to coming home to a "fresh crop of rice"?

WRITING MATTERS

1. Research the options for affordable housing in your community. What options are available to senior citizens or families? Write an essay that summarizes and interprets your findings for your class.
2. Interview a member of your family about the place where they grew up. Compare your findings with the experience of residents of Manilatown.
3. Write a research paper about a project sponsored by HUD in your community. Use the relevant web sites that follow to inform your research.

Mark Applebaum (b. 1967)

Culture Sculpture

Mark Applebaum is a composer of "uncompromising and unmarketable" experimental music, an inventor of sound-sculptures, and a jazz pianist. His solo, chamber, orchestral, choral, and electronic music has been performed throughout the United States, Europe, and Asia. His CDs include Mousetrap Music *(1996),* The Janus ReMixes: Exercises in Auto-Plundering *(1999),* Catfish *(2003), and* Intellectual Property *(2003). He has engaged in numerous intermedia collaborations with neural artists, film-makers, architects, florists, animators, choreographers, and laptop DJs. He is a professor of music composition and theory at Stanford University, where he received the 2003 Walter J. Gores Award for teaching excellence. In addition to composition and theory courses, Applebaum teaches* Art vs. Pop *(an examination and critique of the highbrow/lowbrow paradigm);* Musique Concrète in the Digital Era *(a laboratory seminar for the assembly of scavenged sounds into digital music at Stanford's Center for Computer Research in Music and Acoustics); and* Rock, Sex, & Rebellion *(a survey of rock music with a focus on the transformation of mainstream culture through minority contributions). In "Culture Sculpture," Applebaum asks us to consider the ways in which an individual artist contributes to a local culture, finds a community, and influences world culture.*

Only one person can be the best at something. Ralf Laue of Germany, for example, stacked 555 dominoes on a single supporting domino. According to the *Guinness Book of World Records* this accomplishment has never been equaled. Presuming that you are not Ralf Laue, it seems safe to say that you are not the best domino stacker. You shouldn't feel bad about this; most people are not the best at any one thing. Similarly you mustn't get

The Mouseketier by Mark Applebaum

upset with yourself if you are not the worst person at something. This status seems to be less attractive, but it is an equally exclusive distinction. Guinness has not been particularly scrupulous in its record-keeping of worsts, but suffice it to say, you are probably not listed in its pages as the worst at something.

But that's just you. I am the best and the worst at something. In fact, it is the very same thing. And does anyone care?

I have never been and never will be the world's greatest or worst pianist. I started piano lessons when I was seven. Years later, and after about 8,000 agonizing hours of practice, I could play some moderately demanding classical music and I was reasonably adept as a jazz improviser. Audiences applauded at my concerts and some musicians even looked up to me. These affirmations conferred a respectable social standing within my local music milieu and implied that I was a good pianist. But despite this, I knew that there were just as many pieces that were well beyond my technical and interpretative abilities. And the more I compared myself with my favorite jazz pianists, the more I discovered my own inadequacies. Once, while living in Copenhagen during college, I attended an Oscar Peterson concert. The first half was inspiring; but by the end of the concert my awe had degenerated into a resolve to quit jazz piano. It seemed that I could never join the elite echelon of pros who constituted my musical superheroes and, to tell the truth, when the going got tough, I was uneasy being average.

Thankfully I did not abandon the piano, and my skills improve every day. However, I continue to oscillate between euphoric confidence in my abilities at one moment and the despair of mediocrity in the next. In 1990 I chose to respond to this dilemma. More out of instinct than by design, I invented a new instrument: the *mousetrap.*

5 The *mousetrap* is an electro-acoustic percussion contraption, a musical Frankenstein built out of assorted junk and found objects—threaded rods, nails, wire strings stretched through pulleys and turnbuckles, plastic combs, bronze braising rod blow-torched and twisted, doorstops, shoehorns, ratchets, squeaky steel caster wheels, springs, lead and PVC pipe, corrugated copper gas tubing, toilet tank flotation bulbs, Astroturf, parts from a Volvo gearbox, a metal Schwinn bicycle logo, and mousetraps. These disparate elements are mounted on a soundboard and, assisted by contact pickups, amplified through speakers. To collect parts for the *mousetrap* I rummaged through junkyards, garages, surplus stores, and warehouses. Suspicious hardware store clerks eyed me nervously as I conducted investigations into the acoustical properties of their wares. It was a feeling of accomplishment when, weeks into my research, the same salesmen would excitedly welcome me into the store, giddy with their own epiphanies: "Mark, listen to how this thing sounds when you hit it with this!" My project became an informal and unexpected arts outreach program.

The *mousetrap* turned out to be only the beginning of an obsession, the first in a series of original instruments that I've designed and constructed during more than a decade. Its progeny include the *mini-mouse,* the *midi-mouse,* the *duplex mausphon,* and six *micro mice.* I call these instruments *sound-sculptures* because I am just as concerned with their arresting visual impact as with their astounding sonic quality. The most recent sound-sculpture is the *mouseketier,* so-named for its multi-tier design. I play it with a number of different strikers and gadgets including Japanese chopsticks, knitting needles, combs, thimbles, plectrums, surgical tubing, a violin bow, brushes, various wind-up toys, corrugated Lego rail, and my hands.

Inventing a new instrument provides immediate gratification: one instantly becomes the world's greatest player of that instrument. The problem is that one abruptly realizes that one is also the world's worst player. So the satisfaction that comes from being novel is tempered by the fact that there is no communal standard by which to form a meaningful judgement, no cultural practice. The goal then is to envision—to *invent*—the skills that might constitute virtuosity on a unique instrument. Or, to think of it in historical terms, to develop a classic and then mannerist state of the art from a pre-classic antecedent. There is ample latitude to do this within a culture of one. But it is also a lonely and challenging undertaking in the absence of a community to inform and guide progress.

There are many ways to measure the success of something, but to a considerable—and embarrassing—extent, I measure my success against that of others. As a pianist I look intuitively at the vast community of piano players who provide abundant measuring sticks. Experts can make particularly sensitive measurements, but even the layperson is qualified to make judgements. Most of us, at least those who have participated broadly in Western culture, can make a crude determination of whether a pianist is a beginning, intermediate, or advanced player. Furthermore, we have an approximate idea of what kind of effort and training might nurture the player's progress. We can do this because we are familiar with the cultural practices associated with playing the piano. But what steps should I take to improve myself as a sound-sculpture artist? How do I assess my progress? What are the correct performance techniques? Do these questions even make sense in a culture of one?

When I started to invent instruments I found myself in a cultural vacuum. But I soon discovered compasses by which to navigate the new terrain. First, I certainly did not invent the idea of the sound-sculpture. While my instruments are unique, they might be thought of as contributions to an entire genus of sound-sculptures, some of which inspired mine. From this observation I realized that I was part of a community, that I was complementing a cultural discourse already in progress. It was small not large, marginal not mainstream, but it was a community nevertheless, one that provided ideas for my own development.

10 Second, I drew upon more generic aesthetic models from art and music. I considered samples of art that I admired, those paintings, sculptures, textiles, and architecture that seemed to teach me lessons about form, rhythm, symmetry, and texture. And I considered traditional orchestral and folk instruments and reflected on their timbral features, intonation, dynamic range, and articulation. These were all observations that informed my own approach to building instruments and playing them. As unconventional as my sound-sculptures are, they have a kinship with all musical instruments and this suggests that my work is part of a very expansive community indeed.

And third, having dedicated myself to the development of sound-sculptures for more than a decade, I was able to apprehend the richness of my own history. With each new sound-sculpture I refined the ergonomics, better integrated the electronic components, and improved the soundboard design. With each successive concert I added to a personal but increasingly detailed legacy of performance practice, further broadened my technical facility, and defined an idiomatic method. Compositionally I found myself referring to recent and earlier aesthetic orientations. (In performance I will nostalgically think to myself "Ah, remember how I used to approach the doorstop in the mid-1990s?") It is an autobiographical narrative, but it spans time and thereby provides historical perspective. By looking back, I see that I have come some distance and this distance urges me to look forward.

Some composers might disagree, but having the sound of a doorstop among the range of timbral possibility is, for me, a huge (and now indispensable) advantage. Being able to digitally reverberate that doorstop has its charms too. So in my recent research I have focused on modifying the sounds with a battery of electronic devices. These devices allow me to reverberate the tone, add distortion or echo, change the pitch, and warp the timbre in countless ways. I can accompany myself in performance by recording and playing back live multi-track loops, make them sweep to the left or right in the stereo field, speed them up, or slow them down. Perhaps just a trivial ornamentation at first, the electronics have become a fundamental part of what now might be called a hyper-instrument. There is a subtle performance technique in the use of my electronics, and their integration with the sound-sculptures requires deftness and practice. In my more delusional moments, I think of myself as a super-coordinated human, like a virtuoso hiphop deejay operating his or her playback equipment, or a NASA test pilot finessing complex flight controls.

My current problem is that it is impractical to carry all of my electronic gizmos to every performance. Even though I have developed a clever system by which nonessential, replaceable, and robust pieces fly in my suitcase (usually wrapped in pajamas or sweaters) while the more delicate pieces are crammed into my carry-on luggage, I still bump into the airlines' baggage limits. Consequently, I have one behemoth set-up for local performances, a modest set-up for domestic performances that require travel by airplane, and an even smaller one for performances that necessitate international travel. I think it would be ludicrous to ask a pianist to perform one night on a piano with the customary 88 keys, the next night on a piano with no black notes, and the next night on a piano with no sustain pedal. Yet this is comparable to the musical challenges posed by the frequent changes in the ergonomics and functions of my set-up from performance to performance. As such, I have multiple hyper-instruments to master, not just one.

Practical considerations—mundane things like gravity, money, and air travel—really do have a puissant impact on the music. Even if I was artistically inclined, I can't float around the stage during my performances; neither can I afford to build a sound-sculpture out of gold; and, as mentioned already, my baggage allowance presents another constraint. In fact, the *mouseketier* case was designed first on the basis of the maximum airline baggage dimensions; the instrument came second. In this regard, the culture of air travel, as distant from music as it may seem, has had a direct impact on the physical circumscription of my invention which, in turn, influences the music that I create.

15   I cannot say whether or not my sound-sculptures have had an important impact on the world. They have been seen and heard in concerts throughout the United States, in Europe, and in Asia, and recordings of these instruments may have traveled further. I do know that they have

engendered some fascinating intersections with other artists. Among these were opportunities to use my sound-sculptures in a collaboration with the Merce Cunningham Dance Company; to compose a piece for the Paul Dresher Ensemble that coupled my instruments with traditional ones like violin and bassoon; and to realize my *Concerto for Florist and Ensemble* in a performance that was surely both the best and worst of its genre. The sound-sculptures seem to provoke interesting responses too. Children are particularly attracted to them and display none of the psychological encumbrances that make exploration tentative by adults. I am thrilled when, after a performance, I overhear a bunch of concertgoers—usually young persons— announce that they are headed straight to the garage to build their own sound-sculptures. And perhaps most gratifying, the sound-sculptures have challenged some of my students to build their own instruments and to think about what might constitute virtuosity in a new medium.

With all of this interest in my sound-sculptures, it is clear that one day conservatories of music will contain whole departments dedicated to the training of *mouseketier* players. College students will debate the merits of one *mouseketier* player over another. And the common person on the street will be able to distinguish between beginning, intermediate, and advanced *mouseketier* performers. Okay, I realize that this is probably just a fantasy. But before we dismiss this unlikely scenario entirely, we should keep in mind that all of our traditional instruments were, once upon a time, singular, new, and alien. At some point in our history it was unfathomable that a keyboard instrument such as the piano would enjoy such broad appeal, familiarity, and legitimacy. One need only turn to the percussion instruments of the orchestra to observe a more recent evolution of cultural cachet. The classical orchestra typically included only timpani. The exceptional use of the triangle in Mozart's opera *The Abduction from the Seraglio* was identified by European audiences, in its time, as a transparent reference to exotic Asia Minor. But in my generation, the triangle was simply one of many available percussion instruments in my kindergarten teacher's box of musical tools—and I grew up in Chicago, not Turkey. Similarly, my great-grandparents might have apprehended the xylophone and the marimba as icons of Southeast Asian or Central American cultures; today, however, these are indeed among the prosaic instruments of focus in a Western music education. So goes the fusion, colonization, and evolution of culture.

If not a survival of the fittest instruments, there is a survival of the most popular ones. And if not a natural selection, there is a cultural selection that has bequeathed to us the rich and evolving musical traditions we enjoy today. Conversely, for better and worse, we have lost numerous instruments and instrumental practices, some of which we know of dimly through historical documents and others which we can only imagine. One of our pleasant myths is that the art which has survived throughout history has done so because of its intrinsic greatness. But perhaps its survival simply indicates that it was useful to those who had the agency to insure its longevity. If that is the case, then all of our actions—whether the invention of a new instrument, the writing of a poem, the reading of books and viewing of films, the tasting of food, the consumption of advertising, the practices we keep in business, law, dance, and sport, the ideas we debate in politics and philosophy, the ceremonies we undertake in our religions and in the rituals of our daily lives, the stories that we tell and the memories that we keep alive, the celebration or destruction of traditions, and the growth of new practices—are cultural votes, forces that shape the world that future generations will inherit.

Conversation Starters

Do you believe that the art that survives is intrinsically great? Why or why not?

Reading Matters

1. Why does Applebaum build the mouseketier? Why does he become obsessed with this new instrument?
2. Why are children especially interested in Applebaum's sound sculptures? How does this support Applebaum's belief that play and the ability to express childlike feelings are essential to creativity?
3. How important are practical considerations in Applebaum's performances? How is Applebaum's thinking shaped by practical considerations?
4. Why is Applebaum most gratified that his sound-sculptures have challenged his students to build their own instruments?

Writing Matters

1. What does the success of Applebaum's sound-sculptures suggest about our culture? Write an essay about our culture's values. Use Applebaum's success to illustrate your point or the success of another musician or musical group.
2. Applebaum suggests that art that survives does so because there are practical circumstances that ensure its longevity. Write an essay supporting or challenging Applebaum's idea. Refer to the success of other music that has or has not succeeded because of "cultural votes."
3. Build your own sound-sculpture. Write about the process of collecting your materials, designing the instrument, and sharing it with a group of people. What did you learn about your cultural identity?

Relevant Web Sites

Mark Applebaum <http://www.markapplebaum.com>

The official site for Mark Applebaum, which includes pictures of his sound-sculptures, announcements about upcoming performances, and biographical information.

Michael Shulan

Here Is New York

Michael Shulan is a writer and one of the founders of Here Is New York.

Here Is New York, an exhibition and sale of photographs of the World Trade Center tragedy that four of us organized about a week after 9.11, began on the ground floor of a small four-story building I own with two others at 116 Prince Street in Soho, some fifteen blocks north of Ground Zero. The space, which for twenty years had been a women's clothing shop, had been vacant since August. I was sitting at my laptop in the back when the first plane roared over the building. The idea for the exhibition was sparked by an Ancient Greek poem about despair that I saw written out in magic marker on a sheet of newspaper and stuck up on a wall the following afternoon. By this time the police had closed off the neighborhood and people were wandering about aimlessly in surgical masks. I went back to my loft and dug out a nondescript photograph of the Trade Center which I had acquired sometime earlier in the flea market, and taped it up in the window of the shop.

A day or two later, Gilles Peress, who had been down at Ground Zero photographing for *The New Yorker,* called me on my cell phone and asked what I was doing. I replied that I was in the shop staring at a group of people staring at a photograph, and was thinking about putting up some more. "Do it," he said, simply. We met the following evening with two other friends and colleagues, Alice Rose George and Charles Traub, and quickly devised a plan. In those turbulent days it seemed as if everyone in New York had a camera, and we decided that the exhibition should be as broad and inclusive as possible, open to "anybody and everybody"—not just photojournalists and other professional photographers but bankers, rescue workers, artists, children, and amateurs of every stripe.

The key, we knew, was to act fast. Alice, a photo editor and independent curator, began calling magazines and newspapers and every photographer she knew, asking them to spread the word and send pictures. Gilles suggested that we scan every submission to turn them into digital files and print them with inkjet printers; Charles, a photographer and Chairman of the MFA Department of Photography and the Related Media at the School of Visual Arts, set about rounding up equipment and student volunteers. I visited several galleries with Alice, looking for some appropriate way to hang the pictures, ultimately—inspired by a snapshot I had taken the previous spring of great clouds of laundry suspended from wires above a tiny street in Naples, Italy—finding it in the local hardware store. Since we had decided to sell the prints for $25 each to raise money for the children of victims, I also looked for a charity. We settled on the Children's Aid Society, which had already set up a fund for the children of restaurant workers, illegal immigrants, and others who were not likely to be provided for by other sources. We are very honored to be associated with them.

The exhibition opened on September 25, and by the beginning of the second week there was a long line at the door. We had originally intended to close on October 15, but by then we had been absolutely inundated with pictures, had filled the original storefront and had expanded to another that also was vacant, in the building next door. Over the course of the next month we announced two more closings, but eventually we decided to stay open until Christmas. By December 24 we had sold more than 30,000 prints, had constructed a web site, had sent several exhibitions on the road, and had made commitments to do several others. On January 2, when a crowd began to collect in the street, we decided that we had no choice but to reopen.

5   Here Is New York is a very minor part of the story of 9.11, but in its own small way it became a microcosm of what took place in the disaster's aftermath at Ground Zero and elsewhere in the city. Not an art exhibition in the conventional sense, partly an impromptu memorial, partly a rescue effort, and partly a testimonial of support for those who were actually doing the rescuing, it became a rallying point for the neighborhood and for the community at large. Thousands of photographers selflessly donated pictures; hundreds of thousands of people came to view and to buy them at Prince Street and at our other exhibitions; literally millions of people have looked at them on our web site. None of this would have been possible without the hundreds of highly skilled and dedicated volunteers who have been with Here Is New York since its inception, not a few of whom have continually worked ten- and twelve-hour days, six and seven days a week. Along with the photographers, they deserve most of the credit for Here Is New York's existence. Alice, Gilles, Charles, and I knew from the outset that the exhibition would be powerful, but never for a moment did we think that lines would stretch around the block, disrupting traffic and local businesses. Nor did we imagine that a steady stream of firetrucks and police cars would draw up in front of the building at all hours, the crews who were piling into the storefronts to look at the pictures trailing that horrific smell of Ground Zero

that everyone in Lower Manhattan came to know only too well. We started with the help of some friends and a devoted cadre of Charles's students, but their ranks quickly swelled with photographers, neighbors, artists, housewives, and lawyers—again, "anybody and everybody." They read about the exhibition in the newspaper, saw a report about it on TV, or came to Prince Street to submit pictures. Then they took it upon themselves to scan pictures, color-correct pictures, print pictures, label pictures, hang pictures, sell pictures, ship pictures, and database pictures, as well as to build our web site, network our computers, arrange our exhibitions, program our slideshows, do our contracts and tax filings, work on the production of this book, and do everything else that Here Is New York, by whatever logic, has come to do. We are indebted to them beyond measure. Out of something truly unspeakable has come something truly wonderful: love.

Photography was the perfect medium to express what happened on 9.11, since it is democratic by its very nature and infinitely reproducible. The tragedy at Ground Zero struck all New Yorkers equally, leaving none of us immune to shock or grief. Although the disaster was the lead story in every newspaper in the world, and searing footage of the planes destroying the towers was running on television 24 hours a day, to New Yorkers this wasn't a news story: it was an unabsorbable nightmare. In order to come to grips with all of this imagery that was haunting us, it was essential, we thought, to reclaim it from the media and stare at it without flinching. Terrorism was all too familiar in other parts of the world, but it had rarely happened in the United States, and never on such a scale. Besides announcing that this is the face of our city's tragedy, the title Here Is New York declares that we understand the problem of terrorism to be a global one that respects no geographic or cultural boundaries. After 9.11, New York is Everywhere.

This book contains nearly a thousand of the more than five thousand pictures that some three thousand photographers submitted to the exhibition. It has not been edited to showcase the "best" or the "strongest" images, but to give the most coherent sense of the whole. Here Is New York has by now amassed one of the largest photographic archives in world history devoted to a single event. But whereas after other events of this magnitude one striking picture has sometimes come to stand for, or to symbolize, what happened, the one picture that will probably come to stand for the World Trade Center tragedy will be all of these pictures. What was captured by these photographs—captured with every conceivable kind of apparatus, from Leicas and digital Nikons to homemade pinhole cameras and little plastic gizmos that schoolchildren wear on their wrists—is truly astonishing: not only grief, and shock, and courage, but a beauty that is at once infernal and profoundly uplifting. The pictures speak both to the horror of what happened on 9.11 (and is still happening) and to the way it can and must be countered by us all. They speak not with one voice, but with one purpose, saying that to make sense of this terrifying new phase in our history we must break down the barriers that divide us.

The guiding principle of Here Is New York is a simple one. If one photograph tells *a* story, thousands of photographs tell not only thousands of stories but also perhaps begin to tell *the* story if they are allowed to speak for themselves, to each other, and to the viewer directly, unframed either by glass, metal, or wood, or by preconception or editorial comment. In the political sphere it is this principle, after all, that America's Founding Fathers advanced when they developed the notion of democracy—that wisdom lies not in the vision and will of any one individual, or small group of individuals, but in the collective vision of us all.

10   As with print sales from our exhibitions, the net proceeds from the sale of this book will be donated to the Children's Aid Society and other worthy charities. We hope that it will stand as a living memorial to those who lost their lives on 9.11, as well as a tribute to those who came so valiantly to our aid. It is a testament to the courage and humanity of all New Yorkers. Every picture submitted to Here Is New York shows without question that terrorism can never succeed anywhere.

The entire archive of photographs can be viewed on our web site. Seeing is not only believing. Seeing is *seeing.*

Conversation Starters

Discuss your memories of 9/11. What are the images that you remember? How did these images impact your experience of the tragedy?

Reading Matters

1. What does the author mean when he says "New York Is Everywhere"?
2. Why is photography the perfect medium to express what happened on 9/11?
3. What was captured in the photographs that were displayed at 116 Prince Street? Why was it important that the collection was not edited?
4. How did the origins of the exhibit reflect the sense of community that emerged from 9/11?

Writing Matters

1. Visit the Here Is New York web site and select a photograph that is meaningful to you. Write a story about the photograph and what you think is being expressed.
2. Research the Children's Aid Society and write an essay about their work.
3. Use a camera to document a public event. What impact did your role as photographer have on your experience of the event? Write about the experience of seeing through the lens of the camera.

Relevant Web Sites

Here Is New York <http://www.Hereisnewyork.org>

The official web site of the Here Is New York exhibit. The site provides access to a gallery of photographs taken by both amateur and professional photographers following the tragedy of 9/11.

Chidren's Aid Society WTC Relief Fund
<http://www.uusc.org/news/terreciplist2.html>

Learn more about how the funds raised by "Here Is New York" are being used by the Chidren's Aid Society WTC Relief Fund.

Writing About Culture

1. Write an essay that reflects on your cultural identity and how it has influenced your interactions with the different communities in your life (such as friends, family, work, school).

2. Write a paper that defines culture. Research the topic on the Internet and refer to the relevant readings in this chapter to support your main points.

3. Write an essay that discusses a movie or television show that reflects aspects of your cultural experience.

4. Use the Internet to research a culture that you are interested in and want to understand better. Write a paper to share with your classmates that presents what you have learned.

5. Write an essay that discusses the impact that the Internet has had on our culture.

6. What symbol is most representative of our culture today? Write an essay that discusses this symbol and its impact on popular values. Do you believe the same symbol will be relevant in a decade?

7. Write an essay that explores how people form cultural values.

8. Imagine that you have been asked to assemble a time capsule that will provide future generations with insight into our culture and our notion of community. Write an essay about your selection criteria and the contents of your time capsule.

9. Write an essay that explores the relationships between two distinct cultures.

Work

Graig Kielburger journeys around the world bringing attention to the worldwide abuse of children's rights on behalf of Free the Children. International Rescue Committee Outreach Brochure

Increasing numbers of people are looking to their workplace for a sense of community. In our world of smaller families, with more women working at jobs other than or in addition to mothering and home management, the family no longer necessarily serves as one's primary and stabilizing community. Some corporations and businesses offer employees child care and better health care benefits, realizing that they must provide the support that was previously assumed to be the role of the traditional family. Technology, too, has changed the workplace. While more working people are traveling to do business in our national and international economy, many people can stay at home and work in virtual spaces. The Internet that has brought a democratization of information and services available as well as e-mail make visual and print delivery almost immediate—all have revolutionized the world of work. Finally, service and volunteerism, fundamental aspects of our country's democratic ethic, are developing into essential components of our workforce. Corporations and nonprofit organizations provide technological and economic support to local, national and international communities in need. The selections in "Work" address the challenges and struggles that modern workers face.

The reading selections in the first section, "Reconciling Personal Values and Workplace Expectations" explore the conflicts between an individual's personal identity and values and the expectations and ethics of his or her workplace. The selections ask us to think about how changing attitudes about equality impact how workers are selected and treated in the workplace. For example, through his work as a civil servant and police officer, George Orwell in his classic essay, "Shooting an Elephant," reveals his inner conflict and ethical indecision as he is forced to shoot an innocent elephant and thus confront his assumptions about Imperialism and his relationship with the "natives" whom he is supposed to supervise. Expectations about gender and race are challenged in Maya Angelou's "On the Street Cars" as she reveals her struggle to become the first black woman to be a conductor on the San Francisco trolley cars. The final selection, by veteran computer programmer Ellen Ullman, questions the rigid divisions between programming and serving the needs of the community: "Three programmers, the network guy, me—fifty-eight years of collective technical experience—and the idea of helping people with a computer is a first for any of us." As the selections suggest, all of us face new workplace communities that force us to reflect upon the assumptions that we have about the nature and role of work in our lives.

While the selections in the first section present workplace issues through first-person narrative, the selections in "Revealing the Economic Divide" present serious questions about the growing and increasingly destructive economic divide in our country. With evidence and clarity, Eric Schlosser's "In the Strawberry Fields" presents an ethical argument for protection and fair wage scale for migrant workers who come to work in our fields only because they are paid even less and exploited even more in

Mexico. In a selection from Barbara Ehrenreich's best-selling *Nickel and Dimed*, you will learn about Ehrenreich's experiences traveling around the country, working at the "lowliest" occupations (waitress, housecleaner, department store clerk, etc.) that are mentally and physically challenging but do not pay wages that allow these workers to make ends meet. Ehrenreich realizes and expresses an often unexamined truth: When we take from the poor to have a better life for ourselves, we are putting our communities at great risk. In the face of this economic inequity, Bill Shore, in "A Pioneer of Community Wealth," offers a plan that can begin to reverse the current workplace values. He argues that nonprofit and corporate communities need to create business partnerships that bring profits back to the community.

The final section, "Working Toward Solutions in the Community," opens with a poem, Robert Frost's "Mending Wall." Frost brings deep meanings and irony to the work of two farmers as they mend a perhaps unnecessary common wall that separates their properties. The remaining selections provide you with models of community-based projects with humanitarian goals. The projects include "Kathmandu," which discusses the efforts of the CWIN (Children's Workers in Nepal) to oppose the exploitation of more than 4 million children who live on the streets and work in carpet or garment factories, as domestic servants, or in brothels in India and Thailand. The realistic stories of despair turned to hope emphasize the importance of the work-to-welfare law and encourage others to contribute to its continued success. The final selection, *Bread, Salt and Heart*, is a publication of the International Rescue Committee that was written and produced by a politician and a photographer who volunteered their time to help the people in Kosovo. The publication highlights efforts in Kosovo when almost a half million refugees fled there to escape political persecution in Albania and lets readers know more about the lives of people in crisis and how important volunteer efforts are.

These projects are a testimony to the potential for positive change within many communities that have had to face destructive social, political, and economic forces. We hope that the reading selections in this chapter will help you to realize that although adjusting to the changes in the workplace community is indeed challenging, if we are dedicated to change and to helping the underprivileged, we can develop workplace ethics that will improve the quality of our daily working lives and help others through becoming volunteers when communities face unbearable crisis.

George Orwell (1903–1950)

Shooting an Elephant

George Orwell was born Eric Blair in India. Although comfortable in India, his family returned to England and struggled to send him to be educated at Eton College. However, Orwell decided to forgo a formal education and chose instead a life rich in experiences. He served with the Imperial Police in Burma, fought in the Spanish Civil War, and served as a member of the Home Guard and as a writer for the BBC during World War II. As a journalist, essayist, and novelist, Orwell was "the conscience of his generation" because he confronted the political nightmares of his age in his books; some of the most widely read include Burmese Days *(1934),* Homage to Catalonia *(1938), and* A Collection of Essays *(1946), in which the selection that follows, "Shooting an Elephant," was first anthologized. Orwell is best known for his two brilliantly satirical novels,* Animal Farm *(1945) and* 1984 *(1949). In the following selection, Orwell's position with the Indian Imperial Police forces him to question his personal values and beliefs about work.*

In Moulmein, in Lower Burma, I was hated by large numbers of people—the only time in my life that I have been important enough for this to happen to me. I was sub-divisional police officer of the town, and in an aimless, petty kind of way anti-European feeling was very bitter. No one had the guts to raise a riot, but if a European woman went through the bazaars alone somebody would probably spit betel juice over her dress. As a police officer I was an obvious target and was baited whenever it seemed safe to do so. When a nimble Burman tripped me up on the football field and the referee (another Burman) looked the other way, the crowd yelled with hideous laughter. This happened more than once. In the end the sneering yellow faces of young men that met me everywhere, the insults hooted after me when I was at a safe distance, got badly on my nerves. The young Buddhist priests were the worst of all. There were several thousands of them in the town and none of them seemed to have anything to do except stand on street corners and jeer at Europeans.

All this was perplexing and upsetting. For at that time I had already made up my mind that imperialism was an evil thing and the sooner I chucked up my job and got out of it the better. Theoretically—and secretly, of course—I was all for the Burmese and all against their oppressors, the British. As for the job I was doing, I hated it more bitterly than I can perhaps make clear. In a job like that you see the dirty work of Empire at close quarters. The wretched prisoners huddling in the stinking cages of the lock-ups, the grey, cowed faces of the long-term convicts, the scarred buttocks of the men who had been flogged with bamboos—all these oppressed me with an intolerable sense of guilt. But I could get nothing into perspective. I was young and ill-educated and I had had to think out my problems in the utter silence that is imposed on every Englishman in the East. I did not even know that the British Empire is dying, still less did I know that it is a great deal better than the younger empires that are going to supplant it. All I knew was that I was stuck between my hatred of the empire I served and my rage against the evil-spirited little beasts who tried to make my job impossible. With one part of my mind I thought of the British Raj[1] as an unbreakable tyranny, as something clamped down, in *saecula saeculorum*,[2] upon the will of prostrate peoples; with another part I thought that the greatest joy in the world would be to drive a bayonet into a Buddhist priest's guts. Feelings like these are the normal by-products of imperialism; ask any Anglo-Indian official, if you can catch him off duty.

One day something happened which in a roundabout way was enlightening. It was a tiny incident in itself, but it gave me a better glimpse than I had had before of the real nature of imperialism—the real motives for which despotic governments act. Early one morning the sub-inspector at a police station the other end of the town rang me up on the phone and said that an elephant was ravaging the bazaar. Would I please come and do something about it? I did not know what I could do, but I wanted to see what was happening and I got on to a pony and started out. I took my rifle, an old .44 Winchester and much too small to kill an elephant, but I thought the noise might be useful *in terrorem*. Various Burmans stopped me on the way and told me about the elephant's doings. It was not, of course, a wild elephant, but a tame one which had gone "must."[3] It had been chained up, as tame elephants always are when their attack of "must" is due, but on the previous night it had broken its chain and escaped. Its mahout, the only person who could manage it when it was in that state, had set out in pursuit, but had taken the wrong direction and was now twelve hours' journey away, and in the morning the elephant had suddenly reappeared in the town. The Burmese population had no weapons and were quite helpless against it. It had already destroyed somebody's bamboo hut, killed a cow and raided some fruit-stalls and devoured the stock; also it had met the municipal rubbish van and, when the driver jumped out and took to his heels, had turned the van over and inflicted violences upon it.

The Burmese sub-inspector and some Indian constables were waiting for me in the quarter where the elephant had been seen. It was a very poor

---

[1] the imperial government of British India and Burma
[2] forever and ever
[3] gone into sexual heat

quarter, a labyrinth of squalid bamboo huts, thatched with palm-leaf, winding all over a steep hillside. I remember that it was a cloudy, stuffy morning at the beginning of the rains. We began questioning the people as to where the elephant had gone and, as usual, failed to get any definite information. That is invariably the case in the East; a story always sounds clear enough at a distance, but the nearer you get to the scene of events the vaguer it becomes. Some of the people said that the elephant had gone in one direction, some said that he had gone in another, some professed not even to have heard of any elephant. I had almost made up my mind that the whole story was a pack of lies, when we heard yells a little distance away. There was a loud, scandalized cry of "Go away, child! Go away this instant!" and an old woman with a switch in her hand came round the corner of a hut, violently shooing away a crowd of naked children. Some more women followed, clicking their tongues and exclaiming; evidently there was something that the children ought not to have seen. I rounded the hut and saw a man's dead body sprawling in the mud. He was an Indian, a black Dravidian coolie, almost naked, and he could not have been dead many minutes. The people said that the elephant had come suddenly upon him round the corner of the hut, caught him with its trunk, put its foot on his back and ground him into the earth. This was the rainy season and the ground was soft, and his face had scored a trench a foot deep and a couple of yards long. He was lying on his belly with arms crucified and head sharply twisted to one side. His face was coated with mud, the eyes wide open, the teeth bared and grinning with an expression of unendurable agony. (Never tell me, by the way, that the dead look peaceful. Most of the corpses I have seen looked devilish.) The friction of the great beast's foot had stripped the skin from his back as neatly as one skins a rabbit. As soon as I saw the dead man I sent an orderly to a friend's house nearby to borrow an elephant rifle. I had already sent back the pony, not wanting it to go mad with fright and throw me if it smelt the elephant. The orderly came back in a few minutes with a rifle and five cartridges, and meanwhile some Burmans had arrived and told us that the elephant was in the paddy fields below, only a few hundred yards away. As I started forward practically the whole population of the quarter flocked out of the houses and followed me. They had seen the rifle and were all shouting excitedly that I was going to shoot the elephant. They had not shown much interest in the elephant when he was merely ravaging their homes, but it was different now that he was going to be shot. It was a bit of fun to them, as it would be to an English crowd; besides they wanted the meat. It made me vaguely uneasy. I had no intention of shooting the elephant—I had merely sent for the rifle to defend myself if necessary—and it is always unnerving to have a crowd following you. I marched down the hill, looking and feeling a fool, with the rifle over my shoulder and an ever-growing army of people jostling at my heels. At the bottom, when you got away from the huts, there was a metalled road and beyond that a miry waste of paddy fields a thousand yards across, not yet ploughed but soggy from the first rains and dotted with coarse grass. The elephant was standing eight yards from the road, his left side towards us. He took not the slightest notice of the crowd's approach. He was tearing up bunches of grass, beating them against his knees to clean them and stuffing them into his mouth.

5   I had halted on the road. As soon as I saw the elephant I knew with perfect certainty that I ought not to shoot him. It is a serious matter to shoot a working elephant—it is comparable to destroying a huge and costly piece of machinery—and obviously one ought not to do it if it can possibly be avoided. And at that distance, peacefully eating, the elephant looked no more dangerous than a cow. I thought then and I think now that his attack of "must" was already passing off; in which case he would merely wander harmlessly about until the mahout came back and caught him. Moreover, I did not in the least want to shoot him. I decided that I would watch him for a little while to make sure that he did not turn savage again, and then go home.

But at that moment I glanced round at the crowd that had followed me. It was an immense crowd, two thousand at the least and growing every minute. It blocked the road for a long distance on either side. I looked at the sea of yellow faces above the garish clothes—faces all happy and excited over this bit of fun, all certain that the elephant was going to be shot. They were watching me as they would watch a conjurer about to perform a trick. They did not like me, but with the magical rifle in my hands I was momentarily worth watching. And suddenly I realized that I should have to shoot the elephant after all. The people expected it of me and I had got to do it; I could feel their two thousand wills pressing me forward, irresistibly. And it was at this moment, as I stood there with the rifle in my hands, that I first grasped the hollowness, the futility of the white man's dominion in the East. Here was I, the white man with his gun, standing in front of the unarmed native crowd—seemingly the leading actor of the piece; but in reality I was only an absurd puppet pushed to and fro by the will of those yellow faces behind. I perceived in this moment that when the white man turns tyrant it is his own freedom that he destroys. He becomes a sort of hollow, posing dummy, the conventionalized figure of a sahib. For it is the condition of his rule that he shall spend his life in trying to impress the "natives," and so in every crisis he has got to do what the "natives" expect of him. He wears a mask, and his face grows to fit it. I had got to shoot the elephant. I had committed myself to doing it when I sent for the rifle. A sahib has got to act like a sahib; he has got to appear resolute, to know his own mind and do definite things. To come all that way, rifle in hand, with two thousand people marching at my heels, and then to trail feebly away, having done nothing—no, that was impossible. The crowd would laugh at me. And my whole life, every white man's life in the East, was one long struggle not to be laughed at.

But I did not want to shoot the elephant. I watched him beating his bunch of grass against his knees, with that preoccupied grandmotherly air that elephants have. It seemed to me that it would be murder to shoot him.

At that age I was not squeamish about killing animals, but I had never shot an elephant and never wanted to. (Somehow it always seems worse to kill a *large* animal.) Besides, there was the beast's owner to be considered. Alive, the elephant was worth at least a hundred pounds; dead, he would only be worth the value of his tusks, five pounds, possibly. But I had got to act quickly. I turned to some experienced-looking Burmans who had been there when we arrived, and asked them how the elephant had been behaving. They all said the same thing; he took no notice of you if you left him alone, but he might charge if you went too close to him.

It was perfectly clear to me what I ought to do. I ought to walk up to within, say, twenty-five yards of the elephant and test his behavior. If he charged, I could shoot; if he took no notice of me, it would be safe to leave him until the mahout came back. But also I knew that I was going to do no such thing. I was a poor shot with a rifle and the ground was soft mud into which one would sink at every step. If the elephant charged and I missed him, I should have about as much chance as a toad under a steam-roller. But even then I was not thinking particularly of my own skin, only of the watchful yellow faces behind. For at that moment, with the crowd watching me, I was not afraid in the ordinary sense, as I would have been if I had been alone. A white man mustn't be frightened in front of "natives"; and so, in general, he isn't frightened. The sole thought in my mind was that if anything went wrong those two thousand Burmans would see me pursued, caught, trampled on and reduced to a grinning corpse like the Indian up the hill. And if that happened it was quite probable that some of them would laugh. That would never do. There was only one alternative. I shoved the cartridges into the magazine and lay down on the road to get a better aim.

The crowd grew very still, and a deep, low, happy sigh, as of people who see the theatre curtain go up at last, breathed from innumerable throats. They were going to have their bit of fun after all. The rifle was a beautiful German thing with cross-hair sights. I did not then know that in shooting an elephant one would shoot to cut an imaginary bar running from ear-hole to ear-hole. I ought, therefore, as the elephant was sideways on, to have aimed straight at his ear-hole; actually I aimed several inches in front of this, thinking the brain would be further forward.

10   When I pulled the trigger I did not hear the bang or feel the kick—one never does when a shot goes home—but I heard the devilish roar of glee that went up from the crowd. In that instant, in too short a time, one would have thought, even for the bullet to get there, a mysterious, terrible change had come over the elephant. He neither stirred nor fell, but every line of his body had altered. He looked suddenly stricken, shrunken, immensely old, as though the frightful impact of the bullet had paralysed him without knocking him down. At last, after what seemed a long time—it might have been five seconds, I dare say—he sagged flabbily to his knees. His mouth slobbered. An enormous senility seemed to have settled upon him. One could have imagined him thousands of years old. I fired again into the same spot. At the second shot he did not collapse but climbed with desperate

slowness to his feet and stood weakly upright, with legs sagging and head drooping. I fired a third time. That was the shot that did it for him. You could see the agony of it jolt his whole body and knock the last remnant of strength from his legs. But in falling he seemed for a moment to rise, for as his hind legs collapsed beneath him he seemed to tower upward like a huge rock toppling, his trunk reaching skywards like a tree. He trumpeted, for the first and only time. And then down he came, his belly towards me, with a crash that seemed to shake the ground even where I lay.

I got up. The Burmans were already racing past me across the mud. It was obvious that the elephant would never rise again, but he was not dead. He was breathing very rhythmically with long rattling gasps, his great mound of a side painfully rising and falling. His mouth was wide open—I could see far down into caverns of pale pink throat. I waited a long time for him to die, but his breathing did not weaken. Finally I fired my two remaining shots into the spot where I thought his heart must be. The thick blood welled out of him like red velvet, but still he did not die. His body did not even jerk when the shots hit him, the tortured breathing continued without a pause. He was dying, very slowly and in great agony, but in some world remote from me where not even a bullet could damage him further. I felt that I had got to put an end to that dreadful noise. It seemed dreadful to see the great beast lying there, powerless to move and yet powerless to die, and not even to be able to finish him. I sent back for my small rifle and poured shot after shot into his heart and down his throat. They seemed to make no impression. The tortured gasps continued as steadily as the ticking of a clock.

In the end I could not stand it any longer and went away. I heard later that it took him half an hour to die. Burmans were bringing dahs[4] and baskets even before I left, and I was told they had stripped his body almost to the bones by the afternoon.

Afterwards, of course, there were endless discussions about the shooting of the elephant. The owner was furious, but he was only an Indian and could do nothing. Besides, legally I had done the right thing, for a mad elephant has to be killed, like a mad dog, if its owner fails to control it. Among the Europeans opinion was divided. The older men said I was right, the younger men said it was a damn shame to shoot an elephant for killing a coolie, because an elephant was worth more than any damn Coringhee coolie. And afterwards I was very glad that the coolie had been killed; it put me legally in the right and it gave me a sufficient pretext for shooting the elephant. I often wondered whether any of the others grasped that I had done it solely to avoid looking a fool.

CONVERSATION STARTER

Discuss how you felt during a time when you worked for an institution whose values were different from your own.

---

[4]butcher knives

Reading Matters

1. How does Orwell feel about British Imperialism and his job as a police officer in Burma before he shoots the escaped elephant?
2. Why does Orwell present such a detailed narrative of the incident of shooting the elephant? How does it affect your understanding and evaluation of the incident's meaning and impact?
3. How is Orwell's attitude toward his job and himself changed because he does shoot the elephant? Why does Orwell shoot the elephant?
4. How do the Burmese feel about the British? How do the British Imperialists feel about their role in Burma? What has Orwell learned about "the real nature of imperialism—the real motives for which despotic governments act"?

Writing Matters

1. Orwell felt personal, political, and circumstantial pressures to shoot the elephant. Write an essay that explains why you think he finally did it. Do you think he believed that he made the right decision? Do you think that he made the best decision? What did Orwell learn from his ordeal?
2. Write an essay that explores a work situation that forced you to rethink and reevaluate your own values. What did you learn from the situation? Did you change? How and why?
3. Write an essay that discusses several reasons why this essay is relevant today. How can you apply the lessons that Orwell learned to situations in your own life or in world politics?

Relevant Web Sites

The George Orwell Archive
<http://www.ucl.ac.uk/Library/special-coll/orwell.htm>

This web site from the University College London features the most comprehensive body of research materials relating to the author George Orwell. The archive includes all of Orwell's printed works, including newspaper items, private correspondence, and other private papers in the possession of his widow.

George Orwell <http://www.arlindo-correia.com/101103.html>

This web site provides biographical information as well as links to essays written about the literary and political legacy of George Orwell.

Maya Angelou (b. 1928)

On the Street Cars

Maya Angelou has received critical acclaim for her autobiographical works that chronicle the life of a contemporary woman struggling with chaos and strife. Angelou documents the quest for her identity as a black woman in America and the evolution of her social conscience by relating her personal experiences to the community. Her experience includes working as a dancer, actress, teacher, and screenwriter. Angelou has lectured all over the world, speaking as an advocate of civil rights. Her recent books include Wouldn't Take Nothing for My Journey Now *(1993),* The Complete Collected Poems of Maya Angelou *(1994),* The Challenge of Creative Leadership *(1996), and* A Song Flung to Heaven *(2003). Angelou has earned many scholarships, grants, fellowships, professorships, and honorary degrees. In 1982, she began teaching at Wake Forest University in Winston-Salem, North Carolina, as a professor of American studies.*

In the following selection excerpted from the first book of her memoir, I Know Why the Caged Bird Sings *(1970), Angelou describes the struggle she went through, while still a high school student, to be hired as the first Negro woman to work on the San Francisco trolleys.*

My room had all the cheeriness of a dungeon and the appeal of a tomb. It was going to be impossible to stay there, but leaving held not attraction for me, either. Running away from home would be anti-climactic. But the need for change bull-dozed a road down the center of my mind.

I had it. The answer came to me with the suddenness of a collision. I would go to work. Mother wouldn't be difficult to convince; after all, in school I was a year ahead of my grade and Mother was a firm believer in self-sufficiency. In fact, she'd be pleased to think that I had that much gumption, that much of her in my character. (She liked to speak of herself as the original "do-it-yourself girl.")

Once I had settled on getting a job, all that remained was to decide which kind of job I was most fitted for. My intellectual pride had kept me from selecting typing, shorthand or filing as subjects in school, so office work was ruled out. War plants and shipyards demanded birth certificates, and mine would reveal me to be fifteen, and ineligible for work. So the well-paying defense jobs were also out. Women had replaced men on the streetcars as conductors and motormen, and the thought of sailing up and down the hills of San Francisco in a dark-blue uniform, with a money changer at my belt, caught my fancy.

Mother was as easy as I had anticipated. The world was moving so fast, so much money was being made, so many people were dying in Guam, and Germany, that hordes of strangers become good friends overnight. Life was cheap and death entirely free. How could she have the time to think about my academic career?

5   To her question of what I planned to do, I replied that I would get a job on the streetcars. She rejected the proposal with" "They don't accept colored people on the streetcars."

I would like to claim an immediate fury which was followed by the noble determination to break the restricting tradition. But the truth is, my first reaction was one of disappointment. I'd pictured myself, dressed in a neat blue serge suit, my money changer swinging jauntily at my waist, and a cheery smile for the passengers which would make their own work day brighter.

From disappointment, I gradually ascended the emotional ladder to haughty indignation, and finally to that state of stubbornness where the mind is locked like the jaws of the enlarged building.

I would go to work on the streetcars and wear a blue serge suit. Mother gave me her support with one of her usual terse asides, "That's what you want to do? Then nothing beats a trial but failure. Give it everything you've got. I've told you many times, 'Can't do is like Don't Care.' Neither of them have a home."

Translated, that meant there was nothing a person can't do, and there should be nothing a human being didn't care about. It was the most positive encouragement I could have hoped for.

10   In the offices of the Market Street Railway Company, the receptionist seemed as surprised to see me there as I was surprised to find the interior dingy and the décor drab. Somehow I had expected waxed surfaces and carpeted floors. If I had met no resistance, I might have decided against working for such a poor-mouth-looking concern. As it was, I explained that I had come to see about a job. She asked, was I sent by an agency, and when I replied that I was not, she told me they were only accepting applicants from agencies.

The classified pages of the morning papers had listed advertisements for motorettes and conductorettes and I reminded her of that. She gave me a face full of astonishment that my suspicious nature would not accept.

"I am applying for the job listed in this morning's *Chronicle* and I'd like to be presented to your personnel manager." While I spoke in supercilious accents, and looked at the room as if I had an oil well in my own backyard, my armpits were being pricked by millions of hot pointed needles. She saw her escape and dived into it.

"He's out. He's out for the day. You might call tomorrow and if he's in, I'm sure you can see him." Then she swiveled her chair around on its rusty screws and with that I was supposed to be dismissed.

"May I ask his name?"

15   She half turned, acting surprised to find me still there.

"His name? Whose name?"

"Your personnel manager."

We were firmly joined in the hypocrisy to play out the scene.

"The personnel manager? Oh, he's Mr. Cooper, but I'm not sure you'll find him here tomorrow. He's . . . Oh, but you can try."

20   "Thank you."

"You're welcome."

And I was out the of the musty room and into the even mustier lobby. In the street I saw the receptionist and myself going faithfully through paces that were stale with familiarity, although I had never encountered that kind of situation before and, probably, neither had she. We were like actors who, knowing the play by heart, were still able to cry afresh over the old tragedies and laugh spontaneously at the comic situations.

The miserable little encounter had nothing to do with me, the me of me, any more than it had to do with that silly clerk. The incident was a recurring dream, concocted years before by stupid whites and it eternally came back to haunt us all. The secretary and I were like Hamlet and Laertes in the final scene, where, because of harm done by one ancestor to another, we were bound to duel to the death. Also because the play must end somewhere.

I went further than forgiving the clerk, I accepted her as a fellow victim of the same puppeteer.

25   On the streetcar, I put my fare into the box and the conductorette looked at me with the usual hard eyes of white contempt. "Move into the car, please move on in the car." She patted her money changer.

Her Southern nasal accent sliced my meditation and I looked deep into my thoughts. All lies, all comfortable lies. The receptionist was not innocent and neither was I. The whole charade we had played out in that crummy waiting room had directly to do with me, Black, and her, white.

I wouldn't move into the streetcar but stood on the ledge over the conductor, glaring. My mind shouted so energetically that the announcement made my veins stand out, and my mouth tighten into a prune.

I WOULD HAVE THE JOB. I WOULD BE A CONDUCTORETTE AND SLING A FULL MONEY CHANGER FROM MY BELT. I WOULD.

The next three weeks were a honeycomb of determination with apertures for the days to go in and out. The Negro organizations to whom I appealed for support bounced me back and forth like a shuttlecock on a badminton court. Why did I insist on that particular job? Openings were going begging that paid nearly twice the money. The minor officials with whom I was able to win an audience thought me mad. Possibly I was.

30   Downtown San Francisco became alien and cold, and the streets I had loved in personal familiarity were unknown lanes that twisted with malicious intent. Old buildings, whose gray rococo façades housed my memories of the Forty-Niners, and Diamond Lil, Robert Service, Sutter and Jack London, were then imposing structures viciously joined to keep me out. My trips to the streetcar office were of the frequency of a person on salary. The struggle expanded. I was not longer in conflict only with the Market Street Railway but with the marble lobby of the building which housed its offices, and elevators and their operators.

During this period of strain Mother and I began our first steps on the long path toward adult admiration. She never asked for reports and I didn't offer any details. But every morning she made breakfast, gave me carfare and lunch money, as if I were going to work. She comprehended the perversity of life, that in the struggle lies the joy. That I was no glory seeker was obvious to her, and that I had to exhaust every possibility before giving in was also clear.

On my way out of the house one morning she said, "Life is going to give you just what you put in it. Put your whole heart in everything you do, and pray, then you can wait." Another time she reminded me that "God helps those who help themselves." She had a store of aphorisms which she dished out as the occasion demanded. Strangely, as bored as I was with clichés, her inflection gave them something new, and set me thinking for a little while at least. Later when asked how I got my job, I was never able to say exactly. I only knew that one day, which was tiresomely like all the others before it, I sat in the Railway office, ostensibly waiting to be interviewed. The receptionist called me to her desk and shuffled a bundle of papers to me. They were job application forms. She said they had to be filled in triplicate. I had little time to wonder if I had won or not, for the standard questions reminded me of the necessity for dexterous lying. How old was I? List my previous jobs, starting from the last held and go backward to the first. How much money did I earn, and why did I leave the position? Give two references (not relatives).

Sitting at a side table my mind and I wove a cat's ladder of near truths and total lies. I kept my face blank (an old art) and wrote quickly the fable of Marguerite Johnson, aged nineteen, former companion and driver for Mrs. Annie Henderson (a White Lady) in Stamps, Arkansas.

I was given blood tests, aptitude tests, physical coordination tests, and Rorschachs, then on a blissful day I was hired as the first Negro on the San Francisco streetcars.

35   Mother gave me the money to have my blue serge suit tailored, and I learned to fill out work cards, operate the money changer and punch transfers. The time crowded together and at an End of Days I was swinging on the back of the rackety trolley, smiling sweetly and persuading my charges to "step forward in the car, please."

For one whole semester the streetcars and I shimmied up and scooted down the sheer hills of San Francisco. I lost some of my need for the Black ghetto's shielding-sponge quality, as I clanged and cleared my way down Market Street, with its honky-tonk homes for homeless sailors, past the quiet retreat of Golden Gate Park and along closed undwelled-in-looking dwellings of the Sunset District.

My work shifts were split so haphazardly that it was easy to believe that my superiors had chosen them maliciously. Upon mentioning my suspicions to Mother, she said, "Don't worry about it. You ask them for what you want, and you pay for what you get. And I'm going to show you that it ain't no trouble when you pack double."

She stayed awake to drive me out to the car barn at four thirty in the mornings, or to pick me up when I was relieved just before dawn. Her awareness of life's perils convinced her that while I would be safe on the public conveyances, she "wasn't about to trust a taxi driver with her baby."

When the spring classes began, I resumed my commitment with formal education. I was so much wiser and older, so much more independent, with a bank account and clothes that I had bought for myself, that I was sure that

I had learned and earned the magic formula which would make me a part of the gay life my contemporaries led.

40 Not a bit of it. Within weeks, I realized that my schoolmates and I were on paths moving diametrically away from each other. They were concerned and excited over the approaching football games, but I had in my immediate past raced a car down a dark and foreign Mexican mountain. They concentrated great interest on who was worthy of being student body president, and when the metal bands would be removed from their teeth, while I remembered sleeping for a month in a wrecked automobile and conducting a streetcar in the uneven hours of the morning.

Without willing it, I had gone from being ignorant of being ignorant to being aware of being aware. [And the worst part of my awareness was that I didn't know what I was aware of.] I knew I knew very little, but I was certain that the things I had yet to learn wouldn't be taught to me at George Washington High School.

I began to cut classes, to walk in Golden Gate Park or wander along the shiny counter of the Emporium Department Store. When Mother discovered that I was playing truant, she told me that if I didn't want to go to school one day, if there were not tests being held, and if my school work was up to standard, all I had to do was tell her and I could stay home. She said that she didn't want some white woman calling her up to tell her something about her child that she didn't know. And she didn't want to be put in the position of lying to a white woman because I wasn't woman enough to speak up. That put an end to my truancy, but nothing appeared to lighten the long gloomy day that going to school became.

[To be left alone on the tightrope of youthful unknowing is to experience the excruciating beauty of full freedom and the threat of eternal indecision.] Few, if any, survive their teens. Most surrender to the vague but murderous pressure of adult conformity. It becomes easier to die and avoid conflicts than to maintain a constant battle with the superior forces of maturity.

Until recently each generation found it more expedient to plead guilty to the charge of being young and ignorant, easier to take the punishment meted out by the older generation (which had itself confessed to the same crime short years before). The command to grow up at once was more bearable than the faceless horror of wavering purpose, which was youth.

45 The bright hours when the young rebelled against the descending sun had to give way to twenty-four-hour periods called "days" that were named as well as numbered.

The Black female is assaulted in her tender years by all those common forces of nature at the same time that she is caught in the tripartite crossfire of masculine prejudice, white illogical hate and Black lack of power.

The fact that the adult American Negro female emerges a formidable character is often met with amazement, distaste and even belligerence. It is seldom accepted as an inevitable outcome of the struggle won by survivors and deserves respect if not enthusiastic acceptance.

CONVERSATION STARTER

Share an experience you had overcoming hiring discrimination because of your youth, gender, physical characteristics, ethnic background, or other traits unrelated to your skills and qualifications for the position.

READING MATTERS

1. Why does Maya Angelou decide that she wants to be a streetcar conductor? How and why does she finally succeed?
2. Discuss the scene between Maya Angelou and the secretary at the Railway Company. Why does Angelou say that the encounter "had nothing to do with me"? Why does she compare herself and the secretary to Hamlet and Laertes?
3. How does Angelou's mother feel about her daughter's new job? How does she help to protect Maya?
4. Angelou concludes her essay by referring to "the struggle won by survivors" through which the "American Negro female emerges a formidable character." How do Angelou's work experiences illustrate and clarify the social factors that helped to create her own "formidable character"?

WRITING MATTERS

1. Develop your Conversation Starter discussion into an essay that explores what you have learned from living through work-related situations when you were discriminated against, humiliated, or rejected unjustly.
2. Write an essay in which you argue for or against affirmative action legislation in the job market. Research the topic and include observations and opinions that you have developed at your own job or through learning about your parents' and friends' working lives.
3. Write an essay that explores the similarities and differences in Orwell's and Angelou's attitudes toward work.

RELEVANT WEB SITES

MAYA ANGELOU LINKS AND RESOURCES
<http://ucaswww.mej.uc.edu/ worldfest/about.html>

This site provides biographical information and photographs of Maya Angelou and offers a forum for discussing her work.

MAYA ANGELOU <http://www.empirezine.com/spotlight/maya/maya1.htm>

This web site displays pictures, relevant links, and biographical information on Maya Angelou. It also features excerpts from her books and poetry and has a special forum for discussion.

WOMEN WRITERS OF COLOR
<http://www.voices.cla.umn.edu/wwwsites.html>

Entitled "Voices from the Gaps," this web site shares information on and work by African-American writers as well as Asian-American, Arab-American, Latin-American, and Native-American authors.

Ellen Ullman (b. 1949)

Getting Close to the Machine

Ellen Ullman was born and raised in New York City, where her father owned a business and commercial real estate. She currently lives in San Francisco, where she has been a software engineer, computer programmer, and consultant since 1978. Ullman has written programming and software-related articles for publications such as Byte Magazine, PC World, *and* Datamation. *In 1995 an article she wrote for* Harper's, *"Getting Close to the Machine," led to a book-length work entitled* Close to the Machine *(1997), a personal examination of the lifestyle and work habits of young people intimately involved in the world of creative programming. More recently she has published a novel,* The Bug *(2003). In the following essay, "Getting Close to the Machine," Ullman examines the obsessive communication and thinking styles of those whose demanding technical work takes them "close to the machine"—but a long way from ordinary people.*

I have no idea what time it is. There are no windows in this office and no clock, only the blinking red LED display of a microwave, which flashes 12:00, 12:00, 12:00, 12:00. Joel and I have been programming for days. We have a bug, a stubborn demon of a bug. So the red pulse no-time feels right, like a read-out of our brains, which have somehow synchronized themselves at the same blink rate.

"But what if they select all the text and—"

"—hit Delete."

"Damn! The NULL case!"

5 "And if not we're out of the text field and they hit space—"

"—yeah, like for—"

"—no parameter—"

"Hell!"

"So what if we space-pad?"

10 "I don't know. . . . Wait a minute!"

"Yeah, we could space-pad—"

"—and do space as numeric."

"Yes! We'll call SendKey(space) to—?"

"—the numeric object."

15 "My God! That fixes it!"

"Yeah! That'll work if—"

"—space is numeric!"

"—if space is numeric!"

We lock eyes. We barely breathe. For a slim moment, we are together in a universe where two human beings can simultaneously understand the statement "if space is numeric!"

20   Joel and I started this round of debugging on Friday morning. Sometime later, maybe Friday night, another programmer, Danny, came to work. I suppose it must be Sunday by now because it's been a while since we've seen my client's employees around the office. Along the way, at odd times of day or night that have completely escaped us, we've ordered in three meals of Chinese food, eaten six large pizzas, consumed several beers, had innumerable bottles of fizzy water, and finished two entire bottles of wine. It has occurred to me that if people really knew how software got written, I'm not sure if they'd give their money to a bank or get on an airplane ever again.

What are we working on? An artificial intelligence project to find "subversive" talk over international phone lines? Software for the second start-up of a Silicon Valley executive banished from his first company? A system to help AIDS patients get services across a city? The details escape me just now. We may be helping poor sick people or tuning a set of low-level routines to verify bits on a distributed database protocol—I don't care. I should care; in another part of my being—later, perhaps when we emerge from this room full of computers—I will care very much why and for whom and for what purpose I am writing software. But just now: no. I have passed through a membrane where the real world and its uses no longer matter. I am a software engineer, an independent contractor working for a department of a city government. I've hired Joel and three other programmers to work with me. Down the hall is Danny, a slim guy in wire-rimmed glasses who comes to work with a big, wire-haired dog. Across the bay in his converted backyard shed is Mark, who works on the database. Somewhere, probably asleep by now, is Bill, the network guy. Right now, there are only two things in the universe that matter to us. One, we have some bad bugs to fix. Two, we're supposed to install the system on Monday, which I think is tomorrow.

"Oh, no, no!" moans Joel, who is slumped over his keyboard. "No-o-o-o." It comes out in a long wail. It has the sound of lost love, lifetime regret. We've both been programmers long enough to know that we are at *that place.* If we find one more serious problem we can't solve right away, we will not make it. We won't install. We'll go the terrible, familiar way of all software: we'll be late.

"No, no, no, no. What if the members of the set start with spaces. Oh, God. It won't work."

He is as near to naked despair as has ever been shown to me by anyone not in a film. Here, in *that place,* we have no shame. He has seen me sleeping on the floor, drooling. We have both seen Danny's puffy white midsection— young as he is, it's a pity—when he stripped to his underwear in the heat of the machine room. I have seen Joel's dandruff, light coating of cat fur on his clothes, noticed things about his body I should not. And I'm sure he's seen my sticky hair, noticed how dull I look without make-up, caught sight of other details too intimate to mention. Still, none of this matters anymore. Our bodies were abandoned long ago, reduced to hunger and sleeplessness and the ravages of sitting for hours at a keyboard and a mouse. Our physical selves have been battered away. Now we know each other in one way and one way only: the code.

25   Besides, I know I can now give him pleasure of an order which is rare in my life: I am about to save him from despair.

"No problem," I say evenly. I put my hand on his shoulder, intending a gesture of reassurance. "The parameters *never* start with a space." It is just as I hoped. His despair vanishes. He becomes electric, turns to the keyboard and begins to type at a rapid speed. Now he is gone from me. He is disappearing into the code—now that he knows it will work, now that I have reassured him that, in our universe, the one we created together, space can indeed be forever and reliably numeric.

The connection, the shared thought-stream, is cut. It has all the frustration of being abandoned by a lover just before climax. I know this is not a physical love. He is too young, he works for me; he's a man and I've been tending toward women; in any case, he's too prim and business-schooled for my tastes. I know this sensation is not *real* attraction: it is only the spillover, the excess charge, of the mind back into the abandoned body. *Only*. Ha. This is another real-world thing that does not matter. My entire self wants to melt into this brilliant, electric being who had shared his mind with me for twenty seconds.

Restless, I go into the next room where Danny is slouched at his keyboard. The big, wire-haired dog growls at me. Danny looks up, scowls like his dog, then goes back to typing. I am the designer of this system, his boss on this project. But he's not even trying to hide his contempt. Normal programmer, I think. He has fifteen windows full of code open on his desktop. He has overpopulated his eyes, thoughts, imagination. He is drowning in bugs and I know I could help him, but he wants me dead just at the moment. I am the last-straw irritant.

Talking: Shit! What the hell is wrong with me? Why would I want to *talk* to him? Can't I see that his stack is overflowing?

30   "Joel may have the overlapping controls working" I say.

"Oh, yeah?" He doesn't look up.

"He's been using me as a programming dummy," I say. "Do you want to talk me through the navigation errors?" Navigation errors: bad. You click to go somewhere but get somewhere else. Very, very bad.

"What?" He pretends not to hear me.

"Navigation errors. How are they?"

35   "I'm working on them." Huge, hateful scowl. Contempt that one human being should not express to another under any circumstances. Hostility that should kill me, if I were not used to it, familiar with it, practiced in receiving it. Besides, we are at *that place*. I know that this hateful programmer is all I have between me and the navigation bug. "I'll come back later," I say.

Later: how much later can it get? Daylight can't be far off now. This small shoal of pre-installation madness is washing away even as I wander back down the hall to Joel.

"Yes! It's working!" says Joel, hearing my approach.

He looks up at me. "You were right," he says. The ultimate one programmer can say to another, the accolade given so rarely as to be almost unknown in our species. He looks right at me as he says it: "You were right. As always."

This is beyond rare. *Right:* the thing a programmer desires above, beyond all. *As always:* unspeakable, incalculable gift.

40 "I could not have been right without you," I say. This is true beyond question. "I only opened the door. You figured out how to go through."

I immediately see a certain perfume advertisement: a man holding a violin embraces a woman at a piano. I want to be that ad. I want efficacies of reality to vanish, and I want to be the man with the violin, my programmer to be the woman at the piano. As in the ad, I want the teacher to interrupt the lesson and embrace the student. I want the rules to be broken. Tabu. That is the name of the perfume. I want to do what is taboo. I am the boss, the senior, the employer, the person in charge. So I must not touch him. It is all taboo. Still—

Danny appears in the doorway.

"The navigation bug is fixed. I'm going home."

"I'll test it—"

45 "It's fixed."

He leaves.

It is sometime in the early morning. Joel and I are not sure if the night guard is still on duty. If we leave, we may not get back up the elevator. We leave anyway.

We find ourselves on the street in a light drizzle. He has on a raincoat, one that he usually wears over his too-prim, too-straight, good-biz-school suits. I have on a second-hand-store leather bomber jacket, black beret, boots. Someone walking by might wonder what we were doing together at this still-dark hour of the morning.

"Goodnight," I say. We're still charged with thought energy. I don't dare extend my hand to shake his.

50 "Goodnight," he says.

We stand awkwardly for two beats more. "This will sound strange," he says, "but I hope I don't see you tomorrow."

We stare at each other, still drifting in the wake of our shared mindstream. I know exactly what he means. We will only see each other tomorrow if I find a really bad bug.

"Not strange at all," I say, "I hope I don't see you, either."

I don't see him. The next day, I find a few minor bugs, fix them, and decide the software is good enough. Mind-meld fantasies recede as the system goes live. We install the beginnings of a city-wide registration system for AIDS patients. Instead of carrying around soiled and wrinkled eligibility documents, AIDS clients only have to prove once that they are really sick and really poor. It is an odd system, if I think of it, certifying that people are truly desperate in the face of possible death. Still, this time I'm working on a "good" project, I tell myself. We are *helping* people, say the programmers over and over, nearly in disbelief at their good fortune. Three programmers, the network guy, me—fifty-eight years of collective technical experience—and the idea of helping people with a computer is a first for any of us.

55   Yet I am continually anxious. How do we protect this database full of the names of people with AIDS? Is a million-dollar computer system the best use of continually shrinking funds? It was easier when I didn't have to think about the real-world effect of my work. It was easier—and I got paid more—when I was writing an "abstracted interface to any arbitrary input device." When I was designing a "user interface paradigm," defining a "test-bed methodology." I could disappear into weird passions of logic. I could stay in a world peopled entirely by programmers, other weird logic-dreamers like myself, all caught up in our own inner electricities. It was easier and more valued. In my profession, software engineering, there is something almost shameful in this helpful, social-services system we're building. The whole project smacks of "end users"—those contemptible, oblivious people who just want to use the stuff we write and don't care how we did it.

    "What are you working on?" asked an acquaintance I ran into at a book signing. She's a woman with her own start-up company. Her offices used to be in the loft just below mine, two blocks from South Park, in San Francisco's Multimedia Gulch. She is tall and strikingly attractive; she wears hip, fashionable clothes; her company already has its first million in venture-capital funding. "What are you working on," she wanted to know, "I mean, that isn't under non-D?"

    Under non-D. Nondisclosure. That's the cool thing to be doing: working on a system so new, so just started-up, that you can't talk about it under pain of lawsuit.

    "Oh, not much," I answered, trying to sound breezy. A city-wide network for AIDS service providers: how unhip could I get? If I wanted to do something for people with AIDS, I should make my first ten million in stock options, then attend some fancy party where I wear a red ribbon on my chest. I should be a sponsor for Digital Queers. But actually working on a project for end users? Where my client is a government agency? In the libertarian world of computing, where "creating wealth" is all, I am worse than uncool: I am aiding and abetting the bureaucracy, I am a net consumer of federal taxes—I'm what's wrong with this country.

    "Oh, I'm basically just plugging in other people's software these days. Not much engineering. You know," I waved vaguely, "*plumbing* mostly."

60   My vagueness paid off. The woman winked at me. "Networks," she said.

    "Yeah. Something like that," I said. I was disgusted with myself, but, when she walked away, I was relieved.

    The end users I was so ashamed of came late in the system development process. I didn't meet them until the software was half-written. This is not how these things are supposed to go—the system is not supposed to predate the people who will use it—but it often goes that way anyhow.

The project was eight months old when my client-contact, a project manager in a city department, a business-like woman of fifty, finally set up a meeting. Representatives of several social-service agencies were invited; eight came. A printed agenda was handed around the conference table. The first item was "Review agenda." My programmer-mind whirred at the implication of endless reiteration: Agenda. Review agenda. Agenda. Forever.

"Who dreamed up this stuff?" asked a woman who directed a hospice and home-care agency. "This is all useless!" We had finally come to item four on the agenda: "Review System Specifications." The hospice director waved a big stack of paper—the specifications arrived at by a "task force"—then tossed it across the table. A heavy-set woman apparently of Middle-Eastern descent, she had probably smoked a very large number of cigarettes in the course of her fifty-odd years on earth. Her laugh trailed off into a chesty rumble, which she used as a kind of drum roll to finish off her scorn.

65   The other users were no more impressed. A black woman who ran a shelter—elegant, trailing Kente cloth. She arranged her acres of fabric as some sort of displacement for her boredom; each time I started talking, I seemed to have to speak over a high jangle of her many bracelets set to play as she, ignoring me with something that was not quite hostility, arranged and rearranged herself. A woman who ran a clinic for lesbians, a self-described "femme" with hennaed hair and red fingernails: "Why didn't someone come talk to us first?" she asked. A good question. My client sat shamefaced. A young, handsome black man, assistant to the hospice director, quick and smart: he simply shook his head and kept a skeptical smile on his face. Finally a dentist and a doctor, two white males who looked pale and watery in this sea of diversity: they worried that the system would get in the way of giving services. And around the table they went, complaint by complaint.

I started to panic. Before this meeting, the users existed only in my mind, projections, all mine. They were abstractions, the initiators of tasks that set off remote procedure calls; triggers to a set of logical and machine events that ended in an update to a relational database on a central server. Now I was confronted with their fleshly existence. And now I had to think about the actual existence of the people who used the services delivered by the users' agencies, sick people who were no fools, who would do what they needed to do to get pills, food vouchers, a place to sleep.

I wished, earnestly, I could just replace the abstractions with the actual people. But it was already too late for that. The system pre-existed the people. Screens were prototyped. Data elements were defined. The machine events already had more reality, had been with me longer, than the human beings at the conference table. Immediately, I saw it was a problem not of replacing one reality with another but of two realities. I was there at the edge: the interface of the system, in all its existence, to the people, in all their existence.

I talked, asked questions, but I saw I was operating at a different speed from the people at the table. Notch down, I told myself. *Notch down.* The users were bright, all too sensitive to each other's feelings. Anyone who was the slightest bit cut off was gotten back to sweetly: "You were saying?" Their courtesy was structural, built into their "process." I had to keep my hand over my mouth to keep from jumping in. Notch down, I told myself again. *Slow down.* But it was not working. My brain whirred out a stream of logic-speak: "The agency sees the client records if and only if there is a relationship defined between the agency and the client," I heard myself saying. "By definition, as soon as the client receives services from the agency, the system considers the client to have a relationship with the provider. An internal index is created which represents the relationship." The hospice director closed her eyes to concentrate. She would have smoked if she could have; she looked at me as if through something she had just exhaled.

I took notes, pages of revisions that had to be done immediately or else doom the system to instant disuse. The system had no life without the user, I saw. I'd like to say that I was instantly converted to the notion of real human need, to the impact I would have on the working lives of these people at the table, on the people living with AIDS; I'd like to claim a sudden sense of real-world responsibility. But that would be lying. What I really thought was this: I must save the system.

70   I ran off to call the programmers. Living in my hugely different world from the sick patients, the forbearing service providers, the earnest and caring users at the meeting, I didn't wait to find a regular phone. I went into the next room, took out my cell phone, began punching numbers into it, and hit the "send" button: "We have to talk," I said.

By the time I saw Joel, Danny, and Mark, I had reduced the users' objections to a set of five system changes. I would like to use the word "reduce" like a cook: something boiled down to its essence. But I was aware that the real human essence was already absent from the list I'd prepared. An item like "How will we know if the clients have TB?"—the fear of sitting in a small, poorly ventilated room with someone who has medication-resistant TB, the normal and complicated biological urgency of that question— became a list of data elements to be added to the screens and the database. I tried to communicate some of the sense of the meeting to the programmers. They were interested, but in a mild, backgrounded way. Immediately, they seized the list of changes and, as I watched, they turned them into further abstractions.

"We can add a parameter to the remote procedure call."

"We should check the referential integrity on that."

"Should the code be attached to that control or should it be in global scope?"

75   "Global, because this other object here needs to know about the condition."

"No! No globals. We agreed. No more globals!"

We have entered the code zone. Here thought is telegraphic and exquisitely precise. I feel no need to slow myself down. On the contrary, the faster the better. Joel runs off a stream of detail, and halfway through a sentence, Mark, the database programmer, completes the thought. I mention a screen element, and Danny, who programs the desktop software, thinks of two elements I've forgotten. Mark will later say all bugs are Danny's fault, but, for now, they work together like cheerful little parallel-processing machines, breaking the problem into pieces that they attack simultaneously. Danny will later become the angry programmer scowling at me from behind his broken code, but now he is still a jovial guy with wire-rimmed glasses and a dog that accompanies him everywhere. "Neato," he says to something Mark has proposed, grinning, patting the dog, happy as a clam.

"Should we modify the call to AddUser—"

"—to check for UserType—"

80   "Or should we add a new procedure call—"

"—something like ModifyPermissions."

"But won't that add a new set of data elements that repeat—"

"Yeah, a repeating set—"

"—which we'll have to—"

85   "—renormalize!"

Procedure calls. Relational database normalization. Objects going in and out of scope. Though my mind is racing, I feel calm. It's the spacey calm of satellites speeding over the earth at a thousand miles per second: relative to each other, we float. The images of patients with AIDS recede, the beleaguered service providers are forgotten, the whole grim reality of the epidemic fades. We give ourselves over to the sheer fun of the technical, to the nearly sexual pleasure of the clicking thought-stream.

Some part of me mourns, but I know there is no other way: human needs must cross the line into code. They must pass through this semipermeable membrane where urgency, fear, and hope are filtered out, and only reason travels across. There is no other way. Real, death-inducing viruses do not travel here. Actual human confusions cannot live here. Everything we want accomplished, everything the system is to provide, must be denatured in its crossing to the machine, or else the system will die.

CONVERSATION STARTER

Discuss an experience that you had working with technology when you lost a sense of perspective in the process of creating a program or searching for information. Do you think that one's health and social life can be seriously affected by such activities?

READING MATTERS

1. Why does programming require such intense concentration? Can you think of other activities that require similarly strict and focused concentration?

2. Describe the culture of the programmers. Why does the programmer separate the act of programming from the purpose of the project? What does this tell us about the programmers' attitudes about information?

3. How does the programmers' culture differ from that of the social service agencies? Contrast the values of the programmers and the social service agency.
4. How does Ullman distinguish between low code, high code, and applications? Why does a real programmer want to stay "close to the machine"? How does Ullman contrast computer code language and everyday human language?

WRITING MATTERS

1. Ullman writes, "The system pre-existed the people. Screens were prototyped. Data elements were defined. The machine events already had more reality, had been with me longer, than the human beings at the conference table. Immediately, I saw it was a problem not of replacing one reality with another but of two realities." Write an essay that explains how the programmer tries to resolve this conflict. What are the implications of this conflict for the community and specifically for the users of the software?
2. Write about an experience in which you collaborated on a project. Describe how you felt about working with another person. What impact did the collaboration have on the quality of the final project? Did the process of working collaboratively clarify or change how you see yourself? How?
3. Write an essay that discusses the impact of computers and programmers on the workplace. You can do research into this issue and/or write from your own experiences at work.

RELEVANT WEB SITES

THE NEW WORKPLACE: THE CHANGING NATURE OF WORK, ORGANIZATIONS AND BUSINESS IN THE INFORMATION ECONOMY
<http://www.afsmi.org/journal/sep97/sep-002.htm>

This site provides information and resources on the changing nature of work in the information economy.

WOMEN'S WIRE.COM <http://www.womenswire.com>

This web site provides advice to working women about money, work, and reports on current events, politics, culture, and technology.

Revealing the Economic Divide

Eric Schlosser (b. 1941)

In the Strawberry Fields

Eric Schlosser is an investigative journalist currently working for the Atlantic Monthly. *He won the National Magazine Award for reporting in 1994 for a series of articles in the* Atlantic *about the marijuana enforcement laws, and also received the Sidney Hillman Foundation award in 1995 for his reportage on California's strawberry industry. His first book,* Fast Food Nation *(2000), is an exposé of the impact of the fast food industry on public health in the United States and abroad. He is currently working on an expanded version of an article he wrote for the* Atlantic *entitled "The Prison Industrial Complex." The following selection is from his latest book,* Reefer Madness: Sex, Drugs and Cheap Labor in the American Black Market *(2003).*

One morning in San Diego County, I met a strawberry grower named Doug. We sat and talked in a trailer on the edge of his field. Doug's father and his grandfather had both been sent to an internment camp for Japanese Americans during World War II. Upon their release, the grandfather bought a used truck. At first he worked for other farmers, then he leased some land. He spoke no English and so Doug's father, still a teenager, assumed an important role in the business. The two grew vegetables with success and eventually shifted to strawberries, shipping and processing the fruit as well. On the land where their original farm once stood, there are now condominiums, a park, and a school. Doug grows strawberries a few miles inland. His fields are surrounded by chain-link fences topped with barbed wire. An enormous real estate development, with hundreds of Spanish-style condo units, is creeping up the hills toward his farm. Many of the farmers nearby have already sold their land. Doug has spent most of his life in strawberry fields, learning every aspect of the business firsthand, but now isn't sure he wants his children to do the same.

"Farming's not a glamorous business," Doug said. "Farmers don't have a high status in this community. In fact, we're resented by most people." With all the hassles today from the state and from his neighbors, he sometimes asks himself, "Hey, why do this?" Selling the land would make him instantly rich. Instead, he worries about water costs, about theft, about the strawberries from New Zealand he saw in the market the other day. Rain had wiped out a quarter of his early-season berries, just when the market price was at its peak. Doug cannot understand the hostility toward growers in California. After all, agriculture preserves open land. He thinks Americans don't appreciate how lucky they are to have cheap food. He doesn't understand why anyone would impede strawberry production by limiting his access to migrants. "My workers are helping themselves," he said. "I've picked strawberries, and let me tell you, there is no harder work. I respect these people. They work damn hard. And my jobs are open to anyone who wants to apply." Every so often college kids visit the ranch, convinced that picking strawberries would be a nice way to earn some extra money. Doug laughed. "They don't last an hour out here."

We stepped from the trailer into bright sunshine. Workers moved down the furrows under close supervision. Doug takes great pride in being a third-generation grower. He is smart, well educated, meticulous, and it showed in his field. But I wondered if Doug and his workers would still be there in a few years.

Doug picked a berry and handed it to me, a large Chandler that was brilliantly red. I took a bite. The strawberry was warm and sweet and fragrant, with a slightly bitter aftertaste from the soil.

5   That evening I inadvertently met some of Doug's workers. Ricardo Soto, a young lawyer at CRLA, had brought me to the edge of an avocado orchard to visit a hidden encampment of migrant workers. Perhaps one-third of the farmworkers in northern San Diego County—about 7,000 people— are now homeless. An additional 9,000 of their family members are homeless, too. Many are living outdoors. The shortage of low-income housing became acute in the early 1980s, and large shantytowns began to appear, some containing hundreds of crude shacks. As suburbs encroached on agricultural land in northern San Diego County, wealthy commuters and strawberry pickers became neighbors. At one large shantytown I visited, women were doing their laundry in a stream not far from a walled compound with tennis courts, a pool, and a sign promising country club living. The suburbanites do not like living beside Mexican farmworkers. Instead of providing low-income housing, local authorities have declared states of emergency, passed laws to forbid curbside hiring, and bulldozed many of the large encampments. San Diego growers appalled by the living conditions of their migrants have tried to build farmworker housing near the fields—only to encounter fierce resistance from neighboring homeowners. Although the shantytowns lower nearby property values, permanent farmworker housing might reduce property values even more. "When people find out you want to build housing for your migrants," one grower told me, "they just go ballistic."

The new encampments are smaller and built to avoid detection. At the end of a driveway, near a chain-link fence, I met a young Mixtec who lived in such an encampment. His name was Francisco, and he was eighteen years old. He looked deeply exhausted. He had just picked strawberries for twelve hours at Doug's farm. I asked what he thought of Doug as a boss. "Not bad," he said politely.

The previous year Francisco had picked strawberries from April until July. He had saved $800 during that period and had wired all of it to his mother and father in the village of San Sebastian Tecomaxtlahuaca. This was Francisco's second season in the fields, but he had not seen much of San Diego County. He was too afraid of getting caught. His days were spent at the farm, his nights at the encampment. He picked strawberries six days a week, sometimes seven, for ten or twelve hours a day. "When there's work," Francisco said, "you have to work." Each morning he woke up around four-thirty and walked for half an hour to reach Doug's field.

At dusk, thirteen tired men in dirty clothes approached us. They were all from Francisco's village. They worked together at Doug's farm and stayed at the same encampment. They knew one another's families back home and looked after one another here. The oldest was forty-three and the youngest looked about fifteen. All the men were illegals. All were sick with coughs, but none dared to see a doctor. As the sun dropped behind the hills, clouds of mosquitoes descended, and yet the migrants seemed too tired to notice. They lay on their backs, on their sides, resting on the hard ground as though it were a sofa.

Francisco offered to show me their encampment. We squeezed through a hole in the chain-link fence and through gaps in rusting barbed wire, and climbed a winding path enclosed by tall bushes. It felt like a medieval maze. As we neared the camp, I noticed beer cans and food wrappers littering the ground. We came upon the first shack—short and low, more like a tent, just silver trash bags draped over a wooden frame. A little farther up the path stood three more shacks in a small clearing. They were built of plywood and camouflaged. Branches and leaves had been piled on their roofs. The landowner did not know the migrants lived here, and the encampment would be difficult to find. These migrants were hiding out, like criminals or Viet Cong. Garbage was everywhere. Francisco pointed to his shack, which was about five feet high, five feet wide, and seven feet long. He shared it with two other men. He had a good blanket. But when it rained at night, the roof leaked, and the men would go to work soaking wet the next day and dry off in the sun. Francisco had never lived this way before coming to San Diego. At home he always slept in a bed.

10 Beyond the sheds, bushes crowded the path again, and then it reached another clearing, where two battered lawn chairs had been placed at the edge of the hill. There was a wonderful view of strawberry fields, new houses, and the lights of the freeway in the distance.

Driving back to my motel that night, I thought about the people of Orange County, one of the richest counties in the nation—big on family values, yet bankrupt from financial speculation, unwilling to raise taxes to pay for their own children's education, unwilling to pay off their debts, whining about the injustice of it, and blaming all their problems on illegal immigrants. And I thought about Francisco, their bogeyman, their scapegoat, working ten hours a day at one of the hardest jobs imaginable, and sleeping on the ground every night, for months, so that he could save money and send it home to his parents.

We have been told for years to bow down before "the market." We have placed our faith in the laws of supply and demand. What has been forgotten, or ignored, is that the market rewards only efficiency. Every other human value gets in its way. The market will drive wages down like water, until they reach the lowest possible level. Today that level is being set not in Washington or New York or Sacramento but in the fields of Baja California and the mountain villages of Oaxaca. That level is about five dollars a day. No deity that men have ever worshiped is more ruthless and more hollow than the free market unchecked; there is no reason why shantytowns should not appear on the outskirts of every American city. All those who now consider themselves devotees of the market should take a good look at what is happening in California. Left to its own devices, the free market always seeks a work force that is hungry, desperate, and cheap—a work force that is anything but free.

CONVERSATION STARTER

What do you know about the living conditions of illegal immigrants in the United States? Do you live in an area where there are many illegal immigrants? If you don't, do some research on the Internet about the lifestyle expectations of illegal immigrant workers before reading this selection.

READING MATTERS

1. Schlosser tells us that in 1957 The President's Commission made the employment of illegal immigrant workers illegal. Why did farm owners and construction bosses continue to ignore this law for 20 years? What were the consequences on legal and illegal workers in these types of jobs in this country?
2. Why did the passage of the IRCA have the opposite effect in its attempt to control illegal immigrants in the United States? Why did the *bracero* program also fail and, in fact, encourage more illegal workers in come to work in the United States?
3. What are the advantages and disadvantages of the new guest worker program? Why do Philip L. Martin and Joaquin Avila think that the lives of farm workers can be improved?
4. How has the W.F.W. tried to improve the living conditions of immigrant workers? How successful have they been?

WRITING MATTERS

1. After doing more research on this issue, write an argument that supports or critiques Schlosser's position that conditions will improve for immigrant workers in the United States. In what specific ways can they be improved?
2. Do some research to find out where and how solutions to the problems of immigrant workers have been implemented in this country. Write an essay that presents a plan for helping more immigrant workers.

3. Write a paper that looks at the problem of immigrant workers from a national level. Find out more about why the United States and Mexico have made so little progress in solving the problems of immigrant labor in the United States.

RELEVANT WEB SITES

ERIC SCHLOSSER INTERVIEW
<http://www.bookpage.com/0305bp/eric_schlosser.html>

Jay MacDonald of *Book Page* interviews Eric Schlosser on his book *Reefer Madness,* about America's black market economy and the plight of undocumented workers.

UNDOCUMENTED FARM WORKERS <http://www.ufw.org/FWLegalization.htm>

The official home page of the United Farm Workers Union, this site contains articles on the political struggle for legalization of undocumented farm workers.

Barbara Ehrenreich (b. 1951)

Nickel and Dimed

Activist writer Barbara Ehrenreich holds a Ph.D. from Rockefeller University (1968) and has taught at the UC Berkeley School of Journalism. She has been the recipient of a Guggenheim Fellowship and a MacArthur grant. Her essays and reviews have appeared in many national newspapers magazines, including Harpers, Atlantic Monthly, the Nation, the Progressive, and Time Magazine, where she has been a columnist since 1990. Ehrenreich's recent books include The Worst Years of Our Lives: Irreverent Notes from a Decade of Greed *(1990),* Blood Rites: Origins and History of the Passions of War *(1997),* Nickel and Dimed: On (Not) Getting By in America *(2001), and* Global Woman: Nannies, Maids, and Sex Workers in the New Economy *(2003). The following selection comes from* Nickel and Dimed, *a book about her experience working in underpaid jobs in America's underclass.*

But if it's hard for workers to obey the laws of economics by examining their options and moving on to better jobs, why don't more of them take a stand where they are—demanding better wages and work conditions, either individually or as a group? This is a huge question, probably the subject of many a dissertation in the field of industrial psychology, and here I can only comment on the things I observed. One of these was the co-optative power of management, illustrated by such euphemisms as *associate* and *team member.* At The Maids, the boss—who, as the only male in our midst, exerted a creepy, paternalistic kind of power—had managed to convince some of my coworkers that he was struggling against difficult odds and deserving of their unstinting forbearance. Wal-Mart has a number of more impersonal and probably more effective ways of getting its workers to feel like "associates." There was the profit-sharing plan, with Wal-Mart's stock price posted daily in a prominent spot near the break room. There was the company's much-heralded patriotism, evidenced in the banners over the shopping floor urging workers and customers to contribute to the construction of World War II veterans' memorial (Sam Walton having been one of them). There were "associate" meetings that served as pep rallies, complete with the Wal-Mart cheer: "Gimme a 'W,'" etc.

The chance to identify with a powerful and wealthy entity—the company or the boss—is only the carrot. There is also a stick. What surprised and offended me most about the low-wage workplace (and yes, here all my middle-class privilege is on full display) was the extent to which one is required to surrender one's basic civil rights and—what boils down to the same thing—self-respect. I learned this at the very beginning of my stint as a waitress, when I was warned that my purse could be searched by management at any time. I wasn't carrying stolen salt shakers or anything else of a compromising nature, but still, there's something about the prospect of a purse search that makes a woman feel a few buttons short of fully dressed. After work, I called around and found that this practice is entirely legal: if the purse is on the boss's property—which of course it is—the boss has the right to examine its contents.

Drug testing is another routine indignity. Civil libertarians see it as a violation of our Fourth Amendment freedom from "unreasonable search"; most jobholders and applicants find it simply embarrassing. In some testing protocols, the employee has to strip to her underwear and pee into a cup in the presence of an aide or technician. Mercifully, I got to keep my clothes on and shut the toilet stall door behind me, but even so, urination is a private act and it is degrading to have to perform it at the command of some powerful other. I would add pre-employment personality tests to the list of demeaning intrusions, or at least much of their usual content. Maybe the hypothetical types of questions can be justified—whether you would steal if an opportunity arose or turn in a thieving coworker and so on—but not questions about your "moods of self-pity," whether you are a loner or believe you are usually misunderstood. It is unsettling, at the very least, to give a stranger access to things, like your self-doubts and your urine, that are otherwise shared only in medical or therapeutic situations.

There are other, more direct ways of keeping low-wage employees in their place. Rules against "gossip," or even "talking," make it hard to air your grievances to peers or—should you be so daring—to enlist other workers in a group effort to bring about change, through a union organizing drive, for example. Those who do step out of line often face little unexplained punishments, such as having their schedules or their work assignments unilaterally changed. Or you may be fired; those low-wage workers who work without union contracts, which is the great majority of them, work "at will," meaning at the will of the employer, and are subject to dismissal without explanation. The AFL-CIO estimates that ten thousand workers a year are fired for participating in union organizing drives, and since it is illegal to fire people for union activity, I suspect that these firings are usually justified in terms of unrelated minor infractions. Wal-Mart employees who have bucked the company—by getting involved in a unionization drive or by suing the company for failing to pay overtime—have been fired for breaking the company rule against using profanity.[1]

5 So if low-wage workers do not always behave in an economically rational way, that is, as free agents within a capitalist democracy, it is because they dwell in a place that is neither free nor in any way democratic. When you enter the low-wage workplace—and many of the medium-wage workplaces as well—you check your civil liberties at the door, leave America and all it supposedly stands for behind, and learn to zip your lips for the duration of the shift. The consequences of this routine surrender go beyond the issues of wages and poverty. We can hardly pride ourselves on being the world's preeminent democracy, after all, if large numbers of citizens spend half their waking hours in what amounts, in plain terms, to a dictatorship.

Any dictatorship takes a psychological toll on its subjects. If you are treated as an untrustworthy person—a potential slacker, drug addict, or thief—you may begin to feel less trustworthy yourself. If you are constantly reminded of your lowly position in the social hierarchy, whether by individual managers or by a plethora of impersonal rules, you begin to accept that unfortunate status. To draw for a moment from an entirely different corner of my life, that part of me still attached to the biological sciences, there is ample evidence that animals—rats and monkeys, for example—that are forced into a subordinate status within their social systems adapt their brain chemistry accordingly, becoming "depressed" in humanlike ways. Their behavior is anxious and withdrawn; the level of serotonin (the neurotransmitter boosted by some antidepressants) declines in their brains. And—what is especially relevant here—they avoid fighting even in self-defense.[2]

Humans are, of course, vastly more complicated; even in situations of extreme subordination, we can pump up our self-esteem with thoughts of our families, our religion, our hopes for the future. But as much as any other social animal, and more so than many, we depend for our self-image on the humans immediately around us—to the point of altering our perceptions of the world so as to fit in with theirs.[3] My guess is that the indignities imposed on so many low-wage workers—the drug tests, the constant surveillance, being "reamed out" by managers—are part of what keeps wages low. If you're made to feel unworthy enough, you may come to think that what you're paid is what you are actually worth.

---

[1]Bob Ortega, *In Sam We Trust*, p. 356; "Former Wal-Mart Workers File Overtime Suit in Harrison County," *Charleston Gazette*, January 24, 1999.

[2]See, for example, C. A. Shively, K. Laber-Laird, and R. F. Anton, "Behavior and Physiology of Social Stress and Depression in Female Cynomolgous Monkeys," *Biological Psychiatry* 41:8 (1997), pp. 871–82, and D. C. Blanchard et al., "Visible Burrow System as a Model of Chronic Social Stress: Behavioral and Neuroendocrine Correlates," *Psychoneuroendocrinology* 20:2 (1995), pp. 117–34.

[3]See, for example, chapter 7, "Conformity," in David G. Myers, *Social Psychology* (McGraw-Hill, 1987).

It is hard to imagine any other function for workplace authoritarianism. Managers may truly believe that, without their unremitting efforts, all work would quickly grind to a halt. That is not my impression. While I encountered some cynics and plenty of people who had learned to budget their energy, I never met an actual slacker or, for that matter, a drug addict or thief. On the contrary, I was amazed and sometimes saddened by the pride people took in jobs that rewarded them so meagerly, either in wages or in recognition. Often, in fact, these people experienced management as an obstacle to getting the job done as it should be done. Waitresses chafed at managers' stinginess toward the customers; housecleaners resented the time constraints that sometimes made them cut corners; retail workers wanted the floor to be beautiful, not cluttered with excess stock as management required. Left to themselves, they devised systems of cooperation and work sharing; when there was a crisis, they rose to it. In fact, it was often hard to see what the function of management was, other than to exact obeisance.

There seems to be a vicious cycle at work here, making ours not just an economy but a culture of extreme inequality. Corporate decision makers, and even some two-bit entrepreneurs like my boss at The Maids, occupy an economic position miles above that of the underpaid people whose labor they depend on. For reasons that have more to do with class—and often racial—prejudice than with actual experience, they tend to fear and distrust the category of people from which they recruit their workers. Hence the perceived need for repressive management and intrusive measures like drug and personality testing. But these things cost money—$20,000 or more a year for a manager, $100 a pop for a drug test, and so on—and the high cost of repression results in ever more pressure to hold wages down. The larger society seems to be caught up in a similar cycle: cutting public services for the poor, which are sometimes referred to collectively as the "social wage," while investing ever more heavily in prisons and cops. And in the larger society, too, the cost of repression becomes another factor weighing against the expansion or restoration of needed services. It is a tragic cycle, condemning us to ever deeper inequality, and in the long run, almost no one benefits but the agents of repression themselves.

10   But whatever keeps wages low—and I'm sure my comments have barely scratched the surface—the result is that many people earn far less than they need to live on. How much is that? The Economic Policy Institute recently reviewed dozens of studies of what constitutes a "living wage" and came up with an average figure of $30,000 a year for a family of one adult and two children, which amounts to a wage of $14 an hour. This is not the very minimum such a family could live on; the budget includes health insurance, a telephone, and child care at a licensed center, for example, which are well beyond the reach of millions. But it does not include restaurant meals, video rentals, Internet access, wine and liquor, cigarettes and lottery tickets, or even very much meat. The shocking thing is that the majority of American workers, about 60 percent, earn less than $14 an hour. Many of them get by by teaming up with another wage earner, a spouse or grown

child. Some draw on government help in the form of food stamps, housing vouchers, the earned income tax credit, or—for those coming off welfare in relatively generous states—subsidized child care. But others—single mothers for example—have nothing but their own wages to live on, no matter how many mouths there are to feed.

Employers will look at that $30,000 figure, which is over twice what they currently pay entry-level workers, and see nothing but bankruptcy ahead. Indeed, it is probably impossible for the private sector to provide everyone with an adequate standard of living through wages, or even wages plus benefits, alone: too much of what we need, such as reliable child care, is just too expensive, even for middle-class families. Most civilized nations compensate for the inadequacy of wages by providing relatively generous public services such as health insurance, free or subsidized child care, subsidized housing, and effective public transportation. But the United States, for all its wealth, leaves its citizens to fend for themselves—facing market-based rents, for example, on their wages alone. For millions of Americans, that $10—or even $8 or $6—hourly wage is all there is.

It is common, among the nonpoor, to think of poverty as a sustainable condition—austere, perhaps, but they get by somehow, don't they? They are "always with us." What is harder for the nonpoor to see is poverty as acute distress: The lunch that consists of Doritos or hot dog rolls, leading to faintness before the end of the shift. The "home" that is also a car or a van. The illness or injury that must be "worked through," with gritted teeth, because there's no sick pay or health insurance and the loss of one day's pay will mean no groceries for the next. These experiences are not part of a sustainable lifestyle, even a lifestyle of chronic deprivation and relentless low-level punishment. They are, by almost any standard of subsistence, emergency situations. And that is how we should see the poverty of so many millions of low-wage Americans—as a state of emergency.

In the summer of 2000 I returned—permanently, I have every reason to hope—to my customary place in the socioeconomic spectrum. I go to restaurants, often far finer ones than the places where I worked, and sit down at a table. I sleep in hotel rooms that someone else has cleaned and shop in stores that others will tidy when I leave. To go from the bottom 20 percent to the top 20 percent is to enter a magical world where needs are met, problems are solved, almost without any intermediate effort. If you want to get somewhere fast, you hail a cab. If your aged parents have grown tiresome or incontinent, you put them away where others will deal with their dirty diapers and dementia. If you are part of the upper-middle-class majority that employs a maid or maid service, you return from work to find the house miraculously restored to order—the toilet bowls shit-free and gleaming, the socks that you left on the floor levitated back to their normal dwelling place. Here, sweat is a metaphor for hard work, but seldom its consequence. Hundreds of little things get done, reliably and routinely every day, without anyone's seeming to do them.

The top 20 percent routinely exercises other, far more consequential forms of power in the world. This stratum, which contains what I have termed in an earlier book the "professional-managerial class," is the home of our decision makers, opinion shapers, culture creators—our professors, lawyers, executives, entertainers, politicians, judges, writers, producers, and editors.[4] When they speak, they are listened to. When they complain, someone usually scurries to correct the problem and apologize for it. If they complain often enough, someone far below them in wealth and influence may be chastised or even fired. Political power, too, is concentrated within the top 20 percent, since its members are far more likely than the poor—or even the middle class—to discern the all-too-tiny distinctions between candidates that can make it seem worthwhile to contribute, participate, and vote. In all these ways, the affluent exert inordinate power over the lives of the less affluent, and especially over the lives of the poor, determining what public services will be available, if any, what minimum wage, what laws governing the treatment of labor.

15   So it is alarming, upon returning to the upper middle class from a sojourn, however artificial and temporary, among the poor, to find the rabbit hole close so suddenly and completely behind me. You were *where*, doing *what?* Some odd optical property of our highly polarized and unequal society makes the poor almost invisible to their economic superiors. The poor can see the affluent easily enough—on television, for example, or on the covers of magazines. But the affluent rarely see the poor or, if they do catch sight of them in some public space, rarely know what they're seeing, since—thanks to consignment stores and, yes, Wal-Mart—the poor are usually able to disguise themselves as members of the more comfortable classes. Forty years ago the hot journalistic topic was the "discovery of the poor" in their inner-city and Appalachian "pockets of poverty." Today you are more likely to find commentary on their "disappearance," either as a supposed demographic reality or as a shortcoming of the middle-class imagination.

In a 2000 article on the "disappearing poor," journalist James Fallows reports that, from the vantage point of the Internet's *nouveaux riches*, it is "hard to understand people for whom a million dollars would be a fortune . . . not to mention those for whom $246 is a full week's earnings."[5] Among the reasons he and others have cited for the blindness of the affluent is the fact that they are less and less likely to share spaces and services with the poor. As public schools and other public services deteriorate, those who can afford to do so send their children to private schools and spend their off-hours in private spaces—health clubs, for example, instead of the local park. They don't ride on public buses and subways. They withdraw from mixed neighborhoods into distant suburbs, gated communities, or guarded apartment towers; they shop in stores that, in line with the prevailing "market

---

[4]*Fear of Falling: The Inner Life of the Middle Class* (Pantheon, 1989).
[5]"The Invisible Poor," *New York Times Magazine,* March 19, 2000.

segmentation," are designed to appeal to the affluent alone. Even the affluent young are increasingly unlikely to spend their summers learning how the "other half" lives, as lifeguards, waitresses, or housekeepers at resort hotels. The *New York Times* reports that they now prefer career-relevant activities like summer school or interning in an appropriate professional setting to the "sweaty, low-paid and mind-numbing slots that have long been their lot."[6]

Then, too, the particular political moment favors what almost looks like a "conspiracy of silence" on the subject of poverty and the poor. The Democrats are not eager to find flaws in the period of "unprecedented prosperity" they take credit for; the Republicans have lost interest in the poor now that "welfare-as-we-know-it" has ended. Welfare reform itself is a factor weighing against any close investigation of the conditions of the poor. Both parties heartily endorsed it, and to acknowledge that low-wage work doesn't lift people out of poverty would be to admit that it may have been, in human terms, a catastrophic mistake. In fact, very little is known about the fate of former welfare recipients because the 1996 welfare reform legislation blithely failed to include any provision for monitoring their postwelfare economic condition. Media accounts persistently bright-side the situation, highlighting the occasional success stories and downplaying the acknowledged increase in hunger.[7] And sometimes there seems to be almost deliberate deception. In June 2000, the press rushed to hail a study supposedly showing that Minnesota's welfare-to-work program had sharply reduced poverty and was, as *Time* magazine put it, a "winner."[8] Overlooked in these reports was the fact that the program in question was a pilot project that offered far more generous child care and other subsidies than Minnesota's actual welfare reform program. Perhaps the error can be forgiven—the pilot project, which ended in 1997, had the same name, Minnesota Family Investment Program, as Minnesota's much larger, ongoing welfare reform program.[9]

You would have to read a great many newspapers very carefully, cover to cover, to see the signs of distress. You would find, for example, that in 1999 Massachusetts food pantries reported a 72 percent increase in the demand for their services over the previous year, that Texas food banks were "scrounging" for food, despite donations at or above 1998 levels, as were those in Atlanta.[10] You might learn that in San Diego the Catholic

---

[6]"Summer Work Is Out of Favor with the Young," *New York Times*, June 18, 2000.

[7]The *National Journal* reports that the "good news" is that almost six million people have left the welfare rolls since 1996, while the "rest of the story" includes the problem that "these people sometimes don't have enough to eat" ("Welfare Reform, Act 2," June 24, 2000, pp. 1,978–93).

[8]"Minnesota's Welfare Reform Proves a Winner," *Time*, June 12, 2000.

[9]Center for Law and Social Policy, "Update," Washington, D.C., June 2000.

[10]"Study: More Go Hungry since Welfare Reform," *Boston Herald*, January 21, 2000; "Charity Can't Feed All while Welfare Reforms Implemented," *Houston Chronicle*, January 10, 2000; "Hunger Grows as Food Banks Try to Keep Pace," *Atlanta Journal and Constitution*, November 26, 1999.

Church could no longer, as of January 2000, accept homeless families at its shelter, which happens to be the city's largest, because it was already operating at twice its normal capacity.[11] You would come across news of a study showing that the percentage of Wisconsin food-stamp families in "extreme poverty"—defined as less than 50 percent of the federal poverty line—has tripled in the last decade to more than 30 percent.[12] You might discover that, nationwide, America's food banks are experiencing "a torrent of need which [they] cannot meet" and that, according to a survey conducted by the U.S. Conference of Mayors, 67 percent of the adults requesting emergency food aid are people with jobs.[13]

One reason nobody bothers to pull all these stories together and announce a widespread state of emergency may be that Americans of the newspaper-reading professional middle class are used to thinking of poverty as a consequence of unemployment. During the heyday of downsizing in the Reagan years, it very often was, and it still is for many inner-city residents who have no way of getting to the proliferating entry-level jobs on urban peripheries. When unemployment causes poverty, we know how to state the problem—typically, "the economy isn't growing fast enough"— and we know what the traditional liberal solution is—"full employment." But when we have full or nearly full employment, when jobs are available to any job seeker who can get to them, then the problem goes deeper and begins to cut into that web of expectations that make up the "social contract." According to a recent poll conducted by Jobs for the Future, a Boston-based employment research firm, 94 percent of Americans agree that "people who work full-time should be able to earn enough to keep their families out of poverty."[14] I grew up hearing over and over, to the point of tedium, that "hard work" was the secret of success: "Work hard and you'll get ahead" or "It's hard work that got us where we are." No one said that you could work hard—harder even than you ever thought possible— and still find yourself sinking ever deeper into poverty and debt.

20　　When poor single mothers had the option of remaining out of the labor force on welfare, the middle and upper middle class tended to view them with a certain impatience, if not disgust. The welfare poor were excoriated for their laziness, their persistence in reproducing in unfavorable circumstances, their presumed addictions, and above all for their "dependency." Here they were, content to live off "government handouts" instead of seeking "self-sufficiency," like everyone else, through a job. They needed to get

---

[11]"Rise in Homeless Families Strains San Diego Aid," *Los Angeles Times,* January 24, 2000.

[12]"Hunger Problems Said to Be Getting Worse," *Milwaukee Journal Sentinel,* December 15, 1999.

[13]Deborah Leff, the president and CEO of the hunger-relief organization America's Second Harvest, quoted in the *National Journal,* op. cit.; "Hunger Persists in U.S. despite the Good Times," *Detroit News,* June 15, 2000.

[14]"A National Survey of American Attitudes toward Low-Wage Workers and Welfare Reform," Jobs for the Future, Boston, May 24, 2000.

their act together, learn how to wind an alarm clock, get out there and get to work. But now that government has largely withdrawn its "handouts," now that the overwhelming majority of the poor are out there toiling in Wal-Mart or Wendy's—well, what are we to think of them? Disapproval and condescension no longer apply, so what outlook makes sense?

Guilt, you may be thinking warily. Isn't that what we're supposed to feel? But guilt doesn't go anywhere near far enough; the appropriate emotion is shame—shame at our *own* dependency, in this case, on the underpaid labor of others. When someone works for less pay than she can live on—when, for example, she goes hungry so that you can eat more cheaply and conveniently—then she has made a great sacrifice for you, she has made you a gift of some part of her abilities, her health, and her life. The "working poor," as they are approvingly termed, are in fact the major philanthropists of our society. They neglect their own children so that the children of others will be cared for; they live in substandard housing so that other homes will be shiny and perfect; they endure privation so that inflation will be low and stock prices high. To be a member of the working poor is to be an anonymous donor, a nameless benefactor, to everyone else. As Gail, one of my restaurant coworkers put it, "you give and you give."

Someday, of course—and I will make no predictions as to exactly when—they are bound to tire of getting so little in return and demand to be paid what they're worth. There'll be a lot of anger when that day comes, and strikes and disruption. But the sky will not fall, and we will all be better off for it in the end.

Conversation Starter

Discuss an experience you have had as a low-wage worker. How did you break away from the trap of only working to survive? If you have not had this experience, discuss what you know about someone close to you who was trapped in a "dead-end" job.

Reading Matters

1. How is Ehrenreich's real job different from that of a low-wage worker? Why did her professional studies lead her to conduct the experiment she describes in this selection? Why might she have thought that she needed to go beyond her academic studies to find more answers to the questions she had about wage inequality in the United States?
2. What qualities about the subjects Ehrenreich includes, her style of writing, and the information she includes help you to make a general profile of her audience? Do you think that Ehrenreich and her publisher had a specific audience that they wanted to reach?
3. Ehrenreich contrasts the power of the upper 20 percent of the national population to that of the remaining 80 percent. Why does she believe that the poor remain invisible to the upper middle classes? What does she believe can be done to change this situation? Why does this situa-

tion need to be changed? What do you think that you can do as a member of our society?

4. Why does Ehrenreich argue that the economic status of the poor has declined since welfare reform? Why does she believe that the working poor are the major philanthropists of our society? Do you agree with her position on both of these intertwined issues? Explain your point of view.

WRITING MATTERS

1. Do field research at a local Wal-Mart to better understand its power structure and the lives of its bosses and employees. Interview both the bosses and the workers. Contrast your research findings with Ehrenreich's. Write a paper that discusses your findings and conclude with your personal and intellectual response to this experience.
2. Write a research paper that discusses some of the ways that the managers of major corporations can make their workers' environment safe without treating them like criminals.
3. Write an essay that explains what you think should be done to improve the lives of the working poor. What can you do as an individual? Can you join a community organization that works for the rights of the working poor? What else can you do to change this situation that you encounter in some way everyday in your community?

RELEVANT WEB SITES

NICKEL AND DIMED <http://www.nickelanddimed.net/>

The official web site of the book *Nickel and Dimed,* the site is maintained by the Institute for Policy Studies. It includes book reviews, interviews, letters to the author, relevant articles and news stories, and links to organizations working on wage and equity issues.

NATIONAL PUBLIC RADIO: ONE TOWN, ONE JOB: LOW-WAGE AMERICA <www.npr.org/news/specials/low_wage>

Learn more about the low-income workforce and their struggle to earn a living wage in the United States. This web site documents the year-long series "One Town, One Job: Low-Wage America," special reports by Noah Adams of National Public Radio.

Bill Shore (b. 1957)

A Pioneer of Community Wealth

A former political campaign director turned community activist, Bill Shore earned a law degree from George Washington University. In 1978 he went to work on the campaign staff of Senator Gary Hart, and from 1988 to 1991 he was chief of staff for Senator Robert Kerrey. In 1984 he *founded Share Our Strength, a fund-raising organization designed to help decrease hunger both in Africa and in the United States. Share Our Strength has raised and distributed over $82 million dollars to hunger- and poverty-fighting groups around the world. Shore also founded Community Wealth Ventures, Inc., an advisory group designed to assist corporations and nonprofit organizations in generating wealth within the community through social change enterprises. He has also served on a task force for the President's Summit for America's Future. Shore has written articles on community-related issues for many newspapers and magazines. His books include* Revolution of the Heart: A New Strategy for Creating Wealth and Meaningful Change *(1999) and* The Cathedral Within: Transforming Your Life by Giving Something Back" *(1999), which profiles current community leaders who are dedicated to improving community life at every social level.*

Walla Walla, Washington, is a small city of less than thirty thousand at the foot of the Blue Mountains in the southeast corner of the state. Its entire population could be comfortably seated on one side of an NFL football stadium. It lies so close to the Oregon border that on a map, the second "Walla" almost spills across the state line. You can tell from the names of the surrounding geography that there was a time when life in this territory was not for the timid: Rattlesnake Flat, Ice Harbor Dam, Diamond Peak, Huntsville, Echo. Known today for little more than the Walla Walla Sweet Onion Harvest, it was once the largest city in what was called the Washington Territory.

Built by fur traders on the famous Native American Nez Percé trail, Walla Walla was officially founded in 1856, but it had seen Lewis and Clark's footsteps half a century earlier. The gold rush made it a commercial, banking, and manufacturing center, none of which outlasted the farms that still dominate its economy today. As one of the first areas settled between the Rockies and the Cascades, Walla Walla played a historic role in the development of the Pacific Northwest.

Walla Walla not only attracted the West's earliest pioneers, it bred a few as well. Gary Mulhair was born there in 1941. He spent his boyhood exploring the river valleys and working on farms. He can remember summers irrigating cornfields, pulling the pipes through thick rows of wet and heavy cornstalks and coming out drenched into the cold September air. In the fall, his mother sent him out to find and shell black walnuts that she wanted for cakes and pies. "They're very hard, and after cracking them, scraping the meat out of those was murder," he recalls. "Your fingers would be stained for maybe a week." She expected to receive the amount she'd asked for, often an entire bushel, no matter how hard it was or how long it took. From an early age, he understood that outcomes were what counted, that deliverables are how you measure value.

He stayed through college and eventually journeyed as far as Seattle, some 270 miles west, but no further. He never had to. The region's culture of rugged individualism has been defined by a spirited entrepreneurship and innovation that has changed the course of human history. Gary Mulhair helped do the defining. Many entrepreneurs have been at home there, from Bill Gates at Microsoft to Howard Schultz at Starbucks, as well as hundreds of others who are part of the region's flourishing high-tech economy. But when it came to social entrepreneurship, Gary Mulhair beat them all to the punch.

5   Since 1975, Mulhair has been creating jobs and saving lives through a unique model that is the envy of organizations across the nation. Under his leadership, Seattle's aptly named Pioneer Human Services has become the largest and most self-sustaining human service agency of its kind. He has revolutionized the way human service organizations operate through self-supporting enterprises and programs that integrate jobs, housing, training, and other support services for at-risk individuals. With revenues in excess of $50 million a year, Mulhair has created wealth of a magnitude previously unheard of in the nonprofit world.

He did it the toughest way possible, not by begging for foundation grants or government support, but by manufacturing and selling high-quality products and services with a workforce made up entirely of ex-offenders and former substance abusers. As he explained to the *Seattle Post-Intelligencer*: "These are people who have broken the law, folks most people are frightened of. They've been in prison or they're recovering from alcohol or drugs. They haven't held a job. When they apply for a job they get screened out pretty quickly. . . . We're going to hire people you wouldn't," Mulhair asserts, "but in a year or so, you will—because they'll be citizens."

What Pioneer's success means is that for the first time, a nonprofit organization is not dependent solely upon the charity of others. Its leaders do not have all of their energies diverted and usurped by the relentless demands of fund-raising—the meetings, phone calls, dinners, and events designed to meet and win the hearts of wealthy individual donors. Instead, they can focus on what attracted them to the job in the first place: developing effective programs to help the people they serve. Pioneer has proved that nonprofits can do more than just redistribute wealth, which they are typically quite good at. They can also create wealth, though it is a different kind of wealth—community wealth—that is used to directly benefit the community.

Shattering stereotypes is a fundamentally subversive activity. Initially, Mulhair's role in inventing a new model for nonprofits to grow to scale was so quiet as to be almost unnoticed outside of the Seattle area. Running a factory, building a profitable business, and delivering comprehensive social services to a severely challenged population—all at the same time—is complicated, taxing work. Mulhair couldn't find the time to both do the work and talk about it, so he kept his focus on the former. Gradually, through word of mouth, visitors, and the circulation of a few local press clips, the story of what he'd accomplished began to spread.

I called Gary Mulhair in 1996. I asked him to come to Washington to join in a discussion about redefining civic responsibility with people like Jeff Swartz of Timberland, former New Jersey senator Bill Bradley, and Michael Kennedy from Citizen's Energy. Leaders in various fields who were helping to create this new kind of community wealth did not yet know one another, and were not sharing, collaborating, or even talking. Share Our Strength saw value in playing the simple role of convener.

10 "Why do you want me?" he asked with characteristic reticence. The tone of his voice was stern. I couldn't tell whether he was genuinely curious or whether the question was some kind of test, but I was conscious of choosing my words carefully.

"Because you've been doing what everyone else only talks about."

"Okay," he said, ending the conversation. It meant he would come.

I learned then that Gary doesn't usually say more than he needs to. But when he came to Washington a few months later, he said enough.

Fifty-six years old and neatly if conservatively dressed, he maintains a steady gaze through large round lenses as if searching for the real you and pretty much expecting to find it. He is cautious with his broad smile, but friendly in the way of a small-town pharmacist. You can trust that whatever he's telling you is for your own good. He's given to short declarative statements that you can take or leave.

15 In his plainspoken way, and without the pretense that usually accompanies a Washington presentation, Mulhair described for the group the history of Pioneer, which began in Seattle in 1962 when an attorney named Jack Dalton was released from prison after serving a sentence for embezzling from his clients. "Jack came out of prison," Mulhair explained, "and he realized he was disbarred, disowned, and disenfranchised. He had nothing going for himself except the fact that he had nothing going for himself. Along with half a dozen other former prisoners who were struggling to build new lives, he started a halfway house with a budget of less than a thousand dollars that he raised by going to the very friends from whom he had embezzled. Jack had a lot of chutzpah."

Pioneer now serves more than five thousand clients each year, employing nearly seven hundred people in its programs. Its largest business is a precision light-metal fabricator that has become the sole supplier to Boeing sheet-metal liners for the cargo bays of Boeing aircraft. On a visit there, I walked with Mulhair across a factory floor the size of a football field, listening to him chat with workers whose skills once included forging checks, trafficking cocaine, and burglary. He is able to explain each stage of the production process and how each custom-made machine operates. He describes the flow of water jets, laser cutters, and electrostatic paint machines as the workers move large, flat sheets of plastic and metal among them, cutting them into as many as three hundred precision pieces, depending on the configuration of the plane. "It's like a big jigsaw puzzle."

Thanks to Pioneer, this workforce of ex-offenders has acquired new skills in a first-rate production setting that offers the patience and support few conventional businesses can afford. Operating computer-controlled machine tools to fabricate parts according to designs transmitted electronically by their customers, the employees are held to the most exacting standards. I asked Mulhair what kind of problems they have on the factory floor with a workforce that has such a history as this one, assuming the problems would be fighting and stealing. I assume wrong. "For about half of 'em, there comes a day where they just stop showing up. Problems with authority or what have you. That's about the only difficulty we have. But we can plan for it now and build it into the cost of doing business."

Mulhair is emphatic that quality is not sacrificed. He's got convincing evidence. In 1996, Pioneer's plant became the first nonprofit in the United States to win ISO-9002 certification, a benchmark for quality in the private sector. Even more convincing, Boeing keeps expanding its contract year after year.

In fact, Gary would argue that market forces ensure higher quality. As he told *The Chronicle of Philanthropy:*

> Most of our activities are customer-driven, and it gives us a different relationship with the people we're providing services for than if we were getting government money or foundation money. What you care about when you are talking to a foundation officer is getting his or her money into your organization, and that's input-driven. Our activities are output-driven. . . . I don't think nonprofits in this country have done a very good job of understanding the management side of things, understanding that their businesses should succeed or fail not on how much money they raise, but on how good a job they do. And that means understanding who your customers are and always focusing on satisfying your customers.

20   Pioneer also operates a wholesale food distribution enterprise that reaches four hundred food banks in twenty states. Other businesses include a real estate division that develops and manages more than 500,000 square feet of residential and commercial properties, and the Mezza Café—a 150-seat cafeteria for the corporate headquarters of Starbucks. In 1986, Pioneer bought the St. Regis Hotel in the heart of Seattle's popular Pike Place Market district. Today, it has been transformed into an unusual hybrid, serving tourists on a budget and recovering substance abusers participating in Pioneer's rehabilitation programs.

Ten years ago, 75 percent of Pioneer's revenues came from government, mostly in the form of grants. Today, that has been reduced to 25 percent, and most of that is from government contracts for services. Fifty million dollars in revenue is a lot of money for a nonprofit, and it attracts more. The Ford Foundation just wrote a check for $2.4 million so that Pioneer can continue to acquire other businesses and convert them into sheltered nonprofit workshops. As a result, Pioneer bought Greater Seattle Printing & Mailing in Redmond, Washington, a six-million-dollar business with lots of entry-level jobs, particularly on the mailing and fulfillment side.

There is one fundamental reason that nonprofits have only rarely started or owned businesses for the purpose of generating revenues for growth and sustainability: They only rarely thought they could. It has been a colossal failure of imagination pervasive to the nonprofit sector. That's not to say there are not financial, managerial, and regulatory hurdles to overcome; there are in any business venture. But the limitations on non-profits starting businesses have by and large been self-imposed.

Gary Mulhair managed to get around that. "Growing up in such a small town like Walla Walla made me feel that there were no limitations," he told me over dinner during a visit to New York. "I've never accepted that things had to be just one way or another."

Conversation Starter

What does philanthropy mean to you? Think of examples that you know of from your own experiences, and then look up its definition in the dictionary.

Reading Matters

1. Why is Gary Mulhair an excellent example of the region's individual-ism and entrepreneurship? What idea is Mulhair the first to put into practice? In what ways does he raise money? Why is this nonprofit organization not dependent on the charity of others?
2. Why is Gary Mulhair invited to Washington D.C. in 1996 to meet vari-ous leaders who want to collaborate to develop a new model of creat-ing community wealth? How does Mulhair present himself and what does he tell the leaders in Washington?
3. How does this philosophy of philanthropy differ from the traditional one? Why does Bill Shore think that nonprofits have never tried to gen-erate successful businesses?
4. How does Bill Shore define being a social entrepreneur? What is oper-ational philanthropy? What is unique about his vision?

Writing Matters

1. Write an argument in which you agree or disagree with Bill Shore's plea to business people: "Instead of giving us money, give us work. We'll convert that to jobs and hire the people you won't hire. You will receive products and services you need at a competitive rate."
2. Do a research paper that presents an extended profile with a variety of examples of the contribution that Bill Shore has contributed to the nonprofit sector.
3. Research the Internet and the library to find other organizations that use Shore's model. Write a paper on these organizations: What do they do and how have they been successful? Try to find such an organiza-tion in each region of the country.

Relevant Web Sites

Share Our Strength <http://www.strength.org/learn/founder.htm>

This is the official web site of Share Our Strength, a nonprofit organization committed to mobilizing individuals and industries to lend their talents to raise funds and awareness for the fight against hunger and poverty.

COMMUNITY WEALTH VENTURES, INC <http://www.communitywealth.com/>

This is the official web site of Community Wealth Ventures, Inc., a for-profit subsidiary of Share Our Strength. This organization provides strategic counsel to corporations, foundations, and nonprofit organizations interested in creating community wealth.

Robert Frost (1875–1963)

Mending Wall

Robert Frost was born in San Francisco and raised in the mill town of Lawrence, Massachusetts. He attended Dartmouth College and Harvard University but never completed a degree. Between college studies he held various jobs, including cobbler, editor of a country newspaper, schoolteacher, and farmer. Frost always knew that he was a poet and found public success with the publication of his second book of poems, North of Boston, *in 1914. From that time until his death, Frost became the best known of American poets: He received four Pulitzer Prizes and read at John F. Kennedy's inauguration; in doing so, he affirmed the public nature of poetry. His poem "Mending Wall," published in 1914, explores the complex relationships between neighbors and the ironies involved in working to maintain a wall between properties.*

Something there is that doesn't love a wall,
That sends the frozen-ground-swell under it,
And spills the upper boulders in the sun;
And makes gaps even two can pass abreast.
5 The work of hunters is another thing:
I have come after them and made repair
Where they have left not one stone on a stone,
But they would have the rabbit out of hiding,
To please the yelping dogs. The gaps I mean,
10 No one has seen them made or heard them made,
But at spring mending-time we find them there.
I let my neighbor know beyond the hill;
And on a day we meet to walk the line
And set the wall between us once again.
15 We keep the wall between us as we go.
To each the boulders that have fallen to each.
And some are loaves and some so nearly balls
We have to use a spell to make them balance:
"Stay where you are until our backs are turned!"
20 We wear our fingers rough with handling them.

Oh, just another kind of outdoor game,
One on a side. It comes to little more:
There where it is we do not need the wall:
25   He is all pine and I am apple orchard.
My apple trees will never get across
And eat the cones under his pines, I tell him.
He only says, "Good fences make good neighbors."
Spring is the mischief in me, and I wonder
30   If I could put a notion in his head:
"*Why* do they make good neighbors? Isn't it
Where there are cows? But here there are no cows.
Before I built a wall I'd ask to know
What I was walling in or walling out,
35   And to whom I was like to give offense.
Something there is that doesn't love a wall,
That wants it down." I could say "Elves" to him,
But it's not elves exactly, and I'd rather
He said it for himself. I see him there
40   Bringing a stone grasped firmly by the top
In each hand, like an old-stone savage armed.
He moves in darkness as it seems to me,
Not of woods only and the shade of trees.
He will not go behind his father's saying,
45   And he likes having thought of it so well
He says again, "Good fences make good neighbors."

CONVERSATION STARTER

Discuss the expression, "Good fences make good neighbors."

READING MATTERS

1. Describe the situation in the poem. What is the relationship between the speaker and his neighbor?
2. What do you think the speaker means by "something . . . that doesn't love a wall"? What does the speaker suggest when he says he'd "ask to know/ What I was walling or walling out"? What sort of solution for the problem of walls does his question imply?
3. What kinds of walls, whether psychological, social, or cultural, do we construct within communities? Does the poem help you to answer these questions? How?
4. Frost reflects on community in a poem rather than an essay or a story form. How does the form affect his message? How does poetry add another dimension to your understanding?

Writing Matters

1. Write a dialogue between yourself and the speaker, or yourself and the neighbor on the subject of good neighbors. Or, write a dialogue between the speaker and the neighbor after the fence mending.
2. Write an essay about establishing community using a metaphor to communicate your ideas, or write a dialogue with a neighbor about establishing community.
3. Write an essay that analyzes the theme of the poem; include specific references to the text. Then discuss its implications for establishing a community in a particular political, educational, or social situation.

Relevant Web Sites

Robert Frost <http://www.robertfrost.org>

This tribute web site to Robert Frost includes a biography, selected interviews, a detailed bibliography, and selections of his poetry.

The Academy of American Poets <http://www.poets.org>

Learn more about American poetry at the web site for The Academy of American Poets. Find out about poets, poems, and events throughout the country.

Kathy Torgersen and Carolyn Caddes

Bread, Salt and Heart

Kathy Torgersen has been active in local, county, and congressional politics for more than 20 years. Beginning in 1984 she worked as a precinct organizer for the Betsy Bechtel Supervisorial Campaign. Since then she has successfully managed campaigns for several local candidates, including Betsy Bechtel, Joe Simitian, and Liz Kniss. In 1992 she managed the headquarters for the Anna Eshoo Congressional Campaign and then continued on as Eshoo's finance director during the 1994 and 1996 campaigns. In 1994 Torgersen became a candidate herself and was elected to the Santa Clara County Democratic Central Committee as a delegate.

Torgersen's dedication to community and political activism led her to Albania in 1999 to write a publication for the International Rescue Committee. As a journalist, Torgersen had had experience writing for newspapers, nonprofit organizations, and political campaigns. In addition, she had served on numerous community nonprofit boards and advisory committees, including the Association for Senior Day Health, League of Women Voters, Palo Alto Foundation for Education, Families in Transition, PAUSD PTA Council, PAUSD Tax Advisory Committee and the Palo Alto Endowment Fund.

Carolyn Caddes has worked as a photojournalist for more than 25 years. Her photographs have appeared in the New York Times, San Francisco Chronicle, Los Angeles Times, San Pablo Ave. San Jose Mercury News, *and the* Nikkei Business magazine, *and have been exhibited in numerous galleries, museums, and public buildings. Known widely on the San Francisco peninsula for her landscapes and portraits, Caddes is probably the only photographer who has gained entry into the lives of many of the Silicon Valley giants. Her award-winning book,* Portraits of Success: Impressions of Silicon Valley Pioneers, *captured the electronics subculture with photos of Andy Grove, Steve Jobs, Scott McNealy, Larry Ellison, and numerous others. Caddes studied photography with Roy DeCarava, Yousef Karsh, Mary Ellen Mark, Arnold Newman, and attended photographic classes with Ansel Adams and later assisted at his workshops for five years. In 1997 Caddes completed a second book,* Mountain Dreamers: Visionaries of Sierra Nevada Skiing. *She now is working on a third book, a sequel to* Portraits, *entitled* Silicon Valley Revisited: Founders of the Internet.

Carolyn Caddes joined Kathy Torgerson in November of 1999. Together they traveled into the interior of Albania, staying with families, interviewing refugees, visiting clinics, schools, and refugee camps to create Bread, Salt and Heart. *This booklet captures insights into the way of life in Albania that few westerners have ever seen.*

Bread, Salt & Heart

"Bread, salt and heart" is an Albanian proverb that summarizes the ancient tradition of offering hospitality to travelers and visitors. When almost a half-million refugees fled to Albania during the Kosovo crisis, Albanian families sheltered 60 percent of them.

Stabilizing and Rebuilding Communities
THE INTERNATIONAL RESCUE COMMITTEE (ALBANIA)

Continued

Continued

SEEDS OF THE KOSOVO CRISIS

1913
London Ambassadors Conference grants Kosovo to Serbia

1918
The Kingdom of the Serbs, Croats and Slovens (later to become Yugoslavia) is created

1974
Kosovo acquires autonomy within Yugoslavia

1989
Milosevic (Serb president) removes autonomy from Kosovo

1990–1997
Period of Kosovar persecution and nonviolent resistance

MESSAGE FROM THE COUNTRY DIRECTOR

At the suggestion of Albert Einstein, the International Rescue Committee (IRC) was founded in 1933 to support refugees from Nazism in Germany. Since that beginning, aiding refugees and victims of oppression worldwide has become the driving purpose of the organization. We stay in a country for an average of nine years; and we are committed to staying that long in Albania.

IRC's mission in Albania is to assist the return of the refugees, to contribute toward stabilization and to prepare for future emergencies. Our contribution to stabilization is based on the United Nations High Commissioner for Refugees/European Community Humanitarian Organization (UNHCR/ECHO)-funded Quick-Impact Projects (QIPS) program and the new Community Development Initiative.

IRC has had a leading presence in the Balkan region since the start of the Bosnian war in 1992. Currently, it has programs in Albania, Bosnia, Croatia, Serbia, Montenegro and the former Yugoslav Republic of Macedonia (FYROM).

Our emergency-preparedness program is based on the assumption that this year could bring more war, disorder and displacement to any one of Albania's unstable neighbors.

This publication affords us the opportunity to reach out to English-speaking Albanians, as well as to our supporters, partners and staff, to illustrate what IRC does in Albania. I also would like to thank Kathy Torgersen, Carolyn Caddes and all

Continued

Continued

1998 **Period of violent** **resistance and ethnic** **cleansing**
March 1999 **NATO bombs** **Yugoslavia;** **Kosovars flee** **to Albania**
June 1999 **Bombing stops;** **Yugoslavia withdraws;** **NATO intervenes**
July 1999 **Most refugees** **return to Kosovo**
June 2000 **U.N. Security** **Council will vote on** **extension of NATO's** **Kosovo Force** **(KFOR) mission**

the others who have volunteered their valuable time to produce this report.

Vincenzo Gamberale, Summer 2000

THE CRISIS IN KOSOVO

When 460,000 Kosovar refugees flooded into Albania during 1999, the world held its breath. How would such an impoverished country, whose political system had collapsed in 1997, cope with so massive a human tide?

The Albanian people responded heroically to the unprecedented influx into their small and mountainous country. With centuries of experience enduring hardship and oppression, the Albanians have reserves of strength and resourcefulness unknown to outsiders. Without their efforts, the Kosovo crisis would have been a humanitarian catastrophe. The scale of the influx into Albania exceeded the expectations of the experts. Few people believed that the entire Albanian population of Kosovo would be driven from its homes.

Once the Kosovars had entered Albania and recovered from their exhaustion, they moved to other parts of the country, where they had relatives, friends or a place to stay. An extra half-million people were traveling on Albania's dilapidated road network. It was customary for large groups of refugees to arrive unannounced in a particular area, stay for a few days, then move on. The whole process was self-organized. No agency or government could predict what would happen next or claim to have control of the situation.

THE AFTERMATH

Meanwhile, hundreds of aid agencies were pouring into Albania to help. Millions of dollars were being donated, and thousands of tons of aid were being sent to Albania by road, sea and air—inundating the country's customs service.

By June 1999, the conflict in Kosovo was over, and refugees began making their way home. Again, their actions were spontaneous. According to experts, such a massive population movement—the expulsion and return of a population within a four-month period—was unprecedented.

Continued

Continued

Still, the Kosovo problem has not been resolved. The difficult issue of autonomy has not been addressed, and violent action by extremists is on the increase. More conflict and more refugees are likely to impact Albania in the near future.

RESPONDING TO EMERGENCIES

Chaos! It's the only word to describe what took place when a human tidal wave of Kosovars fleeing ethnic cleansing poured into Albanian refugee camps—no one had been prepared for such numbers.

The refugees were exhausted. They had worn the same clothes for weeks and had nowhere to wash or sleep. Massive amounts of aid were on the way but were held up in the ports. Distribution became an enormous problem.

During these first days, IRC set up a rapid-response team. An emergency meeting between the camp managers and the Kosovar leaders determined that the refugees needed soap, diapers, toothbrushes and toothpaste, utensils, dry clothes and bolts of cloth that could be used as sheets and towels.

The rapid-response team, coordinated by Don Sauer and Flamur Gorica, bought the items locally and rented vans to deliver the supplies. IRC's team served more that 45,000 people—approximately 10 percent of the refugee population in Albania—at a cost of $125,000, or about $3 per person. When the aid supplies finally arrived in the camps, the rapid-response team disbanded. It had done its job.

QUICK-IMPACT PROJECTS

The QIPS program is a partnership between the office of the United Nations High Commissioner for Refugees (UNHCR) and IRC. The main provider of funds for the program was the European Community Humanitarian Organization (ECHO). The program's goal was to rehabilitate sites directly affected by the presence of refugees and to express appreciation to the Albanian government and the people of Albania for their extraordinary generosity during the crisis.

IRC managed an umbrella grant on behalf of UNHCR. The funds were distributed as subgrants to local and international nongovernmental organizations (NGOs) that had submitted proposals. A UNHCR/IRC selection panel decided which groups would receive funds. In addition, IRC was responsible for monitoring all projects. Beginning in July 1999, the QIPS program funded 70 community projects, ranging from rebuilding former collective centers to repairing clinics, community buildings and schools used by the refugees.

Continued

Continued

More than $1.2 million of the grant was allocated to rehabilitate Albanian schools, a high priority of UNHCR. Thirty schools that had enrolled Kosovar children during the crisis and throughout the summer were renovated. Repair work in all 30 schools was finished by the end of 1999, making learning easier for 40,000 students throughout Albania.

IRC'S COMMITMENT TO REBUILDING COMMUNITIES

Sports Palace

Albania's Sports Palace, the largest and most widely used sports venue in the country, is the site of national competitions and training for the Olympic Games.

When the Kosovo crisis erupted in April 1999, the Sports Palace was transformed into a transit center for refugees, an extraordinary gesture of hospitality on Albania's part. For four months, more than 100,000 refugees came through the facility to register and be transferred to a host family or a camp. After the crisis, the Sports Palace was used as a repatriation center for refugees.

To thank the Albanians for their generosity during the crisis, the UNHCR funded a $360,000 subgrant to renovate the Sports Palace. IRC directly implemented the construction work.

Marie Kaculini School

Going to school had been difficult for the 1,200 students at the Marie Kaculini Primary School in Durres. Windows were broken, bathrooms weren't functional, electrical wiring was faulty, and most students worked at broken desks. Through a QIPS subgrant, carried out by Catholic Relief Services (CRS), the school was repaired in only eight weeks.

Naim Frasheri Secondary School

The Naim Frasheri Secondary School was renovated with a $36,000 subgrant to Tolba, an NGO in Gjirokaster. In just 16 days, electrical wiring, windows and bathrooms were repaired, and walls were plastered and painted in time for the beginning of the school year. In November, new desks and chairs arrived for all 540 students.

Valet e Detit School and Handicapped Institution

The Valet e Detit School and Handicapped Institution, home to 33 abandoned children, opened its doors to several disabled and orphaned refugee children during the crisis. After the children left, CRS was given a QIPS subgrant to purchase a new water tank and kitchen stove

Continued

Continued

and to paint the interior of the school. CRS implemented the greatest number of projects under the QIPS program.

SHELTER
ESCAPING THE HORROR
One Family's Story

From behind locked doors and drawn curtains, the Beqiril family watched as the horrors of ethnic cleansing descended on its village in Kosovo. Without warning, soldiers rushed through the streets, killing people, setting fire to homes and gathering up all the young men before marching them off to prison.

A neighbor was pulled from his house and shot as both his daughters watched. Later, the soldiers came back for the girls. "One could only imagine what horrors awaited them," remembered Xufe Beqiril. "It made me terrified for my own daughters. I feared we would be next. I am dying of cancer already. For me, this is nothing, but I couldn't bear to watch what they would do to my children. We decided to save our lives and our souls by running away."

And so, at dawn, the family silently slipped away, becoming part of the massive exodus of people fleeing to safety in Albania. As they passed the burning houses, they heard the screams of people trapped inside. They ran, not knowing where to go.

When they saw soldiers shoving Albanians into buses, the Beqirils joined the crowd and boarded a bus that took them to Prizren, 25 kilometers from the Albanian border. From there, the family began an exhausting six-hour march to the border—without food, water or rest. Strewn along the sides of the road were unrecognizable corpses.

Late that afternoon, exhausted, dehydrated and feverish, the family reached the border; but authorities refused to let them leave Kosovo until they had interrogated Xufe's husband for three hours. On blistered and swollen feet, and clutching her 3-year-old child in her arms, Xufe and her family crossed into Kukes, Albania.

On the other side of the border, the Beqirils collapsed in a field, unable to move. IRC workers and local Albanians found them and offered the family water, food, blankets and fresh fruit from their gardens.

"We were overwhelmed by their hospitality," recalls Xufe. "Only moments before, we were terrified and feared for our lives. Now, we were embraced by caring and concerned people. For a moment, we forgot the horror that had become our lives."

Continued

Continued

ALBANIANS OPEN THEIR HOMES

Musa Thaci calls himself a man with small pockets but a big heart. When he saw the families escaping across the border from Kosovo, his heart ached.

"I understand what it's like to be in need," he reflects. "Everyone in my family is unemployed; we barely get enough to eat on my pension of $60 a month. Even though I have very little, I thought these people needed my help. And my friends and neighbors felt the same way."

During this unprecedented migration, Musa went every day to the Sports Palace, where refugees were being processed, to ask if there was a family he could help. Each time, he was turned down, because his home had only two rooms. Finally, he was introduced to the Beqiril family, and then, 13 people were living under his roof.

The Beqirils stayed with the Thaci family for six months, and Musa says they were welcome to remain longer. "We are a generous people, and our hearts feel better when we can give. I knew they had nothing, and I wouldn't have taken anything from them."

With an IRC subgrant through the host-family program, Musa was able to make badly needed repairs to his home. At last, the leaking roof, the rotted windows and the toilet were fixed. And, for the first time, the installation of a water tank made running water possible.

"We opened our home to help this refugee family, never knowing the opportunity to repair our house would come to us," said Musa. "We did it because it is our tradition to be hospitable. We believe in the old Albanian proverb 'bread, salt and heart,' which means that, even though we are so poor we can put only salt on our bread, we still have heart. We are very thankful to the IRC for the chance to improve our home. Economic conditions are very desperate for us. Without this help, we would not have been able to make these renovations."

IRC AIDS HOST FAMILIES

The sheltering of the refugees who entered Albania last summer was a major challenge. Although camps were set up, the most dramatic response came from the people of Albania, who opened their homes to the Kosovars. An estimated 60 percent of those who fled stayed with Albanians.

IRC subsequently worked out a cost-effective way to help the host families repair and upgrade their homes: Homeowners are contracted to do the construction work. Among the advantages to this approach are that the homeowner and his family work voluntarily, saving at least 50 percent over the cost of using a construction company; all building materials are bought locally, thus stimulating the local economy; and

Continued

Continued

IRC is not required to set up an expensive national distribution-and-storage network.

The average cost of rehabilitating a host-family house is $3,500. IRC field offices—in Elbasan, Fier, Shkodra and Tirana/Durres—are responsible for identifying host families and for monitoring every stage of the program.

Field coordinators identify host families willing to continue to house Kosovars without charging rent. IRC then funds basic roof repairs, rewiring, door-and-window replacements and plumbing to these families' homes.

While the renovations are in progress, IRC field engineers provide technical advice to homeowners, making sure the houses are repaired according to Albania's building regulations.

With an initial grant from the United Kingdom's Department for International Development (DFID), IRC rehabilitated 60 homes, benefiting more than 1,000 people. And through a grant from the Bureau of Population, Refugees, and Migration USA (BPRM), an additional 225 houses are being repaired in five regions of Albania.

FIELD OPERATIONS

Shkodra

Shkodra, one of Albania's oldest cities, was its capital in historical times. Today, it is considered the capital of northern Albania and is of immediate strategic importance to the IRC because of its proximity to the Montenegro border. In preparation for a refugee influx expected this year, plans are under way to renovate the railway station and to establish an emergency-training program for local organizations. Damaged during the crisis last year, the station is likely to become the center of any forthcoming migration.

Other programs in Shkodra include cleaning up and renovating the cultural center (both QIPS projects) and rehabilitating a number of host-family houses.

Elbasan

The metallurgy factory in Elbasan, built by enthusiastic Chinese and Albanian Communists in the 1960s, symbolized a "second liberation." Today, high levels of unemployment, as well as air and water pollution, are the legacies of this failed industrial structure.

Until recently, the main activity of the Elbasan field office has been to implement training programs that diagnose, treat and report incidences of diarrhea and cholera. (Elbasan has been referred to as the cholera epicenter of Europe.) When thousands of Kosovar refugees

Continued

Continued

arrived in Elbasan during the crisis, IRC (Albania) addressed and solved this problem with a grant funded by BPRM.

Other programs in Elbasan include the restoration of the train station by QIPS and two DFID-funded projects: the building of two covered marketplaces in the city center and the construction of a school for Roma (gypsy) children.

Tirana/Durres

The Tirana/Durres field office serves the most densely populated cities in Albania, where most refugees settled during the Kosovo crisis. As the capital of Albania, Tirana is the bustling administrative and political center of the country. Durres is Albania's second-largest city and its main port.

Many public facilities in both cities were rehabilitated by the QIPS program, but the renovation of the Sports Palace in Tirana, used as a refugee processing center during the crisis, was the most ambitious of the QIPS projects. In addition, BPRM funded the renovation of many host-family homes in the Tirana and Durres areas.

The Tirana field office is implementing IRC's first environmental and agricultural projects. A forest is being replanted in a 5-hectare area, and seeds for food crops are being regenerated. Both ventures are being carried out with local NGO partners.

Fier

Renowned for its small oil industry, Fier is an industrial city in the center of southern Albania. Last year, the IRC field office implemented numerous QIPS programs and joined resources with Catholic Relief Services (CRS) to renovate a number of schools in the area. With a continuing focus on education this year, the field office is rehabilitating a school in the Patos area with funds from DFID and is assessing other school-renovation projects.

In addition to the QIPS programs, the Fier field office is renovating houses under the BPRM-funded host-family rehabilitation program. Also under way are studies by IRC water-and-sanitation engineers to determine the feasibility of building water-supply systems in villages that have none.

WATER AND SANITATION

ENSURING A RELIABLE WATER SUPPLY

Although Albania has plentiful amounts of groundwater, its water-supply problems are more dire than almost any other country's in central and southeastern Europe. This is the legacy of the communist period, during which inadequate planning, underinvestment, a chronic lack of funds for repairs and inferior building materials were the norm.

In 1997, Albanians, furious about losing their life savings in the

Continued

Continued

notorious "pyramid" schemes, destroyed much of the state's property. This added to the already poor condition of the country's infrastructure. The Kosovo influx in 1999 depleted resources even further.

With a $2.2 million grant from the European Community Humanitarian Organization (ECHO), IRC is implementing a project that will improve the water supply to Durres, one of the major destinations for refugees during the crisis last year.

Durres is surrounded by reclaimed land that has no natural water supply. The city's water comes from the Fushe Kuqe and Rrushkull Hamallaj communes (40 miles north of Durres), where groundwater is abundant. Although as much as 1,000 liters of water per second were extracted for Durres, villagers in the communes were given an inadequate supply. Consequently, they made many illegal connections to the water main, the result of which was a massive loss of water to Durres.

When these communes are supplied with an alternative and independent source of water, the villagers' illegal connections to the Durres water main will be cut. Wells, pumps and large-diameter pipes are being installed that will yield up to 1,000 liters of water per second. By providing a sustainable water system to the communes of Fushe Kuqe and Rrushkull Hamallaj, an estimated 27 percent more water will be delivered to Durres.

This program is being effected by the Tirana/Durres field office under the technical supervision of IRC's water sanitation department.

PSYCHOSOCIAL AND EDUCATION
COUNSELING YOUNG VICTIMS

Thirteen-year-old Klemend left Kosovo with images of burned corpses, dead animals and terrifying soldiers. His sense of innocence had been destroyed.

Through dynamic peer-counseling and education programs, IRC was able to help Klemend and thousands of other children deal with their psychological trauma.

When the Kosovo crisis erupted in April 1999, USAID and UNICEF gave IRC funds to establish educational and psychosocial programs. These were carried out through a network of centers set up in 18 refugee camps and collective centers in Durres, Shkodra, Tirana, Elbasan and Vlora.

The centers were operated by teams of refugee teachers, youth workers and IRC staff. While teachers taught academic subjects, youth workers organized a wide variety of activities, including storytelling, art projects, puppet shows, sports and a camp newspaper.

Blended into this innovative mix of academic and informal activities were small peer-counseling sessions led by youth workers.

Continued

Continued

Within a safe, confidential environment, refugee children were able to verbalize their experiences and express their feelings of anger and fear. The sessions proved therapeutic, not only for those who spoke, but also for those who listened, since everyone had had a similar experience. Youth workers were trained as peer counselors. They were briefed on basic psychology and were taught the symptoms and treatment of post-traumatic stress disorder.

However, the youth workers' own experiences as refugees gave them an understanding of and empathy for the children even beyond what they had learned in the training program. And by listening to and advising others, the peer counselors were able to help themselves recover from the tragedy of Kosovo as well.

When the children attended camp schools, they were offered numerous opportunities to learn, play and make friends. Not only did this help normalize their lives, but it also helped them begin to recover from their psychological wounds.

Klemend and his family finally returned to Kosovo last July. And because of his positive experience in Albania, Klemend was able to leave behind his feelings of helplessness and despair and to set out with renewed strength and hope.

Klemend's Journal

Most of the refugees who fled Kosovo were women and children; and all were traumatized by the time they reached Albania. IRC helped by providing counseling sessions for the children. One of the activities offered was the opportunity to express in writing what they had experienced. What follows is the account of 13-year-old Klemend, a boy who was forced to leave his home in Kosovo.

"Night fell, and the clock's hands passed midnight. Small children were crying, and the rain was falling. We walked 120 kilometers to the city of Peja, without stopping once. In Peja, the soldiers were looking for young people. Some boys were stopped, taken by the soldiers and pushed into a fire. Later, we saw these young people, and they had been burned and badly beaten. The soldiers also had burned their clothes and identity cards; they were in their underwear.

"The following night, we slept on the road. A cold rain was falling, and I began to cry. I imagined what other children in the world were doing at that moment. I couldn't stand up anymore, because my knees wouldn't support me. I couldn't take off my shoes, because my socks and shoes had stuck to my bleeding feet.

"We spent another night in the rain. I was shivering, as if someone had plugged electricity into me. We got up and followed the road to Decan. My mother couldn't walk at all, so my father, brother and I took turns pushing her in a wheelbarrow.

Continued

Continued

"When we got to Decan, the police stopped us and shot above our heads. They beat and searched us for money. I saw two old people dead in an abandoned cart. I saw someone who had been burned alive in tires. Seeing these things horrified me.

"Eventually, we got to the Albanian border. We saw many dead people and animals along the way. We had been pushing my mother in the wheelbarrow for 150 kilometers. We had run out of food and bread. When we arrived at the border and crossed into Albania, I felt I had been born again. I cried with joy."

HEALING OLD WOUNDS

Psychology in Albania is a relatively new social science. Under communism, the practice and study of psychology was forbidden. The result is a rudimentary system of mental health services that relies almost entirely on medication and institutional psychiatry, rather than on therapy.

The void left by communism has made it necessary to rebuild the practice of psychology from its foundation. In 1994, a faculty of psychology was established at the university in Tirana. The program's first students will graduate this year. IRC supports the psychology department by supplying its books. Readers are able to buy them on the web at www.amazon.com and entering the e-mail address psychclub_alb@hotmail.com.

The most tragic victims of the communist regime were the political prisoners who were tortured for their beliefs. The Albanian Rehabilitation Center for Torture Victims (ARCT) was established in 1994 to counsel them. Its staff has made 10,000 visits to 300 clients.

Bardhyl Belishova, a member of ARCT and a former political prisoner, says of his experience: "I was in prison for 26 years and, during that time, I was tortured every day, as a matter of routine. Eventually, I didn't even notice it. Torture had become the norm, and there was nothing I could do about it."

Through a new program, IRC is helping ARCT train teachers, police, medics, ex-political prisoners and local government staff to deal with victims' post-traumatic stress disorder.

PUBLIC HEALTH
STOPPING EPIDEMICS

Albania's infant mortality rate is the highest in Europe. Although the rate of deaths has dropped steadily for the last four years, it remains elevated, since such easily treated diseases as diarrhea often receive no medical care.

Continued

Continued

IRC is implementing a training program designed to teach the basic methods of diagnosing and treating diarrhea. According to Dr. Arian Pano, IRC's public health and education manager, "The campaign to eradicate diarrheal disease in this country begins with our nurses; they are the primary health-care providers in all isolated villages."

Training began in Elbasan with 250 nurses, most of whom had been practicing alone in remote areas with no opportunity to study new treatments or skills. None of them had attended a professional workshop or refresher course since their university training, usually many years earlier. "What we discovered," Dr. Pano continues, "was that many of the traditional cures for diarrhea were ineffective, and some actually made their young patients worse."

The IRC workshops provide nurses with a clear definition of diarrhea, enabling them to diagnose and treat the disease correctly. Nurses also have learned an effective epidemiological system of reporting; their weekly reports now are standardized and can be passed on to health authorities with confidence.

RAISING AWARENESS

Since the fall of communism, smoking in Albania has increased dramatically, thus becoming a national problem. Legislation to restrict cigarette promotion campaigns does not exist, and the smuggling of cigarettes is rampant. In response, IRC has teamed up with the National Center of Health Education and Promotion and the Association for a Tobacco-Free Albania to conduct the first national survey concerning tobacco use.

The random-sample survey will question 8,000 Albanians in 20 districts about their smoking habits and their knowledge of the impact of tobacco on health. The preliminary data is alarming: In every district surveyed, smoking is increasing rapidly. Fifty percent of the men in the north smoke at least one pack of cigarettes a day. Women, who seldom used tobacco in the past, now are smoking in greater numbers; and even young children have taken up the habit.

A key question on the survey asks individuals why they started to smoke. According to Dr. Roland Shuperka, leader of the project, most men were introduced to tobacco by their fathers or grandfathers, who believe smoking is a symbol of manhood. Others said their doctors advised them to smoke to stop nosebleeds and headaches or to lose weight.

"Even these early findings indicate to us that doctors are grossly misinformed about the harmful effects of smoking," reports Dr. Shuperka. "But that's not surprising, since the medical school curriculum contains nothing about the use of tobacco."

Continued

Continued

Regardless of whether those interviewed were smokers or not, almost all agreed that cigarette sales to children should be banned and that teachers and doctors should set a good example by not smoking. Survey data will be used to assess the population's smoking trends and to determine what the National Center of Health Education and Promotion and the Association for a Tobacco-Free Albania must do to change it.

EMERGENCY PREPAREDNESS
READYING THE RESOURCES

As the 1999 crisis proved, Albanians respond heroically in an emergency. IRC intends to continue to work with the people and to prepare for any future exigency. A conflict in neighboring Montenegro, a resumption of hostilities in Kosovo or outbreaks of disorder in Macedonia are only a few of the events that could lead to further population influxes into Albania this year.

With the goal of familiarizing IRC staff with these and other possibilities, an emergency-preparedness workshop was held last November. The next one, scheduled this spring, will focus on the roles the staff will adopt, if and when another crisis occurs.

Because IRC is aware that its best resource is its local staff, each sector of the organization—public health, psychosocial, shelter, water and sanitation, and education—is preparing detailed plans that outline specialized skills it will provide in the event of an emergency. All appropriate IRC resources, including communications equipment and vehicles, will be made available when necessary.

An important aspect of emergency preparedness is coordination among agencies to share resources and information. To that end, IRC has helped facilitate a number of meetings among NGOs, donors and government agencies.

These meetings are chaired by the United Nations High Commissioner for Refugees (UNHCR). Subcommittees have been formed to coordinate food and logistics, shelter and water, sanitation and health, protection, and psychosocial and security needs. If a refugee emergency does occur this year, IRC and the other leading aid agencies in Albania will be in a position to respond quickly and effectively.

CONTRIBUTIONS
MAKING A DIFFERENCE

The extraordinary generosity of our donors enabled IRC (Albania) to meet the needs of the Kosovars during the crisis and, afterward, to help the people of Albania rehabilitate their homes, public facilities and communities damaged by the migration.

Continued

Continued

In 1999, IRC implemented 107 projects, benefiting 448,381 refugees and Albanians. Beginning last April and continuing through the peak of the crisis, our emergency-response team provided basic survival items to 45,000 people. IRC's psychosocial-and-education team, funded by USAID and UNICEF, stepped in to provide counseling and education to 10,000 refugee children in Albania.

As the crisis subsided over the summer, our shelter sector, with grants from DFID and BPRM, began an innovative program of rehabilitating the homes of more than 200 host families, resulting in far-reaching benefits. Not only has the shelter program improved the living conditions of hundreds of host families and refugees, but it also has upgraded a severely deteriorated housing stock and stimulated the local economy.

The crisis impacted Albania's schools, clinics, community centers, libraries and sports facilities. With $2.7 million from UNHCR and ECHO, and in partnership with numerous NGOs, IRC established the successful QIPS program. Between July and November, the IRC completed 70 projects.

Preventing cholera and diarrhea epidemics, both during and after the crisis, strained Albania's overburdened public-health system. Funded by BPRM, and in cooperation with the Ministry of Health, IRC launched a nurse-training program that focuses on the surveillance, diagnosis and treatment of diarrhea.

IRC's commitment to restore Albania's deteriorated and damaged infrastructure continues this year with a $2.25 million grant from ECHO. The goal of this project is to make a major contribution to the solution of water problems in Durres. DFID has made grants to IRC to build, in the year 2000, a desperately needed school for Roma children in Elbasan and a covered marketplace in its city center. The grant also will be used to renovate a primary school in the Fier area and the railway station in Shkodra.

With a grant from the Dutch organization Stichting Vluchteling (SV), IRC has launched two new programs, one to strengthen local NGOs and the other to support seed production in one of Albania's communes.

As we continue our mission to stabilize and rebuild communities in Albania, we would like to thank the people who made generous donations during and after the Kosovo crisis.

Donors

American Jewish Committee (AJC)

The Anti-Defamation League (ADL)

Bureau of Population, Refugees, and Migration (BPRM)

Department for International Development (DFID)

The David and Lucile Packard Foundation

Continued

Continued

    European Community Humanitarian Organization (ECHO)

    The Ford Foundation

    Kid Connection

    The Markle Foundation

    The Pew Charitable Trusts

    Stitching Vluchteling (SV)

    United States Agency for International Development (USAID)

    United Nations Childrens Fund (UNICEF)

    United Nations High Commissioner for Refugees (UNIHCR)

    The William H. Gates Foundation

    The Woodcock Foundation

    Young Green Foundation

PUBLICATION STAFF

We wish to thank the following professionals, whose contributions of their time and talent have made this publication possible:

Kathy Torgersen	Project manager and copywriter
Carolyn Caddes	Photojournalist
Rupert Wolfe Murray	Editor
Alina Wolfe Murray	Copywriter
Barbara Bennigson	Copy editor
Carroll Harrington	Graphic designer and production director
Andrea Hendrick	Graphic designer and illustrator

Photographs by Carolyn Caddes unless otherwise credited.

ALBANIA: A COUNTRY OF CONTRASTS

1912
Albania wins independence

1913
London Ambassadors Conference recognizes Albanian independence; Kosovo is granted to Serbia

1939
Italy invades Albania

1943
Germany invades Albania

It took a crisis for the world to notice Albania. For half a century, the country was isolated by a ruthless dictator. When 460,000 refugees poured over Albania's border last year, they found a country of extreme contrasts. Its people were extraordinarily generous though impoverished; finally free of communism but naive about capitalism; highly literate but with no opportunity to work; enamored of the West but unwilling to cast off ancient traditions.

Kosovars who fled to Albania were embraced by total strangers who sheltered and fed them, sometimes for months. Aid agencies never had

Continued

Continued

1946 **Communist Party proclaim's People's Republic of Albania**
1948 **Albania breaks relations with Yugoslavia and allies itself with the U.S.S.R.**
1960 **Albania breaks relations with the U.S.S.R. and allies itself with China**
1974 **Albania breaks relations with China and enters a period of extreme isolationism**
1990 **Communist regime begins to crumble**
1992 **Albania holds first free elections**
1997 **Pyramid investment schemes collapse; period of disorder follows**
March–June 1999 **NATO wages bombing campaign against Yugoslavia**

witnessed such a phenomenon; but to Albanians, hospitality is a tradition. On the other hand, many, especially in the north, live by a traditional code of feudal ethics that supersedes the governmental rule of law.

Although the majority of Albanians live in poverty, theirs is a country rich in natural resources. The lack of capital investment and business experience, however, has made the extraction of minerals difficult. And while the country has a great capacity to generate and export hydroelectric power, poor maintenance of its distribution system makes problematic the delivery of electricity to Albania's own cities.

Though Albanians have lived in isolation for almost 50 years, they are a well-educated people. Estimates are that almost 90 percent of the population is literate. Yet, because of high unemployment, many of the country's brightest graduates and professionals have moved to the West in search of better opportunities.

In spite of these obstacles, Albania, in 1999, absorbed the largest human migration since World War II. It was a historic moment, and the world was watching. Now, after years of isolation, and with the help of many European nations and NGOs, Albania is beginning to rebuild its infrastructure. Its dream of being integrated into Europe finally may come true.

INTERNATIONAL RESCUE COMMITTEE

Contact the International Rescue Committee for a copy of the booklet complete with photographs and more information.

International Rescue Committee
122 East 42nd Street
12th floor
New York, New York 10168-1289
Phone: (212) 551-3025
E-mail: debra@interescom.org

CONVERSATION STARTER

Discuss what you know about the International Rescue Committee or other international organizations that help political refugees.

READING MATTERS

1. What is the purpose of this report? What topics does it cover? Why were these topics featured?
2. Why is the report entitled "Bread, Salt and Heart"? How do the pictures help to tell the story of the Albanians' efforts to assist the Kosovo refugees? In what ways is this crisis also a story of rebuilding community?
3. Which pages of the report did you find most effective? Why?
4. What new insights into the human condition did you gain from reading this brochure? Relate the Kosovo crisis to another international situation you have heard about, studied, or experienced.

WRITING MATTERS

1. Research the activities of the International Rescue Committee. Write a paper for your class that highlights some of the humanitarian missions in which the IRC has successfully intervened.
2. Help to produce a report that tells the story of one of the IRC's rescue projects or produce a report for a political organization in your community.
3. There are more than 20 million political refugees worldwide. According to Y2000 statistics, there are 35 million refugees—defined as people forced to flee their countries—or displaced residents (internal refugees), who are forced to flee their homes but not their countries to escape fighting or oppression. Research the issue of political refugees and develop a specific topic that you want to better understand. Write a paper for your class and, if appropriate, for a local community paper or newsletter.

RELEVANT WEB SITES

INTERNATIONAL RESCUE COMMITTEE <www.intrescom.com>

The International Rescue Committee's web site highlights opportunities to provide relief, protection, and resettlement services for refugees and victims of oppression or violent conflict.

CNN <http://www.cnn.com>

This web site from CNN provides online news and information that is updated continuously throughout the day. CNN.com relies heavily on CNN's global team of almost 4,000 news professionals.

Craig Kielburger

Kathmandu

Craig Kielburger was 16 years old when he founded Free the Children, *an international children's organization now active in more than 20 countries. Its mission is to free children from poverty and exploitation and to empower young people to become leaders in their own communities, nationally and internationally. When Craig was only 12 years old, he became the first child advocate for children's rights after reading about the murder of a youth from Pakistan who had been sold into bondage as a carpet weaver. Since then, Craig has traveled to more than 30 countries around the world to visit street and working children and to speak out in defense of children's rights.*

Free the Children *has initiated many projects all over the world, including the opening of schools and rehabilitation centers for children, the creation of alternative sources of revenue for poor families to free children from hazardous work, leadership programs for youth, and projects linking children on an international level. Young people from* Free the Children *have helped to convince members of the business community to adopt codes of conduct regarding child labor, and governments to change laws to better protect children from sexual exploitation.*

A documentary on Craig's work won the 1999 Gold level UNESCO award at the New York Film Festival. Craig has received many awards for his work, including the State of the World Forum Award and the Roosevelt Freedom Medal (with Free the Children*). He was named a Global Leader of Tomorrow at the World Economic Forum.* Kids Can Free the Children *has grown into an influential international children's organization with hundreds of thousands of young people in 35 countries now participating in its activities.* Free the Children *was selected in 2001 by the United Nations and the Office of the Special Representative for Children in Armed Conflict to be the lead NGO coordination youth outreach for the decade of peace and nonviolence toward children.*

The following selection, "Kathmandu," is excerpted from Free the Children *(1998) and captures the struggles that street children in Kathmandu, Nepal, face on a daily basis as well as the efforts of social activists who are trying to improve the working and living conditions of these children.*

Kathmandu, like many Asian cities, is a blend of a rich past and the commercial grime of modern life. Vehicles sometimes share the streets with monkeys and elephants. One day, while we were driving along a main street, all of the cars suddenly swerved to one side and jerked to a stop. Through the ocean of vehicles an elephant was maneuvering its massive feet, taking care not to step on a car or a person. With a load of sugar cane strapped to it back, the mighty beast had made the long trek from a rural village, carrying the farmer's produce to the city market.

The ancient architecture of Kathmandu was impressive. In the city center we found the narrow streets of Durbar Square with its temples and shrines, some dating back to the twelfth century. An earthquake devastated much of Kathmandu in 1933, but these buildings remained, their beautiful exteriors a reminder of the richness of the city's past. One of them was called the "Monkey Temple," after the hundreds of monkeys that had made it their home. Alam had to put his videocamera away after one of them tried to grab it from him.

On a clear day in December, if you can escape the traffic pollution of the city's core, the mountains that ring Kathmandu can draw even the most well-travelled tourist like a magnet. We, however, were not typical visitors. Though we were inspired to draw deep breaths and speak of the potential beauty of a hike through the mountains, our feet were planted firmly on the ground. We had people to meet and work to do. Tourist destinations would have to wait for another time.

The first official meeting was with Child Workers in Nepal (CWIN). Headed by Gauri Pradhan, an outspoken advocate of children's rights, CWIN has worked throughout Nepal to oppose the widespread exploitation of children. It estimates that in a country of 18 million, there are close to four million children under the age of fourteen involved in full-time or part-time labor. This ranges from farm labor to work in carpet and garment factories, to domestic servitude, to the trafficking of young girls out of the country to the brothels of India and Thailand. Of those who attend primary school, more than half drop out.

5   The statistics are staggering. But CWIN is making a difference, especially since the establishment of democracy in the county in 1991. I spoke with Guari and was impressed by the depth of his knowledge. He had worked long and hard on the issue of child labor and had obviously gained a far-reaching insight into the situation in his country.

"Lack of political will," he said, "that's the main obstacle to reform."

"Isn't the public on your side?"

"Yes, but they have to *demand* change. The politicians shout in favor of it at election time, but when it comes to the crunch of making a law, it's all too easy to sidestep the issue."

"Even in a democracy?"

10   He smiled. "Bribes paid to cover up child-labor practices have never really gone away."

We spent much of our time in Nepal with CWIN's project to help the street children of Kathmandu. When we walked at night, we had seen these children hanging out near the hotels, restaurants, and the other spots that tourists frequent. Most of them were nine to fifteen years old, but some were as young as six. We knew them by their appearance—unruly hair, dirty clothes covering their thin bodies, faces often scarred or bearing sores. We knew them by their cheeky actions to draw attention to themselves. I found their pleas for money hard to ignore, though many tourists and most locals found it easy enough. For most it was no more difficult than for the residents of Toronto to pass by the street people begging along Yonge Street.

These kids, known as *kathe* in Nepal, had made the streets their home. They tucked themselves away late at night in whatever bit of vacant space they could find. I was told many of them were abandoned by their parents. In some cases they had been orphaned, or had run away from abusive families. In others, they were on the street begging for money to support their parents, the very people who had sent them out.

CWIN estimates there are fifteen hundred kids on the streets of Kathmandu.

CWIN is one of the few organizations that these street kids can turn to for help. They have set up centers across Kathmandu where kids can go for relief from life on the street. They provide health care and a chance for the children to play together in a safe and friendly environment.

15   In addition, CWIN has established a series of "halfway homes." Here, children come to stay for several months and are encouraged to fit into a routine of keeping themselves and their rooms clean, attending school, eating regular meals. It teaches them self-discipline and habits that with luck will stay with them once they leave. In some instances, the program has been able to reunite kids with their families, or set up adoptions.

I dropped in at several of their projects. Most of the buildings follow the same basic floor plan. A paved area surrounds the building, a place where kids can hang out and play games. By far the most popular was carom, the game Swapan's son had taught me when I was in Calcutta. I joined in a game and flicked around a few discs. They blew me away. It would take a lot more practice to get as good as these guys.

One boy took me on a tour of their facility. There are washrooms with showers and a cooking area, which the kids themselves are responsible for keeping clean. We headed into the main building.

"Here are the bedrooms. Ten beds to a room. A noisy place sometimes." By nine o'clock at night these rooms would be filled with whoever had come in off the street. If the staff ran out of beds, space would be found somewhere in the building. No kid was ever turned away.

"And now for the sick room." Here, the kids come with their many cuts and burns and lesions, often as a result of attacks from older kids. "We don't go to the hospital," the boy said. "They would just turn us away."

20   "Unless they are really sick," one of the staff added, "then we take them to the hospital and make sure they are attended to."

I noticed that many of the staff were in their early twenties. Often they were former street kids who had come to work for CWIN. These young men and women were proof to the kids that it *was* possible to pull themselves out of their miserable circumstances on the street and settle into a new life.

The next stop was a small room that was used as a library. "And we've even got a bank," the boy told me proudly. "We can open an account and keep our money safe from the gangs."

"These kids make maybe one or two U.S. dollars a day," one of the staff told me. "That is a lot of money in Nepal. Lots of times it will get stolen from them. That is why you see kids coming in here with broken bones and knife wounds. Last year a boy was slashed across his temple by an older boy trying to rob him."

"Did he die?" I asked.

25   The CWIN worker nodded.

"And sometimes the police will load them in a truck and dump them by the side of the highway miles out of the city, just to get them off the streets. Other times, they arrest them and send them to jail. Guards and older inmates abuse them, sometimes sexually. AIDS is a very real possibility for some of these kids.

"And when they do have money, a lot waste it. To get away from their troubles they gamble, they buy drugs and alcohol, they sniff glue, they go to prostitution houses."

"At their age?"

He nodded.

30   "But they know that if they hope to stay here they must stop their bad habits. They are not allowed even to swear." He smiled. "That's a difficult one to enforce, but we do our best.

"Many don't like the discipline at first. But they see it is a place where they can get fed for free and are safe. They change. They take pride in this place. The worst possible punishment any of them can receive is to be asked to leave the center."

I had seen evidence of just how much pride they took in what CWIN had provided for them. I had watched a boy that morning with a bucket of red paint and a brush, painting a stone wall. I had seen others sweeping the floors. It was the only home many of them had ever known, a place where they were loved.

We chatted to dozens of kids as we strolled about the center, but one boy in particular stood out. He looked to be no more than eight, and he was playing by himself with a few pieces of Lego in a corner of a roof area. I sat near him, and for a long time neither of us said a word.

He was making a car from the blocks. Now and then I would pick up a loose piece that I thought might be useful and hand it to him. He would take it and try it out. If it didn't work, or he didn't care to use it, he would put it back in pile.

35   I could feel a trust slowly developing between us. It took a while, but eventually he spoke to me, just mumbling a few words at first. He continued working with the Lego, and quietly, one tortured sentence after another, he told his story.

He was born in a small village in the hills of Nepal. When he was a baby, his father deserted him and his mother. Over time his mother remarried and had another child. The new husband turned out to be a drug addict, however, and he eventually passed along the habit to his wife.

One day a stranger showed up in the village. He had come looking for children to buy and take away with him, children he would then resell as labourers. The boy's parents, willing to do anything to support their drug habit, took the man's money and gave him their son.

"I was taken to a tea shop," the boy told us. "My job was to wash the cups and glasses. If I broke one, my master would yell at me and call me stupid, and then beat me up."

After several months, he managed to escape. He ended up on the streets of Kathmandu. The only skill he had was washing teacups. He found a job in another tea shop, but this man turned out to be worse than the first one. Again he was forced into working for nothing but his food.

40 "I tried to escape, many times," he said, his words broken by the painful memories. "Every time, the man beat me. Then I became sick. The man thought I was dying, so he dumped me in the street."

He was discovered by street kids, who told a worker from CWIN they had found a dead boy in a back alley. When the worker showed up, the boy was still alive, though barely. They managed to get him to the hospital, and in time he recovered. A few physical scars remained and many emotional ones.

"They all thought I would die. But I didn't," the boy said proudly. In those words I detected a conviction to fight off the pain he had suffered in the past, to find a way to a better future.

Our translator cautioned us not to be too optimistic. He told us the boy had built a shell around himself. He wouldn't let anyone too close for fear of being hurt again. Any rehabilitation would take a long time.

That afternoon CWIN threw a party to celebrate its ninth anniversary, and invited all the street kids who came to their centers. A tent had been set up with a stage and a microphone. There was music and dancing, and lots of food.

45 The kids loved it. Each center had written a play to be performed by the kids. Some were comic, some serious. They were all big on costumes and props, making great use of what few materials were available to them. There was no shortage of talent, and little stage fright. A favorite scenario was a chase between a policeman and a robber. Of course, the robber always managed to outsmart the cop, much to the delight of an audience who'd experienced more than their share of run-ins with the law.

In one play, a big box was brought on the stage. The robber kept outwitting the cop by disappearing into the box. It was a simple plot, but the audience loved it, laughing uproariously each time the cop was left scratching his head. When it was over, the boy who played the robber bowed to the loudest applause of the afternoon.

When we returned to the relative comfort of "Hotel PLAN," I looked around and saw how trivial were the inconveniences I sometimes had to deal with in my life. I was surprised that some of these heroic young people could laugh and smile as much as they did.

It was New Year's Eve. Tomorrow would be the first day of 1996. A time for celebration? A wild party late into the night? Not for Alam. He ended the year with a bad stomachache. He figured it was all because of some condiments he'd had with his curry that night. According to our guidebook, Nepal is not known for its cuisine. But there were lots of places to indulge in foreign food, so Alam decided to go for an old favourite. The local condiment on the side of his plate seemed innocent enough, but there must have been some bacteria crawling through it, because his normally iron stomach took a beating. Off he went to bed, and slept his way into the new year.

I was left to party by myself. I washed and scrubbed—socks, turtleneck, underwear, everything—and then hung my laundry out to dry, like party banners through "Hotel PLAN." I rocked the place past midnight. It was no Times Square, and I skipped the champagne, but I made the most of it.

50   The next morning Alam was already up and dressed when I awoke. He had even gone off to the market and returned with breakfast.

"Looks like you've made a miraculous recovery," I said sleepily.

"Happy New Year!" He was rather more lively than when he went to bed. "How did you celebrate?"

"I kept it quiet. You know, just some good, clean fun."

Soon we were all set to go. We met up with someone from CWIN who had offered to be our guide and translator for the day.

55   All through Nepal we had seen a type of vehicle that the local people called "tempos." Many of them had a young boy standing on the back bumper as they made their way through the city.

"It would be great if we could talk to some of these children," I said to our guide.

He took us to a street in the centre of Kathmandu. It was here that many of the tempos came to be refueled. We strolled over to where five or six were gathered.

A tempo looks like a cross between a taxi and a minibus, with room to squeeze in eight or ten people. The passengers get on and off through an open doorway at the back. Tempo owners hire young boys (because they are lightweight and cheap labor) to announce the stops, direct the passengers, collect the fares, and stop anyone from jumping off without paying. When the tempos are in motion, the boys stand on the back step and hang on to the frame of the open doorway.

It's not an easy job, or a safe one. Choking gas fumes and black smoke spew out from the tailpipes, even when the tempos are idling. And if one comes to a quick stop or has to swerve suddenly in traffic, the boy could easily be thrown to the street. Stories of legs being run over and bones being broken were common. Boys had been maimed for life and even struck down and killed, all for the sake of a few rupees.

60   Hanging around the tempos, waiting for his workday to begin, was a twelve-year-old boy. The corners of his mouth were raw with infection. On his chin, a section of skin the size of a small coin had been torn away.

"How long have you worked as a tempo helper?" our translator asked.

The boy shifted about uncomfortably, his dirty and hardened feet slipping out of their sandals. He couldn't remember.

"How many hours do you work a day?"

"Twelve."

65   "For how much money?"

"Thirty rupees."

It was less than one U.S. dollar.

"What do you want to do in the future?"

"Buy a tempo," he was quick to answer.

70   "Won't it take a very long time to save that much money?"

"Yes. But I will make more when I am sixteen."

By law, children had to be sixteen to work as tempo helpers, but like a lot of child-labour laws in South Asia, this one was never enforced. In the meantime, because the boy was underage, the driver paid him a lower wage.

His dream of owning a tempo seemed very remote to us. What would become of him? I wondered. I hoped his ambition stayed with him, and that somehow his life as an adult would become better than what he faced as a child.

Farther down the same street, we came upon a young girl sitting on the ground at the roadside, selling oranges and small candies from a broad, flat basket. She was shy at first and reluctant to talk to us, but she whispered to our translator that her parents sent her out each morning with the basket and a collection of items. Whenever cars stopped, perhaps caught in traffic, she would brave the exhaust fumes and hurry from window to window, her basket held high. I could see that in midsummer her work must have been even more torturous. Long hours in the blazing sun, breathing smoke and carbon monoxide, would be a hellish way to spend a childhood. It was a heartbreaking contrast to the carefree summers of most North American children her age.

75 The unfortunate girl also had to take care of her baby sister. The child, less than a year old, squirmed about next to her, whining and trying to get away. The girl kept trying to entertain her, with the hope that she would sit still. She herself was only ten.

We discovered she had gone to school for only two months in her whole life. Like a lot of girls her age, she was expected to take care of younger children in the family. Often girls are kept at home for that reason, and to do household chores. More than 88 percent of Nepalese girls fourteen and under (and more than 60 percent of boys) are illiterate. They are denied an education, because parents see no value in it; girls are expected to marry and take care of the home and raise children.

But that, at least, was better than the fate of many young girls in Nepal, who were being sold by their families and ending up as prostitutes. Up to seven thousand young Nepalese girls are trafficked each year, many sent to the brothels of Bombay and Bangkok and other cities in countries nearby.

I learned that loan sharks arrive in the villages of Nepal to secure girls by lending money to their families. The loan sharks deceive the girls and their parents by telling them they will become waitresses or factory workers, but often they are never seen by their parents again. Those who do manage to escape life in the brothels are shunned and ignored. Many find themselves infected with the AIDS virus.

It is a cruel and hideous crime. Only recently has there been any active campaign to stop it, with some governments being shamed into action. In some cases, raids have been undertaken on the brothels of Bombay, and girls returned to Nepal. The girls are brought to rehabilitation centers where they undergo counselling in an effort to integrate them back into society.

80 We continued a little farther along the street. Before long, we came upon another working child, again a girl, again not yet a teenager. This girl

was seated on the ground beside a stone slab, using a hammer to break up pieces of old brick to be used in the manufacture of new ones. We discovered she worked from dawn to dusk, and earned only food and shelter.

"I have no choice," she said. "I ran away from home. I was beaten. Before this I lived on the street."

"How did you get this job?"

"The lady who owns the quarry gave it to me."

When the owner came out to see why a crowd had gathered, she had a different story.

85   "The girl was dumped here by her parents. I took pity on her. I could have tossed her out on the street. She works a few hours a day, and for her work I provide food and a place to sleep."

As we were leaving, one of the people who had stopped to listen had yet another explanation. "She was a street child," he said. "That is true. But she escaped from a brothel. This is how she got here."

Three different stories, or perhaps the same story with different details. The fact remained that the girl worked long hours breaking bricks for food and shelter, and received not a cent for her labour.

She told our guide that she wanted to be a teacher when she was older. When I looked at her, I could almost picture it. In her eyes was the faraway look of someone who dreamed of a life much better than her own. In her manner was the pride of someone who knew what she was capable of. Perhaps she would find a way to be free of this miserable existence. The chances seemed very slim, but what is anyone's world without hope?

Before leaving Canada I had always assumed that child labour was something hidden, kept out of the public eye, something I would find only in dark alleyways and back streets. I thought we would have to break down doors to get to these children. But within the space of an hour, walking down one street, I had come upon three different instances of child labour, all of them in full view of everyone, including the police and government officials. Yet it continued.

90   Later that day, Alam and I were picked up by a driver to visit a school that PLAN had set up in a village about one hour outside Kathmandu. It was a rough ride, often along narrow roads through mountainous terrain. The village was nestled into thickly forested mountains.

We arrived at the school to find a line of fifty students, each clutching wildflowers to present to us. In some cases they had woven the flowers into chains, and these they hung around our necks. It was a magical welcome.

It was a school holiday, in honor of the King of Nepal's birthday, and many of the students had made long trips on foot to be there. They performed some of their traditional songs and dances for us, then took us on a tour of their schoolroom, stopping to show us the drawings they had done in their art classes—animals, birds, village scenes.

The students obviously took a lot of pride in what they had accomplished. Many of them came from poor farming families, and such opportunities for education, especially for girls, were rare in Nepal. The students had formed clubs, one for boys and one for girls, and had taken their message of the value of education into the communities, going door to door, explaining to parents about what it meant for the futures of the children. They wrote letters to the government, asking that education be given a higher priority. They also did community service, such as explaining to families the importance of good nutrition and how to prevent the spread of disease. In many ways they reminded me of some of my friends back in Canada.

We ended our travel day with a visit to another village not far away. By that time it was almost dusk, and as we walked into the village we were met with a sea of dark faces, many of them children, all with wide, welcoming smiles. We met children amongst them sponsored by people overseas.

95 As long as I could remember, my parents had also sponsored children in other countries. It was a moving experience to meet children like the ones in the pictures and letters that came to our home in Canada.

The families tended gardens along the mountainsides and lived in simple thatched dwellings they call *durahs*. We were guests for supper in one of these homes. The meat dish placed before me was a strange pink mixture that made my eyes widen in dread. I was sure if I stared long enough I would see it twitch. Yet I could not offend our hosts. I ate, and somehow persuaded my stomach to cooperate. Immediately after the meal, I made a quick exit into the fresh air.

We left the village with the sun well below the horizon, and I walked back to our vehicle with a trail of kids tagging behind me.

"I live in Canada," I said, "far, far away." I swooped my hand in the air, making the motions of an airplane. "But first I go back to India."

They laughed and chattered among themselves, probably not understanding a word I had said. But they had made friends with me, and that was the important thing. As our vehicle moved away, the older kids raced after it, slowing to a stop only when they saw there was no chance of catching up.

100 "*Namasto,*" I called for a final time. "Goodbye".

"*Namasto,*" several of them chanted in reply.

When we flew out of Nepal the next day, the flight took us over many similar mountain villages. I wished the children in them were all as hopeful as the ones we had visited.

I knew they probably weren't. As I looked down over the mountain peaks, I realized that the struggles of these children were far more critical than the struggles of tourists I had pictured earlier trekking through the mountains.

It was not mountain climbers I pictured now; it was young girls and boys burdened with the struggles of everyday life.

CONVERSATION STARTER

Share what you know about the lives of children who are exploited as workers in Third World Nations.

READING MATTERS

1. Why is Craig meeting with the CWIN? What role does the organization play in Nepal and in Kathmandu in particular? What are the greatest challenges that the organization faces?
2. How many children in Nepal under the age of 14 are involved in full- or part-time labor? How many street children live in Kathmandu? How do they support themselves? How does the CWIN try to help these children?
3. List several different ways that child laborers are exploited in Kathmandu. Does the selection suggest that the CWIN and other similar types of organizations will be able to help such children to find work that will enable them to develop more stable and fulfilling lives?
4. Do you think that the children who live in the villages of Nepal have more hope for finding meaningful work because they can attend school and have more community support than the street children of Kathmandu? Explain your response.

WRITING MATTERS

1. Do some more research into the exploitation of child laborers in Nepal or in another Third World Nation. Write a paper that presents what you have learned about the conditions that the children work under and any organization or legislation that is helping to improve the children's lives.
2. Volunteer to work at an agency that helps children in Nepal or another Third World Nation to find fair-paying jobs and to attend school. Write an essay that discusses what you have learned from your volunteer experience.
3. Read *Free the Children,* from which this selection is excerpted. Then write an essay about what you learned through studying Kielburger's transformation from a middle-class youth to an activist on behalf of child laborers. What motivated him to change and to develop his new perspective and role? Or, write an essay that presents more information about the lives of children who are forced to work in Third World Nations.

RELEVANT WEB SITES

FREE THE CHILDREN <http://www.freethechildren.org>

The official web site of Free the Children, an international network of children helping children through representation, leadership, and action.

COMMUNITY YOUTH DEVELOPMENT
<http://www.cydjournal.org/2000Winter/kielburger.html>

Learn about Craig Kielburger's perspective on youth activism and the need for intergenerational collaboration through an interview with the *CYD Journal,* published by the Institute for Just Communities (IJC) and the Institute for Sustainable Development, Heller School of Social Policy and Management, Brandeis University.

Writing About Work

1. What benefits do people derive from work, aside from simply providing for basic material needs such as food, shelter, clothing, and transportation? Consider the points of view presented in the readings in this chapter, and then conduct some interviews with family members, friends, or mentors. After finding out more about the various reasons why people work in your community, write a paper that integrates and interprets what you have learned.

2. Write an essay that describes the culture of a particular workplace. How are values expressed by the employers and employees? Why do people choose to work there? How has a sense of community developed at the workplace? Does the sense of community extend beyond the workplace? In what ways is the workplace traditional? In what ways is it nontraditional? In what ways is the workplace community-alienating?

3. How is today's workplace different from how it was 10 years ago? How will it continue to change? Will more people work at home or at an office? What types of work sites will develop in the upcoming years? How much commuting will people do? What will be the role of telecommuting? How will workers establish a sense of community? Write an essay that presents your point of view and predictions. Refer to relevant selections in this chapter; do Internet and/or library research to support your observations and projections.

4. What type of work do you think you are qualified for? Go online and look through the different job sectors: business, nonprofit, public, and private. Read through the employment sections of your local newspaper. Select two different positions that you would like to apply for. Develop a resumé and cover letter for each position. Include the job announcements.

5. What is your ideal career? Do some library or Internet research on your ideal career and interview people in your community who have the type of job that interests you. Do not restrict yourself to traditional jobs. Then write an essay that presents a strategy for reaching your ideal career. Be creative in designing your plans.

6. Do you believe that men and women have equal access to the job market? Do men and women tend to play different roles in the workplace? Do men and women value work for different reasons? Focus on researching one or two of these questions, at the library,

on the Internet, or through conducting interviews. Also consider the relevant selections in this chapter. Then write an essay for your class that presents your point of view on the issue that you have explored.

7. Write an essay that discusses the impact that computers have had and will continue to have on the workplace. How will the skills and resources necessary to be a successful worker change? What will the technology of the workplace be like in ten years?

8. If you were an employer, how would you create an attractive work environment? How would you motivate and inspire your employees? Write an essay that presents your ideal workplace community. What relevant strategies have you learned from the reading selections in this chapter and from your own work experiences?

9. Watch several different contemporary films, each of which presents a unique perspective on work. Then write an essay for your class that explains each film's perspective on work. Also discuss how each perspective has particular relevance for your generation, your particular peer group, or your family's generation.

10. Volunteer to help at a nonprofit organization in your community that serves people who have work-related problems. Write about your experience for your class or for a community newspaper or newsletter. Describe your volunteer experience, what knowledge you gained, and how the experience affected you. Alternatively, develop a web site, brochure, report, or newsletter for a nonprofit community organization that helps people in your community to find jobs or solve problems that arise from workplace situations.

11. Write an essay that discusses what you think will be the consequence of the economic divide in our country. Refer to articles in this chapter, to research you have done, and to personal experience and observation to support your main ideas. Alternatively, write an essay that suggests what needs to be done to eliminate the economic inequality as well as the self-destructive potential that this economic divide nurtures. Again, refer to articles in this chapter, to research you have done, and to personal experience and observation to support your main ideas.

10

Health

Peace Memorial Park in Hiroshima, Japan

Many people take their health for granted, while others feel that their health is a private matter: one to be shared with their doctor, close family members, or friends. How often do we forget to think about how and why the issues related to health, although personal, are also deeply rooted in complex public and community problems? The quality and availability of our health care is determined to a tremendous extent by legislation crafted by local, state, and national government. All citizens need to become more actively involved in the public debates as well as in community meetings, and to learn more about community health resources that are available to them, which they may need if they or a loved one faces a minor or major health problem.

Why, we may ask, have many people adopted passive, frustrated, and/or fearful notions about taking responsibility for their own health care? The articles we have selected for this chapter and the questions and writing prompts that we provide for you to reflect upon should raise your awareness about the changing quality of modern, technologically complex medicine, thus helping you to become more actively engaged in health care issues as well as helping you to realize that no doctor can always be completely certain if he or she has made the right decision for your treatment. As surgeon and writer Atul Gawande says, "Medicine's ground state is uncertainty. And wisdom—for both patient and doctors—is defined by how one copes with it."

The selections we have included ask you to think about many issues. For example, how are the increasing numbers of female doctors changing medical care and how do female doctors with children balance their responsibilities to their professions and to their families? How will genetic engineering affect our future? Can health and happiness be earned through hard work? We certainly hope that you will learn from these readings that you will be making the final decision about your medical treatment—your doctor can only advise you, and that we must all work to raise the standards of health care in our communities for the rich, the middle class, and the poor alike; otherwise, we all will suffer. Health is a community issue.

The selections in the first section of the chapter, "New Realities and Roles for Doctors and Patients," explore the sensitive, complex, and stressful aspects of being a patient and a doctor. In different ways, all of the selections ask us to demystify the god-like power that is associated with doctors. In our first selection, Atul Gawande, in "The Case of the Red Leg" reveals the complexity of diagnosing and curing a young woman with a serious rash on her leg that possibly could lead to its amputation. Through science, intuition, determination, and caring, the patient's leg is saved, and the reader sees how patients, doctors, and parents have to listen to and care for one another's points of view while accepting the risk-taking that sometimes is necessary to cure an unusual disease. The next selection, "The Tennis Partner," by Abraham Verghese, M.D., explores the problems that doctors can have with addictions, and how those addictions can sometimes destroy their professional and personal lives. What leads a doctor to become addicted to an illegal substance? Is it stress? Is it genetic inheritance? This selection is hopeful in that it shows how doctors who have been substance abusers are helping first-timers and one another, using the medical community itself to promote recovery. In our third selection, Julia McMurray, a pediatrician and an advocate for women's health, writes about her own struggle to balance her home life and her professional responsibilities in her essay "Doctor's Daughter." She writes, "I would feel crazed with worry and guilt when a waiting room full of patients were waiting for me at the hospital while I sat helplessly in the pediatrician's office with my sick child. . . ." While life for a woman who also is a physician is never simple, the practice of medicine can benefit from learning about the unique experiences of female doctors.

Our second section, "Solving Today's Health Care Issues," opens with a selection from Greg Crister's best seller, *Fatland America: What Can Be Done?* Crister provides invaluable evidence and advice for how parents and children, schoolteachers, school administrators, and politicians can begin to reverse the frightening trend toward obesity in America. Social activist and community advocate Robert D. Putnam in "Health and Happiness," from his recent book, *Bowling Alone,* introduces another crucial health issue that haunts many of our lives: Can we really find health and happiness through competition, work, and the accumulation of money and material possessions? Putnam provides excellent evidence for his argument that community support from family, friends, and colleagues is more important to any individual's health than material success and the funds to afford excellent medical care. Next, Professor Francis Fukiyama writes about the final ethical issues in medical research in "Policies for the Future," the conclusion of his recent book, *Our Posthuman Future.* The excerpt we have included helps to clarify the potential dangers and advantages, as well as the legal and ethical challenges, of genetic engineering.

Our chapter closes with the section "Building Communities to Address Health Issues." The three pieces exemplify different ways that serious and pervasive health problems have been successfully improved, if not solved, through community support. In the first selection, poet Audre Lorde uses writing *The Cancer Journals* to reach her community and especially to encourage women with breast cancer to break the debilitating silence that surrounds the disease, which makes the painful experience even more isolating and devastating. Her journals give us insight into illness that we may have to face in our private lives and will confront in our public responsibilities. Idealistic community organizations such as the Peace Corps and Americorps are dedicated to helping the underprivileged. Doctors Without Borders (Médecins Sans Frontières–MSF), which has existed since 1971, is one of those organizations. According to Elliott Leyton, author of "The Obliteration of Alienation," those who volunteer to help in the face of crisis after crisis do not see themselves as heroes (although some of us may think that they are). Of his colleagues he says, "They all share in the intoxication of focused collective action. . . . This is disalienation, the antithesis of the programmed numbness that life in a modern industrial city can be, commuting alone to anonymous work with strangers."

We close *Community Matters* with "The One-Thousand Paper Cranes Casebook," which presents an ancient legend in the process of recreating itself in the modern world. The story begins with the death of a schoolgirl who was poisoned by radiation from the bombing of Hiroshima. In their attempts to keep their classmate, Sadako, alive and to memorialize her tragic death, her fellow students folded a thousand paper cranes because a Japanese legend says that this act will ensure an individual's immortality. The story of how Sadako's schoolmates eventually raised the funds to build a memorial for their friend and for the cause of a peaceful world free of the health problems associated with nuclear testing and nuclear war has inspired peace and paper crane folding events around the world. This casebook highlights only a few of the many ways that the legend has been reborn in modern times, and also how a collective global movement for peace can be born from strong local action.

New Realities and Roles for Doctors and Patients

Atul Gawande (b. 1976)

The Case of the Red Leg

Atul Gawande is a surgical resident in Boston and a staff writer on medicine and science for The New Yorker. *A graduate of Harvard Medical School and the Harvard School of Public Health, Gawande's writing has been selected to appear in* The Best American Essays 2002 *and* The Best American Science and Nature Writing 2002. *About Gawande's first book* Complications: A Surgeon's Notes on an Imperfect Science *(2002), Pulitzer prize–winning columnist Ellen Goodman has said, "Atul Gawande is a rare and wonderful storyteller who portrays his profession with bravery and humanity." Gawande has interwoven many themes into his collection of stories about his patients, but his main concern is to "demystify" medicine and to make the public aware that "doctors are not gods."*

With all that we know nowadays about people and diseases and how to diagnose and treat them, it can be hard to see this, hard to grasp how deeply the uncertainty runs. As a doctor, you come to find, however, that the struggle in caring for people is more often with what you do not know than what you do. Medicine's ground state is uncertainty. And wisdom—for both patients and doctors—is defined by how one copes with it.

This is the story of one decision under uncertainty.

It was two o'clock on a Tuesday afternoon in June. I was in the middle of a seven-week stint as the senior surgical resident in the emergency room. I had just finished admitting someone with a gallbladder infection and was attempting to sneak out for a bite to eat when one of the emergency room physicians stopped me with yet another patient to see: a twenty-three-year-old, Eleanor Bratton, with a red and swollen leg. (The names of patients and colleagues have been changed.) "It's probably only a cellulitis"—a simple skin infection—"but it's a bad one," he said. He had started her on some intravenous antibiotics and admitted her to the medical service. But he wanted me to make sure there wasn't anything "surgical" going on—an abscess that needed draining or some such. "Would you mind taking a quick look?" Groan. No. Of course not.

510

She was in the observation units, a separate, quieter ward within the ER where she could get antibiotics pumped into her arm and wait for admitting to find her a bed upstairs. The unit's nine beds are arrayed in a semicircle, each separated by a thin blue curtain, and I found her in Bed 1. She looked fit, athletic, and almost teenage, with blond hair tight in a pony-tail, nails painted gold, and her eyes fixed on a television. There did not seem anything seriously ill about her. She was lying comfortably, a sheet pulled up to her waist, the head of the bed raised. I glanced at her chart and saw that she had good vital signs, no fever, and no past medical problems. I walked up and introduced myself: "Hi, I'm Dr. Gawande. I'm the senior surgical resident down here. How are you doing?"

5   "You're from surgery?" she said, with a look that was part puzzlement and part alarm. I tried to reassure her. The emergency physician was "only being cautious," I said, and having me see her to make sure it was nothing more than a cellulitis. All I wanted to do was ask a few questions and look at her leg. Could she tell me what had been going on? For a moment she said nothing, still trying to compute what to think about all this. Then she let out a sigh and told me the story.

That weekend she had gone back home to Hartford, Connecticut, to attend a wedding. (She had moved to Boston with some girlfriends the year before, after graduating from Ithaca College, and landed work planning con-ferences for a downtown law firm.) The wedding had been grand and she had kicked off her shoes and danced the whole night. The morning after, however, she woke up with her left foot feeling sore. She had a week-old blister on the top of her foot from some cruddy sandals she had worn, and now the skin surrounding the blister was red and puffy. She didn't think too much of this at first. When she showed her foot to her father, he said he thought it looked like a bee sting or maybe like she'd gotten stepped on dancing the night before. By late that afternoon, however, riding back to Boston with her boyfriend, "my foot really began killing me," she said. The redness spread, and during the night she got chills and sweats and a fever of one hundred and three degrees. She took ibuprofen every few hours, which got her temperature down but did nothing for the mounting pain. By morn-ing, the redness reached halfway up her calf, and her foot had swelled to the point that she could barely fit it into a sneaker.

Eleanor hobbled in on her roommate's shoulder to see her internist that afternoon and was diagnosed with a cellulitis. Cellulitis is your garden-variety skin infection, the result of perfectly ordinary bacteria in the envi-ronment getting past the barrier of your skin (through a cut, a puncture wound, a blister, whatever) and proliferating within it. Your skin becomes red, hot, swollen, and painful; you feel sick; fevers are common; and the infection can spread along your skin readily—precisely the findings Eleanor had. The doctor got an X ray to make sure the bone underneath was not infected. Satisfied that it was not, she gave Eleanor a dose of intra-venous antibiotics in the office, a tetanus shot, and a prescription for a week's worth of antibiotic pills. This was generally sufficient treatment for a cellulitis, but not always, the doctor warned. Using an indelible black marker, she traced the border of the redness on Eleanor's calf. If the redness should extend beyond this line, the doctor instructed, she should call. And, regardless, she should return the next day for the infection to be checked.

The next morning, Eleanor said—this morning—she woke up with the rash beyond the black line, a portion stretching to her thigh, and the pain worse than ever. She phoned the doctor, who told her to go to the emergency room. She'd need to be admitted to the hospital for a full course of intravenous antibiotic treatment, the doctor explained.

I asked Eleanor if she had had any pus or drainage from her leg. No. Any ulcers open up in her skin? No. A foul smell or blackening of her skin? No. Any more fevers? Not since two days ago. I let the data roll around in my head. Everything was going for a cellulitis. But something was pricking at me, making me alert.

10   I asked Eleanor if I could see the rash. She pulled back the sheet. The right leg looked fine. The left leg was red—a beefy, uniform, angry red—from her forefoot, across her ankle, up her calf, past the black ink line from the day before, to her knee, with a further tongue of crimson extending to the inside of her thigh. The border was sharp. The skin was hot and tender to the touch. The blister on the top of her foot was tiny. Around it the skin was slightly bruised. Her toes were uninvolved, and she wiggled them for me without difficulty. She had a harder time moving the foot itself—it was thick with edema up through the ankle. She had normal sensation and pulses throughout her leg. She had no ulcers or pus.

Objectively, the rash had the exact appearance of cellulitis, something antibiotics would take care of. But another possibility lodged in my mind now, one that scared the hell out of me. It was not for logical reasons, though. And I knew this perfectly well.

Decisions in medicine are supposed to rest on concrete observations and hard evidence. But just a few weeks before, I had taken care of a patient I could not erase from my mind. He was a healthy fifty-eight-year-old man who had had three or four days of increasing pain in the left side of his chest, under his arm, where he had an abrasion from a fall. (For reasons of confidentiality, some identifying details have been changed.) He went to a community hospital near his home to get it checked out. He was found to have a small and very ordinary skin rash on his chest and was sent home with antibiotic pills for cellulitis. That night the rash spread eight inches. The following morning he spiked a fever of one hundred and two degrees. By the time he returned to the emergency room, the skin involved had become numb and widely blistered. Shortly after, he went into shock. He was transferred to my hospital and we quickly took him to the OR.

He didn't have a cellulitis but instead an extremely rare and horrendously lethal type of infection known as necrotizing fasciitis (fa-shee-EYE-tiss). The tabloids have called it a disease of "flesh-eating bacteria" and the term is not an exaggeration. Opening the skin, we found a massive infection, far worse than what appeared from the outside. All the muscles of the left side of his chest, going around to his back, up to his shoulder, and down to his abdomen, had turned gray and soft and foul with invading bacteria and had to be removed. That first day in the OR, we had had to take even the muscles between his ribs, a procedure called a birdcage thoracotomy. The next day we had to remove his arm. For a while, we actually thought we had saved him. His fevers went away and the plastic surgeons reconstructed his chest and abdominal wall with transfers of muscle and sheets of Gortex. One by one, however, his kidneys, lungs, liver, and heart went into failure, and then he died. It was among the most awful cases I have ever been involved in.

What we know about necrotizing fasciitis is this: it is highly aggressive and rapidly invasive. It kills up to 70 percent of the people who get it. No known antibiotic will stop it. The most common bacterium involved is group A *Streptococcus* (and, in fact, the final cultures from our patient's tissue grew out precisely this). It is an organism that usually causes little more than a strep throat, but in certain strains it has evolved the ability to do far worse. No one knows where these strains come from. As with a cellulitis, they are understood to enter through breaks in the skin. The break can be as large as a surgical incision or as slight as an abrasion. (People have been documented to have gotten the disease from a rug burn, a bug bite, a friendly punch in the arm, a paper cut, a blood draw, a toothpick injury, and chicken pox lesions. In many the entry point is never found at all.) Unlike with a cellulitis, the bacteria invade not only skin but also deep underneath, advancing rapidly along the outer sheaths of muscle (the fascia) and consuming whatever soft tissue (fat, muscle, nerves, connective tissue) they find. Survival is possible only with early and radical excisional surgery, often requiring amputation. To succeed, however, it must be done early. By the time signs of deep invasion are obvious—such as shock, loss of sensation, widespread blistering of the skin—the person is usually unsalvageable.

15   Standing at Eleanor's bedside, bent over examining her leg, I felt a little foolish considering the diagnosis—it was a bit like thinking the ebola virus had walked into the ER. True, in the early stages, a necrotizing fasciitis can look just like a cellulitis, presenting with the same redness, swelling, fever, and high white blood cell count. But there is an old saying taught in medical school: if you hear hoofbeats in Texas, think horses not zebras. Only about a thousand cases of necrotizing fasciitis occur in the entire United States each year, mainly in the elderly and chronically ill—and well over *three million* cases of cellulitis. What's more, Eleanor's fever had gone away; she didn't look unusually ill; and I knew I was letting myself be swayed by a single, recent, anecdotal case. If there were a simple test to tell the two diagnoses apart, that would have been one thing. But there is none. The only way is to go to the operating room, open the skin, and look—not something you want to propose arbitrarily.

Yet here I was. I couldn't help it. I was thinking it.

I pulled the sheets back over Eleanor's legs. "I'll be back in a minute," I said. I went to a phone well out of her earshot and paged Thaddeus Studdert, the general surgeon on call. He called back from the OR and I quickly outlined the facts of the case. I told him the rash was probably just a cellulitis. But then I told him there was still one other possibility that I couldn't get out of my head: a necrotizing fasciitis.

The line went silent for a beat.

"Are you serious?" he said.

20   "Yes," I said, trying not to hedge. I heard an epithet muttered. He'd be right up, he said.

As I hung up the phone, Eleanor's father, a brown-and-gray-haired man in his fifties, came around with a sandwich and soda for her. He had been with her all day, having driven up from Hartford, but when I was seeing her, it turned out, he had been gone getting her lunch. Catching sight of the food, I jumped to tell him not to let her eat or drink "just yet" and with that the cat began crawling out of the bag. It was not the best way to introduce myself. He was immediately taken aback, recognizing that an empty stomach is what we require for patients going to surgery. I tried to smooth matters over, saying that holding off was merely "routine procedure" until we had finished our evaluation. Nevertheless, Eleanor and her father looked on with new dread when Studdert arrived in his scrubs and operating hat to see her.

He had her tell her story again and then uncovered her leg to examine it. He didn't seem too impressed. Talking by ourselves, he told me that the rash looked to him only "like a bad cellulitis." But could he say for sure that it was not necrotizing fasciitis? He could not. It is a reality of medicine that choosing to *not* do something—to not order a test, to not give an antibiotic, to not take a patient to the operating room—is far harder than choosing to do it. Once a possibility has been put in your mind—especially one as horrible as necrotizing fasciitis—the possibility does not easily go away.

Studdert sat down on the edge of her bed. He told Eleanor and her dad that her story, symptoms, and exam all fit with cellulitis and that that was what she most likely had. But there was another, very rare possibility, and, in a quiet and gentle voice, he went on to explain the unquiet and ungentle effects of necrotizing fasciitis. He told them of the "flesh-eating bacteria," the troublingly high death rate, the resistance to treatment by antibiotics alone. "I think it is unlikely you have it," he told Eleanor. "I'd put the chances"—he was guessing here—"at well under five percent." But, he went on, "without a biopsy, we cannot rule it out." He paused for a moment to let her and her father absorb this. Then he started to explain what the procedure involved—how he would take an inch or so of skin plus underlying tissue from the top of her foot, and perhaps from higher up on her leg, and then have a pathologist immediately look at the samples under the microscope.

Eleanor went rigid. "This is crazy," she said. "This doesn't make any sense." She looked frantic, like someone drowning. "Why don't we just wait and see how the antibiotics go?" Studdert explained that this was a disease that you cannot sit on, that you had to catch it early to have any chance of treating it. Eleanor just shook her head and looked down at her covers.

25   Studdert and I both turned to her father to see what he might have to say. He had been silent to this point, standing beside her, his brow knitted, hands gripped behind him, tense, like a man trying to stay upright on a pitching boat. He asked about specifics—how long a biopsy would take (fifteen minutes), what the risks were (a deep wound infection was the biggest one, ironically), whether the scars go away (no), when it would be done if it were done (within the hour). More gingerly, he asked what would happen if the biopsy were positive for the disease. Studdert repeated that he thought the chances were less than 5 percent. But if she had it, he said, we'd have to "remove all the infected tissue." He hesitated before going on. "This can mean an amputation," he said. Eleanor began to cry. "I don't want to do this, Dad." Mr. Bratton swallowed hard, his gaze fixed somewhere miles beyond us.

But in the face of uncertainty, what other than judgment does a physician have—or a patient have, for that matter? Months after seeing Eleanor that spring afternoon, I spoke with her father about the events that had unfolded.

"It felt like it was five minutes from having a swollen foot to being told that she could possibly be losing her life," Mr. Bratton said.

A chef who had owned his own delicatessen for seventeen years and now taught at a culinary arts school in Hartford, he knew no one in Boston. He knew our hospital was affiliated with Harvard, but he knew enough to realize that this did not necessarily mean we were anything special. I was just the resident on duty that day; Studdert was likewise just the surgeon on call. Eleanor had left things to her father now, and he tried to take stock. Some clues were encouraging. Studdert's being in scrubs and an operating hat, having just come from the OR, seemed to suggest experience and know-how. Indeed, it turned out he had seen a number of patients with necrotizing fasciitis before. He was also self-assured, without being bullying, and took time to explain everything. But Bratton was shocked at how young he appeared. (Studdert was, in fact, just thirty-five.)

"This is my daughter we are talking about," Bratton remembered thinking at the time. "Isn't there anybody better than you?" Then he knew what to do. He turned to Studdert and me and spoke softly.

30   "I'd like another opinion," was what he said.

We agreed to the request, and it did not upset us. We were not oblivious to the conundrums here. Eleanor's fever had gone away; she didn't look unusually ill; and likely the biggest reason I had thought of flesh-eating bacteria was that terrible case I had seen a few weeks before. Studdert had put a numeric estimate on the chances of the disease—"well under five percent" he had said—but we both knew it was a stab in the dark (a measure of probability and confidence, but how good is that?) and a vague one at that (how *much* less than 5 percent?). Hearing what someone else might think seemed useful, we both thought.

But, for the Brattons, I had to wonder how useful it would be. If opinions disagreed, then what? And if they did not, wouldn't the same fallibilities and questions remain? Furthermore, the Brattons did not know anyone to call and had to ask if *we* had any ideas.

We suggested calling David Segal, a plastic surgeon on staff who like Studdert had seen such cases before. They agreed. I called Segal and filled him in. He came down within minutes. In the end what he gave Eleanor and her father was mainly confidence, from what I could see.

Segal is a rumpled and complexly haired man, with pen stains on his white coat and glasses that seem too large for his face. He is the only plastic surgeon I know who looks like he has a Ph.D. from M.I.T. (which, as it happens, he does). But he seemed, as Bratton later put it, "not young." And he did not disagree with what Studdert had said. He listened to Eleanor's story and looked carefully at her leg and then said that he too would be surprised if she turned out to have the bacteria. But he agreed that it could not be ruled out. So what else was there but to biopsy?

35   Eleanor and her dad now agreed to go ahead. "Let's get it over with," she said. But then I brought her the surgical consent form to sign. On it, I had written not only that the procedure was a "biopsy of the left lower extremity" but also that the risks included a "possible need for amputation." She cried out when she saw the words. It took her several minutes alone with her father before she could sign. We had her in the operating room almost immediately after. A nurse brought her father to the family waiting area. He tracked her mother down by cell phone. Then he sat and bowed his head, and made some prayers for his child.

The anesthesiologist put Eleanor to sleep. A nurse then painted her leg with antiseptic, from her toes up to her hip. With a small knife, Studdert cut out an inch-long ellipse of skin and tissue from the top of her foot, where the blister was, down to her tendon. The specimen was plopped into a jar of sterile saline and rushed to the pathologist to look at. We then took a second specimen—going deeper now, down into muscle—from the center of the redness in her calf, and this was sent on as well.

At first glance beneath her skin, there was nothing apparent to alarm us. The fat layer was yellow, as it is supposed to be, and the muscle was a healthy glistening red and bled appropriately. When we probed with the tip of a clamp inside the calf incision, however, it slid unnaturally easily along the muscle, as if bacteria had paved a path. This is not a definitive finding, but enough of one that Studdert let out a sudden, disbelieving, "Oh shit." He pulled off his gloves and gown to go see what the pathologist had found, and I followed right behind him, leaving Eleanor asleep in the OR to be watched over by another resident and the anesthesiologist.

An emergent pathology examination is called a frozen section, and the frozen section room was just a few doors down the hallway. The room was small, the size of a kitchen. In the middle of it stood a waist-high laboratory table with a black slate countertop and a canister of liquid nitrogen in which the pathologist had quick-frozen the tissue samples. Along a wall was the microtome that he had used to slice micron-thin sections of the tissue to put on glass slides. We walked in just as he finished preparing the slides. He took them to a microscope and began scanning each one methodically, initially under low power magnification and then under high power. We hovered, no doubt annoyingly, awaiting the diagnosis. Minutes passed in silence.

"I don't know," the pathologist muttered, still staring through the eyepieces. The features he saw were "consistent with necrotizing fasciitis," he said, but he wasn't sure he could clinch the diagnosis. He said he would have to call in a dermatopathologist, a pathologist who specializes in looking at skin and soft tissue. It took twenty minutes before the specialist arrived and another five before he could make his call, our frustration growing. "She's got it," he finally announced grimly. He had detected some tiny patches where the deep tissue had begun to die. No cellulitis could do that, he said.

40   Studdert went to see Eleanor's father. When he walked into the crowded family waiting area, Bratton caught the expression on his face and began yelling, "Don't look at me like that! *Don't look at me like that!*" Studdert took him to a private side room, closed the door behind them, and told him that she appeared to have the disease. He would have to move fast, he said. He was not sure he could save her leg and he was not sure if he could save her life. He would need to open her leg up, see how bad things were, and then go from there. Bratton was overcome, crying and struggling to get out words. Studdert's own eyes were wet. Bratton said to "do what you have to do." Studdert nodded and left. Bratton then called his wife. He told her the news and then gave her a moment to reply. "I will never forget what I heard on the other end of the line," he later said. "Something, some sound, I cannot and will never be able to describe."

Decisions compound themselves, in medicine like in anything else. No sooner have you taken one fork in the road than another and another come upon you. The critical question now was what to do. In the OR, Segal joined Studdert to offer another set of hands. Together they slit open Eleanor's leg, from the base of her toes, across her ankle, to just below her knee, to get a full view of what was going on inside. They pulled the opening wide with retractors.

The disease was grossly visible now. In her foot and most of her calf, the outer, fascial layer of her muscles was gray and dead. A brownish dishwater fluid was seeping out with a faint smell of decay. (Tissue samples and bacterial cultures would later confirm that this was toxic group A *Streptococcus* advancing rapidly up her leg.)

"I thought about a BKA," a below-knee amputation, Studdert says, "even an AKA," an above-knee amputation. No one would have faulted him for doing either. But he found himself balking. "She was such a young girl," he explains. "It may seem harsh to say, but if it was a sixty-year-old man I would've taken the leg without question." This was partly, I think, a purely emotional unwillingness to cut off the limb of a pretty twenty-three-year-old—the kind of sentimentalism that can get you in trouble. But it was also partly instinct again, an instinct that her youth and fundamentally good health might allow him to get by with just removing the most infected tissue ("debridement") and washing out her foot and leg. Was this a good risk to take, with one of the deadliest bacteria known to man loose in her leg? Who knows? But take it he did.

For two hours, using scissors and electrocautery, he and Segal cut and stripped off the necrotic outer layers of her muscle, starting from the webbing of her toes, going up to the tendons of her calf. They took out tissue going three-quarters of the way around. Her skin hung from her leg like open coat flaps. Higher up, inside the thigh, they reached fascia that looked pink-white and fresh, very much alive. They poured two liters of sterile saline through the leg, trying to wash out as much of the bacteria as possible.

45   At the end, Eleanor seemed to be holding steady. Her blood pressure remained normal. Her temperature was ninety-nine degrees. Her oxygen levels were fine. And the worst-looking tissue had been removed from her leg.

But her heart rate was running a bit too fast, one hundred and twenty beats a minute, a sign that the bacteria had provoked a systemic reaction. She was requiring large amounts of intravenous fluid. Her foot looked dead. And her skin was still burning red with infection.

Studdert stood firm with his decision not to take more, but you could see he was uneasy about it. He and Segal conferred and thought of one other thing they could try, an experimental therapy called hyperbaric oxygen. It involved putting Eleanor in one of those pressure chambers they put divers in when they get the bends—a perhaps kooky-sounding notion but not a ludicrous one. Immune cells require oxygen to kill bacteria effectively and putting a person under double or higher atmospheric pressure for a few hours a day increases the oxygen concentration in tissue tremendously. Segal had been impressed by results he had gotten using the therapy in a couple of burn patients with deep wound infections. True, studies had not proven that it would work against necrotizing fasciitis. But suppose it could? Everyone latched onto the treatment immediately. At least it made us feel as if we were doing something about all the infection we were leaving behind.

We did not have a chamber at our hospital, but a hospital across town did. Someone got on the phone and within a few minutes we had a plan for ambulancing Eleanor over with one of our nurses for two hours under 2.5 atmospheres of pressurize oxygen. We left her wound open to drain, laid wet gauze inside it to keep the tissues from desiccating, and wrapped her leg in white bandages. Before sending her over, we wheeled her from the OR to intensive care, where we could make sure she would be stable enough for the trip.

It was eight o'clock at night now. Eleanor woke up nauseated and in pain. But she was sharp-witted enough to surmise from the crowd of nurses and doctors around her that something was wrong.

50   "Oh God, my leg."

She reached down to find it, and for a few panicked moments she wasn't sure she could. Slowly, she convinced herself that she could see it, touch it, feel it, move it. Studdert put his hand on her arm. He explained what he had found, what he had done, and what more there would be to do. She took the information with more grit and fight than I knew she had. Her whole family had now arrived to be with her, and looked as though an SUV had hit them. But Eleanor pulled the sheet back over her leg, took in the monitors flashing their green and orange lights and the IV lines running into her arms, and said, simply, "OK."

The hyperbaric chamber that night was, as she describes it, "like a glass coffin." She lay inside it on a narrow mattress with nowhere to put her arms except straight down or folded across her chest, a panel of thick plexiglass a foot from her face, and an overhead hatch sealed tight with turns of a heavy wheel. As the pressure increased, her ears kept popping, as if she were diving down into a deep ocean. Once the pressure reached a certain point, she would be stuck, the doctors had cautioned. Even if she should start throwing up, they could not get to her, for the pressure could only be released slowly or it would give her the bends and kill her. "One person had a seizure inside," she remembered them telling her. "It took them twenty minutes to get to him." Lying there enclosed, more ill than she'd ever imagined one could be, she felt far away and almost totally alone. It's just me and the bacteria in here, she thought to herself.

The next morning, we took her back to the operating room, to see if the bacteria had spread. They had. The skin over most of her foot and front of her calf was gangrenous and black and had to be cut off. The edges of fascia we had left behind were dead and had to be excised as well. But her muscle was still viable, including in her foot. And the bacteria had not killed anything up in her thigh. She had no further fevers. Her heart rate had normalized. We repacked her wound with wet gauze and sent her back for more hyperbaric oxygen—two hours twice a day.

We ended up operating on her leg four times in four days. At each operation, we had to take a little more tissue, but each time it was less and less. At the third operation, we found the redness of her skin had finally begun to recede. At the fourth operation, the redness was gone and we could see the pink mossy beginnings of new tissue in the maw of her wound. Only then was Studdert confident that not only had Eleanor survived, but her foot and leg had, too.

55 It was a year before I saw Eleanor again. Passing through Hartford, I called in on her at her family's home, a roomy, spic-and-span, putty-colored colonial with a galumphy dog and beds of flowers outside.

Eleanor had moved back home to recover following her twelve days in the hospital, intending to stay only temporarily but instead finding herself nestling in. Returning to a normal life, she said, was taking some getting used to.

Her leg had taken time to heal, not surprisingly. In her final operation, done during her last days in the hospital, we had needed to use a sixty-four-square-inch skin graft, taken from her thigh, to close the wound. "My little burn," she called the result, rolling up the leg of her sweatpants to show me.

It wasn't anything you'd call pretty, but the wound looked remarkably good to my eye. In final form, it was about as broad as my hand and ran from beneath her knee to her toes. Inevitably, the skin color was slightly off, and the wound edges were heaped up. The graft also made her foot and ankle seem wide and bulky. But the wound had no open areas, as there sometimes can be. And the grafted skin was soft and pliant, not at all tight or hard or contracted. Her thigh where the graft had been taken was a bright, cherry red, but still fading gradually.

Recovering the full use of her leg had been a struggle for her. At first, coming home, she found she could not stand, her muscles were so weak and sore. Her leg would collapse right under her. Then, when she'd built the strength back, she found she still could not walk. Nerve damage had given her a severe foot drop. She saw Dr. Studdert and he cautioned her that this was something she might always have. With several months of intense physical therapy, however, she trained herself to walk heel-toe again. By the time of my visit, she was actually jogging. She'd also started back working, taking a job as an assistant at one of the big insurance company headquarters in Hartford.

A year on, Eleanor remained haunted by what happened to her. She still had no idea where the bacteria came from. Perhaps the foot soak and pedicure she had gotten at a small hair-and-nail shop the day before that wedding. Perhaps the grass, outside the wedding reception hall, that she'd danced barefoot through with a conga line. Perhaps somewhere in her own house. Any time she got a cut or a fever, she was stricken with mortal fear. She would not go swimming. She would not immerse herself in a bath. She would not even let the water in the shower cover her feet. Her family was planning a vacation to Florida soon, but the idea of traveling so far from her doctors frightened her.

60   The odds—the seeming randomness—were what disturbed her most. "First, they say the odds of you getting this are nothing—one in two hundred fifty thousand," she said. "But then I got it. Then they say the odds of my beating it are very low. And I beat those odds." Now, when she asked us doctors if she could get the flesh-eating bacteria again, we told her, once more, the odds are improbably low, one in two hundred fifty thousand, just like before.

"I have trouble when I hear something like that. That means nothing to me," she said. She was sitting on her living room sofa as we talked, her hands folded in her lap, the sun rippling through a bay window behind her. "I don't trust that I won't get it again. I don't trust that I won't get anything else that's strange or we've never heard of, or that anyone we know isn't going to get such a thing."

The possibilities and probabilities are all we have to work with in medicine, though. What we are drawn to in this imperfect science, what we in fact covet in our way, is the alterable moment—the fragile but crystalline opportunity for one's know-how, ability, or just gut instinct to change the course of another's life for the better. In the actual situations that present themselves, however—a despondent woman arrives to see you about a newly diagnosed cancer, a victim bleeding from a terrible injury is brought pale and short of breath from the scene, a fellow physician asks for your opinion about a twenty-three-year-old with a red leg—we can never be sure whether we have such a moment or not. Even less clear is whether the actions we choose will prove either wise or helpful. That our efforts succeed at all it still sometimes a shock to me. But they do. Not always, but often enough.

My conversation with Eleanor wandered for a while. We talked about the friends she'd gotten to see now that she was back in Hartford and her boyfriend, who was something called a "fiber-optic electrician" (though what he actually wanted to do, she said, was "high-voltage"), about a movie she had recently gone to, and about how much less squeamish she's discovered herself to be after going through her whole ordeal.

"I feel a lot stronger in some ways," she said. "I feel like there is some kind of purpose, like there has to be some sort of reason that I'm still here.

65   "I think I am also happier as a person"—able to see things in perspective a bit more. "Sometimes," she went on, "I even feel safer. I came through all right, after all."

That May she did go to Florida. It was windless and hot, and one day, off the eastern coast above Pompano, she put one bare foot in the water and then the other. Finally, against all her fears, Eleanor jumped in and went swimming in the ocean.

The water was beautiful, she says.

CONVERSATION STARTER

When you go to the doctor, do you expect that she or he will have the solution to your health problem? Explain your response through reasoning and examples—personal or observed.

READING MATTERS

1. According to Atul, a senior surgical resident, what is the core predicament that doctors face? In what ways does wisdom help doctors to handle complex and sometimes morbid situations? How does this selection illustrate the predicament at the heart of medicine?

2. Select three situations in the selection that you thought reflected the doctors' genuine concern for their patients. Discuss these situations with a group of your peers. Then decide as a group if reading this story gave you more or less confidence and faith in modern medicine and doctors. Share your decision with the class.

3. How do the doctors finally determine that Eleanor has necrotizing fasciitis, a disease that kills 70% of the patients who have it? How do the doctors save not only Eleanor but also her leg?

4. What did you learn about how doctors make decisions about how to treat their patients from reading this story? What does the story suggest about the balance between intuition and science in solving individual cases of illness? How did reading about the complexity of this case help you to better understand the challenges that doctors face?

WRITING MATTERS

1. Write about a complex and challenging medical situation that you or someone close to you has experienced. Explain the problem and discuss how the doctors made their decisions. How did the doctor–patient relationship develop? How important was that relationship in the patient's recovery? What did the patient learn from his or her experience? What did you learn about modern medicine and doctor–patient relationships?

2. Write an essay that explores some of the many ways that technology is changing the ways doctors make decisions and treat patients. You will need to do some research on an aspect of this topic that interests you. Evaluate the positive and negative impacts of technology on this aspect of medicine and health.

3. With technology as an integral part of the process of diagnosing and healing a patient, how does the doctor–patient relationship change? How important is technology in the process of healing? How much of the healing process depends on the patient's faith and belief that his or her doctor cares about his or her recovery? How important are family and friends in the patient's healing process? Do some research on this topic and refer to experiences you have learned about or experienced before you begin to write your essay.

RELEVANT WEB SITES

INTERVIEW WITH ATUL GAWANDE
<http://www.theatlantic.com/unbound/interviews/int2002-05-01.htm>

Read more about Atul Gawande, surgeon and writer, in an interview titled "Under the Microscope" in *The Atlantic* Online.

ATUL GAWANDE ON ATUL GAWANDE <http://slate.msn.com/id/3729/>

Learn about Atul Gawande through his weeklong electronic journal.

Abraham Verghese (b. 1955)

The Tennis Partner

Abraham Verghese was born to Southern Indian and Christian parents. After earning his medical degree in Ethiopia, he moved to the United States to work as an orderly in various hospitals. Verghese completed his medical education in India, and in 1980 he returned to practice medicine in the United States. Trained as a specialist in infectious diseases, he became an expert on AIDS and HIV. Verghese is a talented writer who presents a humanistic and clinical understanding of the impact of AIDS on patients and their loved ones. Currently, he is a Professor of Medicine and Chief of Infectious Diseases at Texas Tech Health Sciences Center in El Paso, Texas. In 1990, Verghese enrolled in the Iowa Writer's Workshop while also practicing medicine at the University's AIDS clinic. His experiences studying writing led him to write about AIDS in his first book, My Own Country: A Doctor's Story *(1994). Verghese began his novel* The Tennis Partner *in 1998, after struggling with how to write about his deep feelings and friendship with his student and tennis partner who was addicted to cocaine. In the excerpt we have selected, you will learn about how many doctors struggle against addictions and how an addiction is a disease, not simply a character weakness.*

He had started rounds at five-thirty in the morning, working his way from one room to the next, writing progress notes as he went. He was at the bedside of his last patient when his beeper went off.

When he saw the number displayed, his throat constricted. A crimson flush spread up his neck, to his cheeks. The elderly woman with Crohn's disease and a short-bowel syndrome, who quite liked this blond, boyish doctor, looked up at him with concern. A minute ago he had been listening to her heart; now she could almost swear she heard his.

He staggered out into the corridor, and stood there, leaning on the chart rack. He took a step in the direction of the stairwell. Then stopped. Then took another step that way. Then turned back.

The flush on his face retreated, taking every drop of color from his skin until it matched the whiteness of the walls. His world and his vision narrowed and he was unaware of the nurse who walked by him.

5 He did not notice that his patient had come out of the bed, pushing her IVAC pump before her, the yellow, white, and clear bags dangling from their hooks. She stood staring at him through the doorway.

With great difficulty he wheeled the charts back to the nurses' station and took up his pen in a peculiar four-fingered, childlike grip. His hand trembling, he brought the progress note he was writing to a close. To anyone but a nurse, his handwriting would have been completely illegible.

He did not answer the page from the phones nearby. Instead, he took the elevator down from the fifth floor to the lobby and walked directly to Dr. Lou Binder's office.

Binder was waiting for the phone to ring. When he saw the intern in his doorway, he stood up. Before the intern could so much as open his mouth, Binder said, "Let's go to the lab."

But the intern could not move. He held Binder's gaze for a second, then his face crumpled, his shoulders sagged, and he slumped into a chair in front of Binder's desk.

10   "What have you done?" Lou asked, softly.

The intern sobbed, but no words came out.

An hour later, the two of them were at the El Paso International Airport, boarding a plane. Dr. Binder had not allowed him to go home for clothes. He had given one of his own jackets to the intern to put over his scrubs. The intern called his girlfriend from a pay phone but again the sobs robbed him of words. "I'm sorry" was all he could manage.

On the plane, a flight attendant had to remind him twice to put on his seat belt. He stared out the window as the plane took off, then made a steep, banking left turn allowing him to see the hospital clearly, and a few blocks beyond it, the Rio Grande, and Juárez, Mexico. The pilot leveled the plane, pointing it east for the one-and-a-half-hour flight to Dallas. Soon, El Paso receded from view, and with it his hopes and dreams. He had tried so hard, he told himself. Then he slapped himself in the face. Binder turned at the sound but was not surprised. "Not hard enough," the intern said aloud, to no one but himself.

In Dallas, Binder walked him over to the gate for the flight to Atlanta, and handed him his ticket. "The Talbott-Marsh clinic is your only chance."

15   The flight attendant collecting boarding passes could tell this was a significant leave-taking. She had a good sense about people, knew how to read the signs, having had years of practice. She was about to say something lighthearted about his scrubs, but decided not to when she looked in the man's face.

Binder watched the intern walk down the jet way. He remained at the window until the plane pulled away from the gate.

In Atlanta, four men awaited him. They introduced themselves: two were surgeons, one was an orthopedist, and one was an anesthesiologist. One of the surgeons was his father's age; the rest looked to be in their thirties or early forties. In the car, one of them said, "You won't believe me, but you'll look back and think of this day as the first day of your real life."

When they arrived at the cluster of buildings in suburban Atlanta that constituted the clinic, he was taken in to meet Dr. Talbott.

Doug Talbott, a big man with thick, silvery hair, came around his desk with an alacrity that belied his seventy years. His handshake was firm, and he took the young man's hand in both of his and led him to one of two armchairs that faced each other next to a fireplace. His smile, under a brigadier's mustache, was warm and unaffected.

20   They sat without speaking, the older man's fingers resting thoughtfully on the side of his face. Despite the scar over his eyebrow and a sunken cheek from what looked like an old orbital fracture, his face was kindly. After a long while, his voice emerged from the depths of his chest, soothing

and with no trace of a Southern drawl, pausing after every sentence, letting each thought hang there before he brought out the next one.

"You have a terrible disease. You need lifelong treatment."

The intern sat, mesmerized, numb, conscious only of the sound of his own breathing.

"I am told I was a world-famous cardiologist," Talbott continues, his gnarled hands moving like delicate wands to punctuate his words. "But I don't know how. I was an alcoholic. When I couldn't swallow alcohol anymore because of the vomiting, the hiatal hernia, I switched to meprobamate, which was not considered addictive. Then Demerol, which was not considered addictive, then Talwin, which was not considered addictive, then Equinil, which was not considered addictive. . . ." He smiled as he recited this, a tale he had told thousands of times, as if the naïveté of his generation of physicians still amazed him.

Talbott had been institutionalized several times, at one point spending a year and a half with psychiatrists who dismissed his alcohol use as a "cover-up for something deeper that you need to lie down on the couch and tell us about." After many relapses, after many rounds with AA, after his oldest son, disgusted with him, beat him over a kitchen table, his wife finally committed him to an asylum for the criminally insane.

25   "When the inmates found out I was a doctor," he said, his eyes twinkling, as if the funny part was coming, "they beat the hell out of me. Broke my face. Cracked my ribs. I remember lying on the floor in my own blood, spitting out fragments of my teeth."

He smiled, and the intern could see the glint of a gold tooth peeking out from behind the mustache. The smile evaporated, leaving in its place an expression of pain that the younger man recognized as the equal of his.

"It was at that moment, lying on the floor, I swore to myself that if I ever got out of that place alive, I would find treatment that was specific for doctors. I would make that my life's mission.

"Sobriety," he said, shaking his head gently, "is the easiest part of recovery. We are only peripherally involved with sobriety here. You can get sobriety in El Paso detox, or the county jail. What you *will* get here is true recovery. This will come from your recognizing that you have a disease, like diabetes. And just like a diabetic taking insulin and monitoring blood sugars, every day for the rest of your life, you will need to monitor and treat your disease.

"Unfortunately, society doesn't understand that you have a disease, a disorder in your forebrain, a genetic defect that makes you so susceptible. *You*—despite being a doctor—don't understand that you have a disease. Instead you see yourself as reprehensible, morally flawed." He leaned forward, as if imparting a secret. "And now, now that they caught you, you feel intense *shame*."

30   That word seemed to pierce the thin veneer of the intern's composure and, his facial muscles drawing up, he began to whimper. Shame was what he had tried to keep bottled in all day, shame had made it difficult to breathe on the plane, made it impossible to eat, and now shame overtook him completely and he boo-hooed like a baby.

The older man leaned back in his chair, his hands forming a steeple in front of his face. He made no effort to intervene. But he observed the young man, felt his grief, watched him weep just as he had watched four thousand or so other doctors over the years weep tears of shame.

He could see their faces clearly. Some were now dead from their disease. He could picture, as if it were a road map, the events that had led them to this state. When they were young college students, they had worked incredibly hard to get into medical school, forgoing the parties, the quick pleasures, in pursuit of the doctor dream. When they were accepted into medical school, and then later, when they graduated and survived the ordeal of internship, they had come to feel special. They had learned to be self-sufficient, and even to think of themselves as invulnerable, as if they had struck a bargain with the Creator in return for caring for the ill. The very qualities that led them to be doctors—compulsiveness, conscientiousness, control over emotions, delayed gratification, fantasies of the future—predisposed them to use drugs. When they did, to the very end, the physician-patient denied his or her patienthood. And when it all came crashing down, what they felt was monstrous, crippling shame.

"Don't confuse shame with guilt," he said eventually. "Shame says, 'I *am* the mistake,' while guilt says, 'I *made* a mistake.' You made a mistake, but you are not a mistake."

The young man composed himself as best he could. Despite what he was hearing, he could still think only of what he had lost, of how he had blown it, of how he was once again in a rehabilitation program. He had been on probation as a student, carefully monitored as an intern, given numerous chances, and now he felt in the pit of his stomach that he had blown the doctor dream, erased his ability to ever get a medical license in any state. What did it matter if he were sober or not—if he couldn't be a doctor, what was the point of any of this?

35   "I know you've been to recovery programs many times before, probably to some good ones, but none that specialized in doctors with addiction. As a physician, you have unique issues that we will address here. Don't get me wrong—the twelve steps are at the core of recovery, wherever you are. But as a doctor, what makes you unique is that your denial is exquisite, a hundredfold more entrenched than non-physicians. Even now as you sit there, you are in massive denial. In the back of your mind, you think that your biggest misfortune was to get caught."

The intern had his head down. He did not try to deny this.

"We'll talk more in the morning," Dr. Talbott said, standing up. "You're lucky to have arrived on the night of our weekly Caduceus Club. We started our first Caduceus Club here in Georgia twenty years ago." He glowed with pride. "We now have seventy-three Caduceus Clubs all over the United States and Canada."

They strolled across the grounds to a large building, the Anchor Hospital. Off to one side were some tennis courts, but if the intern, whose life and livelihood had for so long revolved around tennis, saw the courts, he gave no sign. The two men entered the building through a side door. The intern who had been to so many AA and NA meetings was unprepared for what he saw. Chairs had been pushed to the edges of a large dining hall to form a giant circle, and about a hundred physicians were seated, filling the room with a steady drone, as if this were a medical convention. Everyone was dressed casually, and he saw only one other person dressed in scrubs. His fear and shame rose again as his peers turned to glance at the newcomer with Dr. Talbott. But then, when he realized that every one of them was here for the same reason he was, he felt, for the first time that day, an easing of the weight in his chest. Some of the doctors smiled at him.

"If you think your problems are unique, you get over that in a heartbeat here," his older companion whispered to him, putting an arm on his shoulder. "Terminally unique. Every one of us thought we were terminally unique. We thought that M.D. stood for M. Deity." He sat down and guided the intern to a chair on his right.

40 "Shall we begin?" Dr. Talbott said, and the room quieted. Dr. Talbott nodded to a man sitting on his left.

"Hi, I'm Steve; I'm a neurosuregon and an alcoholic," the man began. He was an intense, dark-haired man, with spidery hands and quick, birdlike movements of his head.

"HI, STEVE!" a chorus of voices said.

"I'm leaving here tomorrow after a four-month stay," he said, beaming. Others looked happy for him. "I feel good, grateful . . . This is my second stay at Talbott-Marsh. I'm looking forward to being with my wife and kids. Lots of issues there, many things she has to forgive me for . . . I'm not going back into practice just yet. Still a few licensing issues that are being sorted out . . . But I'm not worried about that . . ."

"When you look back, Steve," Talbott asked, "what were the factors that made you relapse?"

45 "I stopped communicating," he said quickly. "Hid my feelings, started looking for faults in other people—my wife, my partners, anyone to blame for what I felt. I got on my 'pity pot,' started with the 'stinking thinking,'" he said, using his fingers to make quotation marks in the air, his words tripping over each other. "I was a dry drunk for months before I actually relapsed. I forgot that I had a disease. I thought I could actually take a drink and nothing would happen, no one would know. But I'm on a contract now with my medical society that involves daily Antabuse, urine checks, sponsor visits . . ." He had run out of steam. He added brightly, "One day at a time."

The baton was passed to the left.

"Hi, I'm Judy; I'm an ER physician and a cocaine addict."

"Hi, I'm Todd; I'm a nephrologist and a crack addict."

"Hi, I'm Bob; I'm a radiologist and an alcoholic."

50 Around the room, the litany continued: alcohol, amphetamines, crack, Valium, Lomotil, Xanax. Codeine in many forms. Every specialty

in medicine seemed to be represented, particularly anesthesia. Fentanyl and sufentanil (both very potent narcotics) seemed to be the favorites of the anesthesiologists and surgeons.

It was now the turn of the other man in a scrub suit. He had linebacker shoulders, brown, curly hair, and handsome, movie-star features. The man had sat there with his arms folded, leaning back in his chair, wary of the proceedings. Now he uncrossed his arms.

"I just got in today. From California. I'm a vascular surgeon. I guess I'm here to find out if there is a problem. I'm here for . . . evaluation," he said, looking at Dr. Talbott.

"Tell us what happened, Kurt," Dr. Talbott said.

"I operated early this morning . . . As I was leaving the operating room, the administrator confronted me, along with the head of anesthesia. They said some fentanyl was missing." He shrugged. "I told them I had nothing to do with it—"

55   The other doctors were shifting in their chairs. The momentum of the meeting had been retarded.

"And the reason they suspected you?"

"Allegations at another hospital I go to that I had removed fentanyl. I was under observation, I guess, though no one told me." The silence in the room seemed to weigh on him. "No one has had any complaints about my work, I take good care of my patients—"

"Are you here of your own volition?"

"Well, yeah, I guess. If I didn't agree to come out here for an evaluation, they were going to report me to the medical society. Which meant automatic suspension of my license. Takes away my livelihood. So . . . I said I'd come. I didn't get a chance to pack, or to—"

60   "Tell us, Kurt, how is your marriage?" Talbott interrupted.

"My wife left me two months ago."

"And I understand you have been having a major problem with your finances?"

"I have a lot of debt, if that's what you mean. My partnership dissolved, so I had to set up my own office. But I'm getting back on track. I cover four different hospitals. No one has ever complained about my work—"

"The *work* is the last thing to suffer," an intense older man across the room burst in, unable to keep quiet any longer. He wore half-moon glasses over which he peered at the newcomer. He had a thick Southern accent. "The order in which you dee-stroy your life," he said, holding out his hand and pulling down fingers, "is first family, then you screw your partners, then you screw up your finances, then your health goes. Hell, your job performance is the last thing to go."

65   The burly Californian stirred in his chair. He was embarrassed. If this had been a staff meeting at his own hospital, he would have told this hick to go to hell.

"I should know, son," the man went on, whipping off his glasses, his tone softening, but not much. "I was confronted only when I passed out in the OR and fell face forward into the abdomen I had just opened. In the two years preceding that, I'd lost everything: my family, my friends, my money. I protected my job till the very end, and even when they sent me here, I still didn't think I really had a problem, came here to be ee-valuated . . ."

The surgeon from California was still. He had thought he could finesse his way through this evaluation, get back home in a few days, but it was starting to look more difficult.

"Okay," Dr. Talbott said. "Welcome, Kurt."

Kurt's stay—if he wanted a license to practice medicine—would be more than just a few days.

70   The bouncing ball was coming closer to the young intern from El Paso. He could feel his face getting hot, his mouth getting dry.

All eyes were now on him.

Later that night, in the on-site apartment he was assigned to share with three others, he went to the bathroom to wash up. He saw his face in the mirror above the sink, and he recoiled from it, the sight causing him to sit down on the edge of the tub. The image he had seen was of the person who had betrayed him yet again, a person he loathed.

Despite the stories he had heard that evening, despite the empathy of his new housemates, who had lent him clothes and toiletries, he was, if anything, more fearful. He had a sense of dread, of tremendous apprehension, and it had come to a head when he looked at his reflection.

More than any place he had been through before, he knew that the Talbott-Marsh clinic—if he wanted to practice medicine again—would force him to face that person in the mirror, would make him take down the bricks and mortar he had used to entomb his deepest, darkest secret. Out it would come, bellowing, ferocious and savage after years of confinement, and he would be forced to stand in front of it, puny and defenseless to face its wrath.

75   He raised his head slowly, lifted his chin, until once again his face appeared in the mirror. He ducked, and with an anguished grunt, he slumped to the floor, screwing his eyes shut and covering his face, believing, like a child, that if he closed his eyes and didn't look at the monster, it would go away.

CONVERSATION STARTER

Sometimes we read about or watch shows on television about doctors who become addicted to the drugs that are so readily available to them. What has been your reaction to these types of stories? Explain your response.

READING MATTERS

1. Why is the young intern taken to the Talbott-Marsh Clinic? Why does Dr. Talbott argue that drug addiction is a disease, a genetic disorder in

the forebrain, when he meets the intern? Why does the young intern feel so morally flawed and ashamed? Talbott tells the intern not to mistake shame for guilt. Why?

2. Why did Dr. Talbott start the clinic, and why did he believe that a certain personality profile can make a doctor vulnerable to drug addiction? Despite the many patients that Talbott has treated, why is he still compassionate with the young intern?

3. How are the Caduceus Clubs different from Alcoholics Anonymous (AA) and Narcotics Anonymous (NA)? Why are the basic 12 steps at the core of each program? Look these programs up on the Internet and consider their meaning in relationship to your own values.

4. How does the young intern feel about being at the clinic? How is he treated by the other doctors at the group therapy meeting? Why is he afraid to look at himself in the mirror after the meeting?

Writing Matters

1. Do some research into 12-step programs. Find out about how they were started and why the steps flow the way they do. Interview some people who have attended AA or Alanon meetings. Integrate your research, your interviews, and your personal experiences (if you have had any). The focus of your essay should be to show how and why the 12 steps work, or if they don't, why.

2. Do some research into the percentage of doctors who are addicted to drugs. If possible, interview a doctor who has suffered with drug addiction or find a group leader of a Caduceus Club or another type of group meeting that is specifically for doctors addicted to drugs. Reflect on what you have learned. Has your opinion of doctors in general changed? How and why?

3. Volunteer at a clinic that helps people in recovery from drug addictions. Write a paper for your class about what you have learned about drug addiction and the reasons people turn to drugs. Alternatively, write about a person whom you know well who has suffered from an addiction: alcohol, drugs, an eating disorder, or another obsession—perhaps one related to money. Shape your essay around the person's disorder: how it developed; and how it affected the person's personality and obligations to work, friends and family. Finally, conclude with an evaluation of how this person is doing now and of what you have learned from your experiences with him or her.

Relevant Web Sites

Dr. Abraham Verghese <http://www.texashumanities.org/Verghese.html>

A faculty biography of Dr. Abraham Verghese, Professor of Medicine and Chief of Infectious Diseases at the School of Medicine, is available through the Texas Tech University web site.

Julia McMurray

Doctor's Daughter

Julia McMurray is an Associate Professor of Medicine at the University of Wisconsin. She attended medical school at the University of North Carolina, did her internship and residency at Montefiore Hospital and Medical Center in the Bronx, and had a fellowship at Mount Sinai Medical Center in New York City. McMurray practices at the University Station Clinic in the Internal Medicine Department at the University of Wisconsin. Her special interests are menopause and women's health. McMurray is very active in women's health and has published articles in many medical journals, including the JAMWA *(Journal of American Medical Women's Association) and* Women's Health.

As a small child, I often stood on the stairway in my home, looking up at the pictures of my mother. O.U. School of Medicine, class of 1945. I counted the 69 sepia-toned faces many times, always coming back to my mother's in the oval composite photograph. My mother is one of only three women, and her countenance is serious and composed; the hair in a long, wavy cut typical of the period. In an old picture from the local newspaper, written the year before my birth, my mother is sitting at a desk, wearing a white lab coat, staring out at the camera from her desk at the sexually transmitted diseases clinic where she worked. "Young Doctor Works in Town," reads the headline.

"How come you never worked as a doctor, Mama?" I asked frequently. I often went on rounds with my physician-father in the early morning at the community hospital in the small southern town where we lived. In one minute flat, he could tap a chest, letting the straw-colored liquid rush through the brown rubber tubing to puddle in the glass vacuum bottle on the bed. The nurses stood by at attention, in their starched white dresses and peaked caps. In the small emergency area, my father would casually flip his tie over his shoulder and insert the needle for the lumbar puncture that would diagnose the subarachnoid bleeding in his patient. Afterward, we would drive home to the house, where my mother would be standing in front of the stove, scrambling eggs for my three brothers, who sat watching Saturday morning cartoons. My mother was always home.

"Well, I loved you children and felt you needed me at home. You would start sucking your thumbs or the babysitter would quit." On the day I was born in an army barracks hospital, a psychotic WAC ran amok in the maternity area brandishing a butcher knife. My mother hid me behind her body next to the wall and called my father to come take us home. Later on, a German war bride would sometimes baby-sit for my brother and me in a pinch so my mother could work. After the war, while my father was in fellowship training, there was a job for her at the public health department. The syphilis patients would sit on a long row of stools with their hospital gowns open in the back while she went from one to the other, performing the lumbar punctures for diagnosis or test of cure. It was the last clinical job she ever had.

Such were the stories of my childhood. In the small town near the mountains, my father worked first in solo practice, then with a gradually increasing number of partners. He was on call every second or third night for most of my childhood and was rarely home. The special office phone at home, one that we were never to answer, rang off the hook each call night. Ventricular tachycardia, acute myocardial infarctions, diabetic ketoacidosis, and acute leukemia were never discussed at the dinner table but were nonetheless an integral part of the household. His cotton shirts were ironed every afternoon, and a sandwich was always waiting on the table for the 20-minute lunch break he took every day as he read his mail. On Sunday afternoons, I would go into the office with him while he saw patients. Using his secret name for me, I would pick up the phone and say gleefully, "Doctor McMurray's office, Miss Bird speaking," to neighbors and patients who knew me only as a quiet, well-behaved child.

5   My mother, on the other hand, was at home for us every day after school, cooking dinner in the evenings when my father walked in after rounds. She kept the family in clothes, helped with homework, played music to dance to on rainy afternoons, ferried us all to swimming and music lessons, met with the teacher when my brothers got into trouble at school, and always made it to recitals. She was president of the local mental health society, gave the embarrassing sex talks in schools, and thrilled us all once with a hole-in-one on the golf course. A gifted amateur naturalist, she admonished me not to be squeamish while helping me dissect fish eyes at the lake in the summers. Almost none of the other women in her circle of friends worked; most had never been to college. In the evenings she read all the "Great Books," and she loved nonfiction on almost any subject. I would crawl around her under the covers as she lay reading in bed, feeling the safety and security of her body.

The first crack in her armor of stoicism came when Betty Friedan's *The Feminine Mystique* was published. After reading the book, she refused to cook dinner for 3 days. She looked at me that afternoon and said, "I was smart; I could have done some things." I urged her to work out a way to drive the 3 hours to the nearest medical school in the state in order to get back into practice. But there were four children at home and one demanding, full-time private practice to support. Secretly, I chided my father for what I took to be his inflexibility in this regard; my mother simply said it couldn't be done.

I grew up, did well in school, and was a pre-medicine major in college. My father was emphatic in his support and unambivalent in his enthusiasm for medicine. "It's a great job. Easy, really. You just hang up your shingle and do things any way you like. People will come to see a woman physician. I wish your mother could have done it."

My mother was more cautious. "Whatever you want to do is fine; don't do it for me."

10   "How did you decide to become a doctor?" I once asked.

She responded in her typical low-key way, "I grew up in dust-bowl Oklahoma in the middle of the Depression. We had no money whatsoever. My father ran a garage, but I went to the state university. I was a chemistry major planning on going to pharmacy school, when a local couple urged me to go on to medical school. It was pretty simple, really. I just did it."

When my letter of acceptance came from medical school, she sent me a medical dictionary inscribed, "From one to another." Once in my clinical years, I began using her battered brown medical bag. Medical school was overwhelming, but memories of time spent with my father on house calls and in his office sustained me. I fell in and out of love a half dozen times, married during my residency, and ultimately started a family. My first job was exciting and utterly absorbing. Before the baby came, I was in every morning at 7:00 a.m., staying until late at night. No part-time work for me! Child care would be easy in the city where I lived, and my physician-husband was deeply committed to being involved as a father. It would all work out so easily. Why couldn't my mother have done this? I emulated my father at this point. My profession came first.

When my 4-month-old began reaching for his child care person instead of me and started sucking his thumb, I felt he needed me, as we had needed my mother. I cut back to part-time. Sitting with my child on my lap, I asked my mother, "Couldn't you have worked part-time?" This time, the stories were about the refusal of all the practices in town to hire anyone less than full-time. In fact, the only acceptable full-time jobs for women in her social strata were those of teacher or nurse. It wasn't considered acceptable otherwise.

My second child was born, and life got more complex. I would feel crazed with worry and guilt when a waiting room full of patients were waiting for me at the hospital while I sat helplessly in the pediatrician's office with a sick child. The nannies didn't want to work more than 8 to 10 hours a day, and the consultants always seemed to page me in the late afternoon while I was swinging the children out in the back yard. It was difficult to discuss the cardiac ejection fractions of patients receiving chemotherapy with the children squabbling in the background.

As I contemplated my own difficulties, I seemed to be headed down the same road as my mother and began to think more and more about the mystery of her lost medicine. I couldn't believe things had been so cut and dried, so matter of fact. How could she have avoided the gut-wrenching feelings of guilt, love, and inadequacy that I myself so often felt? And so I became instantly alert one hot summer day, as I sat by a pool with my mother and watched my two small children swim.

15   The question was innocent enough. "So, Mom, just how far did you get in residency exactly? What kind of doctor were you planning to be?"

At her answer I felt a sudden stillness, the sounds of the summer cicadas buzzing loudly in my ears. "I wanted to be a pediatrician, but I got sick."

Sick? My mother was robustly healthy and had not been sick a day in her life. "What do you mean sick, Mother? What kind of sick?"

She answered, "It was stress, I guess." And for the first time she told me the story of how she started in a pediatric residency during the war. Four men, one woman. All the men were married and lived with their families. My mother was given a small room for living quarters on the tuberculosis ward. Being skin-test negative, she was terrified of contracting tuberculosis and asked to be moved. She was then put in a room at the end of the hall in the nurses' quarters. "It was just too much," my mother said in a voice devoid of emotion. She moved to the town where her sister lived, met my father, and married. There it was. A shaky start in the profession: scared, unsupported, possibly unwanted in medicine. The other answer had been in front of me all my life: the demands of mothering, needs of a busy physician-husband, a reluctant profession, and small-town social mores that made employment difficult for a woman physician who wanted a home in addition to a career.

My father retired at the age of 62. After 40 years of working, he told me that he hadn't had a summer off since the third grade. A poem came from him once that said, "I wish I had picked more daisies." Although he would say that he had been more successful than he had ever dreamed, in other moments he would speak of "being sucked dry" by patients or mention fears and anxieties that kept him awake at night, shared with no one. My mother would bask in the glories of her grandchildren and never once mention her lost medicine.

20   As for me, I have come through. I am fortunate to have been able to work part-time and to have a physician-husband willing and able to be fully engaged as a partner in our enterprise of work and home. But the challenges have been formidable and not simply a matter of more child care, more housecleaning help, or take-out food. Children's needs are not always so easily postponed until after hours, and relationships need constant tending. More equal measures of love and work sustain me, options that were not available to my mother.

Indeed, my mother "could have done some things." She earned her career, working hard in difficult times. Because she was one of only three women in a medical school class, there is a temptation to say she was obligated to continue, no matter what. But as this doctors' daughter, I benefited from her choices and her sacrifices. "From one to another," she passed on to me a legacy of competence and a courage tempered with love, a battered brown medical bag and a dictionary. I understand what I did not see before.

Conversation Starter

How do you imagine growing up with a parent who was a doctor? If one or both of your parents were doctors, how do you think their professional lives would affect or did affect your childhood (if your parents actually were doctors)?

Reading Matters

1. How and why did Betty Friedan's *The Feminine Mystique* affect Julia's mother and the way that she raised her daughter? What other situations and values does Julia discuss as influencing the way that she was raised?
2. Why didn't Julia's mother finish her residency? When Julia's mother and father reflect back on their lives, which one is happier? Why? What are the implications of this information?
3. Why doesn't Julia's mother want Julia to go to medical school to please her? Why does Julia go to medical school?
4. Why does Julia's opinion of her mother's decision not to practice medicine change when Julia becomes a mother herself? How are the conditions and expectations of Julia as a mother and a doctor different than they were for her mother?

Writing Matters

1. Visit a medical clinic in your community and set up interviews with an equal number of male and female doctors. When you write your interview questions, your goal should be to learn more about the challenges that women doctors face, especially when they have a family. Do they think of male doctors as being more available to their patients? Do they think that male and female doctors should take equal responsibility in raising their children? Write an essay that integrates what you have learned from your reading, interviewing, and reflection.
2. Write a research paper on the first women to become doctors. Find out why and how they became doctors and what challenges they faced. Conclude with a discussion of how the medical profession is changing because more women are becoming doctors.
3. After doing some research, write a paper that explores whether there are reasons why men make good doctors and women make equally good doctors. Research the issue of whether people prefer to see a doctor of the same gender and how much this seems to matter in selecting and trusting a doctor. Integrate your research, your own experiences, and the experiences of others whom you know well and who have opinions on this topic.

RELEVANT WEB SITES

NATIONAL ORGANIZATION FOR WOMEN (NOW)
<http://www.now.org/index.html>

This is the official web site of the National Organization for Women (NOW), the largest organization of feminist activists in the United States. This site provides information about the organization as well as information about key issues impacting women.

AMERICAN MEDICAL WOMEN'S ASSOCIATION <http://www.amwa-doc.org/>

This is the official web site of the American Medical Women's Association, an organization of 10,000 female physicians and medical students dedicated to serving as the unique voice for women's health and the advancement of women in medicine.

Solving Today's Health Care Issues

Greg Critser

Fatland America: What Can Be Done?

Greg Critser was educated at Occidental College and UCLA and currently lives in Pasadena, California. He is a professional journalist whose work appears regularly in USA Today, *the* Los Angeles Times, *and* Harpers's Magazine. *He has written cover stories on nutrition, health, and medical issues. His writing on obesity earned him a James Feard nomination for the best writing of 1999, and he is frequently interviewed by PBS and other media on the topic of food politics. He researched the topic of obesity in America for four years before writing* Fatland: How Americans Became the Fattest People in the World *(2003). This book presents groundbreaking evidence about the negative impact of food rules in middle-class families, the causes of obesity in economically disadvantaged families, and the role of the public schools in keeping American children obese, as well as some possible solutions for this national epidemic.*

Schools have long offered tremendous promise as possible battlegrounds against childhood obesity. After all, more than 95 percent of American youth between the ages of five and eighteen are enrolled in school. Though school authority has been whittled down substantially over the years, the institution, by sheer dint of its daily presence, still exerts enormous influence on the lives of its subjects. In the early 1980s the Yale obesity expert Kelly Brownell undertook a small-scale intervention at public schools in Fort Myers, Florida, using nutrition education, physical activity training, changes in food service, and behavior modification techniques with a group of overweight children. The students were able to achieve and sustain a notable weight loss of 15 percent. At the time, many hailed the Brownell approach as a possible new standard in the treatment of childhood obesity.

But the Brownell approach fell victim to the cultural politics of the 1980s, namely, the fear that fat children undergoing such treatment would be stigmatized by their peers. Although it is true that some stigmatizing occurs when any group is singled out for special treatment, this objection— and it was voiced widely and vehemently throughout the decade—ignored the most basic truism about fat and stigmatization: The best way to prevent it is to avoid becoming obese in the first place. As the influential— and, it should be noted, very politically sensitive—*International Journal of*

Obesity worried in a review of school programs in 1999, "It is interesting that few studies on school-based treatment of obesity were identified after 1985 . . . Greater awareness of the stigma attached to participating in school-based treatments may have decreased enthusiasm for the programs, *even though they appear to be effective* [emphasis mine]."

Yet the "decreased enthusiasm" seems to be limited to the adults. A more recent survey, based on in-depth interviews with sixty-one overweight adolescents from large inner-city schools, indicated not only that children want such programs, but that they are willing to put up with their possible social ramifications if such a program "was undertaken in a supportive and respectful manner, offered fun activities, was informative, was sensitive to the needs of overweight youth and did not conflict with other activities."

Such interest *by children* has helped launch a new generation of school-based interventions. One of the most promising involves preventive screening. In a study by the University of Houston and Baylor College, scholars looked at how a child's weight in, say, kindergarten would predict that child's chances of becoming obese at a later age. Researchers collated the weights and BMIs of 1013 Mexican American children in a Texas school district. They then tracked the children as they progressed through the system. They found that a kindergarten BMI was highly predictive of obesity at later dates. A child with a low kindergarten BMI at 16.5, for example, would have only a 21 percent chance of becoming obese by fifth grade. A kindergartner with a BMI of 20.9, however, would have a 70 percent chance of becoming an obese fifth grader, while a kindergartner with a BMI of 23.7 would have a 91 percent probability of becoming obese.

5   While the Houston-Baylor study provides schools with one way to assess a child's relative risks, a program in San Jose, California, has carved a potential path toward reducing both current and future obesity rates. The impetus for it flowed from both theoretical and practical concerns. Researchers from Stanford's Departments of Pediatrics and Medicine had long theorized that if sedentary behaviors like TV-viewing and video game–playing were linked to increased obesity, then programs that taught children to reduce such activities might lead to reductions in adiposity. Meanwhile, teachers and parents in the San Jose School District, aware of increasing obesity rates, were looking for ways to deal with the issue. They decided to give the Stanford researchers access.

To find out if their hypothesis held, the researchers recruited 192 third- and fourth-grade students from two socioeconomically matched schools. One school was assigned to implement a program to reduce TV and video game use, the other was not. The means of the intervention was simple: Limit access to TV sets and game machines, teach children to budget their use, then teach them how to become more selective viewers and players. This the researchers sought to inaugurate and support through traditional classroom instruction. Teachers in the intervention school were trained to administer eighteen specialized lessons, each thirty to fifty minutes in length, taught during regular school hours during the first two months of the school year. The first few lessons taught the students how to monitor and report their own TV and game use, followed by a "TV Turnoff." The TV Turnoff challenged children to watch no TV and play no video games for ten days. After the turnoff, students were told to budget their viewing to seven hours per week. The last lessons sought to increase students' ability to be selective, "intelligent viewers," and to become advocates for reducing the use of such media among their peers. At home, each student TV was equipped with an electronic TV time manager, which logged and measured TV time through the use of a personal code, without which the set would not operate.

The results of the intervention surprised even its most enthusiastic and optimistic supporters. After seven months, TV use in the intervention group was down by one third, compared to the control group. Video game use and viewing of videocassettes were down as well. While not an anticipated outcome, the intervention group also "significantly reduced the frequency of children eating meals in a room with a television turned on." And, most important, children in the intervention group, in the words of the researchers, "had statistically significant relative decreases in BMI, triceps skinfold thickness, waist circumference, and waist to hip ratio." The results did not change with ethnicity or level of parental education.

The success of the San Jose experiment posed an intriguing question for its authors. Why did the children lose weight? After all, there were no reports that children had dramatically *increased* high-level activity when not watching TV, and when they *were* watching TV their level of snacking matched that of their more sedentary control group. Three answers emerged. One, children in the intervention group snacked less in toto. Two, they had been exposed to dramatically fewer advertisements for high-calorie foods. And three, they likely sought out and engaged in more low-intensity activity. Whatever the cause, the Stanford researchers concluded, reducing TV, video game, and video use "may be a promising, population-based approach to help prevent childhood obesity."

Jim Hill, at the University of Colorado Health Sciences Center, has come to a similar conclusion about larger interventions. As he and John Peters note in a recent issue of *Obesity Reviews,* "The challenge in changing the environment is not to 'go back in time,' but to engineer physical activity and healthy eating back into our lives in a way that is compatible with our socio-cultural value." As Peters and Hill see it, the challenge is to give everyday people the same cognitive tools—essentially a series of goals and rewards—that the more affluent always have had when it comes to managing weight. Hill and his colleagues have launched a program called "Colorado on the Move," a consortium of government agencies, private foundations, educational institutions, and business with one specific, measurable goal: to increase by 2000 steps a day the average number of steps the average Coloradan takes. To do so, they are underwriting the distribution of low-tech step counters around the state. Hill and his colleagues got the idea after comparing the average number of steps daily by an office worker (3000 to 5000) with the average number of steps by people in the National Weight Control Registry (11,000), the most successful single group to maintain weight loss after several years. Beginning with a modest 2000, Colorado on the Move could eventually encourage large numbers of citizens to take increasingly more steps per day. Already some six thousand people are enrolled in pilot programs.

10   One of the best ways to combat obesity would be to reinvest in traditional public school physical education. Unfortunately, taxpayers have not yet seen fit to do so. (In California in 2001, the legislature was unable to pass even most legislation that would have funded the creation of written standards for all PE courses in the state.) There is the occasional nod and bow toward the need to "do something"—usually when the ever dismal state fitness test results are published every two years—but there is usually little if any follow-up. Many policy makers believe that today's parents have forever separated school and fitness, preferring either to ignore the subject altogether or to fill their kids' sports cravings through private programs. Unfortunately, that means permanent underfunding of public school PE—the only alternative for the less economically advantaged.

    Still, a small core of educators, many of them young PE teachers in some of the nation's most underfunded school districts, have plunged ahead, crafting unique programs specifically targeted at reducing obesity and increasing overall fitness. One of them is Dan Latham, a PE instructor at West Middle School in blue-collar Downey, California. Latham is, in many ways, the kind of fellow that many principals dream about; he is engaging, well-spoken, energetic, and full of ideas—all of which he is convinced he can pull off. When he first arrived at West back in 1991, Latham was struck by how few resources his fellow PE teachers had at hand. "And I was also struck by, frankly, how fat the kids had become." By 1995, he recalls, after-school coaches were coming to him "saying, 'Look I can't get enough kids to make a whole team anymore.'" Later, "we all got together and started talking, and it became clear right away what the enemy was—it was video games. We decided we had to find a way to make PE compute with Nintendo."

    One day Latham had a brainstorm: What if they could create a gym that was one part video parlor and one part health club? He found a 2000-square-foot building on the school lot that was going unused and got the school principal to give him and his buddies permission to rehab it, with the condition that the project would not cost the district any money. Latham raised $50,000 from a local philanthropist for material costs; the labor was donated by "my coaching buddies." To equip the gym, Latham began acquiring stationary bicycles—the fancy kind used in many expensive high-tech urban health clubs. These he had wired into big video screens. On the screens appeared a number of competitive video games—which could only be played as long as the users kept on pedaling. "What we found startled us all—kids who, if you asked them to run a mile outside, would just sort of look at you and hide, they were crazy for it. I have a kid who used to weigh 310 pounds who has already dropped 50 pounds—he laughed and sweated his way through it." By 1999 Latham had raised more than $250,000. His center, which he had dubbed Cyberobics, can now accommodate up to fifty students at a time. "It's always packed," he says. It is also attracting notice. Last year, West Middle School registered big gains on the semiannual California fitness test. Students at West Middle School were number one among schools its size in the category of aerobic capacity. "Next we've gotta get that upper body strength back up," says Latham.

Perhaps the most controversial way to use schools to prevent obesity has been undertaken not by academics and health professionals, but by parents, teachers, and school administrators, who have in recent years fought a high-stakes guerrilla war with the fast-food companies that have come to dominate the school nutrition scene. The most tense battleground is that of soft drink pouring contracts, in which high schools are paid large sums of cash in exchange for an agreement to sell only one kind of soda, usually Pepsi or Coke. Also called exclusivity deals, these contracts can run into the seven-figure range—a great deal of money for any chronically hard-strapped school system. Nationally, there are thousands of such deals in place. They have, in fact, become the norm in most large school districts, with principals—and parents and administrators—justifying the consequent omnipresence of soda (and soda ads) on campus as a way to pay for athletic uniforms and a variety of after-school programs.

Such was the initial justification of most members of the Sacramento school board last year when they considered a lucrative pouring contract from Pepsi. Over a five-year period, the soft drink behemoth promised to pay the board $2.5 million in return for the exclusive right to sell and advertise Pepsi products on Sacramento public school campuses. "Frankly, it was such a done deal that when it came before us, it was expected to be fast-tracked to approval," recalls Mickelle Masoner, a thirteen-year veteran of the school board. But then, after reflection, "it did not feel right to me. After all, we already had some vending machines on campuses, and many parents, and myself as a parent with kids in the district had always felt conflicted about that. I came to believe that this contract would hook us into something long-term that we should not be selling." An associate on the board, Manny Hernandez, soon came to feel the same way. "We looked closely at the contract and saw that we were locking the kids into a long-term cycle that would be skewed to the worst nutritional situation rather than the best."

15   But first Masoner and Hernandez had to convince their fellow board members, who were not wont to give up the $2.5 million in free operating funds. "We decided that we had to make the health case, in very clear terms," Masoner says. At the next board meeting, her fellows heard testimony from the county coroner, who noted that arterial streaking and early signs of bone disease were being seen in children as young as ten years old. The head of the regional dental association presented epidemiological

data indicating that, as he put it, "our area has the worst dental health record in the state." At the next meeting, the board unanimously rejected Pepsi's offer.

But the board did not stop there. The inquiry into the pouring contract had made them curious. And concerned. They decided to look into just how much junk food was present on campus. "What we found was stunning," Masoner says. "Candy and pop were everywhere. In almost any classroom in the district, you could find kids with soda and candy at their desk. Teachers were actually using them as a reward." Presenting all of this at a subsequent meeting, the board voted to present its principals with an ultimatum: They would have ten years to eliminate all high-sugar and high-fat foods from their campuses. The initial reaction was predictably truculent, but, say Masoner and Hernandez, the principals have more than risen to the occasion. By the end of winter break, they had already met the board's first incremental mandate of providing as much bottled water on campus as soda. "The kids were telling us they loved it," says Hernandez.

Even when the contracts themselves go unchallenged, the pouring contract disputes are increasingly fueling a new wave of parental activism. The target is junk food advertising in schools, which in recent years has become ubiquitous. The most common comes in the form of "sponsored educational materials": nutrition curriculum by McDonald's; math lessons using Tootsie Rolls and Domino's Pizza wheel graphics; reading texts that teach first graders to start out by recognizing logos from Pizza Hut and M&Ms. There is even a nutrition guide put out by McDonald's that teaches kids with diabetes how to calculate the number of diabetic "points" (the system advocated by the American Diabetes Association) in a typical McDonald's meal.

In an era when many school districts can't keep up with demand for basic texts, free supplemental materials are hard to turn away. But that is increasingly what is happening, says Andrew Hagelshaw, head of Berkeley's Center for Commercial-Free Public Education. "We are seeing hundreds of groups across the country take this issue on," he says. "The key is the parents. It's like a sleeping giant has been roused. Once they find out this has been happening right under their noses, they are unstoppable. They don't buy the notion that school is about educating consumers. It isn't. It's about educating citizens."

CONVERSATION STARTER

What do you think is causing the pervasive problem of obesity in America? What do you think can be done to solve this problem?

READING MATTERS

1. Considering what you already know about obesity in America, what did you learn that you did not already know from this article? How did it change your understanding of the causes of obesity?

2. Why are so many schoolchildren developing diabetes? In what sense are the schools to blame? Why did the school district in San Antonio, Texas, succeed in helping their children decrease their risk for diabetes? Research suggests that obesity in children is a class issue—that more working class children and adults suffer from obesity. Why do you think this is happening?

3. Leonard Epstein, head of Stanford's Pediatric Weight Control Program, has pioneered a program to decrease obesity in children. How are the guiding principles of his program different from what parents have traditionally been taught about how to get their children involved in exercise and weight control? Why and how does Francine Kaufman, head of Children's Pediatrics in Los Angeles, modify Epstein's approach? Does her approach seem more effective?

4. Why are children more willing to join support groups for obese youth than parents are willing to encourage them to join? Why do the children and youth appreciate the programs and lose weight?

Writing Matters

1. Write an essay that discusses the problems of obesity in children and youth. Find out about what types of programs need to be put into effect in schools in order to help children and youth lose weight and become more active. Propose some solutions for changing the programs and attitudes of teachers, administrators, and schoolchildren to solve the increasingly dangerous problem of obesity.

2. Write an essay that shows how parents are involved in the obesity of their children; then propose working solutions for families in your community that you think would work. Include examples of community and family programs that have been successful.

3. Volunteer to work at a weight control unit of a local clinic. Talk with nurses, doctors, and patients. Write a paper that discusses what you have learned. How effective is the program? How do the children feel about being in the program? Do you intend to continue to volunteer?

Relevant Web Sites

American Obesity Association <http://www.obesity.org/>

The official web site of the American Obesity Association focuses on changing public policy and perceptions about obesity by informing policy makers, media, professionals, and patients on the obesity epidemic.

National Center for Chronic Disease Prevention and Health Promotion <http://www.cdc.gov/nccdphp/dnpa/obesity/>

This government-sponsored web site provides information including a definition of obesity, information regarding body mass index (BMI), obesity trends, contributing factors, health consequences, and resources.

Robert D. Putnam

Health and Happiness

Educated at Swarthmore College, Balliol College at Oxford University, and Yale University, Robert D. Putnam is the Peter and Isabel Malkin Professor of Public Policy at Harvard. He serves as the president of the American Political Science Association and is a fellow of the American Academy of Arts and Sciences. He has been the chairman of Harvard's Department of Government, director of the Center for International Affairs, and dean of the John F. Kennedy School of Government. Putnam has also served on the staff of the National Security Council. He is author or coauthor of eight books and more than 30 scholarly articles published in 10 languages, including Making Democracy Work: Civic Traditions in Modern Italy *(1993),* Disaffected Democracies: What's Troubling the Trilateral Countries? *(2000), and* Better Together: Restoring the American Community *(2004). In the following selection from his study of American community,* Bowling Alone *(2000), Putnam argues for the importance of community and friendship to bolster the health of all citizens, regardless or their class, ethnicity, or religion.*

O f all the domains in which I have traced the consequences of social capital, in none is the importance of social connectedness so well established as in the case of health and well-being. Scientific studies of the effects of social cohesion on physical and mental health can be traced to the seminal work of the nineteenth-century sociologist Émile Durkheim, *Suicide.* Self-destruction is not merely a personal tragedy, he found, but a sociologically predictable consequence of the degree in which one is integrated into society—rarer among married people, rarer in more tightly knit religious communities, rarer in times of national unity, and more frequent when rapid social change disrupts the social fabric. Social connectedness matters to our lives in the most profound way.

In recent decades public health researchers have extended this initial insight to virtually all aspects of health, physical as well as psychological. Dozens of painstaking studies from Alameda (California) to Tecumseh (Michigan) have established beyond reasonable doubt that social connectedness is one of the most powerful determinants of our well-being. The more integrated we are with our community, the less likely we are to experience colds, heart attacks, strokes, cancer, depression, and premature death of all sorts. Such protective effects have been confirmed for close family ties, for friendship networks, for participation in social events, and even for simple affiliation with religious and other civic associations. In other words, both *machers* and *schmoozers* enjoy these remarkable health benefits.

After reviewing dozens of scientific studies, sociologist James House and his colleagues have concluded that the *positive* contributions to health made by social integration and social support rival in strength the *detrimental* contributions of well-established biomedical risk factors like cigarette smoking, obesity, elevated blood pressure, and physical inactivity. Statistically speaking, the evidence for the health consequences of social connectedness is as strong today as was the evidence for the health consequences of smoking at the time of the first surgeon general's report on smoking. If the trends in social disconnection are as pervasive as I argued in section II, then "bowling alone" represents one of the nation's most serious public health challenges.

Although researchers aren't entirely sure why social cohesion matters for health, they have a number of plausible theories. First, social networks furnish tangible assistance, such as money, convalescent care, and transportation, which reduces psychic and physical stress and provides a safety net. If you go to church regularly, and then you slip in the bathtub and miss a Sunday, someone is more likely to notice. Social networks also may reinforce healthy norms—socially isolated people are more likely to smoke, drink, overeat, and engage in other health-damaging behaviors. And socially cohesive communities are best able to organize politically to ensure first-rate medical services.

5   Finally, and most intriguingly, social capital might actually serve as a physiological triggering mechanism, stimulating people's immune systems to fight disease and buffer stress. Research now under way suggests that social isolation has measurable biochemical effects on the body. Animals who have been isolated develop more extensive atherosclerosis (hardening of the arteries) than less isolated animals, and among both animals and humans loneliness appears to decrease the immune response and increase blood pressure. Lisa Berkman, one of the leading researchers in the field, has speculated that social isolation is "a chronically stressful condition to which the organism respond[s] by aging faster."

Some studies have documented the strong correlation between connectedness and health at the community level. Others have zeroed in on individuals, both in natural settings and in experimental conditions. These studies are for the most part careful to account for confounding factors—the panoply of other physiological, economic, institutional, behavioral, and demographic forces that might also affect an individual's health. In many cases these studies are longitudinal: they check on people over many years to get a better understanding of what lifestyle changes might have caused people's health to improve or decline. Thus researchers have been able to show that social isolation *precedes* illness to rule out the possibility that the isolation was caused by illness. Over the last twenty years more than a dozen large studies of this sort in the United States, Scandinavia, and Japan have shown that *people who are socially disconnected are between two and five times more likely to die from all causes, compared with matched individuals who have close ties with family, friends, and the community.*

A recent study by researchers at the Harvard School of Public Health provides an excellent overview of the link between social capital and physical health across the United States. Using survey data from nearly 170,000 individuals in all fifty states, these researchers found, as expected, that people who are African American, lack health insurance, are overweight, smoke, have a low income, or lack a college education are at greater risk for illness than are more socioeconomically advantaged individuals. But these researchers also found an astonishingly strong relationship between poor health and low social capital. States whose residents were most likely to report fair or poor health were the same states in which residents were most likely to distrust others. Moving from a state with a wealth of social capital to a state with very little social capital (low trust, low voluntary group membership) increased one's chances of poor to middling health by roughly 40–70 percent. When the researchers accounted for individual residents' risk factors, the relationship between social capital and individual health remained. Indeed, the researchers concluded that if one wanted to improve one's health, moving to a high-social-capital state would do almost as much good as quitting smoking. These authors' conclusion is complemented by our own analysis. We found a strong positive relationship between a comprehensive index of public health and the Social Capital Index, along with a strong negative correlation between the Social Capital Index and all-cause mortality rates. (See Table 6 for the measure of public health and health care. . . .)

The state-level findings are suggestive, but far more definitive evidence of the benefits of community cohesion is provided by a wealth of studies that examine individual health as a function of individual social-capital resources. Nowhere is the connection better illustrated than in

---

Table 6: Which State Has the Best Health and Health Care?

Morgan-Quitno Healthiest State Rankings (1993–1998):

1. Births of low birth weight as a percent of all births (–)
2. Births to teenage mothers as a percent of live births (–)
3. Percent of mothers receiving late or no prenatal care (–)
4. Death rate (–)
5. Infant mortality rate (–)
6. Estimated age adjusted death rate by cancer (–)
7. Death rate by suicide (–)
8. Percent of population not covered by health insurance (–)
9. Change in percent of population uninsured (–)
10. Health care expenditures as percent of gross state product (–)
11. Per capita personal health expenditures (–)
12. Estimated rate of new cancer cases (–)
13. AIDS rate (–)
14. Sexually transmitted disease rate (–)
15. Percent of population lacking access to primary care (–)
16. Percent of adults who are binge drinkers (–)
17. Percent of adults who smoke (–)
18. Percent of adults overweight (–)
19. Days in past month when physical health was "not good" (–)
20. Community hospitals per 1,000 square miles (+)
21. Beds in community hospitals per 100,000 population (+)
22. Percent of children aged 19–35 months fully immunized (+)
23. Safety belt usage rate (+)

Roseto, Pennsylvania. This small Italian American community has been the subject of nearly forty years of in-depth study, beginning in the 1950s when medical researchers noticed a happy but puzzling phenomenon. Compared with residents of neighboring towns, Rosetans just didn't die of heart attacks. Their (age-adjusted) heart attack rate was less than half that of their neighbors; over a seven-year period not a single Roseto resident under forty-seven had died of a heart attack. The researchers looked for the usual explanations: diet, exercise, weight, smoking, genetic predisposition, and so forth. But none of these explanations held the answer—indeed, Rosetans were actually more likely to have some of these risk factors than were people in neighboring towns. The researchers then began to explore Roseto's social dynamics. The town had been founded in the nineteenth century by people from the same southern Italian village. Through local leadership these immigrants had created a mutual aid society, churches, sports clubs, a labor union, a newspaper, Scout troops, and a park and athletic field. The residents had also developed a tight-knit community where conspicuous displays of wealth were scorned and family values and good behaviors reinforced. Rosetans learned to draw on one another for financial, emotional, and other forms of support. By day they congregated on front porches to watch the comings and goings, and by night they gravitated to local social clubs. In the 1960s the researchers began to suspect that social capital (though they didn't use the term) was the key to Rosetans' healthy hearts. And the researchers worried that as socially mobile young people began to reject the tight-knit Italian folkways, the heart attack rate would begin to rise. Sure enough, by the 1980s Roseto's new generation of adults had a heart attack rate above that of their neighbors in a nearby and demographically similar town.

10   The Roseto story is a particularly vivid and compelling one, but numerous other studies have supported the medical researchers' intuition that social cohesion matters, not just in preventing premature death, but also in preventing disease and speeding recovery. For example, a long-term study in California found that people with the fewest social ties have the highest risk of dying from heart disease, circulatory problems, and cancer (in women), even after accounting for individual health status, socioeconomic factors, and use of preventive health care. Other studies have linked lower death rates with membership in voluntary groups and engagement in cultural activities; church attendance; phone calls and visits with friends and relatives; and general sociability such as holding parties at home, attending union meetings, visiting friends, participating in organized sports, or being members of highly cohesive military units. The connection with social capital persisted even when the studies examined other factors that might influence mortality, such as social class, race, gender, smoking and drinking, obesity, lack of exercise, and (significantly) health problems. In other words, it is not simply that healthy, health-conscious, privileged people (who might happen also to be more socially engaged) tend to live longer.

The broad range of illnesses shown to be affected by social support and the fact that the link is even tighter with death than with sickness tend to suggest that the effect operates at a quite fundamental level of general bodily resistance. What these studies tell us is that social engagement actually has an independent influence on how long we live.

Social networks help you stay healthy. The finding by a team of researchers at Carnegie Mellon University that people with more diverse social ties get fewer colds is by no means unique. For example, stroke victims who had strong support networks functioned better after the stroke, and recovered more physical capacities, than did stroke victims with thin social networks. Older people who are involved with clubs, volunteer work, and local politics consider themselves to be in better general health than do uninvolved people, even after accounting for socioeconomic status, demographics, level of medical care use, and years of retirement.

The bottom line from this multitude of studies: As a rough rule of thumb, if you belong to no groups but decide to join one, you cut your risk of dying over the next year *in half.* If you smoke and belong to no groups, it's a toss-up statistically whether you should stop smoking or start joining. These findings are in some ways heartening: it's easier to join a group than to lose weight, exercise regularly, or quit smoking.

But the findings are sobering, too. . . . There has been a general decline in social participation over the past twenty-five years. [Research also] shows that this same period witnessed a significant decline in self-reported health, despite tremendous gains in medical diagnosis and treatment. Of course, by many objective measures, including life expectancy, Americans are healthier than ever before, but these self-reports indicate that we are feeling worse. These self-reports are in turn closely linked to social connectedness, in the sense that it is precisely less connected Americans who are feeling worse. These facts alone do not *prove* that we are suffering physically from our growing disconnectedness, but taken in conjunction with the more systematic evidence of the health effects of social capital, this evidence is another link in the argument that the erosion of social capital has measurable ill effects.

The remarkable coincidence that during the same years that social connectedness has been declining, depression and even suicide have been increasing. We can also note that this coincidence has deep generational roots, in the sense that the generations most disconnected socially also suffer most from what some public health experts call "Agent Blue." In any given year 10 percent of Americans now suffer from major depression, and depression imposes the fourth largest total burden of any disease on Americans overall. Much research has shown that social connections inhibit depression. Low levels of social support directly predict depression, even controlling for other risk factors, and high levels of social support lessen the severity of symptoms and speed recovery. Social support buffers us from the stresses of daily life. Face-to-face ties seem to be more therapeutic than ties that are geographically distant. In short, even within the single domain of depression, we pay a very high price for our slackening social connectedness.

15   Countless studies document the link between society and psyche: people who have close friends and confidants, friendly neighbors, and supportive co-workers are less likely to experience sadness, loneliness, low self-esteem, and problems with eating and sleeping. Married people are consistently happier than people who are unattached, all else being equal. These findings will hardly surprise most Americans, for in study after study people themselves report that good relationships with family members, friends, or romantic partners—far more than money or fame—are prerequisites for their happiness. The single most common finding from a half century's research on the correlates of life satisfaction, not only in the United States but around the world, is that happiness is best predicted by the breadth and depth of one's social connections.

We can see how social capital ranks as a producer of warm, fuzzy feelings by examining a number of questions from the DDB Needham Life Style survey archives:

"I wish I could leave my present life and do something entirely different."
"I am very satisfied with the way things are going in my life these days."
"If I had my life to live over, I would sure do things differently."
20   "I am much happier now than I ever was before."

Responses to these items are strongly intercorrelated, so I combined them into a single index of happiness with life. Happiness in this sense is correlated with material well-being. Generally speaking, as one rises up the income hierarchy, life contentment increases. So money can buy happiness after all. But not as much as marriage. Controlling for education, age, gender, marital status, income, and civic engagement, the marginal "effect" of marriage on life contentment is equivalent to moving roughly seventy percentiles up the income hierarchy—say, from the fifteenth percentile to the eighty-fifth percentile. In round numbers, getting married is the "happiness equivalent" of quadrupling your annual income.

What about education and contentment? Education has important indirect links to happiness through increased earning power, but controlling for income (as well as age, gender, and the rest), what is the marginal correlation of education itself with life satisfaction? In round numbers the answer is that four additional years of education—attending college, for example—is the "happiness equivalent" of roughly doubling your annual income.

Having assessed in rough-and-ready terms the correlations of financial capital (income), human capital (education), and one form of social capital (marriage) with life contentment, we can now ask equivalent questions about the correlations between happiness and various forms of social interaction. Let us ask about regular club members (those who attend monthly), regular volunteers (those who do so monthly), people who entertain regularly at home (say, monthly), and regular (say, biweekly) churchgoers. The differences are astonishingly large. Regular club attendance, volunteering, entertaining, or church attendance is the happiness equivalent of getting a college degree or more than doubling your income. Civic connections rival marriage and affluence as predictors of life happiness.

If monthly club meetings are good, are daily club meetings thirty times better? The answer is no. [Research] shows what economists might call the "declining marginal productivity" of social interaction with respect to happiness. The biggest happiness returns to volunteering, clubgoing, and entertaining at home appear to come between "never" and "once a month." There is very little gain in happiness after about one club meeting (or party or volunteer effort) every three weeks. After fortnightly encounters, the marginal correlation of additional social interaction with happiness is actually negative—another finding that is consistent with common experience! Churchgoing, on the other hand, is somewhat different, in that at least up through weekly attendance, the more the merrier.

25   This analysis is, of course, phrased intentionally in round numbers, for the underlying calculations are rough and ready. Moreover the direction of causation remains ambiguous. Perhaps happy people are more likely than unhappy people to get married, win raises at work, continue in school, attend church, join clubs, host parties, and so on. My present purpose is merely to illustrate that social connections have profound links with psychological well-being. The Beatles got it right: we "get by with a little help from our friends."

In the decades since the Fab Four topped the charts, life satisfaction among adult Americans has declined steadily. Roughly half the decline in contentment is associated with financial worries, and half is associated with declines in social capital: lower marriage rates and decreasing connectedness to friends and community. Not all segments of the population are equally gloomy. Survey data show that the slump has been greatest among young and middle-aged adults (twenty to fifty-five). People over fifty-five—our familiar friends from the long civic generation—are actually *happier* than were people their age a generation ago.

Some of the generational discrepancy is due to money worries: despite rising prosperity, young and middle-aged people feel less secure financially. But some of the disparity is also due to social connectedness. Young and middle-aged adults today are simply less likely to have friends over, attend church, or go to club meetings than were earlier generations. Psychologist Martin Seligman argues that more of us are feeling down because modern society encourages a belief in personal control and autonomy more than a commitment to duty and common enterprise. This transformation heightens our expectations about what we can achieve through choice and grit and leaves us unprepared to deal with life's inevitable failures. Where once we could fall back on social capital—families, churches, friends—these no longer are strong enough to cushion our fall. In our personal lives as well as in our collective life, the evidence suggests, we are paying a significant price for a quarter century's disengagement from one another.

CONVERSATION STARTER

Why and how do you think your social and family relationships help to keep you a happy person? Think about several incidents when friendships or family members helped you to feel better physically or psychologically or both.

READING MATTERS

1. Why does Putnam begin his article with reference to the ideas of the important book, *Suicide,* by nineteenth century sociologist Émile Durkheim? Why do both men believe "social connectedness matters to our lives in a most profound way"? Many social researchers have completed studies that show that social connectedness can help to fight stress and disease. Explain why you agree or disagree with this claim, illustrating your point of view with several different examples. You can also do some research of you own to help think critically about the claim that links health and happiness.

2. Putnam presents studies that show how serious risk factors to health, such as cigarette smoking, high blood pressure, an inactive lifestyle, and obesity, are less detrimental to an individual's health than the absence of social connections, a life of isolation, and a sense of alienation. Explain why you agree or disagree with Putnam; again use examples to help support your point of view. Does Putnam's perspective on health seem nontraditional in today's world? How does Putnam use the example of the small town of Roseto, Pennsylvania, to support his point of view?

3. Do you agree with Putnam's claim based on various long-term studies that "as a rule of thumb," if you join a group after belonging to none, your risk of dying over the next year will diminish by one half? Explain your point of view. Provide examples for support if you can.

4. Considering Putnam's argument, his supporting evidence, and your life experiences, do you think that social connectedness, a long-term relationship, or marriage is more or less important than wealth? Defend your point of view.

WRITING MATTERS

1. Compose an argument that supports or refutes Putnam's assertion: "The most common finding from a half century's research on the correlates of life satisfaction, not only in the United States but around the world, is that happiness is best predicted by the breath and depth of one's social connections." Do research and reflect on your own experiences and observations to support your thesis.

2. Write an argument to support or refute Putnam's statement: "In round numbers, getting married is the happiness equivalent of quadrupling your annual income." Do some research to learn more about this point

and also consider a marriage as a long-term relationship. Then reflect on the relationships you have observed and those you know about intimately before writing your perspective on this claim.

3. Putnam's thesis can be interpreted as implying that we are paying for the past 25 years of valuing autonomy and individuality as well as success and wealth over developing strong social relationships and other types of support systems. What are the consequences of failure when an individual's striving for wealth and success has no social support? Research this topic before writing your argument. Include evidence from your personal experiences, reading, and observation when appropriate to support your point of view.

Relevant Web Sites

The Saguaro Seminar: Civic Engagement in America
<http://www.ksg.harvard.edu/saguaro/index.htm>

This web site features an ongoing initiative of Professor Robert D. Putnam at the John F. Kennedy School of Government at Harvard University. The project focuses on expanding what we know about our levels of trust and community engagement and on developing strategies and efforts to increase this engagement.

Better Together <http://www.bettertogether.org/index.htm>

The Better Together web site provides interactive ways to celebrate and learn from the ways that Americans are connecting and provides tools and strategies to reconnect with others. Better Together is an initiative of the Saguaro Seminar: Civic Engagement in America at Harvard University. The Saguaro Seminar issued the report "Better Together" in December of 2000, calling for a nationwide campaign to redirect a downward spiral of civic apathy.

Francis Fukuyama (b. 1952)

Policies for the Future

Francis Fukuyama is a world-renowned figure in public policy and international relations who has recently turned his attention to the field of bioethics. Fukuyama received his B.A. in Classics from Cornell University and his Ph.D. in Political Science from Harvard. He has been a policy planner for the RAND corporation and the U.S. Department of State; in 2002 he became a member of the President's Council on Bioethics. Fukuyama has also served as a Public Policy Professor at George Mason University and currently is Professor of International Political Economy at Johns Hopkins University. His books include Trust: The Social Virtues and the Creation of Prosperity *(1995),* The Great Disruption: Human Nature and the Reconstitution of Social Order *(1999), and* Our Posthuman Future: Consequences of the Biotechnology Revolution *(2002), from which the following selection is taken.*

Advances in biotechnology have created gaping holes in the existing regime for the regulation of human biomedicine, which legislatures and administrative agencies around the world have been racing to fill. It is not clear, for example, that the [current] rules for human experimentation . . . apply to embryos outside the womb. The nature of the players and the flow of money within the biomedical and pharmaceutical communities have also changed, with important implications for any future regulatory system.

One thing is reasonably clear: the time when governments could deal with biotech questions by appointing national commissions that brought scientists together with learned theologians, historians, and bioethicists— groups like the National Bioethics Advisory Commission in the United States and the European Group in Ethics in Science and New Technologies— is rapidly drawing to a close. These commissions played a very useful role in doing the preliminary intellectual spadework of thinking through moral and social implications of biomedical research. But it is time to move from thinking to acting, from recommending to legislating. We need institutions with real enforcement powers.

The community of bioethicists that has grown up in tandem with the biotech industry is in many respects a double-edged sword. On the one hand, it has played an extremely useful function by raising doubts and questions about the wisdom and morality of certain technological innovations. On the other hand, many bioethicists have become nothing more than sophisticated (and sophistic) justifiers of whatever it is the scientific community wants to do, having enough knowledge of Catholic theology or Kantian metaphysics to beat back criticisms by anyone coming out of these traditions who might object more strenuously. The Human Genome Project from the beginning devoted 3 percent of its budget to studying the Ethical, Social, and Legal Implications of genetic research. This can be regarded as commendable concern for the ethical dimensions of scientific research, or else as a kind of protection money the scientists have to pay to keep the true ethicists off their backs. In any discussion of cloning, stem cell research, germ-line engineering, and the like, it is usually the professional bioethicist who can be relied on to take the most permissive position of anyone in the room.* But if the ethicist isn't going to tell you that you can't do something, who will?

---

*This phenomenon is a common one and is known as regulatory "capture," whereby the group that is supposed to be overseeing the activities of an industry becomes an agent for the industry. This happens for many reasons, including the dependence of the regulators on the regulatees for money and information. In addition, there are the career incentives that most professional bioethicists face. Scientists do not usually have to worry about winning the respect of ethicists, particularly if they are Nobel Prize winners in molecular biology or physiology. On the other hand, ethicists face an uphill struggle winning the respect of the scientists they must deal with, and are hardly likely to do so if they tell them they are morally wrong or if they depart significantly from the materialist worldview that the scientists hold dear.

A number of countries have in fact moved beyond the stage of national commissions and study groups to actual legislation. One of the first and most contentious policy issues legislators have tried to grapple with concerns the uses that may be made of human embryos. This issue touches on a whole host of medical practices and procedures, both existing today and yet to be developed. These include abortion, in vitro fertilization, preimplantation diagnosis and screening, sex selection, stem cell research, cloning for reproductive and research purposes, and germ-line engineering. There are a huge number of permutations and combinations of possible rules that societies can establish regarding embryos. For example, one can imagine permitting them to be aborted or discarded by in vitro fertilization clinics, yet not created deliberately for research purposes nor selected for sex or other characteristics. Formulation and enforcement of these rules will constitute the substance of any future regulatory system for human biotechnology. There are at present a wide variety of national-level rules regarding human embryos. To date (November 2001), sixteen countries have passed laws regulating human embryo research, including France, Germany, Austria, Switzerland, Norway, Ireland, Poland, Brazil, and Peru (despite the fact that in France abortion is legal). In addition, Hungary, Costa Rica, and Ecuador implicitly restrict research by conferring on embryos a right to life. Finland, Sweden, and Spain permit embryo research, but only on extra embryos left over from in vitro fertilization clinics. Germany's laws are among the most restrictive; since passage of the 1990 Act for the Protection of Embryos (Gesetz zum Schutz von Embryonen), a number of areas have been regulated, including abuse of human embryos, sex selection, artificial modification of human germ-line cells, cloning, and the creation of chimeras and hybrids.

5   Britain in 1990 passed the Fertilisation and Embryology Act, which established one of the most clear-cut legal frameworks in the world for the regulation of embryo research and cloning. This act was thought to ban reproductive cloning while permitting research cloning, though in 2001 a British court ruled reproductive cloning would actually be permitted under a loophole that the government moved quickly to try to close. Given the lack of consensus across the continent on this issue, there has been no action on the European level to regulate embryo research apart from the creation of the European Group on Ethics in Science and New Technologies.

Embryo research is only the beginning of a series of new developments created by technology for which societies have to decide on rules and regulatory institutions. Others that will come up sooner or later include:

- *Preimplantation diagnosis and screening.* This group of technologies, in which multiple embryos are screened genetically for birth defects and other characteristics, is the beginning point of "designer babies" and will arrive much sooner than human germ-line engineering. Indeed, such screening has already been performed for children of parents susceptible to certain genetic diseases. In the future, do we want to permit parents to screen and selectively implant embryos on the basis of sex; intelligence; looks; hair, eye, or skin color; sexual orientation; and other characteristics once they can be identified genetically?

- *Germ-line engineering.* If and when human germ-line engineering arrives, it will raise the same issues as preimplantation diagnosis and screening, but in a more extreme form. Preimplantation diagnosis and screening is limited by the fact that there will always be a limited number of embryos from which to choose, based on the genes of the two parents. Germ-line engineering will expand the possibilities to include virtually any other genetically governed trait, provided it can be identified successfully, including traits that come from other species.

- *The creation of chimeras using human genes.* Geoffrey Bourne, former director of the Emory University primate center, once stated that "it would be very important scientifically to try to produce an ape-human cross." Other researchers have suggested using women as "hosts" for the embryos of chimpanzees or gorillas. One biotech company, Advanced Cell Technology, reported that it had successfully transferred human DNA into a cow's egg and gotten it to grow into a blastocyst before it was destroyed. Scientists have been deterred from doing research in this area for fear of bad publicity, but in the United States such work is not illegal. Will we permit the creation of hybrid creatures using human genes?

10
- *New psychotropic drugs.* In the United States, the Food and Drug Administration (FDA) regulates therapeutic drugs, while the Drug Enforcement Administration (DEA) and the states regulate illegal narcotics such as heroin, cocaine, and marijuana. Societies will have to make decisions on the legality and extent of permissible use of future generations of neuropharmacological agents. In the case of prospective drugs that improve memory or other cognitive skills, they will have to decide on the desirability of enhancement use and how they are to be regulated.

WHERE DO WE DRAW RED LINES?

Regulation is essentially the act of drawing a series of red lines that separate legal from proscribed activities, based on a statute that defines the area in which regulators can exercise some degree of judgment. With the exception of some die-hard libertarians, most people reading the above list of innovations that may be made possible by biotechnology will probably want to see some red lines drawn.

There are certain things that should be banned outright. One of them is reproductive cloning—that is, cloning with the intent of producing a child.

The reasons for this are both moral and practical, and go way beyond the National Bioethics Advisory Commission's concerns that human cloning cannot now be done safely.

The moral reasons have to do with the fact that cloning is a highly unnatural form of reproduction that will establish equally unnatural relationships between parents and children. A cloned child will have a very asymmetrical relationship with his or her parents. He or she will be both child and twin of the parent from whom his or her genes come, but will not be related to the other parent in any way. The unrelated parent will be expected to nurture a younger version of his or her spouse. How will that parent look upon the clone when he or she reaches sexual maturity? Nature . . . is a valid point of reference for our values and should not be discarded as a standard for parent-child relationships lightly. While it is possible to come up with some sympathetic scenarios in which cloning might be justified (for example, a Holocaust surviver with no other way of continuing the family line), they do not constitute a sufficiently strong societal interest to justify a practice that on the whole would be harmful.

Beyond these considerations inherent to cloning itself, there are a number of practical concerns. Cloning is the opening wedge for a series of new technologies that will ultimately lead to designer babies and one that is likely to become feasible much sooner than genetic engineering. If we get used to cloning in the near term, it will be much harder to oppose germ-line engineering for enhancement purposes in the future. It is important to lay down a political marker at an early point to demonstrate that the development of these technologies is not inevitable, and that societies can take some measure of control over the pace and scope of technological advance. There is no strong constituency in favor of cloning in any country. It is also an area where considerable international consensus exists in opposition to the procedure. Cloning therefore represents an important strategic opportunity to establish the possibility of political control over biotechnology.

15 But while a broad-brush ban is appropriate in this case, it will not be a good model for the control of future technologies. Preimplantation diagnosis and screening have begun to be used today to ensure the birth of children free of genetic diseases. The same technology can be used for less laudable purposes, such as sex selection. What we need to do in this case is not ban the procedure but regulate it, drawing red lines not around the procedure itself but within its range of possible uses to distinguish between what is legitimate and what is illegitimate.

One obvious way to draw red lines is to distinguish between therapy and enhancement, directing research toward the former while putting restrictions on the latter. The original purpose of medicine is, after all, to heal the sick, not to turn healthy people into gods. We don't want star athletes to be hobbled by bad knees or town ligaments, but we also don't want them to compete on the basis of who has taken the most steroids. The general principle would allow us to use biotechnologies to, for example, cure genetic diseases like Huntington's chorea or cystic fibrosis, but not to make our children more intelligent or taller.

The distinction between therapy and enhancement has been attacked on the grounds that there is no way to distinguish between the two in theory, and therefore no way of discriminating in practice. There is a long tradition, argued most forcefully in recent years by the French postmodernist thinker Michel Foucault, which maintains that what society considers to be pathology or disease is actually a socially constructed phenomenon in which deviation from some presumed norm is stigmatized. Homosexuality, to take one example, was long considered unnatural and was classified as a psychiatric disorder until the latter part of the twentieth century, when it was depathologized as part of the growing acceptance of gayness in developed societies. Something similar can be said of dwarfism: human heights are distributed normally, and it is not clear at what point in the distribution one becomes a dwarf. If it is legitimate to give growth hormone to a child who is in the bottom 0.5 percentile for height, who's to say that you can't also prescribe it for someone who is in the fifth percentile, or for that matter in the fiftieth? Geneticist Lee Silver makes a similar argument about future genetic engineering, saying that it is impossible to draw a line between therapy and enhancement in an objective manner: "in every case, genetic engineering will be used to add something to a child's genome that didn't exist in the genomes of either of its parents."

While it is the case that certain conditions do not lend themselves to neat distinctions between pathological and normal, it is also true that there is such a thing as health. As Leon Kass has argued, there is a natural functioning to the whole organism that has been determined by the requirements of the species' evolutionary history, one that is not simply an arbitrary social construction. It has often seemed to me that the only people who can argue that there is no difference in principle between disease and health are those who have never been sick: if you have a virus or fracture your leg, you know perfectly well that something is wrong.

And even in the cases where the borderline between sickness and health, therapy and enhancement, is murkier, regulatory agencies are routinely able to make these distinctions in practice. Take the case of Ritalin. . . . The underlying "disease" that Ritalin is supposed to treat, attention deficit–hyperactivity disorder (ADHD), is most likely not a disease at all but simply the label that we put on people who are in the tail of a normal distribution of behavior related to focus and attention. This is in fact a classic case of the social construction of pathology: ADHD was not even in the medial lexicon a couple of generations ago. There is, correspondingly, no neat line between what one might label the therapeutic and enhancement uses of Ritalin. At one end of the distribution, there are children almost anyone would say are so hyperactive that normal functioning is impossible for them, and it is hard to object to treating them with Ritalin. At the other end of the distribution are children who have no trouble whatsoever concentrating or interacting, for whom taking Ritalin might be an enjoyable experience that would give them a high just like any other amphetamine. But they would be taking the drug for enhancement rather than for therapeutic reasons, and thus most people would want to prevent them from doing so. What makes Ritalin controversial is all the children in the middle, who meet some but not all of the diagnostic criteria specified in the *Diagnostic and Statistical Manual of Mental Disorders* for the disease and who nonetheless are prescribed the drug by their family physician.

20   If there was ever a case, in other words, where the distinction between pathology and health in diagnosis, and therapy and enhancement in treatment, is ambiguous, it is ADHD and Ritalin. And yet, regulatory agencies *make and enforce this distinction all the time.* The DEA classifies Ritalin as a Schedule II pharmaceutical that can only be taken for therapeutic purposes with a doctor's prescription; it clamps down on Ritalin's recreational (that is to say, enhancement) use as an amphetamine. That the boundary between therapy and enhancement is unclear does not make the distinction meaningless. My own strong feeling is that the drug is overprescribed in the United States and used in situations in which parents and teachers ought to employ more traditional means of engaging children and shaping their characters. But the current regulatory system, for all its faults, is better than a situation in which Ritalin is either banned altogether or else sold over the counter like cough medicine.

    Regulators are called on all the time to make complex judgments that cannot be held up to precise theoretical scrutiny. What constitutes a "safe" level of heavy metals in the soil, or sulfur dioxide in the atmosphere? How does a regulator justify pushing down the level of a particular toxin in drinking water from fifty to five parts per million, when he or she is trading off health consequences against compliance costs? These decisions are always controversial, but in a sense they are easier to make in practice than in theory. For in practice, a properly functioning democratic political system allows people with a stake in the regulator's decision to push and shove against one another until a compromise is reached.

    Once we agree in principle that we will need a capability to draw red lines, it will not be a fruitful exercise to spend a lot of time arguing precisely where they should be placed. As in other areas of regulation, many of these decisions will have to be made on a trial-and-error basis by administrative agencies, based on knowledge and experience not available to us at present. What is more important is to think about the design of institutions that can make and enforce regulations on, for example, the use of preimplantation diagnosis and screening for therapeutic rather than enhancement purposes, and how those institutions can be extended internationally.

    As noted at the beginning of this chapter, action has to begin with legislatures stepping up to the plate and establishing rules and institutions. This is easier said than done: biotechnology is a technically complex and demanding subject, one moreover that is changing every day, with a wide variety of interest groups pulling in different directions. The politics of biotechnology does not fall into familiar political categories; if one is a conservative Republican or a left-wing Social Democrat, it is not immediately obvious how one should vote on a bill to permit so-called therapeutic cloning or stem cell research. For these reasons many legislators would rather duck the issue, hoping it will get resolved in some other way.

But to not act under conditions of rapid technological change is in effect to make a decision legitimizing that change. If legislators in democratic societies do not face up to their responsibilities, other institutions and actors will make the decisions for them.

25   This is particularly true given the peculiarities of the American political system. In the past, it has been the case that the courts have stepped into controversial areas of social policy when the legislature failed to act to negotiate acceptable political rules. In the absence of the congressional action on an issue like cloning, it is conceivable that the courts at some later point may be tempted or compelled to step into the breach and discover, for example, that human cloning or research on cloning is a constitutionally protected right. This was a very poor approach to the formulation of law and public policy in the past, one that tainted policies, such as the legalization of abortion, that more properly should have been enacted legislatively. On the other hand, if the American people clearly express their will on human cloning through their democratically elected representatives, the courts will be reluctant to thwart their will through discovery of a new right.

If the legislature does act to put further regulatory controls on human biotechnology, it will face large questions concerning the design of the requisite institutions to implement them. The same issue came up for the United States and the European Community in the 1980s when agricultural biotechnology appeared on the scene: Do we use existing regulatory bodies to do the job, or are the new technologies sufficiently different so that entirely new agencies are required? In the American case, the Reagen administration decided that agricultural biotech did not represent a sufficiently radical break with the past to merit regulation on the basis of process rather than product. It therefore decided to leave regulatory authority with existing agencies like the FDA and the Environment Protection Agency (EPA), on the basis of their statutory authority. The Europeans, by contrast, decided to regulate on the basis of process and therefore had to create new regulatory procedures for handling biotech products.

All countries face similar decisions today concerning human biotechnology. In the United States, it would be possible to leave regulatory authority with existing institutions like the FDA, the NIH, or consultative groups like the Recombinant DNA Advisory Committee (RAC). It is prudent to be conservative in the creation of new regulatory institutions and additional layers of bureaucracy. On the other hand, there are a number of reasons for thinking that we need to establish new institutions to deal with the challenges of the coming biotech revolution. Not to do so would be like trying to use the Interstate Commerce Commission, which was responsible for regulating trucks, to oversee civil aviation when that industry came into being, rather than creating a separate Federal Aviation Administration.

Let us consider first the case of the United States. An initial reason that existing U.S. institutions are probably not sufficient to regulate future human biotechnology is the question of their narrow mandate. Human biotechnology differs substantially from agricultural biotechnology insofar as it raises a host of ethical questions related to human dignity and human rights that are not an issue for GMOs. While people object to genetically engineered crops on ethical grounds, the most vociferous complaints have had to do with their possible negative consequences for human health and their environmental impact. This is precisely what existing regulatory institutions like the FDA, the EPA, and the U.S. Department of Agriculture have been set up to do. They can be criticized for having the wrong standards or for not being sufficiently cautious, but they are not operating outside their regulatory mandate when they take on genetically modified foods.

Let us suppose that Congress legislatively distinguishes between therapeutic and enhancement uses of preimplantation diagnosis and screening. The FDA is not set up to make politically sensitive decisions concerning the point at which selection for characteristics like intelligence and height ceases to be therapeutic and becomes enhancing, or whether these characteristics can be considered therapeutic at all. The FDA can disapprove a procedure only on the grounds of effectiveness and safety, but there will be many safe and effective procedures that will nonetheless require regulatory scrutiny. The limits of the FDA's mandate are already evident: it has asserted a right to regulate human cloning on the legally questionable grounds that a cloned child constitutes a medical "product" over which it has authority.

30   One can always try to amend and expand the FDA's charter, but past experience shows that it is very difficult to change the organizational culture of agencies with a long history. Not only will the agency resist taking on new duties, but a shifting mandate will likely mean it will do its old job less well. This implies the need to create a new agency to oversee the approval of new medicines, procedures, and technologies for human health. In addition to having a broader mandate, this new authority would have to have different staffing. It would have to include not just the doctors and scientists who staff the FDA and oversee clinical trials for new drugs, but other societal voices that are prepared to make judgments about the technology's social and ethical implications.

A second reason that existing institutions are probably not sufficient to regulate biotechnology in the future has to do with changes that have taken place in the research community and the biotech/pharmaceutical industry as a whole over the past generation. There was a period up through the early 1990s when virtually all biomedical research in the United States was funded by the NIH or another federal government agency. This meant that the NIH could regulate that research through its own internal rule-making authority, as in the case of rules concerning human experimentation. Government regulators could work hand in glove with committees of scientific insiders, like the RAC, and be reasonably sure that no one in the United States was doing dangerous or ethically questionable research.

None of this holds true any longer. While the federal government remains the largest source of research funding, there is a huge amount of private investment money available to sponsor work in new biotechnologies. The U.S. biotech industry by itself spent nearly $11 billion on research in 2000, employs over 150,000 people, and has doubled in size since 1993. Indeed, the massive government-funded Human Genome Project was upstaged by Craig Venter's privately held Celera Genomics in the race to map the human genome. The first embryonic stem cell lines were cultivated by James Thompson at the University of Wisconsin, using non-government funding in order to comply with the ban on federally funded research that would harm embryos. Many of the participants at a workshop held on the twenty-fifth anniversary of the Asilomar Conference on rDNA concluded that while the RAC had served an important function in its day, it could no longer monitor or police the present-day biotech industry. It has no formal enforcement powers and can bring to bear only the weight of opinion within the elite scientific community. The nature of that community has changed over time as well: there are today many fewer "pure" researchers, with no ties to the biotech industry or commercial interests in certain technologies.

This means that any new regulatory agency not only would have to have a mandate to regulate biotechnology on grounds broader than efficacy and safety but also would have to have statutory authority over all research and development, and not just research that is federally funded. Such an agency, the Human Fertilisation and Embyology Authority, has already been created in Britain for this purpose. Unification of regulatory powers into a single new agency will end the practice of complying with federal funding restrictions by finding private sponsors and, it is hoped, will shed a more uniform light on the whole biotech sector.

What are the prospects for the United States and other countries putting into place a regulatory system of the kind just outlined? There will be formidable political obstacles to creating new institutions. The biotech industry is strongly opposed to regulation (if anything, it would like to see FDA rules loosened), as is, by and large, the community of research scientists. Most would prefer regulation to take place within their own communities, outside the scope of formal law. They are joined in this by advocacy groups representing patients, the elderly, and others with an interest in promoting cures for various diseases, and together these groups form a very powerful political coalition.

35   There are reasons the biotech industry should consider actively promoting the right kind of formal regulation of human biotechnology, however, out of simple long-term self-interest. For that, it needs to look no further than what happened to agricultural biotechnology, which is a good object lesson in the political pitfalls of advancing a new technology too quickly.

At the beginning of the 1990s, Monsanto, a leading innovator in agricultural biotechnology, considered asking the first Bush administration for stronger formal regulatory rules for its genetically engineered products, including labeling requirements. A change of leadership at the top scuttled this initiative, however, on the grounds that there was no scientific evidence of health risks, and the firm introduced a series of new GMOs that were quickly adopted by American farmers. What the company failed to anticipate was the political backlash that arose in Europe against GMOs, and the strict labeling requirements that the European Union imposed in 1997 for genetically modified foods imported into Europe.

Monsanto and other American firms railed at the Europeans for being unscientific and protectionist, but Europe had sufficient market power to enforce its rules on American exporters. American farmers, without a means of separating genetically modified from non–genetically modified foods, found themselves closed out of important export markets. They responded by planting fewer genetically modified crops after 1997 and charging that they had been misled by the biotech industry. In retrospect, Monsanto executives realized that they had made a big mistake by not working earlier to establish an acceptable regulatory environment that would assure consumers of the safety of their products, even if this did not appear to be scientifically necessary.

The history of pharmaceutical regulation was driven by horror stories like the sulfanilamide elixir and thalidomide. It may be the case that regulations concerning human cloning will have to await the birth of a horribly deformed child who is the product of an unsuccessful cloning attempt. The biotech industry needs to consider whether it is better to anticipate such problems now and work toward formulating a system that serves its interests by assuring people of the safety and ethical nature of its products, or wait until there is a huge public outcry following an outrageous accident or horrifying experiment.

THE BEGINNING OF POSTHUMAN HISTORY?

The American regime was built, beginning in 1776, on a foundation of natural right. Constitutional government and a rule of law, by limiting the arbitrary authority of tyrants, would protect the kind of freedom that human beings by nature enjoyed. As Abraham Lincoln pointed out eighty-seven years later, it was also a regime dedicated to the proposition that all men are created equal. There would be an equality of freedom only because there was a natural equality of man; or, to put it more positively, the fact of natural equality demanded an equality of political rights.

40 Critics have pointed out that the United States has never lived up to this ideal of an equality of freedom and has, in its history, excluded entire groups from it. Defenders of the American regime have, more correctly in my view, pointed out that the principle of equal rights has driven a steady expansion in the circle of those entitled to rights. Once it was established that all human beings have natural rights, the big arguments in American political history have been over who falls within that charmed circles of "men" who were said by the Declaration to be created equal. The circle did not initially encompass women, or blacks, or white men without property; however, it was slowly but surely expanded to encompass them in time.

Whether the participants in these arguments recognized it or not, they all had at least an implicit idea of what the "essence" of a human being was and therefore a ground for judging whether one or another individual qualified. Human beings on the surface look, speak, and act very differently from one another, so much of this argument revolved around the question of whether those apparent differences were ones of convention only, or whether they were rooted in nature.

Modern natural science has cooperated to some extent in expanding our view of who qualifies as a human being because it has tended to show that most of the apparent differences between human beings are conventional rather than natural. Where there *are* natural differences, as between men and women, they have been shown to affect nonessential qualities that do not have a bearing on political rights.

So, despite the poor repute in which concepts like natural rights are held by academic philosophers, much of our political world rests on the existence of a stable human "essence" with which we are endowed by nature, or rather, on the fact that we believe such an essence exists.

We may be about to enter into a posthuman future, in which technology will give us the capacity gradually to alter that essence over time. Many embrace this power, under the banner of human freedom. They want to maximize the freedom of parents to choose the kind of children they have, the freedom of scientists to pursue research, and the freedom of entrepreneurs to make use of technology to create wealth.

45 But this freedom will be different from all other freedoms that people have previously enjoyed. Political freedom has heretofore meant the freedom to pursue those ends that our natures had established for us. Those ends are not rigidly determined; human nature is very plastic, and we have an enormous range of choices conformable with that nature. But it is not infinitely malleable, and the elements that remain constant—particularly our species-typical gamut of emotional responses—constitute a safe harbor that allows us to connect, potentially, with all other human beings.

It may be that we are somehow destined to take up this new kind of freedom, or that the next stage of evolution is one in which, as some have suggested, we will deliberately take charge of our own biological makeup rather than leaving it to the blind forces of natural selection. But if we do, we should do it with eyes open. Many assume that the posthuman world will look pretty much like our own—free, equal, prosperous, caring, compassionate—only with better health care, longer lives, and perhaps more intelligence than today.

But the posthuman world could be one that is far more hierarchical and competitive than the one that currently exists, and full of social conflict as a result. It could be one in which any notion of "shared humanity" is lost, because we have mixed human genes with those of so many other species that we no longer have a clear idea of what a human being is. It could be one in which the median person is living well into his or her second century, sitting in a nursing home hoping for an unattainable death. Or it could be the kind of soft tyranny envisioned in *Brave New World*, in which everyone is healthy and happy but has forgotten the meaning of hope, fear, or struggle.

We do not have to accept any of these future worlds under a false banner of liberty, be it that of unlimited reproductive rights or of unfettered scientific inquiry. We do not have to regard ourselves as slaves to inevitable technological progress when that progress does not serve human ends. True freedom means the freedom of political communities to protect the values they hold most dear, and it is that freedom that we need to exercise with regard to the biotechnology revolution today.

CONVERSATION STARTER

Write about your views on biotechnology. Are you concerned that biotechnology is somehow "out of control"? If so, in what ways? Do you think that biotechnology will have a negative effect on humanity and the environment in the future or a positive one overall?

READING MATTERS

1. According to Fukuyama, why is it necessary to move from thinking to acting in our global efforts to control biotechnology? What interests sometimes lead bioethicists to take permissive positions on control of scientific research?
2. What does Fukuyama believe to be the "legitimate" and "illegitimate" uses of technology? What examples does he use? Do you agree with his arguments?
3. What is Fukuyama's position on creating new federal agencies for regulation of biotechnological research? Why does he believe it would be in the best interest for biotech companies to accept such regulations, which they have previously resisted? Is his argument for this approach to regulation convincing?
4. At the end of his essay, Fukuyama makes a distinction between unlimited freedom and "true freedom." What distinction does he draw? Do you believe the distinction he draws is valid?

WRITING MATTERS

1. Fukuyama provides a case history of the drug Ritalin, examining the positive and negative effects of the drug and the current regulations in place to deal with these effects among different types of users. Create a similar case history of a particular product, either a drug or a biotechnical product such as a genetically altered food, and evaluate the success or failure of the current regulations in place.
2. Do some research into an NGO (nongovernmental organization) devoted to limiting biotechnical experimentation in a particular area, such as cloning or other forms of genetic manipulation. Write a paper that discusses how this approach to regulation is different from Fukuyama's and/or complementary to it.

3. Develop your own idea for an agency, program, or organization devoted to heightening awareness about the dangers of a certain kind of biotechnological research and creating workable regulations in this area. How will the decisions related to workable regulations apply to the future of biotechnology? Write up your proposal to share with your classmates.

RELEVANT WEB SITES

DR. FRANCIS FUKUYAMA
<http://apps.sais-jhu.edu/faculty_bios/faculty_bio1.php?ID=20>

A faculty biography of Dr. Francis Fukuyama is available through the Johns Hopkins University web site.

THE PRESIDENT'S COUNCIL ON BIOETHICS
<http:/www.bioethics.gov/about/fukuyama.html>

Learn about Dr. Francis Fukuyama's role as an advisor to the President on ethical issues related to advances in biomedical science and technology.

Audre Lorde (b. 1934)

From *The Cancer Journals*

Born of Caribbean immigrants who settled in New York City, Audre Lorde attended Hunter College and went on to complete an M.A. in Library Science at Columbia University. After attaining the position as Head Librarian at the City University of New York, she moved on to be a poet-in-residence at Tougaloo College in Mississippi. While there, she completed her first book of poetry, The First Cities *(1970), which led to her appointment at Hunter College as a Professor of Poetry. Lorde received many prestigious awards, including The National Endowment for the Arts Grant (1968) and the Creative Arts Public Service Book Award for Poetry (1972). She published 18 books in different genres— poetry, essays collections, and a biography. Her most widely read books include* Zami: A New Spelling of My Name *(1982),* Sister Outsider: Essays and Speeches *(1984), and* The Collected Poems of Audre Lorde *(1997). The selection that follows from* The Cancer Journals *(1980) was written for women who, like Lorde, had to face the crisis of breast cancer. Her intention was to make the impact and complications of the disease more available to women as well as to the public in general. Indeed, her journals have comforted many women and have dispelled many myths about the illness.*

· 1 ·

Each woman responds to the crisis that breast cancer brings to her life out of a whole pattern, which is the design of who she is and how her life has been lived. The weave of her every day existence is the training ground for how she handles crisis. Some women obscure their painful feelings surrounding mastectomy with a blanket of business-as-usual, thus keeping those feelings forever under cover, but expressed elsewhere. For some women, in a valiant effort not to be seen as merely victims, this means an insistence that no such feelings exist and that nothing much has occurred. For some women it means the warrior's painstaking examination of yet another weapon, unwanted but useful.

I am a post-mastectomy woman who believes our feelings need voice in order to be recognized, respected, and of use.

I do not wish any anger and pain and fear about cancer to fossilize into yet another silence, nor to rob me of whatever strength can lie at the core of this experience, openly acknowledged and examined. For other women of all ages, colors, and sexual identities who recognize that imposed silence about any area of our lives is a tool for separation and powerlessness, and for myself, I have tried to voice some of my feelings and thoughts about the travesty of prosthesis, the pain of amputation, the function of cancer in a profit economy, my confrontation with mortality, the strength of women loving, and the power and rewards of self-conscious living.

Breast cancer and mastectomy are not unique experiences, but ones shared by thousands of American women. Each of these women has a particular voice to be raised in what must become a female outcry against all preventable cancers, as well as against the secret fears that allow those cancers to flourish. May these words serve as encouragement for other women to speak and to act out of our experiences with cancer and with other threats of death, for silence has never brought us anything of worth. Most of all, may these words underline the possibilities of self-healing and the richness of living for all women.

5   There is a commonality of isolation and painful reassessment which is shared by all women with breast cancer, whether this commonality is recognized or not. It is not my intention to judge the woman who has chosen the path of prosthesis, of silence and invisibility, the woman who wishes to be "the same as before." She has survived on another kind of courage, and she is not alone. Each of us struggles daily with the pressures of conformity and the loneliness of difference from which those choices seem to offer escape. I only know that those choices do not work for me, nor for other women who, not without fear, have survived cancer by scrutinizing its meaning within our lives, and by attempting to integrate this crisis into useful strengths for change.

•2•

These selected journal entries, which begin 6 months after my modified radical mastectomy for breast cancer and extend beyond the completion of the essays in this book, exemplify the process of integrating this crisis into my life.

1/26/79

I'm not feeling very hopeful these days, about selfhood or anything else. I handle the outward motions of each day while pain fills me like a pus-pocket and every touch threatens to breech the taut membrane that keeps it from flowing through and poisoning my whole existence. Sometimes despair sweeps across my consciousness like luna winds across a barren moonscape. Ironshod horses rage back and forth over every nerve. Oh Seboulisa ma, help me remember what I have paid so much to learn. I could die of difference, or live—myriad selves.

2/5/79
The terrible thing is that nothing goes past me these days, nothing. Each horror remains like a steel vise in my flesh, another magnet to the flame. Buster has joined the rollcall of useless wasteful deaths of young Black people; in the gallery today everywhere ugly images of women offering up distorted bodies for whatever fantasy passes in the name of male art. Gargoyles of pleasure. Beautiful laughing Buster, shot down in a hallway for ninety cents. Shall I unlearn that tongue in which my curse is written?

3/1/79
It is such an effort to find decent food in this place, not to just give up and eat the old poison. But I must tend my body with at least as much care as I tend the compost, particularly now when it seems so beside the point. Is this pain and despair that surround me a result of cancer, or has it just been released by cancer? I feel so unequal to what I always handled before, the abominations outside that echo the pain within. And yes I am completely self-referenced right now because it is the only translation I can trust, and I do believe not until every woman traces her weave back strand by bloody self-referenced strand, will we begin to alter the whole pattern.

4/16/79
10   *The enormity of our task, to turn the world around. It feels like turning my life around, inside out. If I can look directly at my life and my death without flinching I know there is nothing they can ever do to me again. I must be content to see how really little I can do and still do it with an open heart. I can never accept this, like I can't accept that turning my life around is so hard, eating differently, sleeping differently, moving differently, being differently. Like Martha said, I want the old me, bad as before.*

4/22/79
I must let this pain flow through me and pass on. If I resist or try to stop it, it will detonate inside me, shatter me, splatter my pieces against every wall and person that I touch.

5/1/79
Spring comes, and I still feel despair like a pale cloud waiting to consume me, engulf me like another cancer, swallow me into immobility, metabolize me into cells of itself; my body, a barometer. I need to remind myself of the joy, the lightness, the laughter so vital to my living and my health. Otherwise, the other will always be waiting to eat me up into despair again. And that means destruction. I don't know how, but it does.

9/79
There is no room around me in which to be still, to examine and explore what pain is mine alone—no device to separate my struggle within from

my fury at the outside world's viciousness, the stupid brutal lack of consciousness or concern that passes for the way things are. The arrogant blindness of comfortable white women. What is this work all for? What does it matter whether I ever speak again or not? I try. The blood of black women sloshes from coast to coast and Daly says race is of no concern to women. So that means we are either immortal or born to die and no note taken, un-women.

10/3/79
I don't feel like being strong, but do I have a choice? It hurts when even my sisters look at me in the street with cold and silent eyes. I am defined as other in every group I'm a part of. The outsider, both strength and weakness. Yet without community there is certainly no liberation, no future, only the most vulnerable and temporary armistice between me and my oppression.

11/19/79
15 *I want to write rage but all that comes is sadness. We have been sad long enough to make this earth either weep or grow fertile. I am an anachronism, a sport, like the bee that was never meant to fly. Science said so. I am not supposed to exist. I carry death around in my body like a condemnation. But I do live. The bee flies. There must be some way to integrate death into living, neither ignoring it nor giving in to it.*

1/1/80
Faith is the last day of Kwanza, and the name of the war against despair, the battle I fight daily. I become better at it. I want to write about that battle, the skirmishes, the losses, the small yet so important victories that make the sweetness of my life.

1/20/80
The novel is finished at last. It has been a lifeline. I do not have to win in order to know my dreams are valid, I only have to believe in a process of which I am a part. My work kept me alive this past year, my work and the love of women. They are inseparable from each other. In the recognition of the existence of love lies the answer to despair. Work is that recognition given voice and name.

2/18/80
I am 46 years living today and very pleased to be alive, very glad and very happy. Fear and pain and despair do not disappear. They only become slowly less and less important. Although sometimes I still long for a simple orderly life with a hunger sharp as that sudden vegetarian hunger for meat.

4/6/80
Somedays, if bitterness were a whetstone, I could be sharp as grief.

5/30/80

20   *Last spring was another piece of the fall and winter before, a progression from all the pain and sadness of that time, ruminated over. But somehow this summer which is almost upon me feels like a part of my future. Like a brand new time, and I'm pleased to know it, wherever it leads. I feel like another woman, de-chrysalised and become a broader, stretched-out me, strong and excited, a muscle flexed and honed for action.*

6/20/80

I do not forget cancer for very long, ever. That keeps me armed and on my toes, but also with a slight background noise of fear. Carl Simonton's book, Getting Well Again, *has been really helpful to me, even though his smugness infuriates me sometimes. The visualizations and deep relaxing techniques that I learned from it help make me a less anxious person, which seems strange, because in other ways, I live with the constant fear of recurrence of another cancer. But fear and anxiety are not the same at all. One is an appropriate response to a real situation which I can accept and learn to work through just as I work through semi-blindness. But the other, anxiety, is an immobilizing yield to things that go bump in the night, a surrender to namelessness, formlessness, voicelessness, and silence.*

7/10/80

I dreamt I had begun training to change my life, with a teacher who is very shadowy. I was not attending classes, but I was going to learn how to change my whole life, live differently, do everything in a new and different way. I didn't really understand, but I trusted this shadowy teacher. Another younger woman who was there told me she was taking a course in "language crazure," the opposite of discrazure (the cracking and wearing away of rock). I thought it would be very exciting to study the formation and crack and composure of words, so I told my teacher I wanted to take that course. My teacher said okay, but it wasn't going to help me any because I had to learn something else, and I wouldn't get anything new from that class. I replied maybe not, but even though I knew all about rocks, for instance, I still liked studying their composition, and giving a name to the different ingredients of which they were made. It's very exciting to think of me being all the people in this dream.

· 3 ·

I have learned much in the 18 months since my mastectomy. My visions of a future I can create have been honed by the lessons of my limitations. Now I wish to give form with honesty and precision to the pain faith labor and loving which this period of my life has translated into strength for me.

Sometimes fear stalks me like another malignancy, sapping energy and power and attention from my work. A cold becomes sinister; a cough, lung cancer; a bruise, leukemia. Those fears are most powerful when they are not given voice, and close upon their heels comes the fury that I cannot shake them. I am learning to live beyond fear by living through it, and in the process learning to turn fury at my own limitations into some more creative energy. I realize that if I wait until I am no longer afraid to act, write, speak, be, I'll be sending messages on a ouija board, cryptic complaints from the other side. When I dare to be powerful, to use my strength in the service of my vision, then it becomes less important whether or not I am unafraid.

25   As women we were raised to fear. If I cannot banish fear completely, I can learn to count with it less. For then fear becomes not a tyrant against which I waste my energy fighting, but a companion, not particularly desirable, yet one whose knowledge can be useful.

I write so much here about fear because in shaping this introduction to *The Cancer Journals,* I found fear laid across my hands like a steel bar. When I tried to reexamine the 18 months since my mastectomy, some of what I touched was molten despair and waves of mourning—for my lost breast, for time, for the luxury of false power. Not only were these emotions difficult and painful to relive, but they were entwined with the terror that if I opened myself once again to scrutiny, to feeling the pain of loss, of despair, of victories too minor in my eyes to rejoice over, then I might also open myself again to disease. I had to remind myself that I had lived through it all, already. I had known the pain, and survived it. It only remained for me to give it voice, to share it for use, that the pain not be wasted.

Living a self-conscious life, under the pressure of time, I work with the consciousness of death at my shoulder, not constantly, but often enough to leave a mark upon all of my life's decisions and actions. And it does not matter whether this death comes next week or thirty years from now; this consciousness gives my life another breadth. It helps shape the words I speak, the ways I love, my politic of action, the strength of my vision and purpose, the depth of my appreciation of living.

I would lie if I did not also speak of loss. Any amputation is a physical and psychic reality that must be integrated into a new sense of self. The absence of my breast is a recurrent sadness, but certainly not one that dominates my life. I miss it, sometimes piercingly. When other one-breasted women hide behind the mask of prosthesis or the dangerous fantasy of reconstruction, I find little support in the broader female environment for my rejection of what feels like a cosmetic sham. But I believe that socially sanctioned prosthesis is merely another way of keeping women with breast cancer silent and separate from each other. For instance, what would happen if an army of one-breasted women descended upon Congress and demanded that the use of carcinogenic, fat-stored hormones in beef-feed be outlawed?

The lessons of the past 18 months have been many: How do I provide myself with the best physical and psychic nourishment to repair past, and minimize future damage to my body? How do I give voice to my quests so that other women can take what they need from my experiences? How do my experiences with cancer fit into the larger tapestry of my work as a Black woman, into the history of all women? And most of all, how do I fight the despair born of fear and anger and powerlessness which is my greatest internal enemy?

30   I have found that battling despair does not mean closing my eyes to the enormity of the tasks of effecting change, nor ignoring the strength and the barbarity of the forces aligned against us. It means teaching, surviving and fighting with the most important resource I have, myself, and taking joy in that battle. It means, for me, recognizing the enemy outside and the enemy within, and knowing that my work is part of a continuum of women's work, of reclaiming this earth and our power, and knowing that this work did not begin with my birth nor will it end with my death. And it means knowing that within this continuum, my life and my love and my work has particular power and meaning relative to others.

It means trout fishing on the Missisquoi River at dawn and tasting the green silence, and knowing that this beauty too is mine forever.

29 August 1980

CONVERSATION STARTER

Share with your group what you know about the impact of breast cancer on a woman who is ill, on her family, and on her close friends. Do you think that enough people are informed about how to prevent breast cancer and how the disease affects a woman's body and mind?

READING MATTERS

1. Why does Audre Lorde write these cancer journals? What are the dangers of silence and secret fears?
2. Why does Lorde believe that a woman who has suffered from breast cancer must attempt to integrate her crisis into "useful strengths for change"? Have you ever been in a crisis that helped you to develop skills that made you a stronger individual?
3. What universal philosophical issues does Lorde examine in her journal entries?
4. Discuss with your peer writing group one or two of the entries that moved you the most.

WRITING MATTERS

1. Write an essay in which you explain why the silence about breast cancer existed historically and how it has been broken. You will have to do careful research to show how the disease is being defeated and how individuals, health groups, and communities are working to make breast cancer a disease that people understand, know how to treat, and want to cure.

2. Who is the audience for this essay? Write an essay in which you analyze, discuss, and illustrate why and how Lorde constructed this essay for the particular audience she selected.
3. Volunteer to attend a breast cancer support group, and write an essay about your experiences and what you learned. Share your paper with your supervisor as well as with your class and professor.

RELEVANT WEB SITES

AMERICAN CANCER SOCIETY HOME PAGE <http://www.cancer.org>

The American Cancer Society (ACS) is a nationwide, community-based voluntary health organization. The web site provides general information about community programs and services, research, advocacy, public policy, and international programs.

CANCER.GOV <http://www.nci.nih.gov/>

The National Cancer Institute coordinates the National Cancer Program, which conducts and supports research, training, health information dissemination, and other programs with respect to the cause, diagnosis, prevention, treatment, and rehabilitation from cancer; as well as the continuing care of cancer patients and the families of cancer patients.

Elliott Leyton

The Obliteration of Alienation

Canadian anthropologist Elliott Leyton, who has written several studies of serial killings and genocide, became interested in better understanding the famous and well-respected humanitarian group Doctors Without Borders after hearing about their work in the wake of the genocide is Rawanda. Doctors Without Borders (Médecins Sans Frontières, MSF) delivers emergency aid to victims of armed conflict, epidemics, and natural and man-made disasters, and to others who lack health care due to social or geographic isolation. MSF was founded in 1971 by a small group of French doctors who believed that all people have the right to medical care regardless of race, religion, creed, or political affiliation, and that the needs of these people supersede respect for national borders. It was the first nongovernmental organization to both provide emergency medical assistance and publicly bear witness to the plight of the populations they served. A private, nonprofit organization, MSF is at the forefront of emergency health care as well as care for populations suffering from endemic diseases and neglect. It provides primary health care, performs surgery, rehabilitates hospitals and clinics, runs nutrition and sanitation programs, trains local medical personnel, and provides mental health care. Through longer-term programs, MSF treats chronic diseases such as tuberculosis, malaria, sleeping sickness, and AIDS; assists with the medical and psychological problems of marginalized populations including street children and ethnic minorities; and brings health care to remote, isolated areas where resources and training are limited. MSF is based on volunteerism.

Elliot Leyton's book Touched by Fire *(1998) focuses on the 1996 return of the masses of Rawanda victims of genocide who had fled to Zaire. This unique book addresses the triumphs of the exhausted workers who fight against warlords and exploiters. The selection that follows discusses why doctors, nurses, and administrators continue to help in the face of tyranny and despair. Leyton himself writes, "The world can afford a humanitarian ideal, and it cannot afford the brutalization that comes with indifference to catastrophe."*

A primary quality of life in the modern urban, industrial world is alienation. People are brought to work in the cities, packed together in anonymous apartments, often disconnected from family, from neighbourhood, and, more importantly, from themselves. This process of progressive alienation has its roots in modernity, in the industrialization of the economy, the urbanization of the landscape, and the stratification of society that began in the late eighteenth century and reached its fullest flowering in our time.

The Industrial Revolution was one of the great human achievements. On the one hand, it liberated people, freeing them from otherwise unbreakable social commitments to kin and neighbours, as well as from the unthinkable slaveries of caste, race, gender, and class. Anthropologist Eric Wolf wrote that in liberating people, it made them independent actors, directors of their own lives. Yet it also created its own reservoir of anguish. In the industrializing nineteenth century, both conservative and radical social critics were appalled at the new alienation they saw. In the transformed industrial order, people were alienated from "the product of their work which disappeared into the market"; alienated from "their fellow men who had become actual or potential competitors in the market"; and from "themselves to the extent to which they now had to look upon their own capabilities as marketable commodities," no longer the qualities of a full human being.

This alienation of modern industrial man can cut the spirit like a machete. John Berger, writing of an extreme form of this dilemma in *A Seventh Man*—migrant labouring in wealthy Europe—speaks of it as a form of "imprisonment," wherein a man imported for his labour from the Third World is hermetically sealed off from all natural social and sexual intercourse—with his lover, his family, and his home—and is thus transformed into a kind of non-person. Many MSFers also felt like non-persons when trapped in their dull previous lives.

Becoming an MSFer is the opposite of this experience: it is a kind of *dis*alienation. Membership liberates them as human beings, allows them to explore fully their potential as they seize the opportunity to act. With that liberation comes a profound conviction of the purity of what they do, of the moral superiority of their agency and themselves—a belief so powerful, a satisfaction so intense, that it sustains them through whatever they must do. To witness atrocity and fear, to treat vile diseases, to heal terrible wounds, to dig the latrine or deliver clean water are all part of a process in which they confront reality and construct their identities. In acting thus with such purpose and moral clarity, all other dilemmas dissolve. To act without ambivalence or regret, to cut through the mindlessness of conventional life, to revel in what one is and what one does is for them the only way to become whole.

5   MSFers do not of course usually discuss their lives in terms of social philosophy. Yet they consistently allude to the trivialization, even negation, of self that comes with being a replaceable "cog in a machine" in Europe or America. Clive speaks for them all when he reminds us of his gift from MSF—to be permitted to do something of value, to act with confidence, to create his identity, to seize control of his life. Through MSF, he can achieve a kind of internal peace through meaningful labour. He heals himself as he gives the suffering the means to heal, as he sees firsthand the results of setting up a water station, supervising the digging of a latrine. When he works in his characteristic state of total concentration, he is always smiling.

Now they are with MSF, the elite shock troops of the unarmed armies of international aid, the firefighters who are parachuted into a crisis at the first sign of trouble, women and men who routinely go where modern armies and their political masters fear to tread. Now there is no endless waiting as a bureaucracy creeps towards an always meaningless and already outdated decision: MSF makes decisions according to circumstance, and MSF makes them *now*. If they are at home on leave, a packed suitcase sits ready by the door, because the recall could come at any time.

Their work will drain every ounce of their energy. They will eat and sleep when and where they can, but their being is engorged with a sense of purpose that transcends their experience, electrifying their muddy and repellent insect- and reptile-infested environment. We see it all at once on our very first full day in Africa, as we sit in an outbuilding behind MSF's East African Logistics Centre in Nairobi. It is now what the Irish call the edge of dark, and a lone fluorescent bulb on a wall partly illuminates the shadowy room. All we can hear in the background is the song of unfamiliar birds and the sudden onset of this minor rainy season's windswept showers. Leaning over Harry's shoulder we surmise that Zaire, the rotten Empire of the Equator, is indeed imploding and a million refugees are about to pour across the border. What rivets our attention is the clicking of Harry's computer keys, and his rapid switches from Dutch to English on the radio-telephone as MSF struggles to estimate the scale of the disaster. In the main building in front of us, Robert is making a flurry of telephone calls around the world to orchestrate emergency flights into Rwanda. Two rooms away, other MSF workers are on radio-telephones, straining for up-to-the-moment information from their workers in the jungle—"Allo? Allo? Allo?" Lizards wait patiently on the wall and gorge on the insects that swarm the light. Thousands of white-winged moths swirl and dance in front of the outdoor lamps. "Stand by . . . over," sputters through the radio. Nothing else for them will ever be so complete, so focused, so absorbing.

When they arrive at their new posting—into the throat of a flood in Somalia, an epidemic in Cambodia, a plague in the Sudan, or a bloody civil war in what once was Yugoslavia—they become part of a self-confident elite. They lose all sense of alienation, they fuse with both their inner beings and their fellows, and become what they wish to be. We're the best; we don't panic; we know what's going on, and we know what we're doing; we're politically and financially independent; and we tell the others just what we think of them. But most of all we work.

We are back in Rwanda with a million refugees pounding down the road from Zaire. As we leave to check the MSF installations, the inexperienced young woman from a UN relief camp radios in a panic: "The refugees are all here, we don't know if we can handle it!" "Ridiculous!" exclaims MSF nurse Monique. "Don't panic! Everything is fine, at least until tomorrow morning. We're not panicking." Later, as the moving wave of refugees appears below our way station, she phlegmatically announces over the radio-telephone, "Okay, they are coming. We are ready for them."

10   Contact! Not the mindless handing out of food and medicines, but witnessing against evil. Not the soul-less merchandising of public health, but eye and hand contact with the victims of unthinkable deprivation. Their job is clear: Feel the suffering with your hands. Witness, food, water, latrines, medicine!

Contact with the humanity of others and the self's full potential, contact with those who need and feel your human help—the crippled, raped, torn, and traumatized, the victims of ruthless political manipulators. The space around you has become the centre of the world, regardless of whether the eyes of the world are turned in horror on the suffering people before you, as in Rwanda and Zaire in November 1996, or when no one else is watching, as in the unknown wars and genocides in Asia, South America, and Africa. These are the disremembered and unacknowledged tortures, plagues, and famines that only you and your most intimate friends can reach out and touch, and heal. This is the meaning of humanity.

They all share in the intoxication of focused collective action. Make decisions, act to soothe suffering, save lives, to hell with everybody else. A thirsty crowd gathers to watch Clive finish connecting the giant water bladder to its pipes: an audible moan escapes their lips when a tap is turned and a faucet gushes. A few weeks ago, I had thought MSFers were exercising some kind of false modesty when they balked at being called heroes, but now I understand that they are merely experiencing what it is to be fully alive. This is disalienation, the antithesis of the programmed numbness that life in a modern industrial city can be, commuting alone to anonymous work with strangers.

Weeks later, Interhamwe death squads will come with murderous intent to the gate of our emergency team's house in Ruhengeri, but will find the doors too awkward to break, the unarmed MSF guards too stubborn. They will go instead a few metres down the road, drag three Spanish medical workers and an American to the lawn, check their passports to ensure they are the inconvenient foreign witnesses to their genocidal evil, and shoot them on the spot. Only the American will escape death, but his leg will be amputated to save his life. As the death squad flees, it will kill three Rwandan soldiers and many civilians.

This night, around a hurried meal in the MSF compound, an intolerable screeching bursts from the hallway, where rats are fighting for food. Monique runs through the kitchen, past the enormous insects in the air and on the table, and confronts the rats as she would the killers. "Fuck off!" she shouts. Other aid agencies will withdraw from the country immediately after the murders, but MSF workers vote to stay in place for the time being, unarmed, only reminding themselves they are free to leave at any time if they feel insecure.

CONVERSATION STARTER

What do you know about Doctors Without Borders or similar organizations that support the work of doctors, nurses, and administrators in impoverished Third World countries where they need help to control crisis situations in which the health of people in a community is at risk? If you do not know about Doctors Without Borders or similar organizations, do some research to prepare yourself to read the selection that follows.

READING MATTERS

1. How did the Industrial Revolution of the late eighteenth century intensify the sense of alienation that many human beings feel? How did the technological revolution increase feelings of alienation? In what ways do men and women experience their own alienation? In what ways does your lifestyle reflect the alienation of modern life?
2. According to Leyton, how can Doctors Without Borders (or a similar type of group) bring meaning to the life of its members? Why does their job of feeling the suffering and deprivation of others who need help immediately reinforce the meaning of humanity and dispel feelings of modern day alienation? Do you think that in helping others one is also helping oneself?
3. Have you ever experienced the "intoxication of fused collective action"? Discuss your experience and contrast it with a time when you achieved an individual success. Which experience was more rewarding?
4. Why don't Doctors Without Borders see themselves as heroes? Why do they remain unarmed? Why do they survive and thrive on their experiences?

WRITING MATTERS

1. Interview a person who has served in a crisis in a Third World country. Try to learn more about his or her motivation and experiences. Perhaps your interview will help you to understand the feelings and purpose of Doctors Without Borders. Write a paper that integrates what you have learned about their mission and how you feel about this type of work. Would you find such service fulfilling? Would it lessen

your sense of alienation and provide purpose for your life? Discuss your answer.

2. Do some research into other modern theories of alienation. Explain several of the theories and apply them to your own life and the lives of those who are your friends or family members. From what you have learned, write an essay about what can you do to lessen your current sense of alienation. What specific actions might you take? In your essay refer to the theories that you have researched, whenever relevant.

3. Write a profile of someone who has dedicated his or her life to the service of others. What have you learned from your research and writing? What can be done to help people in our country who live in poverty and who are degraded by the quality of their lives? What can be done to help people in Third World countries, where in many cases poverty and disease are constant threats? Who is responsible for helping these people?

RELEVANT WEB SITES

DOCTORS WITHOUT BORDERS <http://www.doctorswithoutborders.org/>

The official web site of *Médecins Sans Frontières* provides detailed information about the organization's efforts to deliver emergency aid to victims of armed conflict, epidemics, and natural and man-made disasters, and to others who lack health care due to social or geographic isolation.

THE NOBEL FOUNDATION
<http://www.nobel.se/peace/laureates/1999/press.html>

The Nobel Foundation, established in 1900 based on the will of Alfred Nobel, manages the assets made available through the will for the awarding of the Nobel Prize and awarded the 1999 Nobel Peace Prize to Médecins Sans Frontières in recognition of the organization's pioneering humanitarian work on several continents.

The One-Thousand Paper Cranes Casebook

Japanese folk belief holds that the crane lives a thousand years, and if we fold one thousand paper cranes, we will have a long life, happiness, and good fortune. Thus the Japanese often fold paper cranes as gifts to friends, relatives, and people who are ill. The following casebook brings together an ancient legend and modern accounts of international community action peace-related projects that reflect back to the symbol and myth of the crane (tsuru). We begin with a Japanese folk tale, "The Legend of the Crane." This legend about an old hunter who frees a trapped crane and is amply rewarded was designed to illustrate the importance of compassion in everyday life as well as to help young people understand the sacred symbolism of the crane. After this story, we present an historical account of the efforts of principals and school children in Japan to raise money for a statue dedicated to peace and to the memory of Sadako Sasaki. Sadako, a 13-year-old girl who died of leukemia brought on by radiation poisoning after the bombing of Hiroshima, has become an international symbol in the struggle for world peace and nuclear disarmament. Before her tragic death, she folded nearly one thousand paper cranes to prolong her life and to bring peace to the world. Next, we include a short account of the creation in 1990 of the Sadako Peace Park in Seattle. Our final selection provides information about the 1996 Sadako/Paper Crane Project and related peace activities by children in the United States and around the world. Subsequent Sadako/ Paper Crane-related activities led to the creation of the World Peace Project, and, among other activities, brought together children from all over the world to create a gigantic paper crane dedicated to the cause of world peace in the Seattle King Dome in 1999.

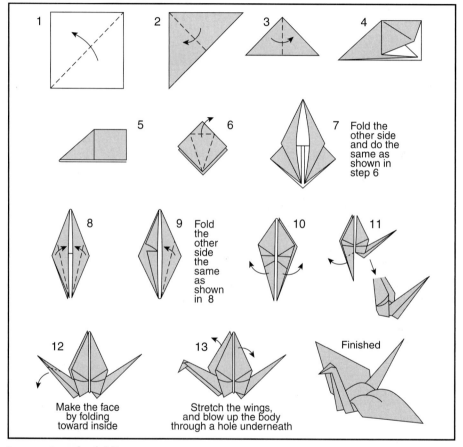

Instructions for folding paper cranes

The Legend of the Crane
Tale from Japanese Folklore

Hungry and cold, an elderly hunter gave up his search for food and started home through a field of tall grasses. He brooded over his empty satchel as he walked, considering how he would comfort his wife when he got home, but his thoughts were interrupted by the sound of someone wailing. Following the cries, he discovered a beautiful crane caught in the thicket. The old man drew his knife and carefully cut away the reeds, setting the crane free.

Later that night, the hunter and his wife were awakened by a lovely young woman who sought refuge from the cold. The elderly couple hurried her inside and prepared her a bed and a bowl of hot rice—the last of their supplies.

In the morning, the young woman rose early to prepare breakfast for her hosts, but there was nothing left to eat. She secured the elderly couple's promise not to disturb her and shut herself into the spare room with a loom. When she emerged, she handed the hunter a beautiful kimono cloth, asking him to sell it. The money he received bought enough food to feed the old people and their guest for many days.

In the meantime, the young woman wove another cloth, again making her hosts vow not to disturb her while she was at the loom. So the winter progressed. The elderly couple soon noticed that the young woman was growing weaker with each cloth she wove. "We have plenty," they told her. "Please do not work so hard!" But she insisted.

5   One night, the sound of the loom indicated that the young woman was very ill. The old hunter couldn't bear it, so he broke their promise and peered into the spare room. He gasped in amazement as he saw a white crane at the loom, plucking her own feathers to weave into the kimono cloth.

Hearing him, the crane turned into a young woman again. "I am the crane you freed from the reeds," she said. "I wanted to repay your kindness. But now that you know the truth, I must leave you." Knowing the old couple was well provided for, the young woman stretched her arms into wings once more and flew away, never to be seen again.

One Thousand Paper Cranes
The Children's Peace Statue

On October 26, 1955, a small article appeared in the Hiroshima Evening Newspaper. It briefly reported the death of a young girl who had suffered the effects of atomic bomb radiation: "The death of Sadako Sasaki is the fourteenth death in Nobori-cho Junior High School this year. She had been sick since last fall with the atomic bomb disease. She was exposed to the atomic bomb ten years ago, and now she is gone. . . . Fourteenth death in this school . . . seventh grader . . . age twelve." The obituary appeared at a time when most of Japan's citizens had come to distance themselves from the horrible memory of war.

Members of the Bamboo Class gathered not long after the funeral to share their grief. Many children felt guilty for not visiting Sadako more often while she was in the hospital, especially after the beginning of their summer vacation. Motivated by their common feelings of remorse, they decided to do something for Sadako.

"What should we do for Sadako?" they asked themselves.

10 "How about a marker in the Peace Park?" suggested one of the girls. "Yes, to remember Sadako and all other children who died because of *Pika*." They all agreed that a marker sounded like a good idea. "But a marker is expensive," someone else said. "How on earth can we raise enough money to buy a marker?" The idea of a marker excited them, but the reality of getting the necessary money to buy one frustrated and discouraged them. The means for seventh-graders to raise a large sum of money were obviously very limited. As an alternative, one student suggested bringing flowers to the gravesite each month to mark the day Sadako died. All agreed that such a remembrance was not only a good idea, but one that was within their limited financial means. Little did they know that fate was already preparing to alter their plans in a most dramatic way.

Sometime after Sadako's death, the Sasakis hosted a small memorial gathering in their Moto-machi home. Mr. Nomura, Sadako's Bamboo Class classmates, and a young Mr. Ichiro Kawamoto were invited, along with Sadako's relatives. Mr. Kawamoto was a conscientious man who devoted much of his time as a volunteer, raising support for disabled victims of the atomic bomb. Many of these individuals were unable to work. Mr. Kawamoto frequently spent his own money to help them.

When the bomb fell on Hiroshima, Mr. Kawamoto had been sixteen years old, and working at the Hiroshima Bay Power Plant. Fortunately, the explosion did not directly affect him because the power plant where he worked was some distance away from the center of the city where the bomb fell. Shortly after the bombing, Mr. Kawamoto went into the devastated area as a member of a volunteer rescue team and did everything he could to help the masses of injured men, women and children. His young, impressionable mind never forgot the images of horror he saw on that day, which changed his whole life. Young Mr. Kawamoto vowed that he would dedicate his life to helping the victims of the atomic bomb.

Mr. Kawamoto had related to Mr. Nomura his idea to build a memorial statue for Sadako and all the children who died of the Atomic Bomb Disease. Mr. Nomura then told Mr. Kawamoto of the upcoming memorial gathering at the Sasakis. As a result, Mr. Kawamoto was invited to Sadako's memorial gathering. He was very eager to come to the Sasakis' house and share his idea with everyone. When it came time for Mr. Kawamoto to address the group, he spoke enthusiastically: "Everyone! I believe if we all work together, we can build a memorial statue for Sadako and all the children who died of *Pika*. No one can do it alone. I need your help. We need each other." With great enthusiasm everyone in the gathering agreed.

The rest of the meeting was something of a miracle. Sadako's former classmates, the Bamboo Class, and others inspired by Mr. Kawamoto's idea, came together in their common desire to build a memorial statue. A dream had now been born.

15   "Where and how will we get the money to build a statue?" someone asked. Mr. Kawamoto fixed a serious eye on all those present. "I've got an idea. In a couple of days, the National Principals' Convention will be held at the City Convention Center. They'll be meeting from November 10th to the 12th. About 2,000 principals from all over Japan will attend. Why don't we make up some flyers and distribute them at the convention? We can use the flyers to tell them about Sadako and ask for support in our cause." Sadako's classmates were impressed with Mr. Kawamoto's idea, because they didn't think that they could raise the money to build even a tombstone. Now they were excited by the idea of building a statue in the Peace Park. Mr. Kawamoto's idea was unanimously accepted by the group. Their enthusiasm was rekindled and now they were prepared to put the plan into effect. But the vital question of how to get 2,000 flyers printed and distributed in time had to be answered immediately. Mr. Kawamoto said, "First, we need to locate a mimograph machine." "You can use our school's mimograph machine." responded Mr. Nomura. Then Mr. Kawamoto looked everybody straight in the eyes and said, "Working as a team we could do it. But there's very little time left before the Principals' Convention, so we must work fast."

Inspired and united by their noble cause, the students immediately put their project into motion. They raised as much cash as they could by pooling their allowance money. Those with artistic ability designed the flyer on the inked, mimeograph plate. Taking turns, they started the time-consuming task of cranking out 2,000 flyers, one at a time, by hand. Mr. Nomura and Mr. Kawamoto did their share, too. But on the first day of the convention, they still had not completed the necessary 2,000 flyers. It was not until late in the evening on November 11th that all the flyers were ready for distribution.

This is what the students had written on the flyer:

LET'S BUILD A STATUE FOR THE CHILDREN
OF THE ATOMIC BOMB:
We learned that school principals from all over Japan would be holding their meeting, and therefore we wish to share with you the following story:
Our dear friend, Sadako Sasaki, died on October 25. Since early childhood she was our closest friend. We studied and played together. But in January of this year the innocent Sadako suddenly became sick. After nine long months in the hospital, she died. Knowing that Sadako was aware of her fatal condition has made us very sad. But there is nothing we can do about it now. We do not want her death to have been in vain, so we hope to build a statue for all the children who died of the Atomic Bomb Disease. We are here today to make our project known to you honorable principals, and to ask you to convey our message to all our fellow junior high school students throughout the country, and encourage them to support us. We came today to make this plea.

Hiroshima Municipal Nobori-cho Junior High School
Seventh Graders
All the Classmates of the Late Sadako Sasaki

The next and the final day of the convention, four boys and four girls from the group were sent to the convention center to distribute the 2,000 flyers. It was a Saturday and the normal school day didn't recess until noon. Forgoing lunch, the eight-member team arrived at the convention center at about 1:15 p.m. They were told by the reception desk that, since the one o'clock session had already begun, they would have to wait until three o'clock, when it would be over.

There was nothing the students could do but wait patiently until the session ended at three o'clock. For this anxious group of young students it was the longest wait of their lives. As three o'clock approached, Mr. Kawamoto arrived to see how things were going and if he could be of any help. He took some time off to help these students. Suddenly the doors to the meeting room swung open and the principals slowly emerged. The eight boys and girls converged on the principals with their flyers. "Please read this. Please. It's important!" Many of the principals were puzzled by this unexpected solicitation. Some ignored the flyers, others put them in their pockets. But quite a few took the time to read them.

One of the principals saw the enlarged picture of Sadako that was held up by one of the students. It was obvious that he was deeply moved by the picture. Handing a contribution to a student, he wished them all good luck with their fundraising. As the last group of principals left the convention center, the young Sadako devotees knew their campaign had been a success. They had a long way to go, but they were on their way and nothing would stop them!

The Circle of Unity Widens

20 In December, in the northern cities of Hokkaido and Tohoku, growing numbers of students who had heard about Sadako's story began to show great interest in the memorial statue project. Many of the principals who had read the flyers informed their students about Sadako's tragedy and passed the flyers around, so their students would get involved.

Coincidentally, the year Sadako died was also the year the Atomic Bomb Museum in Hiroshima Peace Memorial Park opened to the public. As visitors to the museum, many of the school principals were vividly reminded of the devastation caused by the atomic bomb. They responded immediately and emotionally to the pain and suffering the bomb had caused when they saw displays depicting such horrors as black rain that covered Hiroshima after the bombing: men, women and children who had lost their hair to radiation from the bomb; iron beams twisted from the blast; young soldiers with bleeding gums and bodies darkened with purple patches; and the charred remains of homes no longer standing.

The new museum and Sadako's story left a profound impact on the school principals. To motivate their students, they made strong appeals to them to get involved in building the memorial statue. They promoted the virtues of peace, and above all, they used their voices to ask the world never again to use the atomic bomb. Students were so moved when they heard the story of Sadako and the Hiroshima bombing, they immediately decided unanimously to support the fundraising effort to build a statue. As a result, donations started to pour in from many district junior high schools.

By the end of December, the Student Council of Hokkaido Ashibetsu Junior High School had contributed $400. Sadako's classmates were overjoyed and their enthusiasm rose to new heights. They were especially pleased when the Ashibetsu students pledged to contact and encourage other junior high school students in Hokkaido to support the memorial project.

By December 31, contributions totaled over $1,200 and kept coming well into the new year!

25   Encouraged by the outpouring of donations, Sadako's former classmates became more committed and directly involved in the fundraising activities. They formed an official group called *"Kokeshi-no-kai"* or "The Wooden Doll's Association." They gave the association this name in remembrance of the *kokeshi* doll which Sadako had kept at her bedside while in the hospital. The *Kokeshi-no-kai* would include members in addition to the Bamboo Class. In a fundraising effort, members of the *Kokeshi-no-kai* went into the city of Hiroshima and directly solicited contributions.

The circle was widening with each passing day as the *Kokeshi-no-kai* rapidly became a highly recognized group in Hiroshima. It attracted support from elementary schools, junior and senior high schools, as well as many other sources. Because of its rapid growth and success, the representatives of elementary, junior and senior high school student councils formed a new group called "The Hiroshima Children and Students' Council for the Creation of Peace." Sadako's brother, Masahiro, then a ninth grader at Noboricho Junior High School, and Kiyo Ohkura, Sadako's former hospital roommate, also became members of this council.

In March of 1956, the council wrote a letter to all the elementary, junior and senior high schools in the nation. The letter read as follows:

> After a very long and painful hospitalization, Sadako died. Yoshito, a fourth grader, also died of the Atomic Bomb Disease. Sadako was only two years old when the atomic bomb was dropped. Immediately after the bomb exploded, her mother put Sadako on her back and, in fear for their lives, ran to Kusunoki-cho. Fortunately, they both survived. However, about a year ago Sadako was diagnosed with the Atomic Bomb Disease. The official medical term for her condition was "malignant acute marrow leukemia." For nine long and painful months, Sadako struggled with this disease and, finally, she died. Every day of her confinement was an unbearable ordeal, but tough, hopeful Sadako tolerated it without complaint. As friends and classmates of Sadako, we frequently visited her at the Red Cross Hospital,

where she was always in her bed diligently folding paper cranes. When we asked her why she was folding so many cranes, she replied, "What do you think? I want to get better fast." We will never forget the expression on her face. It was one of absolute determination to get better. Our dear, athletic Sadako was determined to get better, so she could start winning races again. While in the hospital Sadako managed to fold more than 1,000 paper cranes. After she died we each received a folded crane as a memento. We took all the remaining cranes and placed them on her face and chest as she lay in the casket. Then we said our final goodbyes.

Even to this very day, there are still many residents of Hiroshima dying one after another as a result of the Atomic Bomb Disease. There are also children like Sadako and Yoshito who survived the atomic bomb without a scratch, attended school like others, only to die eventually because of that hideous bomb. It was not their war, but they were forced to pay the price. Why did this happen to us? The people of Hiroshima were not the only ones injured by the war. Children and students all over the country still suffer from it, and many of them continue to live in pitiful conditions. Our 10,000 older brothers and sisters who were burned to death by the atomic bomb didn't want to die. How horrible must have been their suffering.

Sadako is dead, but to this day she still doesn't have a traditional altar. And her family is forced to live in a cold, drafty shack. Dear Friends! It is our desire to honor the spirit of these children, many of whom were our dearest friends. We are saving our allowances and praying that our dream to build a "Statue for the Children of the Atomic Bomb" will become a reality. To this end, we have banded together in a common cause to secure the financial means to enable us to achieve our goal. You undoubtedly know that a project of such magnitude will be very costly, and this is the problem we must now resolve.

Will you please join us? We desperately need your encouragement and support. We ask you from the bottom of our hearts.

March 1, 1956
The Hiroshima Children and Students' Council
For the Creation of Peace
Masashi Nakamura, Chairperson
Senior at Moto-machi High School,
in the City of Hiroshima

This letter succeeded in uniting the city of Hiroshima with schools from all across the nation. As a result, contributions greatly increased. By the end of August, contributions totaled $360,000; by December when the fundraising campaign officially ended, the council had raised an astounding $450,000.

In the beginning their noble cause seemed like an impossible dream. Now, after so much hard work, dedication and planning, their dream was within reach. They would build a memorial statue. With the final results greatly exceeding all their expectations, the original group who had come together to honor Sadako could not contain their happiness.

Prayer for Peace

With the combined support of more than 3,000 schools, plus thousands of individual contributions, the dream to build the memorial statue finally became a reality. The memorial statue would be called *"Genbaku-no-Ko-no-Zoh"* or "The Statue for the Children of the Atomic Bomb" and Sadako Sasaki would be its model.

30   On May 5, 1958, Children's Day in Japan, the unveiling ceremony of the memorial took place in the Peace Memorial Park in Hiroshima. All of Sadako's former classmates and others who were actively involved in this project were seated around the base of the statue. Nearby were 10,000 excited children and students representing forty-seven schools.

The Sasaki family was seated along with the members of the original *"Kokeshi-no-kai,"* the primary driving force for the memorial project.

The ceremony officially began when Sadako's younger sister Mitsue and younger brother Eiji approached the base of the statue to pull the cord that unveiled the memorial. When the cloth that covered the tall memorial fell to the ground, *Genbaku-no-Ko-no-Zoh* was officially unveiled. Now, the dream of so many had become a reality. Sadako would be remembered forever. On the very top of the statue was the figure of a girl holding a large crane as she looked skyward.

As Mr. and Mrs. Sasaki looked at the sculptured likeness of Sadako atop the memorial statue, they had to restrain themselves from calling out Sadako's name. Silently, they recalled the days when their daughter was a happy, healthy girl.

"Though our Sadako is no longer with us, her spirit lives on, a symbol of peace for all the children of the world!"

35   Engraved in the dark granite at the foot of the statue are the following words:

> This is our cry
> This is our prayer:
> To create peace in the world

These are the words, the prayers and the cries of the victims of the atomic bomb—past and present. They must be heard and remembered by all the people of the world!

To this day, the statue is continually decorated with thousands of paper cranes brought and sent by people throughout the world as symbols of peace. It is an impressive reminder to its visitors that its message is world peace.

Peace must prevail.

(adapted by Jon Ford)

Sadako Peace Park in Seattle and Dr. Floyd Schmoe: A Life of Service

There are peace parks all over the world now, many inspired directly by the Peace Park in Hiroshima, and a number of these natural environments are dedicated to Sadako. A park of particular interest can be found on a small lot in Seattle near the University of Washington. This park was built by Dr. Floyd Schmoe when he was 93 years old. Dr. Schmoe, a peace activist dedicated to helping victims of war and oppression, won the Hiroshima Peace Prize of $5,000 in 1988 and used the money to acquire and clear a vacant lot.

35   From a pile of wrecked cars, garbage, and brush, he built with volunteers a beautiful "Peace Park." The park was dedicated on August 6, 1990, the 45th anniversary of the bombing of Hiroshima. In the park a life-size bronze statue by sculptor Daryl Smith of Sadako Sasaki holds a paper crane aloft. Hundreds of children, many involved with the World Peace Project, visit the park each year and bring paper cranes to the statue to show their hope for world peace. On some days thousands of paper cranes drape Sadako's statue.

A fascinating aspect of this tiny park is the story of its founder, four-time Nobel Prize nominee Dr. Floyd Schmoe. Now 103 years old and in frail health, he is still excited and curious about the world. In his life of service to peace, Dr. Schmoe has traveled to many troubled areas of the world to help people recover from the devastation of war. A Quaker and ardent pacifist throughout his long life, Floyd Schmoe has helped to pick up the pieces that remain after wars have been fought. After volunteering and serving in Europe during World War II as a medic in the Red Cross, he volunteered again to work on a relief train carrying emergency medical and food supplies to Poland after the Armistice was signed. In 1942, he assisted Japanese Americans who were interned by the U.S. government at the beginning of World War II. In 1948, Dr. Schmoe led a project called "Houses for Hiroshima," where volunteers spent five years building houses for the survivors of the bombings of Hiroshima and Nagasaki. Forty years later, in 1988, he received the Hiroshima Peace Prize from the Japanese Government. In 1954, he went to Korea to build homes for those whose homes had been destroyed there in the Korean War; and in 1958, he traveled to the Middle East to help reopen water wells that had been damaged during the Egyptian/Israeli wars. In a recent interview, Schmoe commented that he always has believed that individuals are responsible for what happens in the world: "You feel hopeless sometimes, but the only answer to the hopelessness is to have optimism to expect things to be better—to hope that you in some way can make them better."

Sharon O'Connell

"The Sadako/Paper Crane Project, 1996"

In August of 1995, the Cranes for Peace Project participated in the marking of the 50th anniversary of the dropping of the atomic bombs on Japan and the end of World War II. American children participated by sending a piece of paper to be folded into a crane. The cranes were taken to Japan and placed on the statue of Sadako in the Peace Park in Hiroshima. Anyone who contributed $5 or more received a photo of their sheet of paper folded into a crane. The money contributed was used for expenses related to taking the cranes to Japan or donated to a charity. In 1996 another Cranes Project was initiated, and since then many other related projects have been launched. In the following 1996 activities report, notice that schools in many parts of the world had individual projects that were part of the overall course of action.

Forty-four schools from four countries sent greetings and cranes to Hiroshima for the Sadako Peace Statue Ceremony, which was held this year on July 28th. Akiko Tokai presented the lei of cranes at the statue and described the project at the ceremony. Each crane bore the name of a representative school. Susan Buccola, a teacher from a U.S. Marine Base in Okinawa attended the large Peace Ceremony on Peace Day and presented the beautiful booklet created from pages sent by schools to Mr. Shinichiro Kurose, a principal of Hiroshima Jogaakuin Junior and Senior High School. Mr. Kurose will share this booklet with his students and others in Hiroshima.

Teachers from the forty-four schools responded to an invitation posted on the Internet to have students read the story of Sadako, fold paper cranes, and send them to the Peace Park in Hiroshima, Japan. The invitation was posted once on each of four user groups, LM_Net, Kidsphere, Kidlink and Kid-Lit. . . . Students involved in this project participated in a beautiful kaleidoscope of varied activities. Some schools sent their cranes to the Peace Museum in Hiroshima for the Sadako Children's Statue. Others sent paper cranes to a person who was suffering. Some schools saved one crane for a lei to honor a Hiroshima educator at the 1996 Sadako Children's Statue Ceremony. Some schools created pages for a booklet. The pictures and messages in the booklet represent the faces and hearts of students around the world who join with the children and adults of Hiroshima in saying, "Never again." Seventh-grade students on the Gold Coast of Australia, studying Japanese, folded 1,000 paper cranes for a classmate who was ill. Students in Clarkson Public School, Mississauga, Ontario, Canada, each developed a monologue based on an event in the book, "Sadako and the Thousand Paper Cranes." Students in Camp Kinser, the U.S. Air Force Base in Okinawa, had a cultural exchange with a Japanese primary school.

Students in Cocoa Beach High School, Cocoa Beach, Florida, learned from two Japanese exchange students the art of folding cranes and information about the Peace Park. Students in a Learning Disability class in

Orlando, Florida, read the story and talked about peace. Teacher Pam Bowie, of Des Plaines, Illinois, collaborated with the Peace Museum to create a teacher's guide for a Peace Unit. Students in Berwick Academy, South Berwick, Maine, studied Asia and used the theme of "Peace" along with Earth Day activities.

40   Students in Oxford, Mississippi, learned Japanese through a distance learning project. They hosted fourteen Japanese students for three weeks then went to Japan themselves for one month! Students in Custer School, Broken Bow, Nebraska, sent half of their thousand paper cranes to Bosnia and half to Japan; then [they] sent a few golden cranes to their local hospital. Students in Hatboro, Pennsylvania, read the story of Sadako and many related books. They viewed the Peace Park on the Internet, wrote haiku, tanka and designed peace banners and a huge display for a literary fair. Students of Bucktail High School, Renovo, Pennsylvania, read a play about real victims of the bombing and created their own peace monument. Students in Austin, Texas, filled their school cafeteria with paper cranes—then raised money to send them to Hiroshima.

An Asian student in Dallas, Texas, who speaks no English, taught his classmates to fold paper cranes to participate in this project. Students in Virginia shared their cranes with a terminally ill student. Students in an origami club in Skaneateles, New York, made and sold beautiful origami pins to pay for the mailing of the lei and the booklet. Our deepest gratitude goes to Hiroko Komine, who translated each part of the notebook and to Akiko and Ryoju Tokai, who coordinated our efforts with activities in Hiroshima.

I'm attaching the dedication I wrote for Mr. Kurose. Mr. Kurose, it turns out, is the principal of a Christian school. I didn't know that when I asked him if we could honor him. I simply chose him because I was completely in awe of the work he had put into the Children's International Peace Conference held in his school last year! (He personally raised money for 15 children from many different countries to come to his school to participate in a peace conference for three weeks before Peace Day, 1995.)

DEDICATION OF BOOKLET TO MR. KUROSE

Rollo May contemplated the meaning of the pictures of the earth sent back from the Apollo 7 where astronauts could see the earth without borders. He wrote in "The Cry for Myth, "We cannot turn the clock back . . . , but the control of nuclear energy is the requirement needed to bring us all together. . . . We find ourselves in a new world community; we cannot destroy the parts without destroying the whole. In this bright loveliness we know now that we are truly sisters and brothers, at last in the same family."

Communication through the Internet, also, diminishes the borders which separate citizens of one country from another. Through its power, teachers in four countries easily came together to lend support to the people of Hiroshima in calling for a nuclear free world. Children in the United

States, Canada, Australia and the military base in Okinawa, Japan, read the story "Sadako and the Thousand Paper Cranes" and contemplated the destruction created by the release of an atomic bomb. Children learned to fold paper cranes and raised money to send their paper cranes to the Sadako Children's Statue in Peace Park, Hiroshima, to physically demonstrate their commitment to peace.

45   Many of these students created pages for this notebook. It is their hope that it will be shared with children in Hiroshima. I believe that it is the sincere hope of children that their countries live in peace.

Children are empowered by adults. It is our privilege to present this booklet to Mr. Shinichiro Kurose, Principal of Hiroshima Jogakuin Junior and Senior High School. We feel that he has done a great deal to empower children in their efforts towards peace. We wish to honor his efforts in coordinating the 1995 International High School Summit. It is by meeting "face to face" that children best learn that we are "one family." We congratulate him on his remarkable effort in bringing together children of fifteen countries to solve problems which will help to bring about a peaceful world.

Thank you so much—all of you who helped in small or large ways—to bring this year's Sadako/Paper Crane Project to a successful conclusion!

READING MATTERS

1. What does "One Thousand Paper Cranes" seem to be saying about the relationship between humans and the animal world, as well as about the importance of helping others even when one has one's own problems in life to overcome?

2. How is Sadako transformed from an energetic young girl into a heroic role model for children and an inspiration for world peace?

3. Trace the process by which the "circle of unity widens," leading from the original conception of a marker, to the small group meeting of Sadako's former schoolmates in the Bamboo Class along with the Sasakis, Mr. Nomura, and young Ichiro Kawamoto, to the eventual funding and successful creation of the Sadako statue. How are communications media used to help widen the circle of concern and unity?

4. The three accounts of the peace movement that sprang up around the figure of Sadako and the paper cranes contain brief profiles of and comments by a number of people who were crucial to the success of the movement. Discuss several of the individuals who made a strong impression on you—what qualities do they have in common?

WRITING MATTERS

1. After studying the accounts of activities leading to the development of the peace movement that grew up in response to Sadako and the cranes, write an essay in which you reflect on what can be learned from these narratives about the methods and commitment required for successful long-term community service activities.

2. Often community action projects are given coherence by someone whose life or liberty was lost in service to a particular cause. Write about the contribution and legacy of one such individual.
3. Working separately or with members of a group, create a plan for a peace project that could derive from the figure of Sadako or from some other myth, story, or source of inspiration. How would you go about developing a specific project that made the values of peace visual and dramatic? How would you publicize your efforts using media such as printed articles, flyers, brochures, radio, television, and the Internet?

RELEVANT WEB SITES

WORLD PEACE PROJECT FOR CHILDREN <www.sadako.org/choir.html>

The World Peace Project for Children's web site provides tools to promote world peace by educating children about global matters that concern them and by encouraging positive connections with children in other cultures.

THOUSAND CRANES PEACE NETWORK—A MILLION PAPER CRANES FOR PEACE <http://rosella.apana.org.au/~mlb/cranes/million.htm>

The *Thousand Cranes Peace Network* is made up of groups and individuals who are willing to fold a thousand paper cranes (or as many as they can manage) as a symbol of their hope for and commitment to peace and nonviolence, to be transported to Peace Parks and monuments around the world.

Ideas for Writing

1. What did you learn that was new to you about the relationships between doctors and patients from reading the first three selections in this chapter? Write an essay that discusses three or four of the most valuable insights that you gained. In supporting your points, refer to the essays, to research, to personal experience, and to observation.

2. What is your opinion of health care in your community? Base your answer on research, issues raised in this chapter, as well as your personal experiences and observations.

3. Write an essay that reflects upon the importance of health, basing your ideas on this chapter, health issues that you follow in the news, your personal experiences with your own health and that of friends and family. What have you learned about what it means to be healthy and how to stay healthy?

4. Many of the selections specifically address the importance of community support in remaining healthy. You can respond positively or negatively to one of the essays, or you can write a more general essay that draws on a number of articles in this chapter as well as your personal experience to explain why and to what extent you believe supportive communities are important to health.

5. Write an essay in which you argue for or against a total integration of women into the field of medicine. As Julia McMurray suggests, many women have responsibility for their children and cannot be as devoted to medicine as male doctors. Should more male doctors take care of their children so that women can participate in all specialties of medicine? Do some research to see what fields of medicine are dominated by women and which ones are dominated by men. Does this implicit gender regulation need to be changed? What will make that happen?

6. Watch a film based on a health theme. In your essay, use the first paragraph to briefly summarize the film. Then you have choices about how to develop the essay. You can break down the issues in the film and discuss why each is relevant to yourself and your community. Alternatively, write an argument for or against the persuasive power of the film, or write an essay that discusses how the film brings a new perspective on the health chapter.

7. Write an essay in which you discuss the three articles in this chapter that you found most informative and persuasive. In supporting your three points, refer to research as well as personal experience.

8. Write an essay that explores what you have learned about the relationship between science and intuition or personal support for healing. Refer to specific articles, to research, and to your own experiences to support your main ideas.

9. Write a short story, a series of poems, or a memoir about an experience that you have had that was related to the theme of health and community.

10. Volunteer to work at a community organization that helps people who need supportive services related to health concerns. You can write a profile of the organization for a local newspaper or help the organization by writing a press release, an article for their newsletter, a brochure, or publicity flyer. You might also create a web site or brochure that provides information about a service that supports families, either traditional or nontraditional, within your community. Alternatively, you can volunteer at the organization and then write an informative perspective on the organization and about what you learned through volunteering.

Credits

1. "On the Streetcars" from *I Know Why the Caged Bird Sings* by Maya Angelou, copyright © 1969 and renewed 1997 by Maya Angelou. Used by permission of Random House, Inc.
2. "Culture Sculpture" by Mark Applebaum. Copyright © 2003 Mark Applebaum. Used with permission.
3. "Building a Swan's Nest for Instruction in Rhetoric" by Nora Bacon, *CCC*, Vol. 51, No. 4, June 2000, pp. 589–609. Copyright 2000 by the National Council of Teachers of English. Reprinted with permission.
4. Excerpt from *How to YaYa in Your Neighborhood* by Claudia Barker. Copyright © 1996 Louisiana State University Press. Reprinted by permission.
5. "The Digital Divide" by David Bolt and Ray Crawford. Published by TV Books. Reprinted by permission.
6. "Bread Salt and Heart." Copyright © *The International Rescue Committee.* Reprinted by permission.
7. "The Best Seat in the House" by Melissa Burns. Copyright © 2003 Melissa Burns. Used with permission.
8. "Habitat for Humanity: The Gift of Hope" by Ivanka Choumanova. Copyright © 2003 Ivanka Choumanova. Used with permission.
9. Interview: "The Healing Power of Listening" by Ivanka Choumanova. Copyright © 2003 Ivanka Choumanova. Used with permission.
10. From *The House on Mango Street*. Copyright © 1984 by Sandra Cisneros. Published by Vintage Books, a division of Random House, Inc. and in hardcover by Alfred A. Knopf in 1994. Reprinted by permission of Susan Bergholz Literary Services, New York. All rights reserved.
11. "Volunteering" by Hazel Clarke. Copyright © 2000 Hazel Clarke. Used with permission.
12. "Robotic Iguanas" by Julia Corbett, *Orion Magazine*, March/April 2003. Copyright © 2003 Julia Corbett. Used with permission.
13. From *Fat Land* by Greg Crister. Copyright © 2003 by Greg Crister. Reprinted by permission of Houghton Mifflin Company. All rights reserved.
14. "The Invisible Riot" from *Ecology of Fear* by Mike Davis, Copyright © 1998 by Mike Davis. Reprinted by permission of Henry Holt and Company, LLC.
15. "The Standardized Test and its Implications in the American Classroom" by Elizabeth Derse. Copyright © 2003 Elizabeth Derse. Used with permission.
16. "Total Eclipse" from *Teaching a Stone to Talk: Expeditions and Encounters* by Annie Dillard. Copyright © 1982 by Annie Dillard. Reprinted by permission of HarperCollins Publishers, Inc.

Photo Credits

Index